NONVERBAL COMMUNICATION IN HUMAN INTERACTION

SEVENTH EDITION

Mark L. Knapp
The University of Texas at Austin

Judith A. Hall
Northeastern University

WADSWORTH
CENGAGE Learning

Australia • Brazil • Japan • Korea • Mexico • Singapore • Spain • United Kingdom • United States

WADSWORTH
CENGAGE Learning

Nonverbal Communication in Human
Interaction, Seventh Edition

Mark L. Knapp
Judith A. Hall

Publisher: Lyn Uhl

Executive Editor: Monica Eckman

Development Editor: Kate Scheinman

Assistant Editor: Rebekah Matthews

Editorial Assistant: Colin Solan

Marketing Manager: Erin Mitchell

Marketing Coordinator:
Christine Dobberpuhl

Marketing Communications Manager:
Darlene Macanan

Content Project Management: Pre-Press
PMG

Art Director: Linda Helcher

Print Buyer: Susan Carroll

Permissions Editor: Bob Kauser

Photo Manager: Don Schlotman

Photo Researcher: Nina Smith

Cover Designer: Rokusek Design

Compositor: Pre-Press PMG

For product information and technology assistance,
contact us at
**Cengage Learning Academic Resource Center,
1-800-423-0563**
For permission to use material from this text or product,
submit all requests online at
www.cengage.com/permissions.
Further permissions questions can be e-mailed to
permissionrequest@cengage.com.

Library of Congress Control Number: 2009922302

ISBN-13: 978-0-495-56869-8

ISBN-10: 0-495-56869-4

Wadsworth | Cengage Learning
20 Channel Center
Boston, MA 02210
USA

Cengage Learning products are represented in Canada by
Nelson Education, Ltd.

For your course and learning solutions, visit **www.cengage.com.**

Purchase any of our products at your local college store or at our preferred online store **www.ichapters.com.**

Printed in Canada
2 3 4 5 6 7 12 11 10 09

BRIEF CONTENTS

CONTENTS

PREFACE

Normally, the final thing authors do in a preface is to thank those who have been instrumental in the development of their book. We'd like to depart from that tradition by starting with our heartfelt thanks to the thousands of students and instructors who have used this book and provided feedback during the past 37 years. More than anyone else, you are responsible for the longevity of this book. With this in mind, we undertook this seventh edition by putting what we believe to be instructor and student needs at the forefront of our writing. As with previous editions, we encourage you to let us know whether we have succeeded.

The fact that this book is coauthored is worth noting. One of us represents the field of communication and the other social psychology. This collaboration, which requires the blending of two distinct perspectives, is symbolic of the nonverbal literature we report in this volume. The theory and research addressing nonverbal phenomena comes from scholars with a wide variety of academic backgrounds and perspectives—communication, counseling, psychology, psychiatry, linguistics, sociology, management, speech, and others. Understanding the nature of nonverbal communication is truly an interdisciplinary enterprise.

In revising this book, we retained the features that students and instructors valued from the previous editions while adding and changing other things that we believe will improve the book. In response to instructors and students who asked for more emphasis on how the findings from nonverbal research can be applied, we have given that emphasis in Chapters 12 and 13. We also recognize how important photographs and drawings are in a book like this, so we have continued to use visual representations to aid comprehension of certain nonverbal actions. With an increasing amount of communication that is mediated by some form of technology, we added a section to Chapter 13 that addresses issues related to nonverbal messages and technology.

In every new edition, we incorporate the most recent theory and research while retaining definitive studies from the past. Readers will find that some areas of study have fewer recent references than others. This simply means that there hasn't been a lot of recent research in that area or that the recent work, in our judgment, does not substantially change the conclusions from earlier studies. If something we know about human behavior today was first revealed in a study from 1958, we want readers to know that, and we will maintain the 1958 reference. Research on a particular topic often has an ebb and flow to it. During the 1960s and 1970s, the fear that a worldwide population boom would create terrible problems spawned a lot of research on space, territory, and crowding. In recent years, far less research has been done in this area. The study of gestures, on the other hand, has gone from an area of relatively little research activity during the 1960s and 1970s to an area that is of primary interest to numerous scholars today. To accommodate the explosion of interest in this area, an academic journal, *Gesture,* was initiated in 2001.

As in past editions, extensive bibliographies follow each chapter, and we have tried to retain a writing style that is scientifically accurate as well as interesting to the reader. We are honored that our book serves as both a textbook and a reference work. The *Instructor's Manual* for this book provides the information and imagination necessary for effective classroom learning in nonverbal communication.

The book is divided into five parts. Part One introduces the reader to some fundamental ideas and addresses the following questions: What is nonverbal communication? How do verbal and nonverbal communication interrelate? What difference does a knowledge of nonverbal communication make to your everyday life? Are some people more skilled than others at communicating nonverbally? How did they get that way? With this general perspective in mind, Parts Two, Three, and Four take the reader through the nonverbal elements involved in any interaction: the environment within which the interaction occurs, the physical features of the interactants themselves, and their behavior—gestures, touching, facial expressions, eye gazing, and vocal sounds. Part Five begins with a chapter focused on how all the separate parts of an interaction combine as we seek to accomplish very common goals in daily life—for example, communicating who we are, communicating closeness and distance, communicating varying degrees of status and power, deceiving others, and effectively managing the back-and-forth flow of conversation. The last chapter examines nonverbal communication in the context of advertising, therapy, the classroom, politics, culture, and technology. Throughout the book we repeatedly point out how all interactants involved are likely to play a role in whatever behavior is displayed by a single individual—even though this perspective is not always adequately developed in the research we review.

Several helpful online tools are available for use with this text. The online *Instructor's Resource Manual* includes a sample schedule, chapter objectives, discussion questions, test items, audiovisual resources, exercises, and out-of-class assignments. The companion Web site features student self-quizzes. In addition, you can choose to purchase this text with 4 months of free access to InfoTrac® College Edition, a world-class, online university library that offers the full text of articles from almost 5,000 scholarly journals and popular publications updated daily, going back more than 20 years. Students can also gain instant access to critical-thinking and paper-writing tools through InfoWrite. Your subscription now includes InfoMarks®—instant access to virtual readers drawing from the vast InfoTrac College Edition library and hand selected to work with your books. You can access your online resources at **www.cengage.com/login**, using the access code that came with your book or that you bought online at **www.iChapters.com.** For more information about these online resources, please contact your local Cengage Learning representative.

Each of us would like to thank following reviewers for their input during the development of this edition:

Kathleen Czech, Point Loma Nazarene University
Marcia D. Dixson, Indiana University-Purdue University Fort Wayne
Diane Ferrero-Paluzzi, Iona College
Duane Fish, Northwest College
David Foster, University of Findlay
Sheryl A. Friedley, George Mason University
Bill M. Huddleston, University of North Alabama
Marcy Jones, Grand Valley State University
Erin Kleman, Kent State University
Edith E. LeFebvre, California State University Sacramento
Kathy Lilly, Florida Community College at Jacksonville
Julie Mayberry, Meredith College
David Moss, Mt. San Jacinto College
Narissra Punyanunt-Carter, Texas Tech University
Andrew S. Rancer, The University of Akron
Chris Segrin, University of Arizona
Robert Sidelinger, West Virginia University
Susan J. Szmania, University of Wisconsin–Milwaukee
Rachel Tighe, The University of Virginia's College at Wise
William R. Todd-Mancillas, California State University at Chico
Kristen Treinen, Minnesota State University–Mankato
Mike Wartman, Normandale Community College
Richard West, University of Texas at San Antonio
Susan M. Wieczorek, University of Pittsburgh at Johnstown

Both of us would also like to acknowledge the skills exhibited by the publishing staff who helped us develop this edition: Monica Eckman, executive editor; Kate Scheinman, development editor; Colin Solan, editorial assistant; and Linda Helcher, art director.

AN INTRODUCTION TO THE STUDY OF NONVERBAL COMMUNICATION

What is nonverbal communication? How does nonverbal behavior function in relation to verbal behavior? How does nonverbal communication affect our everyday lives? Do we learn how to perform body language, or is it instinctive? Are some people more skilled at communicating with these face, voice, and body signals? The answers to these fundamental questions are the focus of Part One.

Those of us who keep our eyes open can read volumes into what we see going on around us.

—E. T. Hall

NONVERBAL COMMUNICATION: BASIC PERSPECTIVES

Herr von Osten purchased a horse in Berlin in 1900. When von Osten began training his horse, Hans, to count by tapping his front hoof, he had no idea that Hans would soon become one of the most celebrated horses in history. Hans was a rapid learner and soon progressed from counting to adding, multiplying, dividing, subtracting, and eventually solving problems involving factors and fractions. Even more startling, when von Osten exhibited Hans to public audiences, he counted the size of the crowd or the number wearing eyeglasses. Responding only with taps, Hans could tell time, use a calendar, recall musical pitch, and perform numerous other seemingly fantastic feats. After von Osten taught Hans an alphabet that could be coded into hoofbeats, the horse could answer virtually any question—oral or written. It seemed that Hans, a common horse, had complete comprehension of the German language, the ability to produce the equivalent of words and numerals, and an intelligence beyond that of many human beings.

Even without promotion by the mass media, the word spread quickly, and Hans became known throughout the world. He was soon dubbed "Clever Hans." Because of the profound implications for several scientific fields, and because some skeptics thought a gimmick was involved, an investigating committee was established to decide whether deceit tainted Hans's performances. Professors of psychology and physiology, the director of the Berlin Zoological Garden, a director of a circus, veterinarians, and cavalry officers were appointed to this commission. An experiment with Hans from which von Osten was absent demonstrated no change in the apparent intelligence of the horse. This was sufficient proof for the commission to announce that no trickery was involved.

But the appointment of a second commission was the beginning of the end for Clever Hans. Von Osten was asked to whisper a number into the horse's left ear while another experimenter whispered a number into the horse's right ear. Hans was told to add the two numbers—an answer none of the onlookers, von Osten, or the experimenter knew. Hans failed. And with further tests, he continued to fail. The experimenter, Pfungst, had discovered that Hans could answer a question only if someone in his visual field knew the answer and was attentive to the situation (Pfungst, 1911/1965).

When Hans was given the question, onlookers who knew the answer assumed an expectant posture, increased their body tension, and bent their heads slightly forward. When Hans reached the correct number of taps, the onlookers would relax and make a slight upward movement of their heads, which was Hans's signal to stop tapping. Evidence suggested that Hans could detect head movements as slight as one-fifth of a millimeter. Subsequent experiments found that Hans also would cease tapping as a knowledgeable onlooker raised his or her eyebrows or even showed a dilation of the nostrils.

The story of Clever Hans functions as a vivid introduction to the field of nonverbal communication (Sebeok & Rosenthal, 1981; Sebeok & Umiker-Sebeok, 1980). Hans's cleverness was not in his ability to verbalize or understand verbal commands but in his ability to respond to almost imperceptible and unconscious movements by those surrounding him (Spitz, 1997). A French horse named Clever Bertrand may have developed his cleverness from entirely different but equally subtle signals, although he was not studied scientifically. It is reported that Bertrand could do everything that Hans could do—but Bertrand was blind! Indeed, some of the experiments with Hans had also shown that when auditory cues were added to the visual, Hans's accuracy increased. So Hans's cleverness was not limited to visual cues.

The story of Clever Hans makes two important points regarding the role of nonverbal behavior in human encounters:

1. While we are in the presence of another person, we are constantly giving signals about our attitudes, feelings, and personality.
2. Others may become particularly adept at sensing and interpreting these signals.

This ability is not unlike the perceptiveness or sensitivity to nonverbal cues exhibited by a Clever Carl, Christine, Frank, or Harriet when closing a business deal, presenting an intelligent and industrious image to a professor, knowing when to leave a party, and acting wisely in many other common situations. We also make interpretations about the *absence* of cues, as well as reacting to particular cues. For example, when a nephew does not get his usual greeting kiss from his favorite aunt, he wonders what is wrong. (Perhaps he never noticed the kiss nearly as much as he notices its absence.) As another example, when a doctor tries to act professionally neutral by being somewhat blank and unexpressive, the patient is likely to read the lack of cues as aloofness or disinterest, perhaps even suspecting the doctor of withholding important information. This is a good example of how what we *think* we are communicating may be very different from what we are actually communicating.

The purpose of this book is to expand your conscious awareness of the numerous nonverbal stimuli that you produce and confront in everyday dialogue. Each chapter summarizes behavioral science research in a specific area of nonverbal communication. First, however, let us develop five basic perspectives through which we can view the remaining chapters:

1. Defining nonverbal communication
2. Classifying nonverbal behavior

3. Nonverbal communication in the total communication process
4. The history of nonverbal studies
5. Nonverbal communication in everyday life

PERSPECTIVE 1: DEFINING NONVERBAL COMMUNICATION

To most people, the phrase *nonverbal communication* refers to communication effected by means other than words, assuming words are the verbal element. Like most definitions, this one is generally useful, but it does not account adequately for the complexity of this phenomenon. As long as we understand and appreciate the points listed here, this broad definition should serve us well.

First, we need to understand that separating verbal and nonverbal behavior into two separate and distinct categories is virtually impossible. Consider, for example, the hand movements that make up American Sign Language, a language of the deaf. These gesticulations are mostly linguistic (verbal), yet hand gestures are often considered behavior that is "other than words." McNeill (1992) demonstrated the linguistic qualities of some gestures by noting that different kinds of gestures disappear with different kinds of aphasia—the impairment of the ability to use or comprehend words—namely, those gestures with linguistic functions similar to the specific verbal loss. Conversely, not all spoken words are clearly or singularly verbal; for example, onomatopoeic words, such as *buzz* or *murmur,* and non-propositional speech used by auctioneers and some aphasics.

We also need to understand that our definition does not indicate whether the phrase "by means other than words" refers to the type of signal produced—that is, its *encoding*—or to the perceiver's code for interpreting the symbol, its *decoding*. Generally, when people refer to nonverbal behavior, they are talking about the signals produced, or encoded, to which meaning will be attributed, not the process of attributing meaning. A first step toward understanding the process of attributing meaning to nonverbal behavior is to understand how the brain processes nonverbal stimuli.

PROCESSING NONVERBAL INFORMATION

Currently, many brain researchers believe that the two hemispheres of the brain process different types of information, but each hemisphere does not process each type exclusively. Nonverbal messages may be processed by either hemisphere even though the bulk of the work is probably done by the right side. The left hemisphere processes mainly sequentially ordered, digital, verbal, and linguistic information. Nonverbal messages processed by the left hemisphere may involve symbolic gestures and facial expressions that have a closely linked verbal translation; for example, the speech-independent gestures noted in Chapter 7. The right hemisphere of the brain is normally credited with processing visual/spatial relationships and analogic, or Gestalt, information; and it seems to be the main processing area for some types of gestures and spontaneous, expressive displays of emotion in the face and voice (Buck & VanLear, 2002; Kelly & Goldsmith, 2004). It is important to note, however, that few scientists currently believe that either side of the brain deals *exclusively* with a particular kind of information. In fact, the following case illustrates how adaptable the brain can be.

Bruce Lipstadt had the left hemisphere of his brain removed when he was 5 years old (Koutlak, 1976). Few doctors had hope for the development of his verbal ability, and most thought the operation would paralyze part of his body. Twenty-six years later, Bruce had an IQ of 126—better than 9 out of 10 people. He swam, rode his bike, and got an A in a statistics course. Because his speech was normal, it was assumed the right side took over many of the functions formerly conducted mainly by the left side. Obviously, this does not always happen as a result of operations of this type, especially after puberty. It does suggest that although the right and left hemispheres seem to specialize in processing certain information, they are by no means limited to processing only one type.

Even when information is being processed primarily by one hemisphere, it is unlikely that the other hemisphere is totally inactive. While someone is reading a story, the right hemisphere may be playing a specialized role in understanding a metaphor or appreciating emotional content, while the left side simultaneously works harder at deriving meaning from the complex relations among word concepts and syntax. The different functions of the two brain hemispheres do not seem as clearly differentiated in women as in men, and some left-handed people are known to have hemispheric functions the opposite of those described (Andersen, Garrison, & Andersen, 1979; Iaccino, 1993).

Despite the apparent complexity demonstrated by the brain, much of what is processed by the right hemisphere seems to be what we call *nonverbal phenomena*, and much of what is processed by the left hemisphere is what we categorize as *verbal phenomena*. Obviously, some nonverbal behavior is more closely aligned with verbal behavior than others (e.g., speech-independent gestures, which we will discuss in Chapter 7), and we might expect more left-hemispheric activity in such cases.

AWARENESS AND CONTROL

Thus far, our definition has not addressed the issue of whether the nonverbal behaviors we enact are done with a great deal of awareness or not. Nonverbal behavior, like verbal behavior, is encoded with varying degrees of control and awareness (Lakin, 2006). Sometimes human beings have time to plan their responses, but a great deal of information impinges on their senses, and sometimes it is extremely important to respond rapidly. When this occurs, people are either unaware, or only dimly aware, of why they responded as they did. These responses are linked to a cognitive program that takes place immediately and automatically following the perception of a particular stimulus (Choi, Gray, & Ambady, 2005).

When we use speech-independent gestures, pose for photographs, or select our attire, a high level of awareness and control is usually present. We know what we are doing; we take time to respond, and we enact our behavior according to a conscious plan. Nervous mannerisms, pupil dilation, and mimicking the behavior of an interaction partner are examples of behavior that are often enacted outside of our awareness and control. We may even have an entire array of default verbal and nonverbal behaviors that kick in automatically when, for example, we are introduced to a stranger. We may enact a given behavior without much awareness on some occasions but may do so with a great deal of awareness at other times. For example, we may not realize our tone of voice is signaling our dislike for a person we are talking to, but we are very much aware of using our voice to communicate a sarcastic message.

Decoding nonverbal behavior also may be performed with varying degrees of awareness. Sometimes we perceive a stimulus, such as a man who looks elderly, and this automatically triggers the perception that the man is also walking slowly—whether he is or not. When people say they think a person is lying but cannot explain what behaviors led them to believe that, it may mean there is an out-of-awareness program in their brain that is associated with the deception and triggered by the perception of certain behaviors.

But responses that are out of our awareness and control need not always be that way. Feedback on the accuracy or utility of an automatic process may lead to changing the program or eliminating it. Reading this book may also make you more aware of certain behaviors you have been encoding and decoding.

PERSPECTIVE 2: CLASSIFYING NONVERBAL BEHAVIOR

Another way of defining nonverbal communication is to look at the things people study. The theory and research associated with nonverbal communication focus on three primary units: the environmental structures and conditions within which communication takes place, the physical characteristics of the communicators themselves, and the various behaviors manifested by the communicators. A detailed breakdown of these three features follows.

THE COMMUNICATION ENVIRONMENT

PHYSICAL ENVIRONMENT   Although most of the emphasis in nonverbal research is on the appearance and behavior of the people communicating, increasing attention is being given to the influence of nonhuman factors on human transactions. People change environments to help them accomplish their communicative goals; conversely, environments can affect our moods, choices of words, and actions. Thus, this category concerns those elements that impinge on the human relationship but are not directly a part of it. Environmental factors include the furniture, architectural style, interior decorating, lighting conditions, colors, temperature, additional noises or music, and so on amid which the interaction occurs. Variations in arrangements, materials, shapes, or surfaces of objects in the interacting environment can be extremely influential on the outcome of an interpersonal relationship. This category also includes what might be called *traces of action*. For instance, as you observe cigarette butts, orange peels, and wastepaper left by the person you will soon interact with, you form an impression that will eventually influence your meeting. Perceptions of time and timing make up another important part of the communicative environment. When something occurs, how frequently it occurs, and the tempos or rhythms of actions are clearly a part of the communicative world even though they are not a part of the physical environment per se.

SPATIAL ENVIRONMENT Proxemics is the study of the use and perception of social and personal space. Under this heading is a body of work called *small group ecology,* which concerns itself with how people use and respond to spatial relationships in formal and informal group settings. Such studies deal with seating and spatial arrangements as related to leadership, communication flow, and the task at hand. On an even broader level, some attention has been given to spatial relationships in crowds and densely populated situations. Personal space orientation is sometimes studied in the context of conversation distance and how it varies according to sex, status, roles, cultural orientation, and so forth. The term *territoriality* is also used frequently in the study of proxemics to denote the human tendency to stake out personal territory, or "untouchable space," much as wild animals and birds do.

THE COMMUNICATORS' PHYSICAL CHARACTERISTICS

This category covers things that remain relatively unchanged during the period of interaction. They are influential nonverbal cues that are not visibly movement bound. Included are physique or body shape, general attractiveness, height, weight, hair, skin color or tone, and so forth. Body or breath odors associated with the person are normally considered part of a person's physical appearance. Further, objects associated with the interactants also may affect their physical appearance. These are called *artifacts* and include such things as clothes, eyeglasses, hairpieces, false eyelashes, jewelry, piercings, and accessories such as attaché cases. Physical appearance also includes the various ways people choose to decorate their skin; for example, with tattoos, cosmetics, scars, brands, and paint.

BODY MOVEMENT AND POSITION

Body movement and position typically include gestures; movements of the limbs, hands, head, feet, and legs; facial expressions, such as smiles; eye behavior, including blinking, direction and length of gaze, and pupil dilation; and posture. The furrow of the brow, the slump of a shoulder, and the tilt of a head are all considered body movements and positions. Specifically, the major areas are gestures, posture, touching behavior, facial expressions, and eye behavior.

GESTURES There are many different types of gestures, and many variations of these types, but the most frequently studied are the following:

1. **Speech independent.** When viewed independently of speech, these gestures have a well-known verbal translation in their usage community, usually consisting of a word or two or a phrase. The gestures used to represent "Okay" or "Peace" (also the "V-for-Victory" sign) are examples of speech-independent gestures for large segments of U.S. culture.

2. **Speech related**. These gestures are directly tied to, or accompany, speech and often serve to illustrate what is being said verbally. These movements may accent or emphasize a word or phrase, sketch a path of thought, point to present objects, depict a spatial relationship, depict the rhythm or pacing of an event, draw a picture of a referent, depict a bodily action, or serve as commentary on the regulation and organization of the interactive process.

POSTURE   Posture is normally studied in conjunction with other nonverbal signals to determine the degree of attention or involvement, the degree of status relative to the other interactive partner, or the degree of liking for the other interactant. A forward-leaning posture, for example, has been associated with higher involvement, more liking, and lower status in studies where the interactants did not know each other very well. Posture is also a key indicator of the intensity of some emotional states; for example, the drooping posture associated with sadness or the rigid, tense posture associated with anger. The extent to which the communicators mirror each other's posture may indicate conversational involvement, which sometimes results in greater rapport between the interactants.

TOUCHING BEHAVIOR   Touching may be self-focused or other-focused. Self-focused manipulations, not usually made for purposes of communicating, may reflect a person's particular state or habit. Many are commonly called *nervous mannerisms*. Some of these actions are relics from an earlier time in life, when we first learned how to manage our emotions, develop social contacts, or perform some instructional task. Sometimes we perform these manipulations as we adapt to such learning experiences, and they stay with us when we face similar situations later in life, often as only part of the original movement. Some refer to these types of self-focused manipulation as *adaptors*. These adaptors may involve various manipulations of one's own body such as licking, picking, holding, pinching, and scratching. Object adaptors are manipulations practiced in conjunction with an object, as when a reformed cigarette smoker reaches toward his breast pocket for the nonexistent package of cigarettes. Of course, not all behaviors that reflect habitual actions or an anxious disposition can be traced to earlier adaptations, but they do represent a part of the overall pattern of bodily action.

One of the most potent forms of nonverbal communication occurs when two people touch. Touch can be virtually electric, but it also can irritate or comfort. Touch is a highly ambiguous form of behavior whose meaning often takes more from the context, the nature of the relationship, and the manner of execution than from the configuration of the touch per se. Some researchers are concerned with touching behavior as an important factor in a child's early development, and others are concerned with adult touching behavior.

FACIAL EXPRESSIONS   Most studies of the face are concerned with the configurations that display various emotional states. The six primary affects that receive the most study are anger, sadness, surprise, happiness, fear, and disgust. Facial expressions also can function as regulatory gestures, providing feedback and managing the flow of interaction. In fact, some researchers believe the primary function of the face is to communicate, not to express emotions.

EYE BEHAVIOR   Where we look, when we look, and how long we look during an interaction are the primary foci for studies of gazing. *Gaze* refers to the eye movement we make in the general direction of another's face. Mutual gaze occurs when interactants look into each other's eye area. The dilation and constriction of the pupils is of particular interest to those who study nonverbal communication, because it is sometimes an indicator of interest, attention, or involvement.

VOCAL BEHAVIOR   Vocal behavior deals with how something is said, not what is said. It deals with the range of nonverbal vocal cues surrounding common speech behavior. Generally, a distinction is made between two types of sounds:

1. The sound variations made with the vocal cords during speech that are a function of changes in pitch, duration, loudness, and silence
2. Sounds that result primarily from physiological mechanisms other than the vocal cords; for example, the pharyngeal, oral, or nasal cavities

Most of the research on vocal behavior and its effects on human interaction has focused on pitch level and variability; the duration of sounds, whether they are clipped or drawn out; pauses within the speech stream and the latency of response during turn exchanges; loudness level and variability; resonance; precise or slurred articulation; rate; rhythm; and intruding sounds during speech, such as "uh" or "um." The study of vocal signals encompasses a broad range of interests, from questions focusing on stereotypes associated with certain voices to questions about the effects of vocal behavior on comprehension and persuasion. Thus even specialized sounds such as laughing, belching, yawning, swallowing, moaning, and the like may be of interest to the extent that they may affect the outcome of interaction.

PERSPECTIVE 3: NONVERBAL COMMUNICATION IN THE TOTAL COMMUNICATION PROCESS

Even though this book emphasizes nonverbal communication, it is important not to forget the inseparable nature of verbal and nonverbal signals. Ray Birdwhistell, a pioneer in nonverbal research, reportedly said that studying only nonverbal communication is like studying noncardiac physiology. His point is well taken. It is not easy to dissect human interaction and make one diagnosis that concerns only verbal behavior and another that concerns only nonverbal behavior. The verbal dimension is so intimately woven and subtly represented in so much of what has been previously labeled *non*verbal that the term does not always adequately describe the behavior under study. Some of the most noteworthy scholars associated with nonverbal study refuse to segregate words from gestures, hence these scholars work under the broader terms of *communication* or *face-to-face interaction* (Bavelas & Chovil, 2006). Kendon (1983, pp. 17, 20) puts it this way:

> It is a common observation that, when a person speaks, muscular systems besides those of the lips, tongue, and jaws often become active. . . . Gesticulation is organized as part of the same overall unit of action by which speech is also organized. . . . Gesture and speech are available as two separate modes of representation and are coordinated

because both are being guided by the same overall aim. That aim is to produce a pattern of action that will accomplish the representation of a meaning.

Because verbal and nonverbal systems operate together as part of the larger communication process, efforts to distinguish clearly between the two have not been very successful. One common misconception, for example, assumes that nonverbal behavior is used solely to communicate emotional messages, whereas verbal behavior is for conveying ideas. Words can carry much emotion—we can talk explicitly about emotions, and we also communicate emotion between the lines in verbal nuances. Conversely, nonverbal cues are often used for purposes other than showing emotion; for example, people in conversation use eye movements to help tell each other when it is time to switch speaking turns, and people commonly use hand gestures while talking to help convey their ideas (McNeill, 2000).

We also need to recognize that the ways we attribute meaning to verbal and nonverbal behavior are not all that different either. Nonverbal actions, like verbal ones, may communicate more than one message at a time. For example, the way you nonverbally make it clear to another person that you want to keep talking may simultaneously express your need for dominance over that person and may also express your emotional state. When you grip a child's shoulder during a reprimand, you may increase comprehension and recall, but you may also elicit such a negative reaction that the child fails to obey. A smile can be a part of an emotional expression, an attitudinal message, a self-presentation, or a listener response to manage the interaction. And, like verbal behavior, the meanings attributed to nonverbal behavior may be stereotyped, idiomatic, or ambiguous. Furthermore, the same nonverbal behavior performed in different contexts may, like words, receive different attributions of meaning. For example, looking down at the floor may reflect sadness in one situation and submissiveness or lack of involvement in another. Finally, in an effort to identify the fundamental categories of meaning associated with nonverbal behavior, Mehrabian (1970, 1981) identified a threefold perspective resulting from his extensive testing:

1. **Immediacy**. Sometimes we react to things by evaluating them as positive or negative, good or bad, and so on.
2. **Status**. Sometimes we enact or perceive behaviors that indicate various aspects of status to us, such as strong or weak, superior or subordinate.
3. **Responsiveness**. This third category refers to our perceptions of activity as being slow or fast, active or passive.

In various verbal and nonverbal studies over the past three decades, dimensions similar to Mehrabian's have been reported consistently by investigators from diverse fields studying diverse phenomena. It is reasonable to conclude, therefore, that these three dimensions are basic responses to our environment and are reflected in the way we assign meaning to both verbal *and* nonverbal behavior. Most of this work, however, depends on people translating their reactions to a nonverbal act into verbal descriptors. This issue has already been addressed in our discussion of the way the brain processes different pieces of information. In general, then, like words, nonverbal signals can and do have multiple uses and meanings; like words, nonverbal signals have denotative and connotative meanings; and like words, nonverbal signals play an active role in communicating liking, power, and responsiveness. With these in mind, we can now examine some of the important ways verbal and nonverbal behaviors interrelate during human interaction. Ekman (1965) identified the following: repeating, conflicting, complementing, substituting, accenting/moderating, and regulating.

REPEATING

Nonverbal communication can simply repeat what was said verbally. For instance, if you told a person he or she had to go north to find a parking place and then pointed in the proper direction, this would be repetition.

CONFLICTING

Verbal and nonverbal signals can be at variance with one another in a variety of ways. They may communicate two contradictory messages or two messages that seem incongruous with one another (see Figure 1-1). In both instances, two messages that do not appear to be consistent with one another are perceived. It is quite common, and probably functional, to have mixed feelings about some things. As a result, incongruous verbal and nonverbal messages may be more common than we realize. But it is the more dramatic contradictions we are more likely to notice. Perhaps it is the parent who yells to his or her child in an angry voice, "Of course I love you!" Or the public speaker, who, with trembling hands and knees and beads of perspiration on the brow, claims, "I'm not nervous."

a

b

FIGURE 1-1

(a) Conflicting verbal/nonverbal signals. (b) Is this an aggressive or playful situation? What observations influenced your decision?

Why do these conflicting messages occur? In some cases it is a natural response to a situation in which communicators perceive themselves in a bind. They do not want to tell the truth, and they do not want to lie. As a result, their ambivalence and frustration produce a discrepant message (Bavelas, Black, Chovil, & Mullett, 1990). In other situations, conflicting messages occur because people do an imperfect job of lying. Suppose you have just given a terrible presentation, and you ask me how you did. I may say you did fine, but my voice, face, and body may not support my words. On still other occasions, conflicting messages may be the result of an attempt to communicate sarcasm or irony, saying one thing with words and the opposite with vocal tone and/or facial expression. The term *coy* is used to describe the display of coexisting signals that invite friendly contact with those that signal rejection and withdrawal. We live in a complex world, which makes feelings of ambivalence or mixed emotions a much more common experience than we sometimes acknowledge (Weigert, 1991).

Displays of incongruous or conflicting signals may occur in a variety of ways. Sometimes two nonverbal signals may manifest the discord (e.g., vocal with visual), but usually we are more aware of the contrasting verbal and nonverbal signals (e.g., positive voice/negative words, negative voice/positive words, positive face/ negative words, or negative face/positive words).

When confronted with conflicting messages *that matter to us*, how do we react? Leathers (1979) has identified a common three-step process:

1. The first reaction is confusion and uncertainty.
2. Next, we search for additional information that will clarify the situation.
3. If clarification is not forthcoming, we will probably react with displeasure, hostility, or even withdrawal.

It is not unusual for a person perceiving a conflicting message that is ambiguous to respond with an ambiguous message. Some believe that a constant barrage of conflicting and ambiguous messages can contribute to a psychopathology in the receiver. This may be particularly true when the communicators have a close relationship and the target of the conflicting messages has no one else he or she can turn to for discussion and possible clarification of the confusing messages. Some research finds that parents of disturbed children produce more messages with conflicting cues (Bugental, Love, Kaswan, & April, 1971). Other work suggests that the differences are not in conflicting cues but in negative messages; that is, parents with disturbed children send more negative messages (Beakel & Mehrabian, 1969). The combination of negativity, confusion, and punishment can be very harmful if it is a common style of communication directed toward children. Date rape is another situation in which testimony often centers around the extent to which the signals of rejection were unequivocal or ambiguous.

We do not wish to give the impression that all forms of discrepant messages are harmful. Our daily conversations are probably peppered with instances in which gestures and speech do not exactly match one another; for example, a speaker telling a story about someone climbing up a pipe while simultaneously gesturing as though he or she were climbing a ladder (McNeill, Cassell, & McCullough, 1994). Sometimes these discrepancies go unnoticed, and many are cognitively "resolved" without overtly discussing the mismatch. Even contradictions with more important implications for the conversants may not, in some situations, be considered harmful. Moreover, as stated earlier, discrepancy is *required* for achieving certain effects. Sarcasm, for example, occurs when the words are pleasant and the voice quality is unpleasant; and when our words are unpleasant but the tone of voice is pleasant, we are likely to communicate the message that we are only joking.

Finally, some discrepancies may be helpful in certain situations. In an experiment, teachers used mixed messages while teaching a lesson to sixth-grade pupils. When the teachers combined positive words with a negative nonverbal demeanor, pupils learned more than with any other combination (Woolfolk, 1978). Similarly, a study of doctors talking with patients found that the combination of positive words said in a negative voice tone was associated with the highest levels of patient satisfaction with the visit (Hall, Roter, & Rand, 1981). Possibly the positive verbal/negative nonverbal combination is perceived in classrooms and doctors' offices as "serious and concerned" and therefore makes a better impression.

Some research has questioned whether we trust and believe nonverbal signals more than verbal ones when we are confronted with conflicting messages (Bugental, 1974; Mehrabian, 1972; Stiff, Hale, Garlick, & Rogan, 1990; Burgoon, 1980). It is often assumed that nonverbal signals are more spontaneous, harder to fake, less likely to be manipulated, and hence more believable. It is probably more accurate to say, however, that some nonverbal behaviors are more spontaneous and harder to fake than others and that some people are more proficient than others at nonverbal deception. With two conflicting cues, both of which are nonverbal, we predictably place our reliance on the cues we consider harder to fake. One research team found that people tended to rely primarily on visual cues in visual/auditory discrepancies, but when the discrepancy was great, people tended to rely on the audio signals (DePaulo, Rosenthal, Eisenstat, Rogers, & Finkelstein, 1978).

The credibility of information in messages made up of conflicting signals is also an important factor in determining which cues to believe. If the information being communicated in one channel lacks credibility, we are likely to discount it and look to other channels for the "real" message (Bugental, 1974). Sometimes we are faced with the difficult dilemma of perceiving the meaning communicated by hard-to-fake cues that do not seem credible. If a person says, "This is really great," with a sad tone of voice upon receiving a gift you know was long desired, you are likely to search for other explanations; for example, something else may be bothering the person.

Interestingly, young children seem to give less credence to certain nonverbal cues than adults do when confronted with conflicting verbal and nonverbal messages (Bugental, Kaswan, Love, & Fox, 1970; Bugental, Love, & Gianetto, 1971; Volkmar & Siegel, 1982). Conflicting messages in which the speaker smiled while making a critical statement were interpreted more negatively by children than adults, particularly when the speaker was a woman.

Other work casts a deeper shadow on the theory that we always rely on nonverbal cues in conflicting-message situations. Shapiro (1968) found that student judges differed as to whether they relied on verbal or facial cues when asked to select the affect being communicated by incongruent sketched faces accompanied by written messages. Vande Creek and Watkins (1972) extended Shapiro's work by using real voices and moving pictures. The people in the stimulus examples portrayed inconsistencies in the degree of stress in verbal and nonverbal channels. Again, they found that some respondents tended to rely primarily on verbal cues, some tended to rely on nonverbal cues, and some responded to the degree of stress in general regardless of the channels manifesting it. The cross-cultural research of Solomon and Ali (1975) suggests that familiarity with the verbal language may affect our reliance on verbal or nonverbal cues. They found, for instance, that people who were less familiar with the language used to construct the contradictory message relied on the content for judgments of affective meaning. Those who knew the language well were more apt to rely on the vocal intonation for the affective meaning. So it appears that some people will rely more heavily on the verbal message when verbal and nonverbal cues give conflicting information.

We do not know all the conditions that affect which signals people look to for valid information. As a general rule, people tend to rely on those signals they perceive harder to fake, but this will most likely vary with the situation; so the ultimate impact of verbal, visual, and vocal signals is best determined by a close examination of the people involved and the communication context.

COMPLEMENTING

Nonverbal behavior can modify or elaborate on verbal messages. When the verbal and nonverbal channels are complementary, rather than conflicting, our messages are usually decoded more accurately. Some evidence suggests that complementary nonverbal signals also may be helpful when attempting to recall the verbal message. A student who reflects an attitude of embarrassment when talking to a professor about a poor performance in class assignments is exhibiting nonverbal behavior that complements the verbal. When clarity is of utmost importance, as in a job interview or when making up with a loved one after a fight, we should be especially concerned with making the meanings of verbal and nonverbal behavior complement one another.

SUBSTITUTING

Nonverbal behavior can also substitute for verbal messages. It may indicate more permanent characteristics (sex, age), moderately long-lasting features (personality, attitudes, social group), and relatively short-term states. In the latter case, we may see a dejected and downtrodden executive walk into his or her house after work with a facial expression that substitutes for the statement "I've had a rotten day." With a little practice, people soon learn to identify a wide range of these substitute nonverbal displays—all the way from "It's been a fantastic day!" to "Oh, God, am I miserable!"

Sometimes, when substitute nonverbal behavior does not get the desired response, the communicator tries to verbally clarify the message. Consider the woman who wants her date to stop trying to become physically intimate with her. She may stiffen, stare straight ahead, or act unresponsive and cool. If the suitor still does not stop, she might say something like "Look, Larry, please don't ruin a nice friendship."

ACCENTING AND MODERATING

Nonverbal behavior may accent (amplify) or moderate (tone down) parts of the verbal message. Accenting is much like underlining or *italicizing* written words to emphasize them. Movements of the head and hands are frequently used to accent the verbal message. When a father scolds his son for staying out too late, he may accent a particular phrase with a firm grip on the son's shoulder and an accompanying frown. In some instances, one set of nonverbal cues can accent or moderate other nonverbal cues. For example, by observing other parts of a person's body, the full intensity of a facial expression of emotion is revealed.

REGULATING

Nonverbal behavior is also used to regulate verbal behavior. We do this in two ways:

1. By coordinating our own verbal and nonverbal behavior in the production of our messages
2. By coordinating our verbal and nonverbal message behavior with those of our interaction partners

We regulate the production of our own messages in a variety of ways. Sometimes we use nonverbal signs to segment units of interaction. Posture changes may demarcate a topic change; a gesture may forecast the verbalization of a particular idea; pauses may help organize spoken information into units. When we speak of a series of things, we may communicate discreteness by linear, staccato movements of the arm and hand; for example, "We must consider A, B, and C." When we insert a chopping gesture after each letter, it may suggest a separate consideration of each letter; a single chop after C might indicate either a consideration of all three as a group, or it may indicate C in particular.

We also regulate the flow of verbal and nonverbal behavior between ourselves and an interactant. This may manifest itself in the type of behavior two interactants elicit from one another (e.g., every time one person gets mad and yells, the other behaves in a solicitous manner) or in less obvious ways (e.g., the signals of initiation, continuation, and termination of interaction). The way one person stops talking and another starts in a smooth, synchronized manner may be as important to a satisfactory interaction as the content. After all, we do make judgments about people based on their regulatory skills; for example, we are familiar with the descriptions "Talking to him is like talking to a wall" or "You can't get a word in edgewise with her." When another person frequently interrupts or is inattentive, we may feel this person is making a statement about the relationship, perhaps one of disrespect. There are rules for regulating conversations, but they are generally implicit. It is not written down, but we seem to know that two people should not talk at the same time, that each person should get an equal number of turns at talking if he or she desires, that a question should be answered, and so forth. Wiemann's (1977) research found that relatively minute changes in these regulatory behaviors—interruptions, pauses longer than three seconds, unilateral topic changes, and so on—resulted in sizable variations in how competent a communicator was perceived to be. As listeners, we are apparently attending to and evaluating a host of fleeting, subtle, and habitual features of the speaker's conversational behavior. When children first learn these rules, they use less subtle cues; for example, they tug on clothing, raise a hand, and so on. Children are also less skilled in accomplishing smooth turn taking, as you will have noticed if you have conversed with a young child on the telephone. There are probably differences in the actual behaviors used to manage conversational flow across cultures.

Conversational regulators involve several kinds of nonverbal cues. When we want to indicate that we are finished speaking and the other person can start, we may increase our eye contact with the other person. This is often accompanied by the vocal cues associated with ending declarative or interrogative statements. If the other person still does not figuratively pick up the conversational ball, we might extend silence or interject a "trailer" such as "you know" or "so, ah." To keep another person from speaking in a conversation, we have to keep long pauses from occurring, decrease eye contact, and perhaps raise the volume if the other tries to speak. When we do not want to take a speaking turn, we might give the other some reinforcing head nods, maintain attentive eye contact, and, of course, refrain from speaking when the other begins to yield. When we do want the floor, we might raise our index finger or enact an audible inspiration of breath with a straightening of the posture as if ready to take over. Rapid nodding may signal the other to hurry up and finish; but if we have trouble getting in, we may have to talk simultaneously for a few words or engage in stutter starts that we hope will be more easily observed cues to signal our desire to speak.

Conversational beginnings and endings also act as regulatory points. When we are greeting others, eye contact indicates that the channels are open. A slight head movement and an "eyebrow flash" of recognition—a barely detectable but distinct up-and-down movement of the eyebrows—may be present. The hands are also used in greetings for salutes, waves, handshakes, handslaps, or emblematic signals such as the peace or victory sign, a raised fist, or a thumbs-up. Hands may also perform grooming activities, such as running fingers through the hair, or they may be involved in various touching activities such as kissing, embracing, or hitting another on the arm. The mouth may form a smile or an oval shape, as if ready to start talking (Krivonos & Knapp, 1975).

Saying good-bye in semiformal interviews was shown in one study to elicit many nonverbal behaviors. The most common included the breaking of eye contact more often and for longer periods of time, positioning one's body toward an exit, and leaning forward and nodding. Less frequent, but very noticeable, were accenting behaviors that signaled, "This is the termination of our conversation, and I don't want you to miss it!" These accenters included explosive hand and foot movements, such as raising the hands and/or feet and bringing them down with enough force to make an audible slap while simultaneously using the hands and feet as leverage to catapult the interactant out of his or her seat. A less direct manifestation was placing hands on thighs or knees in a leveraging position, as if preparing to catapult, hoping that the other person picked up the good-bye cue (Knapp, Hart, Friedrich, & Shulman, 1975).

PERSPECTIVE 4: THE HISTORY OF NONVERBAL STUDIES

The scientific study of nonverbal communication is primarily a post-World War II activity. This does not mean we cannot find important early tributaries of knowledge; even ancient Chinese, Greek, and Roman scholars commented on what we today would consider nonverbal behavior. Quintilian's *Institutio Oratoria,* for example, is an important source of information on gesture written in the first century. If we were to trace the history of fields of study—such as animal behavior, anthropology, dance, linguistics, philosophy, psychiatry, psychology, sociology, and speech—we would no doubt find important antecedents for today's work (Asendorpf & Wallbott, 1982; Davis, 1979; DePaulo & Friedman, 1998; Hecht & Ambady, 1999). Nonverbal studies never have been the province of any one particular discipline. In the last half of the 19th century, Delsarte among others attempted to codify and set forth rules for managing both "voice culture" and body movements or gestures (Shawn, 1954). Although Delsarte's "science of applied esthetics" and the elocutionary movement gave way to a less formal, less stylized manner in the 20th century, it represents one of several early attempts to identify various forms of bodily expression. One of the most influential pre-20th-century works was Darwin's *Expression of the Emotions in Man and Animals* in 1872. This work spawned the modern study of facial expressions, and many of Darwin's observations and ideas have been validated by other researchers (Ekman, 1973).

During the first half of the 20th century, there were isolated studies of the voice, physical appearance and dress, and the face. An unsystematic look at the publications during this period suggests that studies of proxemics, the environment, and body movement received even less attention, and the least attention was given to the investigation of eye behavior and touching. Two distinct but noteworthy events occurred during this period: The first involved some controversial scholarship and a scandal; the second concerned a work of extraordinary influence in the study of nonverbal behavior.

In 1925, Kretschmer authored a book, *Physique and Character.* This was followed in 1940 by Sheldon's book *The Variations of Human Physique.* These works were based on the idea that if we precisely measure and analyze a person's body, we can learn much about his or her intelligence, temperament, moral worth, and future achievement. Sheldon's belief that certain characteristics are associated with certain body types—the thin ectomorph, the muscular mesomorph, and the fatty endomorph—is still debated (see Chapter 6). His work was featured on the cover of the popular magazine *Life* in 1951. To develop a catalogue of body types, Sheldon was permitted to photograph freshman students in the nude at Yale, Wellesley, Vassar, Princeton, Smith, Mt. Holyoke, and other colleges (Rosenbaum, 1995). The students were told it was a project involving posture, and thousands complied—including future president George H. W. Bush and future first lady Hillary Rodham Clinton. The photos have reportedly been destroyed, and Sheldon's personal notes have revealed him as drawing racial conclusions from his work. People continue to associate certain characteristics with different body types, but the validity of these perceptions was not proven by Sheldon or any researchers since.

In contrast, Efron's book *Gesture and Environment* (1941) has become a classic because it made three important contributions: Efron's innovative and detailed methods of studying gesture and body language, along with his framework for classifying nonverbal behavior, influenced future generations of scholars. In addition, Efron's work documented the important role of culture in shaping our gestures and body movement, which at the time was contrary to the belief of many—including Adolf Hitler—that people's behavior is not subject to much modification by changing contexts and environments.

The 1950s showed a significant increase in the number of research efforts that delved into nonverbal communication. Some of the milestones of the 1950s included the following:

1. Birdwhistell's *Introduction to Kinesics* appeared in 1952, and Hall's *Silent Language* in 1959. These anthropologists were responsible for taking some of the principles of linguistics and applying them to nonverbal phenomena, providing new labels for the study of body movement (kinesics) and space (proxemics), and launching a program of research in each area.
2. Trager's 1958 delineation of the components of "paralanguage" (see Chapter 11) greatly enhanced the precision with which we classify and study vocal cues.
3. Psychiatrist Jurgen Ruesch and photographer Weldon Kees combined their efforts to produce a popular book titled *Nonverbal Communication: Notes on the Visual Perception of Human Relations* in 1956. This was probably the first book to use the term *nonverbal communication* in its title. Therapists, including Freud, had been interested in nonverbal cues prior to the 1950s, but this work provided additional theoretical insights into the origins, usage, and coding of nonverbal behavior; it also provided extensive visual documentation for the communicative role of environments.
4. Also in 1956, Maslow and Mintz's study of the environmental effects of a "beautiful" room and an "ugly" room was published. This oft-cited study is a highlight in the history of environmental forces impinging on human communication.
5. Frank's comprehensive article "Tactile Communication" appeared in 1957 and suggested a number of testable hypotheses about touching in human interaction.

If the 1950s produced an increase in the number of nonverbal studies, the 1960s must be classified as a nuclear explosion of the topic. Specific areas of the body were the subject of extensive programs of research: Exline's work on eye behavior; Davitz's work on vocal expressions of emotion, which culminated in *The Communication of Emotional Meaning* in 1964; Hess's work on pupil dilation; Sommer's continued exploration of personal space and design; Goldman-Eisler's study of pauses and hesitations in spontaneous speech; and the study of a wide range of body activity by Dittmann, Argyle, Kendon, Scheflen, and Mehrabian. During this time, psychologist Robert Rosenthal and his colleagues brought vividly to our attention the potential impact of nonverbal subtleties when he showed how experimenters can affect the outcome of experiments—and teachers can affect the intellectual growth of their students—through nonverbal behavior (*Experimenter Effects in Behavioral Research*, 1966, and *Pygmalion in the Classroom*, 1968). Perhaps the classic theoretical piece of the 1960s is Ekman and Friesen's article on the origins, usage, and coding of nonverbal behavior (Ekman & Friesen, 1969;

Ekman, 1999). This article distinguished five areas of nonverbal study that served as a guide for their own research and ultimately that of many other researchers. These areas were emblems, illustrators, affect display, regulators, and adaptors.

The 1970s began with a journalist's account of the study of nonverbal communication from the perspective of a handful of researchers. Fast's *Body Language* (1970), a best seller, was followed by a steady stream of books that attempted to make nonverbal findings understandable and usable to the American public. These books, in the interest of simplification and readability, often misrepresented findings when recounting how to make a sale, detect deception, assert one's dominance, obtain a sexual partner, and so on.

Although such books aroused the public's interest in nonverbal communication, they incurred some anticipated fallout (Koivumaki, 1975). Readers were too often left with the idea that reading nonverbal cues was the key to success in any human encounter; some of these books implied that single cues (legs apart) represent single meanings (sexual invitation). Not only is it important to look at nonverbal *clusters* of behavior but also to recognize that nonverbal cues, like verbal ones, rarely have a single denotative meaning. Some of these popularized accounts do not sufficiently remind us that the meaning of a particular behavior is often understood by looking at the context in which the behavior occurs; for example, looking into someone's eyes may reflect affection in one situation and aggression in another.

Another common reaction to such books was the concern that once the nonverbal code was broken we would be totally transparent; people would know everything about us because we could not control these nonverbal signals. As noted earlier, we have varying degrees of conscious control over our nonverbal behavior. Some behavior is very much under our control; other behavior is not, but it may be once awareness is increased. Further, it may be that as soon as someone exhibits an understanding of your body language, you will modify it and make adaptations. We have been studying verbal behavior for more than 2,000 years, and we know much about the impact of certain verbal strategies; but we are still a long way from understanding the totality of verbal behavior.

The 1970s were also a time of summarizing and synthesizing. Ekman's research on the human face (*Emotion in the Human Face*, 1972, with W. V. Friesen and P. Ellsworth); Mehrabian's research on the meaning of nonverbal cues of immediacy, status, and responsiveness (*Nonverbal Communication*, 1972); Scheflen's kinesic research in the framework of general systems theory (*Body Language and Social Order*, 1972); Hess's study of pupil size (*The Tell-Tale Eye*, 1975); Argyle's study of body movement and eye behavior (*Bodily Communication*, 1975; and *Gaze and Mutual Gaze*, with M. Cook, 1976); Montagu's *Touching* (1971); and Birdwhistell's *Kinesics and Context* (1970) were all attempts to bring together the growing literature, or a particular research program, in a single volume.

During the 1980s, some scholars continued to specialize, but others focused on identifying the ways in which a variety of nonverbal signals work together to accomplish common communicative goals; for example, getting someone to do something for you, showing affection, lying to someone, and so forth (Patterson, 1983). It became clear that we could not fully understand the role of nonverbal behavior in accomplishing these goals unless we also looked at the role of co-occurring verbal behavior and tried to develop theories about how various verbal and nonverbal cues interact in the process (Bavelas & Chovil, 2006; Kendon, 1983; Streeck & Knapp, 1992). Thus we are gradually beginning to learn how to put the pieces back together after several decades of separating them to examine them microscopically. This trend is a manifestation of a larger movement to bring our research efforts more in line with the way we know human communication occurs in life's laboratory (Archer, Akert, & Costanzo, 1993; Knapp, 1984; Patterson, 1984). Therefore, nonverbal research continues to change in the following ways:

- From studying noninteractive situations to studying interactive ones
- From studying one person to studying both interactants
- From studying a single point in time to studying changes over time
- From studying single behaviors to studying multiple behaviors
- From the view that we perceive everything that occurs to acknowledging that we need to know more about how people perceive signals during interaction
- From single-meaning and single-intent perspectives to acknowledging that often multiple meanings occur and multiple goals exist
- From a measurement perspective focused almost exclusively on frequency and duration to one that also includes issues related to when and how a behavior occurs
- From attempting to control context by eliminating important and influential elements to attempting to account for such effects
- From studying only face-to-face interaction to examining the role of nonverbal messages in mediated communication with new technologies
- From an overemphasis on studying how strangers interact to one equally concerned about how intimates interact
- From studying only culture or only biology as possible explanations of behavior to examining the roles both play

Such a brief historical view inevitably leaves out many important contributions (see Knapp, 2006). The preceding discussion is simply our attempt to highlight some important developments and depict a general background for current perspectives.

PERSPECTIVE 5: NONVERBAL COMMUNICATION IN EVERYDAY LIFE

Clearly, nonverbal signals are a critical part of all our communicative endeavors. Sometimes nonverbal signals are the most important part of our message. Understanding and effectively using nonverbal behavior is crucial to our success in virtually every social encounter we experience.

First impressions often have a strong impact on any given social interaction and can affect subsequent interactions (Ambady & Skowronski, 2008). We also know that people can make some valid inferences about others based on their initial reading of the other's nonverbal cues (Hall & Andrzejewski, 2008). Thus, each interaction begins with both interactants trying to draw accurate inferences about the other and simultaneously trying to manifest the verbal and nonverbal behavior that will give them the best impression for accomplishing their communicative goals. This process continues as the interaction unfolds.

Nonverbal cues like attire, eye gaze, smiling, posture, distance, listener responses, and the like are just as important as choosing the right words—sometimes more so, as Lieutenant General David McKiernan found out. In June of 2003, the *Boston Globe* reported that he was taken off the list of possible candidates for the top leadership position of Army Chief of Staff because Pentagon officials observed "bad body language." Apparently, McKiernan was standing with his arms crossed and did not respond in positive ways during "applause lines" while listening to a speech given by Secretary of State Donald Rumsfeld in Iraq (*Austin American Statesman*, 2003). Nonverbal messages are no less important in formal job interviews or in ongoing performance on the job, whether it involves public relations, customer service, marketing, advertising, supervision, or leadership (DePaulo, 1992; Hecker & Stewart, 1988; Riggio, 2005). In one study, female job interviewees were subjected to a sexually provocative comment. When they responded with a fake smile (see Chapter 9) in an effort to get through this difficult situation, males who were likely to engage in sexual harassment perceived these smiles as flirtatious and the women as desirable. In addition to their inability to accurately decode these fake smiles, these same men rated nonsmiling women as vulnerable and confused (Woodzicka & LaFrance, 2005).

Some occupations and leadership positions require establishing or implementing policies involving nonverbal messages. Some schools and businesses have rules about hair length, facial hair, or appropriate clothing; sexual harassment cases may hinge on determining the type of touching that occurred; and some airlines, broadcasters, and others have been involved in lawsuits charging discrimination on the basis of physical appearance. The San Francisco City Council was reportedly discussing a ban on certain nonverbal expressions—smirks, raised eyebrows, or loud guffaws—in an effort to restore civility to council debates (Reuters, 2003).

In a remarkable study, the faces of chief executive officers (CEOs) of the 25 highest and 25 lowest performing U.S. companies were rated on their leadership ability and their power-related traits of dominance, maturity, and competence. When any effects due to age, affect, or attractiveness were removed, the highest ratings on leadership and power-related traits were significantly related to their company's profits (Rule & Ambady, 2008).

While the consequences of the preceding studies are unquestionably important, they are not life-threatening. But in nurse–physician interactions during a surgical procedure, effective nonverbal communication can literally make the difference between life and death. One teenager's tragic death was also the result of misreading nonverbal signals: The teen was practicing sign language with his cousin, and some of his gestures were believed by one gang to be signs of a rival gang, so they shot the boy (*Austin American Statesman*, 2000). Other potentially harmful situations involving assault and abuse have been the subject of nonverbal studies.

One study analyzed the appearance and movements of people who walked through one of the highest assault areas in New York City (Grayson & Stein, 1981). Then, prisoners who had knowledge of such matters were asked to view the films of the potential victims and indicate the likelihood of assault. In addition to finding that older people are a prime target, the researchers also found that potential victims tended to move differently. They tended to take long or short strides, not strides of medium length, and their body parts did not seem to move in synchrony; that is, they seemed less graceful and fluid in their movement. A related study, using different methods, found similar results and concluded that any cluster of nonverbal signals indicating a person has the energy to defend oneself and/or the ability to escape with ease reduces vulnerability to attack (Gunns, Johnston, & Hudson, 2002). Other studies have tried to identify nonverbal characteristics that rapists use to select their victims. Some rapists look for women who exhibit passivity, a lack of confidence, and vulnerability; others prefer the exact opposite, wishing to "put an uppity woman in her place." The conclusion seems to recommend a nonverbal demeanor that is confident yet not aggressive (Myers, Templer, & Brown, 1984).

Another study that assessed potentially aggressive acts focused on mothers who abused their children (Givens, 1978). It was noted that even while playing with their children, these mothers communicated their dislike with nonverbal behavior such as turning away, not smiling, and so on. Just as abusive and nonabusive mothers differ in their nonverbal behavior, the children of abusive parents and nonabusive parents differ in theirs (Hecht et al., 1986). Facial expressions of children in response to violence on television may also have some predictive value for identifying aggressive behavior (Ekman et al., 1972). In short, scientists are examining nonverbal signals of both potential perpetrators of violence and the potential victims of that violence (Givens, 2007).

Once a person has been charged with a crime and the trial process begins, we can see several important and influential sources of nonverbal cues (Peskin, 1980; Pryor & Buchanan, 1984). One of this text's authors received a letter from an attorney in Florida seeking information about nonverbal behavior in order to identify the possible effects of an appellate judge making a decision based on the written record of the trial without any nonverbal signals. Because of the important implications of decisions made in courtrooms and the desire to maintain impartial communication, almost every facet of the courtroom process is being analyzed (Searcy, Duck, & Blanck, 2005). Judges are cautioned to minimize possible signs of partiality in their voice and positioning. In one study, mock jurors were very much aware of judges whose nonverbal behavior suggested a lack of involvement in the proceedings and perceived this behavior negatively (Burnett & Badzinski, 2005). Other studies confirm the belief that the attitudes and nonverbal cues enacted by judges do in fact influence the outcome of a trial (Blanck & Rosenthal, 1992). In Chapter 6, several studies are reported concerning the effects of physically attractive witnesses and defendants. In some cases, attorneys and witnesses have been videotaped in pretrial practice sessions to determine whether they are conveying nonverbally any messages they want to avoid. The study of nonverbal behavior is also important to the process of jury selection. Although this attention to nonverbal signals emanating from prospective jurors may indicate a degree of sensitivity that did not previously exist, we need not worry that attorneys or social scientists will become so skilled that they can rig juries (Saks, 1976).

A list of all the situations in which nonverbal communication plays a significant role would be almost endless and would include such areas as dance, theater, music, film, and photography. The nonverbal symbolism of various ceremonies and rituals—the trappings of the marriage ceremony, Christmas decorations, religious rituals, funerals, and so on—provide stimuli which guide the responses of those involved. From this broad array of situations in which nonverbal communication plays a central role, we have selected some areas that we feel are particularly meaningful and have developed them. In Chapter 12 we examine nonverbal behavior used in communicating intimacy, dominance or status, identity, deception, and interaction management. Chapter 13 is devoted to an analysis of nonverbal signals in advertising, politics, education, culture, health care, and technology.

SUMMARY

The term *nonverbal* is commonly used to describe all human communication events that transcend spoken or written words. At the same time, we should realize that these nonverbal events and behaviors can be interpreted through verbal symbols. We also found that any classification scheme that separates things into two discrete categories—verbal/nonverbal, left/right brain, vocal/nonvocal, and so on—will not be able to account for factors that do not seem to fit either category. We might more appropriately think of behaviors as existing on a continuum with some behaviors overlapping two continua.

We encode and decode nonverbal behaviors with varying degrees of awareness and control. There are times when our responses are carefully planned, and we are very much aware of what we are doing; there are other times when our responses occur more automatically, and little conscious planning and awareness is associated with them.

The decoding of nonverbal signals is often done with the right hemisphere of the brain, but a considerable overlapping of functions between right and left hemispheres occurs—especially if one side has to compensate due to surgery or injury on the other hemisphere. The theoretical writings and research on nonverbal communication can be broken down into the following three areas:

1. The communication environment (physical and spatial)
2. The communicator's physical characteristics
3. Body movement and position (gestures, posture, touching, facial expressions, eye behavior, and vocal behavior)

Nonverbal communication should not be studied as an isolated phenomenon but as an inseparable part of the total communication process. The relationship between verbal and nonverbal behavior was illustrated in our discussion of how nonverbal behavior functions in repeating, conflicting with, substituting for, complementing, accenting or moderating, and regulating verbal communication. Nonverbal communication is important because of its role in the total communication system, the tremendous quantity of informational cues it gives in any particular situation, and its use in fundamental areas of our daily life.

This chapter also reviewed some of the historical highlights, noting the current influence of the works of Darwin, Efron, Birdwhistell, Hall, Ruesch and Kees, Mehrabian, Rosenthal, Ekman and Friesen, and others. We reviewed the important roles and shortcomings of the popular literature. The chapter concluded with an account of the prevalence and importance of nonverbal signals in selected areas of our daily life.

QUESTIONS FOR DISCUSSION

1. Identify a situation in which you believe verbal behavior was clearly more important to the outcome of an interaction than nonverbal behavior. Explain why.

2. Identify a situation in which you would give more credibility to a person's verbal behavior when verbal and nonverbal behavior convey different messages.

3. Discuss the most unusual or subtle nonverbal signal or signals you have observed in an interaction partner. What helped you assess their meaning?

4. If you could get an instant and true answer to any question about nonverbal communication, what would your question be?

BIBLIOGRAPHY

Ambady, N., & Skowronski, J. J. (2008). *First impressions*. New York: Guilford.

Andersen, P. A. (2007). *Nonverbal communication: Forms and functions* (2nd ed.). Long Grove, IL: Waveland Press.

Andersen, P. A., Garrison, J. P., & Andersen, J. F. (1979). Implications of a neurophysiological approach for the study of nonverbal communication. *Human Communication Research, 6*, 74–89.

Archer, D., Akert, R., & Costanzo, M. (1993). The accurate perception of nonverbal behavior: Questions of theory and research design. In Blanck, P. D. (Ed.), *Interpersonal expectations: Theory, research, and applications*. Cambridge, MA: Cambridge University Press.

Argyle, M. (1975). *Bodily communication*. London: Methuen.

Argyle, M., & Cook, M. (1976). *Gaze and mutual gaze*. New York: Cambridge University Press.

Asendorpf, J., & Wallbott, H. G. (1982). Contributions of the German "Expression Psychology" to nonverbal communication research. *Journal of Nonverbal Behavior, 6*, 135–147, 199–219; and *7*, 20–32.

Austin American Statesman (June 11, 2003). Next Army chief may be retired general.

Austin American Statesman (June 14, 2000). Teen shot while learning to sign.

Bavelas, J. B., Black, A., Chovil, N., & Mullett, J. (1990). *Equivocal communication*. Newbury Park, CA: Sage.

Bavelas, J. B., & Chovil, N. (2006). Nonverbal and verbal communication: Hand gestures and facial displays as part of language use in face-to-face dialogue. In V. Manusov & M. L. Patterson (Eds.), *The Sage handbook of nonverbal communication*. Mahwah, NJ: Erlbaum.

Beakel, N. G., & Mehrabian, A. (1969). Inconsistent communications and psychopathology. *Journal of Abnormal Psychology, 74*, 126–130.

Beattie, G. (2004). *Visible thought: The new psychology of body language*. New York: Routledge.

Birdwhistell, R. L. (1952). *Introduction to kinesics: An annotation system for analysis of body motion and gesture*. Washington, DC: Foreign Service Institute, U.S. Department of State/Ann Arbor, MI: University Microfilms.

Birdwhistell, R. L. (1970). *Kinesics and context*. Philadelphia: University of Pennsylvania Press.

Blanck, P. D. (Ed.). (1993). *Interpersonal expectations: Theory, research, and applications*. New York: Cambridge University Press.

Blanck, P. D., & Rosenthal, R. (1992). Nonverbal behavior in the courtroom. In R. S. Feldman (Ed.), *Applications of nonverbal behavioral theories and research*. Hillsdale, NJ: Erlbaum.

Buck, R. (1984). *The communication of emotion*. New York: Guilford.

Buck, R., & VanLear, A. (2002). Verbal and nonverbal communication: Distinguishing symbolic, spontaneous, and pseudo-spontaneous nonverbal behavior. *Journal of Communication, 52*, 522–541.

Bugental, D. E. (1974). Interpretations of naturally occurring discrepancies between words and intonation: Modes of inconsistency resolution. *Journal of Personality and Social Psychology, 30*, 125–133.

Bugental, D. E., Kaswan, J. W., Love, L. R., & Fox, M. N. (1970). Child versus adult perception of evaluative messages in verbal, vocal, and visual channels. *Developmental Psychology, 2*, 367–375.

Bugental, D. E., Love, L. R., & Gianetto, R. M. (1971). Perfidious feminine faces. *Journal of Personality and Social Psychology, 17*, 314–318.

Bugental, D. E., Love, L. R., Kaswan, J. W., & April, C. (1971). Verbal–nonverbal conflict in parental messages to normal and disturbed children. *Journal of Abnormal Psychology, 77*, 6–10.

Bull, P. (1983). *Body movement and interpersonal communication*. New York: Wiley.

Burgoon, J. K. (1980). Nonverbal communication research in the 1970s: An overview. In D. Nimmo (Ed.), *Communication yearbook 4*. New Brunswick, NJ: Transaction.

Burgoon, J. K. (2002). Nonverbal signals. In M. L. Knapp & J. A. Daly (Eds.), *Handbook of interpersonal communication* (3rd ed.). Thousand Oaks, CA: Sage.

Burgoon, J. K., Buller, D. B., & Woodall, W. G. (1996). *Nonverbal communication: The unspoken dialogue*. New York: Harper & Row.

Burnett, A., & Badzinski, D. M. (2005). Judge nonverbal communication on trial: Do mock jurors notice? *Journal of Communication, 55*, 209–224.

Cappella, J. N. (1981). Mutual influence in expressive behavior: Adult–adult and infant–adult dyadic interaction. *Psychological Bulletin, 89*, 101–132.

Cappella, J. N., & Palmer, M. T. (Eds.). (1989). *Journal of Language and Social Psychology, 8*, 3–4.

Choi, Y. S., Gray, H. M., & Ambady, N. (2005). The glimpsed world: Unintended communication and unintended perception. In R. R. Hassin, J. S. Uleman, & J. A. Bargh (Eds.), *The new unconscious*. New York: Oxford University Press.

Darwin, C. (1872). *The expression of the emotions in man and animals*. London: John Murray.

Davis, F. (1971). *Inside intuition*. New York: McGraw-Hill.

Davis, M. (1979). The state of the art: Past and present trends in body movement research. In A. Wolfgang (Ed.), *Nonverbal behavior: Applications and cultural implications*. New York: Academic Press.

Davitz, J. R. (1964). *The communication of emotional meaning*. New York: McGraw-Hill.

DePaulo, P. J. (1992). Applications of nonverbal behavior research in marketing and management. In R. S. Feldman (Ed.), *Applications of nonverbal behavioral theories and research*. Hillsdale, NJ: Erlbaum.

DePaulo, B. M., & Friedman, H. S. (1998). Nonverbal communication. In D. T. Gilbert, S. T. Fiske, & G. Lindzey (Eds.), *The handbook of social psychology* (Vol. 2, 4th ed.). New York: McGraw-Hill.

DePaulo, B. M., Rosenthal, R., Eisenstat, R., Rogers, P. L., & Finkelstein, S. (1978). Decoding discrepant nonverbal cues. *Journal of Personality and Social Psychology, 36*, 313–323.

Dittmann, A. T. (1977). The role of body movement in communication. In A. W. Siegman & S. Feldstein (Eds.), *Nonverbal behavior and communication*. Potomac, MD: Erlbaum.

Duncan, S., Jr., & Fiske, D. W. (1977). *Face-to-face interaction: Research, methods, and theory*. Hillsdale, NJ: Erlbaum.

Efron, D. (1941). *Gesture and environment*. New York: King's Crown Press (Republished as *Gesture, race and culture* in 1972). The Hague: Mouton.

Ekman, P. (1965). Communication through nonverbal behavior: A source of information about an interpersonal relationship. In S. S. Tomkins & C. E. Izard (Eds.), *Affect, cognition and personality*. New York: Springer.

Ekman, P. (Ed.). (1973). *Darwin and facial expression: A century of research in review*. New York: Academic Press.

Ekman, P. (1977). What's in a name? *Journal of Communication, 27*, 237–239.

Ekman, P. (1999). Emotional and conversational nonverbal signals. In L. S. Messing & R. Campbell (Eds.), *Gesture, speech, and sign* (pp. 45–55). New York: Oxford University Press.

Ekman, P., & Friesen, W. V. (1969). The repertoire of nonverbal behavior: Categories, origins, usage, and coding. *Semiotica, 1*, 49–98.

Ekman, P., Friesen, W. V., & Ellsworth, P. (1972). *Emotion in the human face*. Elmsford, NY: Pergamon Press.

Ekman, P., Liebert, R. M., Friesen, W. V., Harrison, R., Zlatchin, C., Malmstrom, E. J., & Baron, R. A. (Eds.). (1972). Facial expressions of emotion while watching televised violence as predictors of subsequent aggression. In G. A. Comstock, E. A. Rubinstein, & J. P. Murray (Eds.), *Television and social behavior* (Vol. 5). Washington, DC: U.S. Government Printing Office.

Fast, J. (1970). *Body language*. New York: M. Evans.

Feldman, R. S. (Ed.). (1992). *Applications of nonverbal behavioral theories and research*. Hillsdale, NJ: Erlbaum.

Feldman, R. S., & Rimé, B. (Eds.). (1991). *Fundamentals of nonverbal behavior*. New York: Cambridge University Press.

Frank, L. K. (1957). Tactile communication. *Genetic Psychology Monographs, 56,* 209–255.

Givens, D. B. (1978). Contrasting nonverbal styles in mother–child interaction: Examples from a study of child abuse. *Semiotica, 24,* 33–47.

Givens, D. B. (2007). *Crime signals: How to spot a criminal before you become a victim*. New York: St. Martin's Press.

Goffman, E. (1971). *Relations in public*. New York: Basic.

Goldman-Eisler, F. (1968). *Psycholinguistics: Experiments in spontaneous speech*. New York: Academic Press.

Grayson, B., & Stein, M. I. (1981). Attracting assault: Victims' nonverbal cues. *Journal of Communication, 31,* 68–75.

Gunns, R. E., Johnston, L., & Hudson, S. M. (2002). Victim selection and kinematics: A point-light investigation of vulnerability to attack. *Journal of Nonverbal Behavior, 26,* 129–158.

Hall, E. T. (1959). *The silent language*. Garden City, NY: Doubleday.

Hall, J. A. (1984). *Nonverbal sex differences: Communication accuracy and expressive style*. Baltimore: Johns Hopkins University Press.

Hall, J. A., & Andrzejewski, S. A. (2008). Who draws accurate first impressions? Personality correlates of sensitivity to nonverbal cues. In N. Ambady & J. J. Skowronski (Eds.), *First impressions*. New York: Guilford.

Hall, J. A., Roter, D. L., & Rand, C. S. (1981). Communication of affect between patient and physician. *Journal of Health and Social Behavior, 22,* 18–30.

Harper, R. G., Wiens, A. N., & Matarazzo, J. D. (1978). *Nonverbal communication: The state of the art*. New York: Wiley.

Harrigan, J., Rosenthal, R., & Scherer, K. (Eds.). (2008). *New handbook of methods in nonverbal behavior research*. New York: Oxford University Press.

Harrison, R. P. (1973). Nonverbal communication. In I. deSola Pool, W. Schramm, F. W. Frey,

N. Maccoby, & E. B. Parker (Eds.), *Handbook of communication*. Chicago: Rand McNally.

Harrison, R. P., & Knapp, M. L. (1972). Toward an understanding of nonverbal communication systems. *Journal of Communication, 22,* 339–352.

Hecht, M. A., & Ambady, N. (1999). Nonverbal communication and psychology: Past and future. *New Jersey Journal of Communication, 7,* 1–14.

Hecht, M., Foster, S. H., Dunn, D. J., Williams, J. K., Anderson, D. R., & Pulbratek, D. (1986). Nonverbal behavior of young abused and neglected children. *Communication Education, 35,* 134–142.

Hecker, S., & Stewart, D. W. (Eds.). (1988). *Nonverbal communication in advertising*. Lexington, MA: Lexington.

Hess, E. H. (1975). *The tell-tale eye*. New York: Van Nostrand Reinhold.

Hinde, R. A. (Ed.). (1972). *Non-verbal communication*. New York: Cambridge University Press.

Iaccino, J. F. (1993). *Left brain–right brain differences*. Hillsdale, NJ: Erlbaum.

Jones, S., & LeBaron, C. D. (Eds.). (2002). Special issue: Research on the relationship between verbal and nonverbal communication. *Journal of Communication, 52.*

Kelly, S. D., & Goldsmith, L. H. (2004). Gesture and right hemisphere involvement in evaluating lecture material. *Gesture, 4,* 25–42.

Kendon, A. (1977). *Studies in the behavior of social interaction*. Bloomington: University of Indiana Press.

Kendon, A. (1981). Introduction: Current issues in the study of "nonverbal communication." In A. Kendon (Ed.), *Nonverbal communication, interaction, and gesture*. The Hague: Mouton.

Kendon, A. (1983). Gesture and speech: How they interact. In J. M. Wiemann & R. P. Harrison (Eds.), *Nonverbal interaction*. Beverly Hills, CA: Sage.

Kendon, A. (1989). Nonverbal communication. In E. Barnouw, G. Gerbner, W. Schramm, T. L. Worth, & L. Gross (Eds.), *International encyclopedia of communications* (Vol. 3). New York: Oxford University Press.

Kendon, A., Harris, R. M., & Key, M. R. (Eds.). (1975). *Organization of behavior in face-to-face interaction*. The Hague: Mouton.

Key, M. R. (Ed.). (1980). *The relationship of verbal and nonverbal communication*. The Hague: Mouton.

Knapp, M. L. (1984). The study of nonverbal behavior vis-à-vis human communication theory. In A. Wolfgang (Ed.), *Nonverbal behavior: Perspectives, applications, and intercultural insights*. New York: Hogrefe.

Knapp, M. L. (2006). An historical overview of nonverbal research. In V. Manusov & M. L. Patterson (Eds.), *The Sage handbook of nonverbal communication*. Thousand Oaks, CA: Sage.

Knapp, M. L., Hart, R. P., Friedrich, G. W., & Shulman, G. M. (1975). The rhetoric of goodbye: Verbal and nonverbal correlates of human leave-taking. *Speech Monographs, 40,* 182–198.

Knapp, M. L., Wiemann, J. M., & Daly, J. A. (1978). Nonverbal communication: Issues and appraisal. *Human Communication Research, 4,* 271–280.

Koivumaki, J. H. (1975). Body language taught here. *Journal of Communication, 25,* 26–30.

Koneya, M. (1977). Nonverbal movements or verbal surrogates? *Journal of Communication, 27,* 235–237.

Koutlak, R. (1976, November 7). With half a brain, his IQ is 126, and doctors are dumbfounded. *Chicago Tribune,* pp. 1–6.

Kretschmer, E. (1925). *Physique and character*. New York: Harcourt Brace Jovanovich.

Krivonos, P. D., & Knapp, M. L. (1975). Initiating communication: What do you say when you say hello? *Central States Speech Journal, 26,* 115–125.

Lakin, J. L. (2006). Automatic cognitive processes and nonverbal communication. In V. Manusov & M. L. Patterson (Eds.), *The Sage handbook of nonverbal communication*. Thousand Oaks, CA: Sage.

Leathers, D. G. (1979). The impact of multichannel message inconsistency on verbal and nonverbal decoding behaviors. *Communication Monographs, 46,* 88–100.

Manusov, V. (Ed.) (2005). *The sourcebook of nonverbal measures: Going beyond words*. Mahwah, NJ: Erlbaum.

Manusov, V. & Patterson, M. L. (Eds.). (2006). *The Sage handbook of nonverbal communication*. Thousand Oaks, CA: Sage.

Marsh, P. (1988). *Eye to eye: How people interact*. Topsfield, MA: Salem House.

Maslow, A. H., & Mintz, N. L. (1956). Effects of esthetic surroundings: I. Initial effects of three esthetic conditions upon perceiving "energy" and "well-being" in faces. *Journal of Psychology, 41,* 247–254.

McNeill, D. (1992). *Hand and mind: What gestures reveal about thought*. Chicago: University of Chicago Press.

McNeill, D. (2000). (Ed.). *Language and gesture*. New York: Cambridge University Press.

McNeill, D., Cassell, J., & McCullough, K. E. (1994). Communicative effects of speech-mismatched gestures. *Research on Language and Social Interaction, 27,* 223–237.

Mehrabian, A. (1970). A semantic space for nonverbal behavior. *Journal of Consulting and Clinical Psychology, 35,* 248–257.

Mehrabian, A. (1972). Inconsistent messages and sarcasm. In A. Mehrabian (Ed.), *Nonverbal communication*. Chicago: Aldine-Atherton.

Mehrabian, A. (1972). *Nonverbal communication*. Chicago: Aldine-Atherton.

Mehrabian, A. (1981). *Silent messages* (2nd ed.). Belmont, CA: Wadsworth.

Melbin, M. (1974). Some issues in nonverbal communication. *Semiotica, 10,* 293–304.

Montagu, M. F. A. (1971). *Touching: The human significance of the skin*. New York: Columbia University Press.

Morris, D. (1977). *Manwatching: A field guide to human behavior*. New York: Abrams.

Morris, D. (1985). *Bodywatching*. New York: Crown.

Myers, M. B., Templer, D. I., & Brown, R. (1984). Coping ability of women who become victims of rape. *Journal of Consulting and Clinical Psychology, 52,* 73–78.

Patterson, M. L. (1983). *Nonverbal behavior: A functional perspective*. New York: Springer-Verlag.

Patterson, M. L. (1984). Nonverbal exchange: Past, present, and future. *Journal of Nonverbal Behavior, 8,* 350–359.

Peskin, S. H. (1980). Nonverbal communication in the courtroom. *Trial Diplomacy Journal, 3,* 8–9 (Spring); 6–7, *55* (Summer).

Pfungst, O. (1965). *Clever Hans (the horse of Mr. Von Osten): A contribution to experimental, animal and human psychology* (C. L. Rahn, Trans.). New York: Holt, Rinehart & Winston. (Original work published 1911.)

Polhemus, T. (Ed.). (1978). *The body reader: Social aspects of the human body.* New York: Pantheon.

Poyatos, F. (1980). Interactive functions and limitations of verbal and nonverbal behaviors in natural conversation. *Semiotica, 30,* 211–244.

Poyatos, F. (Ed.). (1992). *Advances in nonverbal communication.* Amsterdam: John Benjamins.

Pryor, B., & Buchanan, R. W. (1984). The effects of a defendant's demeanor on juror perceptions of credibility and guilt. *Journal of Communication, 34,* 92–99.

Quintilian, M. F. (1922/ca. 90 CE). *The institutio oratoria, book XI* (H. E. Butler, Trans.). Cambridge, MA: Harvard University Press.

Reuters. (April 9, 2003). Proposed smirking ban raises eyebrows.

Riggio, R. E. (2005). Business applications of nonverbal communication. In R. E. Riggio & R. S. Feldman (Eds.). *Applications of nonverbal communication.* Mahwah, NJ: Erlbaum.

Riggio, R. E. & Feldman, R. S. (Eds.). (2005). *Applications of nonverbal communication.* Mahwah, NJ: Erlbaum.

Rosenbaum, R. (1995, January 15). The posture photo scandal. *New York Times Magazine,* pp. 26–31, 40, 46, 55–56.

Rosenthal, R. (1966). *Experimenter effects in behavioral research.* New York: Appleton-Century-Crofts.

Rosenthal, R. (1985). Nonverbal cues in the mediation of interpersonal expectancy effects. In A. W. Siegman & S. Feldstein (Eds.), *Multichannel integration of nonverbal behavior* (pp. 105–128). Hillsdale, NJ: Erlbaum.

Rosenthal, R., & Jacobson, L. (1968). *Pygmalion in the classroom.* New York: Holt, Rinehart & Winston.

Ruesch, J., & Kees, W. (1956). *Nonverbal communication: Notes on the visual perception of human relations.* Los Angeles: University of California Press.

Rule, N. O., & Ambady, N. (2008). The face of success: Inferences from chief executive officers' appearance predict company profits. *Psychological Science, 19,* 109–111.

Saks, M. J. (1976). Social scientists can't rig juries. *Psychology Today, 9,* 48–50, 55–57.

Scheflen, A. E. (1972). *Body language and the social order.* Englewood Cliffs, NJ: Prentice-Hall.

Searcy, M., Duck, S., & Blanck, P. (2005). Communication in the courtroom and the "appearance" of justice. In R. E. Riggio & R. S. Feldman (Eds.), *Applications of nonverbal communication.* Mahwah, NJ: Erlbaum.

Sebeok, T. A., Hayes, A. S., & Bateson, M. C. (Eds.). (1964). *Approaches to semiotics.* The Hague: Mouton.

Sebeok, T. A., & Rosenthal, R. (Eds.). (1981). The Clever Hans phenomenon. *Annals of the New York Academy of Sciences, 364.*

Sebeok, T. A., & Umiker-Sebeok, J. (1980). *Speaking of apes: Critical anthology of two-way communication with man.* New York: Plenum.

Shapiro, J. G. (1968). Responsivity to facial and linguistic cues. *Journal of Communication, 18,* 11–17.

Shawn, T. (1954). *Every little movement: A book about Francois Delsarte.* Pittsfield, MA: Eagle Print & Binding Co.

Sheldon, W. H. (1940). *The varieties of human physique.* New York: Harper & Row.

Siegman, A. W., & Feldstein, S. (Eds.). (1985). *Multichannel integrations of nonverbal behavior.* Hillsdale, NJ: Erlbaum.

Siegman, A. W., & Feldstein, S. (Eds.). (1987). *Nonverbal behavior and communication* (2nd ed.). Hillsdale, NJ: Erlbaum.

Solomon, D., & Ali, F. A. (1975). Influence of verbal content and intonation on meaning attributions of first-and-second language speakers. *Journal of Social Psychology, 95,* 3–8.

Sommer, R. (1969). *Personal space.* Englewood Cliffs, NJ: Prentice-Hall.

Spiegel, J., & Machotka, P. (1974). *Messages of the body.* New York: Free Press.

Spitz, H. H. (1997). *Nonconscious movements.* Mahwah, NJ: Erlbaum.

Stiff, J. B., Hale, J. L., Garlick, R., & Rogan, R. G. (1990). Effect of cue incongruence and social normative influences on individual judgments of honesty and deceit. *Southern Communication Journal, 55,* 206–229.

Streeck, J., & Knapp, M. L. (1992). The interaction of visual and verbal features in human communication. In F. Poyatos (Ed.), *Advances in nonverbal communication.* Amsterdam: John Benjamins.

Tickle-Degnen, L., Hall, J., & Rosenthal, R. (1994). Nonverbal behavior. In V. S. Ramachandran (Ed.), *Encyclopedia of human behavior* (Vol. 3). New York: Academic Press.

Trager, G. L. (1958). Paralanguage: A first approximation. *Studies in Linguistics, 13,* 1–12.

Vande Creek, L., & Watkins, J. T. (1972). Responses to incongruent verbal and nonverbal emotional cues. *Journal of Communication, 22,* 311–316.

Volkmar, F. R., & Siegel, A. E. (1982). Responses to consistent and discrepant social communications. In R. S. Feldman (Ed.), *Development of nonverbal behavior in children.* New York: Springer-Verlag.

von Cranach, M., & Vine, I. (Eds.). (1973). *Social communication and movement.* New York: Academic Press.

Weigert, A. (1991). Ambivalence as a social reality. In A. J. Weigert (Ed.), *Mixed emotions: Certain steps toward understanding ambivalence* (pp. 33–58). Albany: SUNY Press.

Weitz, S. (Ed.). (1979). *Nonverbal communication: Readings with commentary* (2nd ed.). New York: Oxford University Press.

Wertz, M. D. (1972). *Toward a theory of nonverbal communication: A critical analysis of Albert Scheflen, Edward Hall, George Mahl and Paul Ekman.* Unpublished doctoral dissertation, University of Michigan.

Wiemann, J. M. (1977). Explication and test of a model of communicative competence. *Human Communication Research, 3,* 195–213.

Wiemann, J. M., & Harrison, R. P. (Eds.). (1983). *Nonverbal interaction.* Beverly Hills, CA: Sage.

Wiener, M., Devoe, S., Rubinow, S., & Geller, J. (1972). Nonverbal behavior and nonverbal communication. *Psychological Review, 79,* 185–214.

Wiener, M., & Mehrabian, A. (1968). *Language within language.* New York: Appleton-Century-Crofts.

Wolfgang, A. (Ed.). (1979). *Nonverbal behavior: Applications and cultural implications.* New York: Academic Press.

Woodzicka, J. A. & LaFrance, M. (2005). Working on a smile: Responding to sexual provocation in the workplace. In R. E. Riggio & R. S. Feldman (Eds.). *Applications of nonverbal communication.* Mahwah, NJ: Erlbaum.

Woolfolk, A. (1978). Student learning and performance under varying conditions of teacher verbal and nonverbal evaluative communication. *Journal of Educational Psychology, 70,* 87–94.

As we look back on a long phylogenetic history, which has determined our present day anatomical, physiological, and biochemical status, it would be simply astounding if it were found not to affect our behavior also.

—T. K. Pitcairn and I. Eibl-Eibesfeldt

THE ROOTS OF NONVERBAL BEHAVIOR

CHAPTER **2**

In 1967, when David Reimer was 8 months old, his genitals were accidentally mutilated when he was being circumcised. Subsequently, on the advice of physicians, David's parents agreed to a surgical sex change and set about raising David as a girl. Nurture, it was believed, would triumph over nature, and David would become "Brenda." Despite 12 years of social, mental, and hormonal conditioning, David never felt he was a girl. His parents gave him dolls, dressed him as a girl, and tried in every way to reinforce his identity as Brenda. But his twin brother expressed what others observed as well: "I recognized Brenda as my sister, but she never, ever acted the part … when I say there was nothing feminine about Brenda … I mean there was *nothing* feminine. She walked like a guy. Sat with her legs apart. She talked about guy things … she played with *my* toys" (Colapinto, 2000, p. 57). It was not that Brenda did not learn what others were teaching her about how to behave like a girl. Nurture played its part. But what surprised everyone involved in this real-life nature/nurture experiment was the powerful influence of genetic, or "hardwired," aspects of sexual identity.

During the 20th century, the question of whether human behavior is influenced more by nature or nurture was hotly debated. For many years the view that all human behavior was the result of learning prevailed. These "behaviorists" believed that any differences between individuals could be erased if they experienced the same environmental stimuli. In short, genetic heritage was presumed to be malleable. Today, the prevailing view seems to reject the either/or approach to the debate. Instead of trying to argue that all of our behavior is primarily guided by nature or nurture, most scientists believe it is wise to assume that there may be both a nature and a nurture component associated with any given behavior we exhibit. No doubt much of our nonverbal behavior has both innate and learned, including imitative, aspects.

Ekman and Friesen (1969), whose work in this area is detailed later, outline three primary sources of our nonverbal behavior:

1. Inherited neurological programs
2. Experience common to all members of the species (e.g., regardless of culture, the hands are used to place food in the mouth)
3. Experience that varies with culture, class, family, or individual

Biological and cultural forces overlap in many important ways. Some common biological processes can be used to communicate—for example, breathing becomes a sigh of relief, grief, or boredom; a hiccup becomes an imitation of a drunk's behavior; audible blowing through one's nose may be interpreted as a snort of scorn; coughing becomes "ahem"; and so on. Later in this chapter, we discuss studies that suggest that some aspects of facial expressions of emotion are inherited and common to members of the human species. These studies, however, do not negate the importance of our cultural learning in manifesting these expressions. The neurological program for any given facial expression can be altered or modified by learned "display rules" specific to our culture, such as men should not cry. Different stimuli may trigger a given facial expression, again depending on one's cultural training. A snake may evoke an expression of fear in one culture and bring out an expression of joy in another, perhaps to those who see it as an important food source. The society we grow up in is also largely responsible for the way we blend two or more emotional expressions, such as showing features of surprise and anger at the same time.

Studies of birds show clearly the joint impact of biology and environment on behavior. The European male robin attacks strange robins that enter his territory during the breeding season. Research using stuffed models has shown that the red breast alone triggers this attack mechanism. The female robin who shares the nest, however, also has a red breast and is not attacked. Thus this aggressive behavior, which is believed to be innate, is modified by certain conditions in the environment or by the situation that calls forth the response. As another example, some birds instinctively sing a song common to their own species without ever having heard another bird sing the song. These birds may, on hearing the songs of their particular group, develop a variation on the melody that reflects a local dialect. It has also been noted that without exposure to mature songs, the young bird's song remains rudimentary and imperfect. And even when a bird is born with its basic song, it may have to learn to whom the call should be addressed, and under what circumstances, and how to recognize signals from other birds. Many of the inherited components of human behavior can be modified similarly. It is like our human predisposition for, or capacity to learn, verbal language (Lenneberg, 1969). Although we are born with the capacity to learn language, it is not learned without cultural training. Children isolated from human contact do not develop linguistic competence. Some nonverbal signals probably depend primarily on inherited neurological programs; others probably depend primarily on environmental learning; and, of course, many behaviors are influenced by both.

Finally, the answer to the nature/nurture issue concerning nonverbal behavior varies with the behavior under consideration. As we see in Chapter 9, there may be multiple origins of facial expressions of emotion. Certain nervous mannerisms or self-touching gestures may be learned primarily as we learn to perform certain tasks and cope with various interpersonal experiences. Some behaviors may be primarily the product of imitating others. Some hand gestures, such as the thumbs-up gesture, are primarily culture specific, but certain patterns of eye gaze seem to have a strong genetic component. The stronger the learned component of nonverbal behavior, the more we would expect to find variations across cultural, class, and ethnic lines. Note, however, that a behavior that varies from group to group may still have a common biological base, after cultural teachings are stripped away. How can we *ever* know that a single behavior or pattern of behavior has a common biological base?

THE DEVELOPMENT OF NONVERBAL BEHAVIOR ACROSS EVOLUTIONARY TIME

Human beings, like other species, have evolved through a process of adaptation to changing conditions. Which nonverbal behaviors have ancient roots in human history? On what basis do social scientists conclude that a behavior or behavioral pattern includes an inherited component? It is not an easy task. Some of our current behavioral displays are only fragments of larger patterns no longer enacted in their entirety; some behaviors now embedded in rituals have little to do with their original function; and some behavior that seems to serve one function may be associated with something completely different; for example, self-grooming may be the result of confusion or frustration in achieving a goal rather than a behavior enacted for self-preservation, courtship, or cleanliness goals. And studying the fossil record is not much help in understanding the biological roots of behavior. Despite the difficulties inherent in any questions of *phylogeny*, the roots of behavior in human evolutionary history, researchers continue to make important discoveries. Real connections to human reproductive success and cross-cultural similarities have been shown for various aspects of facial attractiveness, such as symmetry, as well as the waist–hip ratio (see Chapter 6), which indicates they may have played a role in the evolution of our species (Rhodes & Zebrowitz, 2002; Floyd, 2006).

But the best evidence for inferences about whether a behavior has been inherited and is genetically transmitted to every member of the human species is derived from as many of the following five research perspectives as possible. If we can compile strong evidence in all five of these perspectives, our confidence in a phylogenetic dimension reaches the highest level.

1. Evidence from sensory deprivation—noting the manifestation of a behavior in blind and/or deaf people who could not have learned it through visual or auditory channels
2. Evidence from neonates—observing behaviors displayed within minutes or hours after birth
3. Evidence from identical twins reared in different environments—identifying the behavioral similarities of people whose gene structure is known to be virtually identical and whose learning environment is known to be very different
4. Evidence from nonhuman primates—showing an evolutionary continuity of a behavior up to and including our closest relatives, nonhuman primates
5. Evidence from multicultural studies—observing the manifestation of similar behaviors used for similar purposes in other cultures around the world, both literate and preliterate

Research from each of these perspectives makes up the remainder of this chapter. The nonverbal behavior that has received the most scrutiny in each perspective is the facial expression of emotion. But as Buck and Powers remind us, the origin of any behavioral display by an individual communicator is only part of the story. Evolution may also be responsible for "preattunements" that structure a person's *perceptions* of these behavioral displays. For example, physical attractiveness is perceived with a high degree of consistency, and certain facial expressions of emotion have been decoded accurately in a variety of cultures around the world. According to Buck and Powers (2006, p. 120) this interplay between biologically structured displays and preattunements "creates the basis for the social organization of the species."

Evidence from Sensory Deprivation

Many have observed the early appearance of nonverbal behavior in children. Perhaps the behaviors are learned quickly. To verify such a hypothesis, we need to examine children who, because of being blind and deaf at birth, could not learn such behaviors from visual or auditory cues. Eibl-Eibesfeldt (1973, 1975; Pitcairn & Eibl-Eibesfeldt, 1976) filmed several blind/deaf children between the ages of 2 and 10 and reached conclusions similar to those of others who have systematically compared the behavior of blind/deaf children with sighted/hearing children. His conclusion was that the spontaneous expressions of sadness, crying, laughing, smiling, pouting, anger, surprise, and fear are not significantly different in blind/deaf children. Smiling, crying, and laughing sequences filmed by Eibl-Eibesfeldt are shown in Figure 2-1, Figure 2-2, and Figure 2-3.

Some might argue that such expressions could be learned by blind/deaf children by touching or through a slow reinforcement program. Eibl-Eibesfeldt points out, however, that even babies born with no arms or other severe birth defects because their mothers took the drug thalidomide while they were pregnant, and children who could hardly be taught to raise a spoon to their mouths, showed similar expressions.

Galati and his colleagues (Galati, Sini, Schmidt, & Tinti, 1997; 2001; 2003) found similar results with sighted and congenitally blind children between the ages of 6 months and 5 years. Spontaneous expressions of sadness, anger, joy, fear, disgust, surprise, and interest were filmed and coded with Ekman and Friesen's Facial Action Coding System (see Chapter 9). There were few differences between the expressions of the sighted and blind children, and judges who looked at the faces were able to accurately identify the situations that triggered the expressions for both. Thus, being able to see the facial expressions of others does not seem to provide a significant advantage in being able to make basic facial displays.

In addition to facial expressions, the deaf/blind children studied by Eibl-Eibesfeldt also showed other patterns of movement exhibited by sighted children. They sought contact with others by stretching out one or both hands, wanted to be embraced and caressed when distressed, and, as the pictures in Figure 2-4 reveal, showed a remarkably familiar sequence of refusal gestures.

Eibl-Eibesfeldt also reports some interesting eye patterns of blind children. When he complimented a 10-year-old girl on her piano playing, she looked at him, coyly looked down and away, and then looked at him again. A similar

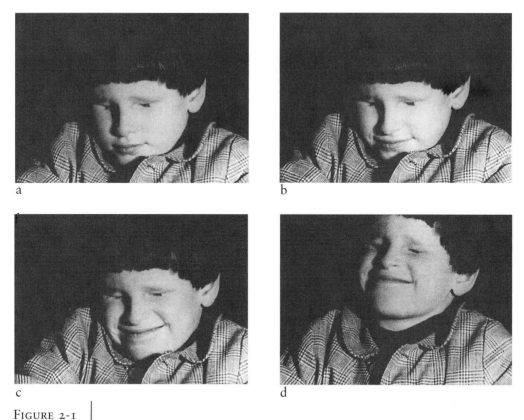

FIGURE 2-1

Eibl-Eibesfeldt's film of a blind/deaf smiling response. The head is lifted and tilted back as the intensity increases.

sequence was recorded for an 11-year-old boy when asked about his girlfriend. This sequence of turning toward and away is also seen in sighted children under similar circumstances. Magnusson (2006) observed some similarities in the way sighted and blind communicators managed conversational turn taking and displayed turn exchange and regulation, like nodding and smiling; but fewer similarities were observed with the congenitally blind than with those whose blindness was the result of an accident.

Naturally, the facial expressions of blind/deaf children and blind children are different in some ways when compared with those of sighted and hearing children. These differences are particularly evident as the children grow older and learn certain display rules by looking at the way others perform expressions. For example, subtle gradations in the onset and passing of expressions were not observed as often in the blind/deaf children; their expressions seemed to quickly appear and suddenly disappear, leaving the face blank. Display rules about the suitable intensity of expressions is another lesson blind/deaf children appear to be less familiar with; for example, how intense crying and laughing should be in various situations. Sighted children also seemed more likely than blind children to learn a display rule

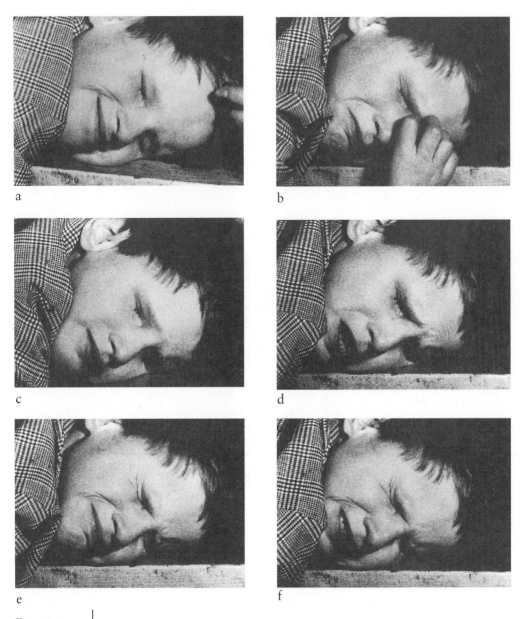

a

b

c

d

e

f

FIGURE 2-2

Blind/deaf crying response filmed by Eibl-Eibesfeldt.

for masking negative emotions (Galati, Miceli, & Sini, 2001; Galati, Sini, Schmidt, & Tinti, 2003). The general absence of facial blends among the blind/deaf suggests that this may also depend on learning. Making voluntary expressions—that is, mimicking facial expressions—is also a learned behavior, and young blind/deaf children do not perform this skill very well. But at least one study suggests that

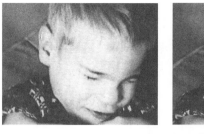
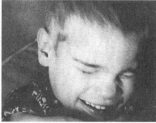
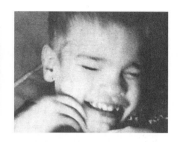

FIGURE 2-3

Laughing response of blind/deaf children filmed by Eibl-Eibesfeldt.

congenital blindness does not prevent adults from producing expressions that are as accurately decoded as those of sighted adults (Galati, Scherer, & Ricci-Bitti, 1997). All of these findings point to a joint role for innate predispositions and social learning.

EVIDENCE FROM INFANTS

Newborn babies seem to have the facial muscle actions necessary to express virtually all the basic affect displays of adults (Oster & Ekman, 1978). Do newborns show affect displays resembling those of adults, and if so, do those displays convey the same emotions? Here the evidence is mixed, partly because of intrinsic difficulties in determining what emotion a baby is experiencing.

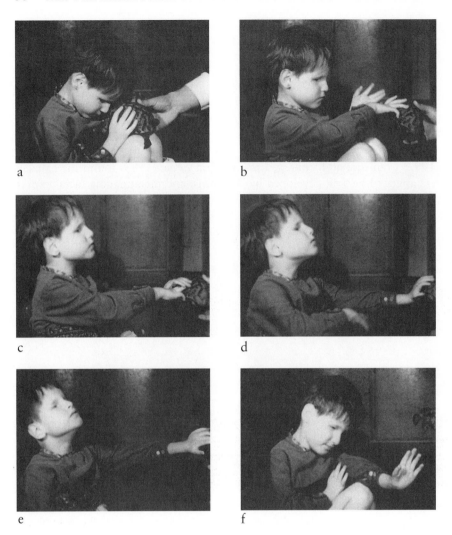

FIGURE 2-4

A blind/deaf child refusing an offer of a tortoise. The child sniffs at the object and pushes it back while simultaneously lifting her head in a movement of withdrawal. Finally, she puts out her hand in a gesture of warding off.

Researchers disagree on one important question: Does an infant's facial repertoire consist of undifferentiated expressions of arousal and distress, which are then shaped by experience, or is a baby born with a biologically based predisposition to display the full repertoire of emotional expressions identified in adults? Much research has been inspired by the latter view, which is embodied in what has become known as *differential emotions theory*, or DET (Izard, 1977; Izard & Malatesta, 1987). DET proposes a strong genetic basis for facial expressions, and thus emotions would produce the same distinctive facial patterns in both infants and adults.

Infants only a few months old do display some expressions consistent with proto-typical emotional displays in adults—specifically expressions for joy, surprise, and interest (Oster, Hegley, & Nagel, 1992). These expressions are also easily recogniz-able by untrained observers as representing those emotions. This does not mean, of course, that the infants were actually experiencing those emotions, only that the facial configurations match the adult prototypes (Camras, 1994). For the negative emotions, however, evidence indicates that discrete expressions corresponding to adults' expressions of emotions such as fear, anger, disgust, and sadness do not exist in young infants (Camras, Sullivan, & Michel, 1993; Oster, Hegley, & Nagel, 1992) even though Stenberg, Campos, and Emde (1983) found the capacity to express anger to be well-developed by 7 months; and the attending facial expres-sion was reliably detected in the absence of contextual information.

Thus, there is not complete support for the claim that infant data confirm the biological roots of discrete facial expressions of emotion. Moreover, it has been pointed out that too much emphasis on finding adults' expressions in infants might lead researchers to make several errors, including the following:

1. They may reach erroneous conclusions about what emotions are actually being felt; just because an infant and an adult show the same expression, we do not know they are feeling the same emotion.
2. They may fail to observe distinctive infant emotional expressions that do not happen to match up with adult expressions (Barrett, 1993; Oster, Hegley, & Nagel, 1992).

All researchers seem to agree, however, that infants' faces convey information about their states; that more research is needed to uncover exactly what is being conveyed and what regularities exist in the developmental unfolding of emotional expression; and that socialization still plays a crucial role.

The study of pain expression in infants and adults also yields information on the biological basis of expression and seems a less debatable topic than the expres-sion of basic emotions. It is easy to argue that the adaptive advantage of being able to engage adult care from the earliest moments of life would lead to the evolution of an innate program for displaying pain (Prkachin & Craig, 1995). Expressions of pain in infants, even in newborns, are highly similar to those observed in adults. These are the five most consistently seen facial movements:

1. A lowered brow
2. Eyes squeezed tightly shut
3. Vertical wrinkles at the side of the nose (the nasolabial furrow)
4. Open lips and mouth
5. A taut, cupped tongue (Grunau & Craig, 1990)

Adults routinely recognize these signs of pain, although evidence also indicates that observers tend to underestimate the extent of pain in both infants and adults (Prkachin & Craig, 1995).

Research on imitation highlights the complex intertwining of biology and socialization in the development of expression. The early ability to imitate others' expressions may be inherited and may ultimately play a role in the development of various facial displays. Meltzoff and Moore (1977, 1983a, 1983b) demonstrated that 12- to 21-day-old infants imitated adults who performed four actions: tongue protrusion, mouth opening, lip protrusion, and sequential finger movement (see Figure 2-5). Subsequent research replicated the findings for tongue protrusion and mouth opening for neonates 0.7 to 71 hours old. Their experiments seem to negate explanations for such behavior based on innate releasing mechanisms similar to those found in many animals and the learning processes based on caregiver behavior. Instead, they argue that infants are born with the ability to use what they call "intermodal equivalencies," which means the infant is able to use the "equivalence between the act seen and the act done as the fundamental basis for generating the behavioral match." Perception and production, then, are closely linked and mediated by a common representational system from birth.

The Meltzoff and Moore research is complemented by other studies (Field, Woodson, Greenberg, & Cohen, 1982) that examined the imitation of specific facial displays of emotion by 2-day-old infants (see Figure 2-6). These findings support those of Meltzoff and Moore and indicate that the ability to discriminate and imitate happy, sad, and surprised facial expressions is one with which children enter their social environment.

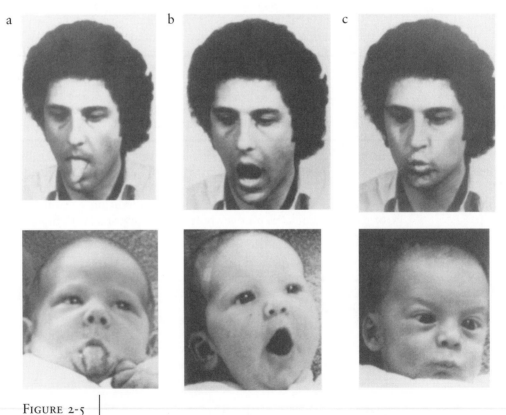

FIGURE 2-5

Sample photographs from videotape recordings of 2- to 3-week-old infants imitating (a) tongue protusion, (b) mouth opening, and (c) lip protrusion demonstrated by an adult experimenter.

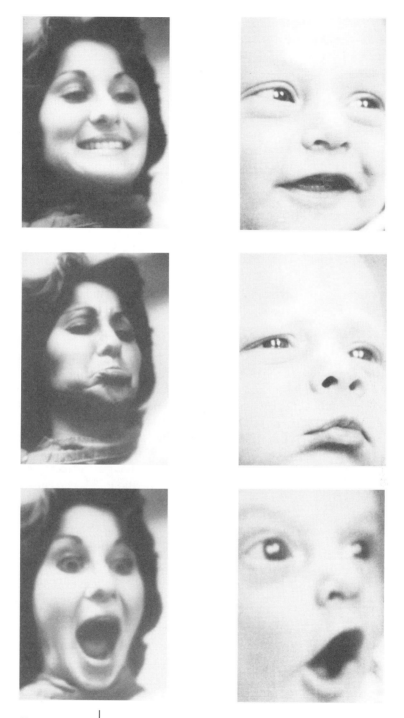

FIGURE 2-6

Sample photographs of model's happy, sad, and surprised expressions and infant's corresponding expressions.

Perhaps even more significant for understanding the early processes of learning and socialization is the finding that 9-month-old infants can imitate behavior from memory after a 24-hour delay (Meltzoff, 1985; Meltzoff, 1988a; Meltzoff & Gopnik, 1989), and 14-month-olds can accurately imitate a sequence of acts after a week's delay (Meltzoff, 1988b). The early integration of cognitive, linguistic, and communicative development is also demonstrated by the infant's ability to process visually the connection between mouth shape and sound; for example, that the "ah" sound comes from a mouth with the lips wide open and the "ee" sound comes from a mouth with corners pulled back (Kuhl & Meltzoff, 1982). In one study, 4- and 6-month-old infants were able to discriminate languages, French and English, from the facial movement they saw on silent videotapes (Weikum, Vouloumanos, Navarra, Soto-Faraco, Sebastián-Gallés, & Werker, 2007).

EVIDENCE FROM TWIN STUDIES

Monozygotic, identical twins are sometimes separated at birth and reared in very different environments. Because their genetic similarity is known, it is possible to compare and contrast their abilities and behavior to determine how much nature and nurture contribute.

Plomin (1989) provided an extensive review of the research using identical and fraternal twins as well as adopted children. This research shows a substantial hereditary influence—usually about 50 percent for identical twins—on such items as job satisfaction; religious interests, attitudes, and values; IQ; vocational interests; reading disability; mental retardation; extraversion; emotionality; sociability; alcoholism; and delinquency and criminal behavior. Extensive studies at the University of Minnesota of identical twins reared apart indicate the amount of genetic influence on a behavior can be high, but it varies with the behavior in question. General intelligence, for example, has a fairly strong genetic influence—50 to 70 percent—whereas personality traits are about 50 percent genetic, occupational interests 40 percent, and social attitudes about 34 percent (Segal, 1999). The genetic influence on behaviors can be substantial, but nongenetic factors such as family and nonfamily environment are responsible for at least half of the variance in most complex behaviors. Even though genes may account for half of the variance associated with a particular behavior, note that this is almost never a highly deterministic, single-gene influence. And just because we have a genetically based predisposition to behave in a particular way does not mean these behaviors are unalterable or that they will even be displayed.

Despite the intriguing results from a variety of behavioral areas, we have almost no systematic research that bears specifically on nonverbal behavior. In one analysis of identical twins reared apart, some statistical evidence showed striking similarities between twins in vocal pitch, tone, and talkativeness (Farber, 1981). Other mannerisms such as posture, laughter, style of walking, head turning, and wrist flicking were also observed as "more alike than any quantifiable trait the observers were able to measure." Farber goes on to say, "Possibly the most interesting observation over the years was that many sets had identical 'body languages'—that is, they unconsciously moved and gestured in the same way, even when they had not had an opportunity for mutual identification" (p. 90).

Researchers at the University of Minnesota Center for Twin and Adoption Research echo these observations (Bouchard, 1984, 1987; Segal, 1999). For example, Segal says,

> One of my favorite tasks was faithfully capturing hand gestures, head positions, foot tapping and energy level in one-hour videotaped sessions of each twin alone, followed by half-hour videotaped sessions of the twins together. Distinctive physical expressions co-occurring in identical twins reared apart suggest that genetic factors are involved. Jerry Levey and Mark Newman, identical [twin] volunteer firemen, held pinky fingers under cans of Budweiser beer long before they met. [See Figure 2-7] Other pairs were notorious for swaying side-to-side while walking, accenting long slender fingers with abundant jewelry, and belting out warm, rich laughter. (pp. 143–144)

When asked to stand against a wall for a series of photographs, identical twins in the University of Minnesota studies frequently assumed the same posture and hand positions; this happened only occasionally with fraternal twins reared apart. One pair of identical male twins reared apart had grown similar beards, had their hair cut similarly, and wore similar shirts and wire-rimmed glasses. Their photo shows them both with thumbs hooked into their pants tops. Another pair of female twins both started crying at the slightest provocation, and it was later learned that each had behaved in this manner since childhood. These unsystematic observations do not prove anything about heredity and nonverbal behavior; they only suggest intriguing avenues for research.

FIGURE 2-7

Identical twins Jerry Levey and Mark Newman were reared apart yet both became volunteer firefighters. For a photograph of how they both hold a beer can with a pinky finger underneath, see N. Segal (1999), Entwined Lives, New York: Dutton, p. 144.

Most of the studies comparing twins reared apart have emphasized responses to paper-and-pencil tests. But it seems reasonable to assume that detailed observational studies will indicate a hereditary influence associated with behavior as well. For example, studies of twins show an inherited component to the trait of extraversion (Pedersen, Plomin, McClearn, & Friberg, 1988; Viken, Rose, Kaprio, & Koskenvuo, 1994), and we know that certain nonverbal behaviors, such as faster speech, are associated with the trait of extraversion. Therefore, it is possible that these and other nonverbal cues related to extraversion are common between identical twins. Twin studies have also shown a strong hereditary basis for social anxiety (Beatty, Marshall, & Rudd, 2001; Beatty, Heisel, Hall, Levine, & LaFrance, 2002). Nonverbal behavior associated with nervousness and tension are logically linked to social anxiety, but we also know learning can play an important role in controlling such behavior. Other relationship styles such as aggressiveness, in which heredity also seems to play an important part, may eventually reveal more about the extent to which nonverbal behavior has an innate foundation. But until more twin studies are done in which nonverbal behavior is the specific focus, we have to rely on tantalizing, but incomplete, anecdotal observations and reasoned inferences.

EVIDENCE FROM NONHUMAN PRIMATES

Human beings are primates, as are apes and monkeys. If we observe our nonhuman primate relatives manifesting behaviors similar to ours in similar situations, we are more confident that such behavior has phylogenetic origins.

For Charles Darwin, evidence of similarities in expressive behavior across different species constituted important support for his theory of evolution. For Darwin, the increasing use of the face, voice, and body for emotional and communicative purposes demonstrated the process of evolutionary advancement. Darwin (1872/1998) wrote:

> With mankind some expressions, such as the bristling of the hair under the influence of extreme terror, or the uncovering of the teeth under that of furious rage, can hardly be understood, except on the belief that man once existed in a much lower and animal-like condition. The community of certain expressions in distinct, though allied species, as in the movements of the same facial muscles during laughter by man and by various monkeys, is rendered somewhat more intelligible if we believe in their descent from a common progenitor. (p. 19)

Among vertebrates, the functionality of a rich repertoire of expressive and signaling behaviors is clearly related to the complexity of a species' social organization. We need only compare the differing number of facial muscles possessed by a lizard to those of a monkey to understand why Darwin considered expression a critical link in the argument for evolution.

Before we begin emphasizing similarities, we should acknowledge some important differences in human and nonhuman primates. Human beings make little use of changes in body color, but we do have an extensive repertoire of gestures that attend our verbal language. Apes, monkeys, and chimpanzees use almost no referential gestures with each other (Pika, Liebal, Call, & Tomasello, 2005; Pika & Mitani, 2006). We also seem to have a greater variety of facial blends, and our response repertoire is not nearly as limited to immediate and direct stimuli. And although other animals are capable of complex acts, the level of complexity, control, and modification shown by the human animal may be hard to match.

Behavioral similarities are often linked to common biological and social problems that confront human and nonhuman primates; for example, mating, grooming, avoiding pain, expressing emotional states, rearing children, cooperating in groups, developing leadership hierarchies, defending, establishing contact, and maintaining relationships. Chimpanzees, like humans, form political alliances to gain power, show empathy for those in distress, do favors for others, and reconcile after a fight with a touch or embrace (de Waal, 2002). Figure 2-8 shows some of these similarities in grooming and bodily contact. Of the many behaviors that might be explored for evolutionary roots (Altmann, 1968; Thorpe, 1972; van Hooff, 1973), we focus on two: facial expressions and eye behavior during greetings.

Studies comparing the facial displays of nonhuman primates and human beings find that the "tense-mouth display" of nonhuman primates (see Figure 2-9) shows social and morphological kinship to anger on human faces. When circumstances trigger a combination of anger and fear, nonhuman primates manifest a threat display (see Figure 2-10 and Figure 2-11). In human beings, this most closely resembles a blend of anger in the mouth—an open-mouthed anger expression—and fear in the eye area (Redican, 1982).

Figure 2-12 provides both written and visual descriptions of probable evolutionary paths for facial displays of anger in three living primates. It shows evolutionary dead ends for some expressions and continuity for others. Chevalier-Skolnikoff has proposed similar phylogenetic chains for expressions of happiness, such as smiling and laughter, and sadness with and without crying (Chevalier-Skolnikoff, 1973; van Hooff, 1972).

Like human beings, nonhuman primates may accompany their emotional facial displays with complementary cues in other body regions; for example, they may display raised hair, muscle tenseness, and the like. Varying degrees of intensity, as well as blending, can also be produced by nonhuman primates (see Figure 2-11).

Extensive studies of different species of macaques also demonstrate a wide variety in the social functions served by particular facial expressions. Thus, even within these closely related monkey species, the same facial expression can be used with different overall frequencies and can have different meanings. For example, there are "remarkable species differences with respect to the exact social meaning of the silent bared-teeth display" or fear grimace (Preuschoft, 1995, p. 201) shown in Figure 2-13. This grimace usually signifies submissiveness and appeasement in species marked by rigid status hierarchies. However, in species in which status differences are weakly expressed, the expression has converged with other expressions—for example, the "play face" shown in Figure 2-14 and the "open-mouthed bared-teeth display," a more extreme version of the grimace—to signify genuinely affiliative and reciprocal social interaction, such as during greeting, grooming, embracing, or huddling, and also to reassure a lower-ranking partner. The likely relation to human smiling has long been noted by primate researchers (van Hooff, 1972). Thus, in species marked by a reduction of power asymmetry and an increased overlap of interests among interactants, there has occurred an "evolutionary emancipation of

FIGURE 2-8

Upper left: A human couple. Upper right: An approximately 4-year-old female with an older male chimpanzee. Middle left: Rhesus monkey mother with child. Middle right: Sonjo children clasping each other in fright. Lower left: Social grooming of vervet monkeys. Lower right: Social grooming among Balinese women.

FIGURE 2-9

A tense-mouth display by an adult female rhesus monkey. Ears are flattened, brows raised, gaze fixed and staring, jaws close together, and lips compressed. Teeth are not prominently exposed, although this animal is highly disposed toward attack. Angry humans display a similar configuration.

FIGURE 2-10

An adult female rhesus macaque *(Macaca mulatta)* displaying a facial threat. Notice that the teeth are not prominently exposed. Ears are flattened against the head, the brow is raised, the gaze is fixed and staring, nostrils are flared, and the upper lip is rounded over the teeth.

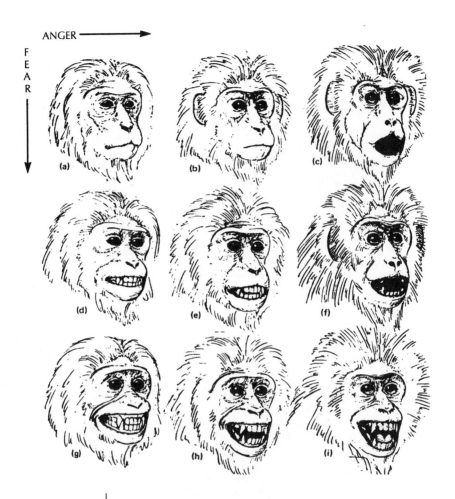

FIGURE 2-11

Facial expressions of *Macaca arctoides* according to intensity and emotion. Note that on the anger axis (top row, left to right) as the monkey becomes increasingly angry, the stare intensifies, the ears are brought forward, the hair is raised over the head and neck, the lips are tightened and contracted, and the mouth is opened. On the fear axis (left column, top to bottom) as the animal's fear increases, the gaze is averted; the ears are drawn back against the head, where they do not show; and the lips are retracted horizontally and vertically, baring the teeth.

Reading left to right, and from top to bottom, these are the expressions: (a) Neutral face. (b) "Stare"; mild, confident threat. (c) "Round-mouthed stare"; intense, confident threat. (d) Slight "grimace"; slight fear. (e) No name; a mild fear-anger blend. (f) "Open-mouthed stare"; moderately confident, intense threat. (g) Extreme "grimace"; extreme fear. (h) Mild "bared-teeth stare"; extreme fear blended with anger. (i) "Bared-teeth stare"; intense fear-anger blend.

Source: From Chevalier-Skolnikoff, 1973; p. 27. Drawn by Eric Stoelting.

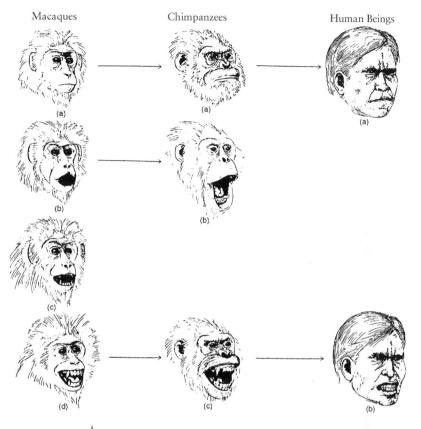

Macaques Chimpanzees Human Beings

FIGURE 2-12

A between-species analysis and probable evolutionary paths for facial expressions of anger.
(a) The closed mouth, Type I Angry Face in humans has an equivalent in both macaques and chimpanzees. In all species, the mouth is closed, eye gaze is direct, and brows are either pulled down and together or raised and lowered, as the macaques do. (b) This anger display has no equivalent in human beings. In macaques and chimpanzees, the mouth is partly opened with lips covering teeth. The macaques' mouth is rounded. Gaze is direct and accompanied by a roar or bark. (c) This anger display is found only in macaques. The common elements are direct gaze, jaws slightly to moderately open, accompanied by a roar or bark. Macaques will raise and lower their brows, and sometimes the lips will not cover the lower teeth. (d) An equivalent of this open mouth, Type II Angry Face in humans is found in all the nonhuman primates identified here. Direct gaze; lower eyelids tensed, often producing a squint; brows lowered and pulled together; jaws moderately open in a rectangular form with teeth showing are all part of the human display. Words often accompany this display, as do screams and shrieks in other species.

Source: From Chevalier-Skolnikoff, 1973; p. 27. Drawn by Eric Stoelting.

FIGURE 2-13

A grimace by an adult female rhesus macaque. Teeth receive a prominent frontal exposure in this and related compound displays.

FIGURE 2-14

A playful chimpanzee (*Pan troglodytes*) displaying the primate equivalent to the human laugh and pleasurable smile.

silent bared-teeth display from its originally fearful motivation" (Preuschoft, 1995, p. 209). Such evidence that the same expression can have a diversity of meanings and functions among macaques should caution researchers of human expressions not to leap to simplistic conclusions about what human expressions mean based on the primate evidence.

Many of our facial expressions have evolved from noncommunicative behaviors such as attacking, moving toward or away from things, self-protective movements, and movements associated with respiration and vision. Chevalier-Skolnikoff (1973, p. 30) argues, for instance, that

> threat postures of most primates contain elements derived from attack (mouth open and ready for biting) and locomotion toward (body musculature tense and ready to advance), while the submissive postures contain elements derived from protective responses (retraction of lips and ears) and locomotion away from the sender.

Thus a behavior such as flight from an enemy, which was originally critical to survival, may eventually become associated with feelings of fear and/or anger. It is possible, then, that an expression of fear and/or anger may appear even if the original behavior (fleeing) is unnecessary; for example, a monkey that feels fearful when approaching a female to copulate. The facial display has, over time, become associated with a particular feeling state and appears when that feeling state is aroused. It is likely that those animals who substituted facial expressions of threat for actual attack and fighting probably had a higher survival rate and, in turn, passed on this tendency to succeeding generations. Similarly, our dependence on signals received visually—rather than through smell, for instance—may have been especially adaptive as our ancestors moved into open areas and increased in physical size.

To this point, our focus has been on our closest living relatives: nonhuman primates. Although these studies may seem most relevant to us, it is worth noting that nonprimates also show discriminable facial displays. The open-mouth display is seen in reptiles, and the flattening of the ears in situations evoking threat or startle is seen in most mammals. Some discriminable facial displays in greeting, grooming, submission, and threat have been identified in fur seals and walruses (Miller, 1975).

We also can look at entire sequences of behavior that may have some genetic components and evolutionary origins. For instance, many factors may affect the way greetings are handled: place, time, relationship between the greeters, and so forth. With so many sources of potential variation, it is noteworthy when we find seemingly invariant patterns. Pitcairn and Eibl-Eibesfeldt (1976) observed the eye behavior of adult human beings, human infants and children, blind persons, and nonhuman primates in greeting rituals and found some remarkable similarities. In each case there was a pattern of looking at the anticipated interaction partner from a distance and looking at them during the greeting at a closer range and as interaction began; then there was a period of looking away prior to reestablishing gaze for interaction. They believe this behavior is a "stream of activity which, once started, must continue to the end" and that there is a strong possibility of a genetic or inherited program behind it.

Eibl-Eibesfeldt's studies of what he calls "basic interaction strategies" in several different cultures led him to conclude that rules related to dominance, bonding affiliation, and the fear of these are at the root of both verbal and nonverbal human behavioral displays, whether in greeting, trying to block aggression, getting the focus of attention, or persuading a partner to give you something. But he acknowledges that cultural teachings and environmental factors may play an enormous role in making these strategies seem very different from one culture to another. Still, his observations of children in various cultures led him to state,

> We can assume there exists a system of universal rules that structure social interactions, verbal and nonverbal alike. These rules could be rooted in certain panhuman dispositions that channel the acquisition of norms, and some norms may even be encoded in reference patterns given to us as phylogenetic adaptations (Eibl-Eibesfeldt, 1988, p. 114).

Although Eibl-Eibesfeldt's view may be perceived as overstated or radically deterministic, given the evidence he provides for behavioral "universality," his observations do open the door for consideration of entire chains or sequences of behavior involved in relating to our fellow human beings that may be rooted in our biological makeup. Cappella (1991), Buck and Powers (2006), and others argue convincingly that a biological foundation for certain *patterns* of interaction—responses of both interactants—in humans also exists.

Evidence from Multicultural Studies

If we can observe human beings in different environments with different cultural guidelines similarly encoding and/or decoding certain nonverbal behaviors, we develop increasing confidence that inherited components of the species may be responsible. Even though multicultural similarities may be attributable to a common human inheritance, such observations are not absolute proof of innateness. It does mean that the cause of similarities across cultures is due to something we all have in common, and it makes a genetic explanation a possible one.

Because human beings around the world share certain biological and social functions, it should not be surprising to find areas of similarity. Eibl-Eibesfeldt (1988) suggests we might find entire sequences of behavior manifesting cross-cultural similarities; for example, coyness, flirting, embarrassment, open-handed greetings, a lowered posture for communicating submission, and so on. In fact, Schiefenhövel (1997) believes his own work and that of Eibl-Eibesfeldt have "clearly proven the existence of universal facial, proxemic, and to a lesser extent, gestural behaviors" (p. 65). Although others may not share the unequivocality of Schiefenhövel's claim, he reminds us of the extensive body of research ethologists have accumulated around the globe that speaks to our common behavioral heritage. But we should not forget the role of culture, which surely will contribute significantly to differences in nonverbal behavior. The circumstances eliciting the behavior will vary, and the cultural norms and rules that govern the management of behavior will differ. Here we detail two behaviors with widespread documentation in a variety of cultures—findings that urge us to look for the possibility of phylogenetic origins: (1) the eyebrow flash and (2) facial expressions of emotion.

Eibl-Eibesfeldt (1972) has identified what he calls the "eyebrow flash." He has observed this rapid raising of the eyebrows—maintained for about one-sixth of a second before lowering—among Europeans, Balinese, Papuans, Samoans, South

FIGURE 2-15
Eyebrow flash during friendly greetings. Filmed by Eibl-Eibesfeldt.

American Indians, Bushmen, and others (see Figure 2-15). Although the eyebrow flash often can be seen in friendly greeting behavior, it has also been seen when people are giving approval or agreeing, seeking confirmation, flirting, thanking, and when beginning and/or emphasizing a statement. The common denominator seems to be a "yes" to social contact, requesting or approving such contact. Smiles and nods sometimes accompany this gesture. The Japanese, however, are reported to suppress it as an indecent behavior. However, other instances of reported eyebrow raising seem to indicate disapproval, indignation, or admonishment. These "no" eyebrow signals are often accompanied by a stare and/or head lift with lowering of the eyelids signaling a cutting off of contact. Because Eibl-Eibesfeldt observed eyebrow lifting in some Old World monkeys, he began speculating on the possible evolutionary development. He reasoned that in both the "yes" and "no" displays, a similar purpose was being served: calling attention to someone or letting someone know for sure that they were being looked at. When we display the expression of surprise, for instance, we raise our eyebrows and call attention to the object of our surprise. It may be a friendly surprise or an annoyed surprise. The evolutionary chain hypothesized by Eibl-Eibesfeldt is presented in Figure 2-16.

Perhaps the most conclusive evidence supporting the universality of facial expressions is found in the work of Ekman and his colleagues (Fridlund, Ekman, & Oster, 1987). Photos of 30 faces expressing happiness, fear, surprise, sadness, anger, and disgust/contempt were presented to people in five diverse, literate cultures. Faces were selected on the basis of meeting specific criteria for facial musculature associated with such expressions. There was generally high agreement among the respondents regarding which faces fit which emotions. Other studies have found results supporting the accuracy of decoding posed facial expressions of emotion. These studies tested people from 21 different countries ranging from Kirghizistan to Malaysia and from Ethiopia to Estonia (Ekman, 1998; Boucher & Carlson, 1980; Ekman, 1972; Izard, 1971; Niit & Valsiner, 1977; Shimoda, Argyle, & Ricci-Bitti, 1978).

Because these people were exposed to the mass media and travelers, we might argue that they learned to recognize aspects of faces in other cultures from these sources. However, Ekman and Friesen's (1971) research with the South Fore in Papua New Guinea and Heider's (1974) work with the Dani in western New Guinea show that these isolated, nonliterate peoples—who were not exposed to the mass media and travelers—decoded the posed expressions comparably to the

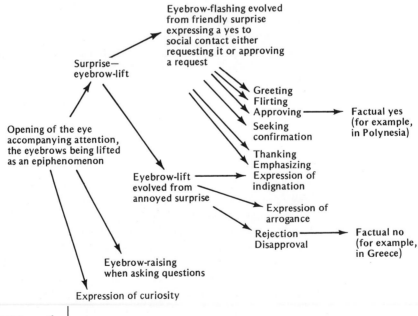

FIGURE 2-16

Eibl-Eibesfeldt's hypothesized evolution of eyebrow movements.

people from literate Eastern and Western cultures. In Ekman's work with the South Fore, stories were told to the subjects who were then asked to select one of three facial photos that reflected the emotion of the story. Distinguishing fear from surprise was the most difficult discrimination to make. Perhaps, as Ekman says, fearful events in this culture are often surprising, too. Interestingly, when Ekman obtained photos of expressions made by these New Guineans and asked Americans to judge them, the Americans accurately decoded all the expressions with high levels of accuracy, with the exception of fear, which was often judged as surprise and vice versa.

Physiological reactions associated with facial expressions have also been established. Ekman, Levenson, and Friesen (1983) found that greater heart rate acceleration and increased skin conductance occurred when people in the United States made negative facial expressions displaying fear, disgust, and anger. Levenson, Ekman, Heider, and Friesen (1992) found the same physiological reactions in the Minangkabau of Sumatra.

Although Ekman program of research is perhaps the most complete, other studies of other cu   port his findings. There does seem to be a universal association betwe   ial muscular patterns and discrete emotions. Note that this i   nt of universality and does not suggest all aspects of facia   as Ekman and Friesen (1969) testify,

[W]e believe that, while   when a particular affect is aroused are the same across cultures,   linked effects, the display rules and the behavioral consequences all ca.   y from one culture to another.

Do these cultural display rules follow a pattern too? Matsumoto (1991) believes two important dimensions of culture will help us predict the display rules for facial expressions in any given culture:

1. *Power distance*, or the extent to which a culture maintains hierarchical, status, and/or power differences among its members
2. *Individualism–collectivism*, or the degree to which a culture encourages individual needs, wishes, desires, and values versus group and collective ones

Matsumoto hypothesizes that members of power-distance cultures will display more emotions in public that preserve status differences. Cultures that stress individualism, according to this theory, will manifest greater differences in public emotional displays between ingroups and outgroups than in collective cultures.

Although the evidence points toward universal recognition of certain emotions from facial expressions (Ekman, 1994), it is important to acknowledge that recognition is nearly unanimous only for expressions of happiness, as indicated by Table 2-1 (also see Russell, 1994). The smile, surely the most salient feature of the happy expressions, may indeed have nearly universal meaning. But even here, we should note that judgment studies like Ekman's ask people to judge "pure" expressions out of context. The social and emotional context of a smile, and the exact combination of facial muscles used, can add many new and even contradictory meanings, as we will discuss in Chapter 9. The claim of universality is not, therefore, that *all* smiles will always be interpreted as happy but that the prototypical

TABLE 2-1 | CORRECT JUDGMENTS OF EMOTION IN FIVE LITERATE CULTURES

	Japan	Brazil	Chile	Argentina	United States
Happiness	87%	97%	90%	94%	97%
Fear	71	77	78	68	88
Surprise	87	82	88	93	91
Anger	63	82	76	72	69
Disgust/Contempt	82	86	85	79	82
Sadness	74	82	90	85	73
Number of Subjects	29	40	119	168	99

Source: From Ekman, 1973; p. 206.

happy expression, involving movements of certain facial muscles, will have a common meaning universally.

The possibility of great variation in the meanings attributed to facial expressions is made even clearer by the remaining emotions in Table 2-1, for which cross-cultural agreement was noticeably less than for expressions of happiness. For these emotions, possibly the biological determinants are weaker or have been more overridden by cultural factors. Russell (1994) demonstrated that recognition scores for people from non-Western cultures are significantly lower than Western subjects for expressions of fear, disgust, and anger. Russell describes the many problems with assessing universality in emotion recognition and cautions that we should not overlook the degree to which cultures do not agree.

As we see in later chapters, there is also evidence that cultures can differ widely in the overall frequency with which specific gestures or expressions are used, as well as in the meanings attributed to those cues. So even though some facial displays of emotion may have a neurologically "hard-wired" component to them, they are also modified by local norms, values, and customs. As a result, these emotional displays can be accurately recognized around the world, although some cultures show more accuracy than others; but all cultures are *most* accurate when judging expressions made by people from their own culture (Elfenbein & Ambady, 2002).

Thus, again, the debate over universality versus cultural specificity cannot be viewed as either/or any more than the nature-versus-nurture debate can be. To illustrate, two cultures might engage in different *amounts* of interpersonal touch, but the meanings *attributed* to various kinds of touches—sexual, friendly, dominant, aggressive, and so forth—may be the same in both. Thus, we would see cultural specificity in terms of usage but universality in terms of meaning. Or different cultures might use the very same hand gesture with the same frequency but may use it to convey very different messages. In this case there would be universality of usage but cultural specificity on meaning.

We have ended this chapter by introducing the idea of differences among cultures in emotional displays and recognition. In Chapter 3 we will expand on the "difference" concept to examine differences among individuals in the ability to send and understand nonverbal cues.

SUMMARY

In this chapter, we examined five different ways researchers accumulate data relevant to questions of genetic and learned behavior. If we had data from each area for a particular behavior, the evidence would be strong. Instead, we have fragments and tantalizing possibilities. The evidence that facial expressions of emotion have an inherited component is, to date, the strongest data we have on any nonverbal behavior. Facial expressions of emotion seem to manifest themselves in children deprived of sight and hearing, in infants, in nonhuman primates, and in literate and preliterate cultures around the world. A genetic component passed on to members of the human species seems probable for this behavior. The innate capacity to perceive various kinds of behaviors and imitate them also has important implications for nonverbal study. And even though little detailed and systematic evidence is available, the possibility that entire sequences of behavior may have a link to inheritance is most intriguing.

We take the point of view that neither nature nor nurture is sufficient to explain the origin of many nonverbal behaviors. In many instances, we inherit a neurological program that gives us the capacity to perform a particular act or sequence of acts; the fact that a particular behavior occurs at all may be genetically based. Our environment and cultural training, however, may be responsible for when the behavior appears, the frequency of its appearance, and the display rules accompanying it.

QUESTIONS FOR DISCUSSION

1. What do you think it means to say that nonverbal behavior is universal? State evidence supporting and not supporting such a claim. What exceptions can you think of?
2. Darwin thought there were many similarities between the nonverbal expressions of humans and those of lower animals. Discuss communication in the animal world. Do you think animals send the same messages via nonverbal behavior that we do?
3. Why, in your opinion, do infants imitate adults' facial movements? Do you think they know what different expressions mean? Why do babies have such expressive faces and voices?
4. The "eyebrow flash" is seen in cultures around the world. Reflect on your own use of this gesture. Do you use it? If so, when do you use it and with what meanings?

BIBLIOGRAPHY

Altmann, S. A. (1968). Primates. In T. A. Sebeok (Ed.), *Animal communication*. Bloomington: Indiana University Press.

Barrett, K. C. (1993). The development of nonverbal communication of emotion: A functionalist perspective. *Journal of Nonverbal Behavior, 17,* 145–169.

Beatty, M. J., Heisel, A. D., Hall, A. E., Levine, T. R., & LaFrance, B. H. (2002). What can we learn from the study of twins about genetic and environmental influences on interpersonal affiliation, aggressiveness, and social anxiety? A meta-analytic study. *Communication Monographs, 69,* 1–18.

Beatty, M. J., Marshall, L. A., & Rudd, J. E. (2001). A twins study of communicative adaptability: Heritability of individual differences. *Quarterly Journal of Speech, 87,* 366–377.

Bouchard, T. J., Jr. (1984). Twins reared apart and together: What they tell us about human diversity. In S. W. Fox (Ed.), *Individuality and determinism*. New York: Plenum.

Bouchard, T. J., Jr. (1987). Diversity, development and determinism: A report on identical twins reared apart. In M. Amelang (Ed.), *Proceedings of the meetings of the German Psychological Association—1986*, Heidelberg, Germany.

Bouchard, T. J., Jr. (1990). Sources of human psychological differences: The Minnesota Study of Twins Reared Apart. *Science, 250,* 223–228.

Boucher, J. D., & Carlson, G. E. (1980). Recognition of facial expression in three cultures. *Journal of Cross-Cultural Psychology, 11,* 263–280.

Brown, D. (1991). *Human universals.* Philadelphia: Temple University Press.

Buck, R., & Powers, S. R. (2006). The biological foundations of social organization: The dynamic emergence of social structure through nonverbal communication. In V. Manusov & M. L. Patterson (Eds.) *The Sage handbook of nonverbal communication.* Thousand Oaks, CA: Sage.

Cairns, R. B. (1976). The ontogeny and phylogeny of social interactions. In M. E. Hahn & E. C. Simmel (Eds.), *Communicative behavior and evolution.* New York: Academic Press.

Camras, L. A. (1994). Two aspects of emotional development: Expression and elicitation. In P. Ekman & R. J. Davidson (Eds.), *The nature of emotion: Fundamental questions.* New York: Oxford University Press.

Camras, L. A., Sullivan, J., & Michel, G. (1993). Do infants express discrete emotions? Adult judgments of facial, vocal, and body actions. *Journal of Nonverbal Behavior, 17,* 171–186.

Cappella, J. N. (1991). The biological origins of automated patterns of human interaction. *Communication Theory, 1,* 4–35.

Charlesworth, W. R., & Kreutzer, M. A. (1973). Facial expressions of infants and children. In P. Ekman (Ed.), *Darwin and facial expression.* New York: Academic Press.

Chevalier-Skolnikoff, S. (1973). Facial expression of emotion in nonhuman primates. In P. Ekman (Ed.), *Darwin and facial expression.* New York: Academic Press.

Colapinto, J. (2000). *As nature made him: The boy who was raised as a girl.* New York: HarperCollins.

Darwin, C. (1998). *The expression of emotion in man and animals* (3rd ed.). New York: Oxford University Press. (Original work published in 1872.)

de Waal, F. B. M. (1999). The end of nature versus nurture. *Scientific American, 281,* 94–99.

de Waal, F. B. M. (2002). Evolutionary psychology: The wheat and the chaff. *Current Directions in Psychological Science, 11,* 187–191.

Eibl-Eibesfeldt, I. (1972). Similarities and differences between cultures in expressive movements. In R. Hinde (Ed.), *Non-verbal communication.* Cambridge, MA: Cambridge University Press.

Eibl-Eibesfeldt, I. (1973). The expressive behavior of the deaf-and-blind born. In M. von Cranach & I. Vine (Eds.), *Social communication and movement.* New York: Academic Press.

Eibl-Eibesfeldt, I. (1975). *Ethology: The biology of behavior* (2nd ed.). New York: Holt, Rinehart & Winston.

Eibl-Eibesfeldt, I. (1988). Social interactions in an ethological, cross-cultural perspective. In F. Poyatos (Ed.), *Cross-cultural perspectives in nonverbal communication.* Toronto: Hogrefe.

Ekman, P. (1972). Universals and cultural differences in facial expressions of emotion. In J. Cole (Ed.), *Nebraska symposium on motivation* (Vol. 19). Lincoln: University of Nebraska Press.

Ekman, P. (1973). Cross-cultural studies of facial expression. In P. Ekman (Ed.), *Darwin and facial expression.* New York: Academic Press.

Ekman, P. (1994). Strong evidence for universals in facial expressions: A reply to Russell's mistaken critique. *Psychological Bulletin, 115,* 268–287.

Ekman, P. (1998). Afterword. Universality of emotional expression? A personal history of the dispute. In C. Darwin, *The expression of emotion in man and animals* (3rd ed.) (pp. 363–393). New York: Oxford University Press.

Ekman, P., & Friesen, W. V. (1969). The repertoire of nonverbal behavior: Categories, origins, usage, and coding. *Semiotica, 1,* 49–98.

Ekman, P., & Friesen, W. V. (1971). Constants across cultures in the face and emotion. *Journal of Personality and Social Psychology, 17,* 124–129.

Ekman, P., Levenson, R. W., & Friesen, W. V. (1983). Autonomic nervous system activity distinguishes between emotions. *Science, 221,* 1208–1210.

Elfenbein, H. A. & Ambady, N. (2002). On the universality and cultural specificity of emotion recognition: A meta-analysis. *Psychological Bulletin, 128,* 203–235.

Farber, S. L. (1981). *Identical twins reared apart: A reanalysis*. New York: Basic.

Field, T. (1982). Individual differences in the expressivity of neonates and young infants. In R. S. Feldman (Ed.). *Development of nonverbal behavior in children*. New York: Springer-Verlag.

Field, T. M., Woodson, R., Greenberg, R., & Cohen, D. (1982). Discrimination and imitation of facial expressions of neonates. *Science, 218,* 179–181.

Floyd, K. (2006). An evolutionary approach to understanding nonverbal communication. In V. Manusov & M. L. Patterson (Eds.) *The Sage handbook of nonverbal communication*. Thousand Oaks, CA: Sage.

Fridlund, A. J., Ekman, P., & Oster, H. (1987). Facial expressions of emotion: Review of literature, 1970–1983. In A. W. Siegman & S. Feldstein (Eds.), *Nonverbal behavior and communication* (2nd ed.). Hillsdale, NJ: Erlbaum.

Galati, D., Miceli, R., & Sini, B. (2001). Judging and coding facial expression of emotions in congenitally blind children. *International Journal of Behavioral Development, 25,* 268–278.

Galati, D., Scherer, K. R., & Ricci-Bitti, P. E. (1997). Voluntary facial expression of emotion: Comparing congenitally blind with normally sighted encoders. *Journal of Personality and Social Psychology, 73,* 1363–1379.

Galati, D., Sini, B., Schmidt, S., & Tinti, C. (2003). Spontaneous facial expressions in congenitally blind and sighted children aged 8–11. *Journal of Visual Impairment & Blindness, 97,* 418–428.

Ghazanfar, A. A., & Logothetis, N. K. (2003). Neuroperception: Facial expressions linked to monkey calls. *Nature, 423,* 937–938.

Grunau, R. V. E., & Craig, K. D. (1990). Facial activity as a measure of neonatal pain perception. In D. C. Tyler & E. J. Krane (Eds.), *Advances in pain research and therapy. Proceedings of the First International Symposium on Pediatric Pain*. New York: Raven.

Hahn, M. E., & Simmel, E. C. (Eds.). (1976). *Communicative behavior and evolution*. New York: Academic Press.

Heider, K. (1974). *Affect display rules in the Dani*. Paper presented at the annual meeting of the American Anthropological Association, New Orleans.

Hinde, R. A. (Ed.). (1972). *Non-verbal communication*. Cambridge, MA: Cambridge University Press.

Hinde, R. A. (1974). *Biological bases of human social behavior*. New York: McGraw-Hill.

Izard, C. E. (1971). *The face of emotion*. New York: Appleton-Century-Crofts.

Izard, C. E. (1977). *Human emotions*. New York: Plenum.

Izard, C. E., & Malatesta, C. (1987). Perspectives on emotional development I: Differential emotions theory of early emotional development. In J. Osofsky (Ed.), *Handbook of infant development*. New York: Wiley.

Kuhl, P. K., & Meltzoff, A. N. (1982). The bimodal perception of speech in infancy. *Science, 218,* 1138–1141.

Lenneberg, E. (1969). *Biological foundations of language*. New York: Wiley.

Levenson, R. W., Ekman, P., Heider, K. & Friesen, W. V. (1992). Emotion and autonomic nervous system activity in the Minangkabau of West Sumatra. *Journal of Personality and Social Psychology, 62,* 972–988.

Magnusson, A.-K. (2006). Nonverbal conversation-regulating signals of the blind adult. *Communication Studies, 57,* 421–433.

Matsumoto, D. (1991). Cultural influences on facial expressions of emotion. *Southern Communication Journal, 56,* 128–137.

Meltzoff, A. N. (1985). Immediate and deferred imitation in fourteen- and twenty-four-month-old infants. *Child Development, 56,* 62–72.

Meltzoff, A. N. (1988a). Infant imitation and memory: Nine-month-olds in immediate and deferred tests. *Child Development, 59,* 217–225.

Meltzoff, A. N. (1988b). Infant imitation after a 1-week delay: Long-term memory for novel acts and multiple stimuli. *Developmental Psychology, 24,* 470–476.

Meltzoff, A. N., & Gopnik, A. (1989). On linking nonverbal imitation, representation, and language learning in the first two years of life. In G. E. Speidel & K. E. Nelson (Eds.), *The many faces of imitation in language learning*. New York: Springer-Verlag.

Meltzoff, A. N., & Moore, M. K. (1977). Imitation of facial and manual gestures by human neonates. *Science, 198,* 75–78.

Meltzoff, A. N., & Moore, M. K. (1983a). Newborn infants imitate adult facial gestures. *Child Development, 54,* 702–709.

Meltzoff, A. N., & Moore, M. K. (1983b). The origins of imitation in infancy: Paradigm, phenomena, and theories. In L. P. Lipsitt (Ed.), *Advances in infancy research* (Vol. 2). Norwood, NJ: Ablex.

Meltzoff, A. N., & Moore, M. K. (1989). Imitation in newborn infants: Exploring the range of gestures imitated and the underlying mechanisms. *Developmental Psychology, 25,* 954–962.

Miller, E. H. A. (1975). A comparative study of facial expressions of two species of pinnepeds. *Behavior, 53,* 268–284.

Niit, T., & Valsiner, J. (1977). Recognition of facial expressions: An experimental investigation of Ekman's model. *Tartu Riikliku Ulikooli Toimetised: Trudy po Psikhologii, 429,* 85–107.

Oster, H. & Ekman, P. (1978). Facial behavior in child development. *Minnesota Symposium on Child Psychology, 11,* 231–276.

Oster, H., Hegley, D., & Nagel, L. (1992). Adult judgments and fine-grained analysis of infant facial expressions: Testing the validity of a priori coding formulas. *Developmental Psychology, 28,* 1115–1131.

Pedersen, N. L., Plomin, R., McClearn, G. E., & Friberg, L. (1988). Neuroticism, extraversion, and related traits in adult twins reared apart and reared together. *Journal of Personality and Social Psychology, 55,* 950–957.

Philippot, P., Feldman, R. S., & Coats, E. J. (1999). *The social context of nonverbal behavior.* New York: Cambridge University Press.

Pika, S., Liebal, K., Call, J., & Tomasello, M. (2005). The gestural communication of apes. *Gesture, 5,* 41–56.

Pika, S., & Mitani, J. (2006). Referential-gestural communication in wild chimpanzees (Pan troglodytes). *Current Biology, 16,* R191–192.

Pitcairn, T. K., & Eibl-Eibesfeldt, I. (1976). Concerning the evolution of nonverbal communication in man. In M. E. Hahn & E. C. Simmel (Eds.), *Communicative behavior and evolution.* New York: Academic Press.

Plomin, R. (1989). Environment and genes: Determinants of behavior. *American Psychologist, 44,* 105–111.

Preuschoft, S. (1995). *'Laughter' and 'smiling' in macaques: An evolutionary perspective.* Utrecht, Netherlands: University of Utrecht.

Prkachin, K. M., & Craig, K. D. (1995). Expressing pain: The communication and interpretation of facial pain signals. *Journal of Nonverbal Behavior, 19,* 191–205.

Redican, W. K. (1982). An evolutionary perspective on human facial displays. In P. Ekman (Ed.), *Emotion in the human face* (2nd ed.). Cambridge, MA: Cambridge University Press.

Rhodes, G., & Zebrowitz, L. A. (Eds.). (2002). *Facial attractiveness.* Westport, CT: Ablex.

Russell, J. A. (1994). Is there universal recognition of emotion from facial expression? A review of the cross-cultural studies. *Psychological Bulletin, 115,* 102–141.

Scherer, K. R., & Wallbott, H. G. (1994). Evidence for universality and cultural variation of differential emotion response patterning. *Journal of Personality and Social Psychology, 66,* 329–340.

Schiefenhövel, W. (1997). Universals in interpersonal interactions. In U. Segerstråle & P. Molnár (Eds.), *Nonverbal communication: Where nature meets culture.* Mahwah, NJ: Erlbaum.

Segal, N. L. (1999). *Entwined lives: Twins and what they tell us about human behavior.* New York: Dutton.

Segerstråle, U., & Molnár, P. (1997). *Nonverbal communication: Where nature meets culture.* Mahwah, NJ: Erlbaum.

Shimoda, K., Argyle, M., & Ricci-Bitti, P. (1978). The intercultural recognition of expressions by three national racial groups: English, Italian, and Japanese. *European Journal of Social Psychology, 8,* 169–179.

Smith, W. J. (1969). Displays and messages in intraspecific communication. *Semiotica, 1,* 357–369.

Spitz, R., & Wolf, K. (1946). The smiling response: A contribution to the ontogenesis of social relations. *Genetic Psychology Monographs, 34*, 57–125.

Stenberg, C. R., Campos, J. J., & Emde, R. N. (1983). The facial expression of anger in seven-month-old infants. *Child Development, 54*, 178–184.

Thorpe, W. H. (1972). The comparison of vocal communication in animals and man. In R. Hinde (Ed.), *Non-verbal communication.* Cambridge, MA: Cambridge University Press.

van Hooff, J. A. R. A. M. (1972). A comparative approach to the phylogeny of laughter and smiling. In R. Hinde (Ed.), *Non-verbal communication.* Cambridge, MA: Cambridge University Press.

van Hooff, J. A. R. A. M. (1973). A structural analysis of the social behaviour of a semi-captive group of chimpanzees. In M. von Cranach & I. Vine (Eds.), *Social communication and movement.* New York: Academic Press.

Viken, R. J., Rose, R. J., Kaprio, J., & Koskenvuo, M. (1994). A developmental genetic analysis of adult personality: Extraversion and neuroticism from 18 to 59 years of age. *Journal of Personality and Social Psychology, 66*, 722–730.

von Cranach, M., & Vine, I. (Eds.). (1978). *Social communication and movement.* New York: Academic Press.

Weikum, W. M., Vouloumanos, A., Navarra, J., Soto-Faraco, S., Sebastián-Gallés, N., & Werker, J. F. (2007). Visual language discrimination in infancy. *Science, 316*, 1159.

The study of nonverbal communication as an interpersonal skill represents a significant shift in the investigation of human social behavior.

—H. S. Friedman

CHAPTER 3

THE ABILITY TO RECEIVE AND SEND NONVERBAL SIGNALS

As you look around, you will readily note that some people seem more socially wise than others. Some people can "get along with anybody"; some we call savvy, tactful, shrewd, or poised. In contrast, some people seem insensitive, awkward, obtuse, or just tuned out. All of these qualities fit into the concept of *social competence*. Social competence is not easy to define, but it has long interested researchers, and *social intelligence* is considered a basic intellectual capacity distinct from other cognitive abilities (Rosenthal, Hall, DiMatteo, Rogers, & Archer, 1979; Sternberg, 1984). *Emotional intelligence* is a related concept involving the ability to judge emotional messages, to regulate our own emotions, and to use emotions wisely to guide thought and action (Matthews, Zeidner, & Roberts, 2002; Salovey & Mayer, 1989).

We definitely know that skill in nonverbal communication is part of social competence. Some people are comparatively more alert to nonverbal cues and better able to identify what these cues mean; some people are also more proficient at expressing their feelings and attitudes nonverbally. Some people try, using nonverbal as well as verbal cues, to project an image of themselves—for example, they want to be seen as cool, reckless, intellectual, sincere, or competent—but they just cannot pull it off convincingly; their performances seem fake or flawed. Others do an excellent job of projecting exactly the image they desire. The social competence that comprises such skill is essential in our daily life, both personal and professional. If we accept the premise that skill in nonverbal communication is important, and that some people are more effective at such communication than others, we may legitimately ask how they became effective, and whether these abilities can be developed in other people.

In this chapter, we focus on the receiving and sending of nonverbal messages, using the terms *skill*, *ability*, and *accuracy* more or less interchangeably. Although nonverbal communication skills are often talked about with reference to judging and expressing emotions, people actually judge and express many other kinds of nonverbal messages, states, and traits as well. We make such inferences and expressions so often in daily life that we are barely aware of doing it.

A person needs to notice characteristics of others in order to interpret them correctly. These can include aspects of physical appearance, including clothing, hairstyle and the like, as well as nonverbal behaviors. Sometimes the noticing by itself is the important thing, independent of whatever interpretations might be made (Hall, Murphy, & Schmid Mast, 2006; Horgan, Schmid Mast, Hall, & Carter, 2004). For example, we might notice and remember that our friend likes dangly earrings, that she often wears blue, or that she might be a bit too plump for the sweater you are thinking of buying her. Sometimes we notice something and make an interpretation right away ("She is jumping up and down at the news —she must be really excited!" or "Whoops, that ring tells me he's married"). Other times, we may notice something but not grasp its meaning until later, as in "Oh, you didn't get your promotion. No wonder you were so quiet at dinner."

Social communication skill does not rest only on nonverbal cues, however. People also need to grasp verbal meanings—literal, metaphoric, and shades of innuendo—and to integrate verbal and nonverbal cues; sarcasm and joking, for example, are expressed through combinations of verbal and nonverbal cues. People also need to understand social contexts and roles: what is and is not expected in a given social situation, how people in particular roles—for example, professors and students—are expected to behave, and what consequences might ensue from violating others' expectations (Bernieri, 2001). The ability to connect a name with a face is yet another skill required in daily life, as is the ability to know whether you have heard a certain voice (see Chapter 11) or seen a certain face before (Leeland, 2008).

The notion of nonverbal skill can be used to gain new insight into other long-established concepts. Empathy, rapport, intuition, and charisma, as well as processes such as social comparison and impression formation, can all be construed in terms of accurate sending or receiving of nonverbal cues among people (Friedman, 1979; Rosenthal, 1979). Kurt Danziger (1976) has argued that social interaction is impossible without a subtle and unspoken—in other words, nonverbal—negotiation of the respective roles to be played by the participants. Usually one person lays claim to a particular role or definition of the relationship, and the other has to go along or else counter with a different role definition. Until the two people tacitly agree on a common understanding, they cannot successfully interact, because they cannot effectively enact the roles of friend–friend, teacher–student, salesperson–customer, doctor–patient, interrogator–suspect, or mother–child. People generally know how to play these roles very well, and they do so without having to think about it consciously; furthermore, people are sensitive to whether roles are being enacted appropriately by others. This subtle negotiation over roles usually goes unnoticed until one person acts "out of role" or inappropriately to the other's unspoken expectations. Then people are likely to become aware that the interaction has become problematic, although they still may not know why. Clearly, the ability to read and send the subtle cues required for role negotiation, and to know when roles are being fulfilled appropriately, is an important social skill.

Although much research has been done on nonverbal abilities, many questions remain unanswered. These include the origins of nonverbal abilities; the role that motivation, and trying hard, plays in accurate judgment and expression; whether skill in receiving and sending are part of one larger skill or are separate skills; and, within the receiving and sending modalities, whether there are many distinct subskills—such as skill in judging emotion, skill in judging personality, skill in judging deception, and so forth—or whether all these can be subsumed under the general concept of accuracy. There are also many methodological issues (Hall, Bernieri, & Carney, 2005), some of which we will touch upon in this chapter.

DEVELOPMENT AND IMPROVEMENT OF NONVERBAL SKILLS

Most of our ability to send and receive nonverbal signals is derived from "on-the-job training," the job being the process of daily living. In short, we learn our nonverbal skills, not always consciously, by imitating and modeling others and by adapting our responses to the coaching, feedback, and advice of others. This process starts in infancy with babies' mimicry of adult facial expressions. Even within the first few days of life, infants can imitate mouth opening and tongue protrusion; within the first few months, imitation extends to lip protrusion, finger movements, brow movements, and even different emotional expressions on the face (see Chapter 2). By 9 months, a mother's facial expressions are not only reciprocated by her baby but also have a clear influence on the baby's affect and play behavior (Field, 1982; Field, Woodson, Greenberg, & Cohen, 1982; Meltzoff & Moore, 1983; Termine & Izard, 1988). Experts believe that an innate repertoire of facial expressions, innate imitative ability, and selective reinforcement by caretakers combine to produce in a child an understanding of the socially agreed on meanings of different nonverbal cues, and that these processes enable people to label emotions in themselves and others (Lewis & Rosenblum, 1978). In Chapters 7 and 9, we discuss nonverbal mimicry further.

That nonverbal and other social skills are strongly rooted in learning seems apparent enough and provides insight into why individuals differ so much in these skills. Among many animals, social interaction is also essential to developing appropriate social behavior later in life. Harlow's famous studies of rhesus macaque monkeys showed that monkeys raised in complete isolation for 6 months and then tested at 2 to 3.5 years of age "displayed aggression even to 1-year-old infants, as no self-respecting socially raised rhesus would" (Harlow & Mears, 1978, p. 272). Even specific communication skills in monkeys have been linked to social experience early in life. Miller and his colleagues found that rhesus monkeys reared in isolation were deficient in facial expression and judgment ability. In an experiment, two monkeys could each avoid an electric shock if one could communicate to the other through facial cues that the shock was imminent (indicated to the expressor monkey by a colored light) so that the other monkey could press a bar in time to cancel the shock for both of them. Monkeys reared in isolation were incapable of producing the necessary expressions and, when put in the role of receiver monkey, proved deficient at reading the fearful facial expressions of the other monkey (Miller, Caul, & Mirsky, 1967).

Feedback from others as we grow up does not have to mention our behavior explicitly; it can be a response *to* our behavior. Feedback, then, may be another person saying, "Well, you don't look happy," or even without making such a statement, treating you like you are an unhappy person. Through feedback we increase our awareness of ourselves and others. We not only learn what behaviors to enact but also how they are performed, with whom, when, where, and with what consequences. You can practice nonverbal sending and receiving frequently, but without regular, accurate feedback, you may not improve your ability. Feedback in the form of telling participants when their nonverbal judgments are right or wrong is one of the more successful methods of improving nonverbal abilities (Ambady, Bernieri, & Richeson, 2000).

Overall, there do appear to be positive effects of training. Studies incorporate a variety of approaches, including teaching the meanings of cues and providing discussion, practice, and feedback as mentioned above. Though the evidence is positive, not much is known about how long such improvements last or about how they impact social functioning (Beck & Feldman, 1989; Costanzo, 1992; Davitz, 1964; Ekman & Friesen, 1975; Elfenbein, 2006; Grinspan, Hemphill, & Nowicki, 2003).

Individuals from one culture have also been successfully trained to understand and enact characteristic nonverbal behaviors of people from a different culture or subculture (Collett, 1971). In Elfenbein's (2006) training study, participants profited the most when learning to judge emotional expressions from a culture dissimilar to their own, perhaps due to the relative novelty of the expressions. One study showed an intriguing connection with training in a different modality: training in keyboard music produced improvements in the ability to decode the meanings of vocal expressions of emotion (Thompson, Schellenberg, & Husain, 2004).

Some kinds of everyday experience may also serve as a form of training. Parents, especially mothers, of toddler-age children were shown to be more accurate in judging nonverbal cues on a standard test than were similar married people without children (Rosenthal et al., 1979). Though this study does not prove cause and effect, it fits with other studies that show positive correlations between experiences requiring communication in the nonverbal medium and performance on tests of decoding nonverbal cues. Furthermore, travel outside one's own country (Swenson & Casmir, 1998) and dance or athletic experience (Pitterman & Nowicki, 2004) are associated with improved ability to decode nonverbal cues. These studies suggest that a person's nonverbal skills benefit from more varied experience in decoding the feelings and reactions of people through nonverbal cues, as would happen when communicating with people who do not speak your language, when spending many hours in the expressive medium of dance, or when reading the cues of teammates and competitors on the playing field.

There have also been efforts to train people's abilities in sending—not just decoding—nonverbal cues, especially using the social-skills model developed by Argyle (1988). According to this model, socially skilled behavior is analogous to skilled motor behavior, such as driving a car. In both kinds of skills, a person makes moves, observes their effect including others' reactions to them (i.e., gets feedback from others about the effect of their moves), and takes corrective action, all with the purpose of obtaining a goal. The different elements of social behavior are seen as hierarchical. The finer, lower-level elements are automatic and habitual; the higher levels are more strategic in nature and therefore are under more direct cognitive control. This kind of training involves more active role-playing and practice than the research described previously. Social-skills training based on this model has been used to train people of low social competence in the effective use of nonverbal cues to make friends; it is also aimed at helping distressed married couples, psychiatric patients, children with learning disabilities, and professionals who need social skills for their occupations (Argyle, Trower, & Bryant, 1974; Hargie, 2006).

A major category of behavior emphasized in social-skills training is reinforcement, the provision of encouragement and reward to others in the course of interaction. Reinforcers can be verbal and nonverbal. Verbal reinforcers include acknowledgment, agreement, and praise; nonverbal reinforcers include the positive use of smiles, head nods, looking at the other, touching, body proximity, certain gestures (e.g., thumbs-up), and an encouraging voice quality.

IS IT GOOD TO HAVE MORE ACCURATE KNOWLEDGE OF NONVERBAL COMMUNICATION?

Students frequently ask whether attempts to learn about and develop skills in non-verbal communication might have negative consequences. They wonder whether we will know too much about others for their own good, and whether those who have this information might use it to manipulate others for self-serving ends; or they worry that is it possible that being expert in reading nonverbal cues will make a person unhappy or unpopular, because that person is able to see through others' lies and insincerity. Though all of these could happen in specific circumstances, there is, thus far, little overall evidence of these negative consequences. In general, we believe that increasing everyone's knowledge of nonverbal cues is a good thing, and that both individuals and society benefit when communication skills are better.

Greater knowledge of cues and more developed skills may also make people less vulnerable to manipulation. But even tactics that work do not work all the time. A good analogy can be drawn from the study of verbal persuasion. People have been studying the art of persuasion for over 2,000 years, yet it does not appear that anyone has become so sophisticated that he or she invariably succeeds in persuading anyone in any situation. Furthermore, it is the nature of human adaptation to change behavior when it becomes unproductive. Whenever people who know more about nonverbal behavior are suspected of using it "against" others, we soon see attempts to expose or counteract the attempted influence. It should also go without saying that each person has the ethical responsibility not to use knowledge for harm.

Interestingly, people seem to be less comfortable with the idea of skilled, conscious use of nonverbal cues than with the idea of skilled use of words, as in persuasion. People seem to want to believe that nonverbal communication is always a spontaneous, and therefore sincere, reflection of feelings or intentions. As long as people believe all nonverbal cues are spontaneous expressions of feeling, they will be less on guard against nonverbal manipulation and, therefore, more vulnerable to it. But nonverbal communication is much more than a spontaneous "readout" of feelings (see Chapter 9). People use nonverbal cues for self-presentation and for a variety of strategic and deliberate, sometimes even dishonest, purposes. The trial lawyer must act convinced of her client's innocence; the therapist must appear sincerely interested and accepting of a client's plight, whatever it might be; a manager needs to be able to produce a smile and a cheerful greeting for his subordinates even when his own mood is less than sunny; and a parent uses nonverbal communication constantly and deliberately to reinforce and direct a child's behavior in socially acceptable ways. Each of us has a multitude of roles to play in life, and a skilled understanding of the nonverbal cues relevant to each role is important for the smooth functioning of society and can serve to keep us in good standing with others.

MEASURING THE ACCURACY OF DECODING AND ENCODING NONVERBAL CUES

Interest in measuring sending (encoding) and receiving (decoding) accuracy goes back to the early decades of the 20th century. Over the years, many researchers have measured accuracy in order to answer a variety of scientific questions. Sometimes the purpose has been to study the encoding and decoding process itself: Can emotions be recognized from nonverbal cues? What cues do people rely on most when making their judgments? Sometimes the goal is to compare accuracy in different communication channels or among different emotions: Is it easier to decode the face than the voice? Which are the hardest messages to send via nonverbal cues? And sometimes the purpose is to compare the accuracy of individuals and groups. It is this last line of research that we emphasize in this chapter. Other chapters in this book take up some of the other questions listed above.

Most research on nonverbal communication skill has focused on the sending and receiving of nonverbal cues reflective of emotions. However, there is much latitude, both theoretically and in practice, in how nonverbal skill is defined and measured (Hall & Bernieri, 2001). The following list shows some of the variety and richness of the information that is sent and received in daily life.

- Interpersonal orientation: "That person was trying to dominate me," or "He didn't seem very threatening."
- Attitudes: "I really like you," or "I could tell that you didn't like that movie."
- Intentions or needs: "She wants to leave," or "She wants attention."
- Physical states: "I'm in pain," or "You look really tired."
- Personality: "She was the most extraverted person I've ever met," or "He is so hostile."
- Personal characteristics: "You don't look a day over 30," or "I bet he's gay."
- Intelligence: "I have to seem really smart to get this job," or "He's not as dumb as he looks."
- Deception and insincerity: "I like this present, I really do," or "I thought she was a big phony."
- Appearance and behavior: "Remember Jenny? She's the one who smiles a lot," or "She's worn the same thing three days in a row!"

The following examples will give you a taste of actual research. Bernieri and his colleagues have studied *rapport* (Bernieri, Gillis, Davis, & Grahe, 1996), which is defined as how much positivity, attentiveness, and coordination are experienced by people toward each other when they interact (Tickle-Degnen & Rosenthal, 1990). Bernieri measured observers' accuracy in rating the degree of rapport felt by opposite-sex dyads interacting on a videotape by comparing these ratings to the degree of rapport reported by the people on the tape. Observers' accuracy was better than the guessing level but was impeded by their reliance on some cues that were not, in fact, indicators of actual rapport. For example, they thought more smiling was a sign of rapport, when in fact it was not.

Another kind of interpersonal accuracy is the ability to recognize what social or identity groups people belong to. Ambady, Hallahan, and Conner (1999) measured the accuracy with which people could identify the sexual orientation (gay/lesbian vs. heterosexual) of people shown speaking for only a few seconds. Accuracy was higher than would be expected by chance, and the less information provided on which to base a judgment, the more accurate gay and lesbian observers were relative to heterosexual observers. Rule and Ambady (2008) further demonstrated that college students had an accuracy rate higher than guessing when shown gay and straight men's faces for only a twentieth of a second!

Using 20-second clips of white undergraduates speaking with black or white experimenters, Richeson and Shelton (2005) found that the speaker's prejudice against blacks was detectable by other undergraduates who rated how positively toned the speaker's behavior was. Accuracy of predicting prejudice was especially high when the rater was black and the video clip showed a white speaking with a black experimenter. In other words, the black student raters seemed to be especially able to discern how the more prejudiced whites spoke to blacks.

A novel kind of accuracy was studied by Carter and Hall (2008), who measured how well people could notice *covariations* between characteristics of people and how they behaved in a group discussion. For example, when observing a group of people talking about living on campus versus living off campus, did the observer notice that those who lived on campus talked more than those who did not? Women's accuracy on this test was higher than men's, and accuracy was higher for observers who had more extraverted and less neurotic personalities.

As one final example, accuracy of judging personality traits can be measured not only from how people behave but also from their *social footprint*. This footprint can include their tastes in music and recreation, their self-representation on personal Web sites, their clothing choices, and the manner in which they decorate and maintain their living or working spaces. Accuracy of judging personality from such footprint cues has been shown to be surprisingly good, as documented in studies of music tastes and living/working spaces, among others (Gosling, Ko, Mannarelli, & Morris, 2002; Rentfrow & Gosling, 2006).

In typical studies of accuracy in judging nonverbal cues, stimuli include videotapes, photographs, or audio recordings of people. The stimuli might show all of the information, as in a full videotape, or the researcher might carve the nonverbal cues up into "channels," such as silent video, face only, voice only, and so on.

For facial encoding, the people who serve as the stimuli are often asked to express a series of emotions or attitudes with their faces, or to tell about an emotional experience, while being videotaped. In the slide-viewing paradigm (Buck, Miller, & Caul, 1974), the researcher shows expressors a series of emotionally arousing slides categorized as scenic, sexual, unpleasant, or unusual. Facial reactions to the slides can then be assessed. Such facial expressions are much more spontaneous than in the previously described methods, because expressors do not know they are being videotaped while watching the slides (or films, in some studies; the issue of posed versus spontaneous behavior is discussed later in this chapter and in Chapter 9).

For vocal encoding, senders may be asked to recite a standard sentence with emotionally neutral content or to recite the alphabet while expressing different emotional/attitudinal states; or to describe a past emotional experience, and thereby re-experience the emotion felt at the time. If, for example, the request is to "talk about a sad experience you have had," the tone of voice you use would reflect how successfully you convey your sadness. If the researcher wants to be sure that verbal cues do not provide the listener with clues as to what message is being conveyed, electronic filtering methods can be applied to make the words unintelligible so that only nonverbal qualities, such as loudness and pitch, remain (see Chapter 11).

The accuracy with which the expressors (also called encoders) have nonverbally conveyed various emotions or messages is often defined in terms of whether people who do not know what the original emotions or messages were can accurately identify them. Thus, Koerner and Fitzpatrick (2003) had spouses deliberately send emotional messages to one another and then scored encoding accuracy by showing the videotapes to a group of naive judges who guessed what emotion was being conveyed. The proportion of judges whose guesses matched the original affective intention was used as the operational definition of encoding accuracy.

The methods described so far involve presenting a set of nonverbal stimuli to perceivers. Such stimuli are often called *thin slices* because they are short excerpts from the ongoing stream of behavior (Ambady, Bernieri, & Richeson, 2000; Ambady & Rosenthal, 1992; Carney, Colvin, & Hall, 2007; Lippa & Dietz, 2000). The thin slices used in research can range in length from a video of people interacting for several minutes down to still facial expressions shown for less than one second (Matsumoto, LeRoux, Wilson-Cohn, Raroque, Kooken, Ekman, Yrizarry, Loewinger, Uchida, Yee, Amo, & Goh, 2000).

There are many advantages to having the stimuli standardized in a set that can be reused with many different perceivers. This is the usual definition of a "test." However, sometimes a researcher wants to investigate nonverbal communication between individuals who are communicating *with* each other; for example, they want to measure the accuracy of communication between husbands and their wives (Noller, 1980) or between subordinates and their bosses (Snodgrass, 1992). Live-interaction studies like these are not standardized in the way that a test would be. Snodgrass studied communication accuracy in dyads in the following manner: After a period of interaction in assigned boss–employee roles, the dyad members indicated their feelings about each other by making a series of ratings, and then both guessed what the other person's feelings were using the same rating scales. Communication accuracy was defined as the correlation between these two sets of ratings, with accurate communication occurring when one person's pattern of guesses matched the pattern of the other person's ratings. Using this method, it is a challenge to separate the skills of encoder (sender) and decoder (receiver), because high accuracy can result if an encoder sends very clear messages about what he or she thinks and feels, or if the decoder is highly sensitive to the cues conveyed by the encoder, or both. However, by showing videotapes of the interactions to a new group of naive judges, it is possible to disentangle these possibilities (Hall, Rosip, Smith LeBeau, Horgan, & Carter, 2006; Snodgrass, Hecht, & Ploutz-Snyder,

1998). But most research has taken the simpler testing approach of showing a standard set of stimuli to all perceivers.

A constant problem in this area of research centers on the question of *criteria*. It is easy to ask decoders to judge what the sender is feeling or communicating, but how do you know whether they are right? If the communication is posed, the criterion can be simply whatever the encoders were asked to pose. If the sender was asked to look happy, a judge would get a correct answer for saying the person looked happy. Using this system, a judge could get an error through no fault of his or her own if the encoder did a poor job of showing the intended emotion. Other criteria have been used, but none is perfect. With the slide-viewing technique, a decoder's answer is scored as correct if he or she correctly identifies which slide the encoder was viewing when the encoder's face was filmed. This method assumes that encoders' faces show an appropriate response; sometimes they do not. Sometimes experts decide on what emotion is being expressed in a stimulus. Sometimes consensus is used, so a correct answer is based on what the majority of judges say. (See Chapter 9 for further discussion of judgment methods.)

STANDARDIZED TESTS OF DECODING ABILITY

Robert Rosenthal and his associates developed a multichannel test of nonverbal decoding ability known as the Profile of Nonverbal Sensitivity, or the PONS test (Rosenthal, Hall, DiMatteo, Rogers, & Archer, 1979). The PONS test is a 45-minute video that contains 220 auditory and visual segments to which viewers are asked to respond. Each segment is a 2-second excerpt from a scene portrayed by a white American woman. Five scenes portray a positive-dominant affect or attitude (e.g., "admiring a baby"); five scenes portray positive-submissive behavior (e.g., "expressing gratitude"); five scenes portray negative-dominant behavior (e.g., "criticizing someone for being late"); and five scenes portray negative-submissive behavior (e.g., "asking forgiveness"). Each scene is presented to viewers in 11 different cue channels, representing the single or combined channels of face, body, and two different kinds of content-masked speech (see Chapter 11 for the description of the methods used to accomplish this). A receiver or viewer obtains a score for particular channels and combinations of channels in addition to a total score. The test has been administered widely to people of different ages, occupations, and nationalities.

Figure 3-1 shows three still photos taken from the PONS test. Each item has two choices: for example, "(a) returning faulty item to a store vs. (b) ordering food in a restaurant" or "(a) talking about one's divorce vs. (b) expressing motherly love." Thus, the PONS test measures the ability to recognize affective or attitudinal states in a situational context.

In contrast, the Diagnostic Analysis of Nonverbal Accuracy, or DANVA (Nowicki & Duke, 1994) is based on recognition of pure emotions—happiness, sadness, fear, and anger—shown out of context; thus it taps into a more unitary kind of knowledge. The DANVA has several versions, including tests of facial, vocal, and postural expressions of adult and child expressors. The facial and postural expressions were generated by asking the encoders to pose the different emotions while a photograph was taken, and the vocal cues were generated by asking encoders

FIGURE 3-1

Still photos from the PONS test.

to say an ambiguous sentence while conveying the four different emotions. The DANVA has been used extensively with children and adults.

A recent addition to these standardized tests is the Japanese and Caucasian Brief Affect Recognition Test, or JACBART (Matsumoto et al., 2000). This test shows still photos of facial expressions of white American and Japanese adults at extremely short exposures—mere fractions of a second. These are "sandwiched" between two neutral expressions of each expressor so that the viewer sees the sequence of neutral–emotion–neutral in rapid succession. The JACBART investigates sensitivity to *micromomentary expressions*, which we discuss further in Chapter 9.

In contrast to these tests, in which expressors act out different scenes or emotions, the Interpersonal Perception Task (IPT) emphasizes more spontaneous behavior. Its developers reasoned that in real life, the things we judge about others are often actual events or relationships (Archer & Akert, 1977; Costanzo & Archer, 1989). For example, a man and woman are interacting with two children: Which is their own child? Two women discuss a tennis game they have just played: Which was the winner? A man tells his life story, then he tells it again quite differently: Which story is true? Figure 3-2 shows some still frames from a preliminary version of the test. In the final audiovisual version of the test, verbal as well as nonverbal information is conveyed by the expressors, but the verbal information is ambiguous enough so that the words alone do not give away the correct answers.

Each item in the IPT has an objectively correct answer; because the scenes are more ecologically valid than items on most such tests, it is believed the IPT measures the subtle and complex skills that people use in everyday life. There is, however, a trade-off in using more naturalistic scenes; for example, the test does not isolate cue channels. The quest for more real-life stimuli in nonverbal decoding tasks continues with two other tests that rely on cues generated in highly naturalistic circumstances (Magill-Evans, Koning, Cameron-Sadava, & Manyk, 1995; Trimboli & Walker, 1993).

One method based on naturalistic stimuli is called the *empathic accuracy paradigm*, in which a person's ability to "mind read" what another person is thinking and feeling at particular moments in a conversation is measured by a later review of the videotape by both parties (Ickes, 2001, 2003; Ickes, Stinson, Bissonnette, & Garcia, 1990).

a

b

FIGURE 3-2

How's your interpersonal perception? In (a), are the two people a couple married two years or strangers posing together? In (b), which woman is the mother of the children? In (c), is the woman waking her husband from a nap, watching an arm wrestling match, or playing with her baby daughter? Answers are given at the end of the chapter.

c

FIGURE 3-2 | *(continued)*

PERSONAL FACTORS INFLUENCING THE ACCURACY OF DECODING NONVERBAL CUES

People can be extremely sensitive to nonverbal cues. In Chapter 1 we showed that students react to very subtle positive and negative expectancy cues from their teachers. Research shows that first impressions of personality, based on superficial observation and no actual interaction, agree impressively among observers and with the targets' own self-descriptions. Thus, people agree on others' sociability or extraversion after the barest exposure to each other, and those ratings are more accurate than would be expected by chance (Albright, Kenny, & Malloy, 1988; Levesque & Kenny, 1993; Marcus & Lehman, 2002). Similarly, observers' ratings of only a few seconds, or thin slices, of behavior can be surprisingly accurate and predictive of other important variables (Ambady et al., 2000). For example, people who watch brief clips of silent video of teachers' classroom behavior agree remarkably on the teachers' qualities, and their ratings predict performance evaluations by the teachers' own students and principal (Ambady & Rosenthal, 1993). Clips a minute long and shorter produce accuracy above chance levels for a variety of personality traits and intelligence (Carney, Colvin, & Hall, 2007; Murphy, Hall, & Colvin, 2003). In the Carney et al. study, clips of 5 seconds were as good as much longer clips for judging some characteristics (e.g., intelligence).

However, the accuracy with which thin slices are judged varies greatly from study to study and depends both on the method used and the construct being judged. Accuracy of distinguishing truth from lies is typically not much above the guessing level (Bond & DePaulo, 2006), while accuracy of judging basic emotions, and also the status difference between two people, is often very high (Biehl, Matsumoto, Ekman, Hearn, Heider, Kudoh, & Ton, 1997; Schmid Mast & Hall, 2004). Comparisons like this must be made with caution, however, because in developing their tests, investigators have great latitude in determining how easy or difficult the items are (by, for example, varying how much information is made available to perceivers). In order to detect individual variations, test developers often strive to make their tests neither too easy nor too difficult.

Self-Appraisals and Explicit Knowledge of Nonverbal Cues

Considering the time required to develop, validate, administer, and score nonverbal tests, you might think it would be cheaper and easier just to ask people to appraise their own skills. Unfortunately, this does not work. People high in sensitivity to nonverbal cues are not necessarily those who appraise their own skills highly (Riggio & Riggio, 2001). Though their accuracy in self-evaluation is above the guessing level (Hall, Andrzejewski, & Yopchick, in press), it is not nearly high enough for self-evaluations to be substituted for tested nonverbal decoding skill. This fairly low self-awareness of skill is entirely consistent with the view of most experts that people's knowledge of nonverbal cues is *tacit*; that is, people process nonverbal cues largely unconsciously, without much awareness of which cues they rely on. Indeed, the cues that people think they use when making nonverbal judgments are often not the ones actually relevant to the judgments they are making (Zuckerman, Koestner, & Driver, 1981; see also earlier discussion of rapport).

Recently, however, it has been shown that people do have some explicit knowledge of nonverbal communication—that is, knowledge they can articulate on a paper-and-pencil test (Rosip & Hall, 2004). The Test of Nonverbal Cue Knowledge (TONCK) measures knowledge with 81 items marked true or false, and the results are scored based on findings established through published research. These scores significantly predict accuracy on the PONS and DANVA nonverbal decoding tests (described above), but the correlations are not large enough to permit the TONCK to be used as a substitute for measuring the actual decoding of cues. However, a test of nonverbal cue knowledge is a good addition to the instruments available for researchers.

Gender

One of the best documented correlates of nonverbal sensitivity is gender. More often than not, girls and women score higher than boys and men on tests of judging the meanings of nonverbal cues (Hall, 1984; McClure, 2000). Women also score higher than men on the TONCK (see above), and they remember people's appearance and nonverbal cues better than men do (Hall, Murphy, & Schmid Mast, 2006; Horgan, Schmid Mast, Hall, & Carter, 2004). The female advantage in decoding the meanings of nonverbal cues is present from grade school on up. Although the difference is not great—about 2 percentage points between average male and female PONS scores, for example—it is extremely consistent. Females scored higher than males in 80 percent of 133 different groups given the PONS test, including a variety of non-U.S. samples (Hall, 1984; Rosenthal et al., 1979). Reviews of research using many other decoding tests have confirmed that this gender difference exists across ages of participants and regardless of whether the encoders are male or female and regardless of which particular test is used (Hall, 1978). It also holds up, with rare exceptions, from culture to culture (Dickey & Knower, 1941; Izard, 1971; Merten, 2005; Rosenthal et al., 1979).

Although these and other studies indicate a superior ability among females to judge nonverbal cues, there are limits and exceptions to a general female advantage. Females are especially good at judging facial cues relative to other channels and when emotion of some sort is being judged (Rosenthal & DePaulo, 1979; Hall, 1978). For the decoding of anger cues, there is some evidence that males may actually have an advantage when the person being judged is male (Rotter & Rotter, 1988; Wagner, MacDonald, & Manstead, 1986). Researchers have shown that women do not have an advantage at judging whether another person is lying (Aamodt & Custer, 2006), or when judging status and dominance (Schmid Mast & Hall, 2004). And, women's advantage is less consistent when the task is Ickes' empathic accuracy paradigm described earlier, involving the ability to guess another person's thoughts and feelings at particular moments in a conversation (Ickes, Gesn, & Graham, 2000). Tasks that possibly show a weaker female advantage are those in which facial expression plays a less significant role. Indeed, in the empathic accuracy paradigm, the most important cues appear to be verbal rather than facial (Gesn & Ickes, 1999; Hall & Schmid Mast, 2007).

Given how widespread the evidence for females' superiority on nonverbal judgment tasks is, it is no surprise that interpersonal sensitivity is part of the common stereotype about women (Briton & Hall, 1995). We think it likely that females' greater skill as interpersonal decoders has been recognized throughout history and contributes to the layperson's notion of "female intuition." The belief that women are more sensitive to nonverbal cues is even present in literature; for example, a passage in George Eliot's *Adam Bede* (1859) describes a scene in which a woman correctly concludes that two young people are in love, based on her observation that the girl trembles in the boy's presence. When asked about this, she replies, "It's on'y the men as have to wait till folks say things afore they find 'em out." Is it a coincidence, we wonder, that the author was a woman? (George Eliot was the pen name of English novelist Mary Ann Evans.) Gender differences in nonverbal communication skill are discussed further in Chapter 12.

AGE

Age also has been studied in relation to decoding skill. Provocative research indicates that infants only a few months old have some ability to discriminate among facial and vocal expressions of emotion (Haviland & Lelwica, 1987; Walker-Andrews, 1997; Walker-Andrews & Lennon, 1991). Of course, it is difficult to assess how much infants understand the cues' *meanings*; discrimination per se does not demonstrate this kind of understanding. But research did find that 7-month-olds showed increased attention to faces that matched auditory tones on emotional quality; for example, they looked more at a joyful face than a sad face when the associated vocal tones were ascending, fast oscillating, high, and pulsing (Phillips, Wagner, Fells, & Lynch, 1990). Thus by this age, infants at least know what facial cues go with what vocal cues.

People generally show a gradually increasing decoding skill from kindergarten until ages 20 to 30 (Dimitrovsky, 1964; Harrigan, 1984; Markham & Adams, 1992; Nowicki & Duke, 1994; Rosenthal et al., 1979). More focused investigations have been able to identify the ages when specific skills are gained; for example, children 6 and 7 years old could not tell smiles of enjoyment from those of nonenjoyment, which differ in muscle movements around the eyes; but children 9 and 10 years old could (Gosselin, Perron, Legault, & Campanella, 2002). The great majority of research into developmental trends has been concerned with judging emotions from nonverbal cues. Recently, McLarney-Vesotski, Bernieri, and Rempala (2006) also found improvements across ages 8, 13, and adult for a test of judging personality traits from short video excerpts.

The trend reverses, however, as a person ages. Numerous studies comparing young adults to older adults show a decline in accuracy in judging nonverbal cues. For example, women averaging 62 years of age scored significantly lower on the multichannel PONS test than women averaging 22 years of age (Lieberman, Rigo, & Campain, 1988), and other researchers have found deficits in adults over 65 compared to younger adults (college aged and in their 20s) for face, body, and voice cues examined separately (Isaacowitz, Löckenhoff, Lane, Wright, Sechrest, Riedel, & Costa, 2007; Ruffman, Henry, Livingstone, & Phillips, 2008).

GENERAL COGNITIVE ABILITY

An important question is whether scores on tests of nonverbal sensitivity reflect a unique ability or a general cognitive skill. If the latter is the case, researchers do not need to develop sensitivity tests but could administer standard cognitive tests, such as IQ tests. In general, although there is a small positive correlation between general cognitive ability and tests of nonverbal sensitivity (Davis & Kraus, 1997), the relation is small enough to suggest that the two abilities are far from synonymous. However, as seen later in this chapter, in children a relation does seem to exist between decoding skill and academic performance, though not one that is large enough to suggest that the skills are interchangeable.

OTHER PERSONAL CORRELATES

Adults who do well on tests of decoding nonverbal cues have been found to exhibit certain personal characteristics, based on much research and many published summaries (e.g., Carney & Harrigan, 2003; Funder & Harris, 1986; Hall et al., 2008; Marsh, Kozak, & Ambady, 2007; Pickett, Gardner, & Knowles, 2004; Rosenthal et al., 1979). High-scoring adults are better adjusted, less hostile and manipulating, more interpersonally democratic and encouraging, more tolerant, more helpful to others, more open to experience, more conscientious, more extraverted, more in need of social inclusion, less shy, less anxious, more likely to believe they control what happens to them (as opposed to luck, fate, or other people; called internal locus of control), more warm, more empathic, more popular, more reported by others to be interpersonally sensitive, and better able to judge others' interpersonal sensitivity. They also perform better in the workplace as rated by supervisors and have more satisfying personal relationships. Nonverbal decoding accuracy has recently been found to predict objective outcomes relevant to workplace success, such as attaining more favorable negotiation outcomes (Elfenbein, Foo, White, Tan, & Aik, 2007) and performing objectively better as a salesperson (Byron, Terranova, & Nowicki, 2007).

Children in preschool and/or elementary school who score higher at decoding face, posture, gesture, or voice tone have been found to be more popular and more socially competent, less anxious, less emotionally disturbed, less aggressive, and less depressed; and they are higher in internal locus of control (e.g., Baum & Nowicki, 1998; Izard, Fine, Schultz, Mostow, Ackerman, & Youngstrom, 2001; Lancelot & Nowicki, 1997; McClure & Nowicki, 2001; Nowicki & Carton, 1997; Nowicki & Duke, 1994; Nowicki & Mitchell, 1998).

A test that consists of black Americans' facial expressions shows an array of correlates among black test-takers (Nowicki, Glanville, & Demertzis, 1998); for example, better decoding scores were associated with higher self-esteem and more internal locus of control in both children and college students. When this test was given along with a corresponding test showing white adult facial expressions to samples of black and white college students, the white participants were less accurate than blacks when judging blacks' expressions, but the two groups did not differ in their accuracy of judging whites' expressions. Subsequent research on white and black school children showed that popularity with peers was related to success in decoding facial expressions of the students' own ethnic group, but not those of the other group (Glanville & Nowicki, 2002).

Children who score higher on nonverbal decoding tests also score higher on academic achievement (Halberstadt & Hall, 1980; Izard, Fine, Schultz, Mostow, Ackerman, & Youngstrom, 2001; Nowicki & Duke, 1994). Several studies suggest that although general cognitive ability may contribute to the ability to understand nonverbal communication, nonverbal skills may in turn influence academic achievement, possibly through their impact on teacher–student relationships. Halberstadt and Hall found that children who scored higher on the PONS test were perceived by their teachers as smarter, even when the pupils' actual academic and IQ scores were controlled statistically. Izard and colleagues found that the ability to understand facial expressions at age 5 predicted teachers' ratings of academic competence at age 9, controlling for objectively tested cognitive ability. It is possible that nonverbally sensitive youngsters create such a good impression that adults attribute cognitive ability to them, which may create a positive, self-fulfilling prophecy in which these children are taught more and are encouraged more, leading to actual gains in academic achievement. One study has found that decoding skill also seems to have a direct role in the learning process. Bernieri (1991) found that high school students who scored higher on the PONS test learned more from a peer in a brief teaching session than did students who scored lower.

Although it is generally difficult to think of any benefits of a large amount of television viewing, Feldman, Coats, and Spielman (1996) hypothesized that children might actually learn to decode emotional expressions from television, where such expressions tend to be plentiful as well as exaggerated. And they were right: elementary school children who watched over 14 hours of television weekly were more accurate in decoding facial expressions of emotion than children who watched 7 or fewer hours.

Certain groups tend to have greater nonverbal decoding ability. The top three groups on the PONS test were actors, students studying nonverbal behavior, and students studying visual arts. Buck's (1976) research on the interpretation of facial expressions found that students who were fine arts majors were better decoders than math and science majors.

Psychologically damaging experiences early in life may also affect accuracy at decoding nonverbal cues. Hodgins and Belch (2000) found that college students who had been exposed to parental violence growing up were worse at judging happy cues than students who had not been, but they did not differ when judging other emotional expressions; and Pollak and Sinha (2002) found that abused and mal-treated children had a lower threshold for identifying anger in facial expressions.

Mental patients score considerably lower than norm groups on the PONS test (Rosenthal et al., 1979). Other studies concur that schizophrenic patients, with both chronic and acute forms of the illness, judge facial and vocal expressions less accurately than unimpaired groups, regardless of whether they are medicated (Edwards, Jackson, & Pattison, 2002; Mandal, Pandey, & Prasad, 1998; Mueser, Penn, Blanchard, & Bellack, 1997). Though groups with various kinds of psycho-logical disturbance often have a generalized decoding deficit, sometimes the deficit is specific; for example, groups with psychopathic personality disorders and other documented antisocial behaviors were selectively worse than control groups when judging fearful facial expressions (Marsh & Blair, 2008), and depressed patients were selectively worse than a control group when decoding sad facial expressions (Surguladze, Young, Senior, Brébion, Travis, & Phillips, 2004).

Examination of error patterns can also be instructive for psychologically im-paired groups. On the PONS test, decrements in decoding ability were found in boys referred to clinics for various kinds of childhood psychopathology (Russell, Stokes, Jones, Czogalik, & Rohleder, 1993). Interestingly, boys with problems of self-control and social incompetence made the majority of their decoding errors on PONS items requiring a judgment about the dominant–submissive dimension of be-havior, consistent with previous findings that aggressive boys tend to see aggres-siveness in neutral stimuli (Dodge & Newman, 1981). Similarly, preschool children who were rated by their teachers as hostile and dependent were biased in their judgments of their classmates' facial expressions; they were more likely to say the expressions were sad or angry and less likely to say they were happy, compared to children who were not hostile and dependent (Barth & Bastiani, 1997).

A group known for having interpersonal communication difficulties is people with autism (Philippot, Feldman, & McGee, 1992). Autism is a disorder largely de-fined in terms of deficient verbal, and especially nonverbal, communication and an extreme inability to relate to other human beings. The neurologist Oliver Sacks has written about Temple Grandin, an autistic academician whose insights greatly illuminate our understanding of the psychological experience of autism. Grandin's understanding of others' feelings and intentions comes from "immense intellectual effort" as opposed to the unconscious, intuitive process used by nonautistic people. Commenting on Grandin's childhood experiences, Sacks writes:

> Something was going on between the other kids, something swift, subtle, constantly changing—an exchange of meanings, a negotiation, a swiftness of understanding

so remarkable that sometimes she wondered if they were all telepathic. She is now aware of the existence of these social signals. She can infer them, she says, but she herself cannot perceive them, cannot participate in this magical communication directly.... This is why she often feels excluded, an alien. (Sacks, 1993, p. 116)

Not surprisingly, individuals with autism—and a milder, related condition, Asperger syndrome—consistently perform worse than normal-functioning people on tests of decoding facial and vocal expressions (Rutherford, Baron-Cohen, & Wheelwright, 2002).

Alcohol consumption, in its extreme form, can also be considered a psychopathology, and alcoholic patients score lower than norm groups on the PONS test (Rosenthal et al., 1979). An intriguing experiment using photographs of six emotions found that when nonalcoholic participants were given alcohol, their decoding accuracy was impaired, especially men's ability to identify anger, disgust, and contempt (Borrill, Rosen, & Summerfield, 1987). Perhaps some of the antisocial behavior of drinkers is linked to an impairment in their sensitivity to these cues.

The PONS test has been administered to people from over 20 nations (Rosenthal et al., 1979). People from countries most similar to the United States in language and culture—relative to modernization, widespread use of communications media, and so on—scored highest. The PONS research therefore offers a synthesis of two opposed positions on the universality of emotional expressions: One states that these are universally used and recognized, the other that nonverbal communication is as culture specific as verbal language itself. The universalist position is supported by the fact that all cultures were able to perform at levels higher than chance on the PONS test. However, the specificity argument is also supported by the fact that groups more culturally similar to that of the person shown in the PONS video were able to extract more accurate meaning from the cues. Elfenbein and Ambady (2002), in a review of many studies, confirmed that people have a slight advantage in accuracy when judging encoders who come from their same culture. (Chapters 2, 9, and 12 offer further discussion of cultural universality and relativity.)

TASK FACTORS AFFECTING NONVERBAL DECODING ACCURACY

You may think the particular channels tested—face, voice, and so on—make a difference in a person's nonverbal receiving accuracy. Generally, judgments of visual channels, especially the face, are more accurate than judgments of the voice, though generalizations like this must be made with caution, because tests of different channels may vary in other methodological ways. Several studies show that emotions and attitudes of liking and disliking are more accurately perceived in the face than in the voice. Although you may be better able to recognize many emotions and attitudes if you get both audio and visual cues, some messages may be more effectively communicated in one mode than in another; for example, vocal cues may be more effective for communicating anxiety and dominance than other communication channels. And studies show that if you are accurate in recognizing facial signals, you will also be accurate in perceiving vocal ones (Zuckerman, Lipets, Koivumaki, & Rosenthal, 1975). Also, accuracy is usually higher if the expressions are posed rather than spontaneous, but if you do well in decoding one of these modalities, you will probably do well in the other (Zuckerman, Hall, DeFrank, &

Rosenthal, 1976). It is clear that some emotional and attitudinal states are more difficult to judge than others. At one extreme, it is very difficult to tell if someone is lying, and at the other, it is very easy to identify posed facial expressions showing basic emotions such as disgust or joy.

We might also speculate, as did the PONS researchers, that the amount of time a receiver was exposed to a nonverbal signal would affect his or her accuracy in identification. The PONS scenes were presented to people with the exposure time varied; for example, $\frac{1}{24}$ of a second, $\frac{3}{24}$ of a second, and so on, up to 2 seconds (Rosenthal et al., 1979). Accuracy did increase as exposure time increased. Research on judgments made of exposures varying between 2 seconds and 5 minutes has shown that more information often does not yield higher accuracy; and when it does, the differences are often not dramatic (Ambady et al., 2000; Carney et al., 2007).

People's moods can influence how they perceive others' behavior. Positive and negative moods produce a bias to see corresponding emotions in others' faces (Niedenthal, Halberstadt, Margolin, & Innes-Ker, 2000; Schiffenbauer, 1974). In general, a sad mood reduces the accuracy of judging others (Ambady & Gray, 2002), which lends support to the argument that sad moods promote a deliberative information-processing style that can detract from accuracy of nonverbal judgments that would otherwise be made in a more automatic, nonanalytic manner.

CHARACTERISTICS OF ACCURATE NONVERBAL SENDERS

When broadly conceived, a definition of nonverbal sending is even more complex than a definition of nonverbal decoding. In a sense, nonverbal sending is everything of an interpersonal nature that we do without words. Indeed, it is inevitable that nonverbal cues will be perceived and interpreted by others—even if a person's intention is to appear neutral or unexpressive. Attempts to control nonverbal cues by trying not to express them at all are likely to be interpreted as dullness, withdrawal, uneasiness, aloofness, or even deceptiveness (DePaulo, 1992). As it is sometimes said, you cannot *not* communicate nonverbally.

A person's nonverbal sending is a mixture of spontaneous cues and more deliberate or intentional ones. The latter are used in daily life to convey a host of impressions of ourselves as nice, smart, youthful, honest, dominant, brave, and so forth. We also use nonverbal communication intentionally as part of our effort to act socially appropriate; for example, to be respectful to authorities, dignified in a fancy restaurant, or polite in the face of disappointment. Children attain these more deliberate self-presentation skills through a long process that combines social experience with their own development of identity; numerous studies testify to developmental trends in these skills (DePaulo, 1992; Harrigan, 1984; Nowicki & Duke, 1994), although we should not underestimate the skill of young children in simulating and masking expressions of emotion (Halberstadt, Grotjohn, Johnson, Furth, & Greig, 1992).

According to DePaulo, success at regulating nonverbal behaviors to promote our public presentation depends on knowledge, skill, practice, experience, confidence, and motivation. The success of nonverbal self-presentation is also limited by the inherent controllability of different nonverbal channels—the face, for example, is believed to be more controllable than voice or body—as well as individual differences among people and the intensity of the reality we might wish to mask; for example, the angrier you are, the harder it will be to act as if everything is fine.

One individual difference that definitely affects self-presentation is spontaneous expressiveness of the sort discussed in relation to the slide-viewing paradigm; for example, a person may not realize how much his or her face reflects the content of a gruesome or romantic scene viewed on television. These differences are observable in infancy and remain stable over the course of development. The spontaneously expressive person has many social advantages, as we outline shortly, but may be handicapped whenever self-presentation calls for application of display rules or deception. It is suggested, for example, that a highly expressive person may not make a good poker player (DePaulo, 1992).

Another factor influencing nonverbal self-presentation involves lasting physical and expressive qualities that bestow a particular demeanor on a person. Thus, for example, the man with thick, bushy eyebrows may look threatening no matter how gentle he actually is. Research finds that some people's demeanors tend to make them look honest or dishonest or pleasant or unpleasant, no matter what they actually feel or do (Wallbott & Scherer, 1986; Zuckerman, DeFrank, Hall, Larrance, & Rosenthal, 1979). Demeanor can work for or against you, depending on your goals; the socially skilled person may learn to complement demeanor with other expressive cues to enhance self-presentation. For example, a person with a babyish face, which others are likely to perceive as honest-looking, may develop a repertoire of "innocent" nonverbal cues to enhance the impression of sincerity.

Most research on nonverbal sending accuracy involves emotions. The person who is spontaneously emotionally expressive tends to be female and reports less ability to control his or her emotions (Tucker & Riggio, 1988). It has been suggested that *not* allowing free expression can take a toll on health and cognitive functioning (Berry & Pennebaker, 1993). People who are less expressive experience a higher level of internal physiological arousal (Buck, 1977; Buck, Miller, & Caul, 1974), and experiments show short-term effects of emotional suppression with negative effects on cardiovascular activity, blood pressure, and memory for stimuli presented during the suppression of emotion (Butler, Egloff, Wilhelm, Smith, Erickson, & Gross, 2003; Richards & Gross, 1999).

Accuracy in expressing emotions deliberately increases through childhood, but then it levels off. Borod, Yecker, and Brickman (2004) compared young, middle-aged, and older adults in their ability to pose several emotions using the face. Clear age effects were observed, with the greatest deficit occurring between the older adult group compared to the other two groups.

The seemingly elusive concept of charisma has been operationally defined as expressiveness, including both spontaneous and more intentional sending. Research with the Affective Communication Test (ACT)—which measures expressiveness through self-reported statements such as "I show that I like someone by hugging or touching that person," "I like being watched by a large group of people," "I don't usually have a neutral facial expression," and "I can easily express emotion over the telephone"—documents that the expressive person is socially influential (Friedman, Prince, Riggio, & DiMatteo, 1980; Friedman & Riggio, 1981; Friedman, Riggio, & Casella, 1988). People who scored as more expressive on the ACT were more likely to have given a lecture, to have been elected to office in a political organization, to influence others' moods, and to be perceived as more likable when meeting new people; in a sample of physicians, they were likely to have more patients than their counterparts who scored as less expressive. High scorers were also more likely to have had acting experience, to have had a job in sales, to desire an occupation that uses social skills—such as counselor, minister, or diplomat—and to be extraverted, affiliative, and dominant. Comparable findings have emerged for a longer self-report instrument designed to measure seven dimensions of social skills (Riggio, 1986).

People can have insight into their spontaneous expressiveness, but research often finds a weak relationship between participants' self-reports of posed encoding skill and their ability to act out emotions on purpose (Riggio, Widaman, & Friedman, 1985; Zuckerman & Larrance, 1979). Studies that actually *measure* people's nonverbal sending abilities, rather than asking for self-reports, have also produced a variety of findings. Females manifest greater encoding skill than males in both posed and spontaneous facial accuracy (Buck, Miller, & Caul, 1974; Friedman, Riggio, & Segall, 1980; Wagner, Buck, & Winterbotham, 1993; Zaidel & Mehrabian, 1969). Possibly contributing to these effects is that females are more successful than males at mimicking facial expressions shown in photographs and on videotape (Berenbaum & Rotter, 1992). However, evidence is mixed on whether a gender difference applies for vocal encoding of emotions. Also, the gender-related difference in sending ability has not been found with children between 4 and 6 years old for spontaneous facial expressions (Buck, 1975). Buck actually found preschool boys to be more accurate senders of spontaneous facial cues than preschool girls, but boys' accuracy declined at ages 4 through 6, perhaps due to socialization pressure related to the male gender role (Buck, 1977).

Just as boys appear to be learning the expression norms for their gender, girls are learning theirs as well. Aside from becoming more facially expressive, girls learn earlier to use nonverbal cues according to "display rules" (see Chapter 9) that dictate what behaviors are socially appropriate. At preschool and elementary school ages, girls showed less negativity than boys after receiving a disappointing gift when in the presence of an adult, although control conditions showed they were no less disappointed than the boys (Cole, 1986; Davis, 1995).

Some personality characteristics also have been associated with accurate senders of nonverbal information. High "self-monitors"—people who are very aware of how they should be acting in various situations and are willing to do so to advance their self-interest—are better able to send emotional information through facial and vocal channels (Snyder, 1974); people who are more extraverted are higher on behavioral measures of expressiveness; and those who are more neurotic are lower on such measures (Riggio & Riggio, 2002). Buck's personality profile for young children shows many of the same characteristics reviewed earlier for decoders (Buck, 1975). Children who are effective senders are extraverted, outgoing, active, popular, and somewhat bossy and impulsive. Ineffective senders tend to play alone and are introverted, passive, shy, controlled, and rated as cooperative. Among adults, highly accurate senders are more dominant and exhibitionistic (Friedman, Riggio, & Segall, 1980); better senders also make an impression of greater expressiveness, confidence, and likability; and among males, they use more fluent speech, more fluent body movements, and more smiles (Riggio & Friedman, 1986).

For many years, clinicians and researchers have noticed expression deficits in individuals with schizophrenia. Compared to individuals without the disorder, these people tend to show reduced facial expressivity, are more likely to show negative than positive expressions, show less congruence between verbal and facial messages, and are less accurate in facial and vocal expressions of affect (Mandal, Pandey, & Prasad, 1998). Individuals with *alexithymia*, or difficulty in identifying one's own emotions, also have reduced facial expressiveness when describing positive or negative events from their past (Wagner & Lee, 2008).

Noller (1980; Noller & Gallois, 1986) studied the accuracy of husbands' and wives' nonverbal communication to each other. Women were better encoders than men, both in terms of perceivers' ability to judge the women accurately and in terms of the women's correct use of the particular cues associated with a given message (e.g., smiling for a positive message, frowning for a negative message). Marital adjustment was related to encoding skill among men. Men in happier marriages sent clearer messages through the face. These husbands were also more likely to offer a correct cue, such as a smile during positive messages, than less happy husbands, whereas less happy husbands used more eyebrow flashes, a cue not associated with a positive message. This research suggests that marital unhappiness might be partly due to the husband's inadequacy in nonverbal communication. Unhappy husbands were, in fact, more accurate in decoding the nonverbal behavior of an unknown married woman than that of their own spouse.

When both spontaneous and posed expressions are obtained from the same people, these two abilities are positively related; that is, if a person's spontaneous facial expression to pleasant stimuli, such as a television comedy scene, and unpleasant stimuli, such as a gory accident scene, were easy to "read," that person would also show skill in performing posed expressions.

PUTTING DECODING AND ENCODING TOGETHER

There are two ways in which decoding and encoding can be considered together. The first way is to ask whether skilled encoders are also skilled decoders. Interestingly, this question has not been definitively answered despite considerable research. Some research finds that the two kinds of skill are positively related, leading to the hypothesis of a "general communication ability" (Zuckerman, Hall, DeFrank, & Rosenthal, 1976). But other researchers have found no relationship, or even a negative relationship, between sending and receiving ability; for example, Lanzetta and Kleck (1970) found that people who were accurate facial senders were poor receivers and vice versa.

Across all the available studies, there is only a weak positive association between encoding and decoding accuracy (DePaulo & Rosenthal, 1979). Researchers do not know what accounts for such variation in results. A negative relation between encoding and decoding skill has been theorized to stem from the childhood socialization experience, in particular, the communication environment within the family (Izard, 1971; Zuckerman, Lipets, Koivumaki, & Rosenthal, 1975). The reasoning goes like this: In a highly expressive family, expression skills will be well developed; but because emotional cues are so clearly sent by other family members, there is no need to fine-tune one's decoding skill, and, therefore, decoding ability remains relatively undeveloped. However, in unexpressive homes, a child's expression skills will be poorly developed, but his or her decoding skill is sharpened, because the child is forced to read minimal or ambiguous cues coming from other family members. The skill developed from reading family members who are just barely showing their feelings is hypothesized to generalize, so that a person from an unexpressive family is predicted to score relatively high on a standard test of decoding nonverbal cues. Using the Family Expressiveness Questionnaire to measure the communication environment in the family, Halberstadt (1983, 1986) found support for the predictions stemming from this theory; namely, that encoding skill would be positively related to greater freedom of emotional expression in the family, and that decoding skill would be negatively related to freedom of emotional expression.

The second way we can consider decoding and encoding together is to acknowledge that they occur together in the communication process. Although we have discussed them as separate skills that can be compared, in real interpersonal interaction, these skills are used together. A person is required to encode and decode simultaneously—to act out or display feelings, reactions, intentions, and attitudes while at the same time noticing the other's cues, forming impressions, interpreting the meanings of expressions, and evaluating feedback from his or her own behavior. This "parallel processing" aspect of interpersonal communication puts many demands on the cognitive system, insofar as it is difficult to allocate attention or effort to all of these tasks at the same time. The process is made somewhat easier by the fact that a certain amount of nonverbal processing is so well learned that it is rather automatic, requiring few cognitive resources (i.e., mental attention). The complex sending and receiving of turn-taking cues in conversation is a good example: We know how to do this without much conscious thought. However, when individuals engage in strategic behavior—as in deliberately trying to persuade someone—or when they suffer from social anxiety, considerable expenditure of cognitive resources is required that can selectively affect either the encoding or decoding process; for example, social anxiety tends to bring a self-focus that would likely detract from one's processing of another person's cues (Patterson, 1995). Indeed, more socially anxious people do score lower on nonverbal decoding tests than less socially anxious people.

ON BEING AN OBSERVER OF NONVERBAL COMMUNICATION

The observation of Expression is by no means easy.

—**Charles Darwin**

As you set out to read the remaining chapters of this book, now seems a good time to reflect on how you can best use the knowledge contained there. You will learn quite a lot about the meanings and functions of nonverbal behaviors conveyed in all cue channels. You will learn that nonverbal cues are major indicators of emotion and play a crucial role in making social impressions and influencing others. You have just learned that people differ markedly in their skills in judging and using nonverbal cues. Although certain groups, such as actors and mental patients, fall at the extremes of skill, a great deal of variation from person to person exists even in the middle, so-called normal range.

The research indicates that there may not be strong general skills; instead, there appear to be distinctive skills in different domains. A person may be skilled at judging emotions in the face but not in the voice; another may have the opposite pattern. Sarah may be good at identifying nonverbal deceptions, whereas Jim specializes in recognizing faces, and Martha can tell who stands where in the pecking order simply from hearing their tone of voice. In short, there are many ways to be accurate in nonverbal communication.

Because so much of a person's time is spent observing other people, either passively as when observing strangers on a train or bus, or actively as when in direct interaction with others, one is wise to try to develop good observational habits. The following list can be useful to observers of any human transaction. At times some of the following information will contribute to observer bias, but the information may be necessary at some point to interpret the observations fully:

1. Find out about the *participants*—age, sex, position or status, relationship to each other, previous history, and the like.
2. Find out about the *setting* of the interaction—kind of environment, relationship of the participants to the environment, and expected behavior in that environment.
3. Find out about the *purposes* of the interaction—what are people's stated as well as hidden goals, compatibility of goals, and so on.
4. Find out about the *social behavior*—who does what to or with whom, form of the behavior, its intensity, who initiates it, apparent objective of the behavior, effect on the other interactants, and so on.
5. Find out about the *frequency* and *duration* of such behavior—when it occurs, how long it lasts, whether it recurs, frequency of recurrence, and how typical such behavior is in the situation.

You will also have to decide whether the cues you see are intentional or unintentional. The term *unintentional* may itself have a range of meaning; a behavior may be truly accidental, or it may have significance not recognized by its enactor. Attributions of intention also may vary depending on the nature of the behavior in question. Some people believe that spoken words are generally designed with some goal in mind, but sometimes people say things unintentionally or without much advance planning. Certain environments cause us to focus or attend to the issue of intention more than others. Take the act of being bumped into by another person: at a crowded football stadium, the question of the person's intent may not even be considered, but being bumped into while walking down an uncrowded hallway may be another matter entirely. A full understanding of the nuances of intentionality poses many difficult barriers (Stamp & Knapp, 1990).

THE FALLIBILITY OF HUMAN PERCEPTION

It is not unusual for several observers of the same event to see several different things, nor is it unusual for one observer to see different things in the same event at different times. Successful observers are wise to take the following into account when considering factors that may contribute to differences in perception.

First, we must recognize that our perceptions are structured by our own cultural conditioning, education, and personal experiences. Adults teach children what they think are critical dimensions of others by what they choose to talk about and make note of. Thus, we form associations that inevitably enter into our observations. For instance, we may be unable to see what we consider to be contradictory traits or behaviors in others; that is, can you conceive of a person who is both quiet and active? Wealthy and accessible? Short and romantic? Another aspect of this internally consistent worldview that may affect our observations concerns preconceptions about what we will see. For example, "My observations will take place in a nursing home. Therefore, the people I will observe will be noncommunicative, sick, and inactive." Social psychological experimentation has produced many demonstrations showing that people see what they expect or wish to see, often without any awareness that they are biasing their observations in this way.

Sometimes we project our own qualities onto the object of our attention; after all, we think, if these qualities are a part of us, they must be true of others. Sometimes such projection stems less from the desire to flatter ourselves than from a distorted worldview, as in bullies who see others as hostile and threatening. We sometimes reverse the process when we want to see ourselves as unique; for example, "I am a rational person, but most people aren't." This interaction between our own needs and desires, or even our temporary emotional states and what we see in others, sometimes causes us to see only what we want to see or causes us to miss what may be obvious to others. This process is known as *selective perception*. Because of these perceptual biases, observers must check their observations against the independent reports of others, or they must check the consistency of their own observations at several different points over an extended period of time.

We must also recognize that our perceptions are influenced by which people we choose to observe. We probably do not use the same criteria for observing our friends and parents as we do when observing strangers. We may attribute more positively perceived behaviors to our friend's personality but attribute negatively perceived behaviors to situational constraints. Familiarity can either assist observation or create observational "noise," but it does affect our perceptions. Furthermore, some phenomena will cause us to zero in on one particular kind of behavior, observing it very closely but missing simultaneous behaviors occurring elsewhere. It might be that the behavior receiving the scrutiny is bigger, more active, or just more interesting. Or it might be that we monitor deviant behavior more closely than normative or expected behavior. When observing a conversation, we cannot possibly attend to everything as it happens. Sometimes we will look for, see, respond to, and interpret a particular set of cues; at other times, the same cues will go unnoticed or be disregarded. Sometimes observers fall prey to the natural tendency to follow conversational speaking turns, viewing only the speaker and missing the behavior of the nonspeakers. And of course, some phenomena are so complex, so minute, or so frequent that observer fatigue becomes a major concern.

Even if two people observe the same event and attach similar meanings to it, they may express their observations differently. Others may suspect, then, that the two observers saw two different things, such as the difference in describing a facial expression as happiness, joy, delight, pleasure, or amusement. Or it might be the difference between saying "She struck him" versus "She pushed him," or between describing a girl as "aggressive" but a boy as "exhibitionistic" when they engage in the same behavior. Hence the language we use to express our perceptions can be an important variable in judging the accuracy of those perceptions.

Finally, we must be aware of the difference between factual, non-evaluative descriptions of behavior and the interpretations we give to these descriptions. At the most basic level, we can say that a successful observer is careful not to confuse pure description with inferences or interpretations about the behavior. Failure at the inference stage is aptly illustrated by the familiar story of the scientist who told his frog to jump, and after a few minutes, the frog jumped. The scientist then amputated one of the frog's hind legs, and again he told the frog to jump. He told the frog to jump several more times, and eventually the frog made a feeble attempt to jump with one hind leg. Then the scientist cut off the other hind leg and repeatedly ordered the frog to jump. When no jumping occurred, the scientist recorded in his log, "Upon amputation of one of the frog's hind legs, it begins to lose its hearing; upon severing both hind legs, the frog becomes totally deaf." This story illustrates clearly the huge gap that can exist between the factual evidence and the interpretations that are made.

When we are judging the meanings of the highly complex behaviors that make up nonverbal communication, it is quite possible to perceive the behaviors accurately but not know, or be wrong about, what they mean. No "dictionary" of nonverbal cue meanings exists in which we can simply look up a cue to find its meaning. Thus, we must constantly be on guard against facile interpretations about meaning. We must also be cautious about assuming cause-and-effect explanations when, in fact, there could be several different paths of causation between one variable and another.

SUMMARY

This chapter dealt with nonverbal skills, how to develop them, and the characteristics of people who have such skills. In the first part of the chapter, we reviewed different definitions of communication skill as well as the major methodologies for measuring sending and receiving skills. We also presented findings on the training of nonverbal skills, using methods such as feedback, observation, and role playing. The second half of the chapter examined traits and conditions associated with effectiveness in nonverbal sending (encoding) and receiving (decoding). Most research in this area has focused on questions of decoding ability. We reviewed a large number of different correlates of accuracy in encoding and decoding nonverbal cues, among which one of the most consistent is the tendency for females to be more accurate communicators as both encoders and decoders.

We also discussed how accuracy in decoding may vary with the channel in which the information is presented, what characteristics the expressors have, and how long we heard or saw the behavior. In spite of these possible variations, some evidence suggests that if you are proficient in decoding one channel, you will be proficient in decoding others; and if you are proficient in decoding posed expressions, you will be proficient in decoding spontaneous ones too. We also presented problems associated with simultaneously encoding and decoding nonverbal cues, as we routinely do in conversation. Evidence is mixed on whether being a good decoder implies being a good encoder. It does not necessarily follow that proficiency in one skill, encoding or decoding, makes a person proficient in the other, although sometimes this is the case.

Finally, we talked about what being a good observer of nonverbal behavior entails. Knowing the most likely meanings of particular cues and cue combinations is important, but so are other factors relating to our attitudes and the context in which observation is taking place.

Answers to Figure 3-2: *a.* strangers posing together, *b.* woman on the left, *c.* playing with her baby daughter.

QUESTIONS FOR DISCUSSION

1. How much insight do you think people have into the cues they use to make judgments about others' states and traits?
2. It has been suggested that abilities to send and receive nonverbal expressions may be inversely related, in part due to the expression norms within families. Is your own family high or low on expressiveness? How might your family's expression norms have influenced your encoding and decoding skills?
3. The ability to decode other people's nonverbal emotional expressions is only one definition of nonverbal sensitivity. Think of some other definitions of nonverbal sensitivity, and analyze why and when they are useful.
4. Are there any moral or ethical issues related to the decoding and encoding of nonverbal cues?
5. Do you think that "too much" knowledge or skill in nonverbal communication could be a bad thing? Argue both for and against this hypothesis.
6. Sometimes it is said that people enact and interpret nonverbal cues "automatically," that is, without analytic thought or intention. For different behaviors and/or skills that you can point to, what do you think are the relative contributions of deliberate intention versus automatic processing?

BIBLIOGRAPHY

Aamodt, M. G., & Custer, H. (2006). Who can best catch a liar? A meta-analysis of individual differences in detecting deception. *Forensic Examiner, 15,* 6–11.

Albright, L., Kenny, D. A., & Malloy, T. E. (1988). Consensus in personality judgments at zero acquaintance. *Journal of Personality and Social Psychology, 55,* 387–395.

Ambady, N., Bernieri, F., & Richeson, J. A. (2000). Toward a histology of social behavior: Judgmental accuracy from thin slices of the behavioral stream. In M. Zanna (Ed.), *Advances in experimental social psychology,* Vol. 32 (pp. 201–271). San Diego: Academic Press.

Ambady, N., & Gray, H. M. (2002). On being sad and mistaken: Mood effects on the accuracy of thin-slice judgments. *Journal of Personality and Social Psychology, 83,* 947–961.

Ambady, N., Hallahan, M., & Conner, B. (1999). Accuracy of judgments of sexual orientation from thin slices of behavior. *Journal of Personality and Social Psychology, 77,* 538–547.

Ambady, N., & Rosenthal, R. (1992). Thin slices of expressive behavior as predictors of interpersonal consequences: A meta-analysis. *Psychological Bulletin, 111,* 256–274.

Ambady, N., & Rosenthal, R. (1993). Half a minute: Predicting teacher evaluations from thin slices of nonverbal behavior and physical attractiveness. *Journal of Personality and Social Psychology, 64,* 431–441.

Ambady, N., & Skowronski, J. J. (Eds.). (2008). *First impressions.* New York: Guilford.

Archer, D., & Akert, R. (1977). Words and everything else: Verbal and nonverbal cues in social interaction. *Journal of Personality and Social Psychology, 35,* 443–449.

Archer, D., & Akert, R. M. (1984). Problems of context and criterion in nonverbal communication: A new look at the accuracy issue. In M. Cook (Ed.), *Issues in person perception*. New York: Methuen.

Argyle, M. (1988). *Bodily communication* (2nd ed.). London: Methuen.

Argyle, M., Trower, P., & Bryant, B. (1974). Explorations in the treatment of personality disorders and neuroses by social skills training. *British Journal of Medical Psychology, 47*, 63–72.

Bales, R. F. (1970). *Personality and interpersonal behavior*. New York: Holt, Rinehart & Winston.

Barth, J. M., & Bastiani, A. (1997). A longitudinal study of emotion recognition and preschool children's social behavior. *Merrill-Palmer Quarterly, 43*, 107–128.

Baum, K. M., & Nowicki, S., Jr. (1998). Perception of emotion: Measuring decoding accuracy of adult prosodic cues varying in intensity. *Journal of Nonverbal Behavior, 22*, 89–107.

Beck, L., & Feldman, R. S. (1989). Enhancing children's decoding of facial expression. *Journal of Nonverbal Behavior, 13*, 269–278.

Beldoch, M. (1964). Sensitivity to expression of emotional meaning in three modes of communication. In J. R. Davitz (Ed.), *The communication of emotional meaning*. New York: McGraw-Hill.

Berenbaum, H., & Rotter, A. (1992). The relationship between spontaneous facial expressions of emotion and voluntary control of facial muscles. *Journal of Nonverbal Behavior, 16*, 179–190.

Bernieri, F. J. (1991). Interpersonal sensitivity in teaching interactions. *Personality and Social Psychology Bulletin, 17*, 98–103.

Bernieri, F. J. (2001). Toward a taxonomy of interpersonal sensitivity. In J. A. Hall & F. J. Bernieri (Eds.), *Interpersonal sensitivity: Theory and measurement*. Mahwah, NJ: Erlbaum.

Bernieri, F. J., Gillis, J. S., Davis, J. M., & Grahe, J. E. (1996). Dyad rapport and the accuracy of its judgment across situations: A lens model analysis. *Journal of Personality and Social Psychology, 71*, 110–129.

Berry, D. S., & Pennebaker, J. W. (1993). Nonverbal and verbal emotional expression and health. *Psychotherapy and Psychosomatics, 59*, 11–19.

Biehl, M., Matsumoto, D., Ekman, P., Hearn, V., Heider, K., Kudoh, T., & Ton, V. (1997). Matsumoto and Ekman's Japanese and Caucasian Facial Expressions of Emotion (JACFEE):

Reliability data and cross-national differences. *Journal of Nonverbal Behavior, 21*, 3–21.

Blair, R. J. R., Mitchell, D. G. V., Peschardt, K. S., Colledge, E., Leonard, R. A., Shine, J. H., Murray, L. K., & Perrett, D. I. (2004). Reduced sensitivity to others' fearful expressions in psychopathic individuals. *Personality and Individual Differences, 37*, 1111–1122.

Bond, C. F., Jr., & DePaulo, B. M. (2006). Accuracy of deception judgments. *Personality and Social Psychology Review, 10*, 214–234.

Borod, J. C., Yecker, S. A., Brickman, A. M., Moreno, C. R., Sliwinski, M., Foldi, N. S. et al. (2004). Changes in posed facial expression of emotion across the adult life span. *Experimental Aging Research, 30*, 305–331.

Borrill, J., Rosen, B. K., & Summerfield, A. B. (1987). The influence of alcohol on judgment of facial expressions of emotion. *British Journal of Medical Psychology, 60*, 71–77.

Boyatzis, C. J., & Satyaprasad, C. (1994). Children's facial and gestural decoding and encoding: Relations between skills and with popularity. *Journal of Nonverbal Behavior, 18*, 37–55.

Briton, N. B., & Hall, J. A. (1995). Beliefs about female and male nonverbal communication. *Sex Roles, 32*, 79–80.

Bruce, V. (1988). *Recognising faces*. Hillsdale, NJ: Erlbaum.

Brunswik, E. (1956). *Perception and the representative design of psychological experiments*. Berkeley: University of California Press.

Buck, R. (1975). Nonverbal communication of affect in children. *Journal of Personality and Social Psychology, 31*, 644–653.

Buck, R. (1976). A test of nonverbal receiving ability: Preliminary studies. *Human Communication Research, 2*, 162–171.

Buck, R. (1977). Nonverbal communication of affect in preschool children: Relationships with personality and skin conductance. *Journal of Personality and Social Psychology, 35*, 225–236.

Buck, R., Miller, R. E., & Caul, W. F. (1974). Sex, personality and physiological variables in the communication of affect via facial expression. *Journal of Personality and Social Psychology, 30*, 587–596.

Buck, R., Savin, V., Miller, R., & Caul, W. (1972). Communication of affect through facial expressions in humans. *Journal of Personality and Social Psychology, 23*, 362–371.

Butler, E. A., Egloff, B., Wilhelm, F. H., Smith, N. C., Erickson, E. A., & Gross, J. J. (2003). The social consequences of expressive suppression. *Emotion, 3*, 48–67.

Byron, K., Terranova, S., & Nowicki, S., Jr. (2007). Nonverbal emotion recognition and salespersons: Linking ability to perceived and actual success. *Journal of Applied Social Psychology, 37*, 2600–2619.

Camras, L. A., Ribordy, S., Hill, J., Martino, S., Spaccarelli, S., & Stefani, R. (1988). Recognition and posing of emotional expressions by abused children and their mothers. *Developmental Psychology, 24*, 776–781.

Carli, L. (1982). *Are women more social and men more task-oriented? A meta-analytic review of sex differences in group interaction, reward allocation, coalition formation, and cooperation in the Prisoner's Dilemma Game*. Unpublished manuscript, University of Massachusetts at Amherst.

Carney, D. R., Colvin, C. R., & Hall, J. A. (2007). A thin slice perspective on the accuracy of first impressions. *Journal of Research in Personality, 41*, 1054–1072.

Carney, D. R., & Harrigan, J. A. (2003). It takes one to know one: Interpersonal sensitivity is related to accurate assessments of others' interpersonal sensitivity. *Emotion, 3*, 194–200.

Carter, J. D., & Hall, J. A. (2008). Individual differences in the accuracy of detecting social covariations: Ecological sensitivity. *Journal of Research in Personality, 42*, 439–455.

Carton, J. S., Kessler, E. A., & Pape, C. L. (1999). Nonverbal decoding skills and relationship well-being in adults. *Journal of Nonverbal Behavior, 23*, 91–100.

Coats, E. J., & Feldman, R. S. (1995). The role of television in the socialization of nonverbal behavioral skills. *Basic and Applied Social Psychology, 17*, 327–341.

Cole, P. M. (1986). Children's spontaneous control of facial expression. *Child Development, 57*, 1309–1321.

Collett, P. (1971). On training Englishmen in the non-verbal behaviour of Arabs: An experiment in intercultural communication. *International Journal of Psychology, 6*, 209–215.

Costanzo, M. (1992). Training students to decode verbal and nonverbal cues: Effects on confidence and performance. *Journal of Educational Psychology, 84*, 308–313.

Costanzo, M., & Archer, D. (1989). Interpreting the expressive behavior of others: The interpersonal perception task. *Journal of Nonverbal Behavior, 13*, 225–245.

Danziger, K. (1976). *Interpersonal communication*. New York: Pergamon.

Davis, T. L. (1995). Gender differences in masking negative emotions: Ability or motivation? *Developmental Psychology, 31*, 660–667.

Davis, M. H., & Kraus, L. A. (1997). Personality and empathic accuracy. In W. Ickes (Ed.), *Empathic accuracy* (pp. 144–168). New York: Guilford.

Davitz, J. R. (1964). *The communication of emotional meaning*. New York: McGraw-Hill.

DePaulo, B. M. (1992). Nonverbal behavior and self-presentation. *Psychological Bulletin, 111*, 203–243.

DePaulo, B. M., & Rosenthal, R. (1979). Ambivalence, discrepancy, and deception in nonverbal communication. In R. Rosenthal (Ed.), *Skill in nonverbal communication: Individual differences*. Cambridge, MA: Oelgeschlager, Gunn & Hain.

Dickey, E. C., & Knower, F. H. (1941). A note on some ethnological differences in recognition of simulated expressions of emotions. *American Journal of Sociology, 47*, 190–193.

DiMatteo, M. R. (1979). Nonverbal skill and the physician–patient relationship. In R. Rosenthal (Ed.), *Skill in nonverbal communication: Individual differences*. Cambridge, MA: Oelgeschlager, Gunn & Hain.

Dimitrovsky, L. (1964). The ability to identify the emotional meaning of vocal expressions at successive age levels. In J. R. Davitz (Ed.), *The communication of emotional meaning*. New York: McGraw-Hill.

Dodge, K. A., & Newman, J. P. (1981). Biased decision-making process in aggressive boys. *Journal of Abnormal Psychology, 60*, 375–379.

Edwards, J., Jackson, H. J., & Pattison, P. E. (2002). Emotion recognition via facial expression and affective prosody in schizophrenia: A methodological review. *Clinical Psychology Review, 22,* 789–832.

Ekman, P., & Friesen, W. V. (1975). *Unmasking the face.* Englewood Cliffs, NJ: Prentice-Hall.

Elfenbein, H. A. (2006). Learning in emotion judgments: Training and the cross-cultural understanding of facial expressions. *Journal of Nonverbal Behavior, 30,* 21–36.

Elfenbein, H. A., & Ambady, N. (2002). On the universality and cultural specificity of emotion recognition: A meta-analysis. *Psychological Bulletin, 128,* 203–235.

Elfenbein, H. A., Foo, M. D., White, J., Tan, H. H., & Aik, V. C. (2007). Reading your counterpart: The benefit of emotion recognition accuracy for effectiveness in negotiation. *Journal of Nonverbal Behavior, 31,* 205–223.

Eliot, G. (1859). *Adam Bede.* New York: Harper & Brothers.

Feldman, R. S., Coats, E. J., & Spielman, D. A. (1996). Television exposure and children's decoding of nonverbal behavior. *Journal of Applied Social Psychology, 26,* 1718–1733.

Field, T. (1982). Individual differences in the expressivity of neonates and young infants. In R. S. Feldman (Ed.), *Development of nonverbal behavior in children.* New York: Springer-Verlag.

Field, T. M., Woodson, R., Greenberg, R., & Cohen, D. (1982). Discrimination and imitation of facial expressions of neonates. *Science, 218,* 179–181.

Friedman, H. S. (1979). The concept of skill in nonverbal communication: Implications for understanding social interaction. In R. Rosenthal (Ed.), *Skill in nonverbal communication: Individual differences.* Cambridge, MA: Oelgeschlager, Gunn & Hain.

Friedman, H. S., Prince, L. M., Riggio, R. E., & DiMatteo, M. R. (1980). Understanding and assessing nonverbal expressiveness: The Affective Communication Test. *Journal of Personality and Social Psychology, 39,* 333–351.

Friedman, H. S., & Riggio, R. E. (1981). Effect of individual differences in nonverbal expressiveness on transmission of emotion. *Journal of Nonverbal Behavior, 6,* 96–104.

Friedman, H. S., Riggio, R. E., & Cassella, D. F. (1988). Nonverbal skills, personal charisma, and initial attraction. *Personality and Social Psychology Bulletin, 14,* 203–211.

Friedman, H. S., Riggio, R. E., & Segall, D. O. (1980). Personality and the enactment of emotion. *Journal of Nonverbal Behavior, 5,* 35–48.

Fujita, B. N., Harper, R. G., & Wiens, A. N. (1980). Encoding–decoding of nonverbal emotional messages: Sex differences in spontaneous and enacted expressions. *Journal of Nonverbal Behavior, 4,* 131–145.

Funder, D. C., & Harris, M. J. (1986). On the several facets of personality assessment: The case of social acuity. *Journal of Personality, 54,* 528–550.

Gesn, P. R., & Ickes, W. (1999). The development of meaning contexts for empathic accuracy: Channel and sequence effects. *Journal of Personality and Social Psychology, 77,* 746–761.

Glanville, D. N., & Nowicki, S. (2002). Facial expression recognition and social competence among African American elementary school children: An examination of ethnic differences. *Journal of Black Psychology, 28,* 318–329.

Gosling, S. D., Ko, S. J., Mannarelli, T., & Morris, M. E. (2002). A room with a cue: Judgments of personality based on offices and bedrooms. *Journal of Personality and Social Psychology, 82,* 379–398.

Gosselin, P., Perron, M., Legault, M., & Campanella, P. (2002). Children's and adults' knowledge of the distinction between enjoyment and nonenjoyment smiles. *Journal of Nonverbal Behavior, 26,* 83–108.

Grinspan, D., Hemphill, A., & Nowicki, S., Jr. (2003). Improving the ability of elementary school-age children to identify emotion in facial expression. *Journal of Genetic Psychology, 164,* 88–100.

Halberstadt, A. G. (1983). Family expressiveness styles and nonverbal communication skills. *Journal of Nonverbal Behavior, 8,* 14–26.

Halberstadt, A. G. (1986). Family socialization of emotional expression and nonverbal communication styles and skills. *Journal of Personality and Social Psychology, 51,* 827–836.

Halberstadt, A. G., Grotjohn, D. K., Johnson, C. A., Furth, M. S., & Greig, M. M. (1992). Children's abilities and strategies in managing the facial display of affect. *Journal of Nonverbal Behavior, 16,* 215–230.

Halberstadt, A. G., & Hall, J. A. (1980). Who's getting the message? Children's nonverbal skill and their evaluation by teachers. *Developmental Psychology, 16,* 564–573.

Hall, J. A. (1978). Gender effects in decoding nonverbal cues. *Psychological Bulletin, 85,* 845–857.

Hall, J. A. (1984). *Nonverbal sex differences: Communication accuracy and expressive style.* Baltimore: Johns Hopkins University Press.

Hall, J. A. (2006). How big are nonverbal sex differences? The case of smiling and sensitivity to nonverbal cues. In K. Dindia & D. J. Canary (Eds.), *Sex differences and similarities in communication,* 2nd ed. (pp. 59–81). Mahwah, NJ: Erlbaum.

Hall, J. A., & Andrzejewski, S. A. (2008). Who draws accurate first impressions? Personal correlates of sensitivity to nonverbal cues. In N. Ambady & J. J. Skowronski (Eds.), *First impressions* (pp. 87–105). New York: Guilford.

Hall, J. A., Andrzejewski, S. A., & Yopchick, J. E. (in press). Psychosocial correlates of interpersonal sensitivity: A meta-analysis. *Journal of Nonverbal Behavior.*

Hall, J. A., & Bernieri, F. J. (Eds.) (2001). *Interpersonal sensitivity: Theory and measurement.* Mahwah, NJ: Erlbaum.

Hall, J. A., Bernieri, F. J., & Carney, D. R. (2005). Nonverbal behavior and interpersonal sensitivity. In J. A. Harrigan, R. Rosenthal, & K. R. Scherer (Eds.), *The new handbook of methods in nonverbal behavior research* (pp. 237–281). Oxford, UK: Oxford University Press.

Hall, J. A., Carter, J. D., & Horgan, T. G. (2001). Status roles and recall of nonverbal cues. *Journal of Nonverbal Behavior, 25,* 79–100.

Hall, J. A., & Halberstadt, A. G. (1997). Subordination and nonverbal sensitivity: A hypothesis in search of support. In M. R. Walsh (Ed.), *Women, men, and gender: Ongoing debates.* New Haven, CT: Yale University Press.

Hall, J. A., Murphy, N. A., & Schmid Mast, M. (2006). Recall of nonverbal cues: Exploring a new definition of interpersonal sensitivity. *Journal of Nonverbal Behavior, 30,* 141–155.

Hall, J. A., Rosip, J. C., Smith LeBeau, L., Horgan, T. G., & Carter, J. D. (2006). Attributing the sources of accuracy in unequal-power dyadic communication: Who is better and why? *Journal of Experimental Social Psychology, 42,* 18–27.

Hall, J. A., & Schmid Mast, M. (2007). Sources of accuracy in the empathic accuracy paradigm. *Emotion, 7,* 438–446.

Hargie, O. (Ed.). (2006). *The handbook of communication skills.* New York: Routledge.

Hargie, O., Saunders, C., & Dickson, D. (1987). *Social skills in interpersonal communication* (2nd ed.). Cambridge, MA: Brookline Books.

Harlow, H. F., & Mears, C. (1978). The nature of complex, unlearned responses. In M. Lewis & L. A. Rosenblum (Eds.), *The development of affect.* New York: Plenum.

Harrigan, J. A. (1984). The effects of task order on children's identification of facial expressions. *Motivation and Emotion, 8,* 157–169.

Haviland, J. M., & Lelwica, M. (1987). The induced affect response: 10-week-old infants' responses to three emotion expressions. *Developmental Psychology, 23,* 97–104.

Henley, N. M. (1977). *Body politics: Power, sex, and nonverbal communication.* Englewood Cliffs, NJ: Prentice-Hall.

Hodgins, H. S., & Belch, C. (2000). Interparental violence and nonverbal abilities. *Journal of Nonverbal Behavior, 24,* 3–24.

Hodgins, H. S., & Zuckerman, M. (1990). The effect of nonverbal sensitivity on social interaction. *Journal of Nonverbal Behavior, 14,* 155–170.

Horgan, T. G., Schmid Mast, M., Hall, J. A., & Carter, J. D. (2004). Gender differences in memory for the appearance of others. *Personality and Social Psychology Bulletin, 30,* 185–196.

Ickes, W. (2001). Measuring empathic accuracy. In J. A. Hall & F. J. Bernieri (Eds.), *Interpersonal sensitivity: Theory and measurement.* Mahwah, NJ: Erlbaum.

Ickes, W. (2003). *Everyday mind reading: Understanding what other people think and feel.* Amherst, NY: Prometheus Books.

Ickes, W., Gesn, P. R., & Graham, T. (2000). Gender differences in empathic accuracy: Differential ability or differential motivation? *Personal Relationships, 7,* 95–109.

Ickes, W., Stinson, L., Bissonnette, V., & Garcia, S. (1990). Naturalistic social cognition: Empathic accuracy in mixed-sex dyads. *Journal of Personality and Social Psychology, 59,* 730–742.

Isaacowitz, D. M., Löckenhoff, C. E., Lane, R. D., Wright, R., Sechrest, L., Riedel, R., & Costa, P. T. (2007). Age differences in recognition of emotion in lexical stimuli and facial expressions. *Psychology and Aging, 22,* 147–159.

Izard, C. E. (1971). *The face of emotion*. New York: Appleton-Century-Crofts.

Izard, C. E., Fine, S., Schultz, D., Mostow, A., Ackerman, B., & Youngstrom, E. (2001). Emotion knowledge as a predictor of social behavior and academic competence in children at risk. *Psychological Science, 12*, 18–23.

Kellogg, W. N., & Eagleson, B. M. (1931). The growth of social perception in different racial groups. *Journal of Educational Psychology, 22*, 374–375.

Knower, F. H. (1945). Studies in the symbolism of voice and action: V. The use of behavioral and tonal symbols as tests of speaking achievement. *Journal of Applied Psychology, 29*, 229–235.

Koerner, A. F., & Fitzpatrick, M. A. (2003). Nonverbal communication and marital adjustment and satisfaction: The role of decoding relationship relevant and relationship irrelevant affect. *Communication Monographs, 69*, 33–51.

Lancelot, C., & Nowicki, S., Jr. (1997). The association between receptive nonverbal processing abilities and internalizing/externalizing problems in girls and boys. *Journal of Genetic Psychology, 158*, 297–302.

Lanzetta, J. T., & Kleck, R. E. (1970). Encoding and decoding nonverbal affect in humans. *Journal of Personality and Social Psychology, 16*, 12–19.

Leeland, K. B. (Ed.). (2008). *Face recognition: New research*. Hauppauge, NY: Nova Science Publishers.

Levesque, M. J., & Kenny, D. A. (1993). Accuracy of behavioral predictions at zero acquaintance: A social relations analysis. *Journal of Personality and Social Psychology, 65*, 1178–1187.

Levy, P. K. (1964). The ability to express and perceive vocal communication of feelings. In J. R. Davitz (Ed.), *The communication of emotional meaning*. New York: McGraw-Hill.

Lewis, M., & Rosenblum, L. A. (Eds.). (1978). *The development of affect*. New York: Plenum.

Lieberman, D. A., Rigo, T. G., & Campain, R. F. (1988). Age-related differences in nonverbal decoding ability. *Communication Quarterly, 36*, 290–297.

Lippa, R. A., & Dietz, J. K. (2000). The relation of gender, personality, and intelligence to judges' accuracy in judging strangers' personality from brief video segments. *Journal of Nonverbal Behavior, 24*, 25–43.

Magill-Evans, J., Koning, C., Cameron-Sadava, A., & Manyk, K. (1995). The Child and Adolescent Social Perception Measure. *Journal of Nonverbal Behavior, 19*, 151–169.

Malone, B. E., & DePaulo, B. M. (2001). Measuring sensibility to deception. In J. A. Hall & F. J. Bernieri (Eds.), *Interpersonal sensitivity: Theory and measurement*. Mahwah, NJ: Erlbaum.

Mandal, M. K., Pandey, R., & Prasad, A. B. (1998). Facial expressions of emotions and schizophrenia: A review. *Schizophrenia Bulletin, 24*, 399–412.

Marangoni, C., Garcia, S., Ickes, W., & Teng, G. (1995). Empathic accuracy in a clinically relevant setting. *Journal of Personality and Social Psychology, 68*, 854–869.

Marcus, D. K., & Lehman, S. J. (2002). Are there sex differences in interpersonal perception at zero acquaintance? A social relations analysis. *Journal of Research in Personality, 36*, 190–207.

Markham, R., & Adams, K. (1992). The effect of type of task on children's identification of facial expressions. *Journal of Nonverbal Behavior, 16*, 21–39.

Marsh, A. A., & Blair, R. J. R. (2008). Deficits in facial affect recognition among antisocial populations: A meta-analysis. *Neuroscience and Biobehavioral Reviews, 32*, 454–465.

Marsh, A. A., Kozak, M. N., & Ambady, N. (2007). Accurate identification of fear facial expressions predicts prosocial behavior. *Emotion, 7*, 239–251.

Matsumoto, D., LeRoux, J., Wilson-Cohn, C., Raroque, J., Kooken, K., Ekman, P., Yrizarry, N., Loewinger, S., Uchida, H., Yee, A., Amo, L., & Goh, A. (2000). A new test to measure emotion recognition ability: Matsumoto and Ekman's Japanese and Caucasian Brief Affect Recognition Test (JACBART). *Journal of Nonverbal Behavior, 24*, 179–209.

Matthews, G., Zeidner, M., & Roberts, R. D. (Eds.). (2002). *Emotional intelligence: Science & myth*. Cambridge, MA: MIT Press.

McClure, E. B. (2000). A meta-analytic review of sex differences in facial expression processing and their development in infants, children, and adolescents. *Psychological Bulletin, 126*, 424–453.

McClure, E. B., & Nowicki, S., Jr. (2001). Associations between social anxiety and nonverbal processing skill in preadolescent boys and girls. *Journal of Nonverbal Behavior, 25*, 3–19.

McLarney-Vesotski, A. R., Bernieri, F., & Rempala, D. (2006). Personality perception: A developmental study. *Journal of Research in Personality*, *40*, 652–674.

Meltzoff, A. N., & Moore, M. K. (1983). Newborn infants imitate adult facial gestures. *Child Development*, *54*, 702–709.

Merten, J. (2005). Culture, gender and the recognition of the basic emotions. *Psychologia*, *48*, 306–316.

Miller, R. E., Caul, W. F., & Mirsky, I. A. (1967). Communication of affects between feral and socially isolated monkeys. *Journal of Personality and Social Psychology*, *7*, 231–239.

Mueser, K. T., Penn, D. L., Blanchard, J. J., & Bellack, A. S. (1997). Affect recognition in schizophrenia: A synthesis of findings across three studies. *Psychiatry*, *60*, 301–308.

Murphy, N. A., Hall, J. A., & Colvin, C. R. (2003). Accurate intelligence assessments in social interaction: Mediators and gender effects. *Journal of Personality*, *71*, 465–493.

Niedenthal, P., Halberstadt, J. B., Margolin, J., & Innes-Ker, A. H. (2000). Emotional state and the detection of change in facial expression of emotion. *European Journal of Social Psychology*, *30*, 211–222.

Noller, P. (1980). Misunderstandings in marital communication: A study of couples' nonverbal communication. *Journal of Personality and Social Psychology*, *39*, 1135–1148.

Noller, P., & Gallois, C. (1986). Sending emotional messages in marriage: Non-verbal behaviour, sex and communication clarity. *British Journal of Social Psychology*, *25*, 287–297.

Nowicki, S., Jr., & Carton, E. (1997). The relation of nonverbal processing ability of faces and voices and children's feelings of depression and competence. *Journal of Genetic Psychology*, *158*, 357–363.

Nowicki, S., Jr., & Duke, M. P. (1994). Individual differences in the nonverbal communication of affect: The Diagnostic Analysis of Nonverbal Accuracy Scale. *Journal of Nonverbal Behavior*, *18*, 9–35.

Nowicki, S., Jr., Glanville, D., & Demertzis, A. (1998). A test of the ability to recognize emotion in the facial expressions of African American adults. *Journal of Black Psychology*, *24*, 335–350.

Nowicki, S., Jr., & Mitchell, J. (1998). Accuracy in identifying affect in child and adult faces and voices

and social competence in preschool children. *Genetic, Social, and General Psychology Monographs*, *124*, 39–59.

Odom, R. D., & Lemond, C. M. (1972). Developmental differences in the perception and production of facial expressions. *Child Development*, *43*, 359–369.

Patterson, M. L. (1995). A parallel process model of nonverbal communication. *Journal of Nonverbal Behavior*, *19*, 3–29.

Philippot, P., Feldman, R. S., & McGee, G. (1992). Nonverbal behavioral skills in an educational context: Typical and atypical populations. In R. S. Feldman (Ed.), *Applications of nonverbal behavioral theories and research*. Hillsdale, NJ: Erlbaum.

Phillips, R. D., Wagner, S. H., Fells, C. A., & Lynch, M. (1990). Do infants recognize emotion in facial expressions? Categorical and "metaphorical" evidence. *Infant Behavior and Development*, *13*, 71–84.

Pickett, C. L., Gardner, W. L., & Knowles, M. (2004). Getting a cue: The need to belong and enhanced sensitivity to social cues. *Personality and Social Psychology Bulletin*, *30*, 1095–1107.

Pitterman, H., & Nowicki, S. Jr. (2004). A test of the ability to identify emotion in human standing and sitting postures: The Diagnostic Analysis of Nonverbal Accuracy – 2 posture test (DANVA2-POS). *Genetic, Social, and General Psychology Monographs*, *130*, 146–162.

Pollak, S. D., & Sinha, P. (2002). Effects of early experience on children's recognition of facial displays of emotion. *Developmental Psychology*, *38*, 784–791.

Rentfrow, P. J., & Gosling, S. D. (2006). Message in a ballad: Personality judgments based on music preferences. *Psychological Science*, *17*, 236–242.

Reynolds, D. J., & Gifford, R. (2001). The sounds and sights of intelligence: A lens model channel analysis. *Personality and Social Psychology Bulletin*, *27*, 187–200.

Richards, J. M., & Gross, J. J. (1999). Composure at any cost? The cognitive consequences of emotional suppression. *Personality and Social Psychology Bulletin*, *25*, 1033–1044.

Richeson, J. A., & Shelton, J. N. (2005). Thin slices of racial bias. *Journal of Nonverbal Behavior*, *29*, 75–86.

Riggio, R. E. (1986). Assessment of basic social skills. *Journal of Personality and Social Psychology, 51,* 649–660.

Riggio, R. E. (2006). Nonverbal skills and abilities. In V. Manusov & M. L. Patterson (Eds.), *The Sage handbook of nonverbal communication* (pp. 79–95). Thousand Oaks, CA: Sage Publications.

Riggio, R. E., & Friedman, H. S. (1986). Impression formation: The role of expressive behavior. *Journal of Personality and Social Psychology, 50,* 421–427.

Riggio, R. E., & Riggio, H. R. (2001). Self-report measurement of interpersonal sensitivity. In J. A. Hall & F. J. Bernieri (Eds.), *Interpersonal sensitivity: Theory and measurement.* Mahwah, NJ: Erlbaum.

Riggio, H. R., & Riggio, R. E. (2002). Emotional expressiveness, extraversion, and neuroticism: A meta-analysis. *Journal of Nonverbal Behavior, 26,* 195–218.

Riggio, R. E., Widaman, K. F., & Friedman, H. S. (1985). Actual and perceived emotional sending and personality correlates. *Journal of Nonverbal Behavior, 9,* 69–83.

Rosenthal, R. (Ed.). (1979). *Skill in nonverbal communication: Individual differences.* Cambridge, MA: Oelgeschlager, Gunn & Hain.

Rosenthal, R., & DePaulo, B. M. (1979). Sex differences in eavesdropping on nonverbal cues. *Journal of Personality and Social Psychology, 37,* 273–285.

Rosenthal, R., Hall, J. A., DiMatteo, M. R., Rogers, P. L., & Archer, D. (1979). *Sensitivity to nonverbal communication: The PONS test.* Baltimore: Johns Hopkins University Press.

Rosip, J. C., & Hall, J. A. (2004). Knowledge of nonverbal cues, gender, and nonverbal decoding accuracy. *Journal of Nonverbal Behavior, 28,* 267–286.

Rotter, N. G., & Rotter, G. S. (1988). Sex differences in the encoding and decoding of negative facial emotions. *Journal of Nonverbal Behavior, 12,* 139–148.

Ruffman, T., Henry, J. D., Livingstone, V., & Phillips, L. H. (2008). A meta-analytic review of emotion recognition and aging: Implications for neuropsychological models of aging. *Neuroscience and Biobehavioral Reviews, 32,* 863–881.

Rule, N. O., & Ambady, N. (2008). Brief exposures: Male sexual orientation is accurately perceived at 50 ms. *Journal of Experimental Social Psychology, 44,* 1100–1105.

Russell, R. L., Stokes, J., Jones, M. E., Czogalik, D., & Rohleder, L. (1993). The role of nonverbal sensitivity in childhood psychopathology. *Journal of Nonverbal Behavior, 17,* 69–83.

Rutherford, M. D., Baron-Cohen, S., & Wheelwright, S. (2002). Reading the mind in the voice: A study with normal adults and adults with Asperger syndrome and high functioning autism. *Journal of Autism & Developmental Disorders, 32,* 189–194.

Sacks, O. (1993, December 27/1994, January 3). An anthropologist on Mars. *The New Yorker,* pp. 106–125.

Salovey, P., & Mayer, J. D. (1989). Emotional intelligence. *Imagination, Cognition, and Personality, 9,* 185–211.

Schiffenbauer, A. (1974). Effect of observer's emotional state on judgments of the emotional state of others. *Journal of Personality and Social Psychology, 30,* 31–35.

Schmid Mast, M., & Hall, J. A. (2004). Who is the boss and who is not? Accuracy of judging status. *Journal of Nonverbal Behavior, 28,* 145–165.

Shapiro, P. N., & Penrod, S. (1986). Meta-analysis of facial identification studies. *Psychological Bulletin, 100,* 139–156.

Snodgrass, S. E. (1992). Further effects of role versus gender on interpersonal sensitivity. *Journal of Personality and Social Psychology, 62,* 154–158.

Snodgrass, S. E., Hecht, M. A., & Ploutz-Snyder, R. (1998). Interpersonal sensitivity: Expressivity or perceptivity? *Journal of Personality and Social Psychology, 74,* 238–249.

Snyder, M. (1974). Self-monitoring of expressive behavior. *Journal of Personality and Social Psychology, 30,* 526–537.

Stamp, G., & Knapp, M. L. (1990). The construct of intent in interpersonal communication. *Quarterly Journal of Speech, 76,* 282–299.

Sternberg, R. (1984). *Beyond I.Q.: A triarchic theory of human intelligence.* Cambridge, UK: Cambridge University Press.

Surguladze, S. A., Young, A. W., Senior, C., Brébion, G., Travis, M. J., & Phillips, M. L. (2004). Recognition accuracy and response bias to happy and sad facial expressions in patients with major depression. *Neuropsychology, 18,* 212–218.

Swenson, J., & Casmir, F. L. (1998). The impact of culture-sameness, gender, foreign travel, and academic background on the ability to interpret facial expression of emotion in others. *Communication Quarterly, 46,* 214–230.

Termine, N. T., & Izard, C. E. (1988). Infants' responses to their mothers' expressions of joy and sadness. *Developmental Psychology, 24,* 223–229.

Thomas, G., & Fletcher, G. J. O. (2003). Mind-reading accuracy in intimate relationships: Assessing the roles of the relationship, the target, and the judge. *Journal of Personality and Social Psychology, 85,* 1079–1094.

Thompson, D. F., & Meltzer, L. (1964). Communication of emotional intent by facial expression. *Journal of Abnormal and Social Psychology, 68,* 129–135.

Thompson, W. F., Schellenberg, E. G., & Husain, G. (2004). Decoding speech prosody: Do music lessons help? *Emotion, 4,* 46–64.

Tickle-Degnen, L., & Rosenthal, R. (1990). The nature of rapport and its nonverbal correlates. *Psychological Inquiry, 1,* 285–293.

Trimboli, A., & Walker, M. (1993). The CAST test of nonverbal sensitivity. *Journal of Language and Social Psychology, 12,* 49–65.

Tucker, J. S., & Riggio, R. E. (1988). The role of social skills in encoding posed and spontaneous facial expressions. *Journal of Nonverbal Behavior, 12,* 87–97.

Wagner, H. L. (1993). On measuring performance in category judgment studies of nonverbal behavior. *Journal of Nonverbal Behavior, 17,* 3–28.

Wagner, H. L., Buck, R., & Winterbotham, M. (1993). Communication of specific emotions: Gender differences in sending accuracy and communication measures. *Journal of Nonverbal Behavior, 17,* 29–53.

Wagner, H., & Lee, V. (2008). Alexithymia and individual differences in emotional expression. *Journal of Research in Personality, 42,* 83–95.

Wagner, H. L., MacDonald, C. J., & Manstead, A. S. R. (1986). Communication of individual emotions by spontaneous facial expressions. *Journal of Personality and Social Psychology, 50,* 737–743.

Walker-Andrews, A. S. (1997). Infants' perception of expressive behaviors: Differentiation of multimodal information. *Psychological Bulletin, 121,* 437–456.

Walker-Andrews, A. S., & Lennon, E. (1991). Infants' discrimination of vocal expressions: Contributions of auditory and visual information. *Infant Behavior and Development, 14,* 131–142.

Wallbott, H. G., & Scherer, K. R. (1986). Cues and channels in emotion recognition. *Journal of Personality and Social Psychology, 51,* 690–699.

Zaidel, S., & Mehrabian, A. (1969). The ability to communicate and infer positive and negative attitudes facially and vocally. *Journal of Experimental Research in Personality, 3,* 233–241.

Zuckerman, M., DeFrank, R. S., Hall. J. A., Larrance, D. T., & Rosenthal, R. (1979). Facial and vocal cues of deception and honesty. *Journal of Experimental Social Psychology, 15,* 378–396.

Zuckerman, M., DePaulo, B. M., & Rosenthal, R. (1981). Verbal and nonverbal communication of deception. In L. Berkowitz (Ed.), *Advances in experimental social psychology* (Vol. 14). New York: Academic Press.

Zuckerman, M., Hall, J. A., DeFrank, R. S., & Rosenthal, R. (1976). Encoding and decoding of spontaneous and posed facial expressions. *Journal of Personality and Social Psychology, 34,* 966–977.

Zuckerman, M., Koestner, R., & Driver, R. (1981). Beliefs about cues associated with deception. *Journal of Nonverbal Behavior, 6,* 105–114.

Zuckerman, M., & Larrance, D. T. (1979). Individual differences in perceived encoding and decoding abilities. In R. Rosenthal (Ed.), *Skill in nonverbal communication: Individual differences.* Cambridge, MA: Oelgeschlager, Gunn & Hain.

Zuckerman, M., Lipets, M. S., Koivumaki, J. H., & Rosenthal, R. (1975). Encoding and decoding nonverbal cues of emotion. *Journal of Personality and Social Psychology, 32,* 1068–1076.

THE COMMUNICATION ENVIRONMENT

The features of the environment within which our interactions take place can exert a powerful influence on that interaction. Lighting, color schemes, furniture, and architecture, among other features, affect what we say and even how often we say it; sometimes we deliberately structure these features in order to obtain certain responses from others. This section of the book also explores the way we affect and are affected by the space we have within communication environments, as a preface to discussing, in Parts Three and Four, the behavior of the people who do the communicating.

Every interior betrays the nonverbal skills of its inhabitants. The choice of materials, the distribution of space, the kind of objects that command attention or demand to be touched—as compared to those that intimidate or repel—have much to say about the preferred sensory modalities of their owners.

—J. Ruesch and W. Kees

THE EFFECTS OF THE ENVIRONMENT ON HUMAN COMMUNICATION

CHAPTER 4

When people communicate with one another, features of the surrounding environment always exert an influence on their interaction. What are these environmental features, and how do they affect us?

First, let us look at a familiar communication environment: the classroom. Modern architects experiment with different designs, but many classes still take place in a rectangular room with straight rows of chairs for student seating. A row of windows along one side of the room may determine the direction students face, and consequently these determine the "front" of the room. It is not uncommon for classroom seats to be permanently attached to the floor for ease of maintenance and tidiness. Classrooms typically have some type of partition, often a desk or lectern, that serves as a boundary between the teacher and students. It is not hard for students and teachers to identify problems encountered in environments designed for learning: poor lighting and acoustics; inadequate climate control; external construction noises; inoperative or nonexistent electrical outlets; immovable seats; gloomy, dull, or distracting color schemes; unpleasant odors; and so on. Both students and teachers recognize that such problems impede the purpose for gathering in these rectangular rooms: to increase knowledge through effective student/teacher communication. The influence of the classroom environment on student and teacher behavior remained relatively unexplored until Sommer (1967, 1969, 1974) took a closer look. He focused his attention on the influence of classroom design on student participation.

Sommer selected several different types of classrooms for his study. He wanted to compare the amount of student participation in these classrooms and to analyze aspects of participatory behavior in each type. He selected seminar rooms with movable chairs, usually arranged in a horseshoe shape; laboratories—complete with Bunsen burners, bottles, and gas valves—that represented an extreme in straight-row seating; a windowless room; and one with an entire wall of windows. Among other things, Sommer concluded the following from his studies:

1. Students and teachers who dislike their learning environment will try to avoid it or change it.
2. In general, the amount of student participation decreases as the number of students in the class increases. The length of a student's participation is also longer in smaller classes.
3. The content of student participation in large classes is more likely to be devoted to questions of clarification or requests to repeat an idea rather than participation focused on the ideas themselves.
4. Participation was most frequent among those students within range of the instructor's eye gaze. In a seminar room, the students sitting directly across from the instructor participated more. A follow-up study by Adams and Biddle (1970) found a zone of participation in the center of the room (see Figure 4-1). This center zone is most likely to occur when the instructor stands in the middle of the room, because it is highly dependent on the instructor's visual contact with the students. If the instructor moved to the side and maintained visual contact with the students in front of him or her, the zone of participation would no longer be in the center. But there is more to this story: Koneya (1973) found that when high-, moderate-, and low-participating students were given a chance to select any seat they desired, high participators were most likely to select seats in the central zone of participation. We can conclude from this that student participation can be facilitated by visual contact with the instructor, but that students who are likely to participate tend to position themselves in seats that are close to the instructor or within the instructor's likely field of gaze. Also note that an instructor's gaze can be used to inhibit communication as well as facilitate it.

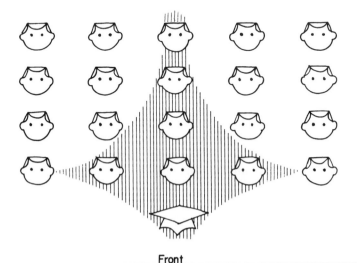

Front

FIGURE 4-1

The zone of class participation.

When students feel they will be punished—or at least not rewarded—for participating, the zone of participation is inoperative.

5. What happens when you take moderate- and low-participating students and deliberately seat them in the zone of participation? Koneya (1973) found that moderate participators increased their participation, but low participators remained low. This suggests that where students sit can alter their classroom participation, but this effect is less likely with low participators. Haber (1982) found that ethnic, racial, and religious minorities at five colleges tended to select seating peripheral to the zone of participation—even when they were a majority at a particular college.

From these studies, we can conclude that classroom seating is not random. Certain types of people gravitate toward seats that are close to the instructor and/or within his or her expected pattern of gaze. The instructor's gazing patterns creates a zone where students are more likely to verbally participate, unless they are students who initially sought seating outside of this zone and were moved within it. Even then, we might find increased participation at some point if a teacher rewards and supports student participation.

The preceding discussion of the classroom is an example of a specific context in which spatial relationships, architecture, and objects surrounding the participants influence the amount and type of interaction that occurs. We will examine other environmental factors that impinge on human communication behavior, but we should remember that the environment is only one element in structuring such behavior. If students, administrators, teachers, secretaries, and custodians want to run a school or university like a prison or a dehumanized bureaucracy, changes in the classroom structure may have very little impact.

Throughout this chapter, we discuss a number of characteristics of environments. Let us initiate our exploration by examining the way we perceive our surroundings, because this can significantly influence the way we feel and the way we choose to communicate.

PERCEPTIONS OF OUR SURROUNDINGS

The number of places in which we communicate with others is limitless: buses, homes, apartments, restaurants, offices, parks, hotels, sports arenas, factories, libraries, movie theaters, museums, and so on. Despite their diversity, we probably evaluate these environments along similar dimensions. Once we perceive our environment in a certain way, we may incorporate such perceptions in the development of the messages we send. And once these messages have been sent, the environmental perceptions of the other person have been altered. Thus we influence and are influenced by our environments.

How do we see our environments? We believe the following six dimensions are central to our perceptions and consequently to how we send and receive messages.

PERCEPTIONS OF FORMALITY

One familiar dimension along which we can classify environments is a formal–informal continuum. Reactions may be based on the objects present, the people present, the functions performed, or any number of other variables. Individual offices may be more formal than a lounge in the same building; a year-end banquet takes on more formality than a "come as you are" party; an evening at home with one other couple may be more informal than an evening with 10 other couples. The greater the formality, the greater the chances that the communication behavior will be less relaxed and more superficial, hesitant, and stylized.

PERCEPTIONS OF WARMTH

Environments that make us feel psychologically warm encourage us to linger, relax, and feel comfortable. It may be some combination of the color of the drapes or walls, paneling, carpeting, texture of the furniture, softness of the chairs, sound-proofing, and so on. Even the exterior of an environment can affect our anticipated feelings of comfort. Students viewed slides of 34 different medical facilities, and the expected quality of care and degree of comfort varied with different types of buildings (Devlin, 2008).

Fast-food chains try to exhibit enough warmth in their decor to seem inviting but enough coldness to encourage rapid turnover. Interestingly, environments that make us feel psychologically warm may also make us feel physically warmer. Students were asked to spend 2 hours studying or reading in a room with a neutral decor, similar to that of a classroom. Then they were asked to read or study in a room that resembled a walk-in meat cooler. Nearly all the students felt the second room was cooler, even though the temperature was actually the same in both rooms. Then the meat cooler room was paneled, carpeted, and equipped with subdued light-ing and other appointments. Another group of students was asked to read or study in each room. This time, the redesigned meat-cooler room was judged to have a higher temperature than the classroom. Again, actual temperatures were the same (Rohles, 1980).

PERCEPTIONS OF PRIVACY

Enclosed environments usually suggest greater privacy, particularly if they accom-modate only a few people. If the possibility of other people's entering and/or over-hearing our conversation is slight, even if we are outdoors, there is a greater feeling of privacy. Personal items such as toilet articles, low or focused lighting, high-density situations, partitions, noise, and other environmental factors can affect perceptions of privacy (Buslig, 1999). With greater privacy, we will probably find close speaking distances and more personal messages designed and adapted for the specific other person rather than people in general.

PERCEPTIONS OF FAMILIARITY

When we meet a new person or encounter an unfamiliar environment, our responses typically are cautious, deliberate, and conventional. Unfamiliar environments are laden with rituals and norms we do not yet know, so we are hesitant to move too quickly. We will probably go slowly until we can associate this unfamiliar environ-ment with one we know. One interpretation for the stereotyped structure of fast-food restaurants is that they allow us, in our mobile society, to readily find a familiar and predictable place that will guarantee minimal demands for active contact with strangers. In unfamiliar environments, the most likely initial topic of conversation will be the environment itself: Have you ever been here before? What is it like? Who comes here?

PERCEPTIONS OF CONSTRAINT

Part of our total reaction to our environment is based on our perception of whether, and how easily, we can leave it. Some students feel confined in their own homes during the school Christmas break. But consider the differences between this 2-week constraint and a permanent live-at-home arrangement. The intensity of these perceptions of constraint is closely related to the space available to us, and the privacy of this space, during the time we are in the environment. Some environments seem to be only temporarily confining, such as an automobile during a long trip, but perceptions of confinement in environments such as prisons, spacecraft, or nursing homes may seem more enduring.

PERCEPTIONS OF DISTANCE

Sometimes our responses within a given environment are influenced by how close or far away we must conduct our communication with another. This may reflect actual physical distance—an office on a different floor, a house in another part of the city—or it may reflect psychological distance, with barriers clearly separating people who are fairly close physically. You may be seated close to someone and still not perceive it as a close environment; for example, interlocking chairs facing the same direction in an airport. When the setting forces us into close quarters with other people not well known to us, such as elevators or crowded buses, we try to increase distance psychologically to reduce threatening feelings of intimacy. We can do this through less eye contact, body tenseness and immobility, cold silence, nervous laughter, jokes about the intimacy, and public conversation directed at all present.

The perceptions just described represent only some of the dimensions along which we can view communication settings. Generally, more intimate communication is associated with informal, unconstrained, private, familiar, close, and warm environments. In everyday situations, however, these dimensions combine in complex ways. The mixture of intimate and nonintimate factors can be seen in an elevator if it is perceived as close, familiar, and temporarily confining but also public, formal, and cold.

REACTING TO ENVIRONMENTS

Once these perceptions are made, how do they affect our reactions? Sometimes the impact of the environment will be slight, but it has the potential to play a significant role in affecting our behavior. In a study of 98 child-care classes for 3- and 4-year-olds, the researcher concluded that perceptions of the physical environment were related to measures of the children's cognitive and social competency, especially for the 3-year-olds (Maxwell, 2007).

Mehrabian (1976) argued that we react emotionally to our surroundings. These emotional reactions can be accounted for in terms of (1) how *aroused* the environment makes us feel, (2) how *pleasurable* we feel, and (3) how *dominant* we feel. *Arousal* refers to how active, stimulated, frenzied, or alert we are. *Dominance* refers to feelings of being in control, importance, and freedom to act in a variety of ways. *Pleasure* refers to feelings of joy, satisfaction, and happiness.

Novel, surprising, and complex environments probably produce higher arousal. Those people less able to screen out unwanted information from the environment inevitably have to respond to more stimuli and, in turn, become more aroused. Although we all probably respond as "screeners" and "nonscreeners" on occasion, some people tend to respond habitually as one or the other. *Nonscreeners* are less selective in what they respond to in any environment. They see, hear, smell, and otherwise sense more stimuli. *Screeners*, in contrast, are selective in what they respond to. They impose a hierarchy of importance on various components in a complex situation. Nonscreeners not only become more aroused than screeners in novel, changing, and sudden situations, they remain aroused longer—even after leaving the arousing environment. That is why nonscreeners are most attracted to environments that are both arousing and pleasurable.

PERCEPTIONS OF TIME

Time is also a part of the communicative environment. At first, it may seem strange to include something as seemingly intangible as time in the same environmental package as chairs, walls, noise, or even weather conditions. However, people in the United States do treat time as something tangible, a commodity that can be divided up, saved, spent, and made. Furthermore, we often project temporal qualities onto objects within our environment; for example, a chair that looks like it has been there "forever" or an elevator that "never seems to be on time."

Time is important to us. It governs when we eat and sleep, it often determines how much we get paid at work, and it sets limits on how much material students can learn in a given class period. Time plays a key role in social interaction as well. It influences our perceptions of people; for example, responsible people are "on time," boring people talk "too long," or a good romantic partner gives us some "time to ourself" (Leonard, 1978; Werner & Baxter, 1994). A course in time management is a staple for anyone expecting to climb the corporate ladder in U.S. organizations. Time plays such an important role in our lives that we often carry the date and time around with us on our wrist or on our cell phones. Most cars have clocks, and some of them even have devices for computing the time it will take to drive from one location to another. We are very much aware of the stress time can create in our lives. We think of a vacation as a retreat to a place where time matters less. Ironically, vacations are usually thought of as a set period of time. Ballard and Seibold (2000) succinctly capture the reciprocal relationship between communication and time when they say, "Communication creates persons' views and understanding of time, yet our sense of time enables and constrains communication in important ways" (p. 219).

Time is perceived very differently in other cultures (Hall, 1959). These varying orientations to time are often a central factor in misunderstandings among members of different cultures. Psychology professor Robert Levine gives this account of his teaching experience in Brazil:

> As I left home for my first day of class, I asked someone the time. It was 9:05 a.m., which allowed me time to relax and look around the campus before my 10 o'clock lecture. After what I judged to be half an hour, I glanced at the clock I was passing. It said 10:20! In a panic, I broke for the classroom, followed by gentle calls of "Hola, professor" and "Tudo bem, professor?" from unhurried students, many of whom, I later realized, were my own. I arrived breathless to find an empty room. Frantically, I asked a passerby the time. "Nine forty-five" was the answer. No, that couldn't be. I asked someone else. "Nine fifty-five." Another said: "Exactly 9:43." The clock in a nearby office read 3:15. I had learned my first lesson about Brazilians: Their timepieces are consistently inaccurate. And nobody minds. My class was scheduled from 10 until noon. Many students came late, some very late . . . none seemed terribly concerned about lateness . . . . The real surprise came at noon . . . only a few students left immediately. Others drifted out during the next fifteen minutes, and some continued asking me questions long after that. (Levine & Wolff, 1985, p. 30)

To understand cultural variations in perceiving time, we must first understand our own culture. We know that our responses are influenced by our experiences with time at several different levels (Cottle, 1976; Friedman, 1990; Hall, 1983; McGrath & Kelly, 1986). Biologically, our bodies seem to be programmed so that "internal clocks" regulate our physical, emotional, and intellectual functioning (Luce, 1971). We also know that people have differing psychological orientations to time. There are important differences among people within this culture regarding their orientations to the past, present, and future. These orientations may represent a long-term style or may be subject to change; for example, a person who "lives for the moment" at one point in his or her life might later adapt to a future-oriented style that involves evaluating today's "moments" in terms of the long-range picture (Gonzalez & Zimbardo, 1985). Different orientations toward time not only affect the way people interact in specific encounters, but they are also used to evaluate more enduring qualities. For example, some people think that being punctual and meeting deadlines are signs not only of successful people but of "good" people.

As we understand more about the environmental stimuli and conditions that trigger time perceptions, we can use this knowledge to construct environments that give off the temporal messages we desire. In social encounters, the following perceptions of time are fundamental:

1. As the location of events
2. As the duration of events
3. As the interval between events
4. As the patterning of intervals

TIME AS LOCATION

Some of our perceptions of time have to do with when something happens, or the timing of an event. The onset of some events is evaluated as well timed; for example, "You hugged me at the exact moment I needed it most." Some are viewed as ill timed; for example, "I don't like eating dinner at 10 P.M." Sometimes our perceptions of when something happens are precise, and sometimes they represent a general time frame. For some, the time to eat lunch is precisely noon; for others it can be anytime between 11 A.M. and 2 P.M. Just as we attribute many different meanings to the timing of events in our lives, we also can communicate multiple meanings as we set deadlines for the occurrence of events in the future. For example, if something is due much sooner than expected, it may mean it is a form of punishment, a reward, very important, or very unimportant.

TIME AS DURATION

Our temporal perceptions also include how long an event lasts. We develop expectations for the proper and improper length of events, but perceptions of duration are not always a reflection of actual duration. An environment with little activity can be perceived as so boring that we feel we have been there "forever." But "time flies when we are having fun."

TIME AS INTERVALS

The periods between events also constitute a way of perceiving time. The rate at which something happens is really a perception of the time since it last occurred. The perceived tempo of our lives is likely to be a reflection of how much or how little time separates each of our activities. We learn to expect certain intervals with certain activities. The phrase "It's been too long since I've seen you" suggests a contact-interval norm associated with close relationships that has been exceeded for this person. Similarly, we may not object to a person's using obscene language, but we may object to the brevity of the intervals between usage.

TIME AS PATTERNS OF INTERVALS

As we observe recurrent sequences of intervals, we begin to sense social rhythms—the regularity–irregularity and order–disorder that make up the cycles of our behavior and routines. Of all our time-bound perceptions, the pattern of intervals is the most complex and the most difficult to articulate to others. Understanding the patterning of intervals is, however, crucial to understanding ourselves as well as understanding our interactions with another person. When we feel in tune with another person, we are focusing on a pleasing perception of interactional synchrony, and when we feel awkward with someone, it may be because their patterning of nonverbal gestures or pauses is very different from ours. The understanding of patterns of intervals in our environment, whether it is a talk–silence pattern or a sunny–cloudy atmospheric pattern, is fundamental to making daily predictions about our lives.

We devote the remainder of this chapter to the characteristics of environments that form the bases of the perceptions just outlined: perceptions of our surroundings and perceptions of time. Each environment has three major components:

1. The natural environment—geography, location, atmospheric conditions
2. The presence or absence of other people
3. Architectural and design features, including movable objects

THE NATURAL ENVIRONMENT

Some of us live in densely populated urban areas, some in smaller towns, some in suburban areas on the outskirts of these cities and towns, and others in rural areas. Within these broad areas, we find other environmental features that affect the nature of human interaction; for example, apartment complexes, neighborhoods, high-rise buildings, and so on. The places we live, play, and work are bound to have an impact on our behavior. The number of people we communicate with can influence our interaction style, but perhaps more important is the number of different people for whom we have to adapt our messages. Some environments are very homogeneous and provide inhabitants with fewer experiences and fewer examples of diverse styles, behavior, and values. The pace of life and the time devoted to developing social and personal relationships may also vary as a function of where we live. In slums or ghettos in urban areas, we often find a social climate that encourages or fosters unconventional and deviant behavior or at least tolerates it. Thus slum areas show a high incidence of juvenile delinquency, prostitution, alcohol and drug addiction, physical and mental disability, and crimes of violence (Krupat, 1985).

Behavioral scientists have also been interested in the effects of barometric pressure. For example, high or rising barometric pressure has been associated with feelings of good health; low or falling barometric pressure is more likely to be linked to feelings of pain or depression. Optimum student behavior and performance have been observed when the barometer was high or rising and on cool days with little wind and precipitation. Increase in positive air ions also seems to increase people's irritability and tension.

The changing seasons seem to have an impact on behavior, too. Even in areas of the United States with minimal seasonal variations in temperature, national routines associated with changing seasons are still followed; for example, taking summer vacations and starting school in the fall. Some of the ways in which our behavior varies with the seasons include the following:

1. Suicide rates and admissions to public mental hospitals rise dramatically in the spring and peak in the summer.
2. College students tend to break up with their dating partners at the beginnings and endings of semesters (May/June, August/September, or December/January).
3. During the summer, people tend to see their friends more often.
4. During the summer, crimes of assault and rape increase.
5. From July to November, people tend to report less happiness but more activity and less boredom.

Temperature and the way it affects human responses is the climatic factor that has received the most scientific attention—specifically, the extent to which hot temperatures increase aggressive motivation and aggressive behavior.

Lengthy periods of extreme heat are often associated with discomfort, irritability, reduced work output, and unfavorable evaluations of strangers. Hot temperatures increased aggressive horn honking for drivers without air conditioning (Kenrick & MacFarlane, 1984). Vrij, van der Steen, and Koppelaar (1994) studied the reactions of police officers to a simulated burglary in which the temperature varied from comfortably cool to hot. When the temperature was hot, officers reported more aggressive and threatening impressions of the suspect and were more likely to draw their weapon. As Anderson (2001) observes, uncomfortably warm temperatures seem to increase the likelihood that ambiguous social interactions will be viewed as aggressive. A simple question like "Is it really necessary that I do that?" may be taken as an aggressive challenge to personal authority that demands some form of retaliation.

An analysis of riots in India over a 22-year period found that most took place during the months when the temperature was between 80 and 90 degrees Fahrenheit (Berke & Wilson, 1951). The National Advisory Commission on Civil Disorders, reporting on riots in the United States, said that hot summer nights added to an already explosive situation that eventually resulted in widespread rioting in ghetto areas: "In most instances, the temperature during the day on which the violence erupted was quite high" (Report of the National Advisory Commission on Civil Disorders, 1968, p. 71; also see Goranson & King, 1970). An analysis of 102 riots in the United States between 1967 and 1971 concluded that the most likely temperature–riot sequence was one in which the temperature rose to between 81 and 85 degrees Fahrenheit and remained within that range for about 7 days preceding the riot. Rotton and Cohen (2003) conducted two studies, each covering 38 years or more, and found annual temperatures associated with various forms of criminal behavior such as assaults, rapes, robberies, burglaries, and larceny—but not murder.

Without any way to relieve the effects of high temperatures, criminal behavior is likely to decrease when extremely high temperatures persist. Very high temperatures lead people to seek ways to relieve their discomfort rather than engage in criminal activity. Riots were less likely to occur as temperatures climbed above 90 degrees Fahrenheit (Baron & Ransberger, 1978; Carlsmith & Anderson, 1979). As Figure 4-2 indicates, assaults in climate-controlled settings tend to increase when

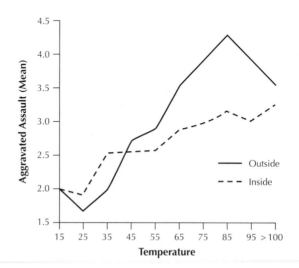

FIGURE 4-2

Aggravated assault as a function of temperature and climate control.

temperatures are extremely high but decrease in outdoor situations without climate-controls (Rotton & Cohn, 2004).

Obviously, the relationship between temperature and aggression is not simple. Probably a number of factors interact with the temperature to increase the chance of aggression: prior provocation; the presence of aggressive models; and negative affect experienced from sources other than temperature, such as poverty and unemployment, perceived ability to leave the environment, the availability of sources to relieve any adverse effects of temperature, and so on. A thorough review of the literature, however, concludes the following:

> Clearly, hot temperatures produce increases in aggressive motives and tendencies. Hotter regions of the world yield more aggression; this is especially apparent when analyses are done within countries. Hotter years, quarters of years, seasons, months, and days all yield relatively more aggressive behaviors such as murders, rapes, assaults, riots, and wife beatings, among others. Finally, those concomitant temperature–aggression studies done in the field also yielded clear evidence that uncomfortably hot temperatures produce increases in aggressive motives and behaviors. (Anderson, 1989, p. 93)

The heat–aggression relationship seems to carry over to our sporting activities as well. An analysis of all major league baseball games between 1986 and 1988 showed a strong correlation between higher temperatures and the number of batters hit by pitched balls (Reifman, Larrick, & Fein, 1991).

Griffitt varied heat and humidity under controlled laboratory conditions for students and confirmed a relationship to interpersonal responses. As temperature and humidity increased, evaluative responses for interpersonal attraction to other students decreased (Griffitt, 1970; Griffitt & Veitch, 1971). There may be more truth than fiction in the familiar explanation for a particularly unpleasant encounter: "Oh, he was just hot and irritable." Note, however, that sometimes unpleasant environmental factors, such as heat or noise, can increase attraction for others. In such cases, the aversive stimulus may function as something both people have in common (Kenrick & Johnson, 1979; Schneider, Lesko, & Garrett, 1980). The extent to which heat and other environmental variables increase or decrease attraction to others depends on how these interact with many other factors, such as the interactants' personalities and the presence or absence of simultaneously occurring rewarding stimuli.

The effects of the moon and sunspots on human behavior have also been studied scientifically. Psychiatrist Arnold Lieber reasoned that human beings, like the earth, are subject to gravitational forces created by different positions of the moon. (Human beings, like the planet itself, are about 80 percent water and 20 percent solids.) He plotted the number of murders in relation to the position of the moon and concluded a strong relationship between the two (Lieber, 1978). But considerable skepticism exists regarding Lieber's theory and similar work, because research of this type shows how two things vary together, *not* that a particular moon position actually *causes* certain behaviors. Several other factors likely are interacting and affecting the two. Two separate analyses of over 37 studies that purportedly linked moon positions and the frequency of psychiatric hospital admissions, suicides, homicides, traffic accidents, and changes in the stock market concluded that a spurious relationship exists between moon phases and these behaviors (Campbell & Beets, 1978; Rotton & Kelly, 1985).

Aside from the influence of high temperatures on aggressive tendencies, we do not have a lot of reliable and valid information on how the natural environment affects our communication behavior. It seems reasonable to believe that various aspects of the natural environment will have an influence, but the exact nature and degree of this influence is still unknown. Most people seem to believe the weather has less impact on their own behavior than it does on others' behavior, that it has less impact on behavior than it does on emotional states, and that it does not have more impact on negative states than on positive ones (Jorgenson, 1981). Kraut and Johnston (1979) found that people walking on the sidewalk smiled more when the weather was sunny and pleasant than when it was rainy and overcast. This difference was much less significant than the effect of being with others; people smiled much more when in interaction than when alone. Thus, compared to more social factors, climate and other environmental variables may have weak influences on our behavior.

OTHER PEOPLE IN THE ENVIRONMENT

Chapter 5 examines the reactions of people to overpopulated environments. For now, we point out that people can be perceived as part of the environment and do have an effect on the behavior of others. These people may be perceived as active or passive participants, depending on the degree to which they are perceived as "involved" in conversations, either speaking or listening. In many situations, these people are seen as active, especially if they are able to overhear what is being said. In some situations, we grant another person or persons the dubious status of "nonperson" and behave accordingly. This may occur in high-density situations, but it is also common with just one other person. Cab drivers, janitors, and children achieve nonperson status with regularity. The presence of nonpersons, of course, allows the uninhibited flow of interaction, because as far as the active participants are concerned, they themselves are the only human interactants present. Parents sometimes talk to others about personal aspects of their child while the child is playing nearby. For the interactants, the child is perceived as "not there." Any relevant verbal or nonverbal responses on the part of the nonperson that are picked up by the interactants immediately strip the person of the nonperson role.

When others are perceived as an active ingredient in the environment, certain kinds of communication may be facilitated or inhibited. The chief difference in communication with active others is that messages must be adapted to multiple audiences rather than to a single one. Even telephone conversations in which a third party can hear only one of the interactants are altered to account for the uninvited listener. Sometimes the existence of these additional audiences presents such a strain or threat that one or both communicators leave the scene. However, the appearance of a third party can provide an opportunity to ease out of a conversation with an undesirable other by "dumping" the focus of the interaction onto this third party and making a polite exit.

The presence of others may increase our motivation to look good in what we say and do, which may be either detrimental, distorting information, or beneficial. The benefits of looking good in the presence of others is exemplified by constructive approaches to conflict. For instance, the presence of others may prohibit overt fighting, albeit temporarily. Others in the environment have ensured a delay, which may act as a cooling-off period or may further frustrate or aggravate the person who has to repress such feelings.

When researchers observed that the home team was usually the winner in sporting events (53 percent of the time in professional baseball, 58 percent in professional football, 60 percent in college football, 67 percent in professional basketball, and 64 percent in professional hockey), it was attributed primarily to the home team's familiarity with the home field or to the visiting team's travel fatigue. Further analysis showed, however, that the primary factor contributing to the home team's victories was the spectators, who seemed to provide psychological support that improved performance. In contrast, unfriendly home crowds may increase performance errors (Schwartz & Barsky, 1977; Thirer & Rampey, 1979). Some analyses of home team performances before supportive fans have suggested a tendency for the home team to "choke" in championship games, but some studies have not shown this to be true for baseball or basketball (Schlenker, Phillips, Boniecki, & Schlenker, 1995). Within the framework of these generalizations, we also may observe that sometimes friendly support is taken for granted; and performance lags, or performers may excel, in response to negative feedback from others. The point to remember, though, is that friendly or unfriendly hometown supporters in the communication environment, as in sporting events, are likely to have a profound effect on performance.

The ways in which groups influence individual performance are too numerous and too large a topic to discuss here. Two examples illustrate the subtlety of some of these effects:

1. In one of social psychology's first experiments, boys wound line on fishing reels faster when others were present performing the same activity, even though there was no competition and no emphasis on speed. Many studies have since found this *social facilitation* effect whereby performance—on simple and well-learned tasks, at least—is enhanced by the mere presence of others.
2. If people feel others are working with them on a joint task, they often slack off without realizing it. This *social loafing* is strongest when people feel their own contributions cannot be tallied or evaluated (Harkins & Szymanski, 1987).

ARCHITECTURAL DESIGN AND MOVABLE OBJECTS

Hall (1966) labeled the architecture and objects in our environment as either fixed feature space or semifixed feature space. *Fixed feature* space refers to space organized by unmoving boundaries, such as in rooms of houses; *semifixed feature* space refers to the arrangement of movable objects, such as tables or chairs. Both can have a strong impact on our communication behavior.

At one time in U.S. history, banks were deliberately designed to project an image of strength and security. The design frequently featured large marble pillars, an abundance of metal bars and doors, uncovered floors, and bare walls. This style generally projected a cold, impersonal image to visitors. Later, bankers perceived the need to change their environment, to create a friendly, warm, "homey" place where people would enjoy sitting down and discussing their financial needs and problems. Bank interiors began to change. Carpeting was added, wood replaced metal, cushioned chairs were added, and potted plants and art were brought in for additional warmth. This is only one example of the recognition that many times, the interior in which interaction occurs can significantly influence the nature of the interaction. Some churches have tried to make their environments more inviting by having greeters, PowerPoint presentations, musicians who sing and play guitars, and the like. Nightclub owners and restauranteurs have long been aware that dim lighting and sound-absorbing surfaces—such as carpets, drapes, and padded ceilings—provide greater intimacy and cause patrons to linger longer than they would in an interior with high illumination and no soundproofing.

The earliest studies to focus on the influence of interior decoration on human responses were conducted by Maslow and Mintz (1956) and Mintz (1956). They selected three rooms for study: one was an "ugly" room, designed to give the impression of a janitor's storeroom in disheveled condition; one was a "beautiful" room, complete with attractive appointments that included carpeting and drapes; and one was an "average" room—a professor's office. People sitting in these rooms were asked to rate a series of negative print photographs (to control for color, shading, and so forth) of faces. The experimenters tried to keep all factors—time of day, odor, noise, type of seating, and experimenter—constant from room to room, so results could be attributed to the type of room.

Results showed that people in the beautiful room gave significantly higher ratings on "energy" and "well-being" to the faces than did participants in the ugly room. Experimenters and subjects alike engaged in various escape behaviors to avoid the ugly room, which was variously described as producing monotony, fatigue, headache, discontent, sleep, irritability, and hostility. The beautiful room, however, produced feelings of pleasure, comfort, enjoyment, importance, energy, and a desire to continue the activity. In this instance, we have a well-controlled study that offers some evidence of the impact of visual–aesthetic surroundings on the nature of human interaction. Similar studies found that students do better on tests, rate teachers higher, and solve problems more effectively in beautiful rooms than in ugly ones (Campbell, 1979; Wollin & Montagre, 1981).

Because at least one study did not find mood or evaluations of others to change with drastic changes in appointments and decor (Kasmar, Griffin, & Mauritzen, 1968), we are reminded that the impact of the environment is only one source of influence on our perceptions. Sometimes it is a powerful force, but sometimes the close relationship between the two parties, an understanding of or tolerance for clutter, positive behavior on the part of the other person, and other factors offset any negative effects emanating from an ugly environment.

Sometimes we get very definite person- or couple-related messages from home environments (see Figure 4-3). The designation of places in the home for certain activities and not for others, the symbolism attached to various objects in the home, and ways of decorating the home may tell us a lot about the nature of a couple's relationship (Altman, Brown, Staples, & Werner, 1992). Sometimes the way a home is decorated reveals whether the inhabitants decorated their home for themselves, for others, for conformity, for comfort, and so on (Sandalla, 1987). When people feel their home decoration expresses their personality, this makes it easier for others to judge aspects of their personality (Hata, 2004).

FIGURE 4-3

Environmental Perception Test: (a) Describe the people who live here. (b) Tell why you would or would not like to meet the people who live here. (c) How much communication takes place here? (d) What topics are mostly likely discussed? (e) Which dimensions listed on pp. 101–103 influenced your perceptions the most? (f) Compare your answers with others.

Lohmann, Arriaga, and Goodfriend (2003) were able to use decorative objects in a home to determine the closeness of the inhabitants' relationship. They asked couples who were either married or living together in a romantic relationship to identify objects in their homes they most wanted visitors to notice and to specify their favorite objects. Each object was also identified as either individually acquired or jointly acquired. Couples completed questionnaires that measured their relationship commitment and closeness. The couples who had greater commitment and closer relationships were also couples who had a higher proportion of jointly acquired objects that they wanted visitors to notice and more jointly acquired favorite objects.

Gosling and colleagues (Gosling, Ko, Mannarelli, & Morris, 2002; Gosling, Gaddis, & Vazire, 2008) were interested in whether personality characteristics could accurately be predicted from a person's office or bedroom. Observers who experienced various offices and bedrooms firsthand indicated the extent to which the environment they saw reflected the person's extraversion, agreeableness, emotional stability, openness to experience, and conscientiousness. The personality profile of the people who worked in the offices and slept in the bedrooms was obtained from their own responses to personality measures. These types of environments seem to have enough signals associated with conscientiousness and openness to experience to enable observers to effectively judge inhabitants with those characteristics, but observers were not as successful in judging other personality characteristics. We may not always be accurate in judging another person's personality characteristics from the way they construct their environment, but that does not stop us from making such judgments. People who judged the personality of characters in a story when the quality of their housekeeping was varied judged the housekeepers with a dirty environment as less agreeable, less conscientious, less intelligent, and less feminine but more open and more neurotic than the clean housekeepers. Whether the housekeeper was male or female did not affect the judgments (Harris and Sachau, 2005).

The way people decorate their rooms may also forecast future behavior. In one study, researchers took photographs of 83 freshman college students' rooms. When the photos of the rooms of students who had dropped out of school a year and a half later were analyzed, it was noted that the dropouts had more decorations reflecting high school and home and fewer related to the university community. Dropouts also seemed to have fewer ways to protect their privacy; their favorite way to combat unwanted noise was to override it with more noise of their own (Vinsel, Brown, Altman, & Foss, 1980).

COLOR

People believe colors can affect behavior. In fact, some believe "prisoner mischief" will vary as a function of the colors surrounding prisoners. For example, the walls of the San Diego city jail were at one time reportedly painted pink, baby blue, and peach on the assumption that pastel colors would have a calming effect on the inmates. In Salem, Oregon, the cell bars of Oregon's correctional institution were painted soft greens, blues, and buffs; some cell doors were painted bright yellow, orange, green, and blue. In addition, the superintendent of the institution said the color schemes would be continually changed to keep it "an exciting place to work and live in." Initial studies of people exposed to environments painted Baker-Miller pink found decreasing heart rates, pulse, and respiration. Subsequent studies in adult and juvenile correctional facilities, psychiatric hospitals, and controlled laboratory studies with undergraduate students supported the belief that this pink color aided in suppressing violent and aggressive behaviors (Pelligrini & Schauss, 1980; Schauss, 1985). In 2005, the sheriff of Mason County, Texas, painted the bars and walls of his five-inmate jail pink and issued pink sheets, pink slippers, and pink jumpsuits to his prisoners. He claims it has led to a 70 percent decrease in repeated offenses (Phinney, 2006).

But not all experiences with pink have been so positive. The county jail in San Jose, California, reportedly painted two holding cells shocking pink in the belief that prisoner hostility would be reduced. Prisoners seemed less hostile for about 15 minutes, but soon the hostility reached a peak; after 3 hours, some prisoners were tearing the paint off the wall. This result is consistent with the research of Smith, Bell, and Fusco (1986) who found pink to be arousing rather than weakening. In fact, any color that is highly saturated and bright is likely to be more arousing and will garner more attention than paler colors (Camgoz, Yener, & Guvenc, 2004; Garber & Hyatt, 2003). When prisoners are allowed to paint their cells with colors they choose, it may have an aggression-reducing effect, but the effect may have more to do with the prisoner's control over the choice of colors than the colors themselves. Nevertheless, the preceding reports show how various institutions have tried, with mixed results, to apply the findings from color research to affect the nature of human interaction in certain environments.

Colors are also believed to influence student learning. Colors that will facilitate, or at least not impede, learning are always a concern during classroom construction. In Munich, Germany, a group of researchers studied the impact of colors on mental growth and social relations ("Blue Is Beautiful," 1973). Children tested in rooms they thought were beautiful scored about 12 points higher on an IQ test than those tested in rooms they thought were ugly. Blue, yellow, yellow green, and orange were considered beautiful; white, black, and brown were considered ugly. The beautifully colored rooms also seemed to stimulate alertness and creativity. In the orange room, psychologists found that positive social reactions, such as friendly words and smiles, increased 53 percent, whereas negative reactions, such as irritability and hostility, decreased 12 percent.

Ball's (1965) summary of the color research prior to 1965 found what others have found since then: that people associate serenity and calm with the colors blue and green, and that red and orange are perceived to be arousing and stimulating. The research of Wexner (1954) and Murray and Deabler (1957) are representative of this tradition. Wexner (see Table 4-1) presented 8 colors and 11 mood-tones to 94 research participants. The results show that a single color is significantly related to some mood-tones; for others, two or more colors may be associated.

It is difficult to know how to interpret this research. First, research participants were asked to judge colors outside of any context, even though the colors we respond to in daily life are perceived within a particular context. Separating color from the objects and forms that give it shape, the surrounding colors, and other contextual features may elicit some learned stereotypes about the relationship of mood and color, but this stereotype may or may not be relevant when given a context. Pink may be your favorite color, but you may still dislike pink hair. Hines (1996) found that residents of four American cities believed red meant danger, warmth, love, strength, and safety; but when these same people were asked to think about red in terms of products, they said red meant Coca-Cola. Because the color red is associated with male dominance and testosterone levels in some nonhuman animals, Hill and Barton (2005) wondered whether the wearing of red would play a role in winning sporting contests. In the 2004 Olympic games, contestants in four combat sports—tae kwon do, boxing, Greco-Roman wrestling, and freestyle wrestling—were randomly assigned red or blue outfits. In all four competitions, the contestants wearing red won significantly more fights. They later compared the performances of five soccer teams that varied the color of their uniforms and found that they won significantly more games when wearing red. The researchers caution, however, that wearing red may only be a favorable factor in winning when the combatants are reasonably matched in skill: Wearing red will not overcome a lack of talent. This might help to explain why every year from 2001 through 2007, the Cincinnati Reds baseball team lost more games than they won.

But red is not the only color believed to affect the outcome of sporting events. A series of studies on the color of uniforms worn by football and hockey players pinpointed the complex ways in which colors may affect behavior. Frank and

TABLE 4.1 | COLORS ASSOCIATED WITH MOODS

Mood-Tone	Color	Number of Times Chosen
Exciting/Stimulating	Red	61
Secure/Comfortable	Blue	41
Distressed/Disturbed/Upset	Orange	34
Tender/Soothing	Blue	41
Protective/Defending	Red	21
	Brown	17
	Blue	15
	Black	15
	Purple	14
Despondent/Dejected/Unhappy/Melancholy	Black	25
	Brown	25
Calm/Peaceful/Serene	Blue	38
	Green	31
Dignified/Stately	Purple	45
Cheerful/Jovial/Joyful	Yellow	40
Defiant/Contrary/Hostile	Red	23
	Orange	21
	Black	18
Powerful/Strong/Masterful	Black	48

Gilovich (1988) began by demonstrating that students rated black uniforms as connoting meanness and aggression more than other colors. Then they examined statistics from actual professional games and found that football and hockey teams wearing black uniforms were penalized more than teams wearing other colors. And when a team changed its color to black from some other color, it began getting more penalties! The researchers then asked whether the effect was caused by the players themselves—maybe they acted meaner and rougher wearing black—or by the stereotyped perceptions of referees. The researchers made experimental films in which they varied the uniforms of players engaging in identical moves and then showed these to subjects acting as referees. These referees did find more instances of penalizable behavior among those suited in black, even though there actually were no differences. However, when the researchers put black uniforms on students, they found evidence that wearing a black uniform produced more aggressive behavior in the wearer. Thus both processes seem to be at work: Players wearing black may be rougher, but people also *perceive* the play of those in black uniforms as rougher. This perception could, of course, make black-suited players even rougher, because of the way people treat them.

We cannot make any conclusive judgments about the impact of color on human interaction from the research to date, but common sense tells us that colors in our environment will affect the way we respond: we simply do not know how or how much.

Sound

Types of sounds and their intensity also seem to affect interpersonal behavior. We may have very different reactions to the drone of several people's voices, the overpowering sound of a nearby jackhammer, or the soothing or stimulating sounds of music.

Most of us are aware of how music can affect our moods, and our selection of music may be designed to match or even change our moods. Depressing music can add to the intensity of an already gloomy mood; uplifting music can enhance a joyful feeling. Beginning with ideas like this, Honeycutt and Eidenmuller (2001) conducted an exploratory study in which they asked couples to work at resolving a source of conflict in their relationship while background music was playing. Some couples experienced music rated as more positive and uplifting, and others experienced negative or dreary music. The results of this study suggest not only that the type of music can affect the verbal and nonverbal behavior of interactants (e.g., agitating music was more likely to be linked to arguments), but the intensity of the music can affect the intensity of the interaction. In a related study, uplifting or annoying music was played for users of a university gym. Following their workout, they were asked to sign up for a helping task that did not involve much effort or commitment or one that did. People exposed to both types of music signed up for the easy task, but significantly more people who heard the uplifting music signed up to help with the more difficult task (North, Tarrant, & Hargreaves, 2004).

Music can also unwittingly affect our consumer behavior. At one British restaurant, diners were exposed to either classical, pop, or no music for 18 evenings. When dining to the sound of classical music, people spent significantly more money (North, Shilcock, & Hargreaves, 2003). Obviously, different types of music are suitable for different environments, and the music that is most effective for an environment is music that is compatible with perceptions of other environmental features. Scientists at the University of Leicester in England displayed four French and four German wines in a local supermarket. The wines from the two countries were similar in price, sweetness, and dryness. For 2 weeks, a tape deck on a nearby shelf alternated each day with either French accordian music or German beer-hall music. Placement of the wine on the shelves was alternated midway through the experiment. Researchers found that sales were clearly linked to the type of music being played: When French music was played, French wines outsold German wines; but when German music was played, German wines outsold French wines. Only about 7 percent of those purchasing wines were willing to acknowledge that the music may have influenced their decision (North, Hargreaves, & McKendrick, 1997).

Glass and Singer (1973) conducted a series of studies on the impact of noise on performance. People were asked to perform a variety of tasks varying in complexity while noises were manipulated by the experimenters. Noise levels were varied: some noise followed a predictable pattern, and some did not. Various noise sources were tested, including typewriters, machinery, and people speaking a foreign language. Although noise alone did not seem to have a substantial effect on performance, deterioration was observed when noise interacted with other factors; for instance, performance decreased when the workload was high and the noise was uncontrollable and unpredictable. Other factors that determine whether noise is a problem or a pleasure include the type of noise—for example, music versus people talking—the volume, the length of time it lasts, and whether the listener is accustomed to it or not. Obviously, some individuals are more influenced by noise than others. Noise-sensitive incoming college students perceived more noise than other students, and these perceptions increased after 7 months into the school year. The noise-sensitive students also received lower grades, felt less secure in their social interactions, and had a greater desire for privacy than did their peers who were less sensitive to noise (Weinstein, 1978).

Lighting

Lighting also helps structure our perceptions of an environment, and these perceptions may influence the type of messages we send. If we enter a dimly lit or candle-lit room, we may talk more softly, sit closer together, and presume that more personal communication will take place (Meer, 1985). When dimly lit university counseling rooms were compared with those that had brighter lighting, students reported feeling more relaxed in the dimly lit rooms. The dimly lit counseling rooms also elicited more self-disclosure from the students and higher ratings of the counselors in those rooms (Miwa and Hanyu, 2006).

When a dimly lit environment is suddenly brightened, it tends to invite less intimate interaction. For example, the flashing of bright lights in nightclubs that previously maintained dim lighting is often a signal that closing time is near to allow patrons some time to make the transition from one mood to another. Carr and Dabbs found that the use of intimate questions in dim lighting with nonintimates caused a significant hesitancy in responding, a significant decrease in eye gaze, and a decrease in the average length of gaze (Carr & Dabbs, 1974). All of these nonverbal behaviors appear to be efforts to create more psychological distance and decrease the perceived inappropriateness of the intimacy created by the lighting and the questions.

The absence of light seems to be a central problem for people who suffer from *seasonal affective disorder* (SAD), a form of depression particularly acute in winter months (Rosenthal, 1993). Therapists have successfully treated those who suffer from SAD by exposing them to extremely bright light for several hours each morning. Artificial lighting that provides a full-range light spectrum, like that of the sun, is most effective in this therapy (Lewy et al., 1998). In view of this need for sunlight, it has been postulated that cities with the lowest amount of annual sunlight might also have the highest suicide rates, but findings do not provide support for this hypothesis (Lester, 1988).

Movable Objects

If we know that the arrangement of certain objects in our environment can help structure communication, it is not surprising that we often try to manipulate objects to elicit specific responses. This was what Attorney General John Ashcroft had in mind when he arranged for the "Spirit of Justice" statue to be covered up with a blue curtain in 2002. The statue, which has been in the Department of Justice since it was built in the 1930s, is a 12-foot-high female; her arms are raised, and a toga is draped over part of her body, but one of her breasts is completely exposed (see Figure 4-4)—and photographs of Ashcroft at press briefings invariably include this statue in the background. The $8,000 curtain provided a neutral background, but the same effect might have been achieved by moving the lectern to the side. With little fanfare, and a new Attorney General, the blue drapes were removed in 2005; but now, Justice Department news conferences are held in another room. Photographers were aware that the statue could add meaning to a photograph. In the 1980s, an image of Attorney General Edwin Meese holding up a report on pornography was captured with the partially nude female statue standing in the background.

Manipulating objects in the environment to communicate particular messages also occurs in personal living spaces. In preparation for an intimate evening at home, a person may light candles; play soft, romantic music; fluff the pillows on the couch; and hide the dirty dishes, clothes, and other unpleasant reminders of daily living.

Employees often use objects to personalize their offices. These signs of personal identity make them feel more satisfied with their work life and provide visitors with information to initiate a conversation. Because the company also wants to

FIGURE 4-4

Attorney General John Ashcroft and the *Spirit of Justice* statue.

communicate its identity, the amount and kinds of personal objects employees display must also be consistent with the image the company wants to project. Objects in our work environment can also be arranged to reflect certain role relationships, to demarcate boundaries, or to encourage greater affiliation. The interior of an executive suite may clearly indicate the perceived status of the inhabitant; for example, expensive paintings, a large desk, plush sofas and chairs, drapes, and so forth display success (Monk, 1994). Such an atmosphere may be inappropriate for a personal counseling situation, but it can be rearranged to make it more conducive to such a purpose. Of course, we sometimes are able to communicate well in seemingly inappropriate settings by blocking out the messages being sent by the environment, as when lovers intimately say good-bye in relatively cold and public airport terminals.

Desks seem to be important objects in the conduct of interpersonal communication. An early experiment in this area, set in a doctor's office, suggests that the presence or absence of a desk may significantly alter the patient's "at ease" state (White, 1953). With the desk separating doctor and patient, only 10 percent of the patients were perceived at ease, whereas removal of the desk increased the percentage of at-ease patients to 55 percent. Student-to-student interaction in classrooms can be constrained by eliminating any possible movement of the student desks or seats (see Figure 4-5). And student–teacher relationships can also be affected by desk placement (Zweigenhaft, 1976). Faculty members were asked to sketch the furniture arrangement of their offices. These sketches were collected and analyzed with other information obtained from the professors, and a schoolwide teacher evaluation was conducted. It was found that 24 of 33 senior faculty members put their desks between themselves and their students, but only 14 of 30 junior faculty members did so. Furthermore, students rated the "unbarricaded" professors as more

FIGURE 4-5

A classroom design with immovable chairs discourages student-to-student interactions.

willing to "encourage the development of different viewpoints by students," ready to give "individual attention to students who need it," and less likely to show "undue favoritism." Because another study did not find the desk barrier related to undesirable experiences in student–professor interactions, we are reminded that other factors may neutralize or override the potentially troublesome effects of the desk barrier (Campbell & Herren, 1978). For example, students expect greater formality in student–teacher relationships in some situations, and the basis for an effective working relationship may have been established outside the professor's office, so the "barrier" is not perceived as such. The podium separating the president's press secretary from the press during White House press briefings also has been perceived both as appropriate and as a barrier to effective communication. During the Nixon administration, press briefings were formal, and the press secretary stood behind a podium. Ron Nessen, President Ford's press secretary, felt that the podium contributed to an unproductive "us and them" feeling, which prompted him to conduct briefings without the obstacle.

Less obvious barriers also exist. For instance, if you find a delicate *objet d'art* placed in front of some books in a bookcase, you may feel hesitant about using the books. Keep in mind that desks and other "barriers" are not inherently good or bad. Should you want to keep a distant, formal relationship, a desk can help create that feeling.

The arrangement of other furniture items can facilitate or inhibit communication. The location of the television set in a room will likely affect the placement of chairs and, in turn, the patterns of conversation in that room. Sommer and Ross found that some residents in a geriatric ward were apathetic and had few friends in spite of a generally cheerful and bright environment. They were able to double the frequency of resident conversations by rearranging the chairs so more of them faced each other (Sommer & Ross, 1958). Even when conversational possibilities have been maximized, not everyone will talk to everyone else. Consider the arrangement of Figure 4-6. Without considering other factors, such as the relationship of the interactants or their knowledge of the subject, we would predict exchanges marked by the arrows to be most frequent. The four people seated on the couch, as well as

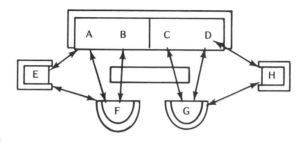

FIGURE 4-6

Conversation flow and furniture arrangement.

Source: From *Public Places and Private Spaces*, by Albert Mehrabian. Copyright © 1976 by Basic Books, Inc. Reprinted by permission of Basic Books, a member of Perseus Books, L.L.C.

persons F and G, will probably talk to each other less frequently. The four on one end are not likely to communicate very often with the four on the other end.

In some environments, people are not expected to linger, so chairs are deliberately designed without comfort in mind. Hotel owners and airport designers are well aware of the "too comfortable" phenomenon. You may have noticed the slightly uncomfortable nature of the 10 degree forward angle of chairs in some fast-food restaurants. This feature encourages customers to eat and move along quickly to provide seats for others. The Port Authority Bus Terminal in New York replaced its old wooden seats with folding plastic seats only 8 inches deep that "require so much concentration to balance that sleeping or even sitting for long is impossible." This was done to keep homeless people from sleeping in the terminal (Rimer, 1989).

Some environments seem to have an unwritten code that virtually prohibits interaction. Lone men entering a movie theater with triple-X–rated movies are likely to enter, sit through, and leave without uttering a word to anyone else.

STRUCTURE AND DESIGN

We pass much of our time in buildings. Most of us spend the day in a dwelling supposedly designed for effective performance of our work; in the evening, we enter another structure supposedly designed for the effective conduct of our personal and family life. The architecture of these buildings can go a long way toward determining who meets whom, where, and perhaps for how long.

The life of domestic animals is controlled through, among other things, the erection of fences, flap doors, litter boxes, or the placement of food and water in particular locations. Although verbal and nonverbal actions help control human situations, manipulation of barriers, openings, and other physical arrangements is also helpful. Meeting places can be appropriately arranged to regulate human traffic and, to a certain extent, the network of communication.

U.S. office buildings often are constructed from a standard plan that reflects a pyramidal organization. A large number of people are under the direction of a few executives at the upper levels. These executives generally have the most space, the most privacy, and the most desirable office locations, usually on the highest floor of the structure. Achieving a height above the masses and occupying a significant amount of space are only two indications of power. Corner offices, large picture windows, and private elevators also are associated with status and power (Monk, 1994). An office next to an important executive may also be a formidable power base. A similar pattern seems to exist in academic settings as well, with the higher-ranking professors normally accorded more space, windows, privacy, and choice of office location (Farrenkopf & Roth, 1980). The offices of top-level executives are often hard to reach, the assumption being that the more complicated the path to get to the executive, the more powerful he or she seems. Figure 4-7 is a hypothetical, but not far-fetched, example of the long and circuitous route to a president's office. To get to the office, the visitor must be screened by a receptionist and a private secretary and, in either or both places, may be asked to sit and wait. So, although the status and power of an executive may be related to his or her inaccessibility, secretaries and receptionists may value open views that allow them to act as lookouts and defenders against unwanted intrusions. It is common for people

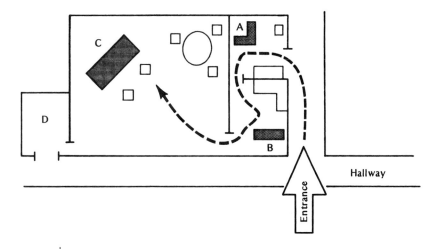

FIGURE 4-7

Getting to the president's office. A = receptionist. B = private secretary. C = president. D = private room with rear exit.

on the lowest rungs of the organizational ladder to find themselves in a large, open "pit." These so-called offices—really only desks, sometimes encompassed by a temporary enclosure—have little or no privacy, and complaints are common. Although privacy is minimal, communication opportunities are plentiful.

Some dormitories are built from floor plans that resemble many office buildings and old hotels. It has been speculated that these corridor-type dorms tend to encourage bureaucratic management, which seems to fit the orderly and uniform structure. Rigid rules are easier to enforce in these structures, and interaction among the residents is discouraged. Compared with suite-type dorms, corridor-type dorms are perceived by residents as more crowded, less private, and more conducive to avoiding others (Baum & Valins, 1979). The sense of community and the resulting responsibility for the living space are difficult to achieve. Lounges are sometimes intended to facilitate such interaction, but their usefulness has been questioned by architects and behavioral scientists. Lounges, like other design features, must be integrated into the entire architectural plan developed from an analysis of *human needs*—not inserted in places where they fit nicely or look good for parents and visitors.

If you look carefully, you can see many environmental structures that inhibit or prohibit communication. Fences separating yards create obvious barriers, even if they are only waist high; locating laundry rooms in dark, isolated areas of apartment buildings and public housing discourages their use, particularly at night; providing access to patios only through a bedroom probably discourages use; and so on.

Other environmental situations seem to facilitate interaction. Homes located in the middle of a block seem to draw more interpersonal exchanges than those located in other positions. Houses with adjacent driveways seem to have a built-in structure that draws the neighbors together and invites communication. The likelihood of interaction between strangers at a bar varies directly with the distance between them. As a rule, a

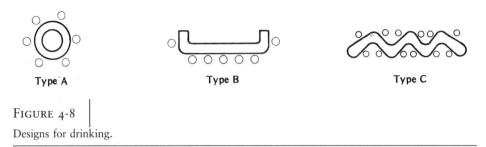

Type A   Type B   Type C

FIGURE 4-8
Designs for drinking.

span of three bar stools is the maximum distance over which patrons will attempt to initiate an encounter. Most bars are not designed for optimum interaction. Note that the three bar designs in Figure 4-8 provide very different opportunities for facing an interaction partner, for mutual eye gaze, and for getting physically close. Most bars are similar to type B, which seems to discourage interaction the most.

Some recent designs for housing the elderly have taken into consideration the need for social contact. In these apartment dwellings, the doors of the apartments on each floor open onto a common entranceway. This greatly increases the probability of social exchange compared to buildings where apartment doors are staggered on either side of a long hallway with no facing doorways. If you want a structure that encourages social interaction, you must have human paths that cross; but if you want people to interact, there must be something that encourages them to linger. Differences in interaction frequency are often related to the distances people must travel between activities. For example, consider this comparison made between two high schools: One was "centralized" with classrooms in one or two buildings, and one was "campus style" with classrooms spread among several buildings. The campus design prompted 5 to 10 percent more interactions in the halls, stairs, and lobbies but 7 to 10 percent fewer interactions in the classrooms than the centralized design. There were 20 percent fewer interactions between students and teachers before and after class in the campus-style high school (Myrick & Marx, 1968). It is no secret that the architecture of a school can affect a student's motivation to learn, a teacher's motivation to teach, how much students and teachers talk to each other, how long they talk, and, to a certain extent, what they talk about. But older school designs were often based on how to maintain strict discipline, emphasize status differences between students and teachers, and minimize informal talking.

Fast-food restaurants also seem to vary regarding how much they contribute to the interactive involvement of their customers. In one study, for example, the behavior of customers at McDonald's showed more involvement than those at Burger King (Eaves & Leathers, 1991). The shorter distance across the tables and the generally less comfortable surroundings seemed to be factors in the greater involvement of the patrons at McDonald's.

Architects and social scientists have even been experimenting with new prison designs. The older structures, which had linear tiers of steel cages, are being replaced with modular units that have fewer inmates and fewer barriers between them and their guards. These new designs, coupled with new ways of managing prisoners, seem to result in more positive behavior on the part of both guards and prisoners, provide more opportunities for rehabilitation, and reduce costs (Cronin, 1992).

Furthermore, an environment's design may encourage or discourage certain *types* of communication; that is, the structure may determine how much interaction takes place and the general content of that interaction. Drew (1971) reports a study of three different designs for nursing stations within a mental hospital. In one, interaction had to take place by opening a door; in another, interaction was conducted through a glass-enclosed counter; and in the third, interaction took place over an open counter. Although substantially more patients entered the nursing station through the door, interactions occurred less frequently than in the other two stations. An average of only 1 interaction per each 15-minute observation period occurred with the door; 5.3 interactions per period occurred in the glass-enclosed counter; and 8.7 occurred with the open counter. Although interaction was higher for the open counter, the author noted a preponderance of social conversation here; the door design seemed to encourage more item requests and permission interactions. In short, the more inaccessible setting decreased interaction frequency and increased task-oriented messages; the more accessible setting increased interaction frequency and increased the amount of small talk.

A more complete analysis of physical proximity and spatial distance appears in Chapter 5, but it is clearly relevant to this discussion on environments as well. Over 60 years ago, Stouffer (1940) made this observation, which holds true today:

> Whether one is seeking to explain why persons go to a particular place to get jobs, why they go to trade at a particular store, why they go to a particular neighborhood to commit a crime, or why they marry a particular spouse they choose, the factor of spatial distance is of obvious significance. (p. 845)

Many studies have confirmed Stouffer's remark. Students tend to develop stronger friendships with students who share their classes, dormitories, apartment buildings, or who sit near them than with others who are geographically distant. Workers tend to develop closer friendships with those who work near them. The effect of proximity seems to be stronger for employees with less status in the organization; managers, however, are more likely to choose their friends at the office according to their status rather than their proximity (Schutte & Light, 1978). Some believe that increased proximity of ethnic groups will assist in reducing prejudice. Although close proximity may bring about positive attitude changes between different ethnic groups, we must exercise caution in generalizing. If the two groups are extremely polarized, or if they perceive no mutual problems or projects requiring cooperation, proximity may have little effect or may even magnify hostilities.

Several studies show an inverse relationship between the distance separating potential marriage partners and the number of marriages. Proximity allows us to obtain more information about the other person. Obviously, obtaining more information about someone may mean we soon learn that we are not attracted to the person; but more often than not, proximity breeds attraction and, in turn, attraction leads to a desire to be in close proximity.

A number of studies have shown how proximity influences friendships. In one study conducted in a townhouse development, most friendships occurred between people who lived within 100 feet of each other. Next-door neighbors became close friends 46 percent of the time; neighbors who lived two or three doors away became close friends 24 percent of the time; and people who lived three or four doors away

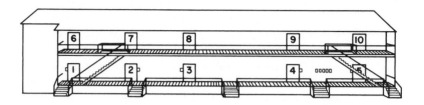

FIGURE 4-9

Design influences the social lives of residents in apartment buildings.

became friends 13 percent of the time (Athanasiou & Yoshioka, 1973). Historically, the most famous study of proximity, friendship choice, and interpersonal contact was conducted by Festinger, Schachter, and Back (1950) in a housing development for married students. Concern for what the authors called "functional distance" led to data clearly demonstrating that architects can have a tremendous influence on the social life of residents in these housing projects. Functional distance is determined by the number of contacts that position and design encourage; for example, factors such as which way apartments face, where exits and entranceways are located, and location of stairways, mailboxes, and the like all have an impact. Figure 4-9 shows the basic design of one type of building studied.

The researchers asked the residents of 17 buildings, with the design of Figure 4-8, which people they saw most often socially and what friendship choices they made. Among the findings from this study, the following are noteworthy:

1. There seemed to be a greater number of friendship choices for those physically close to one another, such as on the same floor or in the same building. It was rare to find a friendship between people separated by more than four or five houses.
2. People living in apartments 1 and 5 gave and received from the upper-floor residents more friendship choices than the people living in any other apartments on the lower floor.
3. Apartments 1 and 6 exchanged more choices than apartments 2 and 7. Similarly, apartments 5 and 10 exchanged more choices than apartments 4 and 9. Although this represented the same physical distance, functional distance differed.
4. Because of the mailboxes, apartment 5 chose more upper-level friends, more of those choices being apartments 9 and 10.

Making friends takes many forms, but functional distance seems to be highly influential, and it is sometimes the result of architectural design.

REGULATING ENVIRONMENTS AND COMMUNICATION

It should be clear by now that our communication is often affected by the social and physical environment. And we have some control over structuring these environments; we can paint our walls a different color, substitute candles for electric lights, and so on. But our communication environments are influenced by others, too. Earlier in this chapter, we noted how architects and furniture designers affect our social interaction, but laws and government regulations also play an important role in creating the environments that affect our communicative behavior. It is important to conclude the chapter with this reminder, because gaining control over the environment that affects our communication may mean becoming a community activist or leader.

Zoning laws, for example, determine whether a part of our environment will be used for industrial, commercial, or residential activity. Zoning laws also determine the population density of an area by defining how many housing units per acre are allowed. Laws prohibiting adult bookstores from operating too close to churches are essentially saying the two environments generate quite different forms of communication and are not likely to happily share the same territory. When business hours of operation are regulated, it affects when streets are empty, when they are crowded, and what segment of the population occupies the street. Some communities have specific laws governing signs and billboards, where they can be placed, their size, materials, and colors that can be used, and so on. Obviously these and similar regulations governing parking areas, parks, display windows, and vending machines impact our social lives.

In addition, there are penal codes that punish loitering, smoking, drinking alcoholic beverages, and other behaviors. Smoking regulations have changed such things as where smokers are allowed to congregate, how long they spend talking after a dinner in a nonsmoking restaurant, whether they go to such restaurants, to whom they speak, and the friendships they develop. The many factors leading to the demise of the neighborhood tavern as a social gathering place prompted Drucker and Gumpert (1996) to say this:

> Public bars, taverns, and pubs have historically provided social centers, supported social and political webs, and provided the site where revolutions were planned, artistic movements launched, friendships formed, and community ties forged. The institution of the English and Irish pub is alive and well, but the American tavern is a dying institution. (p. 289)

SUMMARY

The environment in which people communicate frequently contributes to the overall outcome of their encounters. We have seen that both the frequency and the content of our messages are influenced by various aspects of the setting in which we communicate. We have seen how the environment influences our behavior, but we also know that we can alter environments to elicit certain types of responses. As our knowledge of environments increases, we may deliberately use them to help us obtain desired responses. In many respects, we are products of our environment,

and if we want to change behavior, we need to learn to control the environment in which we interact.

Throughout this chapter, we referred to a number of different types of environments: classrooms, dormitories, offices, prisons, fast-food restaurants, homes, and bars. We suggested several different ways of looking at environments. Mehrabian (1976), following research in other areas of human perception, commented that all environments could profitably be examined by looking at emotional reactions to them. These emotions or feelings, says

Mehrabian, can be plotted on three dimensions: arousing–nonarousing, pleasant–unpleasant, and dominant–submissive. We suggested six perceptual bases for examining environments: formal–informal, warm–cold, private–public, familiar–unfamiliar, constraining–free, and distant–close. We also pointed out that people perceive temporal aspects of their environments: when things happen, how long they last, how much time exists between events, and the pattern or rhythm of events.

Each environment seems to have three major characteristics: 1) the natural environment; 2) the presence or absence of other people; and 3) the architectural design and movable objects, including lighting, sound, color, and general visual-aesthetic appeal. The quality and quantity of the research in each of these areas vary considerably, but it is clear that any analysis of human behavior must account for the influence of environmental features.

QUESTIONS FOR DISCUSSION

1. Select a familiar environment that effectively encourages or discourages human interaction. Now indicate all the changes you would make so this environment would have the exact opposite effect.
2. Assume the role of a stranger entering your own apartment or your family's home. What messages does the environment communicate?
3. The impact of environmental features on human behavior will vary as a function of context, but what features do you think play a large or small role across different contexts? Explain your choices.
4. How do people communicate time-related messages by their behavior?

BIBLIOGRAPHY

Adams, R. S. (1969). Location as a feature of instructional interaction. *Merrill-Palmer Quarterly, 15*, 309–321.

Adams, R. S., & Biddle, B. (1970). *Realities of teaching: Explorations with video tape.* New York: Holt, Rinehart & Winston.

Altman, I., Brown, B. B., Staples, B., & Werner, C. M. (1992). A transactional approach to close relationships: Courtship, weddings, and placemaking. In B. Walsh, K. Craik, & R. Price (Eds.), *Person-environment psychology: Contemporary models and perspectives.* Hillsdale, NJ: Erlbaum.

Altman, I., & Chemers, M. M. (1988). *Culture and environment.* New York: Cambridge University Press.

Altman, I., & Gauvain, M. (1981). A cross-cultural and dialectic analysis of homes. In L. S. Liben, A. H. Patterson, & N. Newcombe (Eds.), *Special representation and behavior across the life span.* New York: Academic Press.

Altman, I., & Low, S. M. (Eds.). (1992). *Place attachment. Human behavior and environment: Advances in theory and research* (Vol. 12). New York: Plenum.

Anderson, C. A. (1989). Temperature and aggression: Ubiquitous effects of heat on occurrence of human violence. *Psychological Bulletin, 106*, 74–96.

Anderson, C. A. (2001). Heat and violence. *Current Directions in Psychological Science, 10*, 33–38.

Anderson, C. A., & Anderson, D. C. (1984). Ambient temperature and violent crime: Tests of the linear and curvilinear hypotheses. *Journal of Personality and Social Psychology, 46*, 91–97.

Anderson, C. A., Anderson, K. B., Dorr, N., DeNeve, K. M., & Flanagan, M. (2000). Temperature and aggression. In M. Zanna (Ed.), *Advances in experimental social psychology,* Vol. 32 (pp. 63–133). New York: Academic Press.

Athanasiou, R., & Yoshioka, G. A. (1973). The spatial character of friendship formation. *Environment and Behavior, 5*, 43–65.

Ball, V. K. (1965). The aesthetics of color: A review of fifty years of experimentation. *Journal of Aesthetics and Art Criticism, 23*, 441–452.

Ballard, D. I., & Seibold, D. R. (2000). Time orientation and temporal variation across work groups: Implications for group and organizational communication. *Western Journal of Communication, 64*, 218–242.

Barker, R. (1968). *Ecological psychology.* Palo Alto, CA: Stanford University Press.

Baron, R. A. (1972). Aggression as a function of ambient temperature and prior anger arousal. *Journal of Personality and Social Psychology, 21*, 183–189.

Baron, R. A., & Bell, P. A. (1975). Aggression and heat: Mediating effects of prior provocation and exposure to an aggressive model. *Journal of Personality and Social Psychology, 31*, 825–832.

Baron, R. A., & Bell, P. A. (1976). Aggression and heat: The influence of ambient temperature, negative affect, and a cooling drink on physical aggression. *Journal of Personality and Social Psychology, 33*, 245–255.

Baron, R. A., & Lawton, S. F. (1972). Environmental influences on aggression: The facilitation of modeling effects by high ambient temperatures. *Psychonomic Science, 26*, 80–82.

Baron, R. A., & Ransberger, V. M. (1978). Ambient temperature and the occurrence of collective violence: The "long hot summer" revisited. *Journal of Personality and Social Psychology, 36*, 351–360.

Baum, A., & Davis, G. E. (1980). Reducing the stress of high-density living: An architectural intervention. *Journal of Personality and Social Psychology, 38*, 471–481.

Baum, A., & Valins, S. (1979). Architectural mediation of residential density and control: Crowding and regulation of social contact. In L. Berkowitz (Ed.), *Advances in experimental social psychology* (Vol. 12). New York: Academic Press.

Baumeister, R. F. (1995). Disputing the effects of championship pressures and home audiences. *Journal of Personality and Social Psychology, 68*, 649–652.

Berke, J., & Wilson, V. (1951). *Watch out for the weather.* New York: Viking.

Birren, F. (1969). *Light, color, and environment.* New York: Van Nostrand Reinhold.

Blake, R. R., Rhead, C. C., Wedge, B., & Mouton, J. S. (1956). Housing architecture and social interaction. *Sociometry, 19*, 133–139.

Blue is beautiful. (1973, September 17). *Time,* p. 66.

Breed, G., & Colaiuta, V. (1974). Looking, blinking, and sitting: Nonverbal dynamics in the classroom. *Journal of Communication, 24*, 75–81.

Buslig, A. L. S. (1999). "Stop" signs regulating privacy with environmental features. In L. Guerrero, J. A. DeVito, & M. L. Hecht (Eds.) *The nonverbal communication reader* (2nd ed.), pp. 241–249. Prospect Heights, IL: Waveland Press.

Byrne, D. (1961). The influence of propinquity and opportunities for interaction on classroom relationships. *Human Relations, 14*, 63–70.

Camgoz, N., Yener, C., & Guvenc, D. (2004). Effects of hue, saturation, and brightness. Part 2: Attention. *Color Research and Application, 29*, 20–28.

Campbell, D. E. (1979). Interior office design and visitor response. *Journal of Applied Psychology, 64*, 648–653.

Campbell, D. E., & Beets, J. L. (1978). Lunacy and the moon. *Psychological Bulletin, 85*, 1123–1129.

Campbell, D. E., & Herren, K. A. (1978). Interior arrangement of the faculty office. *Psychological Reports, 43*, 234.

Canter, D. (1977). *The psychology of place.* London: Architectural Press.

Carlsmith, J. M., & Anderson, C. A. (1979). Ambient temperature and the occurrence of collective violence: A new analysis. *Journal of Personality and Social Psychology, 37*, 337–344.

Carr, S. J., & Dabbs, J. M. (1974). The effect of lighting, distance, and intimacy of topic on verbal and visual behavior. *Sociometry, 37*, 592–600.

Cheek, F. E., Maxwell, R., & Weisman, R. (1971). Carpeting the ward: An exploratory study in environmental psychiatry. *Mental Hygiene, 55*, 109–118.

Cottle, T. J. (1976). *Perceiving time.* New York: Wiley.

Craik, K. (1981). Environmental assessment and situational analysis. In D. Magnusson (Ed.), *Toward a psychology of situations: An interactional perspective.* New York: Erlbaum.

Cronin, M. (1992, May 25). Gilded cages. *Time,* pp. 52–54.

Csikszentmihalyi, M., & Rochberg-Halton, E. (1981). *The meaning of things: Domestic symbols and the self.* New York: Cambridge University Press.

Deutsch, M., & Collins, M. (1951). *Interracial housing: A psychological evaluation of a social experiment.* Minneapolis: University of Minnesota Press.

Devlin, A. S. (2008). Judging a book by its cover: Medical building facades and judgments of care. Environment and Behavior, 40, 307–329.

Doob, L. (1964). *Patterning of time.* New Haven, CT: Yale University Press.

Drew, C. J. (1971). Research on the psychological–behavioral effects of the physical environment. *Review of Educational Research, 41,* 447–463.

Drucker, S. J., & Gumpert, G. (1996). The regulation of public social life: Communication law revisited. *Communication Quarterly, 44,* 280–296.

Duncan, F. (1981). Dormitory architecture influences patterns of student social relations over time. *Environment and Behavior, 13,* 23–41.

Eaves, M. H., & Leathers, D. G. (1991). Context as communication: McDonald's vs. Burger King. *Journal of Applied Communication Research, 19,* 263–289.

Falender, C. A., & Mehrabian, A. (1978). Environmental effects on parent–infant interaction. *Genetic Psychology Monographs, 97* (Pt. 1), 3–41.

Farrenkopf, T., & Roth, V. (1980). The university faculty office as an environment. *Environment and Behavior, 12,* 467–477.

Festinger, L. (1951). Architecture and group membership. *Journal of Social Issues, 1,* 152–163.

Festinger, L., Schachter, S., & Back, K. (1950). *Social pressures in informal groups: A study of human factors in housing.* New York: Harper & Row.

Fraisse, Paul. (1963). *The psychology of time.* New York: Harper & Row.

Frank, M. G., & Gilovich, T. (1988). The dark side of self- and social perception: Black uniforms and aggression in professional sports. *Journal of Personality and Social Psychology, 54,* 74–85.

Fraser, J. T. (1981). A report on the literature of time, 1900–1980. In J. T. Fraser, N. Lawrence, & D. Park (Eds.), *The study of time IV.* New York: Springer-Verlag.

Friedman, W. J. (1990). *About time.* Cambridge, MA: MIT Press.

Gans, H. J. (1961). Planning and social life: Friendship and neighbor relations in suburban communities. *Journal of the American Institute of Planners, 27,* 134–140.

Garber, L. L., Jr., & Hyatt, E. M. (2003). Color as a tool for visual persuasion. In L. M. Scott and R. Batra (Eds.), *Persuasive imagery: A consumer response perspective* (pp. 313–336). Mahwah, NJ: Erlbaum.

Gifford, R. (1987). *Environmental psychology: Principles and practice.* Boston: Allyn & Bacon.

Glass, D., & Singer, J. E. (1973). Experimental studies of uncontrollable and unpredictable noise. *Representative Research in Social Psychology, 4,* 165.

Gonzalez, A., & Zimbardo, P. G. (1985). Time in perspective. *Psychology Today, 19,* 21–26.

Goranson, R. E., & King, D. (1970). *Rioting and daily temperature: Analysis of the U.S. riots in 1967.* Unpublished manuscript, York University, Ontario, Canada.

Gosling, S. D., Gaddis, S., & Vazire, S. (2008). First impressions based on the environments we create and inhabit. In N. Ambady & J. J. Skowronski (Eds.), *First impressions.* New York: Guilford.

Gosling, S. D., Ko, S. J., Mannarelli, T., & Morris, M. E. (2002). A room with a cue: Personality judgments based on offices and bedrooms. *Journal of Personality and Social Psychology, 82,* 379–398.

Griffin, W. V., Mauritzen, J. H., & Kasmar, J. V. (1969). The psychological aspects of the architectural environment: A review. *American Journal of Psychiatry, 125,* 1057–1062.

Griffitt, W. (1970). Environmental effects of interpersonal affective behavior. Ambient effective temperature and attraction. *Journal of Personality and Social Psychology, 15,* 240–244.

Griffitt, W., & Veitch, R. (1971). Hot and crowded: Influence of population density and temperature on interpersonal affective behavior. *Journal of Personality and Social Psychology, 17,* 92–98.

Haber, G. M. (1982). Spatial relations between dominants and marginals. *Social Psychology Quarterly, 45,* 221–228.

Hall, E. T. (1959). *The silent language.* Garden City, NY: Doubleday.

Hall, E. T. (1966). *The hidden dimension.* Garden City, NY: Doubleday.

Hall, E. T. (1983). *The dance of life*. Garden City, NY: Anchor.

Hambrick-Dixon, P. J. (1986). Effects of experimentally imposed noise on task performance of black children attending day care centers near elevated subway trains. *Developmental Psychology, 22*, 259–264.

Harkins, S., & Szymanksi, K. (1987). Social facilitation and social loafing: New wine in old bottles. In C. Hendrick (Ed.), *Review of personality and social psychology* (Vol. 9). Beverly Hills, CA: Sage.

Harris, P. B., & Sachau, D. (2005). Is cleanliness next to godliness? The role of housekeeping in impression formation. *Environment and Behavior, 37*, 81–101.

Hata, T. D. (2004). Inferences about resident's personality in Japanese homes. *North American Journal of Psychology, 6*, 337–348.

Hazard, J. N. (1962). Furniture arrangement as a symbol of judicial roles. *ETC, 19*, 181–188.

Heilweil, M. (Ed.). (1973). Student housing, architecture, and social behavior [Special issue]. *Environment and Behavior, 5*, 375–514.

Hill, R. A., & Barton, R. A. (2005, May 19). Psychology: Red enhances human performance in contests. *Nature, 435*, 293.

Hines, T. (1996). *The total package*. New York: Little, Brown.

Holahan, C. J. (1972). Seating patterns and patient behavior in an experimental dayroom. *Journal of Abnormal Psychology, 80*, 115–124.

Holahan, C. J., Wilcox, B. L., Burnam, M. A., & Culler, R. E. (1978). Social satisfaction and friendship formation as a function of floor level in high-rise student housing. *Journal of Applied Psychology, 63*, 527–529.

Honeycutt, J. M., & Eidenmuller, M. E. (2001). Communication and attribution: An exploration of the effects of music and mood on intimate couples' verbal and nonverbal conflict resolution behaviors. In V. Manusov and J. H. Harvey (Eds.), *Attribution, Communication Behavior, and Close Relationships* (pp. 21–37). New York: Cambridge University Press.

Infante, D. A., & Berg, C. M. (1979). The impact of music modality on the perception of communication situations in video sequences. *Communication Monographs, 46*, 135–141.

Jackson, P. W. (1968). *Life in classrooms*. New York: Holt, Rinehart & Winston.

Johnson, J. D. (1987). Development of the communication and physical environment scale. *Central States Speech Journal, 38*, 35–43.

Jorgenson, D. O. (1981). Perceived causal influence of weather: Rating the weather's influence on affective states and behaviors. *Environment and Behavior, 13*, 239–256.

Kasmar, J. V., Griffin, W. V., & Mauritzen, J. H. (1968). The effect of environmental surroundings on outpatients' mood and perception of psychiatrists. *Journal of Consulting and Clinical Psychology, 32*, 223–226.

Katz, A. M., & Hill, R. (1958). Residential propinquity and marital selection: A review of theory, method, and fact. *Marriage and Family Living, 20*, 327–335.

Kennedy, R. (1943). Premarital residential propinquity. *American Journal of Sociology, 48*, 580–584.

Kenrick, D. T., & Johnson, G. A. (1979). Interpersonal attraction in aversive environments: A problem for the classical conditioning paradigm? *Journal of Personality and Social Psychology, 37*, 572–579.

Kenrick, D. T., & MacFarlane, W. W. (1986). Ambient temperature and horn-honking: A field study of the heat/aggression relationship. *Environment and Behavior, 18*, 179–191.

Koneya, M. (1973). *The relationship between verbal interaction and seat location of members of large groups*. Unpublished doctoral dissertation, Denver University.

Korda, M. (1975, January 13). Office power—You are where you sit. *New York Times*, pp. 36–44.

Kraut, R. E., & Johnston, R. E. (1979). Social and emotional messages of smiling: An ethological approach. *Journal of Personality and Social Psychology, 37*, 1539–1553.

Krupat, E. (1985). *People in cities: The urban environment and its effects*. New York: Cambridge University Press.

Krupat, E., & Kubzansky, P. E. (1987). Designing to deter crime. *Psychology Today, 21*, 58–61.

Lawton, M. P., & Cohen, J. (1974). Environments and the well-being of elderly inner-city residents. *Environment and Behavior, 6*, 194–211.

Leonard, G. (1978). The rhythms of relationships. In G. Leonard (Ed.), *The silent pulse*. New York: Elsevier-Dutton.

Lester, D. (1988). Geographical variables and behavior: XLVIII. Climate and personal violence (suicide and homicide): A cross-cultural study. *Perceptual and Motor Skills, 66*, 602.

Levine, D. W., O'Neal, E. C., Garwood, S. G., & McDonald, P. J. (1980). Classroom ecology: The effects of seating position on grades and participation. *Personality and Social Psychology Bulletin, 6*, 409–412.

Levine, R. (1997). *A geography of time: The temporal misadventures of a social psychologist or how every culture keeps time just a little bit differently*. New York: Basic.

Levine, R., & Wolff, E. (1985). Social time: The heartbeat of a culture. *Psychology Today, 19*, 30.

Lewy, A. J., Bauer, V. K., Cutler, N. L., Sack, R. L., Ahmed, S., Thomas, K. H., et al. (1998). Morning vs. evening light treatment of patients with winter depression. *Archives of General Psychiatry, 55*, 890–896.

Lewy, A. J., Sack, R. L., Miller, L. S., & Hoban, T. M. (1987). Antidepressant and circadian phase-shifting effects of light. *Science, 235*, 352–353.

Lieber, A. L. (1978). *The lunar effect: Biological tides and human emotions*. New York: Anchor/ Doubleday.

Lipman, A. (1968). Building design and social interaction. *The Architect's Journal, 147*, 23–30.

Lohmann, A., Arriaga, X. B., & Goodfriend, W. (2003). Close relationships and placemaking: Do objects in a couple's home reflect couplehood? *Personal Relationships, 10*, 437–449.

Luce, G. G. (1971). *Biological rhythms in human and animal physiology*. New York: Dover.

Maines, David R. (1987). The significance of temporality for the development of sociological theory [Special issue]. *The Sociological Quarterly, 28*(3), 303–311.

Maslow, A. H., & Mintz, N. L. (1956). Effects of esthetic surroundings: I. Initial effects of three esthetic conditions upon perceiving "energy" and "well-being" in faces. *Journal of Psychology, 41*, 247–254.

Maxwell, L. E. (2007). Competency in child care settings: The role of the physical environment. *Environment and Behavior, 39*, 229–245.

McClanahan, L. E., & Risly, T. R. (1975). Design of living environments for nursing home residents: Increasing participation in recreation activities. *Journal of Applied Behavior Analysis, 8*, 261–268.

McCroskey, J. C., & McVetta, W. R. (1978). Classroom seating arrangements: Instructional communication theory versus student preferences. *Communication Education, 27*, 99–110.

McGrath, J. E., & Kelly, J. R. (1986). *Time and human interaction*. New York: Guilford Press.

McLuhan, M. (1976). Inside on the outside or the spaced-out American. *Journal of Communication, 26*, 46–53.

Meer, J. (1985, September). The light touch. *Psychology Today, 19*, 60–67.

Mehrabian, A. (1976). *Public places and private spaces*. New York: Basic.

Mehrabian, A., & Diamond, S. G. (1971). The effects of furniture arrangement, props, and personality on social interaction. *Journal of Personality and Social Psychology, 20*, 18–30.

Mehrabian, A., & Russell, J. A. (1974). The basic emotional impact of environments. *Perceptual and Motor Skills, 38*, 283–301.

Mehrabian, A., & Russell, J. A. (1975). Environmental effects on affiliation among strangers. *Humanitas, 11*, 219–230.

Merton, R. (1948). The social psychology of housing. In W. Dennis (Ed.), *Current trends in social psychology*. Pittsburgh: University of Pittsburgh Press.

Michael, R. P., & Zumpe, D. (1983). Sexual violence in the United States and the role of season. *American Journal of Psychiatry, 140*, 883–886.

Michelson, W. (1971). Some like it hot: Social participation and environmental use as functions of the season. *American Journal of Sociology, 76*, 1072–1083.

Mintz, N. L. (1956). Effects of esthetic surroundings: II. Prolonged and repeated experience in a "beautiful" and "ugly" room. *Journal of Psychology, 41*, 459–466.

Miwa, Y., & Hanyu, K. (2006). The effects of interior design on communication and impressions of a counselor in a counseling room. *Environment and Behavior, 38,* 484–502.

Monk, R. (1994). *The employment of corporate non-verbal status communicators in Western organisations.* Unpublished doctoral dissertation, The Fielding Institute, Santa Barbara, CA.

Moos, R. H. (1976). *The human context: Environmental determinants of behavior.* New York: Wiley.

Moos, R. H., Harris, R., & Schonborn, K. (1969). Psychiatric patients and staff reaction to their physical environment. *Journal of Clinical Psychology, 25,* 322–324.

Moriarty, B. M. (1974). Socioeconomic status and residential location choice. *Environment and Behavior, 6,* 448–469.

Murray, D. C., & Deabler, H. L. (1957). Colors and mood-tones. *Journal of Applied Psychology, 41,* 279–283.

Myrick, R., & Marx, B. S. (1968). *An exploratory study of the relationship between high school building design and student learning.* Washington, DC: U.S. Department of Health, Education and Welfare, Office of Education, Bureau of Research.

Newman, O. (1973). *Defensible space.* New York: Macmillan.

North, A. C., Hargreaves, D. J., & McKendrick, J. (1997, November 13). In-store music affects product choice. *Nature,* p. 132.

North, A. C., Shilcock, A., & Hargreaves, D. J. (2003). The effects of musical style on restaurant customers' spending. *Environment and Behavior, 35,* 712–718.

North, A. C., Tarrant, M., & Hargreaves, D. J. (2004). The effects of music on helping behavior: A field study. *Environment and Behavior, 36,* 266–275.

Oldenburg, R. (1989). *The great good place: Cafes, coffee shops, community centers, beauty parlors, general stores, bars, hangouts, and how they get you through the day.* New York: Pergamon Press.

Osmond, H. (1957). Function as the basis of psychiatric ward design. *Mental Hospitals, 8,* 23–29.

Pelligrini, R. F., & Schauss, A. G. (1980). Muscle strength as a function of exposure to hue differences in visual stimuli: An experiential test of Kinesoid theory. *Journal of Orthomolecular Psychiatry, 2,* 144–147.

Phinney, M. (2006, October 11). Mason County Jail is in the pink, and the offenders are offended. *Austin American Statesman,* B8.

Rapoport, A. (1982). *The meaning of the built environment.* Beverly Hills, CA: Sage.

Reifman, A. S., Larrick, R. P., & Fein, S. (1991). Temper and temperature on the diamond: The heat–aggression relationship in major league baseball. *Personality and Social Psychology Bulletin, 17,* 580–585.

Report of the National Advisory Commission on Civil Disorders (1968). Washington, DC: U.S. Government Printing Office.

Rieber, M. (1965). The effect of music on the activity level of children. *Psychonomic Science, 3,* 325–326.

Rimer, S. (1989, November 18). Doors closing as mood on homeless sours. *New York Times.*

Roethlisberger, F. J., & Dickson, W. J. (1939). *Management and the worker.* Cambridge, MA: Harvard University Press.

Rohles, F. H., Jr. (1967). Environmental psychology: A bucket of worms. *Psychology Today, 1,* 54–62.

Rohles, F. H., Jr. (1980). Temperature or temperament: A psychologist looks at thermal comfort. *ASHRAE Transactions, 86*(1), 541–551.

Rosenfield, P., Lambert, N. M., & Black, A. (1985). Desk arrangement effects on pupil classroom behavior. *Journal of Educational Psychology, 77,* 101–108.

Rosenthal, N. E. (1993). *Winter blues.* New York: Guilford.

Rotton, J., & Cohn, E. G. (2002). Climate, weather, and crime. In R. B. Bechtel & A. Churchman (Eds.), *Handbook of environmental psychology* (pp. 481–498). New York: Wiley.

Rotton, J., & Cohn, E. G. (2003). Global warming and U.S. crime rates: An application of activity theory. *Environment and Behavior, 35,* 802–825.

Rotton, J., & Cohn, E. G. (2004). Outdoor temperature, climate control, and criminal assault: The spatial and temporal ecology of violence. *Environment and Behavior, 36,* 276–306.

Rotton, J., & Kelly, I. W. (1985). Much ado about the full moon: A meta-analysis of lunar-lunacy research. *Psychological Bulletin, 97,* 286–306.

Rubin, Z. (1979). Seasonal rhythms in behavior. *Psychology Today, 12,* 12–16.

Ruesch, J., & Kees, W. (1956). *Nonverbal communication.* Berkeley and Los Angeles: University of California Press.

Russell, J. A., & Mehrabian, A. (1976). Environmental variables in consumer research. *Journal of Consumer Research, 3,* 62–63.

Sandalla, E. (1987). Identity symbolism in housing. *Environment and Behavior, 19,* 569–587.

Schauss, A. G. (1985). The physiological effect of color on the suppression of human aggression: Research on Baker-Miller Pink. *International Journal of Biosocial Research, 7,* 55–64.

Schlenker, B. R., Phillips, S. T., Boniecki, K. A., and Schlenker, D. R. (1995). Championship pressures: Choking or triumphing in one's own territory? *Journal of Personality and Social Psychology, 68,* 632–643.

Schneider, F. W., Lesko, W. A., & Garrett, W. A. (1980). Helping behavior in hot, comfortable, and cold temperatures: A field study. *Environment and Behavior, 12,* 231–240.

Schutte, J. G., & Light, N. M. (1978). The relative importance of proximity and status for friendship choices in social hierarchies. *Social Psychology, 41,* 260–264.

Schwartz, B., & Barsky, S. (1977). The home advantage. *Social Forces, 55,* 641–661.

Schwebel, A. I., & Cherlin, D. L. (1972). Physical and social distancing in teacher–pupil relationships. *Journal of Educational Psychology, 63,* 543–550.

Smith, E., Bell, P. A., & Fusco, M. E. (1986). The influence of color and demand characteristics on muscle strength and affective ratings of the environment. *Journal of General Psychology, 113,* 289–297.

Smith, R. H., Downer, D. B., Lynch, M. T., & Winter, M. (1969). Privacy and interaction within the family as related to dwelling space. *Journal of Marriage and the Family, 31,* 559–566.

Sommer, R. (1967). Classroom ecology. *Journal of Applied Behavioral Science, 3,* 487–503.

Sommer, R. (1969). *Personal space.* Englewood Cliffs, NJ: Prentice-Hall.

Sommer, R. (1972). *Design awareness.* San Francisco: Rinehart Press.

Sommer, R. (1974). *Tight spaces: Hard architecture and how to humanize it.* Englewood Cliffs, NJ: Prentice-Hall.

Sommer, R., & Gilliland, G. W. (1961). Design for friendship. *Canadian Architect, 6,* 59–61.

Sommer, R., & Ross, H. (1958). Social interaction in a geriatric ward. *International Journal of Social Psychiatry, 4,* 128–133.

Stires, L. (1980). Classroom seating location, student grades, and attitudes: Environment or self selection? *Environment and Behavior, 12,* 241–254.

Stokois, D. (1981). Group × place transactions: Some neglected issues in psychological research on settings. In D. Magnusson (Ed.), *Toward a psychology of situations: An interactional perspective.* New York: Erlbaum.

Stouffer, S. A. (1940). Intervening opportunities: A theory relating mobility and distance. *American Sociological Review, 5,* 845–867.

Sundstrom, E. (1986). *Workplaces: The psychology of the physical environment in offices and factories.* New York: Cambridge University Press.

Tars, S., & Appleby, L. (1974). The same child in home and institution. *Environment and Behavior, 5,* 3.

Thirer, J., & Rampey, M. S. (1979). Effects of abusive spectators' behavior on performance of home and visiting intercollegiate basketball teams. *Perceptual and Motor Skills, 48,* 1047–1053.

Todd-Mancillas, W. R. (1982). Classroom environments and nonverbal behavior. In L. L. Barker (Ed.), *Communication in the classroom.* Englewood Cliffs, NJ: Prentice-Hall.

Vinsel, A., Brown, B. B., Altman, I., & Foss, C. (1980). Privacy regulation, territorial displays, and effectiveness of individual functioning. *Journal of Personality and Social Psychology, 39,* 1104–1115.

Vrij, A., van der Steen, J., & Koppelaar, L. (1994). Aggression of police officers as a function of temperature: An experiment with the Fire Arms Training System. *Journal of Community and Applied Social Psychology, 4,* 365–370.

Weinstein, C. S. (1979). The physical environment of the school: A review of research. *Review of Educational Research, 49,* 577–610.

Weinstein, N. D. (1978). Individual differences in reactions to noise: A longitudinal study in a college dormitory. *Journal of Applied Psychology, 63,* 458–466.

Wells, B. W. P. (1965). The psycho-social influence of building environment: Socio-metric findings in large and small office spaces. *Building Spaces, 1,* 153–165.

Werner, C. M., & Baxter, L. A. (1994). Temporal qualities of relationships: Organismic, transactional, and dialectical views. In M. L. Knapp & J. R. Miller (Eds.), *Handbook of interpersonal communication* (2nd ed.). Thousand Oaks, CA: Sage.

Werner, C. M., Irwin, A., & Brown, B. B. (1992). A transactional approach to interpersonal relations: Physical environment, social context, and temporal qualities. *Journal of Social and Personal Relationships, 9,* 297–323.

Wexner, L. B. (1954). The degree to which colors (hues) are associated with mood-tones. *Journal of Applied Psychology, 38,* 432–435.

White, A. G. (1953). The patient sits down: A clinical note. *Psychosomatic Medicine, 15,* 256–257.

Whyte, W. (1949). The social structure of a restaurant. *American Journal of Sociology, 54,* 302–310.

Wilner, D., Walkley, R. P., & Cook, S. W. (1952). Residential proximity and intergroup relations in public housing projects. *Journal of Social Issues, 8,* 45–69.

Wollin, D. D., & Montagre, M. (1981). College classroom environment: Effects of sterility versus amiability on student and teacher performance. *Environment and Behavior, 13,* 707–716.

Wong, H., & Brown, W. (1923). Effects of surroundings upon mental work as measured by Yerkes' multiple choice method. *Journal of Comparative Psychology, 3,* 319–331.

Zerubavel, E. (1981). *Hidden rhythms: Schedules and calendars in social life.* Chicago: University of Chicago Press.

Zweigenhaft, R. (1976). Personal space in the faculty office: Desk placement and the student–faculty interaction. *Journal of Applied Psychology, 61,* 529–532.

Spatial changes give a tone to a communication, accent it, and at times even override the spoken word.

—E. T. Hall

5 | # THE EFFECTS OF TERRITORY AND PERSONAL SPACE ON HUMAN COMMUNICATION

"If you can read this, you're too close," announces a familiar automobile bumper sticker in an attempt to regulate the amount of space between vehicles for traffic safety. Signs reading "Keep Out" and "Authorized Personnel Only" are also attempts to regulate space among human beings. We do not put up signs in daily conversation, but we use other signals to avoid uncomfortable crowding and other perceived invasions of our personal space. Our use of space—our own and others'—can dramatically affect our ability to achieve certain desired communication goals, whether those goals involve romance, diplomacy, or aggression. A fundamental concept in any discussion of human spatial behavior is the notion of territoriality. An understanding of this concept provides a useful perspective for our later examination of conversational space.

THE CONCEPT OF TERRITORIALITY

The term *territoriality* has been used for years in the study of animal and bird behavior. Generally, it means behavior characterized by identification with a geographic area in a way that indicates ownership and often involves defense of this territory against perceived invaders. Some territorial indicators around the home may be particularly strong: Dad's chair, Mom's study, Billy's closet, or Barbara's phone. There are many kinds of territorial behavior, and frequently such behaviors perform useful functions for a given species. For instance, territorial behaviors may help coordinate activities, regulate density, ensure propagation of the species, hold the group together, provide a sense of well-being, and offer hiding places.

Most behavioral scientists agree that territoriality exists in human behavior. It helps regulate social interaction, but it also can be the source of social conflict. Like other animals, the more powerful, dominant humans seem to have control over more territory—as long as the group or societal structure is stable.

Altman (1975) identified three types of territories: (1) primary, (2) secondary, and (3) public. The key distinction is the extent of ownership felt or warranted. *Primary territories* are clearly the exclusive domain of the owner. They are central to the daily functioning of the owner, and they are guarded carefully against intruders. For this reason, the invisible buffer zone surrounding our body also qualifies as a primary territory. It is not stationary and visible, like other territories, but the degree of ownership is extremely high, access to others is often very limited, and the defense against intrusions can be particularly fierce.

Homes or bedrooms often qualify as primary territory. Goffman's (1971) description of *possessional territories*—which include personal effects such as jackets, purses, and even dependent children—also seems to fit the requirements of primary territory. In this same category, Goffman discusses objects that can be claimed temporarily by people; for example, a magazine, television set, or eating utensils. These, however, seem to be more representative of what Altman calls *secondary territories*, which are not as central to the daily life of the owner, nor are they perceived as clearly exclusive to the owner. The neighborhood bar, or those objects like magazines or television sets, are examples of secondary territories. More frequent conflicts are apt to develop over these territories, because the public–private boundary is blurred. The following exchange is an example of this: "Let me watch my program on TV. I was here first." "It's not your TV. You don't own it."

Public territories are available to almost anyone for temporary ownership. Parks, beaches, streets, seats on public transportation, telephone booths, a place in line, or an unobstructed line of vision to see a particular object of interest are examples. The words *temporary occupancy or ownership* are important. A cleaning person who enters our office to clean without our permission might be offensive because permission was not granted, but the intrusion is temporary and job related. It would be a different story, however, if this person occupied the office all day or used it for noncleaning activities, such as eating lunch. The chairs in a classroom are theoretically available to anyone in the class for temporary occupancy, but frequent use or a desirable location can result in greater perceived ownership and territorial behavior (Kaya, 2007).

Territorial behavior seems to be a standard part of our daily contact with others, and it also is evident when sufficient social contact is denied. Altman and Haythorn (1967) analyzed the territorial behavior of socially isolated and non-isolated pairs of men. For 10 days, two individuals lived in a small room with no outside contact while a matched group received outside contacts. The men in the isolated groups showed a gradual increase in territorial behavior and a general pattern of social withdrawal; they desired more time alone. Their territorial behavior first evidenced itself with fixed objects, areas of the room, and personal objects such as beds. Later they began to claim more mobile and less personal objects. When the two men living together were incompatible with respect to dominance and affiliation, this resulted in greater territorial behavior.

TERRITORIALITY: INVASION AND DEFENSE

Instructions to police interrogators sometimes suggest sitting close to the suspect without the intervention of a desk that might provide protection or comfort. This theory of interrogation assumes that invasion of the suspect's personal territory, with little opportunity for defense, will give the officer a psychological advantage. Other examples of human territorial invasion and defense include members of adolescent gangs and ethnic groups who stake out territory in urban areas and defend it against intruders. Preserving national boundaries often underlies international disputes. What happens when somebody invades your territory? For instance, how do you feel when the car behind you is tailgating? When you have to stand in an overpopulated theater lobby or bus? When somebody sits in *your* seat? What do you do? Researchers have asked similar questions, and their answers help us understand further how we treat the objects and space around us.

Obviously, not all territorial encroachments are the same. Lyman and Scott (1967) identify three types:

1. *Violation* involves the unwarranted use of another's territory. This may be done with the eyes (staring at somebody eating in a public restaurant); with the voice or other sounds (somebody talking loudly nearby on their cell phone or construction noise next to a classroom); or with the body (taking up two subway seats).
2. *Invasion* is more all-encompassing and permanent. It is an attempt to take over another's territory. This may be an armed invasion of another country or the act of a wife who has turned her husband's den into her computer room.
3. *Contamination* is defiling another's territory, not by our presence but by what we leave behind. When we take temporary occupancy of a hotel room, for instance, we do not want to find the previous "owner's" toilet articles and soiled sheets. Similarly, we are frequently upset when someone else's dog leaves feces in our yard, or when we find food particles on "our" silverware in restaurants.

Encroachments on our territory do not always produce defensive maneuvers. The intensity of our reaction to territorial encroachment varies depending on a number of factors, including the following:

1. Who violated our territory? We may have very different reactions to friends' or acquaintances' violations as opposed to those of strangers. We may be more inclined to share personal things, including our space, with people we know (Kaya & Weber, 2003). We may also react differently depending on the gender, status, and age of the violator.
2. Why did they violate our territory? If we feel that the violator "knew better," we might react more strongly than if we felt he or she "couldn't help it" or was naive.
3. What type of territory was it? We are more likely to perceive a violation of our primary territory as far more serious than the violation of a secondary or public territory we are occupying, although people sometimes attribute more ownership to secondary and public territories than they deserve.
4. How was the violation accomplished? Was it done in a threatening way? If our body is touched, we may be more aroused and defensive than if someone walks across our yard. On the other hand, sometimes any intrusion, whether made in a threatening manner or not, will be perceived as a threat (Ruback & Kohli, 2005).

5. How long did the encroachment last? If the violation is perceived as temporary, reactions may be less severe.
6. Do we expect further violations in the future? If so, the initial territorial defense may be more intense.
7. Where did the violation occur? The population density and opportunities for negotiating new territorial boundaries will surely affect our reaction.

The two primary methods for territorial defense are *prevention* and *reaction*. *Prevention* is a means of staking out our territory so others recognize it as ours and go elsewhere. A person's mere presence in a place can keep others from entering it. If we stay in a place long enough or often enough, others think we "own" it; for example, a seat in a classroom. Sometimes we ask others to assist us in staking out and defending territory: "Would you hold my seat while I go get some popcorn?" (See Figure 5-1.) Neighbors' help will vary, of course, depending on how urgently their aid is requested, for how long, how important the territory appears, how well they know and are committed to the requester, and so on.

Objects are also used as "territorial markers" to designate "your" spatial area. In places with relatively low density, markers such as umbrellas, coats, notebooks, and so on are often effective; indeed, sometimes these markers will reserve not only a seat in a public area but also an entire table. Markers that appear more personal may be more effective in preventing violations but are also vulnerable to theft. If the marked territory is highly desirable to many others in the immediate area, markers probably will maintain their effectiveness for shorter periods of time. In public territories, it may be more effective to leave several markers, as these areas are

FIGURE 5-1

Marking public territory.

FIGURE 5-2

Seating on a commuter train.

open to nearly everyone. Commuters on trains with a seating arrangement that requires three passengers to sit side by side illustrate how territorial intrusion is sometimes the result of the combined behavior by the protector of the territory and the intruder. Passengers seated on the inside and outside of the three-seat arrangement position their legs, belongings, newspapers, and so on to convey the idea that sitting in the middle seat in "their" territory is forbidden. At the same time, many commuters who could sit in the vacant middle seats with two strangers on each side decide that taking the middle-seat territory is less desirable than standing or sitting on the floor—unless, of course, they are so tired that this is a less desirable course of action (McGeehan, 2005).

Sometimes the uniforms people are wearing identify a territory that can be legitimately used by a particular person. Often we construct fences and grow hedges to demarcate territory. And sometimes we stake out territory simply by the way we conduct our verbal interaction; a special jargon or dialect can warn others that a particular space is reserved for those who "know the language."

If the prevention of territorial violations does not work, how do people react? When people come close to us in face-to-face encounters, we are physiologically aroused, and heart rate and galvanic skin responses increase (Finando, 1973; McBride, King, & James, 1965). Arousal varies with eye gaze and touch as well as distance. Once aroused, we need to label our state as "positive" (liking, love, relief) or "negative" (dislike, embarrassment, stress, anxiety). If the aroused state is labeled positively, according to Patterson (1976), we will reciprocate the behavior; if it is labeled negatively, we will take measures to compensate. If someone is aroused by another person's approach and identifies it as undesirable, we could predict behavior designed to restore the "proper" distance between the interactants: looking away, changing the topic to a less personal one, crossing the arms to form a frontal barrier to the invasion, covering body parts, rubbing the neck to point the elbow sharply toward the invader, and so on.

Russo conducted a 2-year study of invading the territory of female college students seated in a college library (Sommer, 1969/2008). The study compared the responses of those invaded and a similar group that was not invaded. Several different invasion techniques were used: sitting next to subjects, across from them, and so on. The quickest departure or flight was triggered when the researcher sat next to a subject and moved her chair closer by approximately a foot. Other researchers have suggested that when strangers are involved, males feel more stress from frontal invasions, whereas women react more unfavorably to adjacent invasions (Hall, 1984). After approximately 30 minutes, about 70 percent of the people Russo approached at the 1-foot distance moved. From Russo's study, a whole vocabulary of defense was developed. For instance, defensive and offensive displays included the use of position, posture, and gesture. *Position* refers to location in the room; a newcomer to the room will interpret the situation differently if the other person has selected a corner position rather than one in the middle of the room. *Posture* refers to such indicators as whether a person has materials spread out "like he or she owned the place" or whether they are tightly organized. *Gestures* can be used to indicate receptivity or rejection of communication; for example, hostile glances, turning or leaning away, blocking with hands or arms, and so on. Although verbal defense is not a common first reaction, requests or even profanity can be effectively used. Russo's work is summarized by Sommer (1969):

> There were wide individual differences in the ways victims reacted—there is no single reaction to someone's sitting too close; there are defensive gestures, shifts in posture, and attempts to move away. If these fail or are ignored by the invader, or he shifts position too, the victim eventually takes to flight.... There was a dearth of direct verbal responses to the invasions.... Only one of the eighty students asked the invader to move over. (pp. 35–36)

It is worth remembering that the norm of politeness is strong enough to inhibit such direct verbal responses. This demonstrates one important feature of nonverbal communication: It is often "off the record" and can convey messages subtly without provoking confrontation. The person who glares, shuffles papers, or leans away does not have to acknowledge publicly his or her irritation. Barash (1973) conducted a study similar to Russo's, but the library invaders' status was manipulated. Students fled more quickly from the more formally dressed, "high-status" invaders. Knowles (1973) also experimented with a familiar type of invasion: talking to somebody in a hallway leaving other people to decide whether to walk through the conversants or around them. Only 25 percent of the people in this study walked through, but when the conversants were replaced with barrels, 75 percent of the passersby walked through. The fewest intrusions occurred with four-person groups, rather than a dyad, and "high-status" conversants, those older and more formally dressed. This study illustrates that, besides not wanting others to violate our territory, we generally do not want to violate others' territory either, as the mumbled apologies and bowed heads of some of Knowles's invaders testified.

Increasing population density also results in territorial violations. What happens when the population becomes so dense that we cannot exercise the usual territorial behavior?

DENSITY AND CROWDING

During the 1960s, many people were alarmed about the rapidly increasing world population. The first edition of Erlich's (1971) best-selling book, *The Population Bomb*, was published in 1968. It pointed to a rapidly increasing birth rate and predicted the death of hundreds of millions of people due to the effects of an overpopulated world. The growth of urban areas and increasing violence in inner-city areas also fueled concern for the effects of population growth. The central question was this: If worldwide population were to increase dramatically, would there be dire consequences? Some highly publicized research with rats seemed to fully support the fear that in highly dense populations, bad things would happen (Calhoun, 1962).

Calhoun noted that with plenty of food and no danger from predators, Norway rats in a quarter-acre outdoor pen stabilized their population at about 150. His observations, covering 28 months, indicated that spatial relationships are extremely important. He then designed an experiment in which he could maintain a stressful situation through overpopulation while three generations of rats were reared. He labeled this experiment a *behavioral sink*, an area or receptacle where most of the rats exhibited gross distortions of normal behavior. Some of Calhoun's observations are worth noting:

1. Some rats withdrew from social and sexual intercourse completely; others began to mount anything in sight; courtship patterns were totally disrupted, and females were frequently pursued by several males.
2. Nest-building patterns, ordinarily neat, became sloppy or nonexistent.
3. Litters of young rats became mixed; newborn and young rats were stepped on or eaten by invading hyperactive males.
4. Unable to establish spatial territories, dominant males fought over positions near the eating bins; the hyperactive males violated all territorial rights by running around in packs and disregarding any boundaries except those backed by force.
5. Pregnant rats frequently had miscarriages; disorders of the sex organs were numerous; only a fourth of the 558 newborns in the sink survived to be weaned.
6. Aggressive behavior increased significantly.

Can we generalize from rats to people? Some early studies that found moderate correlations between various socially undesirable outcomes such as crime, delinquency, mental and physical disorders, and high population density seemed to suggest so. Others facetiously contended that the only generalization we could make from Calhoun's work was, "Don't crowd rats!" But even this is an overstatement. Judge (2000), who analyzed numerous studies of high density among animal populations, would probably say, "Don't crowd rats with aggressive tendencies." In his own words:

> The individual characteristics and aggressive tendencies of animals that compose populations can influence aggression more so than increasing population density. Even the results of Calhoun's (1962) influential rat studies were dictated by the unique behavior

of a few individuals. The infamous "behavioral sinks" developed when a few dominant adult males established breeding territories in quarter sections of the compartmentalized pens used in the experiments. The remainder of the colony became restricted to single compartments. In colonies in which males did not establish territories or did so in a manner that did not restrict the rest of the colony, no "behavioral sinks" developed (Calhoun, 1962). This outcome of increased density is rarely cited. (p. 144)

Furthermore, nonhuman animals do not always respond to high density in negative or aggressive ways (Freedman, 1979; Judge & de Waal, 1993). In one study, the number of aggressive acts performed by monkeys living in environments of differing densities, from cages to free-ranging activity on an island, were compared (Judge & de Waal, 1997). Aggression was not significantly more prevalent in high-density environments, but coping behavior was. As density increased, the following types of coping behavior also increased: mutual grooming, rapid reconciliation after a fight, and the use of specific facial expressions to indicate the desire to avoid trouble. This tendency to develop ways to cope with high-density life in ways other than aggression is much like the human adaptations reported in the next two sections.

Behavioral sinks are not an inevitable result of unchecked population growth. Stress and aggression among those in high-density situations may also be affected by the amount of space available, the duration of the high-density experience, the ability to enact coping behavior, the extent to which key relationships can be maintained, and other factors. In other words, the widely publicized results of Calhoun's work, which suggested unequivocally harmful consequences of increasing population density, are incorrect. Based on human-density and crowding research conducted thus far, the results are complex and do not lend themselves to a simple "crowding is bad" conclusion.

To understand the effects of population density on human beings, we must first distinguish between the terms *density* and *crowding*. *Density* refers to the number of people per unit of space; *crowding* is a feeling state that may develop in high- or low-density situations. Perceptions of being crowded may be elicited by the following factors:

1. *Environmental factors*, such as reduced space, unwanted noise, the lack of needed resources or the ability to obtain them, and the absence of territorial markers, such as screens and partitions.
2. *Personal factors*, such as gender (males may feel the effects of density more acutely than females); personality characteristics reflecting low self-esteem, dominance, or control; a low desire for social contact; and prior unpleasant experiences with high density.
3. *Social factors*, such as a high frequency of unwanted social contact from many people at close quarters and the inability to change such patterns; inescapable interactions with people from an unfamiliar group; and unpleasant interactions that may be perceived as hostile or competitive.
4. *Goal-related factors*, such as the inability to accomplish what is desired.

The central theme characterizing most of the research in this area is that perceptions of crowding tend to increase as we perceive a decrease in our ability to control and influence our physical and social surroundings. Although the factors in the preceding list may contribute to perceptions of crowding, most high-density situations are characterized by some factors that decrease control and some that do not. Given these conditions, what can we say about the effects of high density and human reactions to it?

THE EFFECTS OF HIGH DENSITY ON HUMAN BEINGS

Definitions of density are complex and varied. Correlational studies have used the number of people per city, per census tract, or per dwelling unit; the number of rooms per dwelling unit; the number of buildings per neighborhood; and so on. Experimental studies sometimes put the same-sized group into different-sized rooms; others vary the number of people in the same room. Laboratory studies that vary density to analyze its effects on perceptions of crowding may have relevance only to those situations in which high density is a temporary condition, such as on elevators, buses, and so on. Few studies have considered the rate at which high density evolves, or whether participants feel they had any control over the development of a high-density situation. To sort through these variations in measurement, the following conclusions seem warranted.

First, it seems clear that increased density does not automatically increase stress or antisocial behavior in human beings. Sometimes we even seek the pleasures of density (see Figure 5-3). Football games and rock concerts are familiar examples.

FIGURE 5-3

A high-density beach.

If we take responsibility for our presence in a highly populated situation, and if we know the condition will terminate in a matter of hours, the chances of negative effects seem to be greatly reduced. Nevertheless, negative effects of density do occur. In one study, classroom density decreased girls' academic achievement and negatively affected boys' behavior (Maxwell, 2003). Other studies have found results—such as aggression, stress, criminal activity, hostility toward others, and a deterioration of mental and physical health—that might fit well into a behavioral-sink theory. However, in most every case, we find other studies that fail to confirm these highly negative effects. Usually, the explanation lies in the fact that the environmental, personal, social, and goal-related factors mentioned earlier could provide a form of control that was influential in offsetting undesirable influences. For example, Altman (1975) cites a study by Rohe and Patterson (1974), which found that if children were provided with enough of the toys they wanted, increased density would not produce the withdrawal and aggression suggested by previous studies. Some high-density neighborhoods that are highly cohesive actually have a lower incidence of mental and physical health problems.

Second, we sometimes blame high density for undesirable effects, either because it is an obvious feature of the situation and has a reputation for causing problems, or because the real causes are things we do not wish to face. Students who took a long time to complete their college registration tended to perceive the large number of students trying to register as the cause for their delays. They did not attribute their delays to forgetting needed forms, filling out forms incorrectly, and not preparing alternative course selections prior to registration (Gochman & Keating, 1980). High density can produce a host of problems, but human beings do not stand by passively in situations that demand a long-term commitment to high density; instead, they try various methods to cope with or offset potentially harmful effects. What are some of the methods of coping?

COPING WITH HIGH DENSITY

City dwellers are often exposed to an overload of information, people, things, problems, and so forth. As a result, they engage in behavior designed to reduce this overload, which sometimes causes outsiders to see them as distant and emotionally detached from others. Here are some of the methods for coping in populated cities:

1. Spending less time with each input; for example, having shorter conversations with people
2. Disregarding low-priority inputs; for example, ignoring the drunk on the sidewalk or not talking to people seen on a commuter train every day
3. Shifting the responsibility for some transactions to others; for example, relieving bus drivers of the responsibility for making change
4. Blocking inputs; for example, using attendants to guard apartment buildings

Nigerian students used nine different strategies to cope with high-density conditions in their residence halls (Amole, 2005). Strategies used to clearly define personal territory and studying in less dense locations were two of the most common.

Now let us shift our attention from spatial relationships in overpopulated conditions to those involved in a two-person conversation.

CONVERSATIONAL DISTANCE

As children, we are exposed to gradually increasing distances for various communication situations. The first few years of life provide a familiarity with what is known as *intimate distance*; the child then learns appropriate conversational distances for an increasing number of acquaintances and friends; and by about age 7, the child may have incorporated the concept of public distance into his or her behavioral repertoire. So by about the third grade, children have learned that conversational distance has meaning. As they age, children will gradually reflect adult norms for their culture as they make spatial adjustments for interactants who are known or unknown, tall or short, higher status or lower status, and so on. What are these adult norms? What are comfortable conversational distances? (See Figure 5-4.)

To answer these questions, first we turn to the astute observations about human spatial behavior made by anthropologist Edward T. Hall (1959; 1966). Hall identified several types of space, but our concern here is with what he called *informal space*. Others have referred to this as *personal space*, but because the space between people is the result of negotiating their personal preferences, it is more appropriately labeled *interpersonal space*. The informal space for each individual expands and contracts under varying circumstances, depending on the type of encounter, the relationship of the communicating persons, their personalities, and many other factors. Hall identified four types of informal space: (1) intimate, (2) casual–personal, (3) social–consultative, and (4) public. According to Hall, *intimate* distances range from actual physical contact to about 18 inches; *casual–personal* extends from 1.5 feet to 4 feet; *social–consultative*, for impersonal business, ranges from 4 to 12 feet; and *public* distance covers the area from 12 feet to the limits of visibility or hearing. Hall was quick to note that these distances are based on his observations of a particular sample of adults from business and professional occupations, primarily white middle-class males native to the northeastern United States, and any generalization to other ethnic and racial groups in the United States should be made with considerable caution.

Sommer (1961) also sought answers to questions about comfortable conversational distance. He studied people who were brought into a room and told to discuss various impersonal topics. Two sofas were placed in the room at various distances, and subjects were observed to see whether they sat opposite or beside one another. It was hypothesized that when they began to sit side by side, it would mean the conversational distance was too far to sit opposite one another on the two couches. From 1 to 3 feet, the subjects sat on different couches facing one another. Beyond 3.5 feet, people sat side by side. If we measure distance "nose to nose," this would make the participants 5.5 feet apart when they started to sit side by side, assuming they were not leaning forward or backward. In a follow-up study, Sommer used chairs, which allowed him to vary side-by-side distance as well as the distance across. Here he found that people chose to sit across from one another until the distance across exceeded the side-by-side distance; they then sat side by side.

How generalizable are these findings? A critical look at this study immediately leads us to question what other variables may affect the distance relationship. For instance, this study was conducted with people who knew each other

FIGURE 5-4

Variations in conversational distance and position.

slightly, were discussing impersonal topics, and were in a large lounge. How would other factors affect the distance relationship? For a long time, researchers have theorized that distance is based on the balance of approach and avoidance forces. What are some of these forces? Burgoon (1978) and Burgoon and Jones (1976) say that the distances we assume in a given conversation are a function of our cultural and personal expectations for appropriate distances. When someone violates these expectations, it garners our attention. Sometimes the violation is so immediately aversive that we flee or become very defensive. On other occasions, we mentally process the nature of the violation and the violator to determine our response. The violation of personal space may be judged to be more positive or more negative than the expected behavior, and we adapt accordingly. When the positive or negative nature of the violation is not clear, we assess our perceptions of the violator. A positive evaluation of the violator should lead to a positive evaluation of the space violation in such cases and vice versa. What are some of these expectations for conversational distance, and how do they develop? What factors lead us to assume certain conversational distances?

Answering these questions is the focus for the remainder of this chapter. Again, however, we must sort through conflicting results due to variations in research methodology and conceptualization of personal space. Logically, we know that conversational distance is the product of both interactants' negotiations. But some research is based on the behavior of a single person; some does not distinguish between actual physical distance and perceptions of distance; some measures distance by floor tiles or space between chair legs and totally ignores the ability of the communicators to vary the "psychological distance" by changes in topic, eye gaze, and body angle; and most research does not distinguish between initial distance and changes that take place over the course of a conversation. Because the methods of measuring personal space vary, we even have to be cautious about results that agree with other studies. Sometimes people complete questionnaires about preferred distances; sometimes they are asked to approach nonhuman objects, such as coat racks and life-sized photographs; sometimes people are unknowingly approached at various distances by others; and sometimes they are asked to arrange miniature dolls, photographs, or silhouettes as if they were in various communication situations. With these factors in mind, we selected the following important sources of variation in conversational distance. They encompass much of what Sommer (2002) called the "best substantiated" findings about personal space.

1. Sex
2. Age
3. Cultural and ethnic background
4. Topic or subject matter
5. Setting for the interaction
6. Physical characteristics
7. Attitudinal and emotional orientation
8. Characteristics of the interpersonal relationship
9. Personality characteristics

SEX

Many studies have looked at sex differences in interpersonal space using all the methodologies listed earlier. Hall (1984) has summarized this research. In naturalistic interaction, settings in which people are interacting more or less naturally and are not aware of being observed, females predominantly choose to interact with others of either sex more closely than males do, as long as the conversations are neutral or friendly. When the conversations are threatening or alienating, females assume a greater conversational distance (Bell, Kline, & Bernard, 1988).

Another way of understanding sex differences in interpersonal distance is to examine how the other person's sex influences the distance set. (The preceding discussion applies only to the influence of one's own sex on that distance.) The research shows very convincingly that people approach females closer than they approach males, and this remains true no matter what kind of methodology is used. When the effects for one's own sex and those for the other's sex are combined, they show that female–female pairs interact most closely, male–male pairs interact most distantly, and mixed-sex pairs set intermediate distances. This pattern shows up frequently in research, especially in Anglo-American samples.

Several theories have been put forth to explain these sex differences in conversational distances. One popular notion is rooted in the different amounts of space children experience. It has been noted, for example, that the same stimuli may cause parents to put male infants on the floor or in a playpen but to hug the females or put them in a nearby high chair. Boys are frequently given toys that seem to encourage activities demanding more space, often away from the confines of the home itself; for example, footballs, cars, trains, and so forth. Girls, in contrast, may receive dolls, dollhouses, and other toys that require less space. Some observational studies have confirmed that young boys at play utilize more space than young girls, but this does not explain those instances in which women want greater interaction distance. The *oppression hypothesis* suggests that women choose a closer interaction distance because people with less status in society are accorded less space, but Atsuko (2003) did not find evidence to support this theory. Using social orientation as the basis for explaining the interaction distances chosen by women has the advantage of explaining both closer and more distant interaction preferences. Women, these theorists argue, are more socially oriented than males, so they should prefer distances that connote warmth, trust, and friendship. Eagly (1987), using social role theory, believes women play a more person-oriented and prosocial role in society, which manifests itself in various kinds of behavior, including interaction distances consistent with that role.

AGE

If distance reflects our general comfort with a person, it seems reasonable to predict that we would interact more closely to people in our own general age range. The exceptions, of course, are the very old and very young who, for various reasons, often elicit interaction at closer quarters. Generally, interaction distance seems to expand gradually from about age 6 to early adolescence, when adult norms seem to be reflected (Aiello & Aiello, 1974). Adults are also more likely to hold older children responsible for understanding adult norms. When 5-year-olds invaded the personal space of people waiting in line to see a movie, they were received positively; but when 10-year-olds were the invaders, they were met with negative responses (Fry & Willis, 1971). Obviously, these reactions are modified by the communicative context, but these studies do suggest that adults expect the norms for conversational distance to be learned before the child is 10. Children are able to decode proxemic meanings before they encode them in their daily interactions, as is true of many behaviors.

CULTURAL AND ETHNIC BACKGROUND

Volumes of folklore and isolated personal observations suggest that spatial relationships in other cultures with different needs and norms may produce very different distances for interacting.

Infants reared in different cultures learn different proxemic patterns. A group of Japanese mothers spent more time than a comparable group of mothers in the United States in close contact with their infants. Mother, father, and infant in Japan usually sleep in the same room. In the Nyansongo culture of Kenya, infants are always in close proximity to a family member, and the infant sleeps in the mother's arms at night (Caudill & Weinstein, 1972). It is not hard to see how such patterns provide a different sense of distance when compared to the patterns of children who are put into a separate room to sleep several times during the day as well as at night.

Hall (1966) used the terms *contact* and *noncontact* to distinguish the behavior of people from different cultural groups. Compared to noncontact cultures, interactants in contact cultures are expected to face one another more directly, interact more closely with one another, touch one another more, look one another in the eye more, and speak in a louder voice. In a study by Watson (1970), contact cultures were Arabs, Latin Americans, and southern Europeans. Noncontact cultures were Asians, Indians, Pakistanis, northern Europeans, and people living in the United States. Studies by Watson and others have found support for these predicted differences, but it is important to remember that these broad cultural norms may or may not manifest themselves in any particular conversation within a culture (Remland, Jones, & Brinkman, 1991). Whether interactants know each other, whether they are arguing, whether they are talking to a person of their same sex, and a host of other factors may sometimes offset these broad cultural tendencies. For example, Sanders, Hakky, and Brizzolara (1985) found few differences between the comfortable conversational space of Egyptian and American males, but Egyptian females were not like their American counterparts. A comfortable interaction distance for male friends of the Egyptian women was nearly as distant as for male strangers. In another study, close seating of two brothers was more comfortable to Saudi students than to American students, but when the interactants were a brother and sister, it was the American students who found a comfort zone in closer interaction distances (Hewitt & Alqahtani, 2003).

Shuter's (1976, 1977) systematic field observations in contact and noncontact cultures reminds us that somewhat different proxemic norms may apply for groups within the larger culture. He found, for instance, significant differences within the so-called Latin American cultural group. Costa Ricans interacted more closely than did Panamanians or Colombians. And contrary to predictions, he found no significant differences in interaction distance and touching for women in Milwaukee, Wisconsin, and Venice, Italy. Italian men did not manifest closer interaction positions or face their interaction partners more directly than German men, but they did engage in more touching.

Variations in proxemic patterns in the United States have been the subject of several research projects. For example, the question of whether black Americans interact at closer distances than white Americans has been studied. Developmental studies show that when entering elementary school, black children may exhibit closer interaction distances than white children, but by the fifth grade, these differences are minimized; and by age 16, black Americans tend to maintain greater conversational distances (Aiello & Thompson, 1980; Halberstadt, 1985). Obviously, the racial composition of the schools and the socioeconomic class of the students will also play an important role in determining comfortable interaction distances. Most studies reveal that interactions involving black and white communicators occur at greater distances than those involving persons of the same race. Another large cultural group in the United States, Hispanic Americans, has also been observed. These studies generally support the prediction that Hispanic Americans interact at closer distances than do Anglo Americans.

Scherer (1974) contended that any differences between blacks and whites, and presumably also Hispanic Americans, may be confounded by socioeconomic factors not attributable to ethnic background. This study found that middle-class children maintained greater conversational distance than lower-class children, but there were no differences between middle-class blacks and whites or lower-class blacks and whites. Because proxemic norms are learned, it is reasonable to assume that people who grow up in the same neighborhood—no matter what their skin color or ethnic heritage—will share more expectations for comfortable conversational distance than those raised in different parts of a city, state, or country.

TOPIC OR SUBJECT MATTER

Erickson (1975) wanted to find out if proxemic shifts forward or backward were associated with any other events in a conversation. By coding co-occurring behavior, he determined that proxemic shifts may mark important segments of the encounter, such as beginnings, endings, and topic changes.

Earlier we noted that in his efforts to examine the limits of conversational distance, Sommer tried to use impersonal topics that would presumably not influence the distances chosen. For intimates, personal topics may demand less conversational distance unless other factors, such as an impersonal setting, neutralize such inclinations.

Leipold's (1963) work demonstrates how anticipated treatment of the same general topic can influence conversational distance. Students entered a room and were given either a negative comment ("Your grade is poor, and you have not done your best"); praise ("You are doing very well, and Mr. Leipold wants to talk to you further"); or a neutral comment ("Mr. Leipold is interested in your feelings about the introductory course"). Students given the negative comment sat farthest from the experimenter; those who were praised sat closest. Following insults, people may want to assume a greater distance than they normally would with that person, particularly if the person giving the insult is perceived as a higher status person (O'Neal, Brunalt, Carifio, Troutwine, & Epstein, 1980). Regardless of topic, very close distances may result in generally less talking (Schulz & Barefoot, 1974).

SETTING FOR THE INTERACTION

Obviously, the social setting makes a great deal of difference in how far we stand from others in conversation. A crowded cocktail party demands a different distance than a comfortable evening in the living room with a spouse or significant other. Lighting, temperature, noise, and available space affect interaction distance. Some authors have hypothesized that as room size increases, people tend to sit closer together. Noisy urban street locations outside an office building may prompt people to stand closer to one another than they do when conversing inside the building. And if the setting is perceived as formal or unfamiliar, we would predict greater distances from unknown others and closer distances to known others.

PHYSICAL CHARACTERISTICS

Height seems to make a difference in the distance people select for interacting. Irrespective of sex, shorter individuals seem to invite smaller interpersonal distances than taller individuals (Caplan & Goldman, 1981). When the two communicators are vastly different in height, the distance has to be adjusted so faces can be seen. Evidence also indicates that obese people are accorded greater interaction distances (Lerner, Venning, & Knapp, 1975).

A series of studies conducted by (Kleck 1969; Kleck & Strenta, 1985) shows that people interacting with stigmatized individuals (a left-leg amputation was simulated with a special wheelchair) choose greater initial speaking distances than with non-stigmatized persons, but that this distance decreases as the length of the interaction increases. Similar results have been found for perceived epileptics and people with facial disfigurations such as scars and port-wine stains. Kleck points out that when people with physical disabilities expect others to behave in a distant manner, they may prepare themselves for such reactions and thereby increase the chances it will happen.

ATTITUDINAL AND EMOTIONAL ORIENTATION

Some experiments have been conducted by telling a person he or she was going to interact with a person who was either "warm and friendly" or "unfriendly." Not surprisingly, greater distances were chosen when interacting with a person perceived to be unfriendly. Similarly, when told to enter into conversation with another person and to behave in a friendly way, people chose closer distances than when told to "let him/her know you aren't friendly." This friendly/unfriendly relationship to distance seems to manifest itself even with preschool children (King, 1966). The number of unfriendly acts was directly related to the distance maintained by the recipient of such acts during free-play situations. The distance could be reduced, however, by putting a prized toy near the aggressive child. In some instances, our anger will cause us to withdraw from others, but if we seek retaliation, we may increase proximity (Meisels & Dosey, 1971).

Variations in our emotional states, such as depression, fatigue, excitement, or joy, can sometimes make vast differences in how close or far away we want to be from others. The traumatic experiences of abused children probably explain why they assumed significantly greater conversational distances than their non-abused peers in one study (Vranic, 2003). This was true for males and females and was exacerbated by frontal approaches by males.

A study reported by Patterson (1968) indicates that we may make a variety of interpersonal judgments about others based on distance. People were told to interview others and secretly rate them on traits of friendliness, aggressiveness, dominance, extraversion, and intelligence. The interviewees were actually confederates who approached the interviewers at different distances and gave standard answers to the questions asked. The mean ratings for all the traits at four different distances were tabulated, and they revealed that the most distant position yielded significantly lower, less favorable ratings. So barring any contradictory information, people choosing closer distances are often seen as warmer, more likeable, more empathic, and more understanding.

When we seek to win another's approval, we reduce conversational distance as opposed to instances when we are deliberately trying to avoid approval. Females seeking approval maintained a mean distance of 57 inches; those trying to avoid approval averaged 94 inches. When the distance was held constant at 5 feet, approval seekers compensated by smiling more and engaging in more gestural activity (Rosenfeld, 1965, 1966).

CHARACTERISTICS OF THE INTERPERSONAL RELATIONSHIP

A number of studies also show that conversational distance varies as a function of our relationship with the other person. Strangers begin conversations at a greater distance than acquaintances, and acquaintances are a bit more distant than friends. In a study of 108 married couples, husbands were asked to walk toward their wives and stop when they got to a comfortable conversational distance. The more dissatisfied the husbands were with their marriage, the greater the distance they chose (Crane, Dollahite, Griffin, & Taylor, 1987). Preschoolers seem to be able to use distance as a criterion for determining liking and disliking also. Like adults, children seem to maintain greater distances with unknown adults, unfriendly or threatening persons, teachers, and endomorphs.

These and other studies suggest that closer relationships are likely to be associated with closer interaction distances. Obviously, there is a point at which we would not expect interactants to get any closer, no matter how close their relationship. And even people who are very close will not always interact at close distances due to the ebb and flow of their relationship, as well as the influence of other distance-altering factors.

PERSONALITY CHARACTERISTICS

Much has been written about the influence of introversion and extraversion on spatial relationships. It is difficult to draw any firm conclusions, but the bulk of the evidence seems to indicate that introverts tend to stand farther away than extroverts and to generally prefer greater interpersonal distances. Other studies suggest that anxiety-prone individuals maintain greater distances, but closer distances are seen when people have a high self-concept, affiliative needs, or when they are low on authoritarianism, high on interdependence, and "self-directed." People with various personality abnormalities can probably be counted on to show greater non-normative spatial behavior, choosing interactive distances both too far away and too close.

In addition to studying human spatial behavior in high-density situations and in conversation, some researchers have examined such questions in the context of small groups, particularly in regard to seating patterns.

SEATING BEHAVIOR AND SPATIAL ARRANGEMENTS IN SMALL GROUPS

The body of work on seating behavior and spatial arrangements in small groups is known as *small group ecology*. Results of these studies show that our seating behavior is not generally accidental or random. Explanations are available for much of it, regardless of whether we are fully conscious of them. The particular position chosen in relation to the other person or persons varies with the task at hand, the degree of relationship between the interactants, the personalities of the two parties, and the amount and kind of space available. We can summarize the findings about seating behavior and spatial positioning under the following categories:

- Leadership
- Dominance
- Task
- Sex and acquaintance
- Introversion–extraversion

LEADERSHIP

It seems to be a norm, in the United States at least, that leaders are expected to be found at the head or foot of the table. In households in which the husband is considered the head of the household, he is likely to be found sitting at one end of a rectangular dinner table. Elected group leaders generally put themselves in the head positions at rectangular tables, and the other group members try to position themselves so they can see the leader. In mock jury deliberations, the man seated on the end position is more likely to be chosen as the leader. The reaction to women who are positioned at the head of a table of men and women has, in the past, been less consistently linked to the leadership role (Porter & Geis, 1981). As long as the group consisted of all women, the one at the head of the table was perceived as the leader. With the recent growth of women in positions of leadership in business and government, we would expect women seated at the end position in groups of men and women to be more consistently chosen as the leader, too.

Howells and Becker (1962) added further support to the idea that a person's position in a group is an important factor in leadership emergence. They reasoned that spatial position determines the flow of communication, which in turn determines leadership emergence. Five-person decision-making groups were examined: Three people sat on one side of a rectangular table, and two sat on the other side. Because previous work suggested that communication usually flows across the table rather than around it, the researchers predicted that the side with two people would be able to influence the most people, or at least talk more, and therefore emerge more often as group leaders. This hypothesis was confirmed.

An experiment by Ward (1968) helps unravel how seating position can create leaders. College males were assigned at random to sit in particular seats at a round table. The experimenters arranged it so that more people were seated around one half of the table than the other; only two people sat at the less populated end, and these two seats were considered visually central, because their occupants would receive more undivided gaze from people at the other, more densely occupied end. As predicted, occupants of these visually central seats received higher ratings of leadership after discussions had taken place. But were they really leaders or just perceived to be? Other research (Taylor & Fiske, 1975) does indicate that the person on whom attention is centered will appear to be an initiator and a person causally responsible for the course of the conversation; but in Ward's study, evidence indicated that those who were visually central actually behaved differently: they talked more. It would be interesting to unravel further the complex routes by which seating position might affect leadership. For example, does the visually central person think, "I'm in a central position; I'd better start acting like a leader"? Or do the attention and subtle cues of the other members of the group trigger leadership behaviors, perhaps without the visually central person even realizing it?

People seem well aware of the different perceptions and communicative potentials associated with different seating positions. When people were asked to select seats to convey different impressions, they chose end positions to convey leadership or dominance, positions with the closest distances to convey interpersonal attraction, and seats that afforded the greatest interpersonal distance, and the least visual accessibility vis-à-vis the end positions, to indicate they did not wish to participate (Reiss & Rosenfeld, 1980).

DOMINANCE

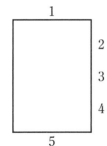

The end positions also seem to carry a status or dominance factor. Russo (1967) found that people rating various seating arrangements on an "equality" dimension stated that one person seated at the head and one on the side indicated more unequal status than if they were seated side by side or both on the ends. In an analysis of talking frequency in small groups, Hare and Bales (1963) noted that people in positions 1, 3, and 5 (see figure) were frequent talkers. Subsequent studies revealed that these people were likely to be dominant personalities, whereas those who avoided the central or focal positions by choosing seats 2 and 4 were more anxious and actually stated they wanted to stay out of the discussion. These self-selection effects demonstrate the importance of conducting randomized studies, such as Ward's (1968) study mentioned earlier. We do not know whether the communication of nondominant persons placed in focal positions would radically change their behavior.

Positions 1, 3, and 5 also were considered positions of leadership, but leadership of different types, depending on the position. The two end positions, positions

1 and 5, attracted *task-oriented leaders*, whereas the middle positions attracted *socioemotional leaders*, those concerned about group relationships and getting everyone to participate.

TASK

The tasks performed in a courtroom are especially important to a defendant, particularly the testimony of witnesses against him or her. In 2006, the two primary defendants in the collapse of the Enron corporation, Skilling and Lay, petitioned the court to give them the ability to face their accusers by moving them from a table that obstructed their view of the witnesses. By law, defendants have a right to face their accusers, a condition that presumably has a positive effect on truth telling.

Seating preferences of students and nonstudents engaged in the accomplishment of different tasks have also been studied (Sommer, 1969; Cook, 1970). In each case, people were asked to imagine sitting at a table with a same-sex friend in each of the following four situations:

1. *Conversation*. Sitting and chatting for a few minutes before class, or before work for nonstudents
2. *Cooperation*. Sitting and studying together for the same exam, or sitting doing a crossword together, or some similar activity for nonstudents
3. *Coaction*. Sitting studying for different exams, or sitting at the same table reading for nonstudents
4. *Competition*. Competing to see who will be the first to solve a series of puzzles

Each person was shown a round table and a rectangular table. Each table had six chairs. The combined results for all the groups surveyed in these two studies are presented in Table 5-1 for rectangular tables and Table 5-2 for circular tables.

There are many similarities among the different groups concerning their order of preference. Conversations before class or work involved primarily corner or "short" opposite seating at rectangular tables and side-by-side seating at round tables. Cooperation seems to elicit a preponderance of side-by-side choices. Coaction—that is, studying for different exams or reading at the same table—necessitated plenty of room between the participants, and the most distant seating positions were generally selected. Most participants wanted to compete in an opposite seating arrangement, however, some students wanted to establish a closer opposite relationship; apparently this would afford them an opportunity to see how the other person was progressing

TABLE 5-1 | SEATING PREFERENCES AT RECTANGULAR TABLES

	x / x□	□ / x	x x □	x□x	x □ / x	x □x
Conversation	45%	36%	12%	1%	4%	2%
Cooperation	23	13	42	8	10	4
Coaction	8	8	10	21	34	19
Competition	6	22	7	40	19	6

TABLE 5-2 | SEATING PREFERENCES AT ROUND TABLES

	x x ◯	x ◯	x ◯ x
Conversation	60%	27%	13%
Cooperation	68	13	19
Coaction	18	32	50
Competition	12	23	65

Source: (Tables 5-1 and 5-2) From "Experiments in orientation and proxemics" by M. Cook, *Human Relations* Vol. 23, pp. 61–76. Copyright © 1975, The Tavistock Institute. Reprinted by permission of Sage Publications.

and would also allow them to use various gestures, body movements, and eye contact to upset their opponents. The more distant opposite position would presumably prevent less spying.

SEX AND ACQUAINTANCE

The nature of a relationship may make a difference in spatial orientation and hence in seating selection. Cook (1970) conducted a questionnaire study and obtained some observational data of people interacting in a restaurant and several bars. People in the questionnaire study were asked to select seating arrangements in the following situations:

- Sitting with a casual friend of the same sex
- Sitting with a casual friend of the opposite sex
- Sitting with a boyfriend or girlfriend

The predominant seating pattern, as stated by questionnaire respondents using a bar as a referent, was corner seating ₓ⬜ for the same-sex friends and casual friends of the opposite sex. However, intimate friends appear to require side-by-side seating ˣˣ⬜. In a restaurant, both nonintimate relationship categories selected predominantly opposite seating ⬜ˣ; but as intimacy increased, other types of seating became more acceptable. Some very practical reasons may be offered for opposite seating in restaurants. For instance, other patrons will not have to sit opposite you, which might create some uncomfortable situations with respect to eye contact and overheard conversation. In addition, you will not poke the other person with your elbow while eating. Actual observations of seating in a restaurant, presented in Table 5-3, seem to validate the questionnaire responses. Most people do select opposite seating in restaurants. However, the observations of people sitting in bars do not agree with the questionnaire study of seating preferences in bars (see Table 5-4). Although questionnaire preferences favored corner seating, actual observations show a marked preference for side-by-side seating. Cook suggests this may have been because the bars he studied were equipped with many seats located against the wall. Supposedly this allowed persons to sit side by side, not have their backs to anyone, and have a good view of the other patrons. Thus, paper-and-pencil preferences were overruled by environmental factors. Nevertheless, this

TABLE 5-3 | OBSERVATIONS OF SEATING BEHAVIOR IN A RESTAURANT

	X / X (opposite short)	X X (side by side)	X / X (diagonal)
Two males	6	0	0
Two females	6	0	1
Male with female	36	7	1
Total	48	7	2

TABLE 5-4 | OBSERVATIONS OF SEATING BEHAVIOR IN THREE BARS

	X X (corner)	X / X (opposite)	X X (side by side)
Bar A			
Two males	7	8	13
Male with female	6	4	21
Total	13	12	34
Bar B			
Two males	1	0	9
Male with female	4	3	20
Total	5	3	29
Bar C			
Two males	0	11	7
Male with female	1	4	10
Total	1	15	17
Overall			
Two males	8	19	29
Male with female	11	11	51
Total	19	30	80

Source: (Tables 5–5 and 5–6) From "Experiments in orientation and proxemics" by M. Cook, *Human Relations* Vol. 23, pp. 61–76. Copyright © 1970, The Tavistock Institute. Reprinted by permission of Sage Publications.

study allows us to conclude that the person's sex and their acquaintance with the other person do have an effect on their actual and preferred seating positions.

INTROVERSION–EXTRAVERSION

We have already discussed the possible influence of introversion and extraversion on conversational distance. Some evidence indicates that this personality variable also affects seating preferences. Extroverts are likely to choose to sit opposite, either across the table or down the length of it, and disregard positions that would put them at an angle. Extroverts may also choose positions that would put them in close physical proximity to another person. Introverts generally choose positions that would keep them more at a distance, visually and physically.

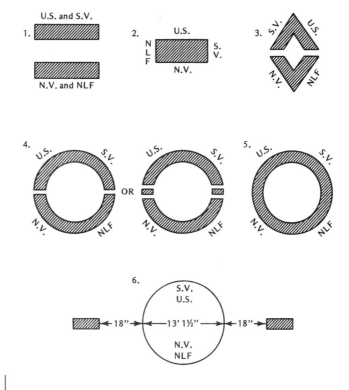

FIGURE 5-5

Proposals for a table to be used at the Paris peace talks, 1968.

Source: From McCroskey, Larson, Knapp (1971). *An Introduction to Interpersonal Communication.* Englewood Cliffs, N.J.: Prentice Hall. Reprinted by permission of Pearson Education.

A discussion of the shape of the negotiating table at the 1968 Paris peace talks that attempted to end the Vietnam War is a most appropriate way to conclude this chapter.

It incorporates elements of territoriality and seating arrangements that are influenced by culture, attitudes, leadership perceptions, and the type of task undertaken. It took negotiators 8 months just to reach an agreement on the shape of the table! The diagrams in Figure 5-5 mark the chronology of the seating proposals.

The United States (U.S.) and South Vietnam (S.V.) wanted a seating arrangement in which only two sides were identified. They did not want to recognize the National Liberation Front (NLF) as an equal party in the negotiations. North Vietnam (N.V.) and the NLF wanted equal status given to all parties, represented by a four-sided table. The final arrangement was such that both parties could claim "victory." The round table minus the dividing lines allowed North Vietnam and NLF to claim all four delegations were equal. The existence of the two secretarial tables (interpreted as dividers), the lack of identifying symbols on the table, and an AA, BB speaking rotation permitted the United States and South Vietnam to claim victory for the two-sided approach. Considering the lives lost during the 8 months needed to arrive at the seating arrangement, we must certainly conclude that proximity and territoriality are far from trivial concerns in some human encounters. (McCroskey, Larson, & Knapp, 1971, p. 98)

SUMMARY

Our perceptions and use of space contribute extensively to the various communication outcomes we seek. Some of our spatial behavior is related to a need to stake out and maintain territory, and territorial behavior can be helpful in regulating social interaction and controlling density; it can also be the source of conflict when territory is disputed or encroached upon without permission. We identified three different types of territories—*primary*, *secondary*, and *public*—and several different levels at which territorial behavior exists: *individual*, *group*, *community*, and *nation*. Although we often think people vigorously defend their territory, the type of defense depends very much on who the intruder is, why the intrusion is taking place, what type of territory is being intruded upon, what type of intrusion occurs—*violation*, *invasion*, or *contamination*—how long the intrusion takes, and where it occurs. We often try to prevent people from moving into our territory by marking it as "ours." This can be achieved by our physical presence, the presence of a friend who agrees to watch our territory, or by using markers—fences, coats, and the like—or a special kind of language. When someone does invade another person's territory, we sometimes find the "owner's" physiological arousal increased, and various defensive maneuvers may be used, such as flight, hostile looks, turning or leaning away, blocking advances with objects or hands and arms, and verbal behavior. Just as people do not like others to invade their territory, we also find they are reluctant to invade the territory of others, often apologizing when it cannot be prevented.

We examined density and crowding in both animal and human interaction. Some animal studies showed undesirable effects from overpopulation. High-density human situations, however, are not always disruptive; sometimes we *want* the company of many people. The best predictor of individually stressful and socially undesirable outcomes seems to be the number of people per room rather than other density measures. When people do feel the stress of a crowded situation, they seek ways to cope with it. We also distinguished between density, or the number of people per unit of space, and crowding, a feeling brought on by the environment, personal, or social factors.

Our examination of spatial behavior in conversations revealed many ways of conceptualizing and measuring this behavior. As a result, some generalizations about conversational space remain tentative. We do know that each of us seeks a comfortable conversational distance that varies depending on age, sex, cultural and ethnic background, setting, attitudes, emotions, topics, physical characteristics, personality, and our relationship with the other person. We also know that conversational distance changes during the course of a conversation.

Finally, we discussed seating arrangements in small groups. Distances and seats chosen do not seem to be accidental. Leaders and dominant personalities tend to choose specific seats, but seating position also can determine a person's role in a group. Seating also varies with the topic at hand, the nature of the relationships among the parties, and certain personality variables.

Questions for Discussion

1. Identify a secondary territory you have experienced in which ownership was disputed. Discuss what happened, why it happened, and how the conflict could have been prevented.

2. What factors are likely to cause a person who comes to the United States from another culture, with different norms for conversational space, to maintain the norms from his or her culture of origin? What factors are likely to cause them to manifest conversational space that is more typical of the United States?

3. When is a woman's purse likely to be perceived as a primary territory? When can it become a secondary territory?

4. Do you think the findings associated with leadership, dominance, and seating behavior apply to females as well as males? Why or why not?

BIBLIOGRAPHY

Aiello, J. R. (1987). Human spatial behavior. In D. Stokols & I. Altman (Eds.), *Handbook of environmental psychology* (Vol. 1, pp. 389–504). New York: Wiley.

Aiello, J. R., & Aiello, T. C. (1974). The development of personal space: Proxemic behavior of children 6 through 16. *Human Ecology, 2,* 177–189.

Aiello, J. R., & Jones, S. E. (1971). Field study of the proxemic behavior of young school children in three subcultural groups. *Journal of Personality and Social Psychology, 19,* 351–356.

Aiello, J. R., & Thompson, D. E. (1980). Personal space, crowding, and spatial behavior in a cultural context. In I. Altman, A. Rapoport, & J. F. Wohlwill (Eds.), *Human behavior and environment* (Vol. 4). New York: Plenum.

Albert, S., & Dabbs, J. M., Jr. (1970). Physical distance and persuasion. *Journal of Personality and Social Psychology, 15,* 265–270.

Allekian, C. I. (1973). Intrusions of territory and personal space: An anxiety-inducing factor for hospitalized persons. *Nursing Research, 22,* 236–241.

Allgeier, A. R., & Byrne, D. (1973). Attraction toward the opposite sex as a determinant of physical proximity. *Journal of Social Psychology, 90,* 213–219.

Altman, I. (1975). *The environment and social behavior.* Monterey, CA: Brooks/Cole.

Altman, I., & Chemers, M. M. (1988). *Culture and environment.* New York: Cambridge University Press.

Altman, I., & Haythorn, W. W. (1967). The ecology of isolated groups. *Behavioral Science, 12,* 169–182.

Amole, D. (2005). Coping strategies for living in student residential facilities in Nigeria. *Environment and Behavior, 37,* 201–219.

Ardrey, R. (1966). *The territorial imperative.* New York: Atheneum Press.

Argyle, M., & Dean, J. (1965). Eye contact, distance and affiliation. *Sociometry, 28,* 289–304.

Atsuko, A. (2003). Gender differences in interpersonal distance: From the viewpoint of oppression hypothesis. *Japanese Journal of Experimental Social Psychology, 42,* 201–218.

Barash, D. P. (1973). Human ethology: Personal space reiterated. *Environment and Behavior, 5,* 67–73.

Baum, A., & Greenberg, C. I. (1975). Waiting for a crowd: The behavioral and perceptual effects of anticipated crowding. *Journal of Personality and Social Psychology, 32,* 671–679.

Baum, A. & Paulus, P. B. (1987). Crowding. In D. Stokols & I. Altman (Eds.), *Handbook of environmental psychology,* (Vol. 1, pp. 533–570). New York: Wiley.

Baum, A., Riess, M., & O'Hara, J. (1974). Architectural variants of reaction to spatial invasion. *Environment and Behavior, 6,* 91–100.

Baxter, J. C. (1970). Interpersonal spacing in natural settings. *Sociometry, 33,* 444–456.

Bechtel, R. B. (1997). *Environment and behavior.* Thousand Oaks, CA: Sage.

Becker, F. D. (1973). Study of spatial markers. *Journal of Personality and Social Psychology, 26,* 439–445.

Bell, P. A., Greene, T. C., Fisher, J. D., & Baum, A. (1996). *Environmental psychology* (4th ed.). Fort Worth, TX: Harcourt Brace.

Bell, P. A., Kline, L. M., & Barnard, W. A. (1988). Friendship and freedom of movement as moderators of sex differences in interpersonal spacing. *Journal of Social Psychology, 128,* 305–310.

Brown, B. B. (1987). Territoriality. In D. Stokols & I. Altman (Eds.), *Handbook of environmental psychology,* (Vol. 1, pp. 505–532). New York: Wiley.

Bull, R. (1985). The general public's reactions to facial disfigurement. In J. A. Graham & A. M. Kligman (Eds.), *The psychology of cosmetic treatments.* New York: Praeger.

Buller, D. B. (1987). Communication apprehension and reactions to proxemic violations. *Journal of Nonverbal Behavior, 11,* 13–25.

Burgoon, J. K. (1978). A communication model of personal space violations: Explication and an initial test. *Human Communication Research, 4,* 129–142.

Burgoon, J. K. (1982). Privacy and communication. In M. Burgoon (Ed.), *Communication yearbook 6.* Beverly Hills, CA: Sage.

Burgoon, J. K. (1983). Nonverbal violations of expectations. In J. M. Wiemann & R. P. Harrison (Eds.), *Nonverbal interaction.* Beverly Hills, CA: Sage.

Burgoon, J. K., & Jones, S. B. (1976). Toward a theory of personal space expectations and their violations. *Human Communication Research, 2,* 131–146.

Calhoun, J. B. (1962). Population density and social pathology. *Scientific American, 206,* 139–148.

Caplan, M. E., & Goldman, M. (1981). Personal space violations as a function of height. *Journal of Social Psychology, 114,* 167–171.

Cappella, J. N. (1986). Violations of distance norms: Reciprocal and compensatory reactions for high and low self-monitors. In M. L. McLaughlin (Ed.), *Communication yearbook 9.* Beverly Hills, CA: Sage.

Carpenter, C. R. (1958). Territoriality: A review of concepts and problems. In A. Roe & G. G. Simpson (Eds.), *Behavior and evolution.* New Haven: Yale University Press.

Caudill, W., & Weinstein, H. (1972). Maternal care and infant behavior in Japan and America. In C. Lavatelli & F. Stendler (Eds.), *Readings in child behavior and development.* New York: Harcourt.

Christian, J. J., & Davis, D. E. (1964). Social and endocrine factors are integrated in the regulation of mammalian populations. *Science, 146,* 1550–1560.

Ciolek, T. M., & Kendon, A. (1980). Environment and the spatial arrangement of conversational encounters. *Sociological Inquiry, 50,* 237–276.

Connolly, P. R. (1975). The perception of personal space among black and white Americans. *Central States Speech Journal, 26,* 21–28.

Cook, M. (1970). Experiments on orientation and proxemics. *Human Relations, 23,* 61–76.

Crane, D. R., Dollahite, D. C., Griffin, W., & Taylor, V. L. (1987). Diagnosing relationships with spatial distance: An empirical test of a clinical principle. *Journal of Marital and Family Therapy, 13,* 307–310.

DeLong, A. J. (1970). Dominance–territorial relations in a small group. *Environment and Behavior, 2,* 190–191.

Drucker, S. J., & Gumpert, G. (1991). Public space and communication: The zoning of public interaction. *Communication Theory, 1,* 294–310.

Eagly, A. H. (1987). *Sex differences in social behavior: A social-role interpretation.* Hillsdale, NJ: Erlbaum.

Edney, J. J. (1974). Human territoriality. *Psychological Bulletin, 31,* 959–975.

Efran, M. G., & Cheyne, J. A. (1974). Affective concomitants of the invasion of shared space: Behavioral, physiological and verbal indicators. *Journal of Personality and Social Psychology, 29,* 219–226.

Erickson, F. (1975). One function of proxemic shifts in face-to-face interaction. In A. Kendon, R. M. Harris, & M. R. Key (Eds.), *Organization of behavior in face-to-face interaction.* Chicago: Aldine.

Erlich, P. R. (1971). *The population bomb.* Ballantine Books: New York.

Esser, A. H. (1971). *Environment and behavior: The use of space by animals and men.* New York: Plenum.

Evans, G. W. (1979). Behavioral and physiological consequences of crowding in humans. *Journal of Applied Social Psychology, 9,* 27–46.

Evans, G. W., & Howard, R. B. (1973). Personal space. *Psychological Bulletin, 80,* 334–344.

Evans, G. W., Lepore, S. J., & Allen, K. M. (2000). Cross-cultural differences in tolerance for crowding: Fact or fiction? *Journal of Personality and Social Psychology, 79,* 204–210.

Felipe, N. J., & Sommer, R. (1966). Invasions of personal space. *Social Problems, 14,* 206–214.

Finando, S. J. (1973). *The effects of distance norm violation on heart rate and length of verbal response.* Unpublished doctoral dissertation, Florida State University.

Fisher, J. D., & Byrne, D. (1975). Too close for comfort: Sex differences in response to invasions of personal space. *Journal of Personality and Social Psychology, 32,* 15–21.

Freedman, J. L. (1975). *Crowding and behavior.* New York: Viking.

Freedman, J. L. (1979). Reconciling apparent differences between the responses of humans and other animals to crowding. *Psychological Review, 86,* 80–85.

Fry, A. M., & Willis, F. N. (1971). Invasion of personal space as a function of the age of the invader. *Psychological Record, 21,* 385–389.

Galle, O. R., Gove, W. R., & McPherson, J. M. (1972). Population density and pathology: What are the relationships for man? *Science, 176,* 23–30.

Gifford, R. (1982). Projected interpersonal distance and orientation choices: Personality, sex, and social situation. *Social Psychology Quarterly, 45,* 145–152.

Gifford, R. (1987). *Environmental psychology: Principles and practice.* Boston: Allyn & Bacon.

Gifford, R., & O'Connor, B. (1986). Nonverbal intimacy: Clarifying the role of seating distance and orientation. *Journal of Nonverbal Behavior, 10,* 207–214.

Gochman, I. R., & Keating, J. P. (1980). Misattributions to crowding: Blaming crowding for non-density caused events. *Journal of Nonverbal Behavior, 4,* 157–175.

Goffman, E. (1971). *Relations in public.* New York: Basic Books.

Greenberg, C. I., & Firestone, I. J. (1977). Compensatory responses to crowding: Effects of personal space intrusion and privacy reduction. *Journal of Personality and Social Psychology, 35,* 637–644.

Guardo, C. J., & Meisels, M. (1971). Child–parent spatial patterns under praise and reproof. *Developmental Psychology, 5,* 365.

Halberstadt, A. G. (1985). Race, socioeconomic status and nonverbal behavior. In A. W. Siegman & S. Feldstein (Eds.), *Multichannel integrations of nonverbal behavior.* Hillsdale, NJ: Erlbaum.

Hall, E. T. (1959). *The silent language.* Garden City, NY: Doubleday.

Hall, E. T. (1966). *The hidden dimension.* Garden City, NY: Doubleday.

Hall, J. A. (1984). *Nonverbal sex differences: Communication accuracy and expressive style.* Baltimore: Johns Hopkins University Press.

Hansen, J. F. (1976). Proxemics and the interpretive processes in human communication. *Semiotica, 17,* 165–179.

Hare, A., & Bales, R. (1963). Seating position and small group interaction. *Sociometry, 26,* 480–486.

Harper, L., & Sanders, K. M. (1975). Preschool children's use of space: Sex differences in outdoor play. *Developmental Psychology, 11,* 119.

Hartnett, J. J., Bailey, K. G., & Hartley, C. S. (1974). Body height, position, and sex as determinants of personal space. *Journal of Psychology, 87,* 129–136.

Hayduk, L. A. (1978). Personal space: An evaluative and orienting overview. *Psychological Bulletin, 85,* 117–134.

Hayduk, L. A. (1994). Personal space: Understanding the simplex model. *Journal of Nonverbal Behavior, 18,* 245–260.

Hearn, G. (1957). Leadership and the spatial factor in small groups. *Journal of Abnormal and Social Psychology, 104,* 269–272.

Hediger, H. P. (1961). The evolution of territorial behavior. In S. L. Washburn (Ed.), *Social life of early man* (pp. 34–57). Chicago: Aldine.

Hewitt, J., & Alqahtani, M. A. (2003). Differences between Saudi and U.S. students in reaction to same- and mixed-sex intimacy shown by others. *Journal of Social Psychology, 143,* 233–242.

Hildreth, A. M., Derogatis, L. R., & McCusker, K. (1971). Body buffer zone and violence: A reassessment and confirmation. *American Journal of Psychiatry, 127,* 1641–1645.

Holland, R. W., Roeder, U-R., van Baaren, R. B., Brandt, A. C., & Hannover, B. (2004). Don't stand so close to me: The effects of self–construal on interpersonal closeness. *Psychological Science, 15,* 237–242.

Hoppe, R. A., Greene, M. S., & Kenney, J. W. (1972). Territorial markers: Additional findings. *Journal of Social Psychology, 88,* 305–306.

Horowitz, M. J. (1965). Human spatial behavior. *American Journal of Psychotherapy, 19,* 20–28.

Horowitz, M. J. (1968). Spatial behavior and psychopathology. *The Journal of Nervous and Mental Disease, 146,* 24–35.

Howells, L. T., & Becker, S. W. (1962). Seating arrangement and leadership emergence. *Journal of Abnormal and Social Psychology, 64,* 148–150.

Hutt, C., & Vaizey, M. J. (1966). Differential effects of group density on social behavior. *Nature, 209,* 1371–1372.

Jones, S. E., & Aiello, J. R. (1973). Proxemic behavior of black and white first, third, and fifth grade children. *Journal of Personality and Social Psychology, 25,* 21–27.

Judge, P. G. (2000). Coping with crowded conditions. In F. Aureli & F. B. M. de Waal (Eds.), *Natural conflict resolution* (pp. 129–154). Berkeley, CA: University of California Press.

Judge, P. G., & de Waal, F. B. M. (1993). Conflict avoidance among rhesus monkeys: Coping with short-term crowding. *Animal Behaviour, 46,* 221–232.

Judge, P. G., & de Waal, F. B. M. (1997). Rhesus monkey behaviour under diverse population densities: Coping with long-term crowding. *Animal Behaviour, 54,* 643–662.

Kaya, N. (2007). Territoriality: Seat preferences in different types of classroom arrangements. *Environment and Behavior, 39,* 859–876.

Kaya, N. & Weber, M. J. (2003). Territorial behavior in residence halls: A cross-cultural study. *Environment and Behavior, 35,* 400–414.

King, M. J. (1966). Interpersonal relations in preschool children and average approach distance. *Journal of Genetic Psychology, 109,* 109–116.

Kinzel, A. S. (1970). Body buffer zone in violent prisoners. *American Journal of Psychiatry, 127,* 59–64.

Kleck, R. E. (1969). Physical stigma and task oriented interaction. *Human Relations, 22,* 51–60.

Kleck, R. E., Buck, P. L., Goller, W. L., London, R. S., Pfeiffer, J. R., & Vukcevic, D. P. (1968). The effect of stigmatizing conditions on the use of personal space. *Psychological Reports, 23,* 111–118.

Kleck, R. E., & Strenta, A. C. (1985). Physical deviance and the perception of social outcomes. In J. A. Graham & A. M. Kligman (Eds.), *The psychology of cosmetic treatments.* New York: Praeger.

Klopfer, P. M. (1969). *Habitats and territories: A study of the use of space by animals.* New York: Basic.

Knowles, E. S. (1973). Boundaries around group interaction: The effect of group size and member status on boundary permeability. *Journal of Personality and Social Psychology, 26,* 327–332.

Knowles, E. S. (1979). An affiliative conflict theory of personal and group spatial behavior. In P. B. Paulus (Ed.), *Psychology of group influence.* Hillsdale, NJ: Erlbaum.

Latta, R. M. (1978). Relation of status incongruence to personal space. *Personality and Social Psychology Bulletin, 4,* 143–146.

Leibman, M. (1970). The effects of sex and race norms on personal space. *Environment and Behavior, 2,* 208–246.

Leipold, W. E. (1963). *Psychological distance in a dyadic interview.* Unpublished doctoral dissertation, University of North Dakota.

LePoire, B. A., Burgoon, J. K., & Parrott, R. (1992). Status and privacy restoring communication in the workplace. *Journal of Applied Communication Research, 20,* 419–436.

Lerner, R. M., Venning, J., & Knapp, J. R. (1975). Age and sex effects on personal space schemata toward body build in late childhood. *Developmental Psychology, 11,* 855–856.

Little, K. B. (1965). Personal space. *Journal of Experimental Social Psychology, 1,* 237–247.

Little, K. B. (1968). Cultural variations in social schemata. *Journal of Personality and Social Psychology, 10,* 1–7.

Loo, C. M. (1973). The effect of spatial density on the social behavior of children. *Journal of Applied Social Psychology, 2,* 372–381.

Lott, D. F., & Sommer, R. (1967). Seating arrangements and status. *Journal of Personality and Social Psychology, 7,* 90–94.

Lyman, S. M., & Scott, M. B. (1967). Territoriality: A neglected sociological dimension. *Social Problems, 15,* 236–249.

Malmberg, T. (1980). *Human territoriality.* The Hague: Mouton.

Maxwell, L. E. (2003). Home and school density effects on elementary school children: The role of spatial density. *Environment and Behavior, 35,* 566–578.

McBride, G., King, M. G., & James, J. W. (1965). Social proximity effects on galvanic skin responses in adult humans. *Journal of Psychology, 61,* 153–157.

McCallum, R., Rusbult, C. E., Hong, G. K., Walden, T. A., & Schopler, J. (1979). Effects of resource availability and importance of behavior on the experience of crowding. *Journal of Personality and Social Psychology, 37,* 1304–1313.

McCroskey, J. C., Larson, C. E., & Knapp, M. L. (1971). *An introduction to interpersonal communication.* Engelwood Cliffs, N.J.: Prentice Hall.

McDowell, K. V. (1972). Violations of personal space. *Canadian Journal of Behavioral Science, 4,* 210–217.

McGeehan, P. (2005, May 31). For train riders, middle seat isn't the center of attention. *The New York Times*, A1, C11.

Mehrabian, A., & Diamond, S. G. (1971). Seating arrangement and conversation. *Sociometry, 34*, 281–289.

Meisels, M., & Dosey, M. (1971). Personal space, anger arousal, and psychological defense. *Journal of Personality, 39*, 333–334.

Meisels, M., & Guardo, C. (1969). Development of personal space schemata. *Child Development, 40*, 1167–1178.

Milgram, S. (1970). The experience of living in cities. *Science, 167*, 1461–1468.

Mitchell, R. (1971). Some social implications of higher density housing. *American Sociological Review, 36*, 18–29.

Moos, R. H., & Kulik, J. (1976). Population density, crowding and the use of space. In R. H. Moos (Ed.), *The human context*. New York: Wiley.

Newman, O. (1972). *Defensible space*. New York: Macmillan.

O'Neal, E. C., Brunalt, M. A., Carifio, M. S., Troutwine, R., & Epstein, J. (1980). Effect of insult upon personal space preferences. *Journal of Nonverbal Behavior, 5*, 56–62.

Pagan, G., & Aiello, J. R. (1982). Development of personal space among Puerto Ricans. *Journal of Nonverbal Behavior, 7*, 59–68.

Pastalan, L., & Carson, D. H. (Eds.). (1970). *Spatial behavior of older people*. Ann Arbor: University of Michigan/Wayne State University Press.

Patterson, M. L. (1968). Spatial factors in social interaction. *Human Relations, 21*, 351–361.

Patterson, M. L. (1975). Personal space–time to burst the bubble? *Man-Environment Systems, 5*, 67.

Patterson, M. L. (1976). An arousal model of interpersonal intimacy. *Psychological Review, 83*, 235–245.

Patterson, M. L. (1978). The role of space in social interaction. In A. W. Siegman & S. Feldstein (Eds.), *Nonverbal behavior and communication*. Hillsdale, NJ: Erlbaum.

Patterson, M. L., & Edinger, J. A. (1987). A functional analysis of space in social interaction. In A. W. Siegman & S. Feldstein (Eds.), *Nonverbal behavior and communication* (2nd ed.). Hillsdale, NJ: Erlbaum.

Patterson, M. L., Mullens, S., & Romano, J. (1971). Compensatory reactions to spatial intrusion. *Sociometry, 34*, 114–121.

Pedersen, D. M., & Shears, L. M. (1973). A review of personal space research in the framework of general system theory. *Psychological Bulletin, 80*, 367–388.

Petschauer, P. W. (1997). *Human space*. New York: Praeger.

Porter, E., Argyle, M., & Salter, V. (1970). What is signalled by proximity? *Perceptual and Motor Skills, 30*, 39–42.

Porter, N., & Geis, F. (1981). Women and nonverbal leadership cues: When seeing is not believing. In C. Mayo & N. M. Henley (Eds.), *Gender and nonverbal behavior*. New York: Springer-Verlag.

Reiss, M., & Rosenfeld, P. (1980). Seating preferences as nonverbal communication: A self-presentational analysis. *Journal of Applied Communication Research, 8*, 22–30.

Remland, M. S., Jones, T. S., and Brinkman, H. (1991). Proxemic and haptic behavior in three European countries. *Journal of Nonverbal Behavior, 15*, 215–232.

Rohe, W., & Patterson, A. H. (1974). *The effects of varied levels of resources and density on behavior in a day care center*. Paper presented at Environmental Design and Research Association, Milwaukee, WI.

Rosenfeld, H. (1965). Effect of approval-seeking induction on interpersonal proximity. *Psychological Reports, 17*, 120–122.

Rosenfeld, H. (1966). Instrumental and affiliative functions of facial and gestural expressions. *Journal of Personality and Social Psychology, 4*, 65–72.

Ruback, R. B. & Kohli, N. (2005). Territoriality at the Magh Mela: The effects of organizational factors and intruder characteristics. *Environment and Behavior, 37*, 178–200.

Russo, N. (1967). Connotation of seating arrangement. *Cornell Journal of Social Relations, 2*, 37–44.

Sanders, J. L., Hakky, U. M., & Brizzolara, M. M. (1985). Personal space amongst Arabs and Americans. *International Journal of Psychology, 20*, 13–17.

Scheflen, A. E. (1975). Micro-territories in human interaction. In A. Kendon, R. M. Harris, &

M. R. Key (Eds.), *Organization of behavior in face-to-face interaction*. Chicago: Aldine.

Scheflen, A. E., & Ashcraft, N. (1976). *Human territories: How we behave in space–time*. Englewood Cliffs, NJ: Prentice-Hall.

Scherer, S. E. (1974). Proxemic behavior of primary school children as a function of their socioeconomic class and subculture. *Journal of Personality and Social Psychology, 29,* 800–805.

Schmidt, D. E., & Keating, J. P. (1979). Human crowding and personal control: An integration of the research. *Psychological Bulletin, 86,* 680–700.

Schulz, R., & Barefoot, J. (1974). Non-verbal responses and affiliative conflict theory. *British Journal of Social and Clinical Psychology, 13,* 237–243.

Shuter, R. (1976). Proxemics and tactility in Latin America. *Journal of Communication, 26,* 46–52.

Shuter, R. (1977). A field study of non verbal communication in Germany, Italy and the United States. *Communication Monographs, 44,* 298–305.

Smith, D. E. (1986). The influence of contextual variables on interpersonal spacing. *Journal of Communication, 29* (Autumn), 34–39.

Smith, M. J., Reinheimer, R. E., & Gabbard-Alley, A. (1981). Crowding, task performance, and communicative interaction in youth and old age. *Human Communication Research, 7,* 259–272.

Sobel, R. S., & Lillith, N. (1975). Determinants of nonstationary personal space invasion. *Journal of Social Psychology, 97,* 39–45.

Sommer, R. (1959). Studies in personal space. *Sociometry, 22,* 247–260.

Sommer, R. (1961). Leadership and group geography. *Sociometry, 24,* 99–110.

Sommer, R. (1962). The distance for comfortable conversation: A further study. *Sociometry, 25,* 111–116.

Sommer, R. (1965). Further studies of small group ecology. *Sociometry, 28,* 337–348.

Sommer, R. (1967). Small group ecology. *Psychological Bulletin, 67,* 145–152.

Sommer, R. (1969/2008). *Personal space*. Englewood Cliffs, NJ: Prentice-Hall.

Sommer, R. (2002). Personal space in a digital age. In R. B. Bechtel and A. Churchman (Eds.), *Handbook of environmental psychology* (pp. 647–660). New York: Wiley.

Sommer, R., & Becker, F. D. (1969). Territorial defense and the good neighbor. *Journal of Personality and Social Psychology, 11,* 85–92.

Sommer, R., & Ross, H. (1958). Social interaction on a geriatrics ward. *International Journal of Social Psychiatry, 4,* 128–133.

Stockdale, J. E. (1978). Crowding: Determinants and effects. In L. Berkowitz (Ed.), *Advances in experimental social psychology* (Vol. 11). New York: Academic Press.

Stokols, D. (1972). On the distinction between density and crowding: Some implications for future research. *Psychological Review, 79,* 275–278.

Stokols, D., Rall, M., Pinner, B., & Schopler, J. (1973). Physical, social, and personal determinants of the perception of crowding. *Environment and Behavior, 5,* 87–117.

Stratton, L. O., Tekippe, D. J., & Flick, G. L. (1973). Personal space and self-concept. *Sociometry, 36,* 424–429.

Strodtbeck, F., & Hook, L. (1961). The social dimensions of a twelve-man jury table. *Sociometry, 24,* 397–415.

Strube, M. J., & Werner, C. (1984). Personal space claims as a function of interpersonal threat: The mediating role of need for control. *Journal of Nonverbal Behavior, 8,* 195–209.

Sundstrom, E. (1978). Crowding as a sequential process: Review of research on the effects of population density on humans. In A. Baum & Y. M. Epstein (Eds.), *Human responses to crowding*. Hillsdale, NJ: Erlbaum.

Sundstrom, E., & Altman, I. (1976). Interpersonal relationships and personal space: Research review and theoretical model. *Human Ecology, 4,* 47–67.

Sundstrom, E., & Sundstrom, M. G. (1977). Personal space invasions: What happens when the invader asks permission? *Environmental Psychology and Nonverbal Behavior, 2,* 76–82.

Sussman, N. M., & Rosenfeld, H. M. (1982). Influence of culture, language, and sex on conversational distance. *Journal of Personality and Social Psychology, 42,* 66–74.

Taylor, R. B. (1988). *Human territorial functioning*. New York: Cambridge University Press.

Taylor, S. E., & Fiske, S. T. (1975). Point of view and perceptions of causality. *Journal of Personality and Social Psychology, 32,* 429–445.

Vine, I. (1975). Territoriality and the spatial regulation of interaction. In A. Kendon, R. M. Harris & M. R. Key (Eds.), *Organization of behavior in face to face interaction*. Chicago: Aldine.

Vranic, A. (2003). Personal space in physically abused children. *Environment and Behavior, 35,* 550–565.

Ward, C. (1968). Seating arrangement and leadership emergence in small discussion groups. *Journal of Social Psychology, 74,* 83–90.

Watson, O. M. (1970). *Proxemic behavior: A cross-cultural study*. The Hague: Mouton.

Watson, O. M. (1972). *Symbolic and expressive uses of space: An introduction to proxemic behavior. Module No. 20.* Reading, MA: Addison-Wesley.

Watson, O. M. (1973). Proxemics. In T. A. Sebeok (Ed.), *Current trends in linguistics*. The Hague: Mouton.

Watson, O. M., & Graves, T. D. (1966). Quantitative research in proxemic behavior. *American Anthropologist, 68,* 971–985.

Williams, J. L. (1971). Personal space and its relation to extroversion–introversion. *Canadian Journal of Behavioral Science, 3,* 156–160.

Willis, F. N. (1966). Initial speaking distance as a function of the speaker's relationship. *Psychonomic Science, 5,* 221–222.

Willis, F. N., Jr., Gier, J. A., & Smith, D. E. (1979). Stepping aside: Correlates of displacement in pedestrians. *Journal of Communication, 29,* 34–39.

Worchel, S. (1986). The influence of contextual variables on interpersonal spacing. *Journal of Nonverbal Behavior, 10,* 230–254.

THE COMMUNICATORS

Much of our nonverbal behavior is characterized by change and movement during a conversation. But some of the nonverbal signals we bring to each interaction remain relatively unchanged during the course of the interaction. These are the individual features of each communicator: skin color, hairstyle, facial features, height, weight, clothes, and so forth. These features affect how others perceive us and how they communicate with us.

By a man's finger-nails, by his coat-sleeve, by his boots, by his trouser-knees, by the callosities of his forefinger and thumb, by his expression, by his shirt-cuffs—by each of these things a man's calling is plainly revealed. That all united should fail to enlighten the competent inquirer in any case is almost unconceivable.

—Sherlock Holmes

THE EFFECTS OF PHYSICAL CHARACTERISTICS ON HUMAN COMMUNICATION

CHAPTER **6**

Picture the following scene: Mr. and Mrs. American wake and prepare to start the day. Mrs. American takes off her nighttime bra and replaces it with a "slightly padded uplift" bra. After removing her cosmetic chin strap, she further pulls herself together with her girdle. Then she begins to "put on her face." This may involve foundation, eyeliner, eye shadow, false eyelashes, mascara, lipstick, and blush. She has removed the hair under her arms and on her legs. She takes a curling iron to her hair. False fingernails, nail polish, and tinted contact lenses precede the deodorant, perfume, and numerous decisions concerning clothes. Mr. American shaves the hair on his face and puts a toupee on his head. He removes his false teeth from a solution used to whiten them, gargles with a breath sweetener, selects his aftershave lotion, puts on his elevator shoes, and begins making his clothing decisions. This hypothetical example represents an extreme, but without a doubt, people do go to great lengths to make themselves attractive. And it is not just an American obsession. Venezuela, a country that has won more international beauty contests than any other country, spends more than a billion dollars each year on cosmetic products, and some teenage girls get a breast enlargement as a coming of age present when they are 15 years old (Pearson, 2006).

Surgery to enhance physical attractiveness is increasing. It may reconstruct a nose; change breast size; eliminate bags, wrinkles, or birthmarks; flatten ears; "tuck" thighs or tummies; vacuum fat from the body by liposuction, or insert fat by lipofilling; or even remove the upper layer of skin via a "chemical peel" or microdermabrasion if it appears too blotchy, red, or rough. Over a million Americans have cosmetic surgery each year, and the American Society of Plastic Surgeons reportedly did 1.2 million procedures on men in 2004 (Heine, 2005). Thousands of adolescents are also having cosmetic surgery. Why do men and women expend so much effort and invest so much money trying to improve their physical attractiveness? Does it influence human interaction?

OUR BODY: ITS GENERAL ATTRACTIVENESS

People care a great deal about appearance. If a friend tells you about someone you have not met, you are likely to ask what the person looks like—you want a face to associate with the information you are receiving. Why? Novelists present intricately detailed descriptions of their characters' appearance. Why? Publishers put photos of book authors on book jackets and in book ads. Why? Most newspapers publish photos of newsmakers. Why must readers *see* the person being discussed in an article on airline deregulation, stock fraud, or the manufacture of computer chips? Because people think they learn things from appearance. We take looks as indicators of a person's background, character, personality, talents, and likely future behavior.

Although it is not uncommon to hear people muse about inner beauty being the only thing that really counts, research suggests that outer beauty, our physical attractiveness, plays an influential role in determining responses for a broad range of interpersonal encounters. The evidence from our culture overwhelmingly supports the notion that *initially* we respond much more favorably to those we perceive as physically attractive than to those we see as unattractive. Numerous studies reveal that physically attractive people are perceived to exceed unattractive people on a wide range of socially desirable evaluations that include success, personality, popularity, sociability, sexuality, persuasiveness, and, often, happiness (Hatfield & Sprecher, 1986; Herman, Zanna, & Higgins, 1986). Even when positive personality traits are not attributed to physically attractive people, such people still seem to have a positive appeal (Timmerman & Hewitt, 1980). Our behavior toward unattractive people seems to be largely negative, however. For example, unattractive patients in hospitals are reportedly visited less, remain hospitalized longer, are judged to be less pleasant, and are less involved with others.

Judgments linked to a person's attractiveness begin early in life. One study found that children as young as 2 to 3 months looked significantly longer at an attractive face (as judged by adults) than at an unattractive one. This tendency occurred regardless of whether the infant's mother was considered attractive or unattractive (Langlois et al., 1987; Slater et al., 1998). Another study found 6-month-old infants able to categorize faces based on their similarities in attractiveness (Ramsey, Langlois, Hoss, Rubenstein, & Griffin, 2004). Cultural guidelines for physical attractiveness are well established by age 6 (Cavior & Lombardi, 1973; Dion & Berscheid, 1972). It is not surprising, then, to find peer popularity and physical attractiveness highly correlated in a number of elementary and secondary schools. The perceptions of attractiveness in a child's world are not limited to his or her peers. Teachers tend to see attractive children as more intelligent, more socially adept, higher in educational potential, and more positive in their attitudes toward school—even when the unattractive children had similar academic performance. As children develop, they are exposed to these attitudes and evaluations made by teachers and parents. Teachers interact less, and less positively, with the so-called unattractive elementary school child. There are many occasions in a child's life when adults ask in a punitive tone of voice, "Who did this?!" If an unattractive child is available, the chances are stronger that he or she will be pointed out as the culprit. As unattractive children grow older, they probably are not discriminated against if their task performance is impressive; but as soon as performance declines, less attractive people receive more sanctions than unattractive ones. Antisocial behavior, such as throwing a brick through a window, was seen differently for attractive and unattractive children (Dion, 1972). The transgression was seen as an enduring trait of the unattractive child but only a temporary problem for the attractive one. The act was also evaluated more negatively for the unattractive child. It does not surprise us, then, to find that juvenile delinquents were also rated as lower on attractiveness. In a study of 9- to 14-year-old boys, differences in perceived physical attractiveness were systematically related to social acceptance (Kleck, Richardson, & Ronald, 1974).

Although much evidence testifies to the existence of a norm that says "what is beautiful is good," physical attractiveness also may be associated with undesirable traits; for example, vanity, egotism, snobbishness, unsympathetic attitudes toward oppressed people, and a greater likelihood of having marital problems (Dermer & Thiel, 1975). These negative attributions, and the knowledge that beautiful people sometimes experience appearance-related problems, suggest all is not perfect for these people. The research to date, however, still suggests it is far better to be attractive than unattractive. In fact, women who were average in looks were rated higher when evaluated from a photograph in which they were posed alongside other women who were attractive. Subsequently, these average-looking women were evaluated from photos of them posed with other average-looking women and were perceived as more attractive by those who had seen them with the attractive women. So it appears that women can boost their attractiveness ratings by being seen with more attractive women, and this association does not seem to decrease the attractive women's ratings (Geiselman, Haight, & Kimata, 1984).

Although there are some who would like us to believe that "everything is beautiful in its own way," there are many reasons to believe that things are often beautiful in the same way to many people. Within the United States, people are constantly exposed to standards for male and female beauty through the mass media, so it is not surprising to find a great deal of agreement on standards for beauty within this culture. But there is also evidence that there may be some inherent standards for physical attractiveness that cut across cultures. Studies involving people from Australia, Austria, China, England, India, Japan, Korea, and Scotland have found significant agreement on facial attractiveness (Etcoff, 1999; Langlois et al., 2000). Dion (2002) points out, however, that agreement is higher when the judges are students from other countries who are studying in the United States and when comparisons are made among different ethnocultural groups within a culture. Agreement is not as high with more geographically isolated groups. Even if there is a universal and biologically based standard for human beauty, cultures may impose certain variations. Nevertheless, participation in global activities like the Miss World contest may affect local standards. Miss World 2001 was Miss Nigeria, but in her home country, she was far too skinny to be considered attractive, even though many young Nigerians reportedly favor the new look.

Common standards for physical attractiveness permeate our culture and are particularly evident in the areas discussed next.

DATING AND MARRIAGE

Physical attractiveness is probably more important to dating partners than it is to friends or married couples, although perceptions of physical attractiveness still can play an important role in marital relationships. Physical attraction may be most important when dating involves short-term goals and more public, rather than private, activities. In recent years, males have become increasingly concerned about their own physical appearance. Men, in fact, often think physical appearance is more influential in women's preferences for them than women indicate. One group of women did, however, place a high value on male physical appearance—those women who are physically attractive and financially independent (Pertschuk, Trisdorfer, & Allison, 1994). Apparently, highly attractive females "want it all," preferring a man who is masculine, is sexy, has an abundance of resources, including money or the potential for it, who will be a loving and caring partner, and who shows a desire to establish a home and raise children (Buss & Shackelford, 2008).

Based on the preceding information, we might suspect that actual dating patterns would reflect the preference for a physically attractive partner. This hypothesis was confirmed by a series of "computer dance" studies at the universities of Texas, Illinois, and Minnesota, in which physical attractiveness superseded a host of other variables in determining liking for one's partner and a desire to date in the future (Walster, Aronson, Abrahams, & Rottmann, 1966). Brislin and Lewis (1968) replicated this study with 58 unacquainted men and women and again found a strong correlation (.89) between "desire to date again" and "physical attractiveness." In addition, this study asked each person whether he or she would like to date anyone else at the dance. Of the 13 other people named, all had previously, and independently, been rated as very attractive.

In light of the many findings that seem to favor the physically attractive, it is worthwhile to note that there are times when the very physically attractive do not enjoy all the benefits. For example, women who had more variable attractiveness ratings—that is, they were not uniformly judged as very attractive or unattractive—were the group most satisfied with their socializing in general with both men and women. They also had as many dates as the most attractive women. Some men did not seek dates with the extremely attractive women because they felt the chances of rejection were high and that the women might perceive their interest as limited to their physical attractiveness (Reis, Nezlek, & Wheeler, 1980; Reis et al., 1982). When less attractive women are in the company of attractive women, this also seems to increase the chances that they will be seen as a good choice for a date.

So it seems that although there is a strong preference for people who are physically attractive, other forces enable those who fall short of the ideal in physical attractiveness to date, marry, and have satisfying relationships. One of these forces that exerts a powerful influence is called the *matching hypothesis*, which argues that each person may be attracted to only the best-looking partners, but reality sets in when actual dates are made. If you select only the best-looking person available, you may face an unwanted rejection, so the tendency is to select a person similar to yourself in physical attractiveness—preferably a little above your self-perceived attractiveness (Hinsz, 1989). Since this hypothesis was presented, other studies have confirmed its validity, including a study of middle-aged married couples. So it seems the least good-looking people must settle for each other after all the very good-looking people choose each other (Kalick & Hamilton, 1986). In fact, one study found evidence to suggest that the greater the match on physical attractiveness for romantic couples at low levels of intimacy, the greater the chances that this couple would develop a more intimate relationship (White, 1980). Even same-sex friends have been rated similarly on physical attractiveness (Cash & Derlega, 1978). Thus we seem to try to maximize the attractiveness of our choice while simultaneously minimizing the possibilities of rejection. If you have high self-esteem, you might seek out highly attractive partners in spite of a considerable gap between your looks and theirs (Berscheid & Walster, 1969). Self-esteem, in this case, will affect the perception of, and possible reaction to, rejection.

Sometimes we observe couples whose physical attractiveness seems to be mismatched. One study suggests that evaluations of males may change dramatically if they are viewed as married to someone very different in general attractiveness (Bar-Tal & Saxe, 1976). Unattractive men who were seen with attractive women were judged, among other things, as making more money, being more successful in their occupations, and being more intelligent than attractive men with attractive partners. Judges must have reasoned that for an unattractive man to marry an attractive woman, he must have offset this imbalance by succeeding in other areas. Unattractive women seen with attractive men, however, did not receive compensating attributions. This study raises the question of what "other resources" unattractive women are perceived to have to offset deficits in physical attractiveness.

Even though physical attractiveness may be valued by both men and women, it seems to play a more dominant role in the perceptions of women by men. Buss (1994) found this gender difference reflected in every one of the 37 different cultures he studied. Women may desire physical characteristics, such as strength or facial attractiveness, but often rank characteristics like ambition, social and economic status, dependability, and stability above physical features—particularly for mate selection.

Physical attractiveness for males and females is also likely to vary with the goals of the relationship. For short-term or casual sexual relationships, both men and women place a high value on physical attractiveness, even though women more than men would also like to have some desirable social and personality characteristics to go along with the physical attractiveness. For long-term relationships, both sexes value other characteristics over physical attractiveness, even though men still rate it as more important. In one study, male college students said they were interested in different characteristics in a woman depending on whether it was a purely sexual relationship or one expected to be long term. A wide range of features associated with physical attractiveness were chosen for the sexual partner, but such features played a far less important role for long-term partners. Female students wanted virtually the same qualities in a long-term relationship as the men—honesty, fidelity, sensitivity, warmth, personality, kindness, character, tenderness, patience, and gentleness—but unlike the men, they also wanted more than mere physical attractiveness for the sexual relationship (Nevid, 1984).

Two physical features of men preferred by women for short-term or casual sexual relationships were features of masculinity in the face—thicker eyebrows,

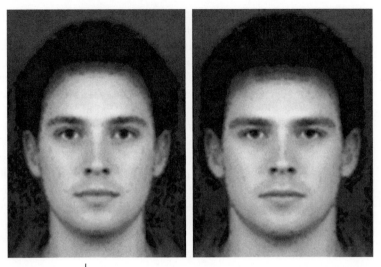

FIGURE 6-1

Left: 50% feminized male composite; right: 50% masculinized male composite.

smaller eyes, thinner lips, and a squarer jaw, as in Figure 6-1—and a high shoulder-to-waist ratio. Broader shoulders and a smaller waist may be perceived as markers of "good genes" (Kruger, 2006; Braun & Bryan, 2006), and these features may be most attractive during periods when conception is most likely (Little, Penton-Voak, Burt, & Perrett, 2002). Apparently the face reveals a lot about a person's sexual attitudes, as well as their suitability as a long-term partner. Boothroyd, Jones, Burt, DeBruine, and Perrett (2008) photographed students and asked them to fill out a questionnaire about their past sexual behavior and their attitudes toward sex. Women were less attracted to men who professed a strong interest in casual sex, but men preferred the faces of females who had a high "sociosexual orientation." In another study, men's testosterone levels were measured and they were asked to fill out a questionnaire dealing with interest in infants. Photos of these men were shown to women who rated their physical attractiveness, their masculinity, the extent to which they perceived them as kind, their potential as a short- or long-term lover, and whether they seemed to like children. Women were skilled at distinguishing the men with high testosterone and those who liked children. Furthermore, they perceived the more masculine faces as attractive for short-term relationships, but were drawn to the faces of the men who scored higher on an interest in children for long-term relationships (Roney, Hanson, Durante, and Maestripieri, 2006).

ON THE JOB

Several studies suggest that physical attractiveness may be an advantage in obtaining a job, or obtaining a more prestigious job, and being hired at a higher salary (Cash, Gillen, & Burns, 1977; Dipboye, Arvey, & Terpstra, 1977; Hamermesh &

Biddle, 1994). Unless the job is deemed inappropriate or irrelevant to the applicant's level of attractiveness, the more attractive applicants are more likely to get the job, assuming all other qualifications are equal. Sometimes attractiveness provides an edge even when the less attractive competitor is more qualified for the position. Once a position has been obtained, less attractive workers may be discriminated against on performance appraisals, unless they maintain a consistently high level of productivity.

Even though both men and women can profit from their physical attractiveness in the workplace, it is not always beneficial. The higher the level of advancement, the more important it is for a person's physical attractiveness to be viewed as "task attractiveness" and not as "social attractiveness." Because physically attractive women are more likely than men to have their physical attractiveness viewed in a social context by men in corporate environments, physically attractive women may dress so their physical beauty is not the immediate focus of attention (Heilman & Saruwatari, 1979). And even though sexual harassment charges brought by unattractive women may garner less credibility with a jury (Seiter & Dunn, 2000), the attractiveness of both parties involved and the gender of jury members are factors that may work against advantages normally associated with physical attractiveness (Wuensch & Moore, 2004).

PERSUADING OTHERS

Getting others to agree with you or do something for you is often based on the extent to which you can demonstrate your knowledge or expertise, as well as your ability to marshal effective supporting arguments (Maddux & Rogers, 1980). But as several research projects show, being physically attractive also may help (Chaiken, 1986). This is especially true when the persuader seeks compliance on relatively low ego-involving topics; when the persuasion involves a relatively short, perhaps one-time, request; and when the effects of initial impressions are crucial to achieving influence. Although most of this research has been done with college students, the association of persuasive effectiveness with physical attractiveness has been documented in the behavior of 10- and 11-year-old children (Dion & Stein, 1978).

One of the earliest studies of physical attractiveness and persuasion used cosmetics to make one woman look more and less attractive. In the unattractive condition, she was rated "repulsive" by independent observers; she wore loose-fitting clothing, her hair was messy, makeup was conspicuously absent, a trace of a mustache was etched on her upper lip, and her complexion was oily and "unwholesome looking." The experimenter suggested to a group of students that they would complete some questionnaires more quickly if a volunteer would read the questions aloud and indicate what they meant. The "volunteer" was either the attractive or unattractive woman. The attractive woman, especially when she stated her desire to influence the audience, was far more effective in modifying the opinions of college students toward issues dealing with higher education (Mills & Aronson, 1965). Other studies also support the influence of physical attractiveness in persuasive situations (Horai, Naccari, & Faloultah, 1974; Widgery, 1974).

The preceding research focused primarily on female communicators, but attractiveness also seems to help male persuaders. Independent assessments of their verbal performance, as well as their ability to obtain signatures on a campus petition, showed attractive men and women outperforming those who were rated as unattractive. In another study, physically attractive men and women were judged to have better sales skills, were treated more cordially, and elicited more willingness by people to contribute to a charitable organization (Reingen & Kernan, 1993). Is the persuasiveness of attractive communicators due solely to their looks, or do they actually have persuasive skills? An examination of previous tests showed attractive students to have higher grades, higher SAT scores, better self-concepts, and better communication skills (Chaiken, 1979). In summary, then, physically attractive persuaders, as compared with unattractive ones, *initially* elicit higher credibility and expectations for a skilled performance, although some evidence indicates that physically attractive people seem to have these skills. But the advantages derived from one's physical attractiveness is probably strongest during the initial stages of a persuasive effort.

SELF-ESTEEM

Does physical attractiveness increase self-esteem? The answer seems to be yes, particularly for women. Women who perceive themselves as physically attractive seem also to perceive greater happiness, self-esteem, and less neuroticism than those who perceive themselves as unattractive (Mathes & Kahn, 1975). As noted earlier, physical attractiveness plays a more important role in men's lives today, so men, too, probably think better of themselves when they feel more attractive. Women aged 18 to 60 who used cosmetics to improve their appearance also reported psychological benefits from doing so. Greater attractiveness for those between the ages of 40 and 60 was perceived as most beneficial for masking the aging process and improving one's physical and mental health (Graham & Jouhar, 1982). And training in the use of cosmetics for elderly women has reportedly had a positive effect on their self-image.

Because physical attractiveness seems to have its greatest impact during the initial stages of a relationship, it is reasonable to assume that attractive men and women whose occupational demands or lifestyles necessitate meeting people in short-term encounters may obtain more self-esteem from their physical attractiveness than an equally attractive person who has a few long-term relationships. Although the self-esteem derived from appearance is important, it is only one factor that makes people feel good about themselves. Sometimes looking good is very important, sometimes it is not. But the knowledge that we can achieve attractiveness when we want to should make us feel much better than the person who is not sure he or she can. Hatfield and Sprecher (1986) point out that there are people who are more likely to give us a boost in self-esteem by positively evaluating our looks. These are people who have a great deal of self-esteem themselves, people who are sexually aroused by us, people who look like us, people who know us, and people who are not likely to compare our looks with media idols.

ANTISOCIAL BEHAVIOR

What happens when attractive and unattractive people are charged with committing a criminal act? Are judges and juries influenced by a person's looks? As expected, a number of studies show that attractive defendants are less likely to be judged guilty and, if convicted, are more likely to receive a shorter sentence (Downs & Lyons, 1991; Efran, 1974; Kulka & Kessler, 1978; Weiten, 1980). The evidence for attractive defendants receiving lighter sentences is stronger than the evidence linking attractiveness to guilt or innocence. Although much of the research is based on the results of simulated juries and cases, Stewart (1980) had the attractiveness of 67 actual defendants rated. The less attractive defendants were charged with more serious crimes and were given longer sentences, but attractiveness did not significantly affect judgments of conviction or acquittal.

Obviously, a defendant's attractiveness is rarely assessed in isolation in the courtroom, and other factors interact with attractiveness; for example, the extent to which the defendant expresses repentance, the degree of commitment jurors have toward impartiality, the extent to which jurors discuss the case, the perceived similarity of jurors and defendant, defendant verbalizations, and the nature of the crime being examined. For some crimes, attractiveness may be a liability for the defendant, as when it is used to commit a crime such as a swindle. For the crime of rape, the relative attractiveness of the victim and the defendant may influence the jury. Attractive rape victims may be perceived as more likely to have provoked the attack (Jacobson, 1981; Seligman, Brickman, & Koulack, 1977).

Once a person has been convicted and sent to prison, some feel that antisocial behavior can sometimes be reduced by radical changes in appearance. It is reported, for instance, that a 19-year-old woman with a face "so deformed that little kids ran away crying" threw a brick through a bank window and waited for police to arrest her. "I was willing to die to get a better face," she said. The judge ordered extensive plastic surgery ("Deformed Brick-Thrower," 1975). The same reasoning launched a massive plastic surgery program for reshaping noses, removing tattoos, tightening sagging skin, disguising ugly scars, reducing extensive ear protrusion, and removing other deformities of convicts at the Kentucky State Reformatory (Watson, 1975). Authorities at this institution reasoned that everyday social ridicule and potential discrimination in hiring might lead to a feeling of rejection and frustration that could manifest itself in antisocial behavior. Similar programs by doctors at the University of Virginia and Johns Hopkins have not shown significant changes in postinstitutionalized behavior for convicts with changes in their appearance. Obviously, appearance is only one factor that might contribute to antisocial behavior.

THE POWER OF PHYSICAL ATTRACTIVENESS: SOME IMPORTANT QUALIFICATIONS

As the preceding sections attest, much research supports the benefits and power of physical attractiveness. No doubt it can be discouraging to the great majority of us who do not perceive ourselves as highly physically attractive. Without ignoring the potentially powerful effects of physical attractiveness in some situations, the goal of this section is to review research that shows that physical attractiveness is not always such a dominant factor in constructive interpersonal outcomes.

THE EFFECTS OF INTERACTION

Methodological issues may provide some comfort to those who perceive themselves as less attractive. Although it is not true of all studies of physical attractiveness, most use frontal facial photographs that had been judged prior to the study by a panel of "experts" to fall into the "beautiful" or "ugly" category. Hence, in most cases we are not reporting results from living, moving, talking human beings in a particular environment, nor are we generally dealing with subtle differences in physical attractiveness that lie between the extremes of beautiful and ugly.

We know little about the socially skilled but homely person whose communicative beauty is greater than perceptions of his or her photographic beauty. We do know that talk can significantly affect perceptions. We also know that interaction behavior and facial beauty are the two primary contributors to overall judgments of physical attractiveness (Riggio, Widaman, Tucker, & Salinas, 1991). When we talk to others, we become a part of the object we are evaluating, and this involvement has the potential to change the way we see our partner. Berg (2004) found that even a 6-minute get-acquainted conversation could significantly affect perceptions of the physical attractiveness of moderately attractive people—positively or negatively. College students' photos were rated prior to a brief interaction and then rated again later, after that interaction. This brief interaction significantly changed perceptions of physical attractiveness, and for most of them—75 percent—the change was positive. An examination of the verbal and nonverbal behavior indicated a variety of behaviors that may have been influential change agents; for example, giving agreement and support, showing interest in the other person, sharing information, and showing a sense of humor. Interaction often elicits information about a person's personality, and that information can significantly change initial perceptions of physical attractiveness not only for physically attractive people but also for neutral and unattractive ones (Lewandowski, Aron, & Gee, 2007).

Many romantic partners tell stories about how their initial perception of their partners' physical attractiveness was not particularly high when compared with their ideal. But they report that continued positive interaction changed this perception. A man who had been married for 20 years told this story about his courtship:

> Initially, I saw her as pretty average in physical attractiveness. I remember telling a friend soon after I met her that she was kind of chunky. But after we dated and I fully appreciated how well we related to each other, I saw her as much more physically attractive. I actually *saw* her differently. Now I can't see her as any less physically attractive.

We also know that people who want to divorce each other find it hard to see their partner as physically attractive in the face of so much negative verbal behavior. Exactly how verbal behavior affects our perceptions of physical attractiveness is not clear at this time, but there are indications that it plays an important role in how we see another person's beauty (Albada, Knapp, & Theune, 2002).

THE EFFECTS OF CONTEXT

The perception of appearance may be relative to the context in which it is judged. For example, we may perceive a popular singer on stage or television as sexy, but the same person in our living room may seem much less glamorous. Similarly, a person who looks good in an isolated rural setting may not look as good in a city environment, where he or she is compared with a far greater variety of potential partners.

Bars also provide a unique context for judging physical attractiveness. One research team wanted to find out if the song about how "all the girls get prettier at closing time" had any validity to it. Pennebaker and collegues (1979) obtained information about the general attractiveness of bar patrons at several different bars at different times leading up to closing time. True to the lyrics of the song, both men and women perceived a significant increase in the attractiveness of others as closing time drew near. Although the gradually dwindling pool of potential partners may have had some effect, research also shows that even moderate alcohol consumption tends to increase the ratings of physical attractiveness of the opposite sex (Jones, Thomas, & Piper, 2003).

Who you associate with may also provide a context that affects your perceived physical attractiveness. Men who rated the attractiveness of middle-aged women tended to give lower ratings when they were in the presence of other men and their rating was made public than they did when in the company of women or when their ratings were kept private (Berman, O'Nan, & Floyd, 1981). Attraction ratings also may vary as a function of the rater's gender. Often the highest evaluations of attractiveness come from the opposite sex.

STEREOTYPES ARE NOT ALWAYS VALID

Even though people often judge another person's physical attractiveness similarly, the self-ratings of the people being judged may be quite different. Thus people we think are physically attractive may not perceive themselves that way and, as a result, may manifest very different characteristics than we think they have. Physically attractive people are typically *perceived* as having a wide range of socially desirable characteristics, and although actual measures do show physically attractive people to be more socially skilled and popular, only a negligible relationship appears to exist between perceptions of a highly attractive persons' personality and mental ability and their actual traits (Feingold, 1992; Eagly, Ashmore, Makhijani, & Longo, 1991).

Judgments of appearance interact with other factors in everyday life. Kniffin and Wilson (2004) have demonstrated that nonphysical traits such as liking, respect, familiarity, and contribution to shared goals can be powerful factors that influence our judgments of physical attractiveness.

CHANGING STANDARDS OVER TIME

Judgments of attractiveness may change over the course of a lifetime. Ratings of facial attractiveness appear to be somewhat stable from about age 16 to age 50, but the overall ratings of attractiveness for both men and women tend to decline as we reach middle and old age, and the decline is more severe for women.

In one study of the effects of time on attractiveness, the high school pictures of 1,300 males and females were rated for attractiveness. The lives of these people were examined 15 years later. Attractive females in high school had husbands with more education and higher salaries, but their own occupational status and income were not significantly different from those of their less attractive counterparts. The least attractive males in high school had more prestigious occupations and more education, and they married women with more education than the men who were judged attractive in high school. Income levels did not differ. The authors speculate that the social ostracism of the less attractive men in high school may have turned their attention to educational achievements that paid off later in life (Udry & Eckland, 1984). Aging also may reveal changes associated with self-esteem and attractiveness. Middle-aged women who had been identified as attractive college students seemed to be less happy, less satisfied with their lives, and less well adjusted than their plainer counterparts (Berscheid & Walster, 1974).

Because appearance can be changed, people judged unattractive are not necessarily doomed to a long list of pitfalls or problems. Changes in makeup and hairstyle have been shown to increase ratings of general attractiveness, as well as ratings of desired personality characteristics (Graham & Jouhar, 1981). Cosmetics have even been used to aid the recovery and adjustment of people recuperating from illnesses.

Now that we have examined the global concept of attractiveness, we can ask, What *specific* aspects of another's appearance do we respond to? Does it make any difference how we perceive our own body and appearance? We focus on the answers to these questions in the remainder of this chapter.

OUR BODY: ITS SPECIFIC FEATURES

THE FACE

Even though the face had long been the specific body feature most commonly examined in studies of physical attractiveness, a basic question remained unanswered: What is facial beauty? Most researchers believed this question could not be answered by measuring facial features and depended instead on people's judgments of general attractiveness. The research by Langlois and Roggman (1990), however, not only pointed the way toward a measure of facial attractiveness but also made a surprising discovery. Contrary to popular belief, Langlois and Roggman found that physically attractive faces approximate the mathematical average of all faces in a particular population. For example, this research would predict that a physically attractive man or woman in a school is one who comes closest to the school average for male or female facial features.

Langlois and Roggman took photographs of 96 college males and 96 college females. These photos were scanned by a video lens connected to a computer that converted each picture into a matrix of tiny digital units with numerical values. The authors divided the male and female faces into three subsets of 32 faces each. From each subset, the computer randomly chose two faces and mathematically averaged their digitized values. It then transformed this information into a composite face of the two individuals. Composite faces then were generated for 4, 8, 16, and 32 members of each set. Ratings by students showed that composite faces were more attractive than virtually any of the individual faces, and the most attractive faces were composites of 16 and 32 faces (see Figure 6-2). Rhodes, Harwood,

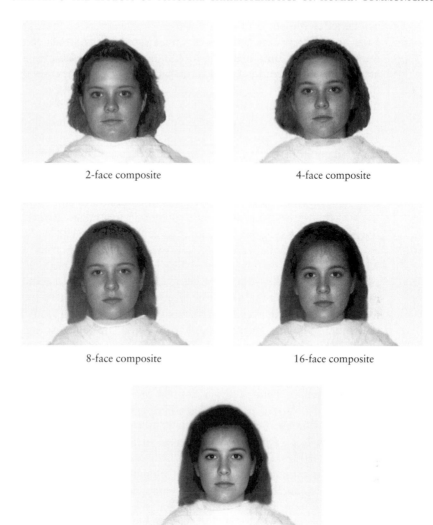

2-face composite

4-face composite

8-face composite

16-face composite

32-face composite

FIGURE 6-2

Progression of mathematically averaged faces, from 2 faces to 32 faces.

Sakiko, Nishitani, and McLean (2002) found that the averaged faces of people within their own culture were also appealing to Chinese and Japanese students.

Langlois and her colleagues acknowledge that in some cases, people are perceived as attractive by large numbers of people even though their features obviously are not the population average. In fact, the most attractive faces are not likely to be average at all. The most attractive faces tend to emphasize those features associated with physically attractive faces. A woman, for example, would have a higher than average forehead, fuller than average lips, shorter than average jaw, and a smaller than average chin and nose. Other female facial features often associated with physical attractiveness are clear skin, high cheekbones, lustrous hair, and big eyes. A woman of any age who has small eyes, a relatively large nose, and wide, thin lips will look older, more masculine, and be seen as less attractive. A powerful jaw and facial hair, although indicators of male facial attractiveness, may need large eyes and a wide smile to avoid being seen as too masculine. This means that extremes of masculinity may not be a good predictor of a dependable and loving relationship partner (Cunningham, Barbee, & Pike, 1990). One study found that during the time of the month when women were more likely to conceive, they were more receptive to men with more rugged, masculine features. During the other 3 weeks of the month, including the menstrual period, women chose faces that were smoother and more feminine (Penton-Voak et al., 1999; Jones, DeBruine, Perrett, Little, Feinberg, & Smith, 2008).

Another promising approach to identifying facial attractiveness is based on the principle of symmetry (Grammer & Thornhill, 1994). Photographs of male and female students were precisely measured at numerous points to determine whether features on one side of the face are equidistant to a midpoint as the same features on the other side of the face. For example, to what extent does the midpoint between the corners of your mouth match up to the midpoint between the corners of your eyes? On perfectly symmetrical faces, all the midpoints meet and roughly form a vertical line. Movie actor Denzel Washington has a very symmetrical face, whereas singer Lyle Lovett does not. Some asymmetry is desirable; otherwise, the face may not look real. Horizontal symmetry was also calculated, and the most symmetrical faces were also those chosen as the most attractive. The researchers believe these results are consistent with findings that show symmetry is also a powerful attractant for other animal and insect species. Symmetry, like averageness, is likely to garner high ratings of facial attractiveness, but neither is a guarantee of the most attractive faces (Cunningham, Barbee, & Philhower, 2002).

Because the face is so central in judgments of attractiveness, it is no surprise that it is the source of stereotyping—often based on glances of one second or less. People have long believed that the face reveals important information about character and personality. Laser and Mathie (1982), for example, engaged an artist to prepare nine charcoal drawings of a male face, varying the thickness of the eyebrows and lips and the shape of the face. People rated these faces with adjectives. The features had marked effects on these ratings: The face with thick eyebrows was seen as less warm, angrier, sterner, less cheerful, and less at ease than those with thin or normal brows; thicker lips connoted warmth and less tension than thinner lips; and narrow faces were seen as more tense and suspicious. But it is important to remember that not all facial stereotypes reflect actual behavior. We will not know if the stereotyped characteristics of people with thick eyebrows and thin lips have any validity until we actually test this hypothesis. One study tested perceptions of baby-faced individuals, who were perceived as more suggestible or persuadable, but this does not seem to be the case (Bachmann & Nurmoja, 2006). People think they can accurately judge intelligence and health from physically attractive faces, but they are not very good at it. This false belief seems to be the result of overgeneralizing based on an accuracy in judging intelligence and health in *unattractive* faces (Zebrowitz & Rhodes, 2004).

Whether a stereotype reflects actual behavior or not, people often act as if it does. As an example, let us continue our examination of baby-faced people. McArthur and her colleagues examined the facial features associated with age and the kinds of interpretations people make of faces that have more or less "youthful" features; in particular, they focussed on the adult with baby-faced features such as a large forehead, short chin, and big eyes. McArthur and Baron (1983) proposed that people correctly differentiate traits that accompany younger age but then incorrectly ascribe these traits—that is, they overgeneralize them—to people with younger-looking faces, even though they are not necessarily young. McArthur and her colleagues found, in support of this, that people rated babyish adult faces as weaker, more submissive, and more intellectually naive than mature-looking faces (Berry & McArthur, 1986).

These investigators also simulated a courtroom trial in which a male defendant was charged with an offense that was marked either by negligence or by deliberate deception; the defendant's appearance was manipulated to be either baby-faced or mature-faced. Subjects acting as jurors more often convicted the baby-faced man for crimes of negligence and the mature-faced man for intentional crimes. This result was predicted based on the earlier finding that adults with babyish features were perceived as more naive and more honest.

Facial babyishness has also been found to affect judgments of attractiveness (Berry, 1991). Facially attractive people are rated higher on characteristics such as honesty, warmth, and sincerity when facial babyishness is high and lower on those same traits when facial babyishness is low. Because all the faces were perceived as attractive, this suggests the possibility of different types of facial attractiveness.

So it seems that a number of social outcomes are consistent with the principle that baby-faced people are more likely to acquire influence, jobs, and judicial convictions when the influence strategies, job descriptions, or alleged crimes fit the characteristics they are expected to have (Zebrowitz, 1997).

In sum, there is no doubt that the way a person's face is structured and contoured creates strong impressions on others. Facial endowment may harm or benefit a person, depending on the stereotypes associated with the features. Future research may be able to tell us to what extent actual personality and ways of expressing ourselves will override initial impressions based on facial stereotypes. We suspect such initial impressions are easily overturned by behavioral evidence. As one example, baby-faced soldiers are not expected to be very brave. As a consequence, when mature-faced and baby-faced soldiers exhibit valor, the baby-faced soldier is more likely to be decorated (Collins & Zebrowitz, 1995).

BODY SHAPE

To add a personal dimension to some of the theory and research in this section, a short Self-Description Test follows. By taking this test, you can gather some data on yourself, which can be compared with that of others who have taken it.

Instructions: Fill in each blank with a word from the suggested list following each statement. For each of the three blanks in each statement, you may select any word from the list of 12 immediately below. An exact word to fit you may not be on the list, but select the words that seem to fit *most closely* with the way you are.

1. I feel _____, _____, and _____ most of the time.

calm	relaxed	complacent
anxious	confident	reticent
cheerful	tense	energetic
contented	impetuous	self-conscious

2. When I study or work, I seem to be _____, _____, and _____.

efficient	sluggish	precise
enthusiastic	competitive	determined
reflective	leisurely	thoughtful
placid	meticulous	cooperative

3. Socially, I am _____, _____, and _____.

outgoing	considerate	argumentative
affable	awkward	shy
tolerant	affected	talkative
gentle-tempered	soft-tempered	hot-tempered

4. I am rather _____, _____, and _____.

active	forgiving	sympathetic
warm	courageous	serious
domineering	suspicious	soft-hearted
introspective	cool	enterprising

5. Other people consider me rather _____, _____, and _____.

generous	optimistic	sensitive
adventurous	affectionate	kind
withdrawn	reckless	cautious
dominant	detached	dependent

6. Underline *one* word out of the three in each of the following lines that most closely describes the way you are:

(a) assertive, relaxed, tense
(b) hot-tempered, cool, warm
(c) withdrawn, sociable, active
(d) confident, tactful, kind
(e) dependent, dominant, detached
(f) enterprising, affable, anxious

This test has been given to numerous individuals in studies on the relationship between certain personality and temperament characteristics and certain body types or builds. Generally, these studies are concerned with a person's physical similarity to three extreme varieties of human physique, shown in Figure 6-3.

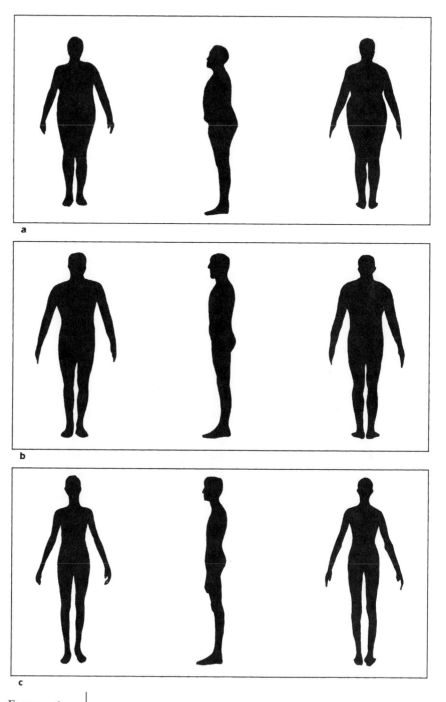

FIGURE 6-3

(a) The endomorph: soft, round, fat; (b) the mesomorph: bony, muscular, athletic;
(c) the ectomorph: tall, thin, fragile.

Because most people do not fit these extremes exactly, a system has been developed for specifying body type based on the assumption that they may have some features of all three types. Let us assume a person's physical characteristics are rated on a scale from 1 to 7, with 7 representing the highest correspondence with one of the three body types. The first number refers to the degree of *endomorphy*, the second to the degree of *mesomorphy*, and the third to the degree of *ectomorphy*. A grossly fat person, then, would be 7/1/1; a broad-shouldered, athletic person would be 1/7/1; and a very skinny person would be 1/1/7. Reportedly, Jackie Gleason was roughly 6/4/1, Muhammad Ali 2/7/1 (in his prime), and Abraham Lincoln 1/5/6.

Now look at the test you took earlier. The test has shown a high correspondence between self-reported temperament characteristics and measures of physique (Cortes & Gatti, 1965). To calculate your score on the Self-Description Test, simply add the number of adjectives you chose from each of the endomorph, mesomorph, and ectomorph categories listed in Table 6-1. If you chose 6 adjectives from the

TABLE 6-1 | THREE PHYSIQUE CATEGORIES AND TEMPERAMENT STEREOTYPES

Endomorphic	Mesomorphic	Ectomorphic
Dependent	Dominant	Detached
Calm	Cheerful	Tense
Relaxed	Confident	Anxious
Complacent	Energetic	Reticent
Contented	Impetuous	Self-conscious
Sluggish	Efficient	Meticulous
Placid	Enthusiastic	Reflective
Leisurely	Competitive	Precise
Cooperative	Determined	Thoughtful
Affable	Outgoing	Considerate
Tolerant	Argumentative	Shy
Affected	Talkative	Awkward
Warm	Active	Cool
Forgiving	Domineering	Suspicious
Sympathetic	Courageous	Introspective
Soft-hearted	Enterprising	Serious
Generous	Adventurous	Cautious
Affectionate	Reckless	Tactful
Kind	Assertive	Sensitive
Sociable	Optimistic	Withdrawn
Soft-tempered	Hot-tempered	Gentle-tempered

endomorph list, 12 from the mesomorph, and 3 from the ectomorph, your temperament score would be 6/12/3. If we assume a high correlation with body features, we would assume you are primarily mesomorphic with a leaning toward endomorphism. The first author of this text was 5/11/5 in 1978, 8/10/3 in 1982, 8/9/4 in 1988, 10/7/4 in 1996, 8/10/3 in 2001, 6/12/3 in 2004, and 10/9/3 in 2008. Although this test is able to make some reasonably accurate predictions about physique for some people, it is, like all predictive tests, based on probabilities and hence less accurate for other people.

We should not assume from this work that the body *causes* temperament traits. The high correspondence between certain temperament traits and body builds may be due to life experiences, environmental factors, self-concept, and a host of other variables, including other people's expectations. If there are clearly defined and generally accepted physique–temperament stereotypes, we can reason that they will have much to do with the way people are perceived and responded to by others and with the personality traits expected of people by others. Wells and Siegel (1961) uncovered some data supporting the existence of such stereotypes. A group of 120 adults were shown silhouette drawings of the endomorph, ectomorph, and mesomorph and were asked to rate them on a set of 24 bipolar adjective scales, such as lazy–energetic, fat–thin, intelligent–unintelligent, and dependent–self-reliant, and so forth. The investigators deliberately chose people who had not attended college, assuming these people would not be contaminated with information from previous studies that might structure their answers. Their results show the following:

1. The *endomorph* was rated fatter, older, shorter (silhouettes were the same height), more old-fashioned, less strong physically, less good looking, more talkative, more warmhearted and sympathetic, more good natured and agreeable, more dependent on others, and more trusting of others.
2. The *mesomorph* was rated stronger, more masculine, better looking, more adventurous, younger, taller, more mature in behavior, and more self-reliant.
3. The *ectomorph* was rated thinner, younger, more ambitious, taller, more suspicious of others, more tense and nervous, less masculine, more stubborn and inclined to be difficult, more pessimistic, and quieter.

Clearly, the evidence shows we do associate certain personality and temperament traits with certain body builds. These expectations may or may not be accurate, but they do exist, and they are a part of the psychological mortar in interpersonal communication. We must recognize these stereotypes as potential stimuli for communication responses so we can deal with them effectively.

As early as kindergarten, children seem to prefer the more muscular mesomorphs to either the thin or fat body types (Johnson & Staffieri, 1971; Lerner & Gellert, 1969; Lerner & Korn, 1972; Lerner & Schroeder, 1971; Staffieri, 1972). Youngsters seem to have a particular aversion to the fat physiques. Older children who select descriptive adjectives for these body types tend to see the mesomorph as "all things good," with ectomorphs and endomorphs attracting a host of unfavorable descriptors. In fact, 10- and 11-year-olds seemed to consider body build as a more important characteristic in judging physical appearance than deformities, disfigurements, and handicaps (Richardson, Goodman, Hastorf, & Dornbusch, 1961). The psychological aversion to chubby figures results in children maintaining a greater physical distance from them (Lerner, Karabenick, & Meisels, 1975; Lerner, Venning, & Knapp, 1975). In turn, we find that chubby children often tend to have a negative perception of their own bodies, which may later generalize to a negative self-image (Walker, 1963). Even the elderly rate the endomorph as a less desirable communication partner, both socially and for working on tasks together (Portnoy, 1993).

Negative reactions to overweight individuals are frequently reported. Such individuals report being discriminated against when seeking to obtain life insurance, adopt children, get jobs, and gain entrance to college (Channing & Mayer, 1966). Although only a small amount of empirical evidence supports the bases of these claims (DeJong & Kleck, 1986), it is safe to say that being excessively overweight in our culture is often a handicap. Researchers who followed 10,000 people between the ages of 16 and 24 for 7 years found obesity meant you were less likely to marry, more likely to have a lower income, and more likely to receive less schooling (Gortmaker, Must, Perrin, Sobol, & Dietz, 1993). People often believe that the inability to lose weight reflects a character flaw. The cultural ideal for U.S. women has tended toward thinness. As a result, women have tended to be more conscious of their weight than have men. In recent years, though, there seem to be more media portrayals—and a generally greater acceptance—of female bodies that are not extremely slender. And men are increasingly concerned about their weight. Another trend in recent years has been toward the development of healthy bodies—"eating right," exercising, and developing muscle strength. These body standards apply to both men and women and will probably constitute some of the features that make up the next cultural standard for the ideal body shape.

Earlier we noted that the mesomorph physique was often rated as better looking. Women say their favorite male physique has a medium-wide upper trunk, a medium-thin lower trunk, and thinner legs—a V-shaped look. The most disliked physique has a thin upper trunk and a wide lower trunk, or a pear-shaped look. Women who see themselves as traditionally feminine and conservative in their lifestyle seem to favor "muscle men"; more "liberated" women liked thinner, more linear bodies; and big women tended to go for big men. The best clue to a woman's favorite male physique, however, is the type of physique belonging to the man who is "most important to her at that time" (Beck, Ward-Hull, & McLear, 1976; Lavrakas, 1975; Pertschuk et al., 1994; Wiggins & Wiggins, 1969). The fact that women tend to like the physique of the man who is currently most important to them suggests that romantic partners are selected for many reasons besides physical attractiveness, and that people can favor an ideal body type but still be happy with a person who does not match that ideal.

Another feature of body shape that seems to play an important role in judgments of a woman's physical attractiveness is the *waist–hip ratio* (Singh, 1993, 1995; Streeter & McBurney, 2003). A waist–hip ratio of .70 means the waist is 70 percent the size of the hips, which is considered the ideal. Singh says early Greek paintings, ancient Indian sculptures, Miss America winners, and *Playboy* centerfolds all show waist–hip ratios very close to the .70 ideal. He has surveyed people of many age groups, cultures, and ethnic groups, and their preferences are for the .70 waist–hip ratio. Women with a lower waist–hip ratio seem to be healthier and more fertile than those with a higher waist–hip ratio. Other research, however, reveals that in a few cultures, women with a greater waist circumference and a higher waist–hip ratio are preferred by males. Some evidence also indicates that women with higher waist–hip ratios and greater waist circumference are more likely to have sons (Manning, Trivers, Singh, & Thornhill, 1999; Yu & Shepard, 1998).

Others argue from their research that the preferred waist–hip ratio will increase as body size and weight increase, even though small and medium waists and hips are preferred regardless of weight (Tassinary & Hansen, 1998; Forestell, Humphrey, & Stewart, 2004). There is no doubt that the waist–hip ratio is one of several features that affect perceptions of female attractiveness, but one study found that the perceived age of a woman's face had a greater overall impact on judgments of physical attractiveness than the waist–hip ratio (Furnham, Disha, & McClelland, 2004). What about men? Singh's research indicates that the ideal waist–hip ratio for men is between .80 and .95.

HEIGHT

Height also influences interpersonal responses. People seem to know that height can be important to their social and work lives. Pediatricians report that parents are often concerned that their child is not as tall as he or she should be at a certain age. Children themselves are asked to focus on height when their teachers tell them to line up by height. Adults seem to overestimate their height, and advertisements for romantic partners often give height as a critical piece of information (Cameron, Oskamp, & Sparks, 1978; Harrison & Saeed, 1977). In some areas of the country, police officers and firefighters are required to meet minimum height requirements. Some applicants, according to newspaper accounts, have actually bludgeoned their heads in the hope that the swelling would make up the difference between their height and the required height!

Height derives its importance from a widespread belief that major deviations from median heights—about 5 feet, 4 inches for women and 5 feet, 9 inches for men—will incur negative judgments from others. Although some may believe it is possible to be "too tall," most negative judgments are thought to be associated with shortness. As Stabler, Whitt, Moreault, D'Ercole, and Underwood (1980) noted, "There is a pervasive social attitude which associates tallness with positive characteristics and assigns negative attributes to shortness." Hall (2006) would concur.

Is there any truth to this? The anecdotal evidence is far more plentiful than the empirical research, and most of the research focuses on men only (Roberts & Herman, 1986). In a study of 956 students in grades 6 through 12, Sandberg, Bukowski, Fung, and Noll (2004) concluded that being too tall or too short had a minimal impact on peer perceptions of social behavior, friendship, or acceptance. Some psychiatrists echo the belief that sometimes short kids are teased, but that they get over it and do not experience lasting psychological problems. And there seems to be little evidence supporting significant differences in the lives of short children whose parents have authorized giving them human growth hormone (HGH) to increase their stature. Still, the belief that tallness is favored in the United States persists, so we will examine three dominant perceptions associated with height: *status*, *attractiveness*, and *competence*.

HEIGHT AND STATUS   Height has long been a metaphor for power and prestige. The taller of the two U.S. presidential candidates has usually won since 1900, with Jimmy Carter and George W. Bush notable exceptions. When Carter debated President Ford, his campaign advisers did not want him to be seen standing next to the 6-foot-1-inch president. Consequently, they asked that the debates be conducted from a sitting position. Ford's advisers refused. The compromise involved placing the lecterns far apart. Further testimony to the stigma associated with shorter people and power is that behavior labeled "competitive" for a taller man is labeled a "Napoleonic complex" for a shorter one. If status and power inhere in taller people, are they also more persuasive? One study indicates they are not (Baker & Redding, 1962). Photographs were taken of the same person, a male, from two different angles: one designed to make him look short, one to make him look tall. These pictures, plus a tape-recorded persuasive speech, were the stimuli for various student groups. Attitude measures indicated no statistically significant difference between the "tall" and "short" speakers.

It is more likely that tallness interacts with other factors, such as general body size, girth, and facial features. In your own experience, you probably can recall some tall individuals who seemed almost frighteningly "overpowering," whereas others of the same height did not have this quality. Science has not yet established a clear-cut relationship between a person's actual height and his or her social status. Nevertheless, the connection is often made when, without any other information, people are asked to make a judgment about height and status. We know of a woman who earned her doctoral degree under a famous psychologist and believed, while she was his student, that he was a tall, imposing figure. Later, she was genuinely surprised to realize he was actually a short man! He had merely *seemed* tall to her.

HEIGHT AND ATTRACTIVENESS   Taller men are frequently perceived as more attractive than shorter men. The ideal male lover is not described as "*short,* dark, and handsome." Male romantic leads in movies are usually either tall or made to look tall by camera angles. Numerous sources attest to the important role of height in perceptions of attractiveness, but obviously we do not make judgments of another's attractiveness based on height alone. Therefore, we can conclude that height is one important feature involved in judgments of attractiveness, but we cannot say that tallness is always associated with the highest judgments of attractiveness. We do know that moviegoers are often taken aback when they learn that a male icon of physical attractiveness and masculinity is much shorter than he is portrayed in his movies.

HEIGHT AND COMPETENCE   Several reports indicate that tall males are perceived as more competent on the job and are rewarded with higher salaries. Before salary becomes an issue, a person has to be hired, and some evidence suggests this is more difficult for a shorter man. In one study, 140 sales recruiters were asked to choose between two men just by reading their applications for employment. The applications were exactly the same except that one listed a height of 6 feet, 1 inch and the other 5 feet, 5 inches. Only 1 percent favored the shorter man (Kurtz, 1969). Another study indicated that men who were selected to advance in corporate training programs were significantly taller than average (Farb, 1978). An analysis of similar studies led Judge and Cable (2004) to conclude that taller people have higher self-esteem, are more likely to be in leadership positions, make more money, and get better performance evaluations at work than shorter people. This was more likely to be the case with men, but there was a strong relationship for women as well.

However, the relationship between height, income, and performance on the job may not be as simple as the preceding studies suggest. For example, actual performance records showed few differences between shorter and taller police officers, but their supervisors felt shorter police officers were more aggressive law enforcers and more likely to be a source of discontent in the police department (Lester & Sheehan, 1980). Persico and Postlewaite (2004) found that taller white male adults did make more money than their shorter colleagues, but when their analysis was controlled for height as a teenager, this difference disappeared. In other words, there was no income gap for short male adults who were not considered short in high school.

BODY IMAGE

So far we have discussed our perceptions of others. An equally important dimension of interpersonal communication is what we think of ourselves. Self-image is the root system from which our overt communication behavior grows. Our overt communication behavior is an extension of the accumulated experiences that have made up our understanding of self. In short, what you are—or rather what you think you are—organizes what you say and do. An important part of your self-image is body image, perhaps the first aspect of self-image formed in young children. Adult males seem to be most satisfied with their bodies when they are somewhat larger than normal; females are most satisfied when their bodies are smaller than normal but when their busts are larger than average. In an effort to test the belief that larger bust sizes were more desirable to others, photographs were taken of three women who artificially altered their bust size. The woman with the smallest bust, about 34 inches, received the highest ratings on competence, ambition, intelligence, morality, and modesty (Kleinke & Staneski, 1980). Sex researchers have frequently noted emotional problems in males stemming from a perceived incongruence between their genital size and the supposed masculine ideal perpetuated by our literary and folklore heritage. More than 71 percent of the women in one survey agreed or strongly agreed that "men seem too concerned with the size and shape of their genitals" (Pertschuk et al., 1994).

As we develop, we learn the cultural ideal of what a body should be. This results in varying degrees of satisfaction with the body, particularly during adolescence. Wolf (1991) and others believe the standards of beauty promulgated in the mass media are oppressive and create an undesirable yearning for often unreasonable goals. A national survey of several thousand adults indicated that between 1972 and 1986, both men's and women's dissatisfaction with their bodies rose sharply. Weight was a major factor of dissatisfaction (Cash, Winstead, & Janda, 1986). Given the fact that about 30 percent of the U.S. population—roughly 59 million people—were considered obese in 2000, dissatisfaction with weight is probably still a concern (Flegal, Carroll, Odgen, & Johnson, 2002). A number of studies show, however, that we are not always accurate in our perceptions of our own body size and weight. In some cases, constant exposure to ideal body images on television contributes to misperceptions of body shape and size (Myers & Biocca, 1992; Bissell & Zhou, 2004). In addition to misjudgments of our own body size and weight, we may also misjudge the body type that is most appealing to the opposite sex. Women seem to think men prefer a thinner woman than men actually report; men seem to think women want a heavier man than women actually report. Men thought that having an attractive face and body build was more important to women than women said it was (Fallon & Rozin, 1985; Pertschuk et al., 1994).

BODY COLOR

We do make some judgments about temporary color changes that show up on people's bodies. On light-skinned people, for example, a pale color may indicate illness, a rosy flush may indicate embarrassment, and a red neck can appear with anger. But in many respects, permanent skin colors have been the most potent body stimulus for determining interpersonal responses in our culture. Some Asian Americans use whitening creams and lotions on their faces, arguing that the desire for pale skin is an ancient Asian tradition associated with delicacy and femininity. Younger Asian Americans wonder if this is really an effort to blend into a culture where there is less discrimination against white-skinned individuals, or even a manifestation of prejudice against those with darker skins. There is no need to review the abuses heaped on black people in America on the basis of skin color alone. These abuses are well documented. The words of a white man who darkened his skin pigmentation and experienced the dramatic and unforgettable life of a black man in America is sufficient reminder:

> When all the talk, all the propaganda has been cut away, the criterion is nothing but the color of skin. My experience proved that. They judged me by no other quality. My skin was dark. That was sufficient reason for them to deny me those rights and freedoms without which life loses its significance and becomes a matter of little more than animal survival.

> I searched for some other answer and found none. I had spent a day without food and water and for no other reason than that my skin was black. I was sitting on a tub in the swamp for no other reason. (Griffin, 1960, pp. 121–122)

As U.S. demographics change, the variety of skin colors manifested by the people around us will continue to increase, and sharp distinctions among people's skin colors will become increasingly difficult to make. Still, there will always be those who want a simple method of classifying their social world, and skin color is easily observed. We can only hope that the number of people who believe skin color to be an accurate gauge for identifying friend and foe will continue to decrease.

The standards for beauty are usually set by the economically dominant group within a society. People in less dominant groups are judged by the standards of the dominant group and, seeing the reward value, may try to mimic the standards of the dominant group. The standards in the United States have traditionally been those associated with the features of the people whose ancestors immigrated here from northern and western Europe. Among other features, they had "white" skin. There is nothing inherently more attractive about "white" skin or the features shared by these Americans who had a northern or western European heritage. In fact, pale skin is more likely to have freckles and is more prone to skin cancer and wrinkles earlier than the skin of many Asians and Africans. In time, the dominant group will change, and no doubt some of the standards for physical attractiveness will change with it.

BODY SMELL

It is obvious that vision and hearing are the most important sensors for social situations in Western societies, but the sense of smell also may influence responses. The scientific study of the human olfactory system is in its infancy, but we know other animals obtain a great deal of information from their sense of smell: the presence of an enemy, territorial markers, finding members of the same species or herd, sexual stimulation, mate selection, and emotional states. Dogs are well known for their ability to sense fear, hate, or friendship in human beings and to track them by only the scent from clothing. The difficulty dogs seem to have in distinguishing between the smells of identical twins prompted Davis (1971) to suggest that we each have an "olfactory signature."

Americans do not seem to rely *consciously* on their sense of smell for much interpersonal information, unless perspiration odor, breath, or some other smell is unusually strong or inappropriate to the situation. It is believed that all of us could enhance our olfactory sensitivity if we learned the words needed to differentiate among various odors. We have a rather limited vocabulary for discussing subtle differences in smells, which in turn may hinder their identification. If it is true that we tend to neglect our olfactory skills, it seems ironic that we spend so much time and money on artificial scents. Each year American men and women spend millions of dollars on deodorants, soaps, mouthwashes, breath mints, perfumes, aftershave lotions, and other products to add to or cover up natural body scents. Publicly, the so-called natural scent seems to have a low priority in our cultural development, but we are not at all reluctant to buy a commercial product that will purportedly make us smell "natural" or sexy.

Artificial scents are not always designed for pleasant reactions. During World War II, scientists developed a noxious-smelling compound they called "Who Me?" This product was put into collapsible plastic tubes and distributed to Chinese children in cities occupied by the Japanese. The children squirted the odorous substance onto the trouser seats of Japanese officers. The foul-smelling result was more than just a temporary irritant—it was nearly impossible to wash out (Russell, 1981). Odors so foul smelling as to be capable of emptying buildings and even incapacitating people may have contemporary applications in law enforcement and the military. The Monell Chemical Senses Center in Philadelphia is reportedly working on just such a product.

What is the role of human odors in daily interaction? Our reactions may be consciously or unconsciously processed, but the message can be quite strong. During heightened emotional arousal, chemical olfactory signals may even assume an importance that rivals the normally dominant visual and auditory channels. Human odors are primarily emitted through glands found in the anal–genital region and in secretory glands in the face, hands, feet, and sometimes across the chest. Odors collect in the mouth and in regions of the body with hair. Several experiments attest to the fact that people are usually able to identify the odors of specific other human beings. These "dirty T-shirt" studies instructed people to wear a cotton T-shirt for periods ranging from 1 day to 1 week and to avoid using any perfumes and deodorants. Seventy-five percent of the people tested were able to sniff out their own T-shirt and those of a male and female stranger; 50 percent of spouses were able to identify their mate's T-shirt. Parents can identify their children, some only 2 hours old, with accuracy rates that sometimes exceed 90 percent; and children are generally able to identify their siblings (Lord & Kasprzak, 1989; Porter, Cernoch, & Balogh, 1985; Porter, Cernoch, & McLaughlin, 1983; Porter & Moore, 1981; Russell, 1976). By the age of 6 weeks, infants respond to the odor on a breast pad from their mother but not from a stranger. One study even found people able to identify gender from hand odors. An important qualification is in order: Although we do seem to be able to identify others by smell, the accuracy rate depends a great deal on how many competing stimuli we have to judge from. It may be much easier to choose a spouse's T-shirt from two than from 20.

Smells not only help us identify people, but may also play a role in relationship development. When unmarried women were asked to select a male's T-shirt that had an odor that they would like to smell if they had to smell it all the time, they selected T-shirts from males who were genetically similar, but not too similar, to their fathers (Jacob, McClintock, Zelano, & Ober, 2002). Major histocompatibility complex (MHC) appears to be a factor. MHC is made up of genes that influence tissue rejection in the immune system, and if a child is conceived with a person who is too similar in MHC, the fetus is at a greater risk of rejection. Animals often use smell to detect MHC differences in potential mates, and now we know humans can, too. Women preferred the smell of male T-shirts that were safely different in MHC from their own, even though women taking birth control pills were not nearly as consistent in selecting safely different MHC based on the smell of male T-shirts (Wedekind & Füri, 1997; Wedekind, Seebeck, Bettens, & Paepke, 1995; Garver-Apgar, Gangestad, Thornhill, Miller, & Olp, 2006).

Homosexual men seem to react differently to male pheromones than heterosexual men and preferred the odors of gay men. Heterosexual men and women, as well as lesbians, did not prefer the odor from homosexual males (Savic, Berglund, & Lindström, 2005; Martins et al., 2005). Heterosexual males also seem to be affected by different odors given off by females at different times in the ovulation cycle. Eighteen strippers (lap dancers) recorded their tips over the course of 60 days. When they were ovulating, they earned $67 an hour; when they were not ovulating or menstruating, they earned $52 an hour; when they were menstruating, they earned $37 an hour. Strippers who were taking a contraceptive pill did not show a peak in earnings during estrus (Miller, Tybur, & Jordan, 2007).

Odor also seems to play a role in synchronizing female menstrual cycles. It was discovered that friends and college roommates moved from an average of 8.5 days apart in their menstrual cycle to less than 5 during the school year. Another experimenter attempted to explain why by taking odor samples from the underarm of a female colleague, which was called "Essence of Genevieve." This odor was dabbed on the upper lips of female volunteers three times a week for 4 months. Another group of women were dabbed with alcohol. The alcohol group showed no change, but the group receiving Essence of Genevieve tended to synchronize their cycles with Genevieve's. This group went from an average of 9.3 days apart in their cycles to 3.4, with 4 women moving to within 1 day of Genevieve's cycle. Subsequent work has examined the role of a man's perspiration odor on women's menstrual cycles. The procedures used in the Essence of Genevieve study were replicated using women whose cycles were longer than normal and shorter than normal. Those whose upper lips were dabbed with the male odor developed cycles closer to normal; the control group did not (Cutler et al., 1986; McClintock, 1971; Russell, 1976; Stern & McClintock, 1998).

In addition to affecting the menstrual cycle, male perspiration also seems to have a positive effect on women's moods in the form of stress reduction and relaxation (Preti, Wysocki, Barnhart, Sondheimer, & Leyden, 2003). The preceding studies are important reminders of the connection between physiological processes and odor. Physicians have long known that people with certain illnesses tend to give off certain odors, but now we are finding that certain physiological processes can be modified by odor. It does not surprise us that such effects take place in the animal or insect worlds, but until recently we have not thought of human behavior in this way. Today, some people even practice aromatherapy, using odors to alleviate anxiety, headaches, and hypertension, for example.

Another source of odor is flatulent air, generally adding a negative or insulting aura to an interpersonal encounter in our culture (Lippman, 1980). In fact, anticipation of expelling flatus may lead to rapid termination of an interpersonal contact. Under certain conditions, however, emission of flatulent air may be used deliberately to draw attention to oneself. The extent to which odors attributed to flatus or unpleasant body odors are evaluated negatively is probably related to the extent to which others believe people are aware of it and whether it is controllable.

The role of odors in human interaction varies considerably from culture to culture. Asians are reported to manifest underarm odor only rarely, but odor seems to play a prominent role in some Arab countries:

> Olfaction occupies a prominent place in Arab life. Not only is it one of the distance-setting mechanisms, but it is a vital part of a complex system of behavior. Arabs consistently breathe on people when they talk. However, this habit is more than a matter of different manners. To the Arab good smells are pleasing and a way of being involved with each other. To smell one's friend is not only nice but desirable, for to deny him your breath is to act ashamed. Americans, on the other hand, trained as they are not to breathe in people's faces, automatically communicate shame in trying to be polite. (Hall, 1966, pp. 159–160)

In addition to human odors, environmental odors also may affect human encounters by setting the mood or bringing back memories associated with the smell. For the first author of this book, a distinct smell is associated with high schools; each time he enters one, it triggers a chain of memories from his own history.

BODY HAIR

The length of a person's hair can dramatically affect perceptions and human interaction. In 1902 the U.S. Commissioner of Indian Affairs sent out an order to forcibly, if necessary, cut all male Indians' hair so they would look "civilized."

Historically, this is only one of many instances in which hair length triggered an undesirable response.

During the 1960s, white males who allowed the hair on their head to grow over their ears and foreheads, and sometimes to their shoulders, found they frequently attracted abuse similar to that leveled at black-skinned individuals. Cases of discrimination in housing, school admittance, jobs, and commercial establishments, to mention a few, were numerous.

The media regularly report stories involving reactions to, or regulations directed toward, human hair, mostly male hair. A small sampling of news stories from 1973 to 2004 illustrates this recurring issue:

AUSTIN, TEXAS (1973) Long hair on boys and men is the "sign of a sissy" and should be banned from American athletic fields, according to the lead article in the May issue of the *Texas High School Coaches Association's* magazine. A head football coach at a junior high school in Houston said God made man to dominate woman and, therefore, meant for man to wear short hair. Simpson told his fellow coaches in the article that "a good hair code will get abnormals out of athletics before they become coaches and bring their 'losers' standards into the coaching profession."

NEW JERSEY (1973) The headmaster of a well-known preparatory school, who sported a beard and a mustache, said about 60 seniors would be suspended if they did not cut their hair to meet regulations on hair grooming. One student reported he was told by the headmaster, "I hold your diploma. Either you get a haircut or [you] don't get your diploma."

CONNECTICUT (1975) A woman was fired from her waitressing job because she refused to shave her legs.

SEOUL, SOUTH KOREA (1980) The national police were ordered to refrain from arresting males because of their long hair. During the first 8 months of the year, 14,911 men were arrested on such a charge.

LUBBOCK, TEXAS (1990) A mother in Texas did not see how the rat-tail hairdo her 11-year-old son had been wearing for 3 years was suddenly in violation of the Lubbock Independent School District's dress code. School officials were enforcing a policy that prohibited boys from having longer than shoulder-length hair, ponytails, rat tails, patterns shaved into their hair, and braids. Her son, a Boy Scout and honor student before his withdrawal, was being tutored at home because he refused to conform to the new policy.

WASHINGTON, D.C. (1994) A woman with a moustache alleged that her facial hair was the reason she was fired.

COLUMBIA, SOUTH CAROLINA (1995) Prisoners at a correctional institution stabbed five guards and took three hostages to protest a policy that would require them to cut their hair.

BASTROP, TEXAS (1996) A state appeals court ruled that school officials were out of bounds when they sent a ponytailed 8-year-old to the equivalent of solitary confinement. The school district's claims that its hair rule was needed to prevent gangs, teach gender identity, and maintain discipline were sheer nonsense, the Third Court of Appeals said. "[The boy] wore the same hairstyle during the previous school year without causing any disruption," the court said. The school district's lawyer said he would recommend the district take the case to the Texas Supreme Court.

HARLINGEN, TEXAS (2004) A 16-year-old student who had several cases of cancer in his family wanted to grow his hair long and donate it to Locks of Love, a non-profit organization that uses donated hair to create custom-fitted hairpieces for children suffering from medical hair loss. School officials said this would violate the policy that forbids males to grow hair that hangs below their shoulders. The school superintendent said that the school district's success is rooted in not making exceptions to the policies in place.

Most of the negative reactions against long hair are directed at males; negative reactions against hair that is too short ("microbuzzes") are more likely to be directed at females. Some men are concerned about baldness as detracting from their own attractiveness, but just as often, women report male baldness does not significantly detract from a male's attractiveness. The motivation for negative responses to these extreme hairstyles by some members of our culture is an interesting question but not our major concern here. The fact that hair length, in and of itself, elicits feelings of either appreciation or repugnance is the important point (see Figure 6-4).

Other body hair also seems to be important in judgments of attractiveness as well. One study that looked at male facial hair from a historical perspective suggests that men sport more facial hair when they want to be more attractive to women, during times when marriage is valued and the competition for brides is intense (Barber, 2001). But another study indicates that male beards may not be much of an asset in obtaining a management-trainee position (Shannon & Stark, 2003). Men with a lot of body hair are attractive to some women and repulsive to others. What about the hair on women's bodies? For years, *Playboy* magazine neatly airbrushed or did not display pubic hair on its models. Even magazines depicting figures in nudist colonies were so well known for such alterations of pubic hair that many subsequently advertised their magazines as "unretouched." But when nude photographs of the pop singer Madonna appeared in two national magazines, many people commented more about the hair under her arms than about her lack of clothing. Some liked the underarm hair, and some did not. Many people in the United States find underarm hair unattractive on women even though this perception is not shared in other countries. And it is reported that the Cacobo Indians of the Amazon rain forest carefully trim and groom their head hair but feel that other body hair is unattractive; they methodically eliminate eyebrows by plucking them. The lack of eyebrows on the Mona Lisa is some evidence that at one time it may have been desirable to pluck them for beauty's sake.

The shape of our bodies, our skin color, our smell, and the hair on our bodies are probably the major factors affecting our responses to personal appearance. Still, many other body features, in any given situation, may play an important role; for

FIGURE 6-4

How do hair length and style influence your perceptions?

example, freckles, moles, acne, and so-called beauty marks. The numerous individuals who have had surgery to improve the appearance of their noses, popularly dubbed "nose jobs," must have felt that a large nose created a sufficiently undesirable impression in face-to-face interaction to have it changed. We now turn to how we alter our body's appearance with clothing, decorations, and artifacts such as eyeglasses, jewelry, piercings, and so forth.

OUR BODY: CLOTHES AND OTHER ARTIFACTS

As early as 1954, Hoult's experiments verified what we take to be common sense today—that you can change people's perceptions of someone by changing that person's clothing. We do not have to look far to find evidence in our daily world to confirm Hoult's finding. The Associated Press once reported that the Lutheran Church believed the attire worn by clergy in the pulpit was responsible for some churchgoers' switching denominations. Many tailors, manufacturers, and sellers of clothes claim to be "wardrobe engineers" who structure their clients' outward appearance to increase their sales, assert their authority, or win more court cases. Career specialists tell us that a job applicant's attire and grooming are important indicators of his or her attitude toward the company and that appropriate dress aids career advancement.

Some research supports the belief that clothes are an important factor in first impressions. Males and females were asked what they notice about people when they first meet them, and they were given 10 characteristics of appearance from which to choose. Females noticed clothes first for both same- and opposite-sex people; males also looked at clothes first for same-sex people, but for members of the opposite sex, clothes took third place behind figure and face ("First Impressions," 1983). Positive first impressions of a person's clothing style are also more likely if the styles of the person being judged and the person doing the judging are similar (Reid, Lancuba, & Morrow, 1997).

School dress codes also provide clear testimony that people believe clothes communicate important messages. The Associated Press reported in 1994 that several Houston-area school districts outlawed what they called the "grunge look." Students were prohibited from wearing baggy pants; untucked shirts; piercings in the lips, nose, and eyebrows; torn or ripped clothing; duster-type coats; or trench coats. Earrings were prohibited for boys, and girls could not wear miniskirts; tank tops; cut-offs; halter tops; strapless garments; or casual pants, dress slacks, or skirts worn on hips. These school administrators, like administrators in other school districts with similar dress and grooming restrictions, wanted to ban clothing that could hide weapons, that might convey gang or drug-related messages, or that seemed sexually provocative, and to encourage clothing that would convey what they believed to be a safe, respectful, and positive learning environment. While many secondary school students agreed with some of these restrictions, they did not perceive others as detracting from a positive learning environment; for example, beards, elongated arm holes on shirts, hair not its natural color, tank tops, and sunglasses.

We can make two important conclusions from the preceding examples: (1) right or wrong, many people believe clothes communicate important messages; and (2) clothing communicates most effectively when it is adapted to the wearer's role and the attendant surroundings. This second conclusion relates to the earlier testimony about how to dress for job interviews and make positive first impressions. It is also supported by research in which well-dressed participants and participants who were dressed sloppily asked strangers for money to make a phone call. When well dressed, those requesting aid received more cooperation in a clean, neatly appointed airport, where most of the people were also well dressed; when participants were poorly dressed, the greatest cooperation was obtained from strangers in a bus station, where the people and surroundings more closely resembled the participant's state of poor dress (Hensley, 1981). Sometimes we are very much aware of what attire fits the situation. Most people know, for example, that the business outfits of working women on television programs are sexier and often inappropriate for women who do not work "on camera" (White, 1995). Other situations are not so clear, as Victoria Clarke, then assistant secretary of defense for public affairs, found out in 2003. She was criticized by some for wearing bright colors while answering questions about the war in Iraq. Some, mainly men, argued that pink is not an appropriate color in a time of war (Givhan, 2003).

Examine the clothing types shown in Figure 6-5. What are your first impressions?

a

b

FIGURE 6-5

Four clothing styles.

Below is a list of 20 characteristics that may be associated with one or more of these clothing types. Check the spaces you think apply to specific clothing types, and compare your impressions with those of your friends, family, and associates.

Males				Females				
1	2	3	4	1	2	3	4	
—	—	—	—	—	—	—	—	1. Has smoked marijuana
—	—	—	—	—	—	—	—	2. Is shy, doesn't talk much
—	—	—	—	—	—	—	—	3. Is a fraternity or sorority member
—	—	—	—	—	—	—	—	4. Is a Democrat
—	—	—	—	—	—	—	—	5. Is involved in athletics
—	—	—	—	—	—	—	—	6. Is married
—	—	—	—	—	—	—	—	7. Is generous
—	—	—	—	—	—	—	—	8. Drives a sports car
—	—	—	—	—	—	—	—	9. Is a Republican
—	—	—	—	—	—	—	—	10. Is vocationally oriented
—	—	—	—	—	—	—	—	11. Is active politically
—	—	—	—	—	—	—	—	12. Is dependable
—	—	—	—	—	—	—	—	13. Listens most to classical music
—	—	—	—	—	—	—	—	14. Lives with parents
—	—	—	—	—	—	—	—	15. Has long hair
—	—	—	—	—	—	—	—	16. Has many friends
—	—	—	—	—	—	—	—	17. Is intelligent
—	—	—	—	—	—	—	—	18. Is religious
—	—	—	—	—	—	—	—	19. Is open-minded
—	—	—	—	—	—	—	—	20. Is older

Did you find any similarities in your responses and those of your peers? Were there any major differences between your responses and the responses of people with distinctly different backgrounds? Later in this chapter, we focus on what specific messages and impressions clothes communicate, but first let us consider the fundamental question: Is clothing, in and of itself, an important factor in communicating?

FUNCTIONS OF CLOTHING

To understand the relationship between clothes and communication, we must be familiar with the various functions clothes can fulfill: decoration, physical and psychological protection, sexual attraction, self-assertion, self-denial, concealment, group identification, persuasion, attitude, ideology, mood reflection or creation, authority, and status or role display (Barnard, 2001). Because some widely accepted cultural rules apply for combining certain colors and styles of dress, clothes may also function to inform the observer of a person's knowledge of such rules. When romantic couples wear similar or matching clothing, the clothing serves as a visible bonding agent for the relationship. Clothing that functions as a means of persuasion has been the subject of numerous studies.

An old but classic study tested the ability of people dressed in "high-status" clothing to get unsuspecting bystanders to violate a traffic light. Lefkowitz, Blake, and Mouton (1955) found pedestrians much more likely to violate a traffic light at an intersection if another person violated it ahead of them, especially if that other person's attire represented a person with social status. Other studies have found that a variety of requests—to make change, accept leaflets, give detailed street directions, return money left in a phone booth, and so on—are more easily accomplished if the requester is dressed to fit the situation or is dressed in what would be considered higher status clothing (Fortenberry, MacLean, Morris, & O'Connell, 1978; Levine, Bluni, & Hochman, 1998). Bickman (1974a, 1974b), for example, had four men stop 153 adults on the streets of Brooklyn and make various requests. The men's clothing varied and included civilian clothing, comprising a sport jacket and tie; a milkman's white uniform; and a guard's uniform, with a badge and insignia but no gun. The men asked pedestrians to pick up a bag, to put a dime in a parking meter for someone else, or to stand on the opposite side of a bus-stop sign. In each case, when dressed in the guard uniform, the men received greater compliance. In fact, 83 percent of those who were asked to put a dime in the parking meter obeyed, even after the person in the guard uniform had left the scene. Uniforms do help people identify the wearer's probable areas of expertise, and this knowledge can be persuasive. In public service announcements, the same woman dressed as a nurse or as a businesswoman asked for contributions to fight leukemia. The nurse was judged to be more knowledgeable and received more pledged contributions (Lawrence & Watson, 1991). Uniformed police officers want their uniform to be persuasive, but it is sometimes difficult because of the different goals associated with their job. It was debated whether the same uniform can communicate approachability and friendliness as well as authoritativeness in enforcing the law (Young, 1999). Lawyers have long known that their clients' manner of dress can have a persuasive impact on the judgments made by a judge or jury. Some defendants have even been encouraged to put on a ring that simulates a wedding ring to offset any prejudice against single people.

CLOTHING AS INFORMATION ABOUT THE PERSON

To make a list of the things invariably communicated by clothes would be impossible; such a list would vary with the demands of each particular situation, ethnic group, time of day and era, region of the country, and so forth. Making the task even harder is the fact that any given item of clothing can be worn in such a way as to convey multiple meanings. The design of a tie may convey sophistication and status, but the way it is knotted or worn—tight or loose, thrown over the shoulder—can send other messages.

Some of the personal attributes communicated by dress include sex, age, nationality, relation to a companion (e.g., matching sweaters), socioeconomic status, identification with a specific group, occupational or official status, mood, personality, attitudes, interests, and values. Clothes also set our expectations for the behavior of the wearer. When the target of our observations is a person well known to us, that knowledge will guide our interpretations of clothing. We may, for example, see radical clothing changes as representing temporary moods rather than lasting personality changes. Obviously, the accuracy of such judgments varies considerably; it is significant to note that the more concrete items such as age, sex, and socioeconomic status are signaled with greater accuracy than more abstract qualities such as attitudes, values, and personality. In recent years, the "message" T-shirt has become a vehicle for communicating some attitudes that might otherwise be more difficult to assess.

EFFECTS OF CLOTHING ON THE WEARER

Up to this point, we have established that clothing communicates a variety of messages, and the people we interact with respond in various ways to those messages. But what about the effect of clothing on the self-image of the wearer? Some authors feel that clothes help satisfy an image of a person's ideal self. Gibbins, in his work with 15- and 16-year-old girls, for instance, found a definite relationship between clothes that were liked and ratings of ideal self. Clothing was a means of communicating messages about the wearer, and liking for a particular outfit was "related to the extent to which this message is similar to the subject's ideal self-image" (Gibbins, 1969). In another fascinating discovery, we see a potential link between clothing and self-concept. High school boys who had higher achievement test scores but who wore clothing deemed "unacceptable" by their peers were found to have lower grade-point averages than those who wore "acceptable" clothing (Hamilton & Warden, 1966). This latter group also found themselves in less conflict and in more school activities. Clothes, then, may encourage or discourage certain patterns of communication. A new outfit may promote feelings of gaiety and happiness, people may feel less efficient in shoes that hurt, and self-consciousness may result from wearing an "inappropriate" outfit, a common feeling for adolescents trying to grapple with their own self-image. Some graduate teaching assistants wear suits to class to distinguish themselves from their students who frequently are almost the same age. Some report that such attire gives them added confidence or assurance in dealing with their students, but their attire seems to have relatively little effect on the perceptions of their students when compared with their behavior (Gorham, Cohen, & Morris, 1999; Roach, 1997).

The mutual effects of clothing on the wearer and on the perceiver were amply demonstrated in a study of the uniforms worn by teams in the National Hockey League and National Football League. In this study, teams with black uniforms ranked near the top of their leagues in penalties, and those teams that switched from nonblack to black uniforms incurred more penalties after the switch. The authors suggest that wearers of black uniforms perceive themselves as more aggressive and that this, coupled with similar perceptions by referees, leads to more penalties (Frank & Gilovich, 1988).

The issue of wearing uniforms to school has gained a great deal of notoriety in recent years. One of the prominent arguments for adopting school uniforms is that the style of dress changes how wearers feel about themselves and, in turn, changes behavior. One large-scale study of 10th-grade students did not find any direct effects of uniforms on substance use, behavioral problems, or attendance but did find a negative effect on achievement (Brunsma & Rockquemore, 1998). For some students, uniforms provide a needed form of structure and control, and they are a symbol of school unity, but it is not realistic to expect uniforms to eliminate most of the offensive behaviors manifested by troubled teens. School uniforms by themselves—without the support of students, teachers, school administrators, and parents—are not likely to accomplish much.

CLOTHING AND PERSONALITY

Rosenfeld and Plax (1977) wanted to determine whether attitudes toward clothing are related to certain personality characteristics. Their study obtained responses from both males and females on a questionnaire about clothing attitudes. A massive battery of personality tests also was given to this group of 371 men and women. The results of these personality tests were then matched with the scores on four dimensions of the clothing questionnaire. These results are listed as follows according to the males and females who scored high or low on each dimension:

1. Clothing consciousness ("The people I know always notice what I wear.")
   - High males were deliberate, guarded, and deferential to authority, custom, and tradition. They did not value beauty, form, and unity very highly, and they believed people were easily manipulated.
   - High females were inhibited, anxious, compliant before authority, kind, sympathetic, and loyal to friends.
   - Low males were aggressive, independent, and did not believe people could be easily manipulated.
   - Low females were forceful, independent, dominant, clear thinking, and had low motivation for heterosexual relationships or for manipulating others.
2. Exhibitionism ("I approve of skimpy bathing suits and wouldn't mind wearing one myself.")
   - High males were aggressive, confident, outgoing, unsympathetic, unaffectionate, moody, impulsive, and had a low self-concept regarding their familial interactions.
   - High females were radical, detached from interpersonal relationships, and had a high opinion of their own self-worth and moral/ethical beliefs.
   - Low males were guarded about self-revelations. They had a low self-concept regarding their familial interactions, and they believed people could be easily manipulated.
   - Low females were timid, sincere, accepting of others, patient, and had a low motivation for heterosexual relationships. They also had feelings of inferiority.

3. Practicality ("When buying clothes, I am more interested in practicality than beauty.")
   - High males were inhibited, cautious, rebellious, dissatisfied, and had a low motivation to make friends, sustain relationships, or gain recognition from authorities.
   - High females were clever, enthusiastic, confident, outgoing, and guarded about personal self-revelations. They had feelings of superiority but did not wish to lead.
   - Low males were success oriented, mature, forceful, serious, analytical, and tried to predict responses of others in various situations.
   - Low females were self-centered, independent, and detached.
4. Designer ("I should love to be a clothes designer.")
   - High males were cooperative, sympathetic, warm, helpful, impulsive, irritable, demanding, and conforming. They worried about their behavior and sought encouragement from others.
   - High females were irrational, uncritical, stereotyped in thinking, quick, expressive, and ebullient.
   - Low males were adventurous, egotistic, dissatisfied, and anxious. They had feelings of superiority and were not highly motivated to form friendships.
   - Low females were efficient, clear thinking, resourceful, persistent, and easily disorganized under pressure. They believed people were easily manipulated, and they were pessimistic about their occupational future.

ARTIFACTS AND BODY DECORATIONS

People adorn themselves with badges, tattoos, masks, earrings, and jewelry, among other things (see Figure 6-6). We must take these artifacts and decorations into consideration in any discussion of clothing, because they are also potential communicative stimuli. A ring worn on a particular finger, a fraternity or sorority pin worn in a particular configuration, and a single earring worn in a particular ear all may communicate something about the nature of a person's relationships and self-image.

We know that people around the world choose to decorate and alter their bodies in a variety of ways. Sometimes the body is scarred, mutilated, or painted. In the case of binding infants' feet or heads, bone structure is reshaped. In our society, we circumcise many male children, and the piercing of various body parts with rings has become increasingly popular with young adults in recent years. The use of tattoos to decorate the body is also widely practiced (Sanders, 1989).

In addition, we know people sometimes react strongly to a particular artifact or decoration, such as eyeglasses or lipstick. And although the initial effect of such features may be strong, the longer the interaction continues, the more co-occurring features and verbal behavior will blend together to form an overall impression.

FIGURE 6-6

People around the world use tattoos to decorate their bodies.

SUMMARY

Appearance and dress are part of the total nonverbal stimuli that influence interpersonal responses, and under some conditions, they are the primary determinants of such responses. Physical attractiveness may be influential in determining whether a person is sought out, and it may have a bearing on whether a person is able to persuade or manipulate others. It is often an important factor in the selection of dates and marriage partners, it may determine whether a defendant is deemed guilty or innocent, and it may even have an effect on whether a prisoner is able to decrease the antisocial behavior responsible for his or her imprisonment. It may be a major factor contributing to how others judge personality, sexuality, popularity, success, and often happiness. Fortunately for some, and unfortunately for others, such judgments begin early in life. Not all children are conventionally beautiful. There are indications that teachers not only make attractiveness judgments about young children but also treat the unattractive ones with fewer and less positive communications. A sizable proportion of the American public still thinks of the ideal man or woman in terms of physical attractiveness.

In spite of the overwhelming evidence that physical attractiveness is a highly desirable quality in interpersonal situations, other factors temper these general findings. For instance, all positive findings for attractiveness are based on probabilities, not certainty. Many less attractive people are not evaluated unfavorably. For example, judgments can be tempered by who people are seen with, the environment in which they are judged, other communicative behavior they engage in, or the time of life at which they are evaluated. In addition, many attractiveness studies have used photographs rather than live, interacting human beings, and we know that the dynamics of interaction influence perceptions.

In addition to the importance of general physical attractiveness in influencing the responses of others, we have some information on stereotyped responses to specific features: general body build, facial appearance, skin color, odor, hair, and clothes. These specific features may have a profound influence on a person's self-image and hence on patterns of communication with others.

The way we clothe our bodies may also communicate important messages in our work and social lives, and it is one of the first things people perceive about us. We can judge age, sex, and socioeconomic status from clothing with more accuracy than we can a person's attitudes or beliefs. Wearing attire that others perceive as similar to theirs, appropriate to the situation, or representative of an expert or authority figure gives a persuasive element to clothing. We also know that clothing and the other ways we decorate our bodies—with jewelry, colors, tattoos, and so on—affect how we feel about ourselves, which in turn affects how we communicate.

QUESTIONS FOR DISCUSSION

1. Can our verbal behavior affect the way people perceive our physical attractiveness? What verbal behavior might cause people to perceive us as less physically attractive? What verbal behavior might make us appear more physically attractive? Do the answers to these questions vary with context? If so, give examples.

2. Do you know romantic couples in which the female is significantly less attractive than the male? If so, develop photos that reflect this difference, and ask people what it is about the female that the male is likely attracted to?

3. Do we see physical attractiveness differently in photos and videos with no sound? Do your own experiment: Obtain ratings of the physical attractiveness of people in photos and the same people shown interacting. They should all interact with the same person and talk about the same subject. How do you explain the differences or the absence of differences?

4. People have been refused employment or fired from their jobs because of perceived problems with their height, weight, odor, skin color, clothing, hair, or general attractiveness. Under what conditions if any do you think such characteristics are legitimate reasons for not hiring a person or for firing an employee?

5. Do you think a person can be physically attractive in one situation but not in another? Test this idea with both males and females by showing photos of the same people in different situations.

BIBLIOGRAPHY

Adams, G. R. (1977). Physical attractiveness research: Toward a developmental social psychology of beauty. *Human Development, 20,* 217–239.

Addison, W. E. (1989). Beardedness as a factor in perceived masculinity. *Perceptual and Motor Skills, 68,* 921–922.

Aiken L. (1963). Relationship of dress to selected measures of personality in undergraduate women. *Journal of Social Psychology, 59,* 119–128.

Albada, K. F., Knapp, M. L., & Theune, K. E. (2002). Interaction appearance theory: Changing perceptions of physical attractiveness through social interaction. *Communication Theory, 12,* 8–40.

Aronson, E., & Golden, B. W. (1962). The effect of relevant and irrelevant aspects of communicator credibility on opinion change. *Journal of Personality, 30,* 135–146.

Bachmann, T., & Nurmoja, M. (2006). Are there affordances of suggestibility in facial appearance? *Journal of Nonverbal Behavior, 30,* 87–92.

Baker, E. E., & Redding, W. C. (1962). The effects of perceived tallness in persuasive speaking: An experiment. *Journal of Communication, 12,* 51–53.

Barber, N. (2001). Mustache fashion covaries with a good marriage market for women. *Journal of Nonverbal Behavior, 25,* 261–272.

Barnard, M. (2001). *Fashion as communication* (2nd ed.). New York: Routledge.

Bar-Tal, D., & Saxe, L. (1976). Perceptions of similarly and dissimilarly attractive couples and individuals. *Journal of Personality and Social Psychology, 33,* 772–781.

Bassett, R. E. (1979). Effects of source attire on judgments of credibility. *Central States Speech Journal, 30,* 282–285.

Beck, S. B., Ward-Hull, C. I., & McLear, P. M. (1976). Variables related to women's somatic preferences of the male and female body. *Journal of Personality and Social Psychology, 34,* 1200–1210.

Berg, R. C. (2004). *Interaction appearance theory and initial interactions.* Unpublished master's thesis, University of Texas.

Berman, P. W., O'Nan, B. A., & Floyd, W. (1981). The double standard of aging and the social situation: Judgments of attractiveness of the middle-aged woman. *Sex Roles, 7,* 87–96.

Berry, D. S. (1991). Attractive faces are not all created equal: Joint effects of facial babyishness and attractiveness on social perception. *Personality and Social Psychology Bulletin, 17,* 523–531.

Berry, D. S., & McArthur, L. Z. (1986). Perceiving character in faces: The impact of age-related craniofacial changes on social perception. *Psychological Bulletin, 100,* 3–18.

Berscheid, E., & Walster, E. H. (1969). *Interpersonal attraction.* Reading, MA: Addison-Wesley.

Berscheid, E., & Walster, E. H. (1974). Physical attractiveness. In L. Berkowitz (Ed.), *Advances in experimental social psychology* (Vol. 7). New York: Academic Press.

Bickman, L. (1971). The effects of social status on the honesty of others. *Journal of Social Psychology, 85,* 87–92.

Bickman, L. (1974a). The social power of a uniform. *Journal of Applied Social Psychology, 4,* 47–61.

Bickman, L. (1974b). Social roles and uniforms: Clothes make the person. *Psychology Today, 7,* 48–51.

Bissell, K. L., & Zhou, P. (2004). Must-see TV or ESPN: Entertainment and sports media exposure and body-image distortion in college women. *Journal of Communication, 54,* 5–21.

Boothroyd, L. G., Jones, B. C., Burt, D. M., DeBruine, L. M., & Perrett, D. I. (2008). Facial correlates of sociosexuality. *Evolution and Human Behavior, 29,* 211–218.

Brain, R. (1979). *The decorated body.* New York: Harper & Row.

Braun, M. F., & Bryan, A. (2006). Female waist-to-hip and male waist-to-shoulder ratios as determinants of romantic partner desirability. *Journal of Social and Personal Relationships, 23,* 805–819.

Brislin, R. W., & Lewis, S. A. (1968). Dating and physical attractiveness: Replication. *Psychological Reports, 22,* 976.

Brunsma, D. L., & Rockquemore, K. A. (1998). Effects of student uniforms on attendance, behavior problems, substance use, and academic achievement. *Journal of Educational Research, 92,* 53–62.

Buss, D. M. (1989). Sex differences in human mate preferences: Evolutionary hypotheses tested in 37 cultures. *Behavioral and Brain Sciences, 12,* 1–14.

Buss, D. M. (1994). *The evolution of desire.* New York: Basic Books.

Buss, D. M., & Shackelford, T. K. (2008). Attractive women want it all: Good genes, economic investment, parenting proclivities, and emotional commitment. *Evolutionary Psychology, 6,* 134–146.

Byrne, D., Ervin, C. R., & Lamberth, J. (1970). Contiguity between the experimental study of attraction and real-life computer dating. *Journal of Personality and Social Psychology, 16,* 157–165.

Cahnman, W. J. (1968). The stigma of obesity. *Sociological Quarterly, 9,* 283–299.

Cameron, C., Oskamp, S., & Sparks, W. (1978). Courtship American style: Newspaper advertisements. *The Family Coordinator, 26,* 27–30.

Cash, T. F., & Derlega, V. J. (1978). The matching hypothesis: Physical attractiveness among same-sexed friends. *Personality and Social Psychology Bulletin, 4,* 240–243.

Cash, T. F., Gillen, B., & Burns, S. (1977). Sexism and "beautism" in personnel consultant decision making. *Journal of Applied Psychology, 62,* 301–310.

Cash, T. F., & Pruzinsky, T. (1990). *Body images: Development, deviance, and change.* New York: Guilford.

Cash, T. F., Winstead, B. A., & Janda, L. H. (1986). The great American shape-up. *Psychology Today, 20,* 30–37.

Cavior, N., & Lombardi, D. H. (1973). Developmental aspects of judgment of physical attractiveness in children. *Developmental Psychology, 8,* 67–71.

Chaiken, S. (1979). Communicator physical attractiveness and persuasion. *Journal of Personality and Social Psychology, 37,* 1387–1397.

Chaiken, S. (1986). Physical appearance and social influence. In C. P. Herman, M. P. Zanna, & E. T. Higgins (Eds.), *Physical appearance, stigma, and social behavior: The Ontario Symposium* (Vol. 3). Hillsdale, NJ: Erlbaum.

Chaikin, A. L., Derlega, V. J., Yoder, J., & Phillips, D. (1974). The effects of appearance on compliance. *Journal of Social Psychology, 92,* 199–200.

Channing, H., & Mayer, J. (1966). Obesity—Its possible effect on college acceptance. *New England Journal of Medicine, 275,* 1172–1174.

Collins, M. A., & Zebrowitz, L. A. (1995). The contributions of appearance to occupational outcomes in civilian and military settings. *Journal of Applied Social Psychology, 25,* 129–163.

Cortes, J. B., & Gatti, F. M. (1965). Physique and self-description of temperament. *Journal of Consulting Psychology, 29,* 432–439.

Cortes, J. B., & Gatti, F. M. (1966). Physique and motivation. *Journal of Consulting Psychology, 30,* 408–414.

Cunningham, M. R., Barbee, A. P., & Philhower, C. L. (2002). Dimensions of facial physical attractiveness: The intersection of biology and culture (pp. 193–238). In G. Rhodes & L. A. Zebrowitz (Eds.), *Facial attractiveness.* Westport, CT: Ablex.

Cunningham, M. R., Barbee, A. R., & Pike, C. L. (1990). What do women want? Facialmetric assessment of multiple motives in the perception of male facial physical attractiveness. *Journal of Personality and Social Psychology, 59,* 61–72.

Cunningham, M. R., Roberts, A. R., Barbee, A. P., Druen, P. B., & Wu, C. H. (1995). "Their ideas of beauty are, on the whole, the same as ours": Consistency and variability in the cross-cultural perception of female physical attractiveness. *Journal of Personality and Social Psychology, 68,* 261–279.

Cutler, W. B., Preti, G., Krieger, A., Huggins, G. R., Garcia, C. R., & Lawley, H. J. (1986). Human axillary secretions influence women's menstrual cycles: The role of donor extract from men. *Hormones and Behavior, 20,* 463–473.

Dannenmaier, W., & Thumin, F. (1964). Authority status as a factor in perceptual distortion of size. *Journal of Social Psychology, 63,* 361–365.

Darley, J. M., & Cooper, J. (1972). The "Clean Gene" phenomenon: The effect of students' appearance on political campaigning. *Journal of Applied Social Psychology, 2,* 24–33.

Davis, F. (1971). *Inside intuition.* New York: McGraw-Hill.

Davis, F. (1992). *Fashion, culture, and identity.* Chicago: University of Chicago Press.

Deformed brick-thrower eyes future with new face. (1975, December 15). *Lafayette Journal and Courier,* p. A-6.

DeJong, W., & Kleck, R. E. (1986). The social psychological effects of overweight. In C. P. Herman, M. P. Zanna, & E. T. Higgins (Eds.), *Physical appearance, stigma, and social behavior: The Ontario Symposium* (Vol. 3). Hillsdale, NJ: Erlbaum.

DeLong, R. R. (1978). Dimensions of visual perceptions of clothing. *Perceptual and Motor Skills, 47,* 907–910.

Dermer, M., & Thiel, D. L. (1975). When beauty may fail. *Journal of Personality and Social Psychology, 31,* 1168–1176.

Dion, K. K. (1972). Physical attractiveness and evaluation of children's transgressions. *Journal of Personality and Social Psychology, 24,* 207–213.

Dion, K. K. (1973). Young children's stereotyping of facial attractiveness. *Developmental Psychology, 9,* 183–188.

Dion, K. K. (2002). Cultural perspectives on facial attractiveness (pp. 239–259). In G. Rhodes & L. A. Zebrowitz (Eds.), *Facial attractiveness.* Westport, CT: Ablex.

Dion, K. K., & Berscheid, E. (1972). Physical attractiveness and peer perception among children. *Sociometry, 37,* 1–12.

Dion, K. K., Berscheid, E., & Walster, E. (1972). What is beautiful is good. *Journal of Personality and Social Psychology, 24,* 285–290.

Dion, K. K., & Stein, S. (1978). Physical attractiveness and interpersonal influence. *Journal of Experimental Social Psychology, 14,* 97–108.

Dipboye, R. L., Arvey, R. D., & Terpstra, D. E. (1977). Sex and physical attractiveness of raters and applicants as determinants of resume evaluations. *Journal of Applied Psychology, 62,* 288–294.

Doty, R. L. (1981). Olfactory communication in humans. *Chemical Senses, 6,* 351–376.

Doty, R. L., Orndorff, M. M., Leyden, J., & Kligman, A. (1978). Communication of gender from human axillary odors: Relationship to perceived intensity and dedonicity. *Behavioral Biology, 23,* 373–380.

Douty, H. I. (1963). Influence of clothing on perception of persons. *Journal of Home Economics, 55,* 197–202.

Downs, A. C., & Lyons, P. M. (1991). Natural observations of the links between attractiveness and initial legal judgments. *Personality and Social Psychology Bulletin, 17,* 541–547.

Eagly, A. H., Ashmore, R. D., Makhijani, M. G., & Longo, L. C. (1991). What is beautiful is good, but … : A meta-analysis of research on the physical attractiveness stereotype. *Psychological Bulletin, 110,* 109–128.

Efran, M. G. (1974). The effect of physical appearance on the judgment of guilt, interpersonal attraction, and severity of recommended punishment in a simulated jury task. *Journal of Experimental Research in Personality, 8,* 45–54.

Etcoff, N. (1999). *Survival of the prettiest.* New York: Random House.

Fallon, A., & Rozin, P. (1985). Sex differences in perceptions of desirable body shape. *Journal of Abnormal Psychology, 94,* 102–105.

Farb, B. (1978). *Humankind.* Boston: Houghton-Mifflin.

Farina, A., Fischer, E., Sherman, S., Smith, W., Groh, T., & Mermin, P. (1977). Physical attractiveness and mental illness. *Journal of Abnormal Psychology, 86,* 510–517.

Feingold, A. (1992). Good-looking people are not what we think. *Psychological Bulletin, 111,* 304–341.

First impressions. (1983, August/September). *Public Opinion,* p. 6.

Flegal, K. M., Carroll, M. D., Ogden, C. L., & Johnson, C. L. (2002). Prevalence and trends in obesity among U.S. adults, 1999–2000. *Journal of the American Medical Association, 288,* 1772–1773.

Flugel, J. (1930). *The psychology of clothes.* London: Hogarth Press.

Forestell, C. A., Humphrey, T. M., & Stewart, S. H. (2004). Involvement of body weight and shape factors in ratings of attractiveness by women: A replication and extension of Tassinary and Hansen (1998). *Personality and Individual Differences, 36,* 295–305.

Fortenberry, J. H., MacLean, J., Morris, P., & O'Connell, M. (1978). Modes of dress as a perceptual cue to deference. *Journal of Personality and Social Psychology, 104,* 139–140.

Frank, M. G., & Gilovich, T. (1988). The dark side of self- and social perception: Black uniforms and aggression in professional sports. *Journal of Personality and Social Psychology, 54,* 74–85.

Freedman, R. (1986). *Beauty bound.* Lexington, MA: Lexington.

Friday, N. (1996). *The power of beauty.* New York: HarperCollins.

Friend, R. M., & Vinson, M. (1974). Leaning over backwards: Jurors' responses to defendants' attractiveness. *Journal of Communication, 24,* 124–129.

Furnham, A., Disha, M., & McClelland, A. (2004). The influence of age of the face and the waist-to-hip ratio on judgments of female attractiveness and traits. *Personality & Individual Differences, 36,* 1171–1185.

Garner, D. M., Garfinkel, P. E., Schwartz, D., & Thompson, M. (1980). Cultural expectations of thinness in women. *Psychological Reports, 47,* 483–491.

Garver-Apgar, C. E., Gangestad, S. W., Thornhill, R., Miller, R. D., & Olp, J. J. (2006). Major histocompatibility complex alleles, sexual responsivity, and unfaithfulness in romantic couples. *Psychological Science, 17,* 830–835.

Geiselman, R. E., Haight, N., & Kimata, L. (1984). Context effects of the perceived physical attractiveness of faces. *Journal of Experimental Social Psychology, 20,* 409–424.

Gibbins, K. (1969). Communication aspects of women's clothes and their relation to fashionability. *British Journal of Social and Clinical Psychology, 8,* 301–312.

Giles, H., & Chavasse, W. (1975). Communication length as a function of dress style and social status. *Perceptual and Motor Skills, 40,* 961–962.

Gillis, J. S., & Avis. W. E. (1980). The male-taller norm in mate selection. *Personality and Social Psychology Bulletin, 6,* 396–401.

Givhan, R. (2003, March 28). Torie Clarke's bold hues raise some cries. *The Washington Post,* C01.

Goldberg, P. A., Gottesdiener, N., & Abramson, P. R. (1975). Another put-down of women? Perceived attractiveness as a function of support for the feminist movement. *Journal of Personality and Social Psychology, 32,* 113–115.

Gorden, W. I., Tengler, C. D., & Infante, D. A. (1982). Women's clothing predispositions as predictors of dress at work, job satisfaction, and career advancement. *Southern Speech Communication Journal, 17,* 422–434.

Gorham, J., Cohen, S. H., & Morris, T. L. (1999). Fashion in the classroom: III. Effects of instructor attire and immediacy in natural classroom interactions. *Communication Quarterly, 47,* 281–299.

Gortmaker, S. L., Must, A., Perrin, J. N., Sobol, A. M., & Dietz, W. H. (1993). Social and economic consequences of overweight in adolescence and young adulthood. *New England Journal of Medicine, 329,* 1008–1012.

Graham, J. A., & Jouhar, A. J. (1980). Cosmetics considered in the context of physical attractiveness: A review. *International Journal of Cosmetic Science, 2,* 77–101.

Graham, J. A., & Jouhar, A. J. (1981). The effects of cosmetics on person perception. *International Journal of Cosmetic Science, 3,* 199–210.

Graham, J. A., & Jouhar, A. J. (1982). *The effects of cosmetics on self perception: How we see ourselves.* Unpublished manuscript, University of Pennsylvania.

Graham, J. A., & Kligman, A. M. (Eds.). (1985). *The psychology of cosmetic treatments.* New York: Praeger.

Grammer, K., & Thornhill, R. (1994). Human (*homo sapiens*) facial attractiveness and sexual selection: The role of symmetry and averageness. *Journal of Comparative Psychology, 108,* 233–242.

Graziano, W. G., Jensen-Campbell, L. A., Shebilske, L. J., & Lundgren, S. R. (1993). Social influence, sex differences, and judgments of beauty: Putting the interpersonal back into interpersonal attraction. *Journal of Personality and Social Psychology, 65,* 522–531.

Griffin, J. H. (1960). *Black like me.* Boston: Houghton Mifflin.

Gurel, L., Wilbur, J. C., & Gurel, L. (1972). Personality correlates of adolescent clothing styles. *Journal of Home Economics, 64,* 42–47.

Halberstadt, J., & Rhodes, G. (2003). It's not just average faces that are attractive: Computer-manipulated averageness makes birds, fish, and automobiles attractive. *Psychonomic Bulletin & Review, 10,* 149–156.

Hall, E. T. (1966). *The hidden dimension.* Garden City, NY: Doubleday.

Hall, S. S. (2006). *Size matters: How height affects the health, happiness, and success of boys—and the men they become.* Boston: Houghton Mifflin.

Hallpike, C. R. (1969). Social hair. *Man, 4,* 256–264.

Hamermesh, D. S., & Biddle, J. E. (1994). Beauty and the labor market. *American Economic Review, 84,* 1174–1194.

Hamid, P. (1972). Some effects of dress cues on observational accuracy: A perceptual estimate and impression formation. *Journal of Social Psychology, 86,* 279–289.

Hamilton, J., & Warden, J. (1966). Student's role in a high school community and his clothing behavior. *Journal of Home Economics, 58,* 789–791.

Harrison, A. A., & Saeed, L. (1977). Let's make a deal: An analysis of revelations and stipulations in Lonely Hearts advertisements. *Journal of Personality and Social Psychology, 35,* 257–274.

Hartmann, G. W. (1949). Clothing: Personal problem and social issue. *Journal of Home Economics, 41,* 295–298.

Hatfield, E., & Sprecher, S. (1986). *Mirror, mirror . . . : The importance of looks in everyday life.* Albany: SUNY Press.

Heilman, M. E., & Saruwatari, L. F. (1979). When beauty is beastly: The effects of appearance and sex on evaluations of job applicants for managerial and nonmanagerial jobs. *Organizational Behavior and Human Performance, 22,* 360–372.

Heine, K. (2005, August 28). Men, plastic surgery's not just for Michael Jackson anymore. *Austin American Statesman,* K14.

Hendricks, S. H., Kelley, E. A., & Eicher, J. B. (1968). Senior girls' appearance and social acceptance. *Journal of Home Economics, 60,* 167–172.

Hensley, W. E. (1981). The effects of attire, location, and sex on aiding behavior: A similarity explanation. *Journal of Nonverbal Behavior, 6,* 3–11.

Herman, C. P., Zanna, M. P., & Higgins, E. T. (Eds.). (1986). *Physical appearance, stigma, and social behavior: The Ontario Symposium* (Vol. 3). Hillsdale, NJ: Erlbaum.

Hinsz, V. B. (1989). Facial resemblance in engaged and married couples. *Journal of Social and Personal Relationships, 6,* 223–229.

Holman, R. H. (1980). A transcription and analysis system for the study of women's clothing. *Semiotica, 32,* 11–34.

Hopson, J. L. (1979). *Scent signals.* New York: William Morrow.

Horai, J., Naccari, N., & Faloultah, E. (1974). The effects of expertise and physical attractiveness upon opinion agreement and liking. *Sociometry, 37,* 601–606.

Hoult, R. (1954). Experimental measurement of clothing as a factor in some social ratings of selected American men. *American Sociological Review, 19,* 324–328.

Hubble, M. A., & Gelso, C. J. (1978). Effect of counselor attire in an initial interview. *Journal of Counseling Psychology, 25,* 581–584.

Iliffe, A. M. (1960). A study of preferences in feminine beauty. *British Journal of Psychology, 51,* 267–273.

Jackson, L. A. (1992). *Physical appearance and gender: Sociobiological and sociocultural perspectives.* Albany: SUNY Press.

Jacob, S., McClintock, M. K., Zelano, B., & Ober, C. (2002). Paternally inherited HLA alleles are associated with women's choice of male odor. *Nature Genetics, 30,* 175–179.

Jacobson, M. B. (1981). Effects of victim's and defendant's physical attractiveness on subjects' judgments in a rape case. *Sex Roles, 7,* 247–255.

Jacobson, S. K., & Berger, C. R. (1974). Communication and justice: Defendant attributes and their effects on the severity of his sentence. *Speech Monographs, 41,* 282–286.

Jensen-Campbell, L. A., Graziano, W. G., & West, S. G. (1995). Dominance, prosocial orientation, and female preferences: Do nice guys really finish last? *Journal of Personality and Social Psychology, 68,* 427–440.

Johnson, B. H., Nagasawa, R. H., & Peters, K. (1977). Clothing style differences: Their effect on the impression of sociability. *Home Economics Research Journal, 6,* 58–63.

Johnson, K. K. P., & Lennon, S. (Eds.). (1999). *Appearance and power.* New York: Oxford University Press.

Johnson, P. A., & Staffieri, J. R. (1971). Stereotypic affective properties of personal names and somatotypes in children. *Developmental Psychology, 5,* 176.

Jones, B. C., DeBruine, L. M., Perrett, D. I., Little, A. C., Feinberg, D. R., & Smith, M. J. L. (2008). Effects of menstrual cycle phase on face preferences. *Archives of Sexual Behavior, 37,* 78–84.

Jones, B. T., Jones, B. C., Thomas, A. P., & Piper, J. (2003). Alcohol consumption increases attractiveness ratings of opposite-sex faces: A possible third route to risky sex. *Addiction, 98,* 1069–1075.

Joseph, N., & Alex, N. (1972). The uniform: A sociological perspective. *American Journal of Sociology, 77,* 719–730.

Joseph, W. B. (1982). The credibility of physically attractive communicators: A review. *Journal of Advertising, 11,* 15–24.

Judge, T. A., & Cable, D. M. (2004). The effects of physical height on workplace success and income: Preliminary test of a theoretical model. *Journal of Applied Psychology, 89,* 428–441.

Kaiser, S. B. (1985). *The social psychology of clothing*. New York: Macmillan.

Kalick, S. M., & Hamilton, T. E. (1986). The matching hypothesis reexamined. *Journal of Personality and Social Psychology, 51*, 673–682.

Kanazawa, S., & Kovar, J. L. (2004). Why beautiful people are more intelligent. *Intelligence, 32*, 227–243.

Keating, C. F. (1985). Gender and the physiognomy of dominance and attractiveness. *Social Psychology Quarterly, 48*, 61–70.

Keating, C. F., Mazur, A., & Segall, M. H. (1977). Facial gestures which influence the perception of status. *Sociometry, 40*, 374–378.

Keating, C. F, Mazur, A., & Segall, M. H. (1981). A cross-cultural exploration of physiognomic traits of dominance and happiness. *Ethology and Sociobiology, 2*, 41–48.

Kenny, C., & Fletcher, D. (1973). Effects of beardedness on person perception. *Perceptual and Motor Skills, 37*, 413–414.

Kenrick, D. T., & Gutierres, S. E. (1980). Contrast effects and judgments of physical attractiveness: When beauty becomes a social problem. *Journal of Personality and Social Psychology, 38*, 131–140.

Keyes, R. (1980). *The height of your life*. New York: Warner.

Kiesler, S. B., & Baral, R. L. (1970). The search for a romantic partner: The effects of self-esteem and physical attractiveness on romantic behavior. In K. J. Gergen & D. Marlowe (Eds.), *Personality and social behavior*. Reading, MA: Addison-Wesley.

Kitson, H. D. (1922). Height and weight as factors in salesmanship. *Journal of Personnel Research, 1*, 289–294.

Kleck, R. E., Richardson, S. A., & Ronald, L. (1974). Physical appearance cues and interpersonal attraction in children. *Child Development, 45*, 305–310.

Kleinke, C. L., & Staneski, R. A. (1980). First impressions of female bust size. *Journal of Social Psychology, 110*, 123–124.

Knapp, M. L. (1985). The study of physical appearance and cosmetics in Western culture. In J. A. Graham & A. M. Kligman (Eds.), *The psychology of cosmetic treatments*. New York: Praeger.

Kniffin, K. M., & Wilson, D. S. (2004). The effect of nonphysical traits on the perception of physical attractiveness: Three naturalistic studies. *Evolution and Human Behavior, 25*, 88–101.

Krebs, D., & Adinolfi, A. A. (1975). Physical attractiveness, social relations, and personality style. *Journal of Personality and Social Psychology, 31*, 107–114.

Kretschmer, E. (1925). *Physique and character*. New York: Harcourt Brace.

Kruger, D. J. (2006). Male facial masculinity influences attributions of personality and reproductive strategy. *Personal Relationships, 13*, 451–463.

Kulka, R. A., & Kessler, J. B. (1978). Is justice really blind? The influence of litigant physical attractiveness on juridical judgment. *Journal of Applied Social Psychology, 8*, 366–381.

Kurtz, D. L. (1969). Physical appearance and stature: Important variables in sales recruiting. *Personnel Journal, 48*, 981–983.

Lakoff, R. T., & Scherr, R. L. (1985). *Face value: The politics of beauty*. London: Routledge & Kegan Paul.

Lambert, S. (1972). Reactions to a stranger as a function of style of dress. *Perceptual and Motor Skills, 35*, 711–712.

Landy, D., & Sigall, H. (1974). Beauty is talent: Task evaluation as a function of the performer's physical attractiveness. *Journal of Personality and Social Psychology, 29*, 299–304.

Langlois, J. H., & Downs, A. C. (1979). Peer relations as a function of physical attractiveness: The eye of the beholder or behavioral reality? *Child Development, 50*, 409–418.

Langlois, J. H., Kalakanis, L. E., Rubenstein, A. J., Larson, A. D., Hallam, M. J., & Smoot, M. T. (2000). Maxims or myths of beauty: A meta-analysis and theoretical review. *Psychological Bulletin, 126*, 390–423.

Langlois, J. H., & Roggman, L. A. (1990). Attractive faces are only average. *Psychological Science, 1*, 115–121.

Langlois, J. H., Roggman, L. A., Casey, R. J., Ritter, J. M., Rieser-Danner, L. A., & Jenkins, V. Y. (1987). Infant preferences for attractive faces: Rudiments of a stereotype? *Developmental Psychology, 23*, 363–369.

Langlois, J. H., Roggman, L. A., & Musselman, L. (1994). What is average and what is not average about attractive faces? *Psychological Science, 5*, 214–220.

Largey, G. P., & Watson, D. R. (1972). The sociology of odors. *American Journal of Sociology, 77,* 1021–1034.

Laser, P. S., & Mathie, V. A. (1982). Face facts: An unbidden role for features in communication. *Journal of Nonverbal Behavior, 7,* 3–19.

Lavrakas, P. J. (1975). Female preferences for male physiques. *Journal of Research in Personality, 9,* 324–334.

Lawrence, S. G., & Watson, M. (1991). Getting others to help: The effectiveness of professional uniforms in charitable fund-raising. *Journal of Applied Communication Research, 19,* 170–185.

Lefkowitz, M., Blake, R., & Mouton, J. (1955). Status factors in pedestrian violation of traffic signals. *Journal of Abnormal and Social Psychology, 51,* 704–706.

Lerner, R. M., & Gellert, E. (1969). Body build identification, preference, and aversion in children. *Developmental Psychology, 1,* 456–462.

Lerner, R. M., Karabenick, S. A., & Meisels, M. (1975). Effects of age and sex on the development of personal space schemata toward body build. *Journal of Genetic Psychology, 127,* 91–101.

Lerner, R. M., Karabenick, S. A., & Stuart, J. L. (1973). Relations among physical attractiveness, body attitudes, and self-concept in male and female college students. *Journal of Psychology, 85,* 119–129.

Lerner, R. M., & Korn, S. J. (1972). The development of body build stereotypes in males. *Child Development, 43,* 908–920.

Lerner, R. M., & Schroeder, C. (1971). Physique identification, preference, and aversion in kindergarten children. *Developmental Psychology, 5,* 538.

Lerner, R. M., Venning, J., & Knapp, J. R. (1975). Age and sex effects on personal space schemata toward body build in late childhood. *Developmental Psychology, 11,* 855–856.

Lester, D., & Sheehan, D. (1980). Attitudes of supervisors toward short police officers. *Psychological Reports, 47,* 462.

Levine, J. M., & McBurney, D. H. (1977). Causes and consequences of effluvia: Body odor awareness and controllability as determinants of interpersonal evaluation. *Personality and Social Psychology Bulletin, 3,* 442–445.

Levine, L. R., Bluni, T. D., & Hochman, S. H. (1998). Attire and charitable behavior. *Psychological Reports, 83,* 15–18.

Lewandowski, G. W., Jr., Aron, A., & Gee, J. (2007). Personality goes a long way: The malleability of opposite-sex physical attractiveness. *Personal Relationships, 14,* 571–585.

Lippman, L. G. (1980). Toward a social psychology of flatulence: The interpersonal regulation of natural gas. *Psychology: A Quarterly Journal of Human Behavior, 17,* 41–50.

Little, A. C., Penton-Voak, I. S., Burt, D. M., & Perrett, D. I. (2002). Evolution and individual differences in the perception of attractiveness: How cyclic hormonal changes in self-perceived attractiveness influence female preferences for male faces (pp. 59–90). In G. Rhodes & L. A. Zebrowitz (Eds.), *Facial attractiveness.* Westport, CT: Ablex.

Long, T. J. (1978). Influence of uniform and religious status on interviewees. *Journal of Counseling Psychology, 25,* 405–409.

Lord, T., & Kasprzak, M. (1989). Identification of self through olfaction. *Perceptual and Motor Skills, 69,* 219–224.

Lurie, A. (1981). *The language of clothes.* New York: Random House.

Maddux, J. E., & Rogers, R. W. (1980). Effects of source expertness, physical attractiveness, and supporting arguments on persuasion: A case of brains over beauty. *Journal of Personality and Social Psychology, 39,* 235–244.

Malloy, J. T. (1975). *Dress for success.* New York: P. H. Wyden.

Malloy, J. T. (1977). *The women's dress for success book.* Chicago: Follet.

Manning, J. T., Trivers, R. L., Singh, D., & Thornhill, R. (1999). The mystery of female beauty. *Nature, 399,* 214–215.

Martin, J. G. (1964). Racial ethnocentrism and judgment of beauty. *Journal of Social Psychology, 63,* 59–63.

Martins, Y., Preti, G., Crabtree, C. R., Runyan, T., Vainius, A. A., & Wysocki, C. (2005). Preference for human body odors is influenced by gender and sexual orientation. *Psychological Science, 16,* 694–701.

Mathes, E. W., & Kahn, A. (1975). Physical attractiveness, happiness, neuroticism, and self-esteem. *Journal of Psychology, 90,* 27–30.

McArthur, L. Z., & Baron, R. M. (1983). Toward an ecological theory of social perception. *Psychological Review, 90,* 215–238.

McBurney, D. H., Levine, J. N., & Cavanaugh, P. H. (1977). Psychophysical and social ratings of human body odor. *Personality and Social Psychology Bulletin, 3,* 135–138.

McClintock, M. K. (1971). Menstrual synchrony and suppression. *Nature, 229,* 244–245.

Miller, G., Tybur, J. M., & Jordan, B. D. (2007). Ovulatory cycle effects on tip earnings by lap dancers: Economic evidence for human estrus? *Evolution and Human Behavior, 28,* 375–381.

Mills, J., & Aronson, E. (1965). Opinion change as a function of the communicators' attractiveness and desire to influence. *Journal of Personality and Social Psychology, 1,* 173–177.

Monetmayor, R. (1978). Men and their bodies: The relationship between body type and behavior. *Journal of Social Issues, 34,* 48–64.

Morris, T. L., Gorham, J., Cohen, S. H., & Huffman, D. (1996). Fashion in the classroom: Effects of attire on student perceptions of instructors in college classes. *Communication Education, 45,* 135–148.

Murstein, B. I. (1972). Physical attractiveness and marital choice. *Journal of Personality and Social Psychology, 23,* 8–12.

Murstein, B. I., & Christy, P. (1976). Physical attractiveness and marriage adjustment in middle-aged couples. *Journal of Personality and Social Psychology, 34,* 537–542.

Murstein, B. I., Gadpaille, W. J., & Byrne, D. (1971). What makes people sexually appealing? *Sexual Behavior, 1,* 75–77.

Myers, P. N., Jr., & Biocca, F. A. (1992). The elastic body image: The effect of television advertising and programming on body image distortions in young women. *Journal of Communication, 42,* 108–133.

Nemmeth, C., & Hyland, R. (1973). A simulated jury study: Characteristics of the defendant and the jurors. *Journal of Social Psychology, 90,* 223–229.

Nevid, J. S. (1984). Sex differences in factors of romantic attraction. *Sex Roles, 2,* 401–411.

Parnell, R. W. (1958). *Behavior and physique: An introduction to practical and applied somatometry.* London: Edward Arnold.

Pearson, N. O. (2006, January 22). In Venezuela, beauty's become a national craze, big business. *Austin American Statesman,* A20.

Pellegrini, R. J. (1973). The virtue of hairiness. *Psychology Today, 6,* 14.

Pellegrini, R. J. (1989). Beardedness as a stimulus variable: Note on methodology and meta-analysis of impression-formation data. *Perceptual and Motor Skills, 69,* 161–162.

Pennebaker, J. W., Dyer, M. A., Caulkins, R. S., Litowitz, D. L., Ackerman, P. L., Anderson, D. B., & McGraw, K. M. (1979). Don't the girls' get prettier at closing time: A country and western application to psychology. *Personality and Social Psychology Bulletin, 5,* 122–125.

Penton-Voak, I. S., Perrett, D. I., Castles, D. L., Kobayashi, T., Burt, D. M., Murray, L. K., & Minamisawa, R. (1999). Menstrual cycle alters face preference. *Nature, 399,* 741–742.

Persico, N., & Postlewaite, A. (2004). The effect of adolescent experience on labor market outcomes: The case of height. *Journal of Political Economy, 112,* 1019–1053.

Pertschuk, M., Trisdorfer, A., & Allison, P. D. (1994). Men's bodies—the survey. *Psychology Today, 27,* 35–36, 39, 72.

Polhemus, T., & Proctor, L. (1978). *Fashion and anti-fashion: An anthropology of clothing and adornment.* London: Thames & Hudson.

Polivy, J., Garner, D. M., & Garfinkel, P. E. (1986). Causes and consequences of the current preference for thin female physiques. In C. P. Herman, M. P. Zanna, & E. T. Higgins (Eds.), *Physical appearance, stigma, and social behavior: The Ontario Symposium* (Vol. 3). Hillsdale, NJ: Erlbaum.

Porter, R. H., Cernoch, J. M., & Balogh, R. D. (1985). Odor signatures and kin recognition. *Physiology and Behavior, 34,* 445–448.

Porter, R. H., Cernoch, J. M., & McLaughlin, F. J. (1983). Maternal recognition of neonates through olfactory cues. *Physiology and Behavior, 30,* 151–154.

Porter, R. H., & Moore, J. D. (1981). Human kin recognition by olfactory cues. *Physiology and Behavior, 27,* 493–495.

Portnoy, E. J. (1993). The impact of body type on perceptions of attractiveness by older individuals. *Communication Reports, 6,* 101–108.

Preti, G., Wysocki, C. J., Barnhart, K. T., Sondheimer, S. J., & Leyden, J. J. (2003). Male axillary extracts contain hormones that affect pulsatile secretion of luteinizing hormone and mood in women recipients. *Biology of Reproduction, 68,* 2107–2113.

Ramsey, J. L., Langlois, J. H., Hoss, R. A., Rubenstein, A. J., & Griffin, A. M. (2004). Origins of a stereotype: Categorization of facial attractiveness by 6-month-old infants. *Developmental Science, 7,* 201–211.

Raymond, B., & Unger, R. (1972). The apparel oft proclaims the man. *Journal of Social Psychology, 87,* 75–82.

Reed, J. A. P. (1973). *Clothing: A symbolic indicator of the self.* Unpublished doctoral dissertation, Purdue University.

Reid, A., Lancuba, V., & Morrow, B. (1997). Clothing style and formation of first impressions. *Perceptual and Motor Skills, 84,* 237–238.

Reingen, P. H., & Kernan, J. B. (1993). Social perception and interpersonal influence: Some consequences of the physical attractiveness stereotype in a personal selling setting. *Journal of Consumer Psychology, 2,* 25–38.

Reis, H. T., Nezlek, J., & Wheeler, L. (1980). Physical attractiveness in social interaction. *Journal of Personality and Social Psychology, 38,* 604–617.

Reis, H. T., Wheeler, L., Spiegel, N., Kernis, M. H., Nezlek, J., & Perri, M. (1982). Physical attractiveness in social interaction: II. Why does appearance affect social experience? *Journal of Personality and Social Psychology, 43,* 979–996.

Rhodes, G., Harwood, K., Sakiko, Y., Nishitani, M., & McLean, I. (2002). The attractiveness of average faces: Cross-cultural evidence and possible biological basis (pp. 35–58). In G. Rhodes & L. A. Zebrowitz (Eds.), *Facial attractiveness.* Westport, CT: Ablex.

Rhodes, G., & Zebrowitz, L. A. (Eds.). (2002). *Facial attractiveness.* Westport, CT: Ablex.

Richardson, S. A., Goodman, N., Hastorf, A., & Dornbusch, S. (1961). Cultural uniformities in relation to physical disabilities. *American Sociological Review, 26,* 241–247.

Riggio, R. E., Widaman, K. F., Tucker, J. S., & Salinas, C. (1991). Beauty is more than skin deep:

Components of attractiveness. *Basic and Applied Psychology, 12,* 423–439.

Roach, K. D. (1997). Effects of graduate teaching assistant attire on student learning, misbehaviors, and ratings of instruction. *Communication Quarterly, 45,* 125–141.

Roach, M. E., & Eicher, J. B. (Eds.). (1965). *Dress, adornment, and the social order.* New York: Wiley.

Roberts, J. V., & Herman, C. P. (1986). The psychology of height: An empirical review. In C. P. Herman, M. P. Zanna, & E. T. Higgins (Eds.), *Physical appearance, stigma, and social behavior: The Ontario Symposium* (Vol. 3). Hillsdale, NJ: Erlbaum.

Roney, J. R., Hanson, K. N., Durante, K. M., and Maestripieri, D. (2006). Reading men's faces: Women's mate attractiveness judgments track men's testosterone and interest in infants. *Proceedings of the Royal Society B, 273,* 2169–2175.

Rosenfeld, L. B., & Plax, T. G. (1977). Clothing as communication. *Journal of Communication, 27,* 24–31.

Rosenthal, T. L., & White, G. M. (1972). On the importance of hair in students' clinical inferences. *Journal of Clinical Psychology, 28,* 43–47.

Rubenstein, A. J., Langlois, J. H., & Roggman, L. A. (2002). What makes a face attractive and why: The role of averageness in defining facial beauty (pp. 1–33). In G. Rhodes & L. A. Zebrowitz (Eds.), *Facial attractiveness.* Westport, CT: Ablex.

Rudofsky, B. (1971). *The unfashionable human body.* Garden City, NY: Doubleday.

Rump, E. E., & Delin, P. S. (1973). Differential accuracy in the status–height phenomenon and an experimenter effect. *Journal of Personality and Social Psychology, 28,* 343–347.

Russell, F. (1981). *The secret war.* Chicago: Time Life.

Russell, M. J. (1976). Human olfactory communication. *Nature, 260,* 520–522.

Ryan, M. S. (1966). *Clothing: A study in human behavior.* New York: Holt, Rinehart & Winston.

Ryckman, R. M., Robbins, M. A., Thornton, B., Kaczor, L. M., Gayton, S. L., & Anderson, C. V. (1991). Public self-consciousness and physique stereotyping. *Personality and Social Psychology Bulletin, 17,* 400–405.

Sandberg, D. E., Bukowski, W. M., Fung, C. M., & Noll, R. B. (2004). Height and social adjustment:

Are extremes a cause for concern and action? *Pediatrics, 114*, 744–750.

Sanders, C. (1989). *The body: The art and culture of tattooing.* Philadelphia: Temple University Press.

Savic, I., Berglund, H., & Lindström (2005), Brain response to putative pheromones in homosexual men. *Proceedings of the National Academy of Sciences, 102*, 7356–7361.

Secord, P. F., Dukes, W. F., & Bevan, W. W. (1954). Personalities in faces: I. An experiment in social perceiving. *Genetic Psychology Monographs, 49*, 231–279.

Seiter, J. S., & Dunn, D. (2000). Beauty and believability in sexual harassment cases: Does physical attractiveness affect perceptions of veracity and the likelihood of being harassed? *Communication Research Reports, 17*, 203–209.

Seligman, C., Brickman, J., & Koulack, D. (1977). Rape and physical attractiveness: Assigning responsibility to victims. *Journal of Personality, 45*, 554–563.

Shannon, M. L., & Stark, C. P. (2003). The influence of physical appearance on personnel selection. *Social Behavior and Personality, 31*, 613–624.

Sheldon, W. H. (1940). *The varieties of human physique.* New York: Harper & Row.

Sheldon, W. H. (1942). *The varieties of temperament.* New York: Harper & Row.

Sheldon, W. H. (1954). *Atlas of man: A guide for somatotyping the adult male at all ages.* New York: Harper & Row.

Shontz, F. C. (1969). *Perceptual and cognitive aspects of body experience.* New York: Academic Press.

Sigall, H., & Landy, D. (1973). Radiating beauty: Effects of having a physically attractive partner on person perception. *Journal of Personality and Social Psychology, 26*, 218–223.

Sigall, H., & Ostrove, N. (1975). Beautiful but dangerous: Effects of offender attractiveness and nature of the crime of juridic judgment. *Journal of Personality and Social Psychology, 31*, 410–414.

Singer, J. E. (1964). The use of manipulative strategies: Machiavellianism and attractiveness. *Sociometry, 27*, 128–151.

Singh, D. (1993). Adaptive significance of female physical attractiveness: Role of waist-to-hip ratio. *Journal of Personality and Social Psychology, 65*, 293–307.

Singh, D. (1995). Female judgment of male attractiveness and desirability for relationships: Role of waist-to-hip ratio and financial status. *Journal of Personality and Social Psychology, 69*, 1089–1101.

Slater, A., Von der Schulennurg, C., Brown, E., Badenoch, M., Butterworth, G., Parsons, S., & Samuels, C. (1998). Newborn infants prefer attractive faces. *Infant Behavior and Development, 21*, 345–354.

Smith, K., & Sines, J. O. (1960). Demonstration of a peculiar odor in the sweat of schizophrenic patients. *Archives of General Psychiatry, 2*, 184–188.

Sobal, J., & Stunkard, A. J. (1989). Socioeconomic status and obesity: A review of the literature. *Psychological Bulletin, 105*, 260–275.

Solender, E. K., & Solender, E. (1976). Minimizing the effect of the unattractive client on the jury: A study of the interaction of physical appearance with assertions and self-experience references. *Human Rights, 5*, 201–214.

Solomon, M. R. (Ed.). (1985). *The psychology of fashion.* New York: Lexington.

Stabler, B., Whitt, K., Moreault, D., D'Ercole, A., & Underwood, L. (1980). Social judgments by children of short stature. *Psychological Reports, 46*, 743–746.

Staffieri, J. R. (1972). Body build and behavioral expectancies in young females. *Developmental Psychology, 6*, 125–127.

Stern, K., & McClintock, M. K. (1998). Regulation of ovulation by human pheromones. *Nature, 392*, 177–179.

Stewart, J. E. (1980). Defendant's attractiveness as a factor in the outcome of criminal trials: An observational study. *Journal of Applied Social Psychology, 10*, 348–361.

Stewart, R. A., Tufton, S. J., & Steel, R. E. (1973). Stereotyping and personality: Sex differences in perception of female physiques. *Perceptual and Motor Skills, 36*, 811–814.

Streeter, S. A., & McBurney, D. H. (2003). Waist–hip ratio and attractiveness: New evidence and a critique of a "critical test." *Evolution and Human Behavior, 24*, 88–98.

Stroebe, W., Insko, C. A., Thompson, V. D., & Layton, B. D. (1971). Effects of physical attractiveness, attitudes similarity, and sex on various aspects of interpersonal attraction. *Journal of Personality and Social Psychology, 79*, 79–91.

Strongman, K. T., & Hart, C. J. (1968). Stereotyped reactions to body build. *Psychological Reports, 23,* 1175–1178.

Suedfeld, P., Bochner, S., & Matas, C. (1971). Petitioner's attire and petition signing by peace demonstrators: A field experiment. *Journal of Applied Social Psychology, 1,* 278–283.

Tassinary, L. G., & Hansen, K. A. (1998). A critical test of the waist-to-hip ratio hypothesis of female physical attractiveness. *Psychological Science, 9,* 150–155.

Tavris, C. (1977). Men and women report their views on masculinity. *Psychology Today, 10,* 34–42, 82.

Thornhill, R., & Gangestad, S. W. (1993). Human facial beauty: Averageness, symmetry, and parasite resistance. *Human Nature, 4,* 237–269.

Timmerman, K., & Hewitt, J. (1980). Examining the halo effect of physical attractiveness. *Perceptual and Motor Skills, 51,* 607–612.

Udry, J. R., & Eckland, B. K. (1984). Benefits of being attractive: Differential payoffs for men and women. *Psychological Reports, 54,* 47–56.

Urbaniak, G. C., & Kilmann, P. R. (2003). Physical attractiveness and the "nice guy paradox": Do nice guys really finish last? *Sex Roles, 49,* 413–426.

Walker, R. N. (1963). Body build and behavior in young children: II. Body build and parents' ratings. *Child Development, 34,* 1–23.

Wallace, P. (1977). Individual discrimination of human by odor. *Physiology and Behavior, 19,* 577–579.

Walster, E., Aronson, V., Abrahams, D., & Rottmann, L. (1966). Importance of physical attractiveness in dating behavior. *Journal of Personality and Social Psychology, 4,* 508–516.

Watson, B. (1975, May 16). Cons get cosmetic surgery. *Lafayette Journal and Courier,* p. A-8.

Wedekind, C., & Füri, S. (1997). Body odour preferences in men and women: Do they aim for specific MHC combinations or simply heterozygosity? *Proceedings, Biological Sciences, 264,* 1471–1479.

Wedekind, C., Seebeck, T., Bettens, F., & Paepke, A. J. (1995). MHC-dependent mate preferences in humans. *Proceedings, Biological Sciences, 260,* 245–249.

Weiten, W. (1980). The attraction–leniency effect in jury research: An examination of external validity. *Journal of Applied Social Psychology, 10,* 340–347.

Wells, W., & Siegel, B. (1961). Stereotyped somatotypes. *Psychological Reports, 8,* 77–78.

White, G. L. (1980). Physical attractiveness and courtship progress. *Journal of Personality and Social Psychology, 39,* 660–668.

White, S. E. (1995). A content analytic technique for measuring the sexiness of women's business attire in media presentations. *Communication Research Reports, 12,* 178–185.

Widgery, R. N. (1974). Sex of receiver and physical attractiveness of source as determinants of initial credibility perceptions. *Western Speech, 38,* 13–17.

Wiener, H. (1966). External chemical messengers: I. Emission and reception in man. *New York State Journal of Medicine, 66,* 3153.

Wiggins, J. S., Wiggins, N., & Conger, J. C. (1968). Correlates of heterosexual somatic preference. *Journal of Personality and Social Psychology, 10,* 82–90.

Wiggins, N., & Wiggins, J. S. (1969). A topological analysis of male preferences for female body types. *Multivariate Behavioral Research, 4,* 89–102.

Wilson, P. R. (1968). Perceptual distortion of height as a function of ascribed academic status. *Journal of Social Psychology, 10,* 97–102.

Wolf, N. (1991). *The beauty myth.* New York: Morrow.

Wuensch, K. L., & Moore, C. H. (2004). Effects of physical attractiveness on evaluations of a male employee's allegation of sexual harassment by his female employer. *Journal of Social Psychology, 144,* 207–217.

Yates, J., & Taylor, J. (1978). Stereotypes for somatotypes: Shared beliefs about Sheldon's physiques. *Psychological Reports, 43,* 777–778.

Young, M. (1999). Dressed to commune, dressed to kill: Changing police imagery in England and Wales. In K. K. P. Johnson and S. J. Lennon (Eds.), *Appearance and power.* New York: Oxford University Press.

Yu, D. W., & Shepard, G. H., Jr. (1998). Is beauty in the eye of the beholder? *Nature, 396,* 321–322.

Zebrowitz, L. A. (1997). *Reading faces.* Boulder, CO: Westview Press.

Zebrowitz, L. A., & Rhodes, G. (2004). Sensitivity to "bad genes" and the anomalous face overgeneralization effect: Cue validity, cue utilization, and accuracy in judging intelligence and health. *Journal of Nonverbal Behavior, 28,* 167–185.

The Communicators' Behavior

Most of our nonverbal behavior involves change or movement. We exhibit different gestures, postures, and body movements during an encounter; sometimes we touch others, and sometimes we do not. Our face, eyes, and voice also are displayed in various patterns. Part Four examines these behaviors individually, but in everyday conversation, these signals work in concert with one another to communicate various messages. The ways various nonverbal signals work together is the subject of Part Five.

We respond to gestures with an extreme alertness and, one might say, in accordance with an elaborate and secret code that is written nowhere, known by none, and understood by all.

—Edward Sapir

THE EFFECTS OF GESTURE AND POSTURE ON HUMAN COMMUNICATION

CHAPTER 7

Sapir's view, quoted above, aptly characterized the prevailing view of gestures during the first part of the 20th century. If he were alive today, his assessment would no doubt be somewhat different. Spoken language and gestures are commonly acknowledged as building blocks of human interaction, both in informal conversation as well as in more formal public discourse. But unlike language, gestures received relatively little scholarly attention until the last part of the 20th century. Kendon (1981a) identified only six scholarly books on gesture published between 1900 and 1979 in the English language. Now, however, gestures are carefully scrutinized by scholars from around the world, and the academic journal *Gesture*, specifically devoted to gesture research, was launched in 2001. As a result, our knowledge of how people use and respond to gestures has greatly increased.

Even though gestures are the primary focus of this chapter, it should be noted that the way people walk and the posture of their bodies may also play an important role in communicating. Several studies have shown that various emotions such as sadness, anger, and happiness can be accurately identified by a person's gait (Janssen Schöllhorn, Lubienetzki, Fölling, Kokenge & Davids, 2008; Montepare, Goldstein, & Clausen, 1987; Montepare & Zebrowitz-McArthur, 1988; Montepare & Zebrowitz, 1993). The amount of arm swing, stride length, heavy-footedness, and walking speed play a central role in these perceptions. We also derive information from a person's posture. For example, Hadjikhani and de Gelder (2003) found that perceptions of fear communicated solely by a person's body, with the expressor's facial features blurred, activated the same areas of a perceiver's brain that are activated when responding to facial expressions of emotion.

Typically, gestures are thought of as arm and hand movements, but head gestures are also well known. In fact, some head gestures seem to transcend culture and language. In some studies, Arabic, Bulgarian, Korean, and African-American speakers all used lateral head movements to accompany expressions of inclusivity, changed their head position for each item on a list, oriented their head toward a specific location when referring to absent or abstract entities, and used head nods to elicit active listening nods from their listeners (McClave, Kim, Tamer, & Mileff, 2007; McClave, 2000). Normally gestures are produced without bodily touch, but touching does occur. For example, a pointing gesture may touch the speaker's own body or that of the listener. The movements involved while actually performing tasks such as grooming, smoking, eating, drawing, or hammering a nail are not considered gestures, but arm and hand movements that allude to and represent the performance of such behaviors are definitely considered gestures. In fact, people whose daily work involves a variety of manual manipulations, like the work of a car mechanic, may develop a gestural repertoire that emanates from this work (Streeck, 2002).

Gestures perform many functions. They may replace speech during dialogue, or when speech is not used at all. They may regulate the flow and rhythm of interaction, maintain attention, add emphasis or clarity to speech, help characterize and make memorable the content of speech, act as forecasters of forthcoming speech, and help speakers access and formulate speech.

Many types of gestures are commonly employed in everyday interaction, and these gestures have been categorized in many ways (McNeill, 2000; Morris, 1977, 1994; Kendon, 2004). This chapter uses a classification system based on the extent to which a gesture is dependent on speech for its meaning. This is a useful distinction, and we can learn a lot about gestures by classifying them as either *speech-independent* or *speech-dependent*. At the same time, however, it is also important to recognize the difficulties in neatly categorizing a behavior which, on the surface, may seem relatively uncomplicated. Take, for example, the head shake (Kendon, 2002). Sometimes we use the head shake as a speech-independent gesture meaning "no," although a side-to-side head wobble in parts of India and Bulgaria means just the opposite. And while a "no" meaning can be communicated without speech, sometimes people will say "no" during the shake. The meaning of the shake has a greater dependence on the accompanying speech when it is used to signal disapproval or doubt, which may occur while saying, "Well, I guess I could talk to him…." In addition, the head shake also accompanies statements to underscore intensity or impossibility, as in "You just wouldn't believe how beautiful she was." The head shake, like all the gestures discussed in this chapter, can be used and interpreted in different ways, depending on the way it is enacted and the context in which it occurs. With this in mind, let us examine those gestures that are less dependent on speech for their meaning.

SPEECH-INDEPENDENT GESTURES

Speech-independent gestures are also known as *emblems* (Ekman, 1976, 1977) or *autonomous gestures* (Kendon, 1984, 1989). They are nonverbal acts that have a direct verbal translation or dictionary definition, usually consisting of a word or two or a phrase. There is high agreement among members of a culture or subculture on the verbal translation of these signals. These gestures are the least dependent on speech for their meaning and most commonly occur as a single gesture. The "ring gesture" in Figure 7-1 is an example of a speech-independent gesture found in several cultures.

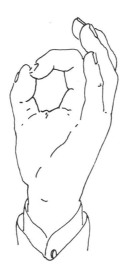

FIGURE 7-1

The ring gesture signifies "A-okay" or "good" in the United States as a speech-independent gesture. It may stand for "zero" or "worthless" in other cultural contexts.

Children are able to decode some of these speech-independent gestures by the time they are 3 years old, and this ability increases dramatically by age 5 (Kumin & Lazar, 1974; Michael & Willis, 1968, 1969). In one study, 4-year-olds of both sexes accurately decoded the emblems for "yes," "no," "come here," "quiet," "good-bye," "two," "I won't listen," "blowing a kiss," "I'm going to sleep," and "I won't do it." None of the 4-year-olds was able to accurately decode "crazy." Generally, children at this age understand and decode accurately more speech-independent gestures than they actually use in their own interactions. However, with prompting and support by caregivers, babies who have not learned to talk can effectively use between 10 and 60 signs to communicate (Acredolo & Goodwyn, 1996).

Adult awareness of speech-independent gestures is about the same as that of word choice. It is a behavior we are usually very conscious of enacting. These gestures often are produced with the hand, but not exclusively. A nose wrinkle may say "I'm disgusted!" or "Phew! It stinks!" To say "I don't know" or "I'm helpless" or "I'm uncertain," we might turn both palms up, shrug the shoulders, or do both simultaneously. Ekman believes that facial emblems differ from facial expressions of emotion by being more stylized and being presented for a longer or shorter duration than the emotional expression. When people talk about their experiences, they may portray certain feelings emblematically by selecting and emphasizing a single feature of a multifeatured facial expression of emotion, for example, smiling to indicate happiness or mechanically dropping the jaw or dramatically raising the eyebrows to indicate surprise.

In some cultures, speech-independent gestures are strung together to form a sequential message, but this is unusual in the United States. Although it could happen if you were on the phone when a visitor enters your office, and you needed to indicate "wait a minute," "come in," and "sit down" in succession. Sometimes an entire system of speech-independent gestures develops, such as with underwater divers, umpires, and television directors. Even though these gestures form a system of signals related to performing a specific task, such systems can grow beyond the boundaries of those tasks. In the sawmills of British Columbia, for example, the noise level made spoken communication very difficult. A system of task-related gestures developed that eventually came to include messages not associated with the tasks of the sawmill (Meissner & Philpott, 1975). Gesture systems not limited to a specific task are known as *sign languages*. Sign language is commonly thought of as a form of communication for the hearing impaired, but sign languages also develop in other contexts. Examples include religious orders in which vows of silence are taken and social situations in which some participants are forbidden to speak, such as has been reported for Armenian wives in the presence of their husbands (Kendon, 1983).

Speech-independent gestures may be used when verbal channels are blocked or fail, but they also are used during verbal interaction. A person may be telling the story of another person's strange behavior and may conclude by making a gesture that communicates "he's crazy." In this case, the circular gesture at the side of the head is a substitute for the statement. This gesture also could be used to complete an utterance: "If you ask me, I think..." In this case, the verbalizations are redundant and unnecessary for understanding the message being communicated. In this example, the speech-independent gesture occurred at the end of a speaker's turn, but others may occur at the beginning. Ekman's study of the "shrug" emblem finds that it occurs most often at the beginning of a speaker's turn (see Figure 7-2).

In an interview observed by Ekman, he noted an emblem that was used for a long time during the interaction and served as the interviewee's commentary on the episode. This "emblematic slip," analogous to a slip of the tongue, occurred when a woman was subjected to a stressful interview by a person whose status kept her from freely expressing her dislike. The woman, unknown to herself or the interviewer, displayed "the finger" on one hand as it rested on the arm of the chair. Listeners may also use speech-independent gestures to comment on or qualify what the speaker is saying. "Yes" and "no" gestures are common listener responses during another's speech.

Thus, even though speech-independent gestures can communicate messages without attendant speech, their meanings are still influenced by context. Giving someone the finger can be humorous or insulting, depending on who performs it, who the target is, and what other behaviors accompany it. Facial expressions and eye movement accompanying speech-independent gestures are likely to expand the range of possible meanings associated with a hand gesture. And it is always possible that the meaning associated with a gesture in the absence of speech will be modified if it is accompanied by speech, including those occasions when the accompanying speech is seemingly redundant. Some of these emblematic gestures are specifically adapted to particular subgroups within a given culture. In the United States, for example, the finger-wag gesture indicating "no-no" is used primarily when adults are addressing children; the "shame on you" gesture seems limited to usage by children (see Figure 7-3).

FIGURE 7-2

The shrug gesture.

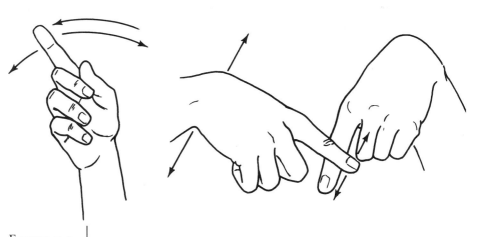

FIGURE 7-3

Finger emblems used in the United States for "no" (left) and "shame on you" (right).

FIGURE 7-4

The thumbs-up gesture by 2008 Presidential candidate John McCain.

Sherzer's (1974) detailed work on the pointed-lip gesture used by the San Blas Cuna of Panama and the thumbs-up gesture used by urban Brazilians illustrates how gestures may have a general meaning that is modified by context. For example, the thumbs-up gesture has a general meaning of "good" or "positive" (see Figure 7-4). Context, however, expands the range of meanings. It can be used to indicate understanding the point of what someone said or did; to acknowledge a favor granted; to greet someone; to indicate knowledge of the next move in an interactional sequence and who is going to perform it; to request permission to carry out an action, as when a customer signals a waiter about the availability of a table; and as a sexual insult.

Sometimes the context does not affect the meaning so much as the slight changes in the way the gesture is performed. When the forefinger is extended, with the rest of the hand in a fist, and is held motionless about 12 inches in front of one's chest, the meaning is "wait a minute." When the finger repeatedly moves up and down, the meaning shifts to one of emphasis or reprimand. When the same finger and hand are put perpendicularly in front of the lips, it means "be quiet."

There are published lists of emblematic gestures for cultures around the world (Armstrong & Wagner, 2003; Axtell, 1991; Barakat, 1973; Creider, 1977; Johnson, Ekman, & Friesen, 1975; Morris, Collett, Marsh, & O'Shaughnessy, 1979; Poggi, 2002; Saitz & Cervenka, 1972; Sparhawk, 1978; Trupin, 1976; Wylie, 1977). Kendon's (1981b) analysis of over 800 emblematic gestures contained in some of these lists revealed three broad categories of meaning that accounted for 80 percent of the speech-independent gestures observed in the United States, Colombia, France, southern Italy, and Kenya and 66 percent of those found in Iran. These categories were 1) *interpersonal control*, 2) *announcement of one's current state or condition*, and 3) *an evaluative response to the actions or appearance of another*. Ekman's studies of five cultures indicate that each has emblematic gestures for greeting and departing, replying, directing locomotion (all forms of interpersonal control), insulting or evaluating another's actions or appearance, referring to a person's physical and affective state, or announcing a person's current condition or state. Some cultures have many emblems in a particular category, such as for evaluations of another's behavior, whereas the emblems in another culture may emphasize other messages.

As yet, no speech-independent gestures have been found that are made the same and have the same meaning in every culture studied. Future research may identify some, however. The most likely candidates are gestures having to do with affirmation and negation, stopping, not knowing, and sleeping, eating, and drinking (i.e., functions all human beings share).

Far more common are examples of gestures of similar form that differ in meaning from culture to culture. From 1877 through 1878, Bulgaria and Russia combined forces to fight Turkey. The alliance discovered a real problem in that the Russian way of saying "no" was to shake the head from side to side, but a very similar Bulgarian gesture, a head sway or wobble, meant "yes" (Jacobson, 1972). The ring gesture, with the thumb and forefinger touching to make a circle (see Figure 7-1), indicates "you're worth zero" in France and Belgium; "money" in Japan; "asshole" in parts of southern Italy; and in Greece and Turkey, it is an insulting or vulgar sexual invitation. Of course, to many U.S. residents, it means "A-okay." Things certainly would not be "A-okay" if the ring gesture was used in cultures that attach other meanings to it.

The thumbs-up gesture pictured in Figure 7-4 is usually decoded as positive, meaning "good" or "okay" in the United States, but in the Middle East, it is an obscene gesture. The thumb inserted between the index and middle finger, the "fig" gesture, is an invitation to have sex in Germany, Holland, and Denmark but is a wish for good luck or protection in Portugal and Brazil (see Figure 7-5). During World War II, Winston Churchill made the "V for victory" gesture world famous, and it continues to mean "victory" in some cultures. But if the palm is facing toward the performer, it is a sexual insult in Great Britain—a meaning former Prime Minister Margaret Thatcher learned the hard way, when she essentially said

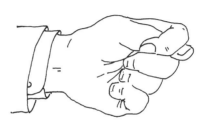

FIGURE 7-5

The "fig" gesture.

FIGURE 7-6

(a) "V" gesture used as an insult in Britain and (b) illustrated by Winston Churchill. (c) Richard Nixon makes the "V for victory" gesture at the 1968 Republican Convention in Miami. (d) People at an anti-Persian Gulf War demonstration in Washington, D.C., using the "V" gesture to signify "peace."

d

FIGURE 7-6 | (continued)

"screw you" to a crowd of people, thinking she was giving a sign meaning victory. In the United States, the British meaning of sexual insult is not associated with the "V" sign facing inward, it simply means "two." Nor is there any distinction the other way—with the palm facing outward—between the "V" for victory and the "V" for peace, a meaning that gained popularity during the anti–Vietnam War protests of the 1960s.

The vertical horn sign pictured in Figure 7-7 is normally decoded "cuckold" in Portugal, Spain, Italy, and places in Central and South America. Students from cultures in which this gesture indicates "your wife has been unfaithful to you, and you are either too stupid to know it or not man enough to satisfy her" would indeed be surprised if they were to attend the University of Texas. Here, and throughout Texas, the horn sign is used to show identification with the university and represents school spirit. It is modeled after longhorn cattle and literally represents the University of Texas Longhorns. Consider the reaction of people who associate the sign with "cuckold" viewing a University of Texas football game with 85,000 fans making the sign vigorously, repeatedly, and in unison! Another sign that is similar, but has the thumb thrust out instead of tucked in, is decoded by many people around the world as "I love you." The origin of this sign is in the American Sign Language (ASL) finger spelling used by deaf communicators.

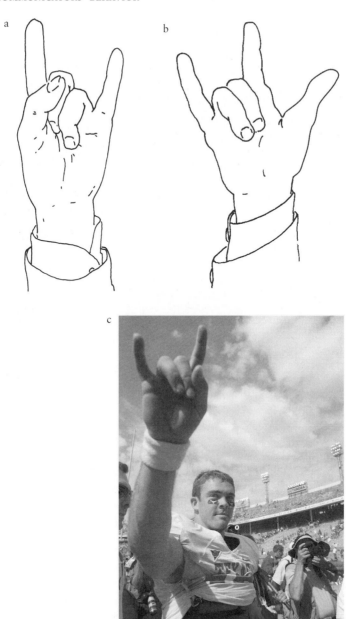

FIGURE 7-7

(a) The vertical horn gesture. (b) The "I love you" sign. (c) University of Texas football player, Colt McCoy, gives the school's "Hook 'em Horns" gesture. (d) Miss America 1995, Heather Whitestore, a former Miss Alabama, walks down the runway and signs "I love you" to the crowd after winning the 74th annual pageant in Atlantic City. (e) The double horn gesture in Naples means "cuckolded."

d

e

FIGURE 7-7 | *(continued)*

Many autonomous gestures have no equivalent in other cultures. In France, for example, one can signal drunkenness by making a fist around the nose and twisting. Many messages have different gestural forms from culture to culture. Notice how the gestures for suicide in Figure 7-8 reflect the most common methods of suicide in each culture. The number of speech-independent gestures used within a culture may vary considerably, from fewer than 100 in the United States to more than 250 identified with Israeli students.

One of the problems in comparing studies of speech-independent gestures across cultures is the lack of a uniform method for identifying them. Johnson, Ekman, and Friesen's study (1975) of American emblematic gestures proposes a systematic procedure that other researchers may want to use. The authors ask members of a particular group or culture to produce emblems associated with a list of verbal statements and phrases. They report that after about 10 or 15 informants have been tested, a great majority of the emblems have been identified. To qualify as a "verified" emblem, at least 70 percent of the encoders must perform the action in a similar way. The emblems similarly encoded are then presented to a group of decoders, who are asked to identify the meaning of the gestures and the extent to which they reflect natural usage in everyday conversation. Gestures used primarily for games like charades normally are not considered "natural."

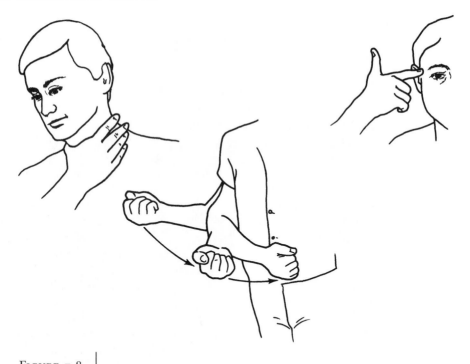

FIGURE 7-8

Cultural variations in suicide gestures: TOP LEFT: the South Fore, Papua New Guinea; BOTTOM: Japan; TOP RIGHT: the United States.

Inventions and performances that require speech are also eliminated. At least 70 percent of the decoders also have to match the encoder's meaning and judge the gesture to be used naturally in everyday communication situations. The index finger pointed at the head can mean "smart" or "stupid" depending on context, but if 70 percent of those in a given community say it means "stupid" without accompanying contextual information, then this is considered a verified emblem for "stupid" among this group. It does not, however, prevent context from changing the meaning.

SPEECH-RELATED GESTURES

Speech-related gestures, sometimes called *illustrators*, are directly tied to or accompany speech. The meanings and functions of these gestures are revealed as we examine how they relate to the attendant spoken language. Attempts to classify the various types of speech-related gestures have used different terminology (Efron, 1941/1972; Ekman, 1977; Kendon, 1989; McNeill, 1992, 2000; Streeck & Knapp, 1992), but four common types emerge:

1. Gestures related to the speaker's referent, concrete or abstract
2. Gestures indicating the speaker's relationship to the referent

3.   Gestures that act as visual punctuation for the speaker's discourse
4.   Gestures that assist in the regulation and organization of the spoken dialogue between two interactants

REFERENT-RELATED GESTURES

As we talk, we use gestures to characterize the content of our speech. Sometimes these movements depict fairly concrete referents, and sometimes vague, abstract ideas are the referent for gestural depiction.

Pointing movements, for instance, can help indicate a specific person, place, or thing being discussed. The referent may be in the immediate conversational environment or may be more distant, as is the case when you say, "And where did you come from before that?" while pointing your finger in the direction of the referred-to place. Gestures that draw the referent's shape or movement, and gestures that depict spatial relationships, can be used to help a listener visualize features associated with concrete referents. When you say, "I had to bend the branch way back" or "she was eating her food like an animal" while illustrating how these events occurred, the gesture bears a close relationship to the concrete semantic content of your speech. When referent-related gestures outline the referent by drawing a picture in space, such as making an hourglass figure to signify a shapely woman, it may be asked whether this is truly speech-related. The test for determining whether such a picture may be speech independent is if 70 percent of the members of the usage community respond with "shapely woman" when shown the gesture portrayal without any speech context.

More abstract referents are characterized when we sketch the path or direction of an idea in the air, when we make a series of circular movements with the hand or arm to suggest we mean more than the specific words used, and when we use expansion and contraction gestures such as those of an accordion player to indicate the breadth of the subject being discussed. Sometimes we represent abstract content via gestural metaphors. For example, cup-shaped gestures in the following sample of discourse (McNeill, 1985) represent containers of what could be supposed. When they spread apart, they seem to convey the idea that anything is possible, and their sudden disappearance suggests that what might have been did not happen:

"Even though one might *[both hands form cups and spread wide apart]* have supposed *[cups vanish abruptly]* …"

GESTURES INDICATING A SPEAKER'S RELATIONSHIP TO THE REFERENT

These gestures comment on the speaker's orientation to the referent rather than characterizing the nature of the thing being talked about. The positioning of the palms can show quite different orientations toward one's own message (see Figure 7-9). For example, palms up show more uncertainty ("I think" or "I'm not sure"), palms down show certainty ("clearly" or "absolutely"), palms out and facing the listener show assertion ("Let me say this" or "Calm down"), and palms facing the speaker allude to embracing a concept ("I've got this great idea …"). Palm positions can have other

FIGURE 7-9

Palm gestures.

speech-related associations, such as a speaker's palms-up gesture when pleading, begging, or even anticipating closeness in greetings.

Oscillating hand movements suggest a speaker is unsure or could go either way. Charles de Gaulle, former president of France, was noted for his grasping gesture, which many felt signified his desire to control the subject under discussion (see Figure 7-10).

FIGURE 7-10

Former French President Charles de Gaulle's characteristic gesture, perceived by many as "grasping for control of an idea."

FIGURE 7-11

Punctuation gestures.

PUNCTUATION GESTURES

Punctuation gestures accent, emphasize, and organize important segments of the discourse. Such a segment may be a single word or a larger utterance unit, such as a summary or a new theme. When these gestures are used to emphasize a particular word or phrase, they often coincide with the primary voice stress. Punctuation gestures can also organize the stream of speech into units. When we speak of a series of things, we may communicate discreteness by rhythmic chopping hand gestures, for example, "We must consider A (gesture), B (gesture), and C (gesture)." Sometimes a single chopping gesture after C indicates C will be considered separately, or it may mean that A, B, and C will be considered as a group. A slight downward movement of the head may accompany the hand gestures. Pounding the hand or fist in the air or on another object also acts as a device for adding emphasis and visually underlining a particular point being made (see Figure 7-11).

Punctuation can, of course, be accomplished with body movements other than the hands. The "eye flash" (not the "eye*brow* flash" discussed in Chapters 2 and 10) is one such display (Bull & Connelly, 1985; Walker & Trimboli, 1983). The momentary widening of a speaker's eyelids, without involving the eyebrows, has been found to occur most often in conjunction with spoken adjectives and is used for emphasis.

INTERACTIVE GESTURES

Thus far, the gesture categories discussed have focused on the content of the speaker's monologue. *Interactive gestures* acknowledge the other interactant relative to the speaker and help regulate and organize the dialogue itself. Because they are directed at the ongoing involvement and shared roles of the interactants, these gestures occur only in the presence of others. The main function of interactive gestures, then, is to include the interaction partner in the dialogue. This is usually done through some form of pointing gesture in the partner's direction. Such gestures probably constitute about 10 to 20 percent of the gestures observed in conversation.

TABLE 7-1 | FUNCTIONS OF INTERACTIVE GESTURES

1. **Delivery Gestures** As a group, these gestures refer to the delivery of information by the speaker to the addressee.

   General delivery gestures mark the standard relation of speaker to addressee; the speaker "hands over" to the addressee new information relevant to his or her main point. A verbal paraphrase is often "Here's my point."

   Shared information gestures mark material that the addressee probably already knows—information that is part of their common ground (Clark & Brennan, 1991). They mean, essentially, "As you know."

   Digression gestures mark information that should be treated by the addressee as an aside from the main point. Analogous to "By the way" or "Back to the main point."

   Elliptical gestures mark information that the addressee should elaborate for himself or herself; the speaker will not provide further details. Analogous to "or whatever."

2. **Citing Gestures** As a group, these gestures refer to a previous contribution by the addressee.

   General citing indicates "as you said earlier," that is, that the point the speaker is now making had been contributed by the addressee.

   Acknowledgment of the addressee's response indicates that the speaker saw or heard that the addressee understood what had been said. Paraphrased, "I see that you understood me."

3. **Seeking Gestures** As a group, these gestures aim to elicit a specific response from the addressee.

   Seeking help requests a word or phrase that the speaker cannot find at the moment. A verbal paraphrase would be "Can you give me the word for …?"

   Seeking agreement asks whether the addressee agrees or disagrees with the point being made. Analogous to "Do you agree?"

   Seeking following asks whether the addressee understands what is being said. Verbal equivalents include "you know?" or "eh?" at the end of a phrase.

4. **Turn Gestures** As a group, these gestures refer to issues around the speaking turn.

   Giving turn hands it over to the other person. As if to say, "Your turn."

   Taking turn accepts the turn from the other person. Paraphrased as "OK, I'll take over."

   Turn open indicates that it is anyone's turn, as if to say "Who's going to talk next?"

Source: From Bavelas, *Research on Language and Social Interaction* 27(3): 213, 1994. Reprinted with permission of Lawrence Erlbaum Associates, Inc.

Bavelas (1994) and her colleagues (Bavelas, Chovil, Lawrie, & Wade, 1992; Bavelas, Chovil, Coates, & Roe 1995) have identified four primary functions served by these gestures:

1. Delivering information
2. Citing a previous contribution by your partner
3. Seeking to solicit a specific response from your partner
4. Referring to issues associated with the exchange of speaking turns

These functions, and certain variations associated with them, are identified in Table 7-1 and illustrated in Figure 7-12. Others have found that the "thinking face" facial

a. General delivery: "Here's my point."

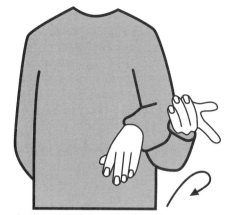

b. Citing: "As you said earlier . . ."

c. Seeking help: "What's the word . . . ?"

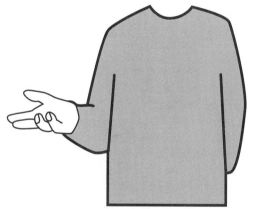

d. Giving turn: "You go ahead."

FIGURE 7-12

Interactive gestures.

gesture also elicits audience coparticipation in word searches and thereby serves the overall inclusion function. The Goodwins (1986) have pointed out that self-touching contributes to a state of conversational disengagement, the opposite of inclusion.

Although the preceding fourfold classification of speech-related gestures is useful for understanding how gestures and speech work together, some gestures may not be limited to a single function. For example, a speaker's relationship with the referent may be highly intense. Some of the gestural displays illuminating this relationship, however, may also emphasize or punctuate certain specific message units. Nevertheless, we must recognize that different types of speech-related gestures exist that may serve different functions for the parties involved. Efron's (1941/1972) cross-cultural comparison shows how helpful gestural distinctions can be. He found that as southern Italians talked, they made extensive use of gestures that had a close resemblance to their referent (e.g., pictorial), whereas eastern European Jews made very little use of such gestures. It seems reasonable that different cultures value different kinds of information, and gestures vary accordingly. Even the number of gestures in all categories may vary from culture to culture.

GESTURE FREQUENCY

The frequency of gesturing can be influenced by several key factors.

1. We would expect to find more gestures in face-to-face communication and when the speaker expects the recipient will see his or her message (Alibali & Don, 2001; Bavelas, Kenwood, Johnson, & Phillips, 2002; Cohen, 1977; Cohen & Harrison, 1973). We do, of course, use some gestures when our listeners cannot see us, for example, when talking on the telephone (see Figure 7-13). Continued communication without visible contact, however, may reduce the number of gestures used. It is curious that we use any gestures when our audience cannot see them. It may be habit, but because some

FIGURE 7-13

Gesture made while speaking on the telephone.

gestures are knowingly used to help communicate ideas, we may continue to use them to maximize the effectiveness of the only channel being used—the voice. In this sense, gestures act as a priming mechanism that activates the entire communicative system and thereby gets the most out of the vocal signals.

2. Gestures are also likely to increase when a speaker is enthusiastic and involved in the topic being discussed.

3. We would expect speakers concerned about their listeners' comprehension of their messages to use more gestures, too—especially in difficult or complex communicative situations, as when the listener is perceived as not paying attention, is not comprehending, or the speaker cannot find the right words to express an idea (Bavelas et al., 2002; Goldin-Meadow, 2003; Holler & Beattie, 2003). Even though exposure to gestures that accompany speech may often facilitate more accurate decoding on the part of the listener, there are some occasions when the contribution is negligible (Krauss, Dushay, Chen, & Rauscher, 1995).

4. Speakers trying to dominate conversations would be expected to use more speech-related gestures.

5. Speech content also plays a role in the number of gestures used. When answering questions about manual activities—such as "Explain how to change a car or bicycle tire," or "Explain how to wrap a box for a present"—we would expect more gestures than when answering questions about visual or abstract images (Feyereisen & Havard, 1999).

6. A communicator's cognitive abilities can affect gesture production. In one study, the rate of gesturing by speakers with a combination of low phonemic fluency and high spatial skill was especially high (Hostetter & Alibali, 2007).

As we note in the next section, speech and gesture are intimately linked, and it would be hard for anyone to abstain completely from gesturing while speaking for very long. Even if it were possible, it would be ill advised, because gestures play an important role in communicating. An experiment reported in a 1931 Soviet publication asked subjects to talk while inhibiting all gestures of the head, hands, face, and body. It is reported that no one was able to carry out the instructions completely, and "the speech...lost its intonation, stress and expressiveness; even the very selection of words needed for the expression of content became labored; there was a jerkiness to the speech, and a reduction of the number of words used" (Dobrogaev, 1931). Without gestures, speakers also would have to increase the number of phrases and words used to describe spatial relations and would probably pause more often (Graham & Heywood, 1976). Rimé (1982) found speakers' fluency to be adversely affected when their gestures were restricted. Furthermore, gesturing helped children learn a new concept and recall information they had previously learned (Cook, Mitchell, & Goldin-Meadow, 2008; Stevanoni & Salmon, 2005). Listeners are also likely to experience a serious loss, because gestures, like speech, are listener-adapted (Beattie & Shovelton, 2006; de Ruiter, 2007). For example, when speakers talk to others who have experienced the event the speaker is talking about, the speaker's gestures are smaller and less precise than when the same event is communicated to people who have not experienced the event (Gerwing & Bavelas, 2004). Since gestures are listener-adapted, it is no surprise that they often facilitate comprehension and help listeners access linguistic cues in their memory (Berger & Popelka, 1971; Church, Garber, & Rogalski, 2007; Rogers, 1978; Woodall & Folger, 1981). Actually, a more accurate statement is that gestures synchronized with and supporting the vocal/verbal stream increase comprehension. This is accomplished through the functions we have outlined: by vivifying ideas, by intensifying points, by maintaining listener attention and focus, and by marking the organizational structure of the discourse. Gestures out of synchrony with the vocal/verbal stream are distracting and interfere with listener comprehension (Woodall & Burgoon, 1981). Experiments conducted by Krauss and his colleagues (Kraus et al., 1995; Krauss, Chen, & Chawla, 1996) argue that gestures may not be aiding listener comprehension by contributing *semantic* information. Instead, they say, speech-related gestures are more likely to aid listener comprehension by getting attention, activating images or motoric representations in the listener's mind, and aiding recall.

THE COORDINATION OF GESTURE, POSTURE, AND SPEECH

Earlier we said that speech-related gestures are tied to, or accompany, speech. That they are connected to speech is easily understood, but the exact nature of that connection is more difficult to understand. Most scholars agree that body movements and gestures are not randomly produced during the stream of speech but are inextricably linked as parts of the same system. The disagreements among scholars in this area focus on how to define coordination, or synchrony, of speech and movement. Must two things happen at exactly the same time to be in sync? Must they happen for the same length of time? If speech and gesture are closely coordinated, does the same part of the brain control both systems? Is there a synchrony of speech and movement between two speakers, as well as within the behavior of a single speaker? This section focuses on the research on these issues. The first part addresses the coordination of a single speaker's speech and movement, and the second examines the coordination of two speakers' behavior.

SELF-SYNCHRONY

In the early 1960s, William S. Condon began a microscopic analysis of the coordination between movement and speech. By examining individual frames of a 16-millimeter film, he was able to match body movements with a speech transcript. This allowed him to observe speech–body orientation accurate to 1/24th of a second. (Condon 1976; Condon & Ogston, 1966) showed that speech and movement are rhythmically coordinated even at the most microscopic levels, for example, in syllables and even smaller sections. This means a change in one behavior, such as the movement of a body part, will coincide or be coordinated with the onset of change in another behavior, such as in a phonological segment, or in some other body part. Just as speech units can be grouped together to form larger units, so can movement units. A sweep of the arm or a turn of the head may occur over an entire phrase of several words, but we may see movements of the face and fingers coordinated with smaller units of speech. At every level, however, the phrases of speech production and the phrases of movement seem closely coordinated. Using digital video annotation, Loehr (2007) examined the rhythmic relationship between the hands, head, and voice of four speakers during spontaneous interaction. He, too, found a complex process of self-synchrony. Stressed syllables often aligned with gestural strokes and even eye blinks.

The smallest idea unit in spoken language is called the *phonemic clause*. This group of words, averaging about five in length, has only one primary stress—indicated by changes in pitch, rhythm, or loudness—and is terminated by a juncture. This unit commonly has shown systematic relationships to body movements. Slight jerks of the head or hand often accompany the primary stress points in the speech of American English speakers. Gestures also seem to peak at the most salient part of the idea unit as well. At the junctures or boundaries, we also find movements of the head or hands that indicate completion or initiation.

Birdwhistell's (1966) analysis of nonverbal activity that accompanies verbal behavior led him to postulate the existence of what he calls *kinesic markers*. These nonverbal behaviors mark a specific oral language behavior. Markers seem to operate at several different levels. For instance, we might see an eye blink at the beginning and end of some words, or a microlateral head sweep may be seen during the expression of a compound word we would hyphenate in the written form. Figure 7-14 shows

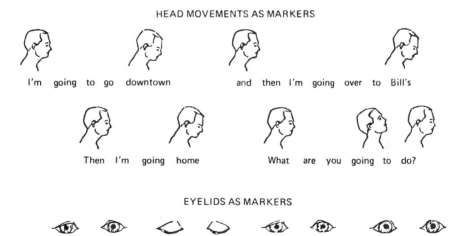

HEAD MOVEMENTS AS MARKERS

I'm going to go downtown   and then I'm going over to Bill's

Then I'm going home   What are you going to do?

EYELIDS AS MARKERS

Then I'm going home   What are you going to do?

HAND MOVEMENTS AS MARKERS

Then I'm going home   What are you going to do?

FIGURE 7-14

Some postural-kinesic markers of syntactic sentences in the United States.

head, hand, and eyelid markers occurring at the end of statements and questions. Similarly, after making a point, speakers may turn the head to one side or tilt, flex, or extend the neck, signaling the transition to another point.

Another level of markers is characterized by gross shifts in postural behavior, involving half the body, indicating or marking a sequence of points or a point of view expressed by the speaker. One marker on this level is simply the shift from leaning back when listening to leaning forward when speaking. The observation that postural shifts mark new stages of interaction or topic shifts, particularly at the beginning or ending of speech segments, has been made by several researchers (Bull & Brown, 1977; Erickson, 1975; Scheflen, 1973). Markers on the next level are frequently complete changes in location, following the presentation of one's total position during an interaction.

Kendon's (1972b, 1980, 1987, 1988, 2004) detailed analyses of speech and body movement confirm the notion of self-synchrony. He also supports the idea of a hierarchy of body movements that acts in conjunction with our speech behavior. Kendon found that the wrist and fingers tended to change positions most often, followed by the forearm, then the upper arm. Elements of the face generally changed more often than the head, and trunk and lower limb movements were rare. The larger units of body movement were related to the larger units of speech, and the smaller body units were related to the smaller verbal units.

Kendon also made some important observations of when movements occur in relation to the speech stream. Some movements accompany speech, but many precede speech units. The time between the speech-preparatory body movement and the onset of speech is apparently related to the size of the impending speech unit, with earlier and more extensive behavior, involving more body parts, for larger speech units. A change in body posture, for instance, may precede a long utterance and may be held for the duration of the utterance. Like other researchers in this area, Kendon believes the hierarchically structured body movements probably convey information about verbal structure and communicative involvement. The positions of the head, limbs, and body sometimes forecast information to a listener, such as length of utterance, change in argument strategy or viewpoint, and the like. The act of forecasting upcoming components of speech through gesture is a crucial function in social interaction. Speakers often shift their gaze to their hands during the production of iconic gestures, thereby calling them to the attention of the listener. Speaker gaze returns to the listener as the speech unit projected by the gesture is completed. In this process, gaze acts as a pointer (Streeck, 1993; Streeck & Knapp, 1992).

The linkage of gestures to speech has also been demonstrated in studies that show how gestures help speakers access and retrieve words from their mental lexicon (Hadar, 1989; Krauss & Hadar, 1999; Krauss et al., 1996; Morrel-Samuels & Krauss, 1992). Hanlon, Brown, and Gerstman (1990) showed that they could improve word retrieval in a picture-naming task by training aphasics to perform gestures just prior to the naming task. This important role of gestures in lexical retrieval and speech production is often overlooked and underemphasized, but it is clear that gestures facilitate both the invention of messages and their organization and delivery.

The preceding research leads us to conclude that speech and gesture are coordinated. But why? It is most likely because they are two components used in the expression of a single unit of content. Both systems are being guided by the same overall purpose, and both systems seem to be under the governance of the same parts of the brain (Cicone, Wapner, Foldi, Zurif, & Gardner, 1979; Kimura, 1976). As Kendon (2000, p. 61) said, "[A]lthough each expresses somewhat different dimensions of the meaning, speech and gesture are co-expressive of a single inclusive ideational complex, and it is this that is the meaning of the utterance." It is not unreasonable, then, to assume a pathological state for people manifesting out-of-sync behavior (Condon, 1980). Nor should it surprise us that gestures and speech both break down in aphasia (McNeill, 1992).

Developmentally, gesture and speech also appear to grow up together (Graham & Kilbreath, 2007). In a related study, Petitto and Marentette (1991) argue that *manual* infant "babbling," rather than oral babbling, may serve as a precursor to language learning. Several other studies indicate that children use more gestures as they develop, just as they use more words, and the nature of that gesticulation varies with the changing nature of speech production (McNeill, 1992). Kendon (1983, p. 25) put it this way:

> There appears to be a shift away from elaborate enactments or pantomimes, which serve instead of speech, toward a more precise coordination, as if gesture is coming to be used more selectively. Gesture is used much less to depict whole scenes. It is brought in only at certain points along the way. There is also an increasing use of abstract, discourse-making gesture; iconic gesture becomes more symbolic and more restricted in the aspects of meaning it is called upon to display.

INTERACTION SYNCHRONY

The preceding section revealed a speech–body movement coordination within the actions of a single speaker. This section provides information about a speech–body movement coordination between two speakers—a kind of social rhythm (Bernieri & Rosenthal, 1991). This behavior has been studied in two ways, which we call *matching* and *meshing*.

MATCHING   Without always being very aware of it, human beings commonly tend to mimic the mannerisms, facial expressions, postures, and other behaviors of the people they interact with. This has been called the "chameleon effect" (Chartrand & Bargh, 1999)—not because people, like chameleons, change colors to match their environment, but because people change their postures, gestures, and mannerisms to match those of their interaction partners. This kind of mimicry can occur completely outside of our conscious awareness, even though matching behavior may also be used intentionally when a person is trying to communicate affiliation. Matching the behavior of our fellow interactant may occur in several different ways. Sometimes a speaker's behavior is followed in kind by the listener when he or she becomes the speaker (Cappella, 1981). Here the matched behavior occurs not simultaneously but in sequence. Chapter 11 reports research that shows how we tend to match our partner's utterance duration, loudness, precision of articulation, latency of response, silence duration, and speech rate. In some instances, the speaker's behavior elicits an offsetting or compensatory behavior from the other interaction partner. For example, if a speaker is leaning

FIGURE 7-15

Postural congruence. The pair facing each other in the foreground are showing matching postures; the pair facing each other in the background are showing mirror-image postures.

toward a listener, and the listener perceives the interaction distance to be too close, the listener is likely to lean back or in other ways increase the interaction distance (see Chapter 5).

Other researchers have been interested in those occasions when both interaction partners exhibit the same behavior at the same time. Postural congruence is one of those frequently matched behaviors. It may involve crossing the legs and/or arms, leaning, head propping, or any number of other positions. Notice the variety of postural congruence in Figures 7-15, 7-16, and 7-17. When the listener's behavior is a mirror image of the speaker's, this form of matching is called *mirroring*.

Postural congruence has been observed to occur during periods of more positive speech, is rated by observers as an indicator of rapport and cooperation, and has been established as an act that is influential in creating rapport (Charney, 1966; LaFrance, 1979, 1985; LaFrance & Broadbent, 1976; Trout & Rosenfeld, 1980). Nonconscious mimicry has also been found to occur more often with people who enter an interaction with the goal to affiliate or establish rapport (Lakin & Chartrand, 2003). Of course, a stronger desire to affiliate makes mimicry more likely (Yabar, Johnston, Miles & Peace, 2006). In one study, a

FIGURE 7-16

Examples of postural congruence through head-propping and leaning.

trained actor selectively mimicked postures and gestures of only some students in an interview situation. In a post-interview assessment of their partner the actor, students who had been mimicked evaluated their partner significantly more favorably and indicated they "identified" with him or that he "thought like me"

FIGURE 7-17

Notice the postural congruence exhibited by cabinet official Joseph Califano and former President Jimmy Carter, 1977.

(Dabbs, 1969). None of the students reported an awareness of the mimicry. Chartrand and Bargh (1999) also found mimicry to increase the degree of liking on the part of an interaction partner. In short, mimicry seems to occur more often when we are other-oriented; for example, when we want to be liked by others, feel concerned about others, seek a closer relationship with others, show dependence on others, and so on.

Bavelas and her colleagues would agree that postural mimicry is most likely to occur when we are other-oriented, but they did not find that it was a sign of rapport or cooperation. Instead, they found that postural mimicry occurred during periods of conversational involvement rather than during cooperation or periods of rapport. Bavelas maintains it is a signal that the participants are talking *with* each other rather than *at* each other, performing symmetrical roles rather than complementary ones. From this perspective, the matching of an interaction partner's nonverbal behavior reflects the moment-to-moment aspects of conversational involvement.

Bavelas has also studied a related phenomenon she calls *motor mimicry*. A common example of motor mimicry is when a person you are near drops a heavy weight on his or her foot. As the injured party reacts in pain, your wincing facial expression seems to register an empathic response (see Figure 7-18). Sometimes we lean in the direction of another person's efforts; sometimes we smile at another's joy. For many years, scholars believed this was a purely empathic reaction based on a vicarious experience. The work of Bavelas and her colleagues does not deny this inner experience, but their research also shows motor mimicry is primarily a communicative phenomenon. Wincing in reaction to another's injury, for example, depended strongly on the visual accessibility of the injured party in Bavelas's experiments. Furthermore, the pattern and timing of the wincer's reaction was determined by eye contact with the victim (Bavelas, Black, Chovil, Lemery, Mullett 1988; Bavelas, Black, Lemery, & Mullett, 1986). In a related study, Kimbara (2008) found that visual accessibility to another interactant during a joint description of previously viewed video clips also led to a greater similarity in the shape of their hand gestures than the same task without visual access to their partner.

This tendency to match and mimic the behavior of others posturally, facially, vocally, and so forth sometimes leads to a condition known as *emotional contagion*, which occurs when an emotional experience is triggered as a result of mimicking someone else's behavior. Two of the essential conditions for this process to occur include strongly felt emotions and communicators who are skilled encoders and decoders (Hatfield, Cacioppo, & Rapson, 1994). Patek, Critton, Myers, and Gallup (2003) found that susceptibility to contagious yawning is related to self-awareness and empathic ability.

MESHING Another way of examining the phenomenon of interaction synchrony has been to observe the ongoing co-occurrence of changes in movement and speech by each of two interactants. In this type of research, changes refer to the initiation, termination, speed, and/or direction of the behaviors under study. Like matching behavior, meshing has also been linked to conversational satisfaction and liking for one's interaction partner (Cappella, 1997).

a

b

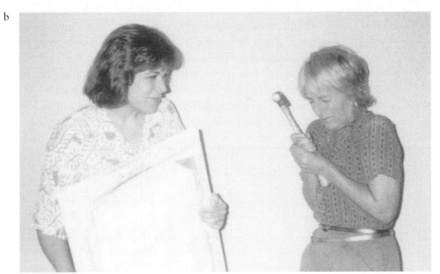

FIGURE 7-18

(a) Former President Ronald Reagan and former Defense Secretary Casper Weinberger exchange similar facial expressions. (b) An onlooker winces in pain as another experiences it.

The study of meshing behavior arose out of Condon's earlier work on self-synchrony. He observed how both interactants seemed to coordinate their actions. One person (Davis, 1971) who viewed his films reported this:

The third film clip Condon showed me was an example of heightened synchrony. A man and a woman—employer and job applicant—sat facing each other in a sequence that at normal speed seemed merely to involve rather a lot of shifting around, as the man first uncrossed and then recrossed his legs and the woman stirred in her chair. But when the film was run through a few frames at a time, their synchrony became clear. In the same frame, the two began to lean toward each other. They stopped at the same split second, both raised their heads, and then they swept backwards together into their chairs, stopping in the same frame. It was very like the elaborate courtship dances of some birds, or—in Condon's favorite analogy—they were like puppets moved by the same set of strings. Condon told me that this kind of heightened synchrony happens often between male and female. During courtship, it's one of the ways in which vast statements can be made between a man and a woman without a word being said. (p. 103)

As Condon suggests, this kind of interaction synchrony may reflect the nature of the ongoing relationship, whether it is the extent of involvement and rapport or the degree of intimate, interpersonal knowledge about the other. In some instances, this relationship is dramatically visible by the kind of synchrony taking place. At other times, the coordination may only be seen in the microscopic analysis of individual film frames. Out-of-sync partners are not likely to value the experience. The fact that out-of-sync experiences tend to stand out for us reminds us how often we operate in synchrony with others. Out-of-sync behavior may reflect decreased listening, a lack of knowledge of one's partner, and so forth. Interaction synchrony may also be a precursor of language learning. Condon and Sander (1974) found babies 12 hours old whose head, hand, elbow, hip, and leg movements tended to correspond to the rhythms of human speech. When the babies were exposed to disconnected speech or to plain tapping sounds, however, the rhythmic pattern was not observed. If this finding is validated by other researchers, it may mean an infant has participated in, and has laid the groundwork for, various linguistic forms and structures long before formal language learning begins (see Bernieri, Reznick, & Rosenthal, 1988).

Sometimes our responses as listeners and the feedback we provide in the form of facial expressions or head movements appear at specific junctures in the speech of our partner. Vocalizations such as "Mmm-hmm," "I see," and the like and head nods and movements of hands and feet tend to occur at the ends of rhythmical units of the speaker's utterance; that is, at pauses within phonemic clauses but mainly at junctures between these clauses. Vocally stressed words also tend to be accompanied by movements. Listener gestures and movements are often indications that the listener understands, appreciates, or anticipates speaker behavior.

Dittmann (1972) noticed that adults sometimes believe children are not listening to them and badger them with questions like "Did you hear me?" Dittmann reasoned that this common adult perception of children may be associated with the absence of what he calls "listener responses" such as head nods, some eyebrow raises, some types of smiles, and verbal acknowledgements such as "yeah," "I see," and so on. His study of children in grades 1, 3, and 5 found these listener responses to be nearly absent except under "the strongest social pull" by the other interactant. Subsequent studies indicated the major deficiencies were in "mmm-hmm" and head-nod responses. By 8th grade, a dramatic increase in these listener responses was found. By early adolescence, peers begin to lengthen their response duration, providing more opportunity for such listener responses. The "response pull" from adult interactants is increasing, and a continuing movement away from a purely self-orientation toward imagining what others are experiencing occurs.

The detailed observations of researchers like Condon, Dittmann, and Kendon offer clear evidence that human interactants do exhibit a speech–body movement interaction synchrony. It is also clear that this synchrony may take place on very microscopic levels. Still, there are questions: How much of this synchrony is due to an ordered relationship between speech and body movements, and how much is due to coincidence? Are there social contexts that intensify the degree of synchrony? How much synchrony is desirable? At least one study suggests that *moderately* rhythmic social interactions are evaluated most positively (Warner, Malloy, Schneider, Knoth, & Wilder, 1987). Is it possible to predict which behaviors will synchronize with which other behaviors at certain times? What is the best method of measuring these minute behavioral changes? (Gatewood & Rosenwein, 1981; McDowall, 1978a, 1978b; Rosenfeld, 1981).

SUMMARY

Although gestures are difficult to define, we often seem to know what movements a person is using to communicate and what movements are merely nervous mannerisms, expressions associated with emotion, and task-related movements. Gestures help us communicate in many ways: They replace speech when we cannot or do not want to talk and help us regulate the back-and-forth flow of interaction. They establish and maintain attention, add emphasis to our speech, and assist in making memorable the content of our speech. Although we do gesture when interaction partners are not visible, such as over the telephone, gestures are more frequent when both interactants are visible to one another. We seem to use more gestures when we are knowledgeable about the topic being discussed, highly motivated to have our listeners understand our message, trying to dominate a conversation, excited and enthusiastic about the topic being discussed, and speaking about manual activities. Gestures also play an important role in word retrieval and speech production. So the absence of gestures may negatively affect the speaker's message as well as a listener's comprehension.

Two major types of gestures were discussed: *speech independent* and *speech related*. *Speech-independent gestures* are operationally defined as gestures that 70 percent of the usage community decodes in a similar way. They have an almost direct verbal definition. We are normally keenly aware of using this type of gesture. Culture affects the number, frequency, and meanings associated with speech-independent gestures. Although no universal gestures of this type have been found—that is, none have the same meaning and form in every culture studied—the most likely candidates would be gestures of affirmation and negation and those meaning "stop," "I don't know," and gestures that indicate sleeping, eating, and drinking. Some speech-independent gestures are culture specific; that is, they are not found in the same form in other cultures. Many gestures have basically the same form but different meanings from culture to culture, and these different meanings are often the source of cross-cultural misunderstandings.

The other major category of gestures is *speech-related gestures*. Some of these gestures characterize the content of speech, and some show the speaker's relationship to the referent by indicating whether the speaker is certain or uncertain, embracing an idea or distancing herself or himself from it, and the like. Some speech-related gestures are used to accent or emphasize speech units. Interactive gestures, unlike the other speech-related gestures, focus on the dialogue rather than the speaker's monologue. Interactive gestures focus on the ongoing involvement of the interactants and their shared roles.

The last part of this chapter examined the coordination and synchrony of speech and body movements. This synchrony between the larger and smaller units of speech and body is called *self-synchrony*. Gesture and speech, then, seem to be different outward manifestations of a process controlled and guided by the same parts of the brain. Gesture and speech both play a role in communicating the same content. In addition to a self-synchrony, interactants also seem to display coordinated exchanges of behavior in many ways that suggest the existence of an interaction synchrony as well. Interaction synchrony can manifest itself through matching behavior—similar behavior occurring at the same time (postural congruence or motor mimicry) or similar behavior occurring in sequence (one speaker raises his or her voice, followed by the next speaker raising his or her voice). Interaction synchrony can also manifest itself in the moment-to-moment coordination of changes in the direction and timing of speech and movement, even though we do not yet know exactly what behaviors will change and how they will change.

QUESTIONS FOR DISCUSSION

1. Spend some time during the day interacting without using hand gestures. What problems did you encounter, if any? What does your experience tell you about the relationship of gestures and speech?

2. Some researchers have found matching behavior to be associated with rapport between the interactants. Can you think of a situation in which rapport would not involve matching behavior? Can you think of a situation in which matching occurred but there was not much rapport?

3. Can you think of any instance in which gestures might pose a challenge to the doctrine of freedom of speech?

4. Select a speech-independent gesture. Discuss the meaning of this gesture when accompanied by different facial expressions and speech.

BIBLIOGRAPHY

Acredolo, L. P., & Goodwyn, S. (1996). *Baby signs.* Chicago: Contemporary.

Alibali, M. W., & Don, L. S. (2001). Children's gestures are meant to be seen. *Gesture, 1,* 113–127.

Allport, G. W., & Vernon, P. E. (1933). *Studies in expressive movement.* Boston: Houghton Mifflin.

Archer, D. (1997). Unspoken diversity: Cultural differences in gestures. *Qualitative Sociology, 20,* 79–105.

Armstrong, N., & Wagner, M. (2003). *Field guide to gestures.* Philadelphia: Quirk Books.

Axtell, R. (1991). *Gestures.* New York: Wiley.

Barakat, R. (1973). Arabic gestures. *Journal of Popular Culture, 6,* 749–792.

Barroso, F., Freedman, N., Grand, S., & van Meel, J. (1978). Evocation of two types of hand movements in information processing. *Journal of Experimental Psychology: Human Perception and Performance, 4,* 321–329.

Barten, S. S. (1979). Development of gesture. In N. R. Smith & M. Franklin (Eds.), *Symbolic functioning in childhood.* Hillsdale, NJ: Erlbaum.

Bavelas, J. B. (1994). Gestures as part of speech: Methodological implications. *Research on Language and Social Interaction, 27,* 201–221.

Bavelas, J. B., Black, A., Chovil, N., Lemery, C. R., & Mullett, J. (1988). Form and function in motor mimicry: Topographic evidence that the primary function is communicative. *Human Communication Research, 14,* 275–299.

Bavelas, J. B., Black, A., Lemery, C. R., & Mullett, J. (1986). "I show you how I feel": Motor mimicry as a communicative act. *Journal of Personality and Social Psychology, 50,* 322–329.

Bavelas, J. B., Chovil, N., Coates, L., & Roe, L. (1995). Gestures specialized for dialogue. *Personality and Social Psychology Bulletin, 21,* 394–405.

Bavelas, J. B., Chovil, N., Lawrie, D. A., & Wade, A. (1992). Interactive gestures. *Discourse Processes*, *15*, 469–489.

Bavelas, J. B., Kenwood, C., Johnson, T., & Phillips, B. (2002). An experimental study of when and how speakers use gestures to communicate. *Gesture*, *2*, 1–17.

Beattie, G. (2004). *Visible thought: The new psychology of body language*. New York: Routledge.

Beattie, G. W., & Beattie, C. A. (1981). Postural congruence in a naturalistic setting. *Semiotica*, *35*, 41–55.

Beattie, G., & Shovelton, H. (2006). When size really matters: How a single semantic feature is represented in the speech and gesture modalities. *Gesture*, *6*, 63–84.

Berger, K. W., & Popelka, G. R. (1971). Extra-facial gestures in relation to speech reading. *Journal of Communication Disorders*, *3*, 302–308.

Bernieri, F. J., Reznick, J. S., & Rosenthal, R. (1988). Synchrony, pseudosynchrony, and dissynchrony: Measuring the entrainment process in mother–infant interactions. *Journal of Personality and Social Psychology*, *54*, 243–253.

Bernieri, F. J., & Rosenthal, R. (1991). Interpersonal coordination: Behavior matching and interactional synchrony. In R. S. Feldman & B. Rimé (Eds.), *Fundamentals of nonverbal behavior*. New York: Cambridge University Press.

Birdwhistell, R. L. (1952). *Introduction to kinesics*. Louisville: University of Louisville Press. (Now available on microfilm only. Ann Arbor, MI: University Microfilms.)

Birdwhistell, R. L. (1955). Background to kinesics. *ETC*, *13*, 10–18.

Birdwhistell, R. L. (1960). Kinesics and communication. In E. Carpenter & M. McLuhan (Eds.), *Explorations in communication*. New York: Beacon.

Birdwhistell, R. L. (1963). Kinesic analysis in the investigation of emotions. In P. Knapp (Ed.), *Expression of the emotions in man*. New York: International Universities Press.

Birdwhistell, R. L. (1966). Some relations between American kinesics and spoken American English. In A. G. Smith (Ed.), *Communication and culture*. New York: Holt, Rinehart & Winston.

Birdwhistell, R. L. (1967). Some body motion elements accompanying spoken American English. In L. Thayer (Ed.), *Communication: Concepts and perspectives* (pp. 53–76). Washington, DC: Spartan.

Birdwhistell, R. L. (1970). *Kinesics and context*. Philadelphia: University of Pennsylvania Press.

Blake, J., & Dolgoy, S. J. (1993). Gestural development and its relation to cognition during the transition to language. *Journal of Nonverbal Behavior*, *17*, 87–102.

Boomer, D. S. (1978). The phonemic clause: Speech unit in human communication. In A. W. Siegman & S. Feldstein (Eds.), *Nonverbal behavior and communication*. Hillsdale, NJ: Erlbaum.

Bremmer, J., & Roodenburg, H. (Eds.). (1991). *A cultural history of gesture*. Ithaca, NY: Cornell University Press.

Bull, P. E. (1987). *Posture and gesture*. New York: Pergamon Press.

Bull, P. E., & Brown, R. (1977). The role of postural change in dyadic conversation. *British Journal of Social and Clinical Psychology*, *16*, 29–33.

Bull, P., & Connelly, G. (1985). Body movements and emphasis in speech. *Journal of Nonverbal Behavior*, *9*, 169–187.

Burgoon, J. K., Stern, L. A., & Dillman, L. (1995). Interpersonal adaptation: *Dyadic interaction patterns*. New York: Cambridge University Press.

Butterworth, B., & Beattie, G. W. (1978). Gesture and silence as indicators of planning in speech. In R. Campbell & P. Smith (Eds.), *Recent advances in psychology of language: Formal and experimental approaches*. New York: Plenum.

Butterworth, B., & Hadar, U. (1989). Gesture, speech and computational stage: A reply to McNeill. *Psychological Review*, *96*, 168–174.

Cappella, J. N. (1981). Mutual influence in expressive behavior: Adult–adult and infant–adult dyadic interaction. *Psychological Bulletin*, *89*, 101–132.

Cappella, J. N. (1997). Behavioral and judged coordination in adult informal social interactions: Vocal and kinesic indicators. *Journal of Personality and Social Psychology*, *72*, 119–131.

Charney, E. J. (1966). Postural configurations in psychotherapy. *Psychosomatic Medicine*, *28*, 305–315.

Chartrand, T. L., & Bargh, J. A. (1999). The chameleon effect: The perception–behavior link and social interaction. *Journal of Personality and Social Psychology, 76*, 893–910.

Church, R. B., Garber, P., & Rogalski, K. (2007). The role of gesture in memory and social communication. *Gesture, 7*, 137–158.

Cicone, M., Wapner, W., Foldi, N., Zurif, E., & Gardner, H. (1979). The relation between gesture and language in aphasic communication. *Brain and Language, 8*, 324–349.

Clark, H. H., & Brennan, S. A. (1991). Grounding in communication. In L. B. Resnick, J. M. Levine, & S. D. Teasely (Eds.), *Perspectives on socially shared cognition*. Washington, DC: American Psychological Association.

Cohen, A. A. (1977). The communicative functions of hand illustrators. *Journal of Communication, 27*, 54–63.

Cohen, A. A., & Harrison, R. P. (1973). Intentionality in the use of hand illustrators in face-to-face communication situations. *Journal of Personality and Social Psychology, 28*, 276–279.

Condon, W. S. (1976). An analysis of behavioral organization. *Sign Language Studies, 13*, 285–318.

Condon, W. S. (1980). The relation of interaction synchrony to cognitive and emotional processes. In M. R. Key (Ed.), *The relationship of verbal and nonverbal communication*. The Hague: Mouton.

Condon, W. S., & Ogston, W. D. (1966). Sound film analysis of normal and pathological behavior patterns. *Journal of Nervous and Mental Disease, 143*, 338–347.

Condon, W. S., & Ogston, W. D. (1967). A segmentation of behavior. *Journal of Psychiatric Research, 5*, 221–235.

Condon, W. S., & Ogston, W. D. (1971). Speech and body motion synchrony of the speaker–hearer. In D. L. Horton & J. J. Jenkins (Eds.), *Perception of language*. Columbus, OH: Merrill.

Condon, W. S., & Sander, L. W. (1974). Neonate movement is synchronized with adult speech: Interaction participation in language acquisition. *Science, 183*, 99–101.

Cook, S. W., Mitchell, Z., & Goldin-Meadow, S. (2008). Gesturing makes learning last. *Cognition, 106*, 1047–1058.

Creider, C. (1977). Toward a description of East African gestures. *Sign Language Studies, 14*, 1–20.

Dabbs, J. M. (1969). Similarity of gestures and interpersonal influence. *Proceedings of the 77th annual convention of the American Psychological Association, 4*, 337–338.

Davis, F. (1971). *Inside intuition*. New York: McGraw-Hill.

de Jorio, A. (2000). *Gesture in Naples and gesture in classical antiquity*. (Translation and Introduction by Adam Kendon. First published in 1832). Bloomington: Indiana University Press.

de Ruiter, J. P. (2007). Postcards from the mind. *Gesture, 7*, 21–38.

Delis, D., Foldi, N. S., Hamby, S., Gardner, H., & Zurif, E. A. (1979). Note on temporal relations between language and gestures. *Brain and Language, 8*, 350–354.

Dittmann, A. T. (1962). The relationship between body movements and moods in interviews. *Journal of Consulting Psychology, 26*, 480.

Dittmann, A. T. (1971). Review of kinesics in context. *Psychiatry, 34*, 334–342.

Dittmann, A. T. (1972). The body movement–speech rhythm relationship as a cue to speech encoding. In A. W. Siegman & B. Pope (Eds.), *Studies in dyadic communication*. New York: Pergamon Press.

Dittmann, A. T. (1987). The role of body movement in communication. In A. W. Siegman & S. Feldstein (Eds.), *Nonverbal behavior and communication* (2nd ed.). Hillsdale, NJ: Erlbaum.

Dittmann, A. T., & Llewellyn, L. G. (1967). The phonemic clause as a unit of speech decoding. *Journal of Personality and Social Psychology, 6*, 341–349.

Dittmann, A. T., & Llewellyn, L. G. (1968). Relationships between vocalizations and head nods as listener responses. *Journal of Personality and Social Psychology, 11*, 98–106.

Dittmann, A. T., & Llewellyn, L. G. (1969). Body movement and speech rhythm in social conversation. *Journal of Personality and Social Psychology, 11*, 98–106.

Dobrogaev, S. M. (1931). The study of reflex in problems of linguistics (M. Kendon, Trans.). In E. A. Marr (Ed.), *Lazykovedenie i materializm* (Vol. 2).

Moscow and Leningrad: State Social Economic Publishing House.

Duffy, R. J., & Duffy, J. R. (1981). Three studies of deficits in pantomimic expression and pantomimic recognition in aphasia. *Journal of Speech and Hearing Research, 46,* 70–84.

Efron, D. (1972). *Gesture, race and culture.* The Hague: Mouton. (Original work published 1941 as *Gesture and environment.* New York: Kings Crown Press).

Ekman, P. (1964). Body position, facial expression, and verbal behavior during interviews. *Journal of Abnormal and Social Psychology, 48,* 295–301.

Ekman, P. (1976). Movements with precise meanings. *Journal of Communication, 26,* 14–26.

Ekman, P. (1977). Biological and cultural contribution to bodily and facial movement. In J. Blacking (Ed.), *The anthropology of the body.* London: Academic Press.

Ekman, P. (1979). About brows. In M. von Cranach, K. Foppa, W. Lepenier, & D. Ploog (Eds.), *Human ethology: Claims and limits of a new discipline.* Cambridge, MA: Cambridge University Press.

Ekman, P. (1999). Emotional and conversational nonverbal signals. In L. S. Messing & R. Campbell (Eds.), *Gesture, speech, and sign* (pp. 45–55). New York: Oxford University Press.

Ekman, P., & Friesen, W. V. (1969). The repertoire of non-verbal behavior: Categories, origins, usage, and coding. *Semiotica, 1,* 49–98.

Ekman, P., & Friesen, W. V. (1972). Hand movements. *Journal of Communication, 22,* 353–374.

Emmorey, K., & Casey, S. (2001). Gesture, thought, and spatial language. *Gesture, 1,* 35–50.

Emmorey, K., & Reilly, J. S. (1995). *Language, gesture, and space.* Mahwah, NJ: Erlbaum.

Erickson, F. (1975). One function of proxemic shifts in face-to-face interaction. In A. Kendon, R. M. Harris & M. R. Key (Eds.), *Organization of behavior in face-to-face interaction.* The Hague: Mouton.

Evans, M. A., & Rubin, K. H. (1979). Hand gestures as a communicative mode in school-aged children. *Journal of Genetic Psychology, 135,* 189–196.

Feyereisen, P. (1987). Gestures and speech, interactions and separations: A reply to McNeill. *Psychological Review, 94,* 493–498.

Feyereisen, P., & Havard, I. (1999). Mental imagery and production of hand gestures while speaking in younger and older adults. *Journal of Nonverbal Behavior, 23,* 153–171.

Feyereisen, P., & Lannoy, J. D. (1991). *Gestures and speech: Psychological investigations.* New York: Cambridge University Press.

Freedman, N. (1972). The analysis of movement behavior during clinical interviews. In A. Siegman & B. Pope (Eds.), *Studies in dyadic communication.* New York: Pergamon Press.

Freedman, N., Blass, T., Rifkin, A., & Quitkin, F. (1973). Body movements and the verbal encoding of aggressive affect. *Journal of Personality and Social Psychology, 26,* 72–85.

Frey, S. (1975). Tonic aspects of behavior in interaction. In A. Kendon, R. M. Harris, & M. R. Key (Eds.), *Organization of behavior in face-to-face interaction.* Chicago: Aldine.

Gatewood, J. B., & Rosenwein, R. (1981). Interactional synchrony: Genuine or spurious? A critique of recent research. *Journal of Nonverbal Behavior, 6,* 12–29.

Gerwing, J., & Bavelas, J. (2004). Linguistic influences on gesture's form. *Gesture, 4,* 157–195.

Givens, D. B. (1977). Shoulder shrugging: A densely communicative expressive behavior. *Semiotica, 19,* 13–28.

Goldin-Meadow, S. (2003). *Hearing gesture: How our hands help us think.* Cambridge, MA: Bellknap Press of Harvard University Press.

Goodglass, H., & Kaplan, E. (1963). Disturbance of gesture and pantomime in aphasia. *Brain, 86,* 702–712.

Goodwin, C. (1981). *Conversational organization.* New York: Academic Press.

Goodwin, C. (1986). Gestures as a resource for the organization of mutual orientation. *Semiotica, 62,* 29–49.

Goodwin, C., & Goodwin, M. H. (1986). Gesture and coparticipation in the activity of searching for a word. *Semiotica, 62,* 51–75.

Graham, J. A., & Argyle, M. A. (1975). A cross-cultural study of the communication of extra-verbal meaning by gestures. *International Journal of Psychology, 10,* 56–67.

Graham, J. A., & Heywood, S. (1976). The effects of elimination of hand gestures and of verbal codability on speech performance. *European Journal of Social Psychology, 5,* 189–195.

Graham, S. A., & Kilbreath, C. S. (2007). It's a sign of the kind: Gestures and words guide infants' inductive inferences. *Developmental Psychology, 43,* 1111–1123.

Hadar, U. (1989). Two types of gesture and their role in speech production. *Journal of Language and Social Psychology, 8,* 221–228.

Hadjikhani, N., & de Gelder, B. (2003). Seeing fearful body expressions activates the fusiform cortex and amygdala. *Current Biology, 13,* 2201–2205.

Hanlon, R. E., Brown, J. W., & Gerstman, L. J. (1990). Enhancement of naming in nonfluent aphasia through gesture. *Brain and Language, 38,* 298–314.

Hatfield, E., Cacioppo, J. T., & Rapson, R. L. (1994). *Emotional contagion.* New York: Cambridge University Press.

Hayes, F. C. (1957). Gestures: A working bibliography. *Southern Folklore Quarterly, 21,* 218–317.

Hess, U., Philippot, P., & Blairy, S. (1999). Mimicry: Facts and fiction. In P. Philippot, R. S. Feldman & E. J. Coats (Eds.), *The social context of nonverbal behavior* (pp. 213–241). New York: Cambridge University Press.

Hewes, G. W. (1957). The anthropology of posture. *Scientific American, 196,* 123–132.

Hewes, G. W. (1974). Gesture language in culture contact. *Sign Language Studies, 4,* 1–34.

Hewes, G. W. (1976). The current status of the gestural theory of language origin. *Annals of the New York Academy of Sciences, 280,* 482–504.

Hinsz, V. B., & Tomhave, J. A. (1991). Smile and (half) the world smiles with you, frown and you frown alone. *Personality and Social Psychology Bulletin, 17,* 586–592.

Holler, J., & Beattie, G. (2003). Pragmatic aspects of representational gestures: Do speakers use them to clarify verbal ambiguity for the listener? *Gesture, 3,* 127–154.

Hostetter, A. B., & Alibali, M. W. (2007). Raise your hand if you're spatial. *Gesture, 7,* 73–95.

Iverson, J. M., Tencer, J. L., & Goldin-Meadow, S. (2000). The relation between gesture and speech in congenitally blind and sighted language-learners. *Journal of Nonverbal Behavior, 24,* 105–130.

Jacobson, R. (1972). Motor signs for yes and no. *Language in Society, 1,* 91–96.

Jaffe, J., & Feldstein, S. (1970). *Rhythms of dialogue.* New York: Academic Press.

Jancovic, M. A., Devoe, S., & Wiener, M. (1975). Age-related changes in hand and arm movements as nonverbal communication: Some conceptualizations and an empirical exploration. *Child Development, 46,* 922–928.

Janssen, D., Schöllhorn, W. I., Lubienetzki, J., Fölling, K., Kokenge, H., & Davids, K. (2008). Recognition of emotions in gait patterns by means of artificial neural nets. *Journal of Nonverbal Behavior, 32,* 79–92.

Johnson, H. G., Ekman, P., & Friesen, W. V. (1975). Communicative body movements: American emblems. *Semiotica, 15,* 335–353.

Kempton, W. (1980). The rhythmic basis of interactional micro-synchrony. In M. R. Key (Ed.), *The relationship of verbal and nonverbal communication.* The Hague: Mouton.

Kendon, A. (1970). Movement coordination in social interaction: Some examples described. *Acta Psychologica, 32,* 101–125.

Kendon, A. (1972a). Review of *Kinesics and context. American Journal of Psychology, 85,* 447–455.

Kendon, A. (1972b). Some relationships between body motion and speech: An analysis of an example. In A. Siegman & B. Pope (Eds.), *Studies in dyadic communication.* New York: Pergamon Press.

Kendon, A. (1975). Gesticulation, speech, and the gesture theory of language origins. *Sign Language Studies, 9,* 349–373.

Kendon, A. (1980). Gesticulation and speech: Two aspects of the process of utterance. In M. R. Key (Ed.), *The relationship of verbal and nonverbal communication.* The Hague: Mouton.

Kendon, A. (1981a). Current issues in "nonverbal communication." In A. Kendon (Ed.), *Nonverbal communication, interaction, and gesture.* The Hague: Mouton.

Kendon, A. (1981b). Geography of gesture. *Semiotica, 37,* 129–163.

Kendon, A. (1983). Gesture and speech: How they interact. In J. M. Wiemann & R. P. Harrison (Eds.), *Nonverbal interaction.* Beverly Hills, CA: Sage.

Kendon, A. (1984). Did gesture have the happiness to escape the curse at the confusion of Babel? In A.

Wolfgang (Ed.), *Nonverbal behavior: Perspectives, applications, intercultural insights*. Toronto: Hogrefe.

Kendon, A. (1987). On gesture: Its complementary relationship with speech. In A. W. Siegman & S. Feldstein (Eds.), *Nonverbal behavior and communication* (2nd ed.). Hillsdale, NJ: Erlbaum.

Kendon, A. (1988). How gestures can become like words. In F. Poyatos (Ed.), *Cross-cultural perspectives in nonverbal communication*. Toronto: Hogrefe.

Kendon, A. (1989). Gesture. *International encyclopedia of communications* (Vol. 2, pp. 217–222). New York: Oxford University Press.

Kendon, A. (1992). Some recent work from Italy on quotable gestures ("emblems"). *Journal of Linguistic Anthropology, 2*, 72–93.

Kendon, A. (1993). Human gesture. In K. R. Gibson & T. Ingold (Eds.), *Tools, language and cognition in human evolution*. New York: Cambridge University Press.

Kendon, A. (1994). Do gestures communicate? A review. *Research on Language and Social Interaction, 27*, 175–200.

Kendon, A. (2000). Language and gesture: Unity or duality? In D. McNeill (Ed.), *Language and gesture*. New York: Cambridge University Press.

Kendon, A. (2002). Some uses of the head shake. *Gesture, 2*, 147–182.

Kendon, A. (2004). *Gesture: visible action as utterance*. New York: Cambridge University Press.

Kimbara, I. (2008). Gesture form convergence in joint description. *Journal of Nonverbal Behavior, 32*, 123–131.

Kimura, D. (1976). The neural basis of language via gesture. In H. Whitaker & H. A. Whitaker (Eds.), *Studies in neurolinguistics* (Vol. 2). New York: Academic Press.

Knapp, R. H. (1965). The language of postural interpretation. *Journal of Social Psychology, 67*, 371–377.

Krauss, R. M., & Hadar, U. (1999). The role of speech-related arm/hand gestures in word retrieval. In L. S. Messing & R. Campbell (Eds.), *Gesture, speech, and sign* (pp. 93–116). New York: Oxford University Press.

Krauss, R. M., Chen, Y., & Chawla, P. (1996). Nonverbal behavior and nonverbal communication:

What do conversational hand gestures tell us? In M. Zanna (Ed.), *Advances in experimental social psychology* (Vol. 28). San Diego, CA: Academic Press.

Krauss, R. M., Dushay, R. A., Chen, Y., & Rauscher, F. (1995). The communicative value of conversational hand gestures. *Journal of Experimental Social Psychology, 31*, 533–552.

Krauss, R. M., Morrel-Samuels, P., & Colasante, C. (1991). Do conversational gestures communicate? *Journal of Personality and Social Psychology, 61*, 743–754.

Krout, M. (1954a). An experimental attempt to determine the significance of unconscious manual symbolic movements. *Journal of General Psychology, 51*, 296–308.

Krout, M. (1954b). An experimental attempt to produce unconscious manual symbolic movements. *Journal of General Psychology, 51*, 121–152.

Kumin, L., & Lazar, M. (1974). Gestural communication in preschool children. *Perceptual and Motor Skills, 38*, 708–710.

LaBarre, W. (1964). Paralinguistics, kinesics, and cultural anthropology. In T. A. Sebeok, A. S. Hayes, & M. C. Bateson (Eds.), *Approaches to semiotics*. The Hague: Mouton.

LaFrance, M. (1979). Nonverbal synchrony and rapport: Analysis by the cross-lag panel technique. *Social Psychology Quarterly, 42*, 66–70.

LaFrance, M. (1985). Postural mirroring and intergroup relations. *Personality and Social Psychology Bulletin, 11*, 207–217.

LaFrance, M., & Broadbent, M. (1976). Group rapport: Posture sharing as a nonverbal indicator. *Group and Organization Studies, 1*, 328–333.

LaFrance, M., & Ickes, W. (1981). Posture mirroring and interactional involvement: Sex and sex typing effects. *Journal of Nonverbal Behavior, 5*, 139–154.

Lakin, J. L., & Chartrand, T. L. (2003). Using nonconscious behavioral mimicry to create affiliation and rapport. *Psychological Science, 14*, 334–339.

Lakin, J. L., Jefferis, V. E., Cheng, C. M., & Chartrand, T. L. (2003). The chameleon effect as social glue: Evidence for the evolutionary significance of nonconscious mimicry. *Journal of Nonverbal Behavior, 27*, 145–162.

Loehr, D. (2007). Aspects of rhythm in gesture and speech. *Gesture, 7*, 179–214.

Mallery, G. (1972). *Sign language among North American Indians compared with that among other peoples and deaf-mutes*. The Hague: Mouton. (Original work published Washington, DC: Smithsonian Institution Bureau of Ethnology, 1880).

Markel, N. N. (1975). Coverbal behavior associated with conversation turns. In A. Kendon, R. M. Harris, & M. R. Key (Eds.), *Organization of behavior in face-to-face interaction*. Chicago: Aldine.

Matsumoto, D., & Kudoh, T. (1987). Cultural similarities and differences in the semantic dimensions of body postures. *Journal of Nonverbal Behavior, 11*, 166–179.

Maurer, R. E., & Tindall, J. H. (1983). Effect of postural congruence on client's perception of counselor empathy. *Journal of Counseling Psychology, 30*, 158–163.

McClave, E. (2000). Linguistic functions of head movements in the context of speech. *Journal of Pragmatics, 32*, 855–878.

McClave, E., Kim, H., Tamer, R., & Mileff, M. (2007). Head movements in the context of speech in Arabic, Bulgarian, Korean, and African-American vernacular English. *Gesture, 7*, 343–390.

McDowall, J. J. (1978a). Interactional synchrony: A reappraisal. *Journal of Personality and Social Psychology, 36*, 963–975.

McDowall, J. J. (1978b). Microanalysis of filmed movement: The reliability of boundary detection by observers. *Environmental Psychology and Nonverbal Behavior, 3*, 77–88.

McNeill, D. (1985). So you think gestures are nonverbal? *Psychological Review, 92*, 350–371.

McNeill, D. (1986). Iconic gestures of children and adults. *Semiotica, 62*, 107–128.

McNeill, D. (1992). *Hand and mind*. Chicago: Chicago University Press.

McNeill, D. (2000). *Language and gesture*. New York: Cambridge University Press.

McNeill, D., Cassell, J., & McCullough, K. (1994). Communicative effects of speech-mismatched gestures. *Research on Language and Social Interaction, 27*, 223–237.

McNeill, D., & Levy, E. (1982). Conceptual representations in language activity and gesture. In R. J. Jarvella & W. Klein (Eds.), *Speech, place, and action: Studies in deixis and related topics*. Chichester, UK: Wiley.

McNeil, N. M., Alibali, M. W., & Evans, J. L. (2000). The role of gesture in children's comprehension of spoken language: Now they need it, now they don't. *Journal of Nonverbal Behavior, 24*, 131–150.

Meissner, M., & Philpott, S. B. (1975). The sign language of sawmill workers in British Columbia. *Sign Language Studies, 9*, 291–308.

Meltzoff, A. N., & Moore, M. K. (1989). Imitation in newborn infants: Exploring the range of gestures imitated and the underlying mechanisms. *Developmental Psychology, 25*, 954–962.

Messing, L. S., & Campbell, R. (Eds.). (1999). *Gesture, speech, and sign*. New York: Oxford University Press.

Michael, G., & Willis, F. N. (1968). The development of gestures as a function of social class, education and sex. *Psychological Record, 18*, 515–519.

Michael, G., & Willis, F. N. (1969). The development of gestures in three subcultural groups. *Journal of Social Psychology, 79*, 35–41.

Montepare, J. M., Goldstein, S. B., & Clausen, A. (1987). The identification of emotions from gait information. *Journal of Nonverbal Behavior, 11*, 33–41.

Montepare, J. M., & Zebrowitz, L. A. (1993). A cross-cultural comparison of impressions created by age-related variations in gait. *Journal of Nonverbal Behavior, 17*, 55–68.

Montepare, J. M., & Zebrowitz-McArthur, L. (1988). Impressions of people created by age-related qualities of their gaits. *Journal of Personality and Social Psychology, 55*, 547–556.

Morrel-Samuels, P., & Krauss, R. M. (1992). Word familiarity predicts temporal asynchrony of hand gestures and speech. *Journal of Experimental Psychology: Learning, Memory and Cognition, 18*, 615–662.

Morris, D. (1977). *Manwatching: A field guide to human behavior*. New York: Abrams.

Morris, D. (1994). *Bodytalk: The meaning of human gestures*. New York: Crown.

Morris, D., Collett, P., Marsh, P., & O'Shaughnessy, M. (1979). *Gestures: Their origins and distribution*. London: Jonathon Cape.

Morsbach, H. (1988). Nonverbal communication and hierarchical relationships: The case of bowing in Japan. In F. Poyatos (Ed.), *Cross-cultural perspectives in nonverbal communication.* Toronto: Hogrefe.

Nicoladis, E. (2002). Some gestures develop in conjunction with spoken language development and others don't: Evidence from bilingual preschoolers. *Journal of Nonverbal Behavior, 26,* 241–266.

Patek, S. M., Critton, S. R., Myers, T. E., & Gallup, G. G., Jr. (2003). Contagious yawning: The role of self-awareness and mental state attribution. *Cognitive Brain Research, 17,* 223–227.

Pelose, G. C. (1987). The functions of behavioral synchrony and speech rhythm in conversation. In S. J. Sigman (Ed.), *Research on language and social interaction* (Vol. 20). Edmonton, Alberta: Boreal.

Peterson, L. N., & Kirshner, H. S. (1981). Gestural impairment and gestural ability in aphasia: A review. *Brain and Language, 14,* 333–348.

Petitto, L. A., & Marentette, P. F. (1991, March 22). Babbling in the manual mode: Evidence for the ontogeny of language. *Science, 251,* 1493–1496.

Pickett, L. (1974). An assessment of gestural and pantomimic deficit in aphasic patients. *Acta Symbolica, 65,* 69–86.

Poggi, I. (2002). Symbolic gestures: The case of the Italian gestionary. *Gesture, 2,* 71–98.

Poyatos, F. (1975). Gesture inventories: Fieldwork methodology and problems. *Semiotica, 13,* 199–227.

Rimé, B. (1982). The elimination of visible behaviour from social interactions: Effects on verbal, nonverbal and interpersonal behaviour. *European Journal of Social Psychology, 12,* 113–129.

Rimé, B., & Schiaratura, L. (1991). Gesture and speech. In R. Feldman & B. Rimé (Eds.), *Fundamentals of nonverbal behavior.* New York: Cambridge University Press.

Riseborough, M. G. (1985). Physiographic gestures as decoding facilitators: Three experiments exploring a neglected facet of communication. *Journal of Nonverbal Behavior, 5,* 172–183.

Rogers, W. T. (1978). The contribution of kinesic illustrators toward the comprehension of verbal behavior within utterances. *Human Communication Research, 5,* 54–62.

Rosenberg, B. G., & Langer, J. (1965). A study of postural-gestural communication. *Journal of Personality and Social Psychology, 2,* 593–597.

Rosenfeld, H. M. (1967). Nonverbal reciprocation of approval: An experimental analysis. *Journal of Experimental Social Psychology, 3,* 102–111.

Rosenfeld, H. M. (1981). Whither interactional synchrony? In K. Bloom (Ed.), *Prospective issues in infant research.* Hillsdale, NJ: Erlbaum.

Rosenfeld, H. M. (1987). Conversational control functions of nonverbal behavior. In A. W. Siegman & S. Feldstein (Eds.), *Nonverbal behavior and communication* (2nd ed.). Hillsdale, NJ: Erlbaum.

Rosenfeld, H. M., & Hancks, M. (1980). The nonverbal context of verbal listener responses. In M. R. Key (Ed.), *The relationship of verbal and nonverbal communication.* The Hague: Mouton.

Saitz, R. L., & Cervenka, E. J. (1972). *Handbook of gestures: Colombia and the United States.* The Hague: Mouton.

Sapir, E. (1949). The unconscious patterning of behavior in society. In D. G. Mandelbaum (Ed.), *Selected writings of Edward Sapir in language, culture, and personality.* Berkeley: University of California Press.

Scheflen, A. (1973). *Communicational structure: Analysis of a psychotherapy transaction.* Bloomington: University of Indiana Press.

Scheflen, A. E. (1964). The significance of posture in communication systems. *Psychiatry, 27,* 316–331.

Scheflen, A. E., & Scheflen, A. (1972). *Body language and the social order.* Englewood Cliffs, NJ: Prentice-Hall.

Schegloff, E. A. (1984). On some gestures' relation to talk. In J. M. Anderson & J. Heritage (Eds.), *Structures of social action: Studies in conversational analyses.* New York: Cambridge University Press.

Sherzer, J. (1974). Verbal and nonverbal deixis: The pointed-lip gesture among the San Blas Cuna. *Language in Society, 2,* 117–131.

Sousa-Poza, J. F., Rohrberg, R., & Mercure, A. (1979). Effects of type of information (abstract–concrete) and field dependence on asymmetry of hand movements during speech. *Perceptual and Motor Skills, 48,* 1323–1330.

Sparhawk, C. M. (1978). Contrastive identificational features of Persian gesture. *Semiotica, 24,* 49–86.

Stevanoni, E., & Salmon, K. (2005). Giving memory a hand: Instructing children to gesture enhances their event recall. *Journal of Nonverbal Behavior, 29,* 217–233.

Stokoe, W. C. (1980). Sign language and sign languages. *Annual Review of Anthropology, 9,* 365–390.

Streeck, J. (1988). The significance of gesture: How it is established. *Papers in Pragmatics, 2,* 25–59.

Streeck, J. (1993). Gesture as communication: I. Its coordination with gaze and speech. *Communication Monographs, 60,* 275–299.

Streeck, J. (1994). Gesture as communication: II. The audience as coauthor. *Research on Language and Social Interaction, 27,* 239–267.

Streeck, J. (2002). A body and its gestures. *Gesture, 2,* 19–44.

Streeck, J., & Knapp, M. L. (1992). The interaction of visual and verbal features in human communication. In F. Poyatos (Ed.), *Advances in nonverbal communication.* Amsterdam: Benjamins.

Tabensky, A. (2001). Gesture and speech rephrasings in conversation. *Gesture, 1,* 213–235.

Taylor, A. (1975). Nonverbal communication systems in native North America. *Semiotica, 13,* 329–374.

Teodorrson, S. T. (1980). Autonomy and linguistic status of non-speech language forms. *Journal of Psycholinguistic Research, 9,* 121–145.

Trout, D. L., & Rosenfeld, H. M. (1980). The effect of postural lean and body congruence on the judgment of psychotherapeutic rapport. *Journal of Nonverbal Behavior, 4,* 176–190.

Trupin, C. M. (1976). *Linguistics and gesture: An application of linguistic theory to the study of emblems.* Unpublished doctoral dissertation, University of Michigan.

van de Koppel, J. M. H., de Bok-Huurman, J. F. H., & Moezelaar, M. J. M. (1988). Understanding gestures in another culture: A study with children from the Dutch Antilles and the Netherlands. In F. Poyatos (Ed.), *Cross-cultural perspectives in nonverbal communication.* Toronto: Hogrefe.

Varney, N. R. (1978). Linguistic correlates of pantomime recognition in asphasic patients. *Journal of Neurology, Neurosurgery and Psychiatry, 41,* 546–568.

Walker, M. B., & Trimboli, C. (1983). The expressive functions of the eye flash. *Journal of Nonverbal Behavior, 8,* 3–13.

Warner, R. M., Malloy, D., Schneider, K., Knoth, R., & Wilder, B. (1987). Rhythmic organization of social interaction and observer ratings of positive affect and involvement. *Journal of Nonverbal Behavior, 11,* 57–74.

Washabaugh, W., Woodward, J., & DeSantis, S. (1978). Providence Island sign language: A context dependent language. *Anthropological Linguistics, 20,* 95–109.

Webb, J. T. (1972). Interview synchrony: An investigation of two speech rate measures. In A. W. Siegman & B. Pope (Eds.), *Studies in dyadic communication.* New York: Pergamon Press.

Wilkinson, L. C., & Rembold, K. L. (1981). The form and function of children's gestures accompanying verbal directives. In P. S. Dale & D. Ingram (Eds.), *Child language: An international perspective.* Baltimore: University Park Press.

Wolff, P., & Gustein, J. (1972). Effects of induced motor gestures on vocal output. *Journal of Communication, 22,* 277–288.

Woodall, W. G., & Burgoon, J. K. (1981). The effects of nonverbal synchrony on message comprehension and persuasiveness. *Journal of Nonverbal Behavior, 5,* 207–223.

Woodall, W. G., & Folger, J. P. (1981). Encoding specificity and nonverbal cue content: An expansion of episodic memory research. *Communication Monographs, 48,* 39–53.

Wundt, W. (1973). *The language of gestures.* The Hague: Mouton. (Original work published 1900).

Wylie, L. (1977). *Beaux gestes: A guide to French body talk.* Cambridge, MA: The Undergraduate Press.

Yabar, Y., Johnston, L., Miles, L., & Peace, V. (2006). Implicit behavioral mimicry: Investigating the impact of group membership. *Journal of Nonverbal Behavior, 30,* 97–113.

We often talk about the way we talk, and we frequently try to see the way we see, but for some reason we have rarely touched on the way we touch.
—Desmond Morris

8 THE EFFECTS OF TOUCH ON HUMAN COMMUNICATION

The scene is a university library, but it could just as easily be the local supermarket, bank, or restaurant. What happens takes about half a second and is not noticed by those experiencing it. Remarkably, however, this event affects their evaluation of their experience in the library. What could be so mysterious and so powerful?

The answer begins with three researchers at Purdue University (Fisher, Rytting, & Heslin, 1976), who wanted to investigate systematically the effects of a brief, seemingly accidental touch in a nonintimate context. They had male and female clerks return library cards to some students by placing their hand directly over the student's palm, making physical contact; other students were not touched. Outside the library, a researcher approached the students and asked questions about their feelings toward the library clerk and the library in general. Students who were touched, especially the females, evaluated the clerk and the library significantly more favorably than those who were not touched. This was true for students who were aware of being touched and those who were not.

Awareness of the power of a seemingly insignificant touch may be one reason why politicians are so eager to shake hands, or "press the flesh." Touch serves many functions and conveys many messages. It is a crucial aspect of most human relationships, both intimate personal. The act of touching is like any other message we communicate: it may elicit negative reactions as well as positive ones, depending on the configuration of the touch, the people involved, and the circumstances. We know that sometimes people get tense, anxious, or uncomfortable when touched. We know that when touching is perceived as inappropriate for the relationship, it can produce aggressive reactions, including touching back in the form of slapping or hitting. Some people seem to evaluate almost all touching negatively. In some cases, this dislike for touching may be related to early experiences with touch. What do we know about touching as it occurs throughout the life span?

TOUCHING AND HUMAN DEVELOPMENT

Tactile communication is probably the most basic and primitive form of communication. In fact, tactile sensitivity may be the first sensory process to become functional, and it is the most developed sense at birth. In fetal life, the child begins to respond to vibrations of the mother's pulsating heartbeat, which impinge on the child's entire body and are magnified by the amniotic fluid. In one sense, our first input about what life itself will be like comes from the sense of touch.

Research shows that touch is critical to normal physiological growth in newborns. Maternal licking of rat pups stimulates growth hormone production, and massage with pressure stimulates weight gain in preterm infants and continues to be associated with mental and motor development a year later (Field, 1998). Parent–infant bonding may also be fostered by tactile contact during a critical period in the first hours after birth, but the research on this is mixed (Hertenstein, Verkamp, Kerestes, & Holmes, 2006).

Infants gain knowledge of themselves and the world around them through tactile explorations with their mouths and hands. Some common touch experiences include the obstetrician's hands and the parents' or caregivers' hands that change diapers, feed, bathe, rock, and give comfort. During early childhood, words accompany touch until the child associates the two; then words may replace touch entirely. For example, a mother may gently stroke or pat an infant to console him or her. As the child grows older, a mother may stroke and pat the child while murmuring encouraging words. Eventually, instead of touching the child, the mother may simply call from another room, "It's all right, Mommy's here." As words replace touch, an intimate closeness may still be present because of the earlier associations.

Gender differences show up early. After 6 months of age, girls are not only allowed but are encouraged to spend more time touching and staying near their parents than boys. Harrison-Speake and Willis (1995) gathered adults' views on the appropriateness of different kinds of parental touch with children of different ages. Clear norms were evident: Touch was seen as increasingly inappropriate as children grew from toddlers to young teenagers, especially for fathers and for boys. White respondents were more approving of parental touch than were African-American respondents, regardless of the kind of touch, the child's age, or the gender of the child or parent.

Several observations of touching behavior have been made in the context of the developing child's school experiences. In one study, preschool boys tended to touch their male teachers more than their female teachers; preschool girls touched teachers of both sexes about equally. The teachers themselves usually touched children of their own sex more (Perdue & Connor, 1978). Willis and his colleagues (Willis & Hoffman, 1975; Willis & Reeves, 1976) observed children in elementary school and junior high school. From kindergarten through 6th grade, the amount of touching steadily declined but still surpassed most reports of adult touching. This same trend occurred in junior high, with about half as much touching as in the primary grades. The most touching occurred between same-sex dyads. African-American children, especially African-American females, tended to exhibit more touching behavior. Although touching in the primary grades is more often initiated with the hands, junior high students showed much more shoulder-to-shoulder and elbow-to-elbow touching. Junior high females began to show more aggressive touching, and junior high boys were touched in more places, primarily because of the play fighting so common at that age. During adolescence, tactile experiences with members of the same sex, and then the opposite sex, become increasingly important.

The use of touch to communicate emotional and relational messages to the elderly may be crucial, particularly as the reliance on verbal and cognitive messages wanes. Although we seem to give the aged in the United States a greater license to touch others, it is not clear how much others touch them. No doubt the infirmities of age require more touching, but it may make a big difference whether this increased touching is merely functional and professional or whether it expresses affection. Observations of touching in four homes for the elderly revealed that in such places, females tend to initiate more touching than do males. And, as in childhood, same-sex touch is more likely than touch between members of the opposite sex (Rinck, Willis, & Dean, 1980).

Early tactile experiences seem crucial to later mental and emotional adjustment. Youngsters who have little physical contact during infancy may be slower to learn to walk and talk, and some instances of difficulties and retardation in reading and speech are also associated with early deprivation of, and confusion in, tactile communication. Physical violence in adults may also be related to deprivation of touch during infancy.

Ashley Montagu (1971) cited many animal and human studies to support the theory that tactile satisfaction during infancy and childhood is of fundamental importance to subsequent healthy behavioral development. He maintained that it is not possible to handle a child too much, as "there is every reason to believe that, just as the salamander's brain and nervous system develops more fully in response to peripheral stimulation, so does the brain and nervous system of the human being" (p. 188). Harlow's (1958) famous "surrogate mother" experiments offer supporting evidence from the animal world for the importance of touch for infants. Harlow constructed a monkey mother figure out of wire that could provide milk and protection; then he constructed another one out of sponge rubber and terry cloth that did not provide milk. Because infant monkeys consistently chose the terry cloth mother, Harlow concluded that contact comfort was a more important part of the mother–child relationship for monkeys than was sustenance per se. Psychologically, nursing was less important as a food source and more important as a source of reassuring touch.

WHO TOUCHES WHOM, WHERE, WHEN, AND HOW MUCH?

The amount and kind of contact experienced in adulthood varies considerably with the age, personality, sex, situation, culture, and relationship of the parties involved. We explore these factors briefly here (see Chapter 12 for more discussion of gender, dominance, and culture). There are reports of married couples who either have so little to say to each other, or who find it so difficult to establish closeness through verbal contact, that physical contact during sexual encounters becomes a primary mode of communication for establishing closeness. Many factors in the development of American society have led to a common expectation that touching is conducted only in extremely personal and intimate relationships, which leads to the belief that all touching is somehow sensuous in nature. The irony is that long-term intimates probably touch each other less, and less intimately, than those who are either working to establish a romantic relationship or working to restore one that is losing intimacy (Emmers & Dindia, 1995; Guerrero & Andersen, 1991; McDaniel & Andersen, 1998). For intimates in long-established romantic relationships, the quality of touch has likely replaced the quantity needed to initially establish the relationship as an intimate one. In married relations also, people are more likely to reciprocate touch than in dating relationships (Guerrero & Andersen, 1994).

For some individuals, the contact occurring in a crowded commuter train or theater lobby is very uncomfortable, especially opposite-sex contacts for women and same-sex contacts for men. Explanations for such feelings are numerous. Some children grow up learning not to touch a multitude of animate and inanimate objects. They are told not to touch their own body and later not to touch the body of their dating partner. Care is taken so children do not see their parents touch one another intimately. Touching is associated with admonitions of "not nice" or "bad" and is punished accordingly. Because of such experiences, some people become nontouchers in any situation.

Several studies have tried to identify the personality characteristics of people who enjoy touching and those who do not (Andersen, Andersen, & Lustig, 1987; Deethardt & Hines, 1983). Sometimes these studies rely on self-reports of touch avoidance and reactions to touch. Fortunately, the self-description of oneself as touch avoidant or not has proved to be quite valid in many studies. Touch avoiders stand farther from others, respond negatively to touch in a live interaction, touch their relationship partners less in public, tend to have lower self-esteem, and are more likely to be Protestant than Jewish (Andersen, 2005). Nontouchers, when compared with touchers, report more anxiety and tension in their lives, less satisfaction with their bodies, and more suspicion of others; they are also more socially withdrawn and more likely to be rigid or authoritarian in their beliefs. Men are also more likely to describe themselves as touch avoidant than women are. Dorros, Hanzal, and Segrin (2008) found that adults who reported a more positive attitude toward touch had personalities that were more agreeable, more open to experience, and less neurotic than those who had a more negative attitude.

Certain situations have a facilitating or inhibiting effect on touching behavior. Several studies have demonstrated that in public places, where most observational research is done, touching can be quite infrequent. As an example, Hall and Veccia (1990) observed 4,500 pairs of people in public places and found that only 15 percent were already touching or had been touched during the observation period. Similarly, Remland, Jones, and Brinkman (1991) observed dyads in public places in several European locations and found that people touched in only 9 percent of the interactions observed.

Henley (1977) gathered people's opinions on touch patterns and concluded that people think that the likelihood of touch is increased in the following situations, which imply underlying themes of power, intimacy, and emotion:

1. Giving information or advice rather than asking for it
2. Giving an order rather than responding to it
3. Asking a favor rather than agreeing to do one
4. Trying to persuade rather than being persuaded
5. Participating in a deep, rather than casual, conversation

6. Interacting at a party rather than at work
7. Communicating excitement rather than receiving it from another
8. Receiving messages of worry from another rather than sending such messages

Greetings and departures at airport terminals are communicative situations that reflect a higher incidence of touching than would normally be expected. In one study, 60 percent of the people observed in greetings touched; another study reported that 83 percent of the participants touched (Greenbaum & Rosenfeld, 1980; Heslin & Boss, 1980). Heslin and Boss found that extended embraces and greater intimacy of touch were more likely to occur during departures than greetings. The stronger the emotion, as reflected in facial expressions, and the closer the perceived relationship, the greater the chances of increased touching. Actual relationship closeness, such as in romantic relationships as opposed to friendships, has in fact been shown to predict the amount of interpersonal touching in public (Afifi & Johnson, 1999; Guerrero, 1997). The term *tie signs* refers to behaviors, including touching, that signal the nature of a relationship (Goffman, 1971).

Another situation likely to show a higher incidence of touch than normally found in public settings involves team sports. In one study, the touching behavior of bowlers during league play was observed and found to be far more frequent than observations during normal social interaction (Smith, Willis, & Gier, 1980). Similarly, Kneidinger, Maple, and Tross (2001) counted touches made on the field during college baseball and softball games and found a high touching rate, averaging more than 20 touches per inning.

Anthropologists and travelers, as well as researchers, have noted that touch patterns differ according to culture and nationality. Some cultures seem very tactile, and others are more "hands off" (DiBiase & Gunnoe, 2004; McDaniel & Andersen, 1998). We explore this topic further in Chapter 13, but let us note here that cultures can differ in overall quantity of touch, the contextual rules that determine when and how people touch, and in the meanings expressed by touch. Research has not progressed far in mapping out these sources of variation. A strong likelihood is that most touches have common meanings in different cultures, but the norms for who can touch whom and when follow local customs. Most of our knowledge about the psychology of touch and other nonverbal behaviors is based on the study of white Americans.

Gender and relationships influence touching patterns. In his classic study, Jourard (1966) asked what parts of the body people think are touched most often. He administered a questionnaire to students, who indicated which of 24 body parts they had seen or touched on others, or that others had seen or touched on them, within the previous 12 months. The other people were specified as mother, father, same-sex friend, and opposite-sex friend. Among other findings, Jourard's study found that females were perceived as considerably more accessible to touch by all of the people specified than males were. Opposite-sex friends and mothers were reported as doing the most touching. Many fathers were recalled as touching not much more than the hands of the subjects. The likelihood of opposite-sex touching of course depends greatly on the relationship between the parties, and this kind of touch is more likely when intimacy and familiarity are high (Stier & Hall, 1984).

Jourard's data were gathered over 50 years ago. A replication of this study more than a decade later revealed about the same results—with one exception (Rosenfeld,

Kartus, & Ray, 1976). It seems that both males and females are perceived as even more accessible to opposite-sex friends than they were in the preceding decade, with increased touching reported for body parts normally considered more intimate, such as chest, stomach, hips, and thighs. When people are asked to recall where they have been touched and how often, there is always the possibility that these recollections will not be accurate. Jones (1991) found that the number of body parts actually contacted was consistently fewer than those anticipated or recalled by students filling out a questionnaire. In the area of touching, expectations about which touches *should* occur seem to exert an important influence on questionnaire responses.

We pursue the topic of gender differences in touch further in Chapter 12. Suffice it to say here that the observation of gender differences in nonverbal behavior raises many interesting questions about determinants. Henley (1977) proposed the hypothesis that gender differences in touch, as well as several other nonverbal behaviors, are closely tied to gender differences in dominance and power, with the general hypothesis being that differences between men and women parallel differences between powerful and weak people in society at large. The evidence supporting Henley's hypothesis is extremely mixed and is undermined by the very inconsistent evidence of systematic differences in nonverbal behavior, including touching, according to the dominance–power dimension (Hall, Coats, & Smith LeBeau, 2005; see Chapter 12).

DIFFERENT TYPES OF TOUCHING BEHAVIOR

Argyle (1975) listed the following kinds of bodily contact as most common in Western culture*:

Type of Touch	Bodily Areas Typically Involved
Patting	Head, back
Slapping	Face, hand, buttocks
Punching	Face, chest
Pinching	Cheek
Stroking	Hair, face, upper body, knee, genitals
Shaking	Hands, shoulders
Kissing	Mouth, cheek, breasts, hand, foot, genitals
Licking	Face, genitals
Holding	Hand, arm, knee, genitals
Guiding	Hand, arm
Embracing	Shoulder, body
Linking	Arms
Laying on	Hands
Kicking	Legs, buttocks
Grooming	Hair, face
Tickling	Almost anywhere

*We made the following alterations to the original list: (1) we changed *bottom* to *buttocks*; (2) added *genitals* to four categories; (3) and added *shoulders* to the "Shaking" category.

Morris (1977) reported on field observations that led to the naming of 457 types of body contact, falling into 14 major types of public body contact occurring between two people. Some of these forms of touch can be seen in Figure 8-1. Sometimes the specific nature of a relationship can be deduced by observing the way touching is enacted. Morris's major categories of nonaggressive touching include the following:

1. *The Handshake.* The strength of the tie or desired tie between the participants can often be observed by watching the nonshaking hand.
2. *The Body-Guide.* Here, touching is a substitute for pointing. The person guiding the other's body is frequently the person in charge during that encounter.
3. *The Pat.* Morris says that when adults pat other adults, it is often a condescending gesture or a sexual one. The well-known exception is the congratulatory pat, often on the buttocks, following a successful performance in men's team sports.
4. *The Arm-Link.* This may be used for support when one person is infirm, but it is also frequently used to indicate a close relationship. The person in charge, says Morris, is less likely to be the person grasping the other's arm.
5. *The Shoulder Embrace.* This half-embrace is used in male–female romantic relationships as well as to signify "buddies" in male–male relationships.
6. *The Full Embrace or Hug.* This gesture frequently occurs during moments of intense emotion, sporting events, romance, greetings, and farewells. It is also used ritualistically to show a relationship closer than a handshake would indicate.
7. *The Hand-in-Hand.* When adults hold hands with children, it is designed for support, to keep the child close, or to protect the child. As adults, hand holding suggests an equality within the relationship, because both parties are performing the same act. It is often thought of in opposite-sex relationships, but same-sex hand holding is not uncommon, even between males (e.g., children, high-contact cultures).
8. *The Waist Embrace.* According to Morris, the waist embrace is frequently substituted for the full embrace when the participants wish to signal more intimacy than hand holding or a shoulder embrace yet still remain mobile.
9. *The Kiss.* The location, pressure, duration, and openness of a kiss help signal the closeness or desired closeness of a particular moment.
10. *The Hand-to-Head.* Given the highly vulnerable nature of the head area, letting someone touch us on the head shows a trusting, often intimate, relationship.
11. *The Head-to-Head.* Two people touching heads renders them incapable of regarding other ongoing activities in a normal manner, so this is usually thought of as an agreement by both parties to shut out the rest of the world—a condition especially common to young lovers.
12. *The Caress.* This signal is associated with romantic feelings for a partner, although like any signal, it can be used by nonintimates who are trying to deceive others about the depth of their relationship.
13. *The Body Support.* Parents often support children by carrying, lifting, or letting them sit in their laps. Such support may be sought among adults in playful situations, or when one person feels physically helpless.

FIGURE 8-1

Some common forms of touch. (a) Full embrace. (b) Shoulder embrace. (c) Arm-link. (d) Kiss. (e) Head-to-head.

14. *The Mock Attack*. Aggressive-looking behaviors are sometimes performed in a nonaggressive manner; for example, arm punches, hair rufflings, pushes, pinches, ear nibbles, and so forth. We sometimes allow or even encourage such gestures with friends to show the range of behavioral understanding between us. And sometimes these mock-attack touches are substitutes for more loving touches that may be too embarrassing, such as in the case of some fathers wishing to show love for their sons.

Another method of categorizing the various types of touching was undertaken by Heslin and Alper (1983). This taxonomy is based on the functions of the messages communicated and ranges from less personal to more personal types of touch. Accidental touches and aggressive touches seem to be a part of the intimacy continuum but are not presented in this list.

1. *Functional/Professional*. The communicative intent of this impersonal, often cold and businesslike touching is to accomplish some task or to perform some service. The other person is considered an object or nonperson to keep any intimate or sexual messages from interfering with the task at hand. Examples of such situations may include a golf pro with a student, a tailor with a customer, or a physician with a patient.

2. *Social/Polite*. This type of touching affirms the other person's identity as a member of the same species, operating by essentially the same rules of conduct as functional or professional touch. Although the other is treated as a person, there is still very little perceived involvement between the interactants. The handshake is the best example of this type of touching. Although the handshake is only about 150 years old, it was preceded by a handclasp, which goes back at least as far as ancient Rome.

3. *Friendship/Warmth*. This kind of touching behavior begins to recognize more of the other person's uniqueness and expresses a liking for that person. It is oriented toward the other person as a friend. However, this type of touch may engender uneasiness, because it can be misunderstood as intimate or sexual touching. Private situations may exacerbate this problem, so it probably will take place in public if the toucher anticipates the possibility of misinterpretation.

4. *Love/Intimacy*. When we lay a hand on the cheek of a person, or when we fully embrace that person, we are probably expressing an emotional attachment or attraction through touch. The other person is the object of feelings of intimacy or love. The various kinds of touching at this point are probably the least stereotyped and the most adapted to the specific other person.

5. *Sexual Arousal*. Although sexual arousal is sometimes an integral part of love and intimacy, it also may have characteristics distinct from that category. Here we are primarily looking at touch as an experience of physical attraction only. The other person is, in common parlance, a sex object.

Morris (1971) proposed that heterosexual couples in Western culture normally go through a sequence of steps, similar to courtship patterns in other animal species, on the road to sexual intimacy. Notice that each step, aside from the first three, involves some kind of touching: eye to body, eye to eye, voice to voice, hand to hand, arm to shoulder, arm to waist, mouth to mouth, hand to head, hand to body, mouth to breast, hand to genitals, and genitals to genitals or mouth to genitals.

According to Morris, these steps generally follow the same order, although with variations. One form of skipping steps, beyond what would be expected, is found in socially formalized types of bodily contact; for example, a ritualized greeting kiss or a hand-to-hand introduction. In this case, the context alters the meaning so that anyone would understand the innocuous nature of the touch. Also, it is important to remember that designations such as "eye to eye" or "hand to body" are not very specific and can contain many variations based on stylistic features of the touch, such as duration, speed, pressure, and so on. It is a challenge to researchers to develop observational systems that are sensitive to such nuances.

Indeed, it is a challenge to study touch at all. Because people do not touch much in public, at least in Western societies (see Chapter 13 for more on culture), observers must wait long periods, and observe a great many people, to see many touches. Furthermore, the private settings in which touch occurs more often tend to be ones to which researchers do not have access. Therefore naturalistic observation is more difficult and time-consuming than for other kinds of nonverbal behavior. For this reason, touch researchers use self-report methodology relatively more. To demonstrate effects of touch, other challenges arise. Often, to create experimental control, experimenters will train helpers (called "confederates") to deliberately engage in the behavior, or not, as in the library study mentioned earlier. Experiments are an important way of studying the impact of specific behaviors. Lewis, Derlega, Shankar, Cochard, and Finkel (1997) offer a valuable caution about the use of confederates who are expected to control their behavior precisely. Despite training, confederates may have difficulty controlling one behavior, such as touch, without simultaneously changing other behaviors, such as smiling and gazing. It is sometimes hard, therefore, to know which behavioral cue was crucial in influencing the recipient of the cues. A critical reader is wise to consider possible confounding effects of unintended cues when evaluating research with these designs.

THE MEANINGS AND IMPACT OF INTERPERSONAL TOUCH

Data gathered by Jones and Yarbrough (1985) indicate a wide range of meanings associated with touch. In their study, 39 male and female university students recorded the details of each touch experience over a 3-day period. Over 1,500 acts of social touching were analyzed. The following discussion incorporates their findings, along with others.

TOUCH AS POSITIVE AFFECT

Positive touching may involve support, reassurance, appreciation, affection, sexual attraction, or, if the touch is sustained, it may send a message of inclusion (i.e., "We're together"). Some kinds of touching behavior from nurses, if it is perceived as comforting and relaxing, would fit into the category of positive touching. Back rubs and massages may also express positive feelings from a friend but may be perceived as task related when performed by a professional massage therapist. Psychotherapists, too, recognize the importance of performing touch in such a way that it communicates positive regard but not too much intimacy. If touch is perceived as an indication of interpersonal warmth, it may bring forth other related behaviors, for example, increased verbal output of patients and improved patient attitudes toward nurses (Aguilera, 1967; Pattison, 1973). The enhanced positive affect that can be produced by even fleeting touches may generalize to the entire local environment, as found in the library study described at the beginning of this chapter and in the consumer studies of Hornik (1991, 1992), in which shoppers touched by student greeters evaluated the store more favorably.

TOUCH AS NEGATIVE AFFECT

The students in Jones and Yarbrough's study did not report many touches in this category, but we clearly perceive some touches as an expression of negative attitudes and emotions. An expression of anger or frustration may be conveyed by hitting, slapping, or tightly squeezing another's arm so the person cannot escape. Generally, negative touch is much more likely among young children than among adults.

TOUCH AND DISCRETE EMOTIONS

Touch can do more than convey generalized positive and negative affect; it can convey discrete emotions. Hertenstein, Keltner, App, Bulleit, and Jaskolka (2006) videotaped participants (touchers) while they tried to convey different emotions just by touching the hand and forearm of another person (recipients). Viewers who watched the video were able to identify, at levels better than guessing, the emotions of anger, fear, happiness, disgust, love, sympathy, and disgust. Analysis of the videos provided insight into how these emotions were conveyed. For example, sympathy was expressed with stroking and patting, anger with hitting and squeezing, and disgust with a pushing motion. There were also differences in intensity and duration.

Unlike other nonverbal cues, touch can be experienced both by seeing it and by receiving it. Hertenstein, Keltner, and colleagues (2006) also asked the original recipients of the touch to guess what emotion was the toucher was trying to convey. They could not see the touches, because the touching was done while their arm was sticking through a curtain—they could only *feel* the touches. Anger, fear, disgust, sympathy, love, and gratitude could be identified at better than guessing levels; but some other emotions could not be accurately identified by those receiving them, such as embarrassment, envy, happiness, and surprise.

People can also identify discrete emotions on another person's face by *feeling* that person's face with their hands, as a blind person might do—another connection between touch and emotion. Even normally sighted individuals with no special experience in doing this decoded six emotions at levels well above guessing, with the highest accuracy for happiness, sadness, and surprise (Lederman, Klatzky, Abramowicz, Salsman, Kitada, & Hamilton, 2007).

TOUCH AS PLAY

Sometimes we interpret the touching we give and receive as attempts to reduce the seriousness of a message—whether it is affection or aggression. When one person goes through the motions of landing a knockout punch on the other person, then stops the forward movement of the fist just as it makes contact with the other person's skin, the message is "I'm not fighting, I'm playing." An accompanying smile or laugh may further reinforce this message. The ultimate in playful touch is tickling, a phenomenon first addressed by psychologists nearly a century ago and discussed even by Charles Darwin. One question is why we cannot tickle ourselves, and whether the "other" who does the tickling must be human or could as easily be a mechanical device. According to Harris and Christenfeld (1997, 1999), a machine can tickle as well as a person provided there is an element of unpredictability to it.

Touch as Influence

When the goal of the touch is to persuade the other to do something, touch is associated with influence. Jones and Yarbrough called these "compliance touches." Waitresses who touched diners got bigger tips (Crusco & Wetzel, 1984), and customers who were touched briefly by their waitress drank more alcohol compared to their partners than customers who were not touched (Kaufman & Mahoney, 1999). Customers in stores who were touched by a greeter spent more time shopping and bought more (Hornik, 1991, 1992). Psychologists who touched students on the shoulder when requesting help obtained greater compliance (Patterson, Powell, & Lenihan, 1986), and people who were touched after agreeing to fill out a survey answered a significantly larger number of items than people who agreed but were not touched (Nannberg & Hansen, 1994). In one study, people were touched on the arm for one second or less by a stranger who asked them to hold on to a very active, large dog for 10 minutes while the stranger went into a pharmacy (Guéguen & Fischer-Lokou, 2002); even this very slight tactile contact produced a greater willingness to hold on to the dog. Similarly, a female confederate asking for a cigarette from female strangers was more likely to get one if she touched the stranger slightly on the forearm (Joule & Gúeguen, 2007). In that study, unlike Fisher and colleagues' (1976) library study described at the beginning of the chapter, compliance was greater among those who remembered being touched. Even without a direct request, being touched can increase helpfulness; when a toucher walked away and then dropped his possessions as if by accident, the person who was touched was more helpful (Guéguen & Fischer-Lokou, 2003). The psychological mechanism accounting for such effects is likely to be positive affect and the personal bonding that may be implied (nonconsciously) by even a fleeting and seemingly insignificant touch between strangers. These findings suggest that one could try to use touch manipulatively; for example, waitpersons might deliberately touch their customers to get bigger tips. Such efforts would of course backfire if the touch recipients did not like the touch, or if they perceived a manipulative intent.

Aside from using touch to achieve discrete goals, such as bigger tips or a favor, people may also use touch for more general impression-management purposes; for example, to convey the impression of strength, dominance, or self-confidence. Barack Obama often grips another person's upper arm with one hand while shaking hands with the other. He may do this to convey an aura of being in control, though he could also intend to convey warmth and friendliness. Whatever the motive, the recipient might interpret it as either a welcome expression of solidarity or as an offensive act of interpersonal control. Touch exemplifies the ambiguous nature of much nonverbal communication: it is hard to know what the toucher's intention is, and the toucher may not be able to predict the recipient's reaction.

TOUCH AS INTERACTION MANAGEMENT

We try to structure or control conversations, or elements of conversations, in many ways. These "management touches" may guide someone without interrupting verbal conversation; get someone's attention by touching or tugging at that person's arm, or tapping him or her on the shoulder; indicate or mark the beginning (greeting) or end (good-bye) of a conversation; or fulfill some ritualistic function, such as touching a baby's head at a baptism.

TOUCH AS PHYSIOLOGICAL STIMULUS

Obviously, touch is preeminently important at all stages of sexual interaction. Touch is also a strong but complex stimulus in more mundane interactions. When people are in experiments in which they are forewarned that they will be touched in a professional, innocuous manner, researchers find predictable heart rate decreases (Drescher, Gantt, & Whitehead, 1980), which is said to demonstrate that touch is intrinsically calming and relates to the evolutionary importance of mother–infant bonding. However, when touch is unexpected and/or unexplained, the heart rate goes up; for example, when females were touched unexpectedly on the wrist for 10 seconds by a male experimenter, a significant increase in heart rate was found; and, moreover, all subjects showed increases in blood pressure in this condition compared to a no-touch condition and a condition in which touch was expected, such as taking a pulse (Nilsen & Vrana, 1998). Such research underscores that the impact of touch depends on social–contextual factors and on the interpretations given to the touch.

TOUCH AS INTERPERSONAL RESPONSIVENESS

Sometimes the meanings attributed to touch concern the level of involvement, responsiveness, or activity of the communicator (Afifi & Johnson, 1999). Sometimes touch simply means that the intensity of the interaction, or the interactants' level of involvement in the conversation, is high. Interpersonal responsiveness may be perceived as positive affect when it is mutually felt, or when one person feels he or she contributed to the other's behavior. Probably more than any other nonverbal behavior, acts of touch that are perceived as deliberate are extremely salient in interaction; they are almost certain to be noticed and are likely to produce strong reactions, either positive or negative.

TOUCH AS TASK RELATED

There are times when we need to help someone get out of a car, or our hands touch as the result of passing something back and forth. These touches, associated with the performance of a task, are similar to what Heslin called "functional/

professional touch." As with any other message, the two communicators may not share a similar meaning for the touch—or one person may deliberately try to mislead another. A not unfamiliar example of the latter deception is when one person touches another in a joking context but intends the touch to be a step toward intimacy. Such a blending of functions has also occurred in studies, such as the library touch study described earlier: the touch occurred during task performance, while handing the library card to the patron, but the effect was positive–emotional.

Touch as Healing

A miraculous cure is one that cannot be explained by recognized medical or physiological therapy. Throughout recorded history, wondrous healings of the sick and infirm by religious workers, royalty, and other charismatic persons have had interpersonal touch as a major ingredient. Jesus was said to heal by touch, and he was often described as being surrounded by crowds hoping for his touch. The French and English kings were widely believed to be able to accomplish healing by the laying on of hands. Edward I of England is documented to have touched 938 of his subjects suffering from scrofula in the 28th year of his reign (Older, 1982). In later centuries, including our own, healing touch became the province of ministers and of others who attribute the healing touch to the power of God. The healing power of touch in so-called miraculous cases has not been studied in a controlled way that could establish its effectiveness or the mechanisms by which it may work. Although it may be difficult to rule out the power of God or some unknown physical forces, Older (1982) attributes inexplicable cures to psychological factors:

- The patient feels a great need for improvement.
- The patient has profound trust in the healer's powers.
- The patient is part of a group that increases pressure and adds encouragement.
- There is a shared, irrational belief system, usually of a religious nature.
- Emotions are at a high pitch in the patient and in any onlookers.

Currently, the medical and nursing professions have shown renewed interest in touching as a form of therapy (Borelli & Heidt, 1981; Kerr, Wasserman, & Moore, 2007; Krieger, 1987). Some touch therapies involving what researchers call "light touch" have been shown to reduce pain (Kerr et al., 2007). Massage, long known for its relaxing and pleasurable properties, also has positive effects on other outcomes such as brain activity, attentiveness and alertness, pain relief, anxiety and depression, stress hormones, sleep, appetite, pulmonary function in asthmatic children, immune function, weight gain in preterm infants, and other clinical indicators of health (Field, 1998, 2001; Field, Diego, & Hernandez-Reif, 2007). It has been suggested that parasympathetic nervous system activity may be the mechanism underlying massage's favorable impact: the pressure stimulates the vagal nerve, which lowers physiological arousal and stress hormones. Even a single massage-therapy session has beneficial effects on anxiety, blood pressure, and heart rate (Moyer, Rounds, & Hannum, 2004).

The beneficial effects of touch may partially underlie the beneficial physiological and psychological effects of having pets, because relationships with pets typically entail high levels of touching (Allen, 2003). Because touch can be so comforting and physiologically beneficial, researchers in one study were surprised at how little supportive touching took place between parents and their children with cancer during painful medical procedures, such as a lumbar puncture. Based on videotape analysis, over one-quarter of the children received no supportive touch when they needed it most (Peterson, Cline, Foster, Penner, Parrott, & Keller, 2007).

Mental health professionals and physicians debate whether touch should be incorporated into the therapeutic process (Hetherington, 1998; Smith, Clance, & Imes, 1998; Young, 2007). Risk of sexual involvement, or simply risk that clients will take offense, is weighed against the potential value of human physical contact during stressful moments. Certainly therapists, and medical doctors as well, need to be highly sensitive to the responses that clients may have to being touched.

According to some, especially in the nursing profession, healing can be accomplished even without any actual touch. The method called "therapeutic touch," or "TT" for short, has been widely claimed as effective for many physical conditions when used by practitioners who strongly endorse the concept. The TT practitioner moves the hands *above*, not on, the patient's body, and in so doing supposedly influences the energy field surrounding the patient, with therapeutic benefit. Believers and skeptics have debated whether this method is any better than a simple placebo, but little empirical research has been conducted to settle the issue. However, a study published in a prestigious medical journal casts serious doubt on one of TT's basic principles—that the experienced TT practitioner can detect the energy emanating from another person's body (Rosa, Rosa, Sarner, & Barrett, 1998). Experienced TT practitioners serving as subjects were told that the experimenter would hold her own hand over one of the subject's hands—blocked from the subject's view by a screen—and all the subject had to do was guess which hand the experimenter's hand was above. Much to the subjects' surprise, "guess" was an apt word, because in fact, their accuracy was no better than chance, meaning they could not detect an energy field around the experimenter's hand. Thus, this well controlled study strongly suggested that TT adherents are guided more by faith than by science. (Interestingly, the young scientist who conducted and coauthored this research was a 4th grader conducting a school science project!)

TOUCH AS SYMBOLISM

Perhaps because touch outside of intimate relationships is so infrequent, it is highly salient when it occurs. Touch can be so fraught with meaning that the act of touch itself comes to represent the significance of the relationship, ritual, or occasion. The touch shown in Figure 8-2 between Israeli leader Yitzhak Rabin and Palestinian leader Yasir Arafat on the day they announced an Israeli–Palestinian reconciliation says more than words could. Ironically, that same handshake apparently sparked Rabin's assassin to plan the prime minister's death ("With a Handshake," 1995).

Sometimes, the symbolism of a touch is experienced at a very personal level through one's own experience of touch. We are all familiar with photographs of screaming fans reaching out to touch a famous rock star. Even in everyday situations, people often find value in touching someone who is important to them. They might say proudly, "I shook so-and-so's hand!" The vicarious symbolic

FIGURE 8-2

Rabin and Arafat shaking hands.

power of touch is sometimes evident even when the actual touch is one step re-moved from the actual person, as when one can touch or possess a remnant or other souvenir of the important person. Even an autograph fits this description, because the important person has touched the pen and paper. Certainly, through-out the history of Christianity, it has been very meaningful to claim to own a piece of a saint's body or clothing.

Figure 8-3 vividly portrays an audience reaching out to touch President Bush. One study of touch patterns in a state legislature noted that though the governor was touched by many, he was not seen to touch anyone during the observation period (Goldstein & Jeffords, 1981). The daughter of the Buddhist Panchen Lama, a holy man second in importance to the Dalai Lama, recollected a trip to Tibet when she was 7 years old: "They told me that there were people lining the road for fifty miles. Thousands and thousands of people, all wanting to touch me" (Hilton, 2004). On another trip, at age 17, she told of being exhausted by the crowds surrounding her. But, she said, "I can't complain, because it makes them so happy to see me and to touch me." But she had to ask her bodyguards to stop them from lifting up her skirt to get to her legs.

Touching in these scenarios gives the toucher the feeling of acquiring some-thing important: something has "rubbed off" on them. It does not always seem to matter whether the significant other person is the toucher or the recipient. What is rubbed off can vary, too. Sometimes it is vicarious power: the person is somehow more important among peers after touching a famous person. Other times, what is gained is less definable though no less important: We might say that one feels one has acquired some piece of the other's essence through touch. Whatever the

FIGURE 8-3

The audience is eager to touch President Bush after one of his speeches.

valuable quality possessed by the other, people feel they have gained a bit of it through even a very minor touch. This somewhat magical way of thinking has its reverse side, too, when we feel contaminated by touching or being touched by undesirable people. It is surely no coincidence that members of the lowest caste in traditional Hindu society in India were called "Untouchables."

CONTEXTUAL FACTORS IN THE MEANING OF INTERPERSONAL TOUCH

The meanings of touch depend on many environmental, personal, and contextual variables, as previous sections have made clear. Indeed, it is likely that much of the time, the meaning of touch derives from such qualifying variables and not from the nature of the touch *per se*. Often, touch intensifies ongoing emotional experiences rather than conveying specific meanings or messages. The relationship between the interactants provides important context for interpreting the meaning of touch. A touch on the arm, which might be interpreted as a social/polite or merely friendly gesture between strangers, may acquire sexual overtones if a friendly relationship already exists. An embrace may take on different intimacy connotations if displayed by two men versus two women (Floyd, 1999), or if two men embrace on the sports field versus in a bar (Kneidinger et al., 2001).

Interpretations of touch are also related to other contextual variables such as duration, the specific form of the touch, other cues, and other contextual features, singly and in combination; for example, a touch might seem more intimate if it is accompanied by other signals, such as prolonged gaze, or if the touch is held an instant too long, if the environment is private, and so forth. A brief shoulder touch by waitpersons to their customers resulted in bigger tips, but especially if it was opposite-gender touching in a bar (Hubbard, Tsuji, Williams, & Seatriz, 2003). Friendship/warmth touching may be more likely to occur in public settings between people who are not intimate, because the same kind of contact in private is more likely to take on connotations of love or sexual intimacy. Certain parts of the body connote greater intimacy than other parts, but intimacy is also linked to the manner of touch. For instance, a touch and release on any part of the body is likely to be perceived as less intimate than a touch and hold.

Men and women may also attribute different meanings to similar types of touch. In a hospital study by Whitcher and Fisher (1979), female nurses touched patients during an explanation of procedures prior to surgery. Females reacted positively, showing lower anxiety, more positive preoperative behavior, and more favorable postoperative physiological responses. But men who were touched in the same way reacted less positively. A similar result was obtained by Lewis, Derlega, Nichols, Shankar, Drury, and Hawkins (1995), who obtained ratings of photographic representations of nurses touching or not touching patients at the bedside. Men who looked at the photos rated both male and female nurses as more supportive if they did not touch the patient, whereas women viewers thought the nurses were more supportive if they did.

Heslin, Nguyen, and Nguyen (1983) found that men and women responded differently in a questionnaire study regarding people from whom touching would be considered the greatest invasion of privacy. Women indicated that touch from a stranger would be the greatest invasion of privacy, whereas men felt that touch from a same-sex person would be the greatest invasion of privacy. Men reported themselves to be as comfortable with touch from women strangers as they were with touch from women friends! Both men and women agreed that the most pleasant type of touch was stroking in sexual areas by an opposite-sex friend. But the second most pleasant type of touch reported by women was for a male friend to stroke nonsexual areas, whereas the second most pleasant type of touch by men was for a female stranger to stroke sexual areas.

Marital status influences how men and women interpret different kinds of touches. Over 300 individuals who were in an intimate relationship, either married or not, reported on what it meant to them when their significant other touched them on various parts of the body (Hanzal, Segrin, & Dorros, 2008). Confirming results found by Nguyen, Heslin, and Nguyen (1976), unmarried men found more pleasantness and warmth or love in being touched than unmarried women did, but this pattern was reversed among those who were married—in this group, the women found greater reward in being touched. Moreover, this result was not due to the difference in age between the unmarried and married groups.

TOUCH CAN BE A POWERFUL UNCONSCIOUS FORCE IN INTERACTION

As studies cited earlier indicate, being touched can influence our perceptions, moods, and behaviors even when it is fleeting, subtle, and possibly even unnoticed. But just as the influence of touch can be unconscious on the part of the person being touched, so too can it be unconscious on the part of the *toucher*. A most vivid demonstration of this point can be found in the phenomenon called *facilitated communication*, a technique developed for improving the communication of individuals with autism, mental retardation, and physical diseases that impair motor abilities and communication, such as cerebral palsy. Facilitated communication was hailed on several continents as a breakthrough in the ability of speech-impaired individuals to communicate, and it became widely practiced and taught in the 1980s and 1990s (Jacobson, Mulick, & Schwartz 1995; Spitz, 1997).

How does facilitated communication work? The technique is based on close tactile contact between the facilitator and the communicator, as well as a close psychological relationship in which trust is established. The facilitator holds and steadies the communicator's hands while the communicator types words or sentences on a keyboard. Using this method, many communication-impaired clients typed out highly revealing, often eloquent accounts of their feelings and thoughts. To many observers, it seemed that at last individuals with impairments could overcome their isolation and break out of their terrible enforced silence. Or so it seemed.

Unfortunately, facilitated communication proved not to reveal the impaired communicators' thoughts, but rather the thoughts of the facilitators themselves. Research showed that the communicators were able to answer questions only when their facilitator knew the question and its answer, and communicators' responses often seemed much too verbally advanced for their intellectual level. In fact, communicators could even type out answers to questions when they were not looking at the keyboard (Kezuka, 1997; Spitz, 1997). Proceeding against a wave of protest by those who believed in the system, researchers persisted in conducting controlled experiments that ultimately revealed that often the facilitated communication effects were due to the facilitator's unconsciously guiding the communicator's hand to type out what was in the facilitator's mind. Research showed that when facilitators were fed incorrect information about the communicator's background, and then had to ask the communicator about those same facts, the "answers" given reflected the misinformation, not the true answers (Burgess, Kirsch, Shane, Niederauer, Graham, & Bacon, 1998). Kezuka (1997), using mechanical methods of determining physical force exerted by the facilitators, demonstrated that facilitators did indeed use tiny muscle movements of their hand, and sometimes facial and other cues, to influence the position of the communicator's hand. Thus, the facilitators were the real communicators.

What makes facilitated communication fascinating and important for behavioral science is the fact that, in all likelihood, the great majority of facilitators were not frauds or charlatans but sincere believers (Spitz, 1997). Needless to say, the exposure of the true nature of facilitated communication was a great disappointment to those who believed in it. However, the actual—that is, unconscious—mechanism of its effect is no less astonishing than the original claims. How could the facilitators be expressing their own thoughts without being aware of it?

But this is not the first phenomenon involving unconscious movement that has been documented. In the 19th century, great interest was paid to pendulums purported to swing in response to mysterious forces. Forked sticks called *dowsing rods* are said to suddenly point downward when the person using them walks over a place where there is underground water (Vogt & Hyman, 2000). And furniture has suddenly moved or turned, supposedly under the influence of spirits (Spitz, 1997). In all of these cases, there were no supernatural forces at work, only strong expectancies that produced motor responses that were out of awareness. We can also include on this list Clever Hans, the brilliant horse described in Chapter 1. Hans's brilliance was not that he could read and do math—he could not, of course—but that he noticed and acted on minute physical movements made by people who knew the answers. These unwitting accomplices, like the facilitated communicators, were completely unaware that their movements were producing the horse's responses. Indeed, like the people with impairments in the facilitated communication paradigm, Clever Hans could not "answer" questions correctly unless the questioner or some other onlooker knew the correct response. All of these phenomena rest on what Wegner, Fuller, and Sparrow (2003) call "authorship confusion"—attributing the source of action to the wrong person or agent.

SELF-TOUCHING

People also communicate nonverbally through self-touching that includes nail chewing, skin picking, twirling the hair, hand wringing, lip biting, holding, stroking, and self-grooming activities. It is not clear what psychological functions are served by these actions, though researchers generally agree that they are more an out-of-awareness expression of personal needs than reflective of intentional communication—more "signs" than "signals." However, intentional communication sometimes involves self-touching, as when a sexual come-on includes self-stroking. Various kinds of self-touching, or self-touching used in different circumstances, may serve different functions. Figure 8-4 shows several kinds of self-touching.

Morris (1971) offered a list of different kinds of self-touching:

1. *Shielding Actions.* These behaviors usually involve reducing input or output, for example, covering the mouth or ears with the hand(s).
2. *Cleaning Actions.* Sometimes we bring our hands up to our head to scratch, rub, pick, or wipe—for literal cleaning. But sometimes similar self-touching is used for attending to our appearance; for example, hair grooming, clothes straightening, and other types of preening. Observations and subsequent interviews with people in public restrooms found women engaging in more of this behavior than men. People in the process of building an intimate relationship did more preening than those whose intimate relationship had been established for some time (Daly, Hogg, Sacks, Smith, & Zimring, 1983).
3. *Specialized Signals.* These gestures are used to communicate specific messages, such as cupping the ear with the hand to signal an inability to hear, or holding a hand under the chin to signal "I have had it up to here."

FIGURE 8-4
Self-touching.

4. *Self-Intimacies*. Self-intimacies, according to Morris, are comforting actions that represent unconsciously reproduced acts of being touched by someone else. They may involve holding one's own hands, arm folding, leg crossing, masturbation, and so on. Some, he maintains, are more likely to be performed by women than men, for example, the head-lowered-on-to-the-shoulder posture and leg hugging. Thus self-touching can be a substitute for comfort that might otherwise be provided by others.

Some self-touching behaviors are what Ekman and Friesen called *adaptors* or *self-manipulators*. As the term implies, they are behavioral adaptations in response to certain situations. There is consensus that adaptors are generally associated with negative feelings. Some useful classifications exist for different types of adaptors, which include both the probable referent for the behavior—self, other, or object—and the type of behavior, such as scratching or rubbing.

Research on psychiatric patients has found that self-adaptors increase as a person's psychological discomfort, anxiety, or depression increase (Ekman & Friesen, 1972; Freedman, 1972; Freedman, Blass, Rifkin, & Quitkin, 1973; Freedman & Hoffman, 1967; Waxer, 1977). If, however, the anxiety level is too high, a person may freeze, engaging in little movement at all. The finding that self-adaptors also were associated with guilt feelings in the patients studied illuminates one aspect of the deception research we review in Chapter 12. Ekman and Friesen also discovered picking and scratching self-adaptors to be related to a person's hostility and suspiciousness. Theoretically, this picking and scratching is a manifestation of aggression against oneself or aggression felt for another person that is directed inward. Other speculations and hypotheses about self-adaptors include the possibility that rubbing is used to give self-assurance, that covering the eyes is associated with shame or guilt, that self-grooming shows concern for one's self-presentation, or that self-touching is an outlet for nervous energy.

A number of studies have indicated that self-touching is associated with situational anxiety or stress. This is the case in baboons as well as in people (Castles, Whitens, & Aureli, 1999). Ekman and Friesen (1974) asked people to watch one of two films, one highly stressful and the other quite pleasant. Viewers were then instructed to describe the film as pleasant to an interviewer. Thus, those watching the stressful film were trying to deceive, which in itself can be considered stressful. Participants in the second group engaged in more self-touch than those simply describing the pleasant film as pleasant. In a study of physician–patient communication, patients were more likely to touch their bodies when talking about conflictual hidden agendas than when talking about the primary complaint (Shreve, Harrigan, Kues, & Kagas, 1988).

Interracial interaction is another context in which stress can produce self-touching. Olson and Fazio (2007) coded any kind of self-manipulation—such as scratching the head, playing with the hair, or kneading the hands—by white participants when interacting with black and white confederates. The participants' general racial attitudes were measured, as well as their attitudes about the particular black confederate they interacted with. When these two kinds of attitudes were discordant—such as when their general attitude was negative, but their attitude toward the particular black confederate was positive—participants engaged in significantly higher levels of self-touching. This study well illustrates the complexity of interpreting the meaning of nonverbal communication. Though some authors have emphasized prejudiced individuals' communication of hostile attitudes through nonverbal behaviors, this study reminds us that nonverbal behavior can also be a sign of discomfort or internal conflict, and not due to interpersonal negativity per se.

Self-touching is also greater in people who are chronically anxious, a variable known as *trait anxiety*, such as among people who are shy but also have a desire to be sociable (Cheek & Buss, 1981). When trait anxiety is measured indirectly, using a reaction-time task, it predicts self-touching and other behavioral signs of anxiety better than an explicit self-report does. Perhaps on an explicit self-report, highly anxious people deny their anxiety or are not fully aware of it (Egloff & Schmukle, 2002). An interesting question is whether the self-touching associated with anxiety is simply an indicator that anxiety is occurring, or whether such touching actually relieves stress.

Another source of body-focused movements is cognitive, or information-processing, demand. When engaged in a monologue, people touched themselves more than when simply sitting still, and in Heaven and McBrayer's (2000) study, people touched themselves more when answering questions about a passage they heard than when simply listening to it. When asked to read the names of colors that were printed in contradictory colors, such as the word *red* printed in blue, people touched themselves more than if they were given color-consistent color names to read (Kenner, 1993). These results suggest that mental concentration and stress can be a cause of self-touching.

Though not much direct evidence exists for how aware people are of their self-touching, it is generally assumed that, compared to some other nonverbal behaviors, self-touching is low in awareness. Hall, Murphy, and Schmid Mast (2007) found that, indeed, when asked how much of several nonverbal behaviors they engaged in during a videotaped interaction, people were least accurate in remembering how much they had engaged in self-touching, though they did remember their self-touching at levels better than chance.

The concept of adaptors can be extended to behaviors other than self-touching. Such behaviors are theorized to have been learned in conjunction with our early experiences with interpersonal relations: giving and taking from another, attacking or protecting, establishing closeness or withdrawing, and so forth. Ekman believes that restless movements of the hands and feet, which have typically been considered indicators of anxiety, may be residues of adaptors necessary for flight from an interaction.

Object-adaptors involve the manipulation of objects for no obvious functional purpose but they may be derived from the performance of some instrumental task, for example, writing with a pencil or smoking. Some people engage in these mannerisms more than others. Although people are typically unaware of performing self-adaptor behaviors, they are probably more aware of object-adaptors. These movements are often learned later in life, and fewer social taboos seem to be associated with them. As with self-adaptors, object-adaptors are likely to be associated with anxiety, stress, or cognitive load.

Because there are social constraints on displaying some self-adaptors, they are more often seen when a person is alone. At any rate, in public we would not expect to see the full act. As an example, alone you might pick your nose without inhibition, but when around other people, you may just touch your nose or rub it casually. Although adaptors are typically not intended for use in communication, they may be triggered by verbal behavior in a situation associated with conditions that were present when the adaptive habit was first learned.

Individual and group differences in self-touching have been found. In a study of children from four countries, those from England and Australia engaged in significantly less self-touching during experimental tasks than did Italian children and French-speaking children in Belgium. Possibly, touching of other people may parallel these self-touching differences across these cultures. Also in those samples, significant individual variation was revealed, meaning that some children were consistently more likely to touch themselves during a variety of experimental tasks (Kenner, 1993). Another group difference relates to gender: women touch themselves in interpersonal interaction more than men do (Hall, 1984). It is not clear to what extent this may reflect greater social anxiety or arousal on the part of females, a heightened self-consciousness about appearance, or the simple fact that women's clothes and hair often demand readjustment.

SUMMARY

Our first information about ourselves, others, and our environment probably comes from touching. The act of touching or being touched can have a powerful impact on our response to a situation, even if that touch was unintentional. In some cases, touching is the most effective method for communicating; in others, it can elicit negative or hostile reactions. The meanings we attach to touching behavior vary according to what body part is touched, how long the touch lasts, the strength of the touch, the method of the touch, and the frequency of the touch. Touch also means different things in different environments—institutions, airports, and so on—and varies with communicators' age, gender, culture, personality, and relationship. Indications are that children in the U.S. touch more than adults do, but there seems to be a decreasing amount of touch from kindergarten through junior high school. Investigators agree that early experiences with touch are crucial for later adjustment.

The common types of interpersonal touching and self-touching may communicate a variety of messages that include influence, positive affect, negative affect, play, interpersonal responsiveness, interaction management, and task requirements. Touch can have powerful symbolism, and its possible healing and therapeutic power has received much attention throughout history and in modern research laboratories. Touching can also intensify whatever emotional experience is occurring. Touch can be a powerful source of behavioral influence, and both the toucher and the recipient of touch may be unaware of its occurrence and effects.

QUESTIONS FOR DISCUSSION

1. Think of a person you know personally who does not like touching or being touched. What analysis can you offer for this person's characteristic? How much do you think it reflects personal history and personality versus social and cultural norms?

2. What do you think about the ethics of using touch to achieve compliance or a favor from someone? Is it different from using persuasive language or using other forms of nonverbal communication, such as smiling or generally "being nice"?

3. Most studies find that touch is a rather infrequent event. Do you think this is correct? Discuss exceptions to this generalization. Why do you think touch might seem to be not very common?

4. Sometimes people are eager to touch others because they gain something of psychological value by doing so, yet people often feel violated by being touched. Discuss these different perspectives on the phenomenon of touch.

5. It has been suggested that sometimes a woman's friendly intention touch is misperceived by a man as being a sexual invitation. Have you ever had such an experience? Do you think this is a true phenomenon?

6. For a day, pay close attention to your own and others' use of self-touching. Try to analyze the circumstances under which people engage in this behavior. Note what brings it on, what situations it occurs in, and what kind of people do it more or do it less. What kind of psychological function do you think self-touching serves?

BIBLIOGRAPHY

Afifi, W. A., & Johnson, M. L. (1999). The use and interpretation of tie signs in a public setting: Relationship and sex differences. *Journal of Social and Personal Relationships, 16,* 9–38.

Aguilera, D. C. (1967). Relationships between physical contact and verbal interaction between nurses and patients. *Journal of Psychiatric Nursing, 5,* 5–21.

Alagna, F. J., Whitcher, S. J., Fisher, J. D., & Wicas, E. A. (1969). Evaluative reaction to interpersonal touch in a counseling interview. *Journal of Counseling Psychology, 26,* 465–472.

Allen, K. (2003). Are pets a healthy pleasure? The influence of pets on blood pressure. *Current Directions in Psychological Science, 12,* 236–239.

Andersen, P. A. (2005). The Touch Avoidance Measure. In V. Manusov (Ed.), *The sourcebook of nonverbal measures* (pp. 57–65). Mahwah, NJ: Erlbaum.

Andersen, J. F., Andersen, P. A., & Lustig, M. W. (1987). Opposite-sex touch avoidance: A national replication and extension. *Journal of Nonverbal Behavior, 11,* 89–109.

Andersen, P. A., & Leibowitz, K. (1978). The development and nature of the construct touch avoidance. *Environmental Psychology and Nonverbal Behavior, 3,* 89–106.

Argyle, M. (1975). *Bodily communication.* New York: International Universities Press.

Barnlund, D. C. (1975). Communicative styles in two cultures: Japan and the United States. In A. Kendon, R. M. Harris, & M. R. Key (Eds.), *Organization of behavior in face-to-face interaction.* The Hague: Mouton.

Barroso, F., & Feld, J. K. (1986). Self-touching and attentional processes: The role of task difficulty, selection stage, and sex differences. *Journal of Nonverbal Behavior, 10,* 51–64.

Blondis, M., & Barbara, J. (1982). *Nonverbal communication in nursing: Back to the human touch.* New York: Wiley Medical.

Borelli, M., & Heidt, P. (1981). *Therapeutic touch: A book of readings.* New York: Springer.

Brownlee, J., & Bakeman, R. (1981). Hitting in toddler–peer interaction. *Child Development, 52,* 1076–1079.

Burgess, C. A., Kirsch, I., Shane, H., Niederauer, K. L., Graham, S. M., & Bacon, A. (1998). Facilitated communication as an ideomotor response. *Psychological Science, 9,* 71–74.

Burgoon, J. K. (1991). Relational message interpretations of touch, conversational distance, and posture. *Journal of Nonverbal Behavior, 15,* 233–259.

Casler, L. (1965). The effects of extra tactile stimulation on a group of institutionalized infants. *Genetic Psychology Monographs, 71,* 137–175.

Castles, D. L., Whitens, A., & Aureli, F. (1999). Social anxiety, relationships and self-directed behaviour among wild female olive baboons. *Animal Behavior, 58,* 1207–1215.

Cheek, J. M., & Buss, A. H. (1981). Shyness and sociability. *Journal of Personality and Social Psychology, 41,* 330–339.

Cooper, C. L., & Bowles, D. (1973). Physical encounter and self-disclosure. *Psychological Reports, 33,* 451–454.

Cooper, V. W. (1987). The tactile communication system: State of the art and research perspectives.

In B. Dervin & M. J. Voigt (Eds.), *Progress in communication sciences* (Vol. 8). Norwood, NJ: Ablex.

Crusco, A. H., & Wetzel, C. G. (1984). The Midas touch: The effects of interpersonal touch on restaurant tipping. *Personality and Social Psychology Bulletin, 10*, 512–517.

Daly, J. A., Hogg, E., Sacks, D., Smith, M., & Zimring, L. (1983). Sex and relationship affect social self-grooming. *Journal of Nonverbal Behavior, 7*, 183–189.

Deethardt, J. F., & Hines, D. G. (1983). Tactile communication and personality differences. *Journal of Nonverbal Behavior, 8*, 143–156.

DiBiase, R., & Gunnoe, J. (2004). Gender and culture differences in touching behavior. *Journal of Social Psychology, 144*, 49–62.

Dorros, S., Hanzal, A., & Segrin, C. (2008). The Big Five personality traits and perceptions of touch to intimate and nonintimate body regions. *Journal of Research in Personality, 42*, 1067–1073.

Drescher, V. M., Gantt, W. H., & Whitehead, W. E. (1980). Heart rate response to touch. *Psychosomatic Medicine, 42*, 559–565.

Dresslar, F. B. (1984). Studies in the psychology of touch. *American Journal of Psychology, 6*, 313–368.

Egloff, B., & Schmukle, S. C. (2002). Predictive validity of an implicit association test for assessing anxiety. *Journal of Personality and Social Psychology, 83*, 1441–1455.

Ekman, P., & Friesen, W. V. (1972). Hand movements. *Journal of Communication, 22*, 353–374.

Ekman, P., & Friesen, W. V. (1974). Detecting deception from the body or face. *Journal of Personality and Social Psychology, 29*, 288–298.

Emmers, T. M., & Dindia, K. (1995). The effect of relational stage and intimacy on touch: An extension of Guerrero and Andersen. *Personal Relationships, 2*, 225–236.

Field, T (1998). Touch therapy effects on development. *International Journal of Behavioral Development, 22*, 779–797.

Field, T. (1999). American adolescents touch each other less and are more aggressive toward their peers as compared with French adolescents. *Adolescence, 34*, 753–758.

Field, T. (2001). *Touch*. Cambridge, MA: MIT Press.

Field, T., Diego, M., & Hernandez-Reif, M. (2007). Massage therapy research. *Developmental Review, 27*, 75–89.

Fisher, J. D., Rytting, M., & Heslin, R. (1976). Hands touching hands: Affective and evaluative effects of an interpersonal touch. *Sociometry, 39*, 416–421.

Floyd, K. (1999). All touches are not created equal: Effects of form and duration on observers' interpretations of an embrace. *Journal of Nonverbal Behavior, 23*, 283–299.

Forden, C. (1981). The influence of sex-role expectations on the perception of touch. *Sex Roles, 7*, 889–894.

Frank, L. K. (1957). Tactile communication. *Genetic Psychology Monographs, 56*, 209–255.

Freedman, N. (1972). The analysis of movement behavior during the clinical interview. In A. W. Siegman & B. Pope (Eds.), *Studies in dyadic communication*. New York: Pergamon Press.

Freedman, N., Blass, T., Rifkin, A., & Quitkin, F. (1973). Body movements and the verbal encoding of aggressive affect. *Journal of Personality and Social Psychology, 26*, 72–85.

Freedman, N., & Hoffman, S. P. (1967). Kinetic behavior in altered clinical states: Approach to objective analysis of motor behavior during clinical interviews. *Perceptual and Motor Skills, 24*, 527–539.

Goffman, E. (1971). *Relations in public*. New York: Basic Books.

Goldberg, M. A., & Katz, B. (1990). The effect of nonreciprocated and reciprocated touch on power/dominance perception. *Journal of Social Behavior and Personality, 5*, 379–386.

Goldberg, S., & Rosenthal, R. (1986). Self-touching behavior in the job interview: Antecedents and consequences. *Journal of Nonverbal Behavior, 10*, 65–80.

Goldstein, A. G., & Jeffords, J. (1981). Status and touching behavior. *Bulletin of the Psychonomic Society, 17*, 79–81.

Greenbaum, P. E., & Rosenfeld, H. M. (1980). Varieties of touching in greetings: Sequential structure and sex-related differences. *Journal of Nonverbal Behavior, 5*, 13–25.

Guéguen, N., & Fischer-Lokou, J. (2002). An evaluation of touch on a large request: A field setting. *Psychological Reports, 90*, 267–269.

Guéguen, N., & Fischer-Lokou, J. (2003). Tactile contact and spontaneous help: An evaluation in a natural setting. *Journal of Social Psychology, 143*, 785–787.

Guerrero, L. K. (1997). Nonverbal involvement across interactions with same-sex friends, opposite-sex friends and romantic partners: Consistency or change? *Journal of Social and Personal Relationships, 14*, 31–58.

Guerrero, L. K., & Andersen, P. A. (1991). The waxing and waning of relational intimacy: Touch as a function of relational stage, gender and touch avoidance. *Journal of Social and Personal Relationships, 8*, 147–165.

Guerrero, L. K., & Andersen, P. A. (1994). Patterns of matching and initiation: Touch behavior and touch avoidance across romantic relationship stages. *Journal of Nonverbal Behavior, 18*, 137–153.

Halberstadt, A. G. (1985). Race, socioeconomic status, and nonverbal behavior. In A. W. Siegman and S. Feldstein (Eds.), *Multichannel integrations of nonverbal behavior*. Hillsdale, NJ: Erlbaum.

Hall, E. T. (1966). *The hidden dimension*. New York: Doubleday Anchor.

Hall, J. A. (1984). *Nonverbal sex differences: Communication accuracy and expressive style*. Baltimore: Johns Hopkins University Press.

Hall, J. A. (1996). Touch, status, and gender at professional meetings. *Journal of Nonverbal Behavior, 20*, 23–44.

Hall, J. A., Coats, E. J., & Smith LeBeau, L. (2004). *Nonverbal behavior and the vertical dimension of social relations: A meta-analysis*. Manuscript submitted for publication.

Hall, J. A., Murphy, N. A., & Schmid Mast, M. (2007). Nonverbal self-accuracy in interpersonal interaction. *Personality and Social Psychology Bulletin, 33*, 1675–1685.

Hall, J. A., & Veccia, E. M. (1990). More "touching" observations: New insights on men, women, and interpersonal touch. *Journal of Personality and Social Psychology, 59*, 1155–1162.

Hanzal, A., Segrin, C., & Dorros, S. M. (2008). The role of marital status and age on men's and women's reactions to touch from a relational partner. *Journal of Nonverbal Behavior, 32*, 21–35.

Harlow, H. F. (1958). The nature of love. *American Psychologist, 13*, 678–685.

Harrigan, J. A., Lucic, K. S., Kay, D., McLaney, A., & Rosenthal, R. (1991). Effect of expresser role and type of self-touching on observers' perceptions. *Journal of Applied Social Psychology, 21*, 585–609.

Harris, C. R., & Christenfeld, N. (1997). Humour, tickle, and the Darwin-Hecker hypothesis. *Cognition & Emotion, 11*, 103–110.

Harris, C. R., & Christenfeld, N. (1999). Can a machine tickle? *Psychonomic Bulletin and Review, 6*, 504–510.

Harrison-Speake, K., & Willis, F. N. (1995). Ratings of the appropriateness of touch among family members. *Journal of Nonverbal Behavior, 19*, 85–100.

Heaven, L., & McBrayer, D. (2000). External motivators of self-touching behavior. *Perceptual and Motor Skills, 90*, 338–342.

Heller, M. A., & Schiff, W. (Eds.). (1991). *The psychology of touch*. Hillsdale, NJ: Erlbaum.

Henley, N. (1973a). Status and sex: Some touching observations. *Bulletin of the Psychonomic Society, 2*, 91–93.

Henley, N. (1973–1974). Power, sex and nonverbal communication. *Berkeley Journal of Sociology, 18*, 1–26.

Henley, N. (1977). *Body politics: Power, sex, and nonverbal communication*. Englewood Cliffs, NJ: Prentice-Hall.

Hertenstein, M. J., Keltner, D., App, B., Bulleit, B. A., & Jaskolka, A. R. (2006). Touch communicates distinct emotions. *Emotion, 6*, 528–533.

Hertenstein, M. J., Verkamp, J. M., Kerestes, A. M., & Holmes, R. M. (2006). The communicative functions of touch in humans, nonhuman primates, and rats: A review and synthesis of the empirical research. *Genetic, Social, and General Psychology Monographs, 132*(1), 5–94.

Heslin, R., & Alper, T. (1983). Touch: A bonding gesture. In J. M. Wiemann & R. P. Harrison (Eds.), *Nonverbal interaction*. Beverly Hills, CA: Sage.

Heslin, R., & Boss, D. (1980). Nonverbal intimacy in airport arrival and departure. *Personality and Social Psychology Bulletin, 6*, 248–252.

Heslin, R., Nguyen, T. D., & Nguyen, M. L. (1983). Meaning of touch: The case of touch from a stranger or same-sex person. *Journal of Nonverbal Behavior, 7,* 147–157.

Hetherington, A. (1998). The use and abuse of touch in therapy and counselling. *Counselling Psychology Quarterly, 11,* 361–364.

Hilton, I. (2004, March 29). The Buddha's daughter. *The New Yorker,* pp. 42–50.

Hollender, M. H., & Mercer, A. J. (1976). Wish to be held and wish to hold in men and women. *Archives of General Psychiatry, 33,* 49–51.

Hornik, J. (1991). Shopping time and purchasing behavior as a result of in-store tactile stimulation. *Perceptual and Motor Skills, 73,* 969–970.

Hornik, J. (1992). Tactile stimulation and consumer response. *Journal of Consumer Research, 19,* 449–458.

Hubbard, A. S. E, Tsuji, A. A., Williams, C., & Seatriz, V., Jr. (2003). Effects of touch on gratuities received in same-gender and cross-gender dyads. *Journal of Applied Social Psychology, 33,* 2427–2438.

Hutchinson, K. L., & Davidson, C. A. (1990). Body accessibility re-revisited: The 60s, 70s, and 80s. *Journal of Social Behavior and Personality, 5,* 341–352.

Jacobson, J. W., Mulick, J. A., & Schwartz, A. A. (1995). A history of facilitated communication: Science, pseudoscience, and antiscience. *American Psychologist, 50,* 750–765.

Jones, S. (1991). Problems of validity in questionnaire studies of nonverbal behavior: Jourard's tactile body-accessibility scale. *Southern Communication Journal, 56,* 83–95.

Jones, S. E. (1986). Sex differences in touch communication. *Western Journal of Speech Communication, 50,* 227–241.

Jones, S. E. (1994). *The right touch: Understanding and using the language of physical contact.* Cresskill, NJ: Hampton Press.

Jones, S. E., & Yarbrough, A. E. (1985). A naturalistic study of the meanings of touch. *Communication Monographs, 52,* 19–56.

Joule, R., & Guéguen, N. (2007). Touch, compliance, and awareness of tactile contact. *Perceptual and Motor Skills, 104,* 581–588.

Jourard, S. M. (1966). An exploratory study of body-accessibility. *British Journal of Social and Clinical Psychology, 26,* 235–242.

Jourard, S. M., & Rubin, J. E. (1968). Self-disclosure and touching: A study of two modes of interpersonal encounter and their interrelation. *Journal of Humanistic Psychology, 8,* 39–48.

Kauffman, L. E. (1971). Tacesics, the study of touch: A model for proxemic analysis. *Semiotica, 14,* 149–161.

Kaufman, D., & Mahoney, J. M. (1999). The effect of waitresses' touch on alcohol consumption in dyads. *Journal of Social Psychology, 139,* 261–267.

Kenner, A. N. (1984). The effect of task differences, attention and personality on the frequency of body-focused hand movements. *Journal of Nonverbal Behavior, 8,* 159–171.

Kenner, A. N. (1993). A cross-cultural study of body-focused hand movement. *Journal of Nonverbal Behavior, 17,* 263–279.

Kerr, C. E., Wasserman, R. H., & Moore, C. I. (2007). Cortical dynamics as a therapeutic mechanism for touch healing. *Journal of Alternative and Complementary Medicine, 13,* 59–66.

Kezuka, E. (1997). The role of touch in facilitated communication. *Journal of Autism and Developmental Disorders, 27,* 571–593.

Kneidinger, L. M., Maple, T. L., & Tross, S. A. (2001). Touching behavior in sport: Functional components, analysis of sex differences, and ethological considerations. *Journal of Nonverbal Behavior, 25,* 43–62.

Krieger, D. (1987). *Living the therapeutic touch: Healing as a lifestyle.* New York: Dodd, Mead.

Krout, M. (1954a). An experimental attempt to determine the significance of unconscious manual symbolic movements. *Journal of General Psychology, 51,* 296–308.

Krout, M. (1954b). An experimental attempt to produce unconscious manual symbolic movements. *Journal of General Psychology, 51,* 121–152.

Lederman, S. J., Klatzky, R. L., Abramowicz, A., Salsman, K., Kitada, R., & Hamilton, C. (2007). Haptic recognition of static and dynamic expressions of emotion in the live face. *Psychological Science, 18,* 158–164.

Lewis, R. J., Derlega, V. J., Nichols, B., Shankar, A., Drury, K. K., & Hawkins, L. (1995). Sex differences in observers' reactions to a nurse's use of touch. *Journal of Nonverbal Behavior, 19*, 101–113.

Lewis, R. J., Derlega, V. J., Shankar, A., Cochard, E., & Finkel, L. (1997). Nonverbal correlates of confederates' touch: Confounds in touch research. *Journal of Social Behavior and Personality, 12*, 821–830.

Lockard, J. S., & Adams, R. M. (1980). Courtship behaviors in public: Different age/sex roles. *Ethology and Sociobiology, 1*, 245–253.

Lomranz, J., & Shapira, A. (1974). Communicative patterns of self-disclosure and touching behavior. *Journal of Psychology, 88*, 223–227.

Maier, R. A., & Ernest, R. C. (1978). Sex differences in the perception of touching. *Perceptual and Motor Skills, 46*, 577–578.

Maines, D. R. (1977). Tactile relationships in the subway as affected by racial, sexual, and crowded seating situations. *Environmental Psychology and Nonverbal Behavior, 2*, 100–108.

Major, B. (1981). Gender patterns in touching behavior. In C. Mayo & N. M. Henley (Eds.), *Gender and nonverbal behavior*. New York: Springer-Verlag.

Major, B., & Heslin, R. (1982). Perceptions of same-sex and cross-sex touching: It's better to give than to receive. *Journal of Nonverbal Behavior, 6*, 148–162.

Major, B., Schmidlin, A. M., & Williams, L. (1990). Gender patterns in touch: The impact of age and setting. *Journal of Personality and Social Psychology, 58*, 634–643.

McCorkle, R. (1974). Effects of touch on seriously ill patients. *Nursing Research, 23*, 125–132.

McCormick, N. B., & Jones, A. J. (1989). Gender differences in nonverbal flirtation. *Journal of Sex Education and Therapy, 15*, 271–282.

McDaniel, E., & Andersen, P. A. (1998). International patterns of interpersonal tactile communication: A field study. *Journal of Nonverbal Behavior, 22*, 59–73.

Montagu, A. (1971). *Touching: The human significance of the skin*. New York: Columbia University Press.

Morris, D. (1971). *Intimate behaviour*. New York: Random House.

Morris, D. (1977). *Manwatching*. New York: Abrams.

Morry, M. M., & Enzle, M. E. (1994). Effect of gender dominance expectancies for knowledge on self-touching during conversations. *Social Behavior and Personality, 22*, 123–129.

Moyer, C. A., Rounds, J., & Hannum, J. W. (2004). A meta-analysis of massage therapy research. *Psychological Bulletin, 130*, 3–18.

Murphy, A. J. (1972). Effect of body contact on performance of a simple cognitive task. *British Journal of Social and Clinical Psychology, 11*, 402–408.

Nannberg, J. C., & Hansen, C. H. (1994). Post-compliance touch: An incentive for task performance. *Journal of Social Psychology, 134*, 301–307.

Nguyen, M. L., Heslin, R., & Nguyen, T. (1976). The meaning of touch: Sex and marital status differences. *Representative Research in Social Psychology, 7*, 13–18.

Nguyen, T., Heslin, R., & Nguyen, M. L. (1975). The meanings of touch: Sex differences. *Journal of Communication, 25*, 92–103.

Nilsen, W. J., & Vrana, S. R. (1998). Some touching situations: The relationship between gender and contextual variables in cardiovascular responses to human touch. *Annals of Behavioral Medicine, 20*, 270–276.

Older, J. (1982). *Touching is healing: A revolutionary breakthrough in medicine*. New York: Stein and Day.

Olson, M. A., & Fazio, R. H. (2007). Discordant evaluations of blacks affect nonverbal behavior. *Personality and Social Psychology Bulletin, 33*, 1214–1224.

Patterson, M. L., Powell, J. L., & Lenihan, M. G. (1986). Touch, compliance, and interpersonal affect. *Journal of Nonverbal Behavior, 10*, 41–50.

Pattison, J. E. (1973). Effects of touch on self-exploration and the therapeutic relationship. *Journal of Consulting and Clinical Psychology, 40*, 170–175.

Perdue, V. P., & Connor, J. M. (1978). Patterns of touching between preschool children and male and female teachers. *Child Development, 49*, 1258–1262.

Perper, T. (1989). Theories and observations on sexual selection and female choice in human beings. *Medical Anthropology, 11*, 409–454.

Peterson, A. M., Cline, R. J. W., Foster, T. S., Penner, L. A, Parrott, R. L., Keller, C. M., Naughton, M. C., Taub, J. W., Ruckdeschel, J. C., & Albrecht, T. L. (2007). Parents' interpersonal distance and touch behavior and child pain and distress during painful pediatric oncology procedures. *Journal of Nonverbal Behavior, 31*, 79–97.

Pisano, M. D., Wall, S. M., & Foster, A. (1986). Perceptions of nonreciprocal touch in romantic relationships. *Journal of Nonverbal Behavior, 10*, 29–40.

Regan, P. C., Jerry, D., Narvaez, M., & Johnson, D. (1999). Public displays of affection among Asian and Latino heterosexual couples. *Psychological Reports, 84*, 1201–1202.

Remland, M. S., Jones, T. S., & Brinkman, H. (1991). Proxemic and haptic behavior in three European countries. *Journal of Nonverbal Behavior, 15*, 215–232.

Rinck, C. M., Willis, F. N., & Dean, L. M. (1980). Interpersonal touch among residents of homes for the elderly. *Journal of Communication, 30*, 44–47.

Roese, N. J., Olson, J. M., Borenstein, M. N., Martin, A., & Shores, A. L. (1992). Same-sex touching behavior: The moderating role of homophobic attitudes. *Journal of Nonverbal Behavior, 16*, 249–259.

Rosa, L., Rosa, E., Sarner, L., & Barrett, S. (1998). A close look at Therapeutic Touch. *Journal of the American Medical Association, 279*, 1005–1010.

Rosenfeld, L. B., Kartus, S., & Ray, C. (1976). Body accessibility revisited. *Journal of Communication, 26*, 27–30.

Shreve, E. G., Harrigan, J. A., Kues, J. R., & Kagas, D. K. (1988). Nonverbal expressions of anxiety in physician-patient interactions. *Psychiatry, 51*, 378–384.

Shuter, R. (1976). Proxemics and tactility in Latin America. *Journal of Communication, 26*, 46–52.

Sigelman, C. K., & Adams, R. M. (1990). Family interactions in public: Parent–child distance and touch. *Journal of Nonverbal Behavior, 14*, 63–75.

Silverman, A. F., Pressman, M. E., & Bartel, H. W. (1973). Self-esteem and tactile communication. *Journal of Humanistic Psychology, 13*, 73–77.

Silverthorne, C., Micklewright, J., O'Donnell, M., & Gibson, R. (1976). Attribution of personal characteristics as a function of the degree of touch on initial contact and sex. *Sex Roles, 2*, 185–193.

Smith, D. E., Willis, F. N., & Gier, J. A. (1980). Success and interpersonal touch in a competitive setting. *Journal of Nonverbal Behavior, 5*, 26–34.

Smith, E. W. L., Clance, P. R., & Imes, S. (1998). *Touch in psychotherapy: Theory, research, and practice.* New York: Guilford.

Spitz, H. H. (1997). *Nonconscious movements: From mystical messages to facilitated communication.* Mahwah, NJ: Erlbaum.

Spitz, R. (1945). Hospitalism: Genesis of psychiatric conditions in early childhood. *Psychoanalytic Study of the Child, 1*, 53–74.

Stier, D. S., & Hall, J. A. (1984). Gender differences in touch: An empirical and theoretical review. *Journal of Personality and Social Psychology, 47*, 440–459.

Summerhayes, D., & Suchner, R. (1978). Power implications of touch in male–female relationships. *Sex Roles, 4*, 103–110.

Sussman, N. M., & Rosenfeld, H. M. (1978). Touch, justification, and sex: Influences on the aversiveness of spatial violations. *Journal of Social Psychology, 106*, 215–222.

Thayer, S. (1982). Social touching. In W. Schiff & E. Foulke (Eds.), *Tactual perception: A sourcebook.* New York: Cambridge University Press.

Thayer, S. (1986). History and strategies of research on social touch. *Journal of Nonverbal Behavior, 10*, 12–28.

Vogt, E. Z., & Hyman, R. (2000). *Water witching U.S.A.* (2nd ed.). Chicago: University of Chicago Press.

Watson, W. H. (1975). The meanings of touch: Geriatric nursing. *Journal of Communication, 25*, 104–112.

Waxer, P. H. (1977). Nonverbal cues for anxiety: An examination of emotional leakage. *Journal of Abnormal Psychology, 86*, 306–314.

Wegner, D. M., Fuller, V. A., & Sparrow, B. (2003). Clever hands: Uncontrolled intelligence in facilitated communication. *Journal of Personality and Social Psychology, 85*, 5–19.

Whitcher, S. J., & Fisher, J. D. (1979). Multidimensional reaction to therapeutic touch in a hospital setting. *Journal of Personality and Social Psychology, 37*, 87–96.

Williams, S. J., & Willis, F. N. (1978). Interpersonal touch among preschool children at play. *Psychological Record, 28,* 501–508.

Williams, T. (1966). Cultural structuring of tactile experience in a Borneo society. *The American Anthropologist, 68,* 27–39.

Willis, F. N., Jr., & Briggs, L. F. (1992). Relationship and touch in public settings. *Journal of Nonverbal Behavior, 16,* 55–63.

Willis, F. N., & Hamm, H. K. (1980). The use of interpersonal touch in securing compliance. *Journal of Nonverbal Behavior, 5,* 49–55.

Willis, F. N., & Hoffman, G. E. (1975). Development of tactile patterns in relation to age, sex, and race. *Developmental Psychology, 11,* 866.

Willis, F. N., & Rawdon, V. A. (1994). Gender and national differences in attitudes toward same-gender touch. *Perceptual and Motor Skills, 78,* 1027–1034.

Willis, F. N., & Reeves, D. L. (1976). Touch interactions in junior high students in relation to sex and race. *Developmental Psychology, 12,* 91–92.

Willis, F. N., Reeves, D. L., & Buchanan, D. R. (1976). Interpersonal touch in high school relative to sex and race. *Perceptual and Motor Skills, 43,* 843–847.

With a handshake, Rabin's fate was sealed. (1995, November 19). *New York Times.*

Young, C. (2007). The power of touch in psychotherapy. *International Journal of Psychotherapy, 11,* 15–24.

Your face, my thane, is a book where men
May read strange matters.
—Shakespeare, Macbeth, Act I

THE EFFECTS OF THE FACE ON HUMAN COMMUNICATION

CHAPTER **9**

The face is rich in communicative potential. It is a primary site for communication of emotional states, it reflects interpersonal attitudes, it provides nonverbal feedback on the comments of others, and some scholars say it is the primary source of communicative information next to human speech. For these reasons, and because of the face's visibility, we pay a great deal of attention to the messages we receive from the faces of others. Frequently, we rely heavily on facial cues when making important interpersonal judgments. This begins when, as infants, we take special interest in the huge face peering over our crib and tending to our needs. Most of the research on facial expressions and various components of the face has focused on the display and interpretation of emotional signals. Although this is the major focus of this chapter, we also emphasize that the face may be the basis for judging another person's personality, and it can—and does—provide information on much more than our emotional state.

THE FACE AND PERSONALITY JUDGMENTS

The human face and its features come in many sizes and shapes. As reviewed in Chapter 6, people have long believed that certain personality or character traits can be judged from the shape or features of a person's face. For example, high foreheads are believed to reveal intelligence, thin lips conscientiousness, thick lips sexiness, and so on (Secord, Dukes, & Bevan, 1959). *Facial primacy*, or the tendency to give more weight to the face than to other communication channels, may stem in part from these facial stereotypes.

But facial primacy probably stems even more from the *dynamic* nature of the face—its ability to make practically an infinite number of expressions. Many different muscles are used routinely in making facial expressions (Rinn, 1984). The look of a person's face is due in part to the genetic blueprint that endows it with certain physical features, in part to transient moods that stimulate the muscles to move in distinctive ways, and in part to the lingering imprint of chronically held expressions that seem to set in and become virtually permanent over the years. The dynamic face is the subject of the present chapter.

People make personality attributions based on facial expressions (Knutson, 1996). For example, the person who smiles at us warmly upon introduction is immediately perceived to be nice. Likewise, we think a sour-faced old man is mean and selfish. Little research exists on the validity of such stereotypes, and certainly the person with the warm smile might be a cutthroat manipulator, and the mean-looking man may be a tenderhearted soul. One study supporting the validity of facial expression stereotypes found that college students believe facially expressive individuals are more confident and likable, and indeed, in a sample of college women, those with more expressive faces were more extraverted, according to several self-report scales (Riggio & Friedman, 1986). Thus, there can be truth in stereotypes.

Another study lending support to the validity of facial expression stereotypes was done by Harker and Keltner (2001). The more women's faces showed positive emotional expression in their college yearbook pictures, the more observers of the pictures thought the women would be rewarding to interact with. And indeed, the women who had more positive expressions had more affiliative personalities and reported experiencing more positive affect, not only at age 21, but also decades later, and they were more likely to be married by age 27 than women who had less positive yearbook photos.

Research does not always support the validity of facial expression stereotypes, however. Gifford (1994) studied self-reported personality, others' impressions of personality, and various nonverbal cues emitted during interaction. Although smiling was positively related to observers' impressions of extraversion, agreeableness, and ingenuousness, smiling was not related to the targets' own personality ratings for any of these traits.

THE FACE AND INTERACTION MANAGEMENT

Our faces also are used to facilitate and inhibit responses in daily interaction. Parts of the face are used to:

1. Open and close channels of communication
2. Complement or qualify verbal and/or nonverbal responses
3. Replace speech

Behaviors can, of course, serve several functions simultaneously. For example, a yawn may replace the spoken message "I'm bored" and may serve to shut down the channels of communication.

CHANNEL CONTROL

When we want a speaking turn, we sometimes open our mouths in readiness to talk, which is often accompanied by an inspiration of breath. Others notice such signals and decide whether to ignore or respect them. As noted in Chapter 2, the eyebrow flash found in greeting rituals, which is frequently accompanied by a smile, is another facial cue that signals a desire to interact. Interestingly, smiles also are found in situations in which there is a desire to close the channels of communication, for example, a smile of appeasement as a person backs away from someone threatening physical harm. Smiling and winking, at least in popular stereotypes, also are used to flirt with others—an invitation that not only opens the channels of communication but also suggests the type of interaction desired. Facial behaviors associated with flirtation seem to be similar in form across different cultures (Eibl-Eibesfeldt, 1974).

Although we usually think of smiles as showing emotion or attitudes, they actually have many complex functions. Brunner (1979) showed that smiles serve as "listener responses" or "back channels" in conversation, in that they signal attentiveness and involvement just as head nods, "uh-huh," and "yeah" do. These smiles do not indicate joy or happiness in the sender but are meant to facilitate and encourage the other person's speech. These cues achieve channel control by keeping channels open.

COMPLEMENTING OR QUALIFYING OTHER BEHAVIOR

In normal conversational give and take, there are instances when we wish to underline, magnify, minimize, or contradict messages. The speaker or listener may give these signals. A sad verbal message may acquire added emphasis with eyebrow movements that normally accompany the expression of sadness. A smile may temper a message otherwise interpreted as negative. The hand emblem for "A-okay" may be accompanied by a wink, leaving little doubt that approval is being communicated. Thus, facial cues can combine with other cues to avoid confusion and magnify or qualify our messages.

REPLACING SPOKEN MESSAGES

Ekman and Friesen (1975) identified what they call "facial emblems." Like hand emblems, these displays have a fairly consistent verbal translation. Facial emblems are different from the actual emotional expressions in that the sender is trying to talk *about* an emotion while indicating he or she is not actually feeling it. These facial emblems usually occur in contexts not likely to trigger the actual emotion; they are usually held for a longer or shorter time than the actual expression and are usually performed by using only part of the face. When you drop your jaw and hold your mouth open without displaying other features of the surprise expression, you may be saying that the other person's comment is surprising or that you were dumbfounded by what was said. Widened eyes without other features of the surprise and fear expressions may serve the same purpose as a verbal "Wow!" If you want to comment nonverbally on your disgust for a situation, a nose wrinkle or raising one side of your upper lip should get your message across. Sometimes one or both eyebrows communicate "I'm puzzled" or "I doubt that." Other facial messages with common verbal translations that are not associated with expressions of emotion include the "You know what I mean" wink and sticking your tongue out to convey insult or disapproval (Smith, Chase, & Lieblich, 1974).

Facial movements play an important role in managing conversation (Bavelas & Chovil, 1997; Chovil, 1991/1992). According to Chovil, the most frequent function is *syntactic display*. Syntactic facial displays act as markers, functioning as visible punctuation for words and clauses; they are directed toward the organizational structure of the conversation to mark beginnings, endings, restarts, continuations, and emphasis. Raising and lowering the eyebrows is a central activity in syntactic displays. Facial actions made by the speaker that are directly connected with the content of what is being said are called *semantic displays*. These may be redundant with the verbal behavior, or they may involve additional commentary on the spoken words, such as personal reactions to what is being said. The face also provides *listener responses*, as mentioned earlier. These are primarily facial displays that facilitate the flow of interaction but also include those that give personal reactions and seemingly empathic displays in the form of mimicry.

Although the preceding discussion provides an overview of how the face is used in managing the interaction, it does not sufficiently reflect the complexity a thorough analysis requires. For instance, we did not deal with concomitant gaze behavior and other subtle movements such as head tilts. We talked about smiles as if there were only one variety. Brannigan and Humphries (1972) have identified nine smiles, representing various types and degrees of intensity, many of which seem to occur in distinctly separate situations. Ekman and Friesen, using an anatomically based coding system we will describe shortly, have found over 100 distinctly different human smiles. Most recently, researchers have distinguished between smiles that are more and less likely to be indicative of true positive affect, as discussed later in this chapter.

THE FACE AND EXPRESSIONS OF EMOTION

The intellectual roots of our modern interest in facial expression stem from the mid-19th century. Charles Darwin's *Expression of the Emotions in Man and Animals* (1872), although not as famous as his other writings on natural selection, was a major work of theory and empirical observation that largely focused on the face (Ekman & Oster, 1982). To Darwin, the study of emotional expression was closely tied to his case for evolution, for he held that the capacity to communicate through nonverbal signals had evolved just as the brain and skeleton had. The face becomes increasingly mobile as one moves up the phylogenetic ladder. In many animals, the face is a fixed mask with little to no capacity for mobility, but in primates we see a great variety of expressions (Redican, 1982). Because it would support his theory of evolution, Darwin considered it extremely important to document similarities in the nature of emotional expression across species and across human cultures.

Several strands of contemporary facial research can be traced to Darwin's insights, including conducting judgment studies to find out what meanings observers ascribe to different expressions, undertaking cross-cultural studies, studying the movements of particular facial muscles, and testing the hypothesis that making facial expressions can intensify the expressor's experience of emotion. We review each of these topics here.

DISPLAY RULES AND FACIAL EMOTION EXPRESSION

Consider the following situations:

1. A student who feels sure he is doing "C" work is told by his instructor that he is doing "A" work. His immediate reaction is total surprise, probably followed by glee. But how does he react? His face shows mild surprise, and he comments that he thought he was doing pretty good work in the course.

2. A poker player draws her fourth ace in a game with no wild cards. Her face would lead the other players to believe she was unmoved.
3. A woman receives a holiday present that she likes, but it is nothing spectacular. Her facial expression and comments, however, lead the giver to believe it was the only thing she ever wanted in her entire life.
4. The husband of a fledgling executive is forced to attend the boss's party and is told explicitly that his behavior will have a profound impact on the promotion of his spouse. He is nervous and also annoyed. But, according to those who describe the party later, Mr. Fledgling was the life of the party—happy, carefree, and relaxed.

These four examples illustrate certain *display rules* we tend to follow (Ekman & Friesen, 1969). The student illustrated a *deintensified affect*—strong surprise was made to look like mild surprise. The poker player was trying to *neutralize her feelings* to make it appear there was no emotion at all. The person reacting to the holiday present tried to make mild happiness appear to be strong happiness—an *overintensification of the affect*. Mr. Fledgling was trying to *mask feelings* of tension or annoyance with happiness and confidence. These display rules are learned, but we do not always use them at a conscious level of awareness. We learn culturally prescribed norms for when and how much emotion to display; we also develop personal display rules based on our needs or perhaps the demands of our occupation, for example, as politicians or salespersons. We learn that some affect displays are appropriate in some places but not others, for some status and role positions but not others, and for one sex but not the other.

The existence of display rules helps explain why some anthropologists have believed that emotions are expressed in sharply different ways from culture to culture. For example, in one society, people may weep and moan at a funeral; in another they may celebrate with a feast and dance. However, the underlying emotion, grief, is experienced and likely expressed similarly in private. The difference is that in public, the cultural norms—display rules—regulate behavior. In one society, the rule says "Show how sad you are," but in another the rule says "Affirm social bonds" or "Show hope for the future."

The topic of deception is taken up in a later chapter, but here let us say that the face, along with other nonverbal cues, can certainly be used to deceive others about our feelings and thoughts. The line between deception and display rules can be fuzzy, but in general it can be said that display rules, because they are shared, reflect a collective understanding of socially appropriate behavior, whereas deception is generally considered to be done for a person's own self-advantage and to the disadvantage of others. Therefore, basing our nonverbal behavior on display rules tends to be looked on with approval, as an indication of social skill or maturity, whereas deception is generally disapproved of.

Display rules do not always have to be socially defined and shared. People can have their own idiosyncratic "rules" for expression. Ekman and Friesen (1975) developed a classification system for various styles of facial expressions. The styles are heavily based on personal display rules and represent extremes. A style may be displayed in a less extreme fashion in some situations, or at certain times in the person's life, but some people manifest a given style with consistency. These styles include the following:

1. *The Withholder*. The face inhibits expressions of actual feeling states. There is little facial movement.
2. *The Revealer*. This style is the opposite of the Withholder. The face of the person who "lets it all hang out" leaves little doubt how the person feels—continually.
3. *The Unwitting Expressor*. This pattern usually pertains to a limited number of expressions that a person thought were masked, hence this person might ask, incredulously, "How did you know I was angry?"
4. *The Blanked Expressor*. In this style, the person is convinced an emotion is being portrayed, but others see only a blank face.
5. *The Substitute Expressor*. Here, the facial expression shows an emotion other than the one the person thinks is being displayed.
6. *The Frozen-Affect Expressor*. This style manifests at least part of an emotional display at all times. Some people are born with a facial configuration that in a relaxed, neutral state shows the downturned mouth associated with sadness; others habitually experience an emotion so much that traces of the emotional display are permanently etched into the face. (This is an idea that Darwin proposed.)

Self-presentational desires can also produce distinctive styles of facial expression. Former President Clinton often used a smile we call his "brave smile" (Figure 9-1). It

FIGURE 9-1

Former President Clinton's "brave" smile.

is not a pure expression of happiness, as our discussion of blends and "felt" smiles later in this chapter makes clear. Rather, we think Clinton was trying to convey a complex mixture of pride, determination, concern, and modesty with the combination of the paradoxically down-turned mouth, the set chin, and the "smile wrinkles" around the eyes.

The preceding discussion of display rules and styles of emotional facial expression demonstrates that we have considerable control over our facial expressions, and this control is manifested in a variety of ways. Although we can successfully present facial messages that we do not feel, sometimes we lie imperfectly by enacting an expression at the wrong time; enacting it too often or for too long, as when we insincerely display a smile too long; or using various facial muscles inappropriately. These factors may help us separate genuine emotions from pseudoexpressions of emotion on the face. People undeniably are aware of the communicative potential of the face and tend to monitor it carefully by inhibiting or exhibiting when desired. With the constant feedback we receive about our facial expressions, we become rather proficient at controlling them, and we are also more accurate in reporting our facial expressions than other head or body movements (Hall, Murphy, & Schmid Mast, 2007). As Ekman and Friesen (1969) put it,

> Although we usually are aware of our facial affect displays, they may occur with or without a deliberate intention to communicate. Similarly, inhibition of facial display, control of facial display, or dissimulation of an affect (looking cool even when tense) may or may not be intentional. Because we have such good feedback about our facial behavior, we usually are aware of what happens the moment we change facial movements. (p. 76)

As these comments imply, the distinction between spontaneous, unintentional facial displays of emotion and deliberate, posed displays may be quite difficult to make in practice, both by an observer and by the expressing person him or herself.

The way we experience emotions can be quite complex. Sometimes we move rapidly from one emotion to another. For example, people reporting the feeling of jealousy indicate that the "jealous flash may move from shock and numbness to desolate pain to rage and anger to moral outrage in a very brief time" (Ellis & Weinstein, 1986). Sometimes we are not sure what emotion we are feeling, and at other times, we seem to feel many emotions at once. Simultaneously felt emotions may even be contradictory, as when one is both attracted and repulsed by a grisly accident scene. When we experience more than one emotion, we sometimes try to control one while we deal with the other. These are only some of the many ways we experience emotions (Ellis, 1991).

Because emotional experience is complex, understanding emotion through facial expression is correspondingly difficult. People do not always portray pure or single emotional states, in which all the parts of the face show a single emotion. Instead, the face conveys multiple emotions. These are called *affect blends* and may appear on the face in numerous ways. For example, one emotion is suggested by one facial area, and another is suggested by another area, as when brows are raised as in surprise and lips are pressed as in anger. Or two different emotions are shown in one part of the face, as when one brow is raised as in surprise, and the other is lowered as in anger. Such displays may merely confuse a viewer, or they may convey a new meaning that is different from either of the elements. The brows just described might, for example, convey skepticism.

Figure 9-2 shows two examples of facial blends. One photograph shows a blend of happiness, evidenced by a smiling movement in the mouth area, and also surprise, evidenced by the raised eyebrows and forehead, wide eyes, and a slight dropping of the jaw. Such an expression could occur if you thought you were going to get an F on an exam, but you received an A instead. In the other photograph, the eyebrow, forehead, and eye area show anger while the mouth shows sadness. This combination might occur if your instructor told you that your grade on an exam you considered unfair was an F. You feel sad about the low grade and angry at the instructor.

A final note about the complexity of faces concerns what Haggard and Isaacs (1966) called "micromomentary facial expressions." While searching for indications of nonverbal communication between therapist and patient, they ran films at slow motion and noticed that the expression on the patient's face would sometimes change dramatically—from a smile to a grimace to a smile, for example—within a few frames of the film. Further analysis revealed that when they ran the films at 4 frames per second, instead of the normal 24 frames per second, 2.5 times as many changes of expression could be discerned. One hypothesis is that these micromomentary expressions reveal actual emotional states but are condensed in time because of repressive processes. They are often incompatible with both the apparent expression and the patient's words. One patient, saying nice things about a friend, had a seemingly pleasant facial expression; however, slow-motion film showed a wave of anger cross her face. Although agreeing that micromomentary expressions may show conflict,

FIGURE 9-2

Facial blends.

repression, or efforts to conceal an emotion, Ekman, Friesen, and Ellsworth (1982b) actually found them to be "very rare events" based on extensive analysis of facial movements. However, this does not mean they do not have an impact, possibly a subliminal one, when they occur.

THE FACIAL EMOTION CONTROVERSY

One tradition, originating with Darwin and associated today with the work of Paul Ekman and Carroll Izard, emphasizes the close connection between facial displays of emotion and concurrently felt emotions with a corresponding emphasis on emotion-expressive display linkages as being biologically grounded. This approach has fueled ambitious programs of cross-cultural research on the recognition of facial expression, as discussed in Chapter 2 and also later in this chapter. A simplistic version of such a theoretical position would hold that a given emotion always produces a certain expression, which could be a single muscle movement or a complex pattern of movements and conversely that this expression always signifies the occurrence of its associated emotion. According to such a view, facial expressions are always a *readout*—an honest, unpremeditated, uncontrolled indication of internal emotional states.

A bit of reflection on everyday experience should make the reader skeptical of such a view, however, and indeed it is unlikely that any theorist holds such an extreme position. As we discussed in the previous section, people can feign emotions by willfully putting on different expressions. They also are sensitive to situations in which it would be inappropriate to show certain expressions; for example, a winner who shows too much happiness could be seen as gloating. A rising tide of research now shows that a purely spontaneous nonverbal readout of emotional states may be a rarer event than some think (Bonanno & Keltner, 2004; Russell, Bachorowski, & Fernández-Dols, 2003). The term "loosely coupled" is used to describe emotion and expression systems that coincide only occasionally or under certain circumstances.

Many studies support the argument that expressions are not a perfect window into emotional experience. Researchers have sought situations for study in which the experience of an emotion can be confirmed, so they can see what expressions are produced. People bowling with friends have been observed in the United States and Spain. After a good roll, and at other moments when they reported feeling happy, bowlers smiled much more when facing their friends than when facing the pins. Similarly, soccer fans watching a match on television smiled much more during happy moments when orienting directly to their friends than during happy moments when they were not interacting with them directly. During their noninteractive happy moments, they showed expressions indicative of several different emotions not shown in the interactive happy moments (Fernández-Dols & Ruiz-Belda, 1997; Kraut & Johnston, 1979; Ruiz-Belda, Fernández-Dols, Carrera, & Barchard, 2003). Thus, a person can be very happy yet not show it in a prototypically "happy" facial expression.

Further evidence that facial expression and experienced emotion are only loosely coupled, and that the nature of the social situation is a strong determinant of what is displayed on the face, is that facial *motor mimicry*—displaying what another person is feeling, such as wincing after a friend stubs his toe—decreases when no one is there to see the facial display (Bavelas, Black, Lemery, & Mullett, 1986; Chovil, 1991). Furthermore, college students watching emotionally provoking slides were more facially expressive when they watched with a friend as opposed to a watching with a stranger (Wagner & Smith, 1991), and college students recounting positive and negative experiences showed facial expressions that inconsistently matched their reported affect (Lee & Wagner, 2002). At the Olympic Games, gold medal winners were filmed at three moments: while standing behind the podium away from public view, while standing on the podium interacting with authorities and the public, and while standing on the podium facing the flagpoles and listening to their national anthem (Fernández-Dols & Ruiz-Belda, 1995). Although their feelings of happiness probably did not vary across these three closely spaced periods, the winners smiled the most during the public-interactive period, suggesting again that facial expression is not due solely to the emotion being experienced.

Audience effects such as these may even occur when a person is alone and behaving "spontaneously," for even then a person may respond to fantasies of social interaction. In support of this notion, Fridlund (1991) found that college students watching a pleasant film smiled more when watching with a friend than when watching alone. But students who watched the film in a different room from their friend but aware that the friend was watching the same film also smiled more than students who watched the film alone. Thus, even the *imagined* presence or experience of others may serve to stimulate or facilitate facial displays.

Fridlund's *behavioral ecology theory* of facial expression asserts that facial expressions are virtually never simply emotional and are, instead, always enacted for social purposes (Fridlund, 1994, 1997). In Fridlund's view, spontaneous expression of emotion would not have been a selected trait during evolution, because it would too often not serve the expressor's interest, and it could possibly even serve the interests of rivals by depriving the expressor of the ability to deceive. Fridlund's argument that facial expressions are meant to *communicate* rather than to simply *reveal* is consistent with many examples of functional expressive behavior in the animal kingdom, as well as with everyday observation of human interaction.

However, most researchers appear not to accept the extreme position that facial expressions are mainly messages and are hardly ever purely spontaneous windows into one's emotional life. There are certainly many instances where our faces show feelings without our being aware of it—sometimes feelings we would very much have wanted to conceal. The fact that audience presence effects can sometimes work in reverse, with people showing *more* facial expression when alone than with others present rather than less, suggests that people do indeed make spontaneous emotional expressions (Buck, 1984, 1991; Wagner & Lee, 1999). Facial expressions are not always put on only for social purposes.

Thus far, the approach described for testing whether expressions match inner feelings involves comparing expressions in different social circumstances. Another way of asking this question is to compare people's expressions to what they say about their emotional states. When viewers were asked about their emotions during neutral or scary film excerpts, almost no matching occurred (Fernández-Dols & Ruiz-Belda,

1997)—only two of 35 viewers who reported a basic emotion showed the expression that theoretically should have been produced by that emotion, and three showed expressions that suggested entirely different emotions from those reported.

Similarly, a study of actors' expressions in Hollywood movies first obtained good agreement from viewers on which emotions were being expressed in over 100 scenes and then conducted a detailed analysis of the actors' faces (Carroll & Russell, 1997). Only for happy episodes did the expected "happy" pattern of facial movements occur. For other emotions, although particular expected movements— such as lowered brows in angry episodes—occurred more often than chance might dictate, little evidence supported the idea that whole prototypical patterns of expression would occur. Considering that actors are likely to make *more* stereo-typed expressions than people in real life, these results give a strong indication that the face and emotion do not necessarily have a close correspondence.

MEASURING THE FACE

ANATOMICAL DESCRIPTION For many years, descriptions of facial movements tended to be impressionistic or idiosyncratic (Ekman, 1982; Rinn, 1984). This changed dramatically with the work of Carroll Izard (1979) and of Paul Ekman and Wallace Friesen (1978), who independently developed precise systems for de-scribing facial action based on muscle movements. Izard's work has focused on in-fant expressions; the Ekman-Friesen Facial Action Coding System (FACS) has been applied more generally and appears to be the most widely adopted. In this context, the term "widely" is relative, because learning a system comprehensive enough to describe nearly any combination of muscle movements requires many hours of training and practice and is extremely time consuming to apply. Consequently, use of the method is limited to dedicated facial researchers.

Ekman and Friesen developed the FACS by painstakingly, and sometimes pain-fully, learning how to move all their facial muscles and by studying anatomy texts. They studied the faces of other people who had learned how to control specific muscles and considered what movements an observer could reliably distinguish— important because observers would be the data gatherers. As a consequence, a trained observer could identify which muscles were moving, and these were called "action units." Sometimes an action unit involves more than one muscle, if those muscles always work in tandem or if an observer cannot see the difference. Altogether, the FACS can identify over 40 distinct action units in the face. For illus-tration, Figure 9-3 presents the action units identified by Ekman (1979) for the brow and forehead. Altogether, seven different muscles can influence this region of the face.

The FACS allows emotion researchers to describe objectively what move-ments have occurred on the face, and further work with this system allows a face to be categorized as showing a given emotion based on extensive data relating those movements to other criteria, mainly observers' judgments of facial expres-sions. Through years of collecting such judgments, Ekman and his colleagues de-veloped a catalogue of prototypical movements associated with seven different judged emotions. For example, Ekman and Friesen (1978) determined that in the

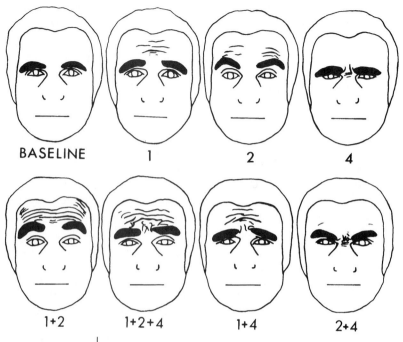

BASELINE   1   2   4

1+2   1+2+4   1+4   2+4

FIGURE 9-3

Action units for the brow/forehead.

Source: From P. Ekman, "About Brows: Emotional and Conversational Signals" in J. Aschoff, M. von Cranach, K. Foppa, W. Lepenies, & D. Ploog (Eds.), *Human Ethology*, p. 174. Cambridge, UK: Cambridge University Press, 1979. Reprinted by permission of Cambridge University Press.

brow/forehead region (shown in Figure 9-3), action units 1 or 1 + 4 occur in sadness, along with associated movements across the rest of the face. In surprise, we see 1 + 2; in fear, 1 + 2 + 4; in anger, 4; and so forth.

Recall that we discussed the role of the face in interaction management. Ekman tells us how the brow/forehead area contributes to these conversational signals as well:

- Accent a word, 1 + 2 (Actor Woody Allen uses 1 + 4 for this, according to Ekman.)
- Underline a phrase, 1 + 2 or 4
- Punctuate, like a "visual comma," 1 + 2 or 4
- Question mark, 1 + 2 or 4
- Word search, 4
- Listener response (back channel), 1 + 2
- Indicate lack of understanding, 4

We have gone into detail on the brow/forehead area to give you a feel for how the system works. Although the method is laborious to apply, the results can be very interesting and lessons derived from it can be possibly quite useful in daily life. For example, facial muscle movements can reveal the occurrence of pain and can even distinguish among different pain sources, such as pain from immersion of the hand in cold water, from electric shock, and from surgery or other physical trauma (LeResche, 1982; Patrick, Craig, & Prkachin, 1986). The facial signs of pain, measured in both infants and adults, include a tightening of the muscles surrounding the eyes, which narrows the eyes and raises the cheeks; the corrugator and other forehead muscles lower the eyebrows and wrinkle the bridge of the nose; and the levator muscles raise the upper lip and may produce wrinkles at the side of the nose (Prkachin & Craig, 1995). The faces of terminal cancer patients differ according to the stage of disease progression. In the early stages, signs of fear are more prominent ("whole eye tension combined with tension... in the lower eyelid"), but these give way to signs of sadness (in the brow/forehead region) in the late stage (Antonoff & Spilka, 1984–1985).

Some of the most subtle and fascinating work studying facial muscle movements concerns different kinds of smiles, referred to as *Duchenne smiles* and *non-Duchenne smiles* after the 19th-century neurologist who first described them. The muscle called the *zygomatic major*, which stretches out the lips when we smile, is the common denominator. Ekman has shown that the frequency, duration, and intensity of action by the zygomatic major differentiated among facial displays made by people watching different kinds of films, and it also correlated with how much happiness people said they felt while viewing them (Ekman, Friesen, & Ancoli, 1980). However, other muscles besides the zygomatic major are crucial to understanding what the smile really means. Darwin proposed that in a "felt" or genuinely happy (Duchenne) smile, the orbicularis oculi muscle—the muscle that gives you crow's feet at the corner of your eyes—is involved, but that it is not involved in a phony or mechanical (non-Duchenne) smile. Figure 9-4 shows the difference between "felt" and "unfelt" smiles.

In another study, student nurses were shown either a pleasant or a stressful film, and those shown the stressful film were asked to act as though the film were pleasant. Thus, those who were watching the stressful film had to lie about their experience. The smiles of those who saw the pleasant film were found to be felt, happy smiles with no muscular activity associated with any of the negative emotions. Those trying to look pleasant while watching the stressful film showed more "masking" smiles, involving the zygomatic major but not the orbicularis oculi, and they also showed more movements of the 10 or so muscles associated with fear, disgust, contempt, sadness, or anger (Ekman, Friesen, & O'Sullivan, 1988). Can you tell which face in Figure 9-5 displays the felt smile? (See the end of the chapter for the answer.)

In another demonstration of the value of such precise muscle coding, Matsumoto and Willingham (2006) analyzed the expressions of athletes in the 2004 Olympic judo competition. Compared to silver medal winners, both gold and bronze medal winners showed many more Duchenne (felt) smiles than the silver medal winners, especially the open-mouthed variety, when receiving their medals and when on the podium. Although we might have expected the silver medalists to be happier than bronze winners, apparently coming in second felt like a defeat, whereas coming in third felt like a victory over the many other athletes who did not win any medal at all.

The distinction between felt and unfelt smiles has been supported in numerous studies, even among infants as young as 10 months of age (Ekman, Davidson, & Friesen, 1990; Ekman & Friesen, 1982; Fox & Davidson, 1988). Aside from the

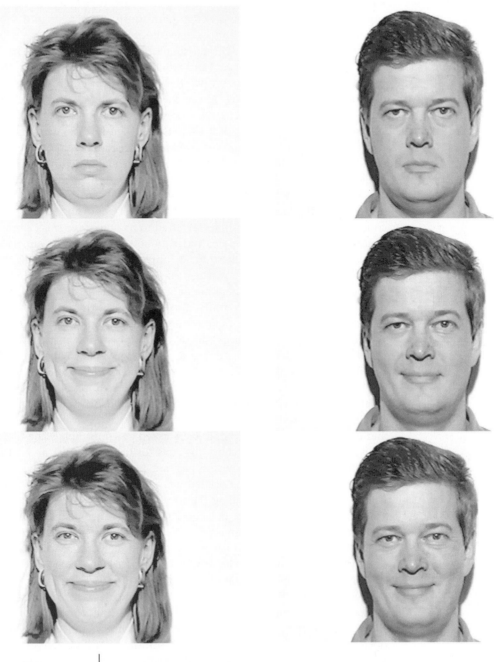

FIGURE 9-4

Neutral face, "unfelt" smile, and "felt" smile.

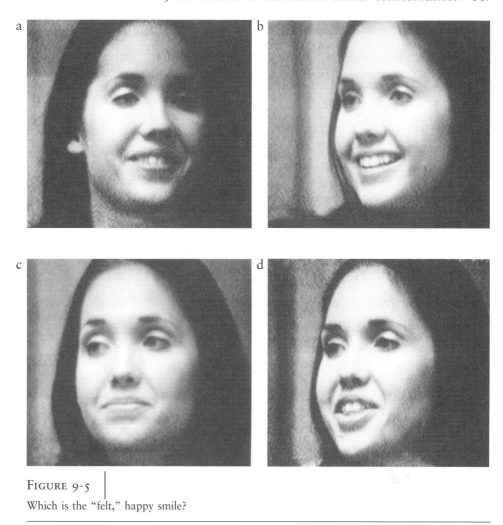

FIGURE 9-5

Which is the "felt," happy smile?

involvement of the eye muscle, Duchenne smiles are of less variable duration and have a smoother quality than unfelt smiles. Moreover, the two kinds of smiles can be distinguished from one another by naive viewers, even children as young as 9 years old (Frank, Ekman, & Friesen, 1993; Gosselin, Perron, Legault, & Campanella, 2002; Scherer & Ceschi, 2000), although not always with high levels of accuracy (Hess & Kleck, 1990).

The distinction between felt and unfelt smiles, although very important, is still a probabilistic one. This means that in any particular instance, there may be uncertainty about the smile's true meaning. Although it may be unlikely that a smile involving only the mouth is a true expression of pleasure or happiness, it is possible for a smile involving the eye muscles, a so-called felt smile, to be feigned by someone who is aware that such a smile is more convincing than the mouth-only kind. The fact that a felt smile display can be posed, as in Figure 9-4, underscores this point.

AUTOMATED FACIAL MEASUREMENT   Because anatomical description of the face, such as that used in the FACS, is so time consuming to learn and employ, there is strong interest in developing computer programs that can recognize emotions and describe facial movement. This is a major challenge because of the many possible muscle movements and the existence of great differences between individual faces in shape and musculature. The challenge is especially great for stimuli that are not standardized in terms of head position and other movement parameters. Early systems were not very practical, because they required attaching small dots to the face to serve as landmarks for the computerized analysis (Kaiser & Wehrle, 1992). Automated systems that can analyze movement under more natural circumstances and in real time are currently being developed and have very promising validity as tested against trained human coders for recognizing discrete emotions (Cohn & Ekman, 2005). Eventually such automated systems will contribute greatly to research on facial expression.

Another approach that eliminates human judgment is based on the fact that different emotions produce distinctive facial movements, even when the movements are too slight to be seen with the naked eye. Electrodes attached to the face measure electromyographic (EMG) responses, that is, electrical activity indicative of an incipient muscle movement. Most consistent are results showing that the zygomatic muscle, which expands the mouth, responds under happy conditions, and the corrugator muscle between the brows responds under sad, angry, and fearful conditions (Matsumoto, Keltner, Shiota, O'Sullivan, & Frank, 2008). Studies that use EMG recordings have shown that facial muscles respond in predictable ways to simply seeing others' emotional expressions (Blairy, Herrera, & Hess, 1999; Dimberg, 1982; Lundqvist, 1995). Thus, the face responds with corrugator activity to seeing angry expressions and with zygomatic major activity to seeing happy expressions. The face also responds in mimicking fashion to facial expressions of sadness and disgust. This process of unconscious mimicry may in turn contribute to one's own emotions through facial feedback, as we explain later.

MEASUREMENT BY SIMPLE OBSERVATION   Although much is to be gained from the FACS's fine-grained anatomical analysis and EMG technology, researchers most often employ less highly trained human observers for their facial measurement and judgment tasks. Observers are frequently asked to count the frequency of facial expressions, rate their intensity, or time their duration, either with or without a period of training (Kring & Sloan, 2007). As long as adequate interobserver agreement is obtained, these simpler approaches can have high validity. For example, Sato and Yoshikawa (2007) studied unconscious mimicry of facial expressions by unobtrusively videotaping participants while they watched videos of faces that were posing either angry or happy expressions. In this study, untrained observers were just as good as trained FACS coders at distinguishing which kind of video the participants were watching.

MEASURING EMOTION RECOGNITION

Emotions can be identified at levels much higher than chance from posed facial expressions, as Ekman and colleagues have shown (1987), and also from spontaneously expressed facial displays (Tcherkassof, Bollon, Dubois, Pansu, & Adam, 2007), though accuracy is lower for spontaneous expressions than for posed ones. But before going further, measurement issues must be discussed.

  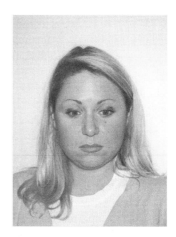

FIGURE 9-6

How should these facial expressions be read?

THE RESPONSE FORMAT   Examine the three faces shown in Figure 9-6, then consider the following methods of measuring your accuracy.

1. In the space provided, write in the emotion being expressed in each of the faces you observed.

    A. _____ B. _____ C. _____

2. From the choices given, select the one emotion that best describes Face A, Face B, and Face C.

Face A	Face B	Face C
Rage	Happiness	Sadness
Anger	Joy	Despair
Wrath	Delight	Solemnity
Indignation	Amusement	Despondency
Resentment	Pleasure	Melancholy

3. From the following list, select the term that best describes Face A, Face B, and Face C: Happiness, Sadness, Surprise, Fear, Anger.

    This exercise illustrates one of the many problems involved in testing the accuracy of judgments about facial expressions or other nonverbal cues. In this case, judgment accuracy would depend a great deal on which set of instructions the judge received. The first testing condition, involving a free response from the judge, will produce a wide range of responses, and researchers will be faced with the problem of deciding whether the judge's label corresponds with their own "correct" label for the emotion. The labels used by the experimenters or expressors and those used by the judges may be different, but both may respond the same way to the actual emotion in real life or may be thinking of the same emotion.

In the second testing condition, the discrimination task is too difficult, because the emotions listed in each category are too much alike. We can predict low accuracy for judges given these instructions, because different perceivers will make slightly different construals. In contrast, the last set of instructions is the opposite of the second set—the discrimination task may be too easy. Because the emotion categories are discrete, we can predict high accuracy for the third condition.

Accuracy is also influenced by biases in judgment patterns. Consider a facial judgment task with equal numbers of sad, happy, and angry faces. If a judge guesses "happy" all the time, to state the extreme case, he or she would score as very accurate on happy faces, and we might conclude that such a judge is an excellent judge of happiness. But obviously the judge has no differential accuracy, because she or he gave only one answer to all the items. For the same reason, the low accuracy obtained by such a judge on the other emotions is less an index of actual accuracy than of rating bias. Researchers who employ multiple-choice tests have fortunately developed ways of scoring that take rating bias into account (Wagner, 1993). And of course we must keep in mind what level of accuracy would be expected on the basis of guessing alone: with four choices, this level would be 25 percent, with three, 33 percent, and so on. Therefore any given level of accuracy cannot be evaluated in absolute terms but rather must be appraised in terms of how much higher or lower it is than the guessing level.

Aside from these methodological factors, other factors also influence the levels of accuracy that will be obtained by a researcher. For example, the duration of exposure to the facial expressions will likely have an impact, though accuracy can be obtained with surprisingly short exposures (see Ambady, Bernieri, & Richeson, 2000; Matsumoto et al., 2000).

CREATING THE FACIAL STIMULUS   Researchers use various methods to elicit the emotional expressions that observers are asked to identify. Some simply describe a situation and tell the actor to behave as if he or she were in that situation, others give a list of emotions and tell the actor to portray them, and others gather examples of facial expressions of people in real situations that are not posed or acted. One early study (Dunlap, 1927) went to an almost comic extreme: A camera was set up in a laboratory, ready to catch the subject's expressions at the proper moment. To elicit an expression of pain, the experimenter bent the subject's finger backward forcibly; to produce a startled look, the experimenter fired a pistol behind the subject at an unexpected moment; apprehension was elicited by telling the subject the pistol would be fired again, close to his ear, on the count of three—at the count of two, the photo was taken. Amusement was captured when the experimenter told the subject some jokes; disgust resulted from the subject's smelling a test tube containing tissues of a dead rat; and finally—unbelievably—to elicit an expression of grief, a subject was hypnotized and was told several members of his family had been killed in a car wreck! "Unfortunately," says the experimenter, "the camera could not catch intense grief because the subject bowed his head and cried," so he had to settle for an expression of "mild grief" to be used in the study.

The idea of presenting subjects with a controlled stimulus and then observing their reactions, although carried to an extreme in Dunlap's study, still underlies much research on spontaneous expressions. Expressors are shown slides or films that differ in their content—funny, disgusting, sexy, heartwarming, and so forth—while a video camera unobtrusively records their facial reactions. Judges later observe the expressors' faces and try to guess which slide or film each subject had been viewing (Buck, 1979; Zuckerman, Hall, DeFrank, & Rosenthal, 1976). This method can capture completely unpremeditated expressions. However, because expressors are not in a truly communicative situation, their behavior may be no more generalizable to real social interaction than are expressors' attempts to pose various emotions on the command of the experimenter. Another method, asking subjects to reexperience an emotional event and then talk about it, has been used sometimes as a more natural alternative that blends some elements of deliberate and spontaneous communication (Halberstadt, 1986).

CONTEXT OR NOT?   Though researchers might present faces of strangers out of context, contextual factors obviously influence accuracy. Prior exposure to a face is one such factor. If you are familiar with the face, and have seen it express other emotions, you are more likely to correctly identify another emotion you have not seen before.

Several studies make it clear that additional knowledge concerning the context in which a particular facial expression occurs will affect how people judge the emotion expressed. Context can be visual, as when observers are shown the situation, including people who may be in it; or context can be narrative, as when observers are told a background story and then shown a facial expression of a person supposedly in the story. Observers can label facial expressions of emotion without any knowledge of the context in which they occur, but co-occurring perceptions of the social context, the environment, and other people will surely affect their judgments.

Although a number of investigators have pursued the question of whether context or expression dominates perceptions, the issue is far from resolved (Fernández-Dols & Carroll, 1997). Perhaps the study cited most often regarding the influence of context in face judging is the classic one by Munn (1940). Facial expressions taken from popular magazines were shown with and without background context. The background information was very helpful in accurately identifying these facial expressions, as were verbal cues describing the situation.

Another classic demonstration of context effects is Cline's (1956) study of line drawings to test the effect of seeing another face as part of the total context. He found that the expression on one face influenced interpretation of the other face. When the smiling face was paired with a glum face, the smiling face was seen as that of a vicious, gloating, taunting bully. When paired with a frowning face, the smiling face seemed peaceful, friendly, and happy.

Thus, the context in which a facial expression is embedded can influence our interpretation of the expression. Sometimes the question is asked in terms of which matters more, expression or context (see the review by Fernández-Dols & Carroll, 1997), but this is too simplistic an approach. Often a judgment depends not on which source of information wins out in observers' judgments, but rather on whether the two sources of information can be meaningfully integrated. Sometimes this is done by reinterpreting the information from one source, for example, by deciding that a "sad" story context might actually produce angry feelings, too. Other times, a true integration is made, as when a facial expression of "fear" plus a context of "anger" produces the overall interpretation of "pain" (Carroll & Russell, 1996).

EMOTIONS INFERRED FROM THE FACE

Many factors influence how emotions are inferred from the face, but the compelling fact remains that they *can* be inferred, and often with extremely high levels of accuracy. Some emotions are more likely to be confused, but six "basic" emotions—happiness, anger, sadness, disgust, surprise, and fear—are judged with very high accuracy among observers in many studies. In one large database, the ordering of accuracy from highest to lowest followed the list just given, but the emotions differed in how accuracy was influenced by how long the expression was shown (Calvo & Lundqvist, 2008). Happiness was equally easy to judge across exposures ranging from 25 to 500 milliseconds—that is, up to a half a second—but all of the other emotions showed increases as the exposures got longer.

Figures 9-7 to 9-12 show these six basic emotions with a description of their characteristic facial actions, each of which can also be described in terms of which action units are involved. These expressions are recognized at high levels not only in the United States but also around the globe (see Chapters 2 and 3; Ekman, Sorenson, & Friesen, 1969; Izard, 1971). More recently, Biehl and colleagues (1997) demonstrated that seven emotions shown on the faces of both Japanese and Caucasian individuals were judged with high levels of agreement by viewers in Hungary, Japan, Poland, Sumatra, and by Caucasians and recently immigrated Vietnamese in the United States.

We can argue that in today's world of global media exposure, such a result is not at all surprising. Ekman and his colleagues set about to find out how remote tribal people in New Guinea, who had not been exposed to Western facial expression norms, would respond. Even in New Guinea, photos of U.S. citizens' faces showing these six basic emotions—fear, surprise, anger, happiness, sadness, and disgust—were judged correctly for the most part. Moreover, some New Guineans were photographed while showing how they would react in different situations, such as "you feel sad because your child died," and U.S. respondents later guessed with great accuracy which scenario was being communicated (Ekman & Friesen, 1971).

Most cross-cultural research has dealt with depictions of the face showing very pure configurations for the major emotions. However, as noted earlier, facial expressions can be complex blends, with different muscles simultaneously showing elements of different emotions. The question of whether cross-cultural universality also applies to secondary, more subtle expressions led Ekman and a team of colleagues to introduce a new methodology into the cross-cultural research. These researchers obtained ratings of faces on a variety of emotions from subjects in 10 places around the world, including Estonia, Sumatra, Scotland, Japan, Italy, and Hong Kong. There was dramatic agreement across cultures not only on the

 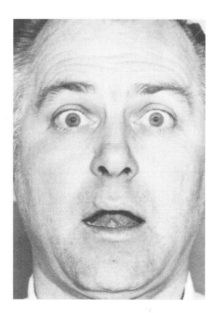

FIGURE 9-7

Surprise: The brows are raised so they are curved and high. The skin below the brow is stretched, and horizontal wrinkles go across the forehead. The eyelids are opened: the upper lid is raised, and the lower lid is drawn down; the white of the eye—the sclera—shows above the iris and often below as well. The jaw drops open so the lips and teeth are parted, but there is no tension or stretching of the mouth.

 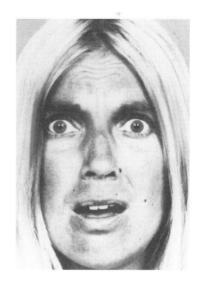

FIGURE 9-8

Fear: The brows are raised and drawn together. The wrinkles in the forehead are in the center, not across the entire forehead. The upper eyelid is raised, exposing the sclera, and the lower eyelid is tensed and drawn up. The mouth is open, and the lips are either tensed slightly and drawn back or stretched and drawn back.

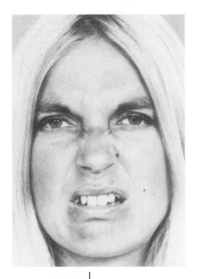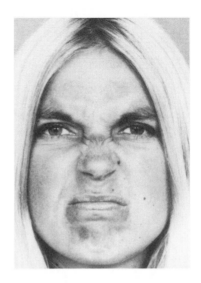

FIGURE 9-9

Disgust: The upper lip is raised. The lower lip is also raised and pushed up to the upper lip, or is lowered and slightly protruding. The nose is wrinkled, and the cheeks are raised. Lines show below the lower lid, and the lid is pushed up but not tense. The brow is lowered, lowering the upper lid.

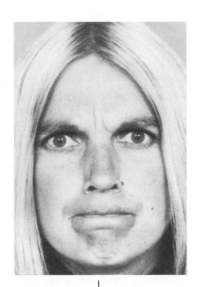

FIGURE 9-10

Anger: The brows are lowered and drawn together, and vertical lines appear between them. The lower lids are tensed and may or may not be raised. The upper lids are tensed and may or may not be lowered by the action of the brow. The eyes have a hard stare and may have a bulging appearance. The lips are in either of two basic positions: pressed firmly together, with the corners straight or down, or open and tensed in a squarish shape, as if shouting. The nostrils may be dilated, but this is not essential to the anger facial expression and may also occur in sadness. There is ambiguity unless anger is registered in all three facial areas.

FIGURE 9-11

Happiness: The corners of the lips are drawn back and up. The mouth may or may not be parted, with teeth exposed or not. A wrinkle, the nasolabial fold, runs down from the nose to the outer edge beyond the lip corners. The cheeks are raised. The lower eyelids show wrinkles below them and may be raised but not tense. Crow's-feet wrinkles go outward from the outer corners of the eyes (covered by hair in these photographs).

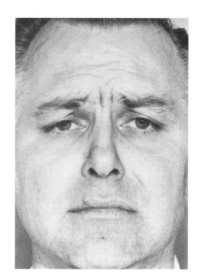

FIGURE 9-12

Sadness: The inner corners of the eyebrows are drawn up. The skin below the eyebrows is triangulated, with the inner corner up. The upper eyelid inner corners are raised. The corners of the lips are down, or the lips are trembling.

primary emotion being shown by the faces but also on the secondary emotion (Ekman et al., 1987).

Although accurate recognition of certain emotions is generally well above chance everywhere it has been tested, variability still exists between individuals and from place to place, and we discussed research on differences between individuals in Chapter 3. Variation from place to place is still being investigated. Russell (1994) found that facial expressions, mainly of Westerners' faces, were more accurately recognized by other Western groups than by non-Western groups. An *in-group advantage* has been documented, showing that people have an advantage when judging cues expressed by members of their own cultural, national, or ethnic group (Elfenbein & Ambady, 2002, 2003). One reason for such an advantage is the existence of "emotion dialects," or culturally learned ways of expressing different emotional messages through nonverbal cues. Such dialects, when shared between senders and receivers, promote accurate judgments. Elfenbein and Ambady (2003) measured accuracy in judging photographs of mainland Chinese people in China and Caucasian Americans expressing different emotions through the face. The groups whose accuracy was tested were mainland Chinese people in China, mainland Chinese people in the U.S., Chinese Americans—that is, U.S. citizens of Chinese extraction—and non-Asian U.S. citizens. These four groups' accuracy conformed exactly to the authors' "dialect" predictions: the more the group was familiar with mainland Chinese expressions, the better they were on Chinese compared to Caucasian expressions; and the more the group was familiar with American expressions, the better they were on Caucasian compared to Chinese expressions. In addition, an analysis of how long the Chinese-Americans' families had been in the United States showed that the longer the families had been in the country, the better they were at judging Caucasian compared to Chinese faces. These data lend strong support to the emotion dialects concept.

Although researchers do not agree on how many "basic" emotions there are, most research describing facial movements associated with emotion has concentrated on the six shown in Figures 9-7 to 9-12. Recently, attention has turned to other expressions. "Contempt" has been found to have a universally recognizable expression: a slight tightening and raising of the corner of the lip on one side (Ekman et al., 1987). "Threat" is conveyed by several facial signals, as shown in Figure 9-13. The faces are ordered so that decreasing ratings of perceived threat go from left to right in each row, with the highest ratings occurring for the face on the upper left and the lowest ratings occurring for the face on the lower right (Tipples, 2007). V-shaped brows, wide eyes, open mouth, and down-turned mouth all produced higher threat ratings. Facial signs for "anxiety" have been shown to include increased blinking and more facial movements associated with fear, such as a horizontal mouth stretch and more facial movements overall (Harrigan & O'Connell, 1996). "Pride" in its prototypical form includes a small smile in conjunction with other cues: head tilted back slightly, expanded posture, and hands on the hips (Tracy & Robins, 2004, 2007). "Embarrassment" has been shown to be signaled by looking down, shifting the eyes, turning the head away, touching the face, and engaging in "controlled smiles," which are smiles a person tries to counter with other facial movements (Keltner, 1995). Keltner has also studied the temporal ordering and relative duration of the components of facial embarrassment (Figure 9-14).

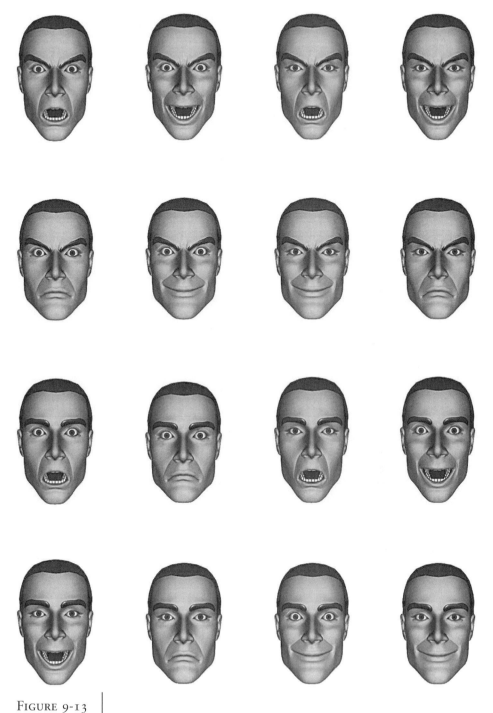

FIGURE 9-13

Facial stimuli in which four cues to threat are manipulated.
Source: From Tipples, J. (2007). Wide eyes and an open mouth enhance facial threat.
Cognition and Emotion, 21, 535–557.

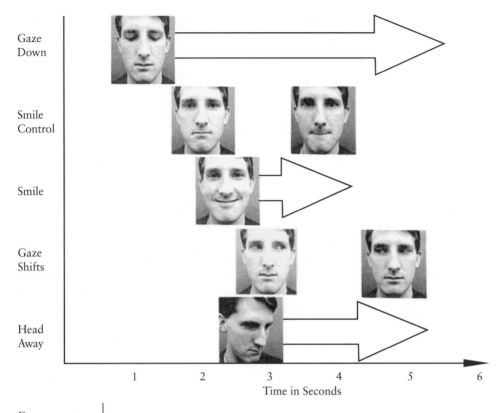

Gaze
Down

Smile
Control

Smile

Gaze
Shifts

Head
Away

1   2   3   4   5   6

Time in Seconds

FIGURE 9-14

Prototypical embarrassment response. The mean duration of each action is equal to the interval, beginning with the leftmost edge of the photograph and ending with the end of the arrow.

PHYSIOLOGY AND THE FACE

INTERNALIZERS AND EXTERNALIZERS

We all have at least one friend with a face that remains as still as a rock, no matter how much excitement swirls around him or her. We also have friends with faces that seem as sensitive as a butterfly's wings to every shift of the emotional winds. What we may not know is that these differences, aside from being quite real and enduring, also are associated with differences in physiological functioning. The "internalizers," those who show little facial expression, experience high physiological reactivity on measures such as heart rate and electrodermal responding; the "externalizers," the expressive ones, show the opposite pattern (Buck, Savin, Miller, & Caul, 1972; Lanzetta & Kleck, 1970; Notarius & Levenson, 1979). Most theorizing about this relationship has pointed to learned factors; for example, the notion that society encourages people to suppress their overt emotional reactions, and that individuals who do so must experience their emotions or arousal in some other way, perhaps through internal activation of the nervous system. The metaphor of discharge can be applied: the emotion is released, either externally or internally (Notarius & Levenson, 1979). However, research on newborns finds a similar negative relationship between expressiveness and physiological response, suggesting that temperamental factors may also be at work (Field, 1982).

FACIAL EXPRESSION AND HEALTH

Given these differences, it is intriguing to consider a possible connection between expressiveness and physical health. Could restraining the outward expression of emotion be damaging to health? Friedman and his colleagues (Friedman & Booth-Kewley, 1987; Friedman, Hall, & Harris, 1985) pursued this idea and found that, as predicted, a "repressed" style of expression was related to indications of coronary artery disease and even to the actual occurrence of a heart attack. King and Emmons (1990) found some support for the hypothesis that *ambivalence* over emotional expression would be associated with poorer health. Malatesta, Jonas, and Izard (1987) found that women who showed less expression on their face when talking about an angry experience had more arthritis symptoms, and women who showed less facial expression during a sad account had more skin problems. Promising evidence for a relation of emotional expression/suppression to health comes from research on *alexithymia*, a term used to describe patients who have a pronounced inability to describe their own emotions. These patients are deficient in facial expressiveness and also seem to suffer from a disproportionate number of psychosomatic ailments (Buck, 1993).

FACIAL FEEDBACK

Adding to the complexity and fascination regarding the relation between the face and physiology is the *facial feedback hypothesis* put forth by Darwin, who believed that if an emotion is freely expressed it will be intensified. The facial feedback hypothesis states that expressions on the face can intensify emotional experience via direct connections between facial muscles and emotion centers in the brain, even without any conscious awareness of what the face is showing.

Is the facial feedback hypothesis valid? The idea that emotions can be regulated via facial behavior—that we can create authentic emotional experience from inauthentic outward expressions—has important ramifications for child rearing, psychotherapy, and many other domains (Izard, 1990). The facial feedback hypothesis has been debated at length, for although a majority of studies support it, many of those studies are potentially flawed (Matsumoto, 1987). A typical experiment asks subjects to pose their faces in various ways and then measures their emotional state through self-report (Laird, 1974; Tourangeau & Ellsworth, 1979). The flaw in such a study is that expressors may realize their posed expression is meant to look like fear or happiness. If this happens, it is no surprise that they obediently report feeling those emotions.

Fortunately, studies exist that do not share this problem. Some studies measure reactions objectively and not in terms of expressors' self-reports. For example, posing a strong reaction to electric shocks, as opposed to posing no reaction, produced relative increases in physiological reaction via electrodermal measures, suggesting that more pain was experienced; posing a strong reaction also led to subjective reports of more pain (Lanzetta, Cartwright-Smith, & Kleck, 1976).

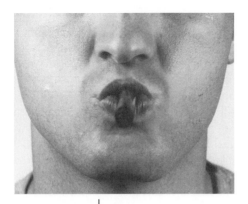
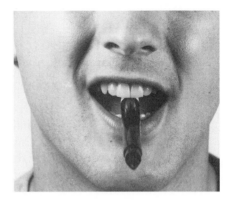

FIGURE 9-15

Illustration of the technique used to contract the different facial muscles: *left*, lips condition; *right*, teeth condition.

In a particularly well designed study, a group of investigators disguised the purpose of the facial posing by telling participants they were helping develop ways for persons with disabilities to hold a writing implement; it could be held between the teeth, which naturally expands the lips, or it could be held by the lips, which of course contracts them. Figure 9-15 illustrates these mouth positions. Unknown to the participants, these two manipulations differ in whether the "smiling" muscles around the mouth are activated. Those holding the pen between their teeth, which activates the smiling muscles, rated cartoons as funnier than the other participants did (Strack, Martin, & Stepper, 1988). Thus the position of the facial muscles can indeed "feed back" to influence the expressor's emotional state. Subsequent research using this same pencil-in-the-teeth paradigm showed, furthermore, that inducing expressors to activate their eye-corner muscles as well as their mouth-widening muscles, to produce Duchenne smiles, produced higher levels of enjoyment when viewing positive video clips than occurred when expressors made non-Duchenne smiles (Soussignan, 2002). This makes sense when you consider that the Duchenne smile is said to reflect more genuine positive emotion than the non-Duchenne smile.

Ekman and his colleagues, in a facial feedback experiment, also demonstrated that moving particular facial muscles on command, as well as "reliving" past emotional experiences, produces specific patterns of reaction in the autonomic nervous system (Ekman, Levenson, & Friesen, 1983). Heart rate and finger temperature increased more in anger than in happiness, and anger and fear were similar in terms of heart rate increases but differed in finger temperature. Perhaps these results translate into the familiar feelings of being flushed or hot when angry and of having cold hands when afraid.

Strack and Neumann (2000) extended the facial feedback phenomenon beyond emotional responses to the kinds of judgments we make about others. Under the guise of studying how working on a computer produces tension, participants were asked to furrow their brows, or not, while doing a computer judgment task. On the task, participants made ratings of how famous various celebrities and noncelebrities were. Those who maintained the furrowed brow rated the individuals as less famous than those in the control group, perhaps because the furrowed brow unconsciously put them in a skeptical frame of mind.

Though most feedback studies have involved the face, other body parts can also produce feedback effects. In one study, researchers manipulated upright versus slumped postures using differently designed chairs and showed that if participants were upright rather than slumped when hearing that they had performed well on an earlier task, they experienced more pride in their performance (Stepper & Strack, 1993).

Not much is known about the exact mechanisms that produce psychological changes, such as emotions, following face and body movement. Although well designed studies can rule out a cognitive explanation—that is, that people simply report the feelings they know their movements suggest—the nature of the physiological mechanism is still an open question. Although most investigators assume feedback occurs through the nervous system, a novel theory called the *vascular theory of emotional efference* holds that certain facial movements and breathing patterns change the temperature of the blood flowing into the brain, which then influences affective state, suggesting that perhaps cooler blood produces more positive affect (McIntosh, Zajonc, Vig, & Emerick, 1997; Zajonc, 1985).

Thus it appears that our own expressions, whether deliberately put on or spontaneously mimicked in response to others' expressions, can produce corresponding emotions or can intensify or deintensify experiences already in progress. The process of "emotional contagion" (Hatfield, Cacioppo, & Rapson, 1994) may contribute to our ability to experience empathy and understand others' emotional states. Indeed, when Surakka and Hietanen (1998) showed the "felt" and "unfelt" smiles shown in Figure 9-4 to viewers, they found that EMG recordings of both eye and cheek muscles were stronger for those who saw the felt smiles and that more pleasure was subsequently experienced by those who saw those smiles.

Though mimicry of other's facial expressions can occur entirely without awareness, mimicry is not, however, immune to social influences. In a good demonstration of this, facial EMG responses—specifically, the zygomatic major responding to a happy facial expression and the corrugator responding to a sad facial expression—occurred only when the participants had acquired positive associations to the target person by being told she had traits such as niceness and likeability. When the target person had negative traits, such as being "deceitful" and "aggressive," participants' faces showed no mimicking activity (Likowski, Mühlberger, Seibt, Pauli, & Weyers, 2008).

Researchers studying the face and physiology also have discovered that posed and spontaneous facial expressions are controlled by different pathways within the brain. This has been demonstrated by certain forms of brain injury that result in a person's losing the ability to produce facial expressions deliberately but not losing the capacity to laugh, cry, frown, and so on when genuinely experiencing an emotion; the reverse form of disability also exists (Rinn, 1984). When brain damage occurs, facial expressiveness is especially impaired when the damage is to the right hemisphere of the brain, which is considered the more nonverbal hemisphere (Buck & Duffy, 1980). Researchers have found that the left side of a person's face tends to be more expressive (Borod, Koff, Yecker, Santschi, & Schmidt, 1998; Nicholls, Wolfgang, Clode, & Lindell, 2002; Skinner & Mullen, 1991), because the left half of the face is controlled by the right hemisphere. However, consistent with the notion of separate neural pathways, this asymmetry is present only for posed expressions; spontaneous, more genuine ones tend to be symmetrical (Ekman, Hager, & Friesen, 1981; Skinner & Mullen, 1991). Perhaps now you will think differently about your friend with the crooked smile!

Thus far we have mostly examined the face in terms of what its movements mean. But researchers also have asked broader questions about real-world correlates of facial expression.

THE SOCIAL IMPACT OF FACIAL EXPRESSIONS

Facial expressions, both intended and spontaneous, exert many influences on other people. In this section, we present only a sampling of this research. The strong impact of facial expressions takes on special significance, because people have a great deal of control over their faces. Most discussions of the face center on emotions and how the face reveals what emotions are being felt. But several times we have mentioned posed versus spontaneous expressions. By its very nature, a posed expression means that people need not actually feel what they are showing, so the face becomes a tool of self-presentation, used to create a desirable image in the eyes of others, and of social influence, producing desirable impressions in someone else. Ironically, people may be particularly vulnerable to manipulation by others' faces, because people are likely to assume the face is an honest window into another's true feelings, when this might not be the case.

An important application of knowledge of facial expressions occurs in the helping professions. One such application is ascertaining the existence and severity of mental disorders. Ekman, Matsumoto, and Friesen (1997) showed that more contempt and more "unfelt" happy expressions at the time of hospital admission were related to less improvement at discharge, and that different diagnostic groups showed different facial emotion patterns: people with major depression showed more sadness and disgust; people in a manic condition showed more "felt" and "unfelt" happiness and less anger, disgust, and sadness; and people with schizophrenia showed fear and low levels of all the other coded emotions. Fridlund, Ekman, and Oster (1987) similarly showed that depressed individuals had sadder and less expressive faces than others.

In an even more precise and revealing investigation of depressive individuals' expressions, Reed, Sayette, and Cohn (2007) asked how such individuals would handle a situation in which a positive stimulus—in this case, a video clip of the comedian Chris Rock—could not be avoided. Would they be unmoved by the stimulus, or would they respond with happy feelings and expressions, the same as individuals with no depressive tendencies? The answer was some of both. The video affected all participants equally in terms of self-rated happiness and number of elicited smiles. However, participants with current depression symptoms and a depression history were five times more likely to try to control their smiles with additional muscle movements than other participants (see Figure 9-16). It was as though these individuals were fighting off the urge to smile.

The patient's face may not be the only face that is important in a clinical situation, however. There is reason to believe that physicians' and therapists' facial expressions have an impact on patients. Ambady, Koo, Rosenthal, and Winograd (2002) found that the facial expressions of physical therapists predicted changes in

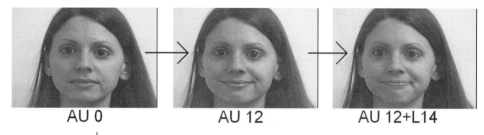

FIGURE 9-16

Depressed person's response to a funny film: Neutral, to smile, to smile control. Numbers refer to which muscle action units were activated.
Source: From Reed, L. I., Sayette, M. A., & Cohn, J. F. (2007). Impact of depression on response to comedy: A dynamic facial coding analysis. *Journal of Abnormal Psychology, 116,* 804–809.

elderly patients' physical and psychological functioning over the course of treatment. Facial "distancing," not smiling and not looking at the patient, was associated with decreases in functioning; but facial expressiveness—that is, smiling, nodding, and frowning—was associated with increases in functioning.

The faces of depressed mothers may similarly be an influential stimulus. Extensive work has been conducted on the interaction between mothers who have depression and their infants (Field, 2002; Lundy, Field, & Pickens, 1996). Infants of depressed mothers have less expressive faces than other infants, do not orient as well visually to adults, and show more facial negativity. Research shows that adults' smiles and other expressions influence babies' moods and responses to the environment (Cappella, 1981). In Field's (2002) study, the depressed mothers displayed the same kinds of behaviors that were then seen in their infants, such as more negative facial expressions and less looking around, as well as less vocalization and less tactile stimulation.

Savitsky, Izard, Kotsch, and Christy (1974) were interested in whether facial expressions of emotion by a victim would have any effect on the aggressor's behavior. When individuals thought they were controlling the amount of electric shock that another person, the victim, would get, they gave more shocks to victims who responded with expressions of happiness and smiles and fewer to victims who displayed expressions of anger.

Facial expressions also influence perceptions of trustworthiness. Krumhuber and colleagues (2007) manipulated a video of several potential "partners" in a game in which people could choose to cooperate or not, where cooperation implied trust and where mutual cooperation would result in higher monetary rewards for both. The partners' faces showed either an authentic-looking smile, an inauthentic-looking smile, or a neutral expression. Participants chose the authentically smiling person to cooperate with, rating that person the most trustworthy.

Although defendants' faces are scrutinized closely in the courtroom, their faces are not the only influential ones. In a cleverly designed experiment, Hart (1995) obtained videotapes of judges reading standard instructions to juries in real trials, and he also found out how those judges personally leaned in terms of guilt or innocence. These videotapes were then spliced onto a *different* trial, and the whole sequence was shown to groups of role-playing jurors. Thus these jurors were being "instructed" by judges who were known to be biased, although about a different case. Jurors' verdicts of guilt and innocence were significantly influenced by the judges' facial expressions and voice tone, thus demonstrating that judges' expressions can influence jurors even though the judges are supposed to remain impartial in their behavior.

There has been much interest and debate about whether children can give accurate eyewitness reports, for example, when being interviewed about possible sexual abuse. In an interview situation, it appears that the interviewer's facial expressions, combined with body movements, can influence a child's responses. In a study by Almerigogna, Ost, Akehurst, and Fluck (2008), an adult quizzed a child about what the child could remember from a learning exercise the previous week. When the interviewer smiled and refrained from fidgeting, the children gave more accurate and honest answers than when the adult fidgeted and did not smile. Furthermore, children in the nonsmiling-fidgeting situation were more likely to falsely report being touched by the teacher in that exercise when asked a leading question.

Interactions between service providers and customers provide yet another forum in which facial expressions can have impact. In an experiment in which role-playing "customers" watched videos of hotel clerks interacting with someone who was checking in, the clerk who displayed a smile that appeared authentic received higher customer satisfaction ratings than the clerk whose smile appeared inauthentic—but only when the clerk was performing her tasks competently. When the clerk made errors, the kind of smile had no impact (Grandey, Fisk, Mattila, Jansen, & Sideman, 2008). Thus the context was an important qualifier of whether the smile mattered.

The possibility that facial expressions are related to discrimination against women was the topic of Butler and Geis's (1990) study of male and female leaders in groups. Each group had a male or female leader who had, unknown to the group members, been trained to offer identical suggestions and arguments. However, the group members, who were the subjects of study, displayed more pleased responses (smiling and nodding) and fewer displeased responses (furrowed brow, mouth tightening, head shaking) when listening to the male leader than when listening to the female leader. Group members were apparently unaware of their gender-biased behavior or denied it, for they later revealed no gender bias in written evaluations of the leaders. The potential importance of this finding in real groups is obvious: subtle signals of devaluation sent by audience members could undermine a female leader's performance and could even create negativity in audience members who were not initially biased against her.

Another connection between the face and sex discrimination was made by Archer's discovery of the "face-ism" or facial prominence phenomenon: in magazine and newspaper pictures, proportionately more of the picture is devoted to men's faces, whereas pictures of women show more of the body. Archer, Iritani, Kimes, and Barrios (1983) found this pattern in publications from 11 different cultures and in artwork over 6 centuries, as well as in people's amateur drawings. Both Archer and later researchers (Zuckerman, 1986) have made the case that face-ism is a form of devaluing women. Consistent with the view that depicting less of the face devalues the person in the picture, Zuckerman and

Kieffer (1994) demonstrated that face-ism favoring whites over blacks also exists in magazines and art, when the artists are white, and the higher the status of the person shown in magazine photos, the larger the proportional depiction of the subject's face. Consistent with this, Matthews (2007) found higher facial prominence in magazine photographs of individuals who had intellectually oriented as opposed to physically oriented occupations, especially if the person in the photograph was a man.

The smile is a profoundly influential social cue that has been studied in many contexts. People reciprocate smiles quite predictably (Hinsz & Tomhave, 1991; Jorgenson, 1978). You can imagine how, after returning someone's smile, facial feedback or attributional processes ("I just smiled at Jim. I must really like him!") could produce real changes in your emotional state or your attitude toward the smiler. Smiles are positive reinforcers that can change behavior just as other, more traditional reinforcers can. Receiving a smile from one stranger can make you more helpful toward a different stranger (Gúeguen & de Gail, 2003; Solomon, Solomon, Arnone, Maur, Reda, & Roth, 1981), and receiving a smile from your waitperson can lead you to leave a larger tip (Tidd & Lockard, 1978).

Angry faces are a potent stimulus, too. In a series of experiments, Hansen and Hansen (1988) compared people's ability to pick out an angry face in a crowd of happy faces to their ability to pick out a happy face in a crowd of angry faces. As they predicted, picking out the angry face was faster and more error free than picking out the happy face. Perhaps our survival as a species has some relation to our sensitivity to threats.

The influence exerted on us by others' facial expressions is not limited to those faces that we consciously see and take note of. Unconscious, subliminal perception effects have been uncovered. Murphy and Zajonc (1993) showed people a happy or an angry face for only 4 milliseconds, an interval much too short to allow for conscious perception of the faces, followed by unfamiliar stimuli—in this case, written Chinese characters. When the experimenters asked the participants how much they liked each Chinese character, they found that characters preceded by a happy face were liked more than those preceded by an angry face. More recently, Dimberg, Thunberg, and Elmehed (2000) found that subliminally exposing people to happy or angry facial expressions produced corresponding facial movements according to EMG measurements. In this case, both the stimulus (the faces seen) and the response (the small facial movements picked up by EMG recording) occurred unconsciously. The almost uncanny sensitivity of human beings to facial expressions undoubtedly plays an important role in our adaptation to social life.

SUMMARY

The face is a multimessage system. It can communicate information regarding personality, interest and responsiveness during interaction, emotional states, and how people want to present themselves to others. Although we know that people associate certain personality characteristics with certain expressions and facial features, we do not yet know how accurate these impressions are. We know the face is used as a conversational regulator that opens and closes communication channels, complements and qualifies other behaviors, and replaces spoken messages.

Facial expressions are very complex entities to deal with. Of all the areas of the body, the face seems to elicit the best external and internal feedback, which makes it easy for us to follow a variety of facial display rules. Not all facial displays represent single emotions; some are blends of several emotions. Sometimes we show aspects of an emotional display when we are not actually feeling emotional, as with facial emblems that represent commentary on emotions. Other times the emotion we are feeling is not very predictably shown on the face. The question of how often the face spontaneously reveals emotional experiences in daily life is hotly contested.

We noted some measurement issues involved in the study of facial expressions: the complexity of the decisions observers are asked to make, simulated as opposed to real expressions, the method of presenting the face to the observer—films, photos, and the like—knowledge of the context, and others. Naturally, all these factors may impinge on our accuracy in identifying facial expressions of emotion.

Accuracy in judging the face tends to be high, at least when prototypical expressions are presented. Furthermore, certain basic emotions have been found to be accurately judged in cultures around the world: anger, fear, disgust, sadness, happiness, surprise, and contempt. To understand what the face actually does during the expression of emotion, anatomically based coding systems, such as the Facial Action Coding System (FACS), have been developed; these systems can identify which muscles are involved in different kinds of expressions.

A psychophysiological approach has added much to our understanding of facial behavior. People with more expressive faces have less activity in their autonomic nervous systems than less expressive people; this is interesting partly because of its health implications. Under certain circumstances, facial movements can influence the emotions felt by the expressor; thus the face may not only read out emotions but also may actually produce them. Studies of minute facial movements show that people unconsciously mimic the facial expressions of others, even those expressions too quick to be consciously perceived. And researchers are finding out more about which activities of the brain and nervous system are associated with different emotions. We concluded with a sampling of studies showing that facial expressions can have a strong impact on the people in our social environment.

(Answer to Figure 9-5: b. All the others have traces of disgust or sadness.)

QUESTIONS FOR DISCUSSION

1. Facial expressions can show emotions, but they also are used for conversation management. Give examples of each, and state which function you consider the most important.
2. Consider men's and women's nonverbal behavior. Does the concept of display rules help you explain any differences between the sexes?
3. As noted in the chapter, the distinction between a feigned or posed facial display and an authentic or spontaneous one may be hard to make. Discuss the issue of intentionality in facial expressions. Is it important to be able to make such a distinction? Do you think you can make such a distinction yourself, and if so, how do you think you do it?

4. The chapter gives examples of how the face is a potent influence on others. Think of some other examples of this, and discuss whether the face is more or less influential than other nonverbal channels in terms of its social impact.
5. Can you think of any occasions when you might have experienced intensification, or even creation, of an emotion as a result of facial feedback?
6. Some people are more aware of the expressions that occur on their faces than other people. Discuss this phenomenon. What kind of people do you think are more self-observant than others? What impact do you think this kind of self-accuracy has?

BIBLIOGRAPHY

Abelson, R. P., & Sermat, V. (1962). Multidimensional scaling of facial expressions. *Journal of Experimental Psychology, 63*, 546–551.

Ambady, N., Bernieri, F. J., & Richeson, J. (2000). Toward a histology of social behavior: Judgmental accuracy from thin slices of the behavioral stream. In M. P. Zanna (Ed.), *Advances in experimental social psychology* (Vol. 32, pp. 201–271). San Diego: Academic Press.

Ambady, N., Koo, J., Rosenthal, R., & Winograd, C. H. (2002). Physical therapists' nonverbal communication predicts geriatric patients' health outcomes. *Psychology and Aging, 17*, 443–452.

Andrew, R. J. (1965). The origins of facial expression. *Scientific American, 213*, 88–89.

Antonoff, S. R., & Spilka, B. (1984–1985). Patterning of facial expressions among terminal cancer patients. *Omega, 15*, 101–108.

Archer, D., Iritani, B., Kimes, D. D., & Barrios, M. (1983). Face-ism: Five studies of sex differences in facial prominence. *Journal of Personality and Social Psychology, 45*, 725–735.

Bartlett, M. S., Hager, J. C., Ekman, P., & Sejnowski, T. J. (1999). Measuring facial expressions by computer image analysis. *Psychophysiology, 36*, 253–263.

Bavelas, J. B., Black, A., Lemery, C. R., & Mullett, J. (1986). "I show how you feel": Motor mimicry as a communicative act. *Journal of Personality and Social Psychology, 50*, 322–329.

Bavelas, J. B., & Chovil, N. (1997). Faces in dialogue. In J. A. Russell & J. M. Fernández-Dols (Eds.), *The psychology of facial expression*. Paris: Cambridge University Press.

Biehl, M., Matsumoto, D., Ekman, P., Hearn, V., Heider, K., Kudoh, T., & Ton, V. (1997). Matsumoto and Ekman's Japanese and Caucasian Facial Expressions of Emotion (JACFEE): Reliability data and cross-national differences. *Journal of Nonverbal Behavior, 21*, 3–21.

Blairy, S., Herrera, P., & Hess, U. (1999). Mimicry and the judgment of emotional facial expressions. *Journal of Nonverbal Behavior, 23*, 5–41.

Bonanno, G. A., & Keltner, D. (2004). The coherence of emotion systems: Comparing "on-line" measures of appraisal and facial expressions and self-report. *Cognition and Emotion, 18*, 431–444.

Borod, J. C., Koff, E., Yecker, S., Santschi, C., & Schmidt, J. M. (1998). Facial asymmetry during emotional expression: Gender, valence, and measurement technique. *Neuropsychologia, 36*, 1209–1215.

Brannigan, C. R., & Humphries, D. A. (1972). Human nonverbal behavior, a means of communication. In N. Blurton Jones (Ed.), *Ethological studies of child behavior*. New York: Cambridge University Press.

Brunner, L. J. (1979). Smiles can be back channels. *Journal of Personality and Social Psychology, 37*, 728–73.

Buck, R. (1979). Measuring individual differences in the nonverbal communication of affect: The slide-viewing paradigm. *Human Communication Research, 6*, 47–57.

Buck, R. (1984). *The communication of emotion*. New York: Guilford.

Buck, R. (1988). Nonverbal communication: Spontaneous and symbolic aspects. *American Behavioral Scientist, 31*, 341–35.

Buck, R. (1991). Social factors in facial display and communication: A reply to Chovil and others. *Journal of Nonverbal Behavior, 15*, 155–161.

Buck, R. (1993). Emotional communication, emotional competence, and physical illness: A developmental–interactionist view. In H. C. Traue & J. W. Pennebaker (Eds.), *Emotion, inhibition, and health*. Seattle: Hogrefe & Hubner.

Buck, R. (1994). Social and emotional functions in facial expression and communication: The readout hypothesis. *Biological Psychology, 38*, 95–115.

Buck, R., & Duffy, R. (1980). Nonverbal communication of affect in brain-damaged patients. *Cortex, 16*, 351–362.

Buck, R., Savin, V., Miller, R. E., & Caul, W. F. (1972). Nonverbal communication of affect in humans. *Journal of Personality and Social Psychology, 23*, 362–371.

Bugental, D. E., Love, L. R., & Gianetto, R. M. (1971). Perfidious feminine faces. *Journal of Personality and Social Psychology, 17*, 314–318.

Butler, D., & Geis, F. L. (1990). Nonverbal affect responses to male and female leaders: Implications for leadership evaluations. *Journal of Personality and Social Psychology, 58,* 48–59.

Calvo, M. G., & Lundqvist, D. (2008). Facial expressions of emotion (KDEF): Identification under different display-duration conditions. *Behavior Research Methods, 40,* 109–115.

Cappella, J. N. (1981). Mutual influence in expressive behavior: Adult–adult and infant–adult dyadic interaction. *Psychological Bulletin, 89,* 101–132.

Carroll, J. M., & Russell, J. A. (1996). Do facial expressions signal specific emotions? Judging emotion from the face in context. *Journal of Personality and Social Psychology, 70,* 205–218.

Carroll, J. M., & Russell, J. A. (1997). Facial expressions in Hollywood's portrayal of emotion. *Journal of Personality and Social Psychology, 72,* 164–176.

Chovil, N. (1991). Social determinants of facial displays. *Journal of Nonverbal Behavior, 15,* 141–15.

Chovil, N. (1991/1992). Discourse-oriented facial displays in conversation. *Research on Language and Social Interaction, 25,* 163–19.

Cline, M. (1956). The influence of social context on the perception of faces. *Journal of Personality, 25,* 142–158.

Cohn, J. F., & Ekman, P. (2005). Measuring facial action. In J. A. Harrigan, R. Rosenthal, & K. R. Scherer (Eds.), *The new handbook of methods in nonverbal behavior research* (pp. 10–64). Oxford, UK: Oxford University Press.

Coleman, J. D. (1949). Facial expressions of emotions. *Psychological Monographs, 63* (1, Whole No. 296).

Darwin, C. R. (1872). *The expression of the emotions in man and animals.* London: John Murray.

Del Giudice, M., & Colle, L. (2007). Differences between children and adults in the recognition of enjoyment smiles. *Developmental Psychology, 43,* 796–803.

Dimberg, U. (1982). Facial reaction to facial expressions. *Psychophysiology, 19,* 643–647.

Dimberg, U., Thunberg, M., & Elmehed, K. (2000). Unconscious facial reactions to emotional facial expressions. *Psychological Science, 11,* 86–89.

Duclos, S. E., Laird, J. D., Schneider, E., Sexter, M., Stern, L., & Van Lighten, O. (1989). Emotion-specific effects of facial expressions and postures on emotional experience. *Journal of Personality and Social Psychology, 57,* 100–108.

Dunlap, K. (1927). The role of eye muscles and mouth muscles in the expression of the emotions. *Genetic Psychology Monographs, 2,* 199–233.

Eibl-Eibesfeldt, I. (1974). *Love and hate: The natural history of behavior patterns.* New York: Schocken.

Ekman, P. (Ed.). (1973). *Darwin and facial expression.* New York: Academic Press.

Ekman, P. (1979). About brows: Emotional and conversational signals. In V. von Cranach, K. Foppa, W. Lepenies, & D. Ploog (Eds.), *Human ethology.* Cambridge, UK: Cambridge University Press.

Ekman, P. (1982). Methods for measuring facial action. In K. R. Scherer & P. Ekman (Eds.), *Handbook of methods in nonverbal behavior research.* Cambridge, UK: Cambridge University Press.

Ekman, P., Davidson, R. J., & Friesen, W. V. (1990). The Duchenne smile: Emotional expression and brain physiology: II. *Journal of Personality and Social Psychology, 58,* 342–353.

Ekman, P., & Friesen, W. V. (1969). The repertoire of nonverbal behavior: Categories, origins, usage, and coding. *Semiotica, 1,* 49–98.

Ekman, P., & Friesen, W. V. (1971). Constants across cultures in the face and emotion. *Journal of Personality and Social Psychology, 17,* 124–129.

Ekman, P., & Friesen, W. V. (1975). *Unmasking the face.* Englewood Cliffs, NJ: Prentice-Hall.

Ekman, P., & Friesen, W. V. (1978). *The Facial Action Coding System: A technique for the measurement of facial movement.* Palo Alto: Consulting Psychologists Press.

Ekman, P., & Friesen, W. V. (1982). Felt, false, and miserable smiles. *Journal of Nonverbal Behavior, 6,* 238–252.

Ekman, P., & Friesen, W. V. (1986). A new pan-cultural facial expression of emotion. *Motivation and Emotion, 10,* 159–168.

Ekman, P., Friesen, W. V., & Ancoli, S. (1980). Facial signs of emotional experience. *Journal of Personality and Social Psychology, 39,* 1125–113.

Ekman, P., Friesen, W. V., & Ellsworth, P. (1982a). Does the face provide accurate information? In P. Ekman (Ed.), *Emotion in the human face* (2nd ed.). Cambridge, UK: Cambridge University Press.

Ekman, P., Friesen, W. V., & Ellsworth, P. (1982b). Methodological decisions. In P. Ekman (Ed.), *Emotion in the human face* (2nd ed.). Cambridge, UK: Cambridge University Press.

Ekman, P., Friesen, W. V., & Ellsworth, P. (1982c). What are the relative contributions of facial behavior and contextual information to the judgment of emotion? In P. Ekman (Ed.), *Emotion in the human face* (2nd ed.). Cambridge, UK: Cambridge University Press.

Ekman, P., Friesen, W. V., & O'Sullivan, M. (1988). Smiles when lying. *Journal of Personality and Social Psychology, 54,* 414–420.

Ekman, P., Friesen, W. V., O'Sullivan, M., Chan, A., Diacoyanni-Tarlatzis, I., Heider, K., Krause, R., LeCompte, W. A., Pitcairn, T., Ricci-Bitti, P. E., Scherer, K., Tomita, M., & Tzavaras, A. (1987). Universals and cultural differences in the judgments of facial expressions of emotion. *Journal of Personality and Social Psychology, 53,* 712–717.

Ekman, P., Hager, J. C., & Friesen, W. V. (1981). The symmetry of emotional and deliberate facial actions. *Psychophysiology, 18,* 101–106.

Ekman, P., Levenson, R. W., & Friesen, W. V. (1983). Autonomic nervous system activity distinguishes among emotions. *Science, 221,* 1208–1210.

Ekman, P., Matsumoto, D., & Friesen, W. V. (1997). Facial expression in affective disorders. In P. Ekman & E. Rosenberg (Eds.), *What the face reveals: Basic and applied studies of spontaneous expression using the Facial Action Coding System (FACS).* New York: Oxford University Press.

Ekman, P., & Oster, H. (1982). Review of research, 1970–1980. In P. Ekman (Ed.), *Emotion in the human face* (2nd ed.). Cambridge, UK: Cambridge University Press.

Ekman, P., & Rosenberg, E. (Eds.). (1997). *What the face reveals: Basic and applied studies of spontaneous expression using the Facial Action Coding System (FACS).* New York: Oxford University Press.

Ekman, P., Sorenson, E. R., & Friesen, W. V. (1969). Pan-cultural elements in facial displays of emotions. *Science, 164,* 86–88.

Elfenbein, H. A., & Ambady, N. (2002). On the universality and cultural specificity of emotion recognition: A meta-analysis. *Psychological Bulletin, 128,* 203–235.

Elfenbein, H. A., & Ambady, N. (2003). When familiarity breeds accuracy: Cultural exposure and facial emotion recognition. *Journal of Personality and Social Psychology, 85,* 276–290.

Ellis, C. (1991). Sociological introspection and emotional experience. *Symbolic Interaction, 14,* 23–50.

Feleky, A. M. (1914). The expression of emotions. *Psychological Review, 21,* 33–41.

Fernández-Dols, J. M., & Carroll, J. M. (1997). Is the meaning perceived in facial expression independent of its context? In J. A. Russell & J. M. Fernández-Dols (Eds.), *The psychology of facial expression.* Paris: Cambridge University Press.

Fernández-Dols, J. M., & Ruiz-Belda, M. A. (1995). Are smiles a sign of happiness? Gold medal winners at the Olympic Games. *Journal of Personality and Social Psychology, 69,* 1113–1119.

Fernández-Dols, J. M., & Ruiz-Belda, M. A. (1997). Spontaneous facial behavior during intense emotional episodes: Artistic truth and optical truth. In J. A. Russell & J. M. Fernández-Dols (Eds.), *The psychology of facial expression* (pp. 255–274). New York: Cambridge University Press.

Fernández-Dols, J. M., Sanchez, F., Carrera, P., & Ruiz-Belda, M A. (1997). Are spontaneous expressions and emotions linked? An experimental test of coherence. *Journal of Nonverbal Behavior, 21,* 163–177.

Field, T. (1982). Individual differences in the expressivity of neonates and young infants. In R. S. Feldman (Ed.), *Development of nonverbal behavior in children.* New York: Springer-Verlag.

Field, T. (2002). Early interactions between infants and their postpartum depressed mothers. *Infant Behavior & Development, 25,* 25–29.

Fox, N. A., & Davidson, R. J. (1988). Patterns of brain electrical activity during facial signs of emotion in 10-month-old infants. *Developmental Psychology, 14,* 230–236.

Frank, M. G., Ekman, P., & Friesen, W. V. (1993). Behavioral markers and recognizability of the smile of enjoyment. *Journal of Personality and Social Psychology, 64,* 83–93.

Frank, M. G., & Stennett, J. (2001). The forced-choice paradigm and the perception of facial expressions of emotion. *Journal of Personality and Social Psychology, 80,* 75–85.

Fridlund, A. J. (1991). Sociality of solitary smiling: Potentiation by an implicit audience. *Journal of Personality and Social Psychology, 60,* 229–240.

Fridlund, A. J. (1994). *Human facial expression: An evolutionary view.* San Diego: Academic Press. Fridlund, A. J. (1997). The new ethology of human facial expressions. In J. A. Russell & J. M. Fernández-Dols (Eds.), *The psychology of facial expression.* Paris: Cambridge University Press.

Fridlund, A. J., Ekman, P., & Oster, H. (1987). Facial expressions of emotion: Review of literature, 1970–1983. In A. W. Siegman & S. Feldstein (Eds.), *Nonverbal behavior and communication* (2nd ed.). Hillsdale, NJ: Erlbaum.

Friedman, H. S., & Booth-Kewley, S. (1987). Personality, Type A behavior, and coronary heart disease: The role of emotional expression. *Journal of Personality and Social Psychology, 53,* 783–792.

Friedman, H. S., DiMatteo, M. R., & Mertz, T. I. (1980). Nonverbal communication on television news: The facial expressions of broadcasters during coverage of a presidential election campaign. *Personality and Social Psychology Bulletin, 6,* 427–435.

Friedman, H. S., Hall, J. A., & Harris, M. J. (1985). Type A behavior, nonverbal expressive style, and health. *Journal of Personality and Social Psychology, 48,* 1299–1315.

Gifford, R. (1994). A lens-mapping framework for understanding the encoding and decoding of interpersonal dispositions in nonverbal behavior. *Journal of Personality and Social Psychology, 66,* 398–412.

Gosselin, P., Perron, M., Legault, M., & Campanella, P. (2002). Children's and adults' knowledge of the distinction between enjoyment and nonenjoyment smiles. *Journal of Nonverbal Behavior, 26,* 83–108.

Grandey, A. A., Fisk, G. M., Mattila, A. S., Jansen, K. J., & Sideman, L. A. (2005). Is "service with a smile" enough? Authenticity of positive displays during service encounters. *Organizational Behavior and Human Decision Processes, 96,* 38–55.

Guégen, N., & de Gail, M. (2003). The effect of smiling on helping behavior: Smiling and Good Samaritan behavior. *Communication Reports, 16,* 133–140.

Hager, J. C., & Ekman, P. (1985). The asymmetry of facial actions is inconsistent with models of hemispheric specialization. *Psychophysiology, 22,* 307–318.

Haggard, E. A., & Isaacs, F. S. (1966). Micro-momentary facial expressions as indicators of ego mechanisms in psychotherapy. In L. A. Gottschalk & A. H. Auerback (Eds.), *Methods of research in psychotherapy.* New York: Appleton-Century-Crofts.

Halberstadt, A. G. (1986). Family socialization of emotional expression and nonverbal communication styles and skills. *Journal of Personality and Social Psychology, 51,* 827–836.

Hall, J. A. (1984). *Nonverbal sex differences: Communication accuracy and expressive style.* Baltimore: Johns Hopkins University Press.

Hall, J. A., Murphy, N. A., & Schmid Mast, M. (2007). Nonverbal self-accuracy in interpersonal interaction. *Personality and Social Psychology Bulletin, 33,* 1675–1685.

Hansen, C. H., & Hansen, R. D. (1988). Finding the face in the crowd: An anger superiority effect. *Journal of Personality and Social Psychology, 54,* 917–924.

Harker, L., & Keltner, D. (2001). Expressions of positive emotion in women's college yearbook pictures and their relationship to personality and life outcomes across adulthood. *Journal of Personality and Social Psychology, 80,* 112–124.

Harrigan, J. A., & O'Connell, D. M. (1996). How do you look when feeling anxious? Facial displays of anxiety. *Personality and Individual Differences, 21,* 205–212.

Hart, A. J. (1995). Naturally occurring expectation effects. *Journal of Personality and Social Psychology, 68,* 109–115.

Hatfield, E., Cacioppo, J. T., & Rapson, R. (1994). *Emotional contagion.* Cambridge, UK: Cambridge University Press.

Hess, U., & Kleck, R. E. (1990). Differentiating emotion elicited and deliberate emotional facial expressions. *European Journal of Social Psychology, 20,* 369–385.

Hinsz, V. B., & Tomhave, J. A. (1991). Smile and (half) the world smiles with you, frown and you frown alone. *Personality and Social Psychology Bulletin, 17,* 586–592.

Izard, C. E. (1971). *The face of emotion.* New York: Appleton-Century-Crofts.

Izard, C. E. (1979). *The maximally discriminative facial movement coding system.* Unpublished manuscript, University of Delaware.

Izard, C. E. (1990). Facial expressions and the regulation of emotions. *Journal of Personality and Social Psychology, 58,* 487–498.

Jones, S. S., Collins, K., & Hong, H. (1991). An audience effect on smile production in 10-month-old infants. *Psychological Science, 2,* 45–49.

Jorgenson, D. O. (1978). Nonverbal assessment of attitudinal affect with the smile-return technique. *Journal of Social Psychology, 106,* 173–179.

Kaiser, S., & Wehrle, T. (1992). Automated coding of facial behavior in human–computer interactions with FACS. *Journal of Nonverbal Behavior, 16,* 65–140.

Katsikitis, M. (Ed.). (2002). *The human face: Measurement and meaning.* Dordrecht, NL: Kluwer.

Keltner, D. (1995). Signs of appeasement: Evidence for the distinct displays of embarrassment, amusement, and shame. *Journal of Personality and Social Psychology, 68,* 441–454.

King, L. A., & Emmons, R. A. (1990). Conflict over emotional expression: Psychological and physical correlates. *Journal of Personality and Social Psychology, 58,* 864–877.

Knutson, B. (1996). Facial expressions of emotion influence interpersonal trait inferences. *Journal of Nonverbal Behavior, 20,* 165–182.

Kraut, R. E., & Johnston, R. E. (1979). Social and emotional messages of smiling: An ethological approach. *Journal of Personality and Social Psychology, 37,* 1539–1553.

Kring, A. M., & Sloan, D. M. (2007). The Facial Expression Coding System (FACES): Development, validation, and utility. *Psychological Assessment, 19,* 210–224.

Krumhuber, E., Manstead, A. S. R., Cosker, D., Marshall, D., Rosin, P. L., & Kappas, A. (2007). Facial dynamics as indicators of trustworthiness and cooperative behavior. *Emotion, 7,* 730–735.

Laird, J. D. (1974). Self-attribution of emotion: The effects of expressive behavior on the quality of emotional experience. *Journal of Personality and Social Psychology, 24,* 475–486.

Lanzetta, J. T., Cartwright-Smith, J., & Kleck, R. E. (1976). Effects of nonverbal dissimulation of emotional experience and autonomic arousal. *Journal of Personality and Social Psychology, 33,* 354–370.

Lanzetta, J. T., & Kleck, R. E. (1970). Encoding and decoding of nonverbal affect in humans. *Journal of Personality and Social Psychology, 16,* 12–19.

Lee, V., & Wagner, H. (2002). The effect of social presence on the facial and verbal expression of emotion and the interrelations among emotion components. *Journal of Nonverbal Behavior, 26,* 3–25.

LeResche, L. (1982). Facial expression in pain: A study of candid photographs. *Journal of Nonverbal Behavior, 7,* 46–56.

Likowski, K. U., Mühlberger, A., Seibt, B., Pauli, P., & Weyers, P. (2008). Modulation of facial mimicry by attitudes. *Journal of Experimental Social Psychology, 44,* 1065–1072.

Lundqvist, D., Esteves, F., & Ohman, A. (1999). The face of wrath: Critical features for conveying facial threat. *Cognition and Emotion, 13,* 691–711.

Lundqvist, L. O. (1995). Facial EMG reactions to facial expressions: A case of facial emotional contagion? *Scandinavian Journal of Psychology, 36,* 130–141.

Lundy, B., Field, T., & Pickens, J. (1996). Newborns of mothers with depressive symptoms are less expressive. *Infant Behavior and Development, 19,* 419–424.

Malatesta, C. Z., Jonas, R., & Izard, C. E. (1987). The relation between low facial expressibility during emotional arousal and somatic symptoms. *British Journal of Medical Psychology, 60,* 169–180.

Matsumoto, D. (1987). The role of facial response in the experience of emotion: More methodological problems and a meta-analysis. *Journal of Personality and Social Psychology, 52,* 769–774.

Matsumoto, D. (1989). Face, culture, and judgments of anger and fear: Do the eyes have it? *Journal of Nonverbal Behavior, 13,* 171–188.

Matsumoto, D. (1992). American-Japanese cultural differences in the recognition of universal facial expressions. *Journal of Cross-Cultural Psychology, 23,* 72–84.

Matsumoto, D., & Ekman, P. (1989). American-Japanese cultural differences in intensity ratings of facial expressions of emotion. *Motivation and Emotion, 13,* 143–157.

Matsumoto, D., Keltner, D., Shiota, M. N., O'Sullivan, M., & Frank, M. (2008). Facial expressions of emotion. In M. Lewis, J. M. Haviland-Jones, & L. Feldman Barrett (Eds.), *Handbook of emotions* (3rd ed., pp. 211–234). New York: Guilford.

Matsumoto, D., LeRoux, J., Wilson-Cohn, C., Raroque, J., Kooken, K., Ekman, P., Yrizarry, N., Loewinger, S., Uchida, H., Yee, A., Amo, L., & Goh, A. (2000). A new test to measure emotion recognition ability: Matsumoto and Ekman's Japanese and Caucasian Brief Affect Recognition Test (JACBART). *Journal of Nonverbal Behavior*, 24, 179–209.

Matsumoto, D., & Willingham, B. (2006). The thrill of victory and the agony of defeat: Spontaneous expressions of medal winners of the 2004 Athens Olympic Games. *Journal of Personality and Social Psychology*, 91, 568–581.

Matthews, J. L. (2007). Hidden sexism: Facial prominence and its connections to gender and occupational status in popular print media. *Sex Roles*, 57, 515–525.

McIntosh, D. N., Zajonc, R. B., Vig, P. S., & Emerick, S. W. (1997). Facial movement, breathing, temperature, and affect: Implications of the Vascular Theory of Emotional Efference. *Cognition and Emotion*, 11, 171–195.

Mullen, B. (1986). Newscasters' facial expressions and voting behavior of viewers: Can a smile elect a president? *Journal of Personality and Social Psychology*, 51, 291–295.

Munn, N. L. (1940). The effect of knowledge of the situation upon the judgment of emotion from facial expression. *Journal of Abnormal and Social Psychology*, 35, 324–338.

Murphy, S. T., & Zajonc, R. B. (1993). Affect, cognition, and awareness: Affective priming with optimal and suboptimal stimulus exposures. *Journal of Personality and Social Psychology*, 64, 723–739.

Nicholls, M. E. R., Wolfgang, B. J., Clode, D., & Lindell, A. K. (2002). The effect of left and right poses on the expression of facial emotion. *Neuropsychologia*, 40, 1662–1665.

Notarius, C. I., & Levenson, R. W. (1979). Expressive tendencies and physiological response to stress. *Journal of Personality and Social Psychology*, 37, 1204–1210.

Osgood, C. E. (1966). Dimensionality of the semantic space for communication via facial expressions. *Scandinavian Journal of Psychology*, 7, 1–30.

Papa, A., & Bonanno, G. A. (2008). Smiling in the face of adversity: The interpersonal and intrapersonal functions of smiling. *Emotion*, 8, 1–12.

Patrick, C. J., Craig, K. D., & Prkachin, K. M. (1986). Observer judgments of acute pain: Facial action determinants. *Journal of Personality and Social Psychology*, 50, 1291–1298.

Prkachin, K. M., & Craig, K. D. (1995). Expressing pain: The communication and interpretation of facial pain signals. *Journal of Nonverbal Behavior*, 19, 191–205.

Redican, W. K. (1982). An evolutionary perspective on human facial displays. In P. Ekman (Ed.), *Emotion in the human face* (2nd ed.). Cambridge, UK: Cambridge University Press.

Reed, L. I., Sayette, M. A., & Cohn, J. F. (2007). Impact of depression on response to comedy: A dynamic facial coding analysis. *Journal of Abnormal Psychology*, 116, 804–809.

Riggio, R. E., & Friedman, H. S. (1986). Impression formation: The role of expressive behavior. *Journal of Personality and Social Psychology*, 50, 421–427.

Rinn, W. E. (1984). The neuropsychology of facial expression: A review of the neurological and psychological mechanisms for producing facial expressions. *Psychological Bulletin*, 95, 52–77.

Rozin, P., Lowery, U., & Ebert, R. (1994). Varieties of disgust faces and the structure of disgust. *Journal of Personality and Social Psychology*, 66, 870–881.

Ruiz-Belda, M., Fernández-Dols, J., Carrera, P., & Barchard, K. (2003). Spontaneous facial expressions of happy bowlers and soccer fans. *Cognition and Emotion*, 17, 315–326.

Russell, J. A. (1994). Is there universal recognition of emotion from facial expression? *Psychological Bulletin*, 115, 102–141.

Russell, J. A., Bachorowski, J., & Fernández-Dols, J. (2003). Facial and vocal expressions of emotion. *Annual Review of Psychology*, 54, 329–349.

Russell, J. A., & Fernández-Dols, J. M. (1997). *The psychology of facial expression*. Paris: Cambridge University Press.

Sato, W., & Yoshikawa, S. (2007). Spontaneous facial mimicry in response to dynamic facial expressions. *Cognition*, 104, 1–18.

Savitsky, J. C., Izard, C. E., Kotsch, W. E., & Christy, L. (1974). Aggressor's response to the victim's facial expression of emotion. *Journal of Research on Personality, 7,* 346–357.

Savitsky, J. C., & Sim, M. E. (1974). Trading emotions: Equity theory of reward and punishment. *Journal of Communication, 24,* 140–146.

Scherer, K. R., & Ceschi, G. (2000). Criteria for emotion recognition from verbal and nonverbal expression: Studying baggage loss in the airport. *Personality and Social Psychology Bulletin, 26,* 327–339.

Secord, P. F., Dukes, W. F., & Bevan, W. (1959). Personalities in faces: I. An experiment in social perceiving. *Genetic Psychology Monographs, 49,* 231–279.

Skinner, M., & Mullen, B. (1991). Facial asymmetry in emotional expression: A meta-analysis of research. *British Journal of Social Psychology, 30,* 113–124.

Smith, W. J., Chase, J., & Lieblich, A. K. (1974). Tongue showing: A facial display of humans and other primate species. *Semiotica, 11,* 201–246.

Solomon, H., Solomon, L. Z., Arnone, M. M., Maur, B. J., Reda, R. M., & Roth, E. O. (1981). Anonymity and helping. *Journal of Social Psychology, 113,* 37–43.

Soussignan, R. (2002). Duchenne smile, emotional experience, and autonomic reactivity: A test of the facial feedback hypothesis. *Emotion, 2,* 52–74.

Spitz, R. A., & Wolf, K. M. (1946). The smiling response: A contribution to the ontogenesis of social relations. *Genetic Psychology Monographs, 34,* 57–125.

Stepper, S., & Strack, F. (1993). Proprioceptive determinants of emotional and nonemotional feelings. *Journal of Personality and Social Psychology, 64,* 211–220.

Strack, F., Martin, L. L., & Stepper, S. (1988). Inhibiting and facilitating conditions of the human smile: A nonobtrusive test of the facial feedback hypothesis. *Journal of Personality and Social Psychology, 54,* 768–777.

Strack, F., & Neumann, R. (2000). Furrowing the brow may undermine perceived fame: The role of facial feedback in judgments of celebrity. *Personality and Social Psychology Bulletin, 26,* 762–768.

Surakka, V., & Hietanen, J. K. (1998). Facial and emotional reactions to Duchenne and non-Duchenne smiles. *International Journal of Psychophysiology, 29,* 23–33.

Tcherkassof, A., Bollon, T., Dubois, M., Pansu, P., & Adam, J. (2007). Facial expressions of emotions: A methodological contribution to the study of spontaneous and dynamic emotional faces. *European Journal of Social Psychology, 37,* 1325–1345.

Tidd, K., & Lockard, J. (1978). Monetary significance of the affiliative smile: A case of reciprocal altruism. *Bulletin of the Psychonomic Society, 11,* 344–346.

Tipples, J. (2007). Wide eyes and an open mouth enhance facial threat. Cognition and *Emotion, 21,* 535–557.

Tomkins, S. S. (1962–1963). *Affect, imagery, consciousness* (Vols. 1 and 2). New York: Springer.

Tourangeau, R., & Ellsworth, P. C. (1979). The role of facial response in the experience of emotion. *Journal of Personality and Social Psychology, 37,* 1519–1531.

Tracy, J. L., & Robins, R. W. (2004). Show your pride: Evidence for a discrete emotion expression. *Psychological Science, 15,* 194–197.

Tracy, J. L., & Robins, R. W. (2007). The prototypical pride expression: Development of a nonverbal behavior coding system. *Emotion, 7,* 789–801.

Wagner, H. L. (1993). On measuring performance in category judgment studies of nonverbal behavior. *Journal of Nonverbal Behavior, 17,* 3–28.

Wagner, H., & Lee, V. (1999). Facial behavior alone and in the presence of others. In P. Philoppot, R. S. Feldman, & E. J. Coats (Eds.), *The social context of nonverbal behavior.* Cambridge, UK: Cambridge University Press.

Wagner, H. L., & Smith, J. (1991). Facial expressions in the presence of friends and strangers. *Journal of Nonverbal Behavior, 15,* 201–214.

Zajonc, R. B. (1985). Emotion and facial efference: A theory reclaimed. *Science, 228,* 15–21.

Zuckerman, M. (1986). On the meaning and implications of facial prominence. *Journal of Nonverbal Behavior, 10,* 215–229.

Zuckerman, M., Hall, J. A., DeFrank, R. S., & Rosenthal, R. (1976). Encoding and decoding of spontaneous and posed facial expressions. *Journal of Personality and Social Psychology, 34,* 966–977.

Zuckerman, M., & Kieffer, S. C. (1994). Race differences in face-ism: Does facial prominence imply dominance? *Journal of Personality and Social Psychology, 66,* 86–92.

He speaketh not; and yet there lies
A conversation in his eyes.
—Henry Wadsworth Longfellow

CHAPTER **10** | # THE EFFECTS OF EYE BEHAVIOR ON HUMAN COMMUNICATION

Throughout history, we have been preoccupied with the eye and its effects on human behavior. Do you recall the last time you heard or read one of these phrases?

"It was an icy stare."

"He's got shifty eyes."

"Did you see the gleam in his eye?"

"We're seeing eye to eye now."

"His eyes shot daggers across the room."

"She could kill with a glance."

It is common to associate various eye movements with a wide range of human emotions or traits: downward glances are associated with modesty; wide eyes with frankness, wonder, naïveté, or terror; generally immobile facial muscles and a rather constant stare with coldness; and eyes rolled upward with fatigue or to suggest that another's behavior is a bit weird. What attribution would you make about the eye shown in Figure 10-1?

In addition, our society has established a number of eye-related norms. For example, we must not look too long at strangers in public places, we must not make eye contact for too long, and we are not supposed to look at various parts of the body except under certain conditions, and so on.

Fascination with eyes has led to the exploration of almost every conceivable feature of the eyes and the areas surrounding them. We look at eye size, color, position, eyebrows, and wrinkles around the eyes. Eye rings are found mainly in other animals, but some speculate that human eyebrows are residual "rings," to be raised during surprise or fear and lowered for focus during threat and anger. Eye "patches" are the colored eyelids sometimes seen in primates, but these are not a part of the natural human communicative repertoire, although women often use eyeliner and eye shadow to achieve a similar effect. Another nonhuman feature that has received scholarly attention is "eyespots," eye-shaped images located on

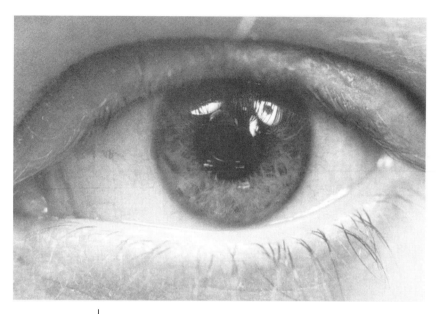

FIGURE 10-1

The human eye.

various parts of some animals' bodies. These can be seen on peacock feathers, butterflies, and certain fish.

Researchers have examined the degree to which eyes open or close as a reflection of various emotional states. Some feel that excessive blinking may be associated with various stages of anxiety—as if attempting to cut off reality. Psychiatrists report that some patients blink up to 100 times per minute; normal blinking, needed to lubricate and protect the eyeball, occurs about 6 to 10 times per minute in adults. Some evidence shows that when a person is attentive to objects in the environment, or deep in concentrated thought, the blinking rate decreases.

Further diversity in the significance of the eyes comes from research on eye color. Blue eyes are a genetically based marker for inhibition and shyness (Rosenberg & Kagan, 1987). Some eye-related behaviors occur without much conscious awareness, such as the crinkles around the eyes when a person is feeling genuine enjoyment, but others are used very deliberately. An example of the latter is the "eye flash," in which the eyelids are briefly opened without the accompanying involvement of the eyebrows, for less than a second, used to emphasize particular words, usually adjectives (Walker & Trimboli, 1983). The eye*brow* flash is yet another, but quite different gesture, discussed in depth in Chapter 2.

Of the many eye-related topics of inquiry, this chapter focuses on two: The first is known by such terms as *eye contact, mutual glances, visual interaction, gazing,* or *line of regard.* The second concerns pupil dilation and constriction under various social conditions.

GAZE AND MUTUAL GAZE

We begin by looking at the terminology we will be using: *gaze* and *mutual gaze* (Argyle & Cook, 1976; Kleinke, 1986; Rutter, 1984). *Gaze* refers to an individual's looking at another person; *mutual gaze* refers to a situation in which two interactants are looking at each other, usually in the region of the face (see Figure 10-2). Eye contact—that is, looking specifically in each other's eyes—does not seem to be reliably distinguished by receivers or observers from gazing at the area surrounding the eyes (von Cranach & Ellgring, 1973). In fact, much of what is considered "looking someone in the eye" is a series of rapid, repeated scans of several parts of the face. Indeed, if someone did look fixedly without moving the eyes, the impression would be one of vacant staring. Gaze and mutual gazing can be reliably assessed by observers. At a distance of 3 meters, face-directed gazing can be distinguished, and shifting the direction of the gaze by 1 centimeter can reliably be detected from a distance of 1 meter. Furthermore, people tend to be accurate in reporting their own amount of gaze directed at a partner in interaction (Hall, Murphy, & Schmid Mast, 2007).

We know that we do not look at the other person the entire time we are talking to him or her, nor do we avert our gaze 100 percent of the time. What are considered normal gazing patterns? Obviously, the answer varies according to the background and personalities of the participants, the topic, the other person's gazing patterns, objects of mutual interest in the environment, and so on. The speaker's fluency also affects gazing patterns. During fluent speech, speakers tend to look at listeners much more than during hesitant speech. We will discuss some of these factors in more detail later in this chapter. Keeping such qualifications in mind, we can get a general idea of

FIGURE 10-2

Mutual gaze.

TABLE 10-1 | AMOUNT OF GAZING IN TWO-PERSON CONVERSATIONS

	(%)	(%)	(%)	(%)	(%) Mutual	Average Length of Gaze	Average Length of Mutual Gaze
Nielsen	50*	8–73	38	62	—	—	—
Argyle & Ingham	61	—	41	75	31	2.95 sec.	1.18 sec.

*Percentages reflect the amount of time gazing relative to the total interaction time.

normal gazing patterns from two studies of focused interaction between two people, shown in Table 10-1. The table shows that, on average, people gaze about half the time; that there is a huge range, indicating notable individual differences, in the amount of other-directed gaze; and that people gaze more while listening than while talking.

FUNCTIONS OF GAZING

Kendon (1967) identified four functions of gazing: (1) *regulatory*—responses may be demanded or suppressed by looking; (2) *monitoring*—people may look at their partner to indicate the conclusions of thought units and to check their partner's attentiveness and reactions; (3) *cognitive*—people tend to look away when having difficulty processing information or deciding what to say; and (4) *expressive*—the degree and nature of involvement or emotional arousal may be revealed through looking.

Our discussion follows a similar pattern, as gazing has been shown to serve several important functions:

1. Regulating the flow of communication
2. Monitoring feedback
3. Reflecting cognitive activity
4. Expressing emotions
5. Communicating the nature of the interpersonal relationship

These functions do not operate independently; that is, visual behavior not only sends information, it is also one of the primary methods for collecting it. Looking at the other person as you finish an utterance may not only tell the other it is his or her turn to speak, it is also an occasion to monitor feedback regarding the utterance.

REGULATING THE FLOW OF COMMUNICATION

Visual contact occurs when we want to signal that the communication channel is open. In some instances, eye gaze establishes a virtual *obligation* to interact. When you seek visual contact with your server at a restaurant, you are essentially indicating that the communication channel is open and that you want to say something to him or her. You may recall instances when an instructor asked the class a question, and you were sure you did not know the answer. Establishing eye contact with the instructor was the last thing you wanted to do. Police use this knowledge to identify drivers who may be engaged in illegal activity because they consider drivers who avoid eye contact to be suspicious. People routinely use gaze avoidance to prevent unwanted social interactions. As long as we can avoid eye gaze in a seemingly natural way, it is much easier to avoid interaction.

When passing unknown others in a public place, we typically acknowledge them with a brief glance, but this initial glance is followed by the avoidance of gaze unless further contact is desired, or unless the other person signals a desire for further contact by gazing back or by smiling. A length of gaze that exceeds this acknowledgment glance is likely to signal a desire to initiate a conversation (Cary, 1978a), and violation of this "civil inattention" norm, a term coined by Goffman (1963), can produce negative feelings in the recipients (Zuckerman, Miserandino, & Bernieri, 1983). When you want to disavow social contact, your eye gaze will likely diminish. Thus we see mutual gazing in greeting sequences and greatly diminished gazing when we wish to bring an encounter to a halt.

Within a conversation, gazing at the other can command a nonverbal, as well as verbal, response. Because speakers gaze less than listeners, it is the speaker's gazing that determines moments of mutual looking. During these moments, it is highly likely that the listener will respond with a "listener response," also called a "back-channel response," that signifies attention (Bavelas, Coates, & Johnson, 2002). These responses can include smiles and other facial expressions, sounds such as "mm-hmm," and nods. Thus, the speaker's behavior is an important determinant of the timing of these responses. However, gazing is not the only determinant: listener responses also occur when people do not see each other, as when talking on the telephone.

In addition to opening and closing the channel of communication and commanding responses from the other, eye behavior also regulates the flow of communication by providing turn-taking signals. Speakers generally look less often than listeners. But speakers do seem to glance during grammatical breaks, at the end of a thought unit or idea, and at the end of the utterance. Although glances at these junctures can signal the other person to assume the speaking role, we also use these glances to obtain feedback, to see how we are being received, and to see if the other will let us continue. This feedback function is addressed in the next section. The speaker–listener pattern is often choreographed as follows: As the speaker comes to the end of an utterance or thought unit, eye gaze toward the listener will continue as the listener assumes the speaking role; the listener will maintain gaze until the speaking role is assumed, when he or she will look away.

Research on naturally emerging and appointed leaders in three-person male groups has found that the leader controls the flow of conversation using this cue pattern: The leader shows an increased tendency to engage in prolonged gaze at someone when he is done with a speaking turn, as if inviting, or possibly instructing, that person to take the floor. Thus, leaders do not only keep the floor for themselves more than others (Schmid Mast, 2002), they also orchestrate who gets the floor and when (Kalma, 1992).

A speaker's gaze at the completion of an utterance may help signal the yielding of a speaking turn, but listener-directed gazes do not always accompany the smooth exchange of speaking turns (Beattie, 1978a; Rutter, Stephenson, & White, 1978). On the other hand, sometimes the speaker glances at the listener when yielding a speaking turn, and the listener delays a response or fails to respond. Further, when a speaker begins an anticipated lengthy response, he or she is likely to delay gazing at the other beyond what would normally be expected. This pattern of adult gazing and looking away during speech seems to have its roots in early childhood development. Observations of the gazing patterns of 3- to 4-month-old infants and their parents revealed temporal similarities between their looking-at and looking-away sequence and the vocalizing and pausing sequences in adult conversations (Jaffe, Stern, & Peery, 1973).

MONITORING FEEDBACK

When people seek feedback concerning the reactions of others, they gaze at the other person. If the other person is looking back, it is usually interpreted as a sign of attention to what is being said. Listener facial expressions and gazing suggest not only attention but also whether or not the listener is interested in what is being said. Being seen is a profound form of social acknowledgment, and its lack—the experience of having others "look right through you"—undermines a person's very existence as a social being. A child on a playground who demands to be watched by his or her parent while doing feats on the jungle gym is not simply asking for added safety or security. Far more importantly, the parent's gaze *infuses meaning* into the child's actions. Without a witness, the actions feel pointless or even unreal. A chronic feeling of being invisible is sometimes reported by people with borderline personality disorder. And people in low-status service occupations, such as janitors and hotel maids, often feel that a lack of visual acknowledgment by the people they serve is dehumanizing. On the other hand, under some circumstances being seen—especially in the sense of being *watched*—can feel like a violation of privacy and can be very uncomfortable, especially when one cannot look back at the person watching.

People's need to have visual contact with others is undoubtedly central to the phenomenon known as *emotional contagion,* whereby one person's mood or emotion is influenced by another's mood or emotion via subtle and mostly unconscious processes (Hatfield, Cacioppo, & Rapson, 1994). When people must communicate without seeing one another, a number of adaptations take place to compensate for this loss of information. For example, they engage in more verbal back-channel responses, such as "uh-huh" (Boyle, Anderson, & Newlands, 1994).

Effective monitoring via gaze may have important practical consequences. In studies of physician–patient interaction, those physicians who engaged in more patient-directed gaze were more accurate at recognizing the patients' degree of psychosocial distress (Bensing, Kerssens, & van der Pasch, 1995), and a relation between engaging in more patient-directed gaze and obtaining more psychosocial information from the patient was found (van Dulmen, Verhaak, & Bilo, 1997).

Monitoring of others' reactions during group discussions is crucial to planning responsive statements and maintaining group harmony and morale. Crosby, Monin, and Richardson (2008) showed that when a white member of a group made an offensive statement about blacks, visual attention was shifted to the black member of the group, but only when listeners thought he could hear the offensive remark. Presumably, group members want to know how the affected person reacts before deciding how to respond themselves. Effective monitoring of group members via gaze has been shown to be higher in women than men: women spread their gaze more evenly around a group than men do (Koch, Baehne, Kruse, Zimmermann, & Zumbach, 2008).

REFLECTING COGNITIVE ACTIVITY

Both listeners and speakers have a tendency to avoid gazing at others when trying to process difficult or complex ideas. This averted gaze, which may include closing the eyes, reflects a shift in attention from external to internal matters, as well as an effort to exclude external stimulation. People avoid gaze more on reflective questions than factual ones and on more difficult questions—more difficult in factual content or in terms of the length of the temporal search required, as in "Name a professor you currently have" versus "Name a professor you had two semesters ago" (Glenberg, Schroeder, & Robertson, 1998). Furthermore, when participants were required to answer factual questions, either with their eyes closed or while looking directly at the experimenter, performance was better in the eyes-closed condition, thus demonstrating the functional utility of excluding external stimulation while engaging in difficult cognitive activity.

The nature of cognitive activity can also influence leftward or rightward eye movements. When a person moves his or her eyes in a particular direction, it is thought to reflect activity in the *opposite* hemisphere of the brain: Left hemisphere activity, often involving intellectual and linguistic tasks, is associated with rightward glances, whereas right hemisphere activity, often involving spatial or emotional processing, is associated with leftward glances (Ehrlichman & Weinberger, 1978; Weisz & Adam, 1993; Wilbur & Roberts-Wilbur, 1985). Studies show that electroencephalic activity increases in the hemisphere opposite the direction of the eye movement, and such activity can actually be stimulated by the movements. Individuals vary in their leftward or rightward eye-movement tendencies, with left movers being more susceptible to hypnosis, less scientifically oriented, more involved with feelings and inner experience, more creative, and more prone to psychosomatic symptoms and the psychological defenses of repression and denial.

EXPRESSING EMOTIONS

Sometimes a glance at the eye area provides us with a good deal of information about the emotion being expressed. For example, if we see tears, we certainly would conclude a person is emotionally moved, although without other cues, we may not know whether the tears reflect grief, physical pain, frustration, joy, anger, or some complex blend of emotions. And as we indicate later, downcast or averted eyes are often associated with feelings of sadness, shame, or embarrassment. The extensive studies of Paul Ekman and Wallace Friesen have given us valuable insights into facial configurations for six common, "basic" emotions, shown in the photographs here. The descriptions shown pertain to the brow and eye area, and the eye photographs are from Ekman and Friesen's collection. As the photographs suggest, it may be difficult to judge what emotion is being expressed without being able to see the brows. Similarly, some expressions may be ambiguous unless the entire face can be seen. Also, in everyday interaction we are likely to see facial blends, in which the eyes tell one story, and other parts of the face tell another.

SURPRISE Brows are raised so they are curved and high. Skin below the brow is stretched. Eyelids are opened; the upper lid is raised, and the lower lid is drawn down; and the white of the eye shows above the iris, and often below as well.

FEAR Brows are raised and drawn together. The upper eyelid is raised, exposing the white of the eye, called the *sclera*, and the lower eyelid is tensed and drawn up.

DISGUST Disgust is shown primarily in the lower face and in the lower eyelids. Lines show below the lower lid, and the lid is pushed up but not tense. The brow is lowered, lowering the upper lid.

ANGER The brows are lowered and drawn together, and vertical lines appear between them. The lower lid is tensed and may or may not be raised. The upper lid is tensed and may or may not be lowered by the action of the brow. The eyes have a hard stare and may have a bulging appearance.

HAPPINESS Happiness is shown primarily in the lower face and lower eyelids. The lower eyelid shows wrinkles below it and may be raised but is not tense. Crow's-feet wrinkles go outward from the outer corners of the eyes.

SADNESS The inner corners of the eyebrows are drawn up. The skin below the eyebrow is triangulated, with the inner corner up. The upper-eyelid inner corner is raised.

Many of these conclusions were confirmed in the experimental study of Knoll, Attkiss, and Persing (2008), who used digital imaging software to make numerous subtle changes to the brows and lids of a woman's eyes in a photograph. Observers who rated the altered photographs were very sensitive to these changes; for example, either raising the lower lid slightly or adding tiny crows' feet at the corner of the eyes produced strong impressions of happiness. In this study, in addition to studying the basic emotions, the investigators were interested in what makes eyes look tired. Raters' impressions of tiredness were independently conveyed by a more evident expanse of upper lid, more total eyebrow elevation, a hooded or droopy-looking upper lid, and upper lid depression (see Figure 10-3).

Do the eyes display emotion better or worse than other parts of the face? Ekman, Friesen, and Tomkins (1971) demonstrated that the eyes were better than the brows, forehead, or lower face for the accurate perception of fear but were less accurate for anger and disgust. Baron-Cohen, Wheelwright, and Jolliffe (1997) tested university students' accuracy at identifying 16 emotional states, posed by an actress, by evaluating each area separately: the eye area, including brows; the mouth area; and the whole face. The authors included "basic" emotions such as angry, afraid, and happy and "nonbasic" states such as admiring, flirtatious, arrogant, and

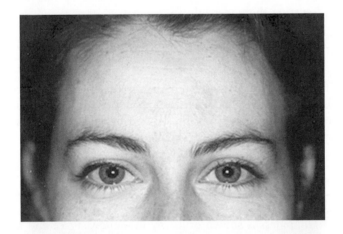

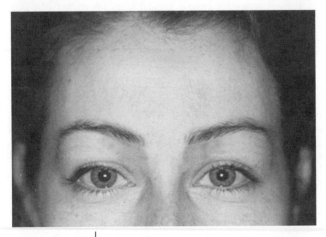

FIGURE 10-3

Neutral eyes (first photograph) compared to eyes perceived as tired (remaining photographs).

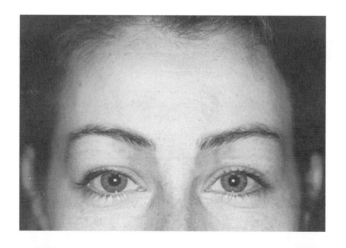

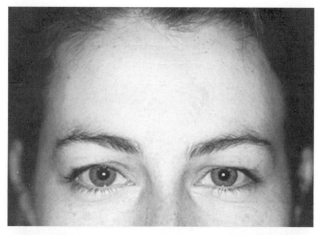

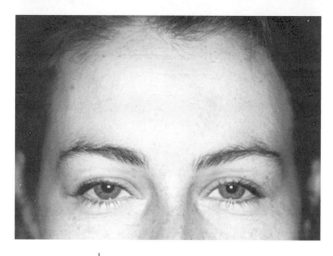

FIGURE 10-3   (continued)

thoughtful. The eye region was not quite as accurately judged as the whole face for the basic emotions but was indistinguishable for the nonbasic states (see Figure 10-4). Can you identify the emotions posed by the actress in this study? (Answers are at the end of the chapter). Both the eyes and the whole face were judged much more accurately than the mouth. Consistent with the research by Ekman and colleagues (1971), accuracy for the mouth region, although not superior to the eye region, was similar to that of the eye region for distinguishing disgust and anger and much lower than the eye region for distinguishing fear.

Most research on recognizing facial expressions of emotion presents faces with direct forward gaze. However, it has been shown that the direction in which the eyes are gazing has an influence on judgments of emotion in the face (Adams & Kleck, 2003, 2005). In one of the studies, a face shown with the eyes gazing directly forward made viewers more likely to see approach-orientation emotions, such as anger and joy, in the faces; but a face with an averted gaze made them

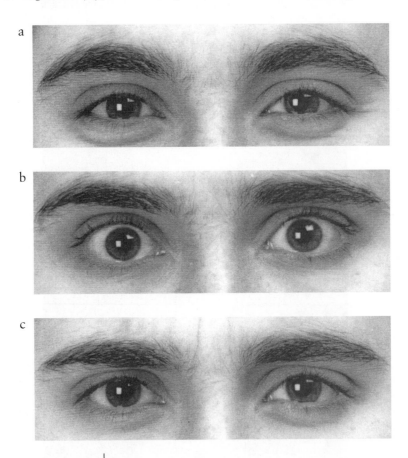

FIGURE 10-4

Can you judge the emotions in these eyes? (a) happy or surprised, (b) angry or afraid, (c) sad or disgusted, (d) distressed or sad, (e) arrogant or guilty, (f) thoughtful or arrogant, (g) flirting or happy, (h) guilty or arrogant. (See answers at end of chapter.)

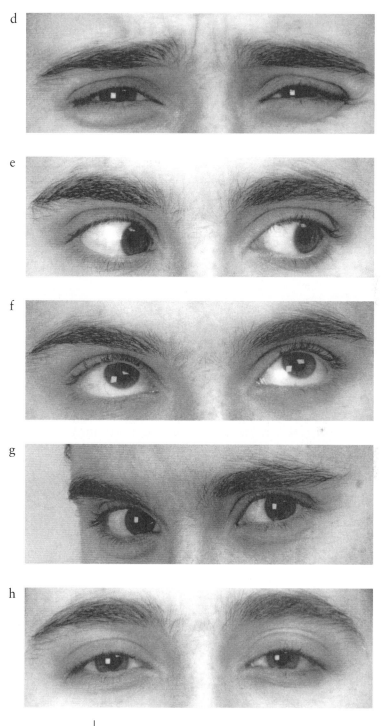

FIGURE 10-4 | *(continued)*

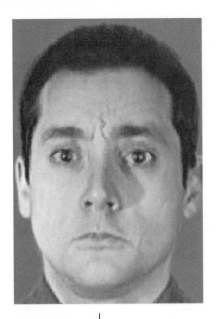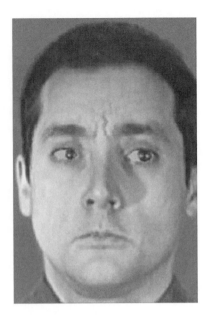

FIGURE 10-5

The ambiguous fear-anger blend is judged differently depending on the direction of gaze.

more likely to see avoidance-orientation emotions, such as fear and sadness. In another study, identical facial blends of fear and anger were presented to viewers with direct versus averted gaze; more anger was attributed to the face that had direct gaze, and more fear was attributed to the face that had averted gaze. Thus, when the expression was ambiguous, gaze direction alone influenced emotional perception (see Figure 10-5).

COMMUNICATING THE NATURE OF THE INTERPERSONAL RELATIONSHIP

Gazing and mutual gazing are often indicative of the nature of the relationship between two interactants. Relationships characterized by different status or dominance levels may be reflected in the eye patterns; one example was given earlier—the way the leader in a group seems to pick the next speaker by gazing at him or her. Another indicator of status or dominance is the *visual dominance ratio*—the ratio of the percentage of *speaking* time spent looking at the other to the percentage of *listening* time spent looking at the other. People with higher status or dominance gaze relatively more while speaking and relatively less while listening, compared to people with lower status or dominance.

Although subtle patterns such as these distinguish people with higher and lower dominance, a simple measure of overall gazing does not, according to numerous studies (as reviewed by Hall, Coats, & Smith LeBeau, 2005). On the other hand, stereotypes about gazing and dominance indicate a belief in such an association. When asked to imagine how much gazing people of high or low dominance would display, either in terms of personality or rank in a workplace, participants thought the higher dominant person would gaze more (Carney, Hall, & Smith LeBeau, 2005). And across many studies, when shown video excerpts of people gazing different amounts, viewers attributed higher dominance to those who gazed more (Hall et al., 2005).

Several studies testify that we gaze more at people and things perceived as rewarding. Efran and Broughton (1966) found that males gazed more at other males with whom they had engaged in a friendly conversation preceding an experiment and with those who nodded and smiled during the person's presentation. Exline and Eldridge (1967) found that the same verbal communication was decoded as being more favorable when associated with more gaze than when presented with less gaze. Exline and Winters (1965) reported that people avoided the eyes of an interviewer and disliked him after he had commented unfavorably on their performance. Self-relevance influences responses to gaze, too. Faces are considered more likable if the eyes are shown shifting towards the viewer than if the eyes are shown shifting away (Mason, Tatkow, & Macrae, 2005).

Mehrabian (1972) asked a group of people to imagine they liked a person and to engage this person in conversation. Even in this role-playing situation, increased gazing was associated with increased liking. Mutual liking, revealed in the form of participants' rating of rapport, was similarly related to gazing when interactants debated a controversial topic (Bernieri, Gillis, Davis, & Grahe, 1996). Interestingly, when engaging in a more cooperative discussion, eye contact was not related to rapport judgments.

Increased gazing is often considered in the context of a courtship relationship. The maintenance of mutual gaze longer than otherwise expected is a primary way of signaling desire for heightened intimacy. In movies, we can almost always predict when a first kiss is coming, because the characters share a longer than expected mutual gaze. An increased amount of gaze can both signal a wish for more involvement and be an indication that heightened involvement has occurred. Indeed, several sources confirm an increase in gazing between two people who are seeking to develop a more intimate relationship. Rubin's (1970) analysis of engaged couples indicated more mutual gaze, and Kleinke, Bustos, Meeker, and Staneski (1973) found that longer glances or reciprocated glances were perceived as an indicator of a longer relationship. It may be that the amount of gazing increases as relationships become more intimate, but it may also be true that after maintaining an intimate relationship for years, gazing returns to levels below those observed during more intense stages of the relationship's development.

Argyle and Dean (1965) proposed an intimacy equilibrium model to help explain why and how much people gaze in an interpersonal interaction. This model suggests that intimacy is a function of the amount of eye gazing, physical proximity, intimacy of topic, and amount of smiling. Thus, gaze is part of a network of other behaviors that have important relations to each other in a total system reflective of the overall psychological intimacy in a given interaction. Clearly, other variables might be inserted into the equation; for example, body orientation, the form of address used, tone of voice, other facial expressions, forward lean, and the like. The central idea behind this proposal is that as one component of the model is changed, one or more of the other components also will change in the opposite direction, as a form of compensation to keep the overall intimacy or stimulation at a constant, desired level.

For example, if one person looks too much, the other may look less, move farther away, smile less, talk less about intimate matters, and so on to reestablish the initial desired level of intimacy. Also, when one person is forced to increase the implied intimacy of a behavior—for example, by standing close to another in a crowded elevator—the other will compensate by gazing less, talking about impersonal topics, and so forth.

Cross-cultural research shows that in societies that emphasize a greater amount of physical contact between mothers and infants, mutual gaze between them is lower than in societies where the norms prescribe more physical autonomy and distance. Here again is evidence of a compensatory mechanism, whereby the crucial psychological connection between mothers and infants is maintained in different but equivalent ways. The same trade-off between physical contact and mutual gaze has also been observed in chimpanzee mother–infant interactions (Bard, Myowa-Yamakoshi, Tomonaga, Tanaka, Costall, & Matsuzawa, 2005).

Although this compensatory model has received extensive support, there are many occasions when, rather than counter or offset the other's behavior, people will *reciprocate* it; for example, gazing will elicit gazing, and smiling will elicit smiling. This can be seen in personal interactions as well as between strangers, and glancing at a passing stranger is likely to produce a glance in return (Patterson, Webb, & Schwartz, 2002; Patterson, Iizuka, Tubbs, Ansel, Tsutsumi, & Anson, 2007).

Several scholars have proposed alternatives to the intimacy equilibrium model (Cappella & Greene, 1982; Patterson, 1976) in an attempt to accommodate both compensation and reciprocation. These theories argue that our tendency to exchange the same behavior (that is, to reciprocate) or to offset the other's behavior (to compensate) is a result of the type and amount of arousal we feel and desire. A general rule suggests that we tend to reciprocate or match another's nonverbal behavior when the other's behavior is perceived by us as congruent with our expectations and preferences, or when we want to initiate an upward or downward spiral in intimacy. When our partner's behavior is not congruent with our expectations and preferences, we are more likely to enact compensatory or offsetting behavior. (See also Chapter 12.)

When the relationship between the two communicators is characterized by negative attitudes, we might see a decrease in gazing and mutual gazing, but not always. This is because gaze, like touch, can sometimes serve more to intensify or highlight whatever feeling or intention is present at the moment than to communicate a specific message. Also, gaze does not occur in isolation from other cues—a threatening stare and a long, loving look may both be long, but the rest of the face is likely to be doing quite different things!

To illustrate one of the preceding points, satisfied married couples in one study tended to look at each other *less* than couples who were dissatisfied with their relationship, with this being particularly true when negative messages were exchanged (Noller, 1980). Increased gazing served to emphasize the confrontational nature of the relationship while simultaneously providing a way to monitor the other's reactions during critical moments. This is a good example of how the immediate context can never be ignored when interpreting the meaning of nonverbal behavior.

A hostile or aggressive orientation may also trigger the use of staring to produce anxiety in others. A gaze of longer than 10 seconds is likely to induce irritation, if not outright discomfort, in many situations. In one study, drivers sped away more quickly from an intersection when stared at by a pedestrian (Ellsworth,

Carlsmith, & Henson, 1972). Several studies confirm that mutual gaze is physiologically arousing. We can express our hostility toward another by visually and verbally ignoring him or her, especially when the other person knows we are deliberately doing so. But we can insult another person by looking at that person too much, that is, by not according him or her the public anonymity that each of us requires at times. Sometimes you can elicit aggressive behavior from others just because you happen to look too long at their behavior. Sometimes threats and aggressive action can be elicited in zoo monkeys by human beings who stare at them too long.

Thus, if we are looking for a unifying thread to link gazing patterns motivated by positive and negative feelings toward the other, it would seem to be this: People tend to look at those with whom they are interpersonally involved. Gazing motivated by hostility or affection *both* suggest an interest and involvement in the interpersonal relationship. We must rely on contextual information, and other verbal and nonverbal cues, to decide whether to interpret extended gazing positively or negatively.

CONDITIONS INFLUENCING GAZING PATTERNS

DISTANCE

As suggested by intimacy equilibrium theory, gazing and mutual gazing often increase as the people interacting increase the physical distance between them. In this case, gazing psychologically reduces the distance between communicators and allows for better monitoring. Similarly, there may be less visual contact when the two parties feel too close in terms of physical distance, especially if they are not well acquainted. Reducing one's gaze in this situation, then, increases the psychological distance. Several studies by Aiello and colleagues found that extending the conversational distances to as much as 10 feet produced a steady increase in gazing for men, but for women, being more than 6 feet from their interactant brought a sharp decline in their gazing (Aiello, 1972, 1977a). It is probable that because women prefer closer interaction distances (see Chapter 5), they may find it difficult to define interactions at relatively great distances as normal and friendly, and they may react by ceasing their attempts to maintain involvement.

PHYSICAL CHARACTERISTICS

We would think that when interacting with a person who was perceived as disabled or stigmatized in some way, such as identified as an epileptic or made to look like an amputee, gaze would be less frequent. However, Kleck (1968) found that the amount of gazing between normal and disabled interactants did not differ significantly from interactions between those considered normal. Possible explanations are that in such situations, the normal person is seeking information that might suggest the proper mode of behavior, or the disabled person is a novel stimulus that arouses curiosity. These factors would counteract any tendency to avoid eye gaze. A subsequent study, however, found that when a strong possibility arose that a nondisabled person would have to engage a disabled person in conversation, gaze avoidance increased. When conversation was not expected, people without disabilities tended to stare more at people with disabilities than those without (Thompson, 1982).

PERSONAL CHARACTERISTICS AND PERSONALITY

Some patterns have emerged in the relations between gazing patterns and personality traits. In actual interaction, of course, gaze patterns reflect the message sender's mood, intent, and stable disposition as well as reflecting situational factors. There are definitely stereotypes about gaze and personality. Kleck and Nuessle (1968) showed a film of people looking at their partners either 15 or 80 percent of the time to observers, who were asked to select characteristics that typified the interactants. Those who looked at their partner only 15 percent of the time were labeled as cold, pessimistic, cautious, defensive, immature, evasive, submissive, indifferent, and sensitive; those who looked 80 percent of the time were seen as friendly, self-confident, natural, mature, and sincere. Napieralski, Brooks, and Droney (1995) presented viewers with 1-minute videotaped interactions in which the target person gazed for 5, 30, or 50 seconds at an interviewer. The less a person gazed, the more state anxiety and trait anxiety were attributed to that person by viewers.

Dependent individuals seem to use eye behavior not only to communicate more positive attitudes but also to elicit such attitudes when they are not forthcoming (Exline & Messick, 1967). Dependent males directed more gaze towards a listener who provided them with few, as opposed to many, social reinforcers, whereas dominant males decreased their eye gaze with listeners who reinforced less. Kalma (1993) distinguished between two personality styles relating to dominance: *sociable dominance* and *aggressive dominance*. The sociably dominant person agrees strongly with statements such as "I have no problem talking in front of a group" and "No doubt I'll make a good leader." The aggressively dominant person agrees strongly with statements such as "I quickly feel aggressive with people" and "I find it important to get my way." In an experimental setting, Kalma observed people who varied on these dominance styles and found that the sociably dominant person engaged in more mutual gaze, whereas the aggressively dominant person engaged in more looking around; that is, they showed lack of interest in others.

A particular kind of social dominance is sexual harassment. Male college students' proclivity to sexually harass women was measured using a questionnaire that asked how likely they would be to exploit a woman under varying hypothetical circumstances, such as rewarding her in return for sexual favors. Videotapes that were surreptitiously made of the same men interacting at a later date with a subordinate female revealed that, among other behaviors, the men more likely to harass engaged in more direct eye contact with the woman (Murphy, Driscoll, & Kelly, 1999).

Self-esteem and self-confidence are associated with gazing patterns. A study of attributions found that interviewees were rated by observers as having increasingly lower self-esteem as their gazing decreased (Droney & Brooks, 1993). Variations in gazing at another person during positive and negative feedback may indeed be related to self-esteem. When receiving favorable feedback on their performance, people with high self-esteem tended to gaze more, and negative feedback reduced their gazing behavior. But the pattern was reversed for those with low self-esteem. These people gazed more during feedback that criticized their performance than during feedback that complimented it (Greene & Frandsen, 1979).

Intelligence is also a trait people display in social interaction. Evidence shows that people who score higher on standard tests of cognitive ability, such as an IQ test, engage in more interpersonal gaze and responsiveness, and that perceivers who watch these people on videotape can use these cues to accurately judge intelligence levels (Murphy, Hall, & Colvin, 2003).

Other personality traits—as measured by self-report of the gazers, not as attributed by observers—have been associated with more gazing. Such traits include extraversion, agreeableness, and openness (Berry & Hansen, 2000; Mobbs, 1968), although some studies do not find correlations between gaze and personality. Gifford (1994), for example, failed to find associations between interpersonal gazing and trait measures of ambitiousness, gregariousness, warmth, unassumingness, laziness, aloofness, coldness, and arrogance.

Shyness is related to gazing behavior, but this correlation can depend on whether the shy person is of a sociable or unsociable type. In a laboratory experiment, Cheek and Buss (1981) classified college students on both a shyness scale and a sociability scale and observed them in a get-acquainted session. Although shy individuals engaged in less gazing overall, and in more self-touching and less talking, this effect was mainly present if the person was both shy (e.g., "I am socially somewhat awkward"; "I feel inhibited in social situations") *and* sociable (e.g., "I like to be with people"; "I prefer working with others rather than alone"). Thus the behavioral deficits associated with shyness appear mainly in shy people who crave social interaction; shy people who would just as soon be left alone behaved much like people who were not shy in terms of their gazing.

Social anxiety, another related concept, is also associated with less gazing; in one study in which socially anxious people were asked to present a viewpoint to two confederates, the socially anxious ones were especially likely to reduce gaze toward a confederate with opposing views compared to one with agreeing views (Farabee, Holcom, Ramsey, & Cole, 1993). In an experiment in which participants had choices of which face to look at on a computer screen, Mansell, Clark, Ehlers, and Chen (1999) found that socially anxious people whose anxiety was heightened by being told they would be giving a public talk avoided faces that showed emotional expressions, preferring to give their visual attention to neutral-expression faces. Under such circumstances, the socially anxious person may have an especially strong need to avoid the arousal engendered by emotional faces, which in turn may be related to a history of finding emotionally charged social interactions to be aversive. Highly anxious individuals also avert their eyes sooner from an extended facial display of anger compared to less anxious individuals (Rohner, 2002). However, when negative facial expressions are very intense, more trait-anxious individuals look at them more (Mogg, Garner, & Bradley, 2007). The term *gaze cuing* refers to the automatic tendency to look in the direction of someone else's gaze. This effect is especially pronounced when the target person's face looks fearful. When viewers saw a fearful face with eyes averted, as though the target person was looking at something frightening in the environment, their own gaze shifted in that direction more than was the case when the averted eyes were shown on a happy face (Putnam, Hermans, & van Honk, 2006). Furthermore, this effect is especially notable for viewers who are high on trait anxiety: highly anxious individuals are especially quick to use gaze direction as a cue when the gazer has a fearful facial expression, suggesting that anxiety makes a person especially visually attuned and responsive to evidence of threat in their environment (Fox, Mathews, Calder, & Yiend, 2007; Mathews, Fox, Yield, & Calder, 2003; Putnam et al., 2006).

Finally, males and females differ in the use of gaze. As shown in many studies, females look at others during interaction more than males do on almost all measures of gaze frequency, duration, and reciprocity—and such differences have been observed in infancy and early childhood as well as in adulthood (Hall, 1984; Leeb & Rejskind, 2004). In addition, women are gazed at more than men are by others in interaction. (Sex differences are discussed further in Chapter 12.)

PSYCHOPATHOLOGY

A number of research studies find special gazing patterns, usually less gaze, in some psychopathological conditions. For example, depressed patients are characterized by nonspecific gaze patterns and looking-down behaviors that revert to more normal patterns with clinical improvement (Schelde & Hertz, 1994). Mothers with depressive symptoms spend less time gazing at their infants, and their infants respond by averting gaze more than control infants (Field, 1995). Paranoid schizophrenic patients show a deficit in judging the gaze direction of others, which is consistent with everyday conceptions of paranoia: paranoid individuals are more likely than comparison subjects to perceive another as looking at them, when the person is actually looking away (Rosse, Kendrick, Wyatt, Isaac, & Deutsch, 1994).

Clinicians and researchers on autism cite gaze aversion, among other social interaction deficits, as a characteristic of their autistic patients (Adrien et al., 1993; Hutt & Ounsted, 1966; Walters, Barrett, & Feinstein, 1990). Autistic individuals also suffer deficits in the ability to detect the direction of another's gaze (Senju, Yaguchi, Tojo, & Hasegawa, 2003), to monitor a speaker's gaze direction, and to direct someone else's gaze via the pointing gesture (Baron-Cohen et al., 1997). Baron-Cohen, Wheelwright, Hill, Raste, and Plumb (2001) reported that individuals with autism or Asperger syndrome, a condition related to autism, were less accurate overall than normally functioning participants in judging emotions from the eye region of the face. And Baron-Cohen and colleagues (1997) also found that the patients were especially impaired for nonbasic—that is, more complex—expressions, and when the eye region alone was being judged as opposed to the full face. (See Figure 10-4 for the eye expressions used in this study.) Gaze measurement confirmed that individuals with autism fail to use information from the eye region when making emotion judgments (Spezio, Adolphs, Hurley, & Piven, 2007), a deficit that directly impacts their ability to distinguish genuine from posed smiles, for which attention to the eye region is necessary (Boraston, Corden, Miles, Skuse, & Blakemore, 2008).

One theory to account for these deficits holds that individuals with autism find direct gaze to be overwhelmingly arousing, and they avoid it for that reason. Using an experimental method that varied the direction of a poser's gaze (looking at or away from the camera), while zooming the image in larger to suggest an approaching person, Kylliäinen and Hietanen (2006) found that autistic children's skin conductance (a measure of physiological arousal) was greater in the direct gaze compared to averted gaze condition; but for control children, there was no difference. Thus, the hypothesis that gaze is aversively arousing for autistic children was supported.

Another promising, and likely related, new avenue of insight involves the role of the neuropeptide oxytocin in the ability of humans, both those with and without psychopathology, to develop social attachments and to be sensitive and responsive socially. Especially relevant to the present chapter is the study of Guastella, Mitchell, and Dadds (2007), who found that experimental administration of oxytocin to male college students via nasal inhalation caused them to give added attention to the eye region of faces shown to them in photographs. The authors suggested that oxytocin administration might have therapeutic benefits for groups such as those with schizophrenia and autism, who have chronic difficulties in social communication (see Chapter 3).

TOPICS AND TASKS

Common sense suggests that the topic being discussed and the task at hand affect the amount of gazing. We would expect, for instance, more gazing when the topic is happy rather than sad. And we would expect interactants who have not developed an intimate relationship to gaze less when discussing intimate topics, assuming other factors, such as the need for affiliation or inclusion, are controlled. People also may gaze differently during competitive tasks and cooperative tasks. In one study, cooperators used longer gazes and mutual gazes to signal trust, liking, and honesty. Gazes also were used to aid coordination. Competitors, however, seemed to use frequent, short gazes to assess their partner's intentions while not giving away their own (Foddy, 1978).

Discussing topics that cause embarrassment, humiliation, shame, or guilt might be expected to engender less gazing at the other person. Looking away during such situations may be an effort to insulate oneself against threats, arguments, information, or even affection from the other party. When subjects were caused to fail at an anagram task and were publicly criticized for their work, they not only reported feeling embarrassed, but the amount of gaze slipped from 30 percent to 18 percent (Modigliani, 1971). When people want to hide some aspect of their inner feelings, they may try to avoid visual contact—for example, in situations where they are trying to deceive a partner. Exline, Thibaut, Hickey, and Gumpert (1970) designed a fascinating, although possibly ethically unsound, experiment. A paid confederate induced research participants to cheat on an experimental task. Later, the experimenter interviewed the participants with the supposed purpose of understanding and evaluating their problem-solving methods. With some participants, the experimenter grew increasingly suspicious during the interview and finally accused the participant of cheating and demanded an explanation. Participants included both those who scored high and low on tests of Machiavellianism, a characteristic of a person who uses cunning and shrewdness to achieve a goal without much regard for how unscrupulous the means might be. Figure 10-6 shows that high Machiavellian participants used gazing to present the appearance of innocence after being accused of cheating; low Machiavellian participants, in contrast, continued to look away.

In the study by Bensing and colleagues mentioned earlier, physicians' average levels of gaze at patients were much greater when the patients were talking about social and emotional topics than when talking about more physiological problems, and levels were also high when the physicians were verbally conveying empathy or psychosocial interest. Patients were also more satisfied with their visits when the physicians gazed more.

Persuasion is another communicative task we often undertake. We know that gazing can add emphasis to a particular point, but Mehrabian and Williams (1969)

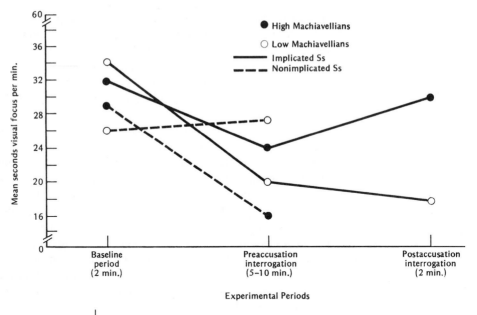

FIGURE 10-6

Gazing, Machiavellianism, and deception.

found that a person trying to be persuasive gazes more overall. And research shows that listeners judge speakers who gaze more as more persuasive, informed, truthful, sincere, and credible. Also, compliance with a request can be enhanced if the requester engages in more gazing within an appropriate range (Guéguen & Jacob, 2002).

The application of such findings in a simulated courtroom situation found that witnesses who testified while looking slightly downward, rather than directly at their questioner, were judged less credible—and the defendant for whom they were testifying was more likely to be judged guilty (Hemsley & Doob, 1978). In another important study, actors reenacted the actual verbal performances of surgery students during medical school oral examinations, using a nonverbal style marked either by direct gaze and a moderate speech rate or by indirect gaze and a slower speech rate. Surgery faculty from 46 medical institutions who judged the competency of these reenacted oral examinations gave significantly higher scores to the actor who used direct gaze and a moderate rate of speech, even though the answers were the same as in the other condition (Rowland-Morin, Burchard, Garb, & Coe, 1991). It is clear from these studies that in real-life situations, the presence or absence of gaze can have a profound impact, yet the impact can be highly unfair or damaging. We would not want to be the honest witness, the sincere speaker, or the competent medical student who had the misfortune to gaze less than expected.

CULTURAL BACKGROUND AND RACIAL ATTITUDES

Eye behavior also varies according to the environment in which we learn social norms. Sometimes gazing patterns show differences between "contact" cultures, such as Arab cultures, and "noncontact" cultures, such as northern European cultures (see Chapters 5, 8, and 13). Sometimes *where* we observe gaze behavior reveals differences among cultures, that is, looking more in public places. Sometimes cultural rules dictate whom you should or should not look at. One report says that in Kenya, conversations between some men and their mothers-in-law are conducted by each party turning his or her back to the other. We may find different patterns within our own culture. Whites are found to gaze significantly more at their partners than blacks do, and this difference may be especially pronounced with authority figures—a tendency that could create cross-racial misunderstanding. Some research shows blacks' and whites' changing gazing patterns in cross-racial encounters, but the research is not consistent (Fehr & Exline, 1987; Halberstadt, 1985). Such findings underscore the variety of factors that may influence gaze in each encounter, and our cultural inclinations may be suppressed, neutralized, or emphasized by other forces attendant to the situation. Although cultural experiences may alter gazing patterns and the total amount of gaze, we may also find that perceived extremes in gaze elicit similar meanings in different cultures. For instance, too much gazing may signal anger, threat, or disrespect; too little may signal dishonesty, inattention, or shyness.

Because people often enact nonverbal behavior without conscious awareness, psychologists have suggested that nonverbal cues may sometimes be subtle indicators of social attitudes, especially those that may be denied or not consciously acknowledged, such as negative feelings toward minority groups (Crosby, Bromley, & Saxe, 1980; Word, Zanna, & Cooper, 1974). Dovidio, Kawakami, Johnson, Johnson, and Howard (1997) predicted that the amount of gaze directed by interviewees toward black versus white interviewers would be related to the interviewees' racial prejudice, as measured by an implicit attitudes task, based on reaction time when associating negative words to different racial groups. As predicted, interviewees who had displayed more racial bias on the implicit task gazed less at the black than the white interviewer and also blinked more, as predicted—blinking being associated with negative arousal and tension. The nonverbal cues were not related to explicit, and more reactive, paper-and-pencil reports of prejudice.

PUPIL DILATION AND CONSTRICTION

Most of us are aware that the pupils of the eyes constrict in the presence of bright light and dilate in the absence of light. In the early 1960s, however, Eckhard Hess and colleagues stimulated the interest of the scientific community in pupil dilation and constriction as a possible indicator of mental and emotional states. At one point, dozens of universities were conducting pupil-dilation research, and advertising agencies were testing magazine ads, package designs, television pilot films, and television commercials using the results of Hess's pupil dilation measures.

In an early experiment, Hess and Polt (1960) presented five pictures to male and female subjects. Males' pupils dilated more than females' pupils in response to pictures of female nudes; females' pupils dilated more than males' to pictures of a partially clothed "muscle man," a woman with a baby, and a baby alone. Thus it seemed pupil dilation and interest in the stimulus were related. Hess, Seltzer, and Shlien (1965) found that pupils of male homosexuals dilated more when viewing pictures of males than the pupils of heterosexual males, whose pupils dilated in response to female pictures. Studies since then have had similar results. Barlow (1969) preselected subjects who actively supported either liberal or conservative candidates. He photographed the pupil of the right eye while they watched slides of political figures and found what seemed to be a perfect correlation between pupillary response and political attitudes, with dilation occurring for photographs of liked candidates and constriction occurring for disliked candidates.

Several of Hess's studies suggested that pupil response might be a bidirectional index of attitudes: pupils dilate for positive attitudes and constrict for negative ones. His oft-cited finding in support of this theory was the constriction of the pupils of subjects who viewed pictures of concentration camp victims, dead soldiers, and a murdered gangster. In Hess's (1975a) words, "The changes in emotions and mental activity revealed by changes in pupil size are clearly associated with changes in attitude." Hess (Hess, 1975b; Hess & Petrovich, 1987) continued to advocate this position, although he acknowledged the need for more research on the pupil's reaction to negative stimuli.

Hensley (1990) attempted to replicate Hess's work and obtained the responses of over 500 students to the photographs of models with constricted and dilated pupils used by Hess. The students evaluated the photos on 22 characteristics, including attractiveness, social skills, persuasiveness, friendliness, and outgoingness. No statistically significant differences were found between responses to photos of models with constricted pupils and those with dilated pupils on any of the 22 characteristics, raising doubts about the strength of Hess's claim.

Woodmansee (1970) tried to improve on Hess's methodology and measuring instruments and found no support for pupil dilation and constriction as an index of attitudes toward African Americans. Hays and Plax (1971) found that their subjects' pupils dilated when they received supportive statements, such as "I am very much interested in your speech," but constriction did not follow nonsupportive statements such as "I disagree completely with the development of your speech." Some research has found pupil dilation in response to both positive *and* negative feedback (Janisse & Peavler, 1974; Partala & Surakka, 2003). Other research has found dilation of the pupil to be associated with arousal, attentiveness, interest, and perceptual orientation but not to be an attitudinal index. Thus the intriguing hypothesis that pupils can be used as bidirectional indicators of attitudes appears not to be viable.

Pupil-size research is difficult to do, in part because many stimuli can cause variations in pupil size. Tightening muscles anywhere on the body, anticipation of a loud noise, drugs, eyelid closure, and mental effort all alter pupil size. People also have varying absolute pupil sizes. Children, for instance, have larger absolute pupil sizes than adults. With so many sources of variation, it is difficult to state positively that the dilation is exclusively due to an attitudinal orientation.

Another approach to studying pupil size is to investigate its impact on a viewer. Hess cited a study that showed photographs, like those in Figure 10-7, where a woman's pupils were retouched to appear large in one photo and smaller in the other. Although male subjects did not tend to pick either picture as consistently more friendly or attractive, they tended to associate positive attributes with the woman who had larger pupils and negative attributes with the one with smaller pupils. Recently, several studies have shown that observers are sensitive to pupils of different sizes, and the impact is especially pronounced in the context of a sad

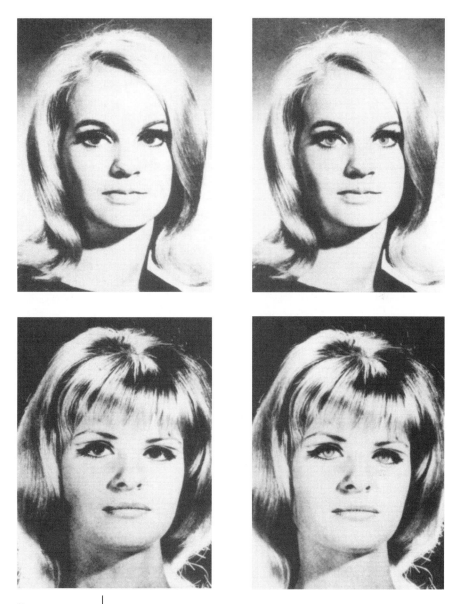

FIGURE 10-7
Some of Hess's stimulus photos with pupil dilation varied.

facial expression. In a study that varied three levels of pupil size, observers "saw" more intensity and more negativity when a sad face had smaller pupils (Harrison, Wilson, & Critchley, 2007).

One study suggested that pupil dilation may be influential in selecting interaction partners or even dates. Stass and Willis (1967) dealt with live subjects rather than pictures. Subjects were told they would be in an experiment and that they had to choose a partner who was trustworthy, pleasant, and easy to talk to on an intimate basis. They were taken to a room where two other individuals waited. The two waiting had previously been independently rated as about the same in general attractiveness. Eye gazing and pupil dilation, through use of a drug, were varied. Once the naive subject left the waiting room, the experimenter asked him or her to choose one of the two people and to give reasons for the choice. Gazing was an overwhelming factor in choice making, but pupil dilation also was a factor. A few people mentioned visual contact as a reason for their choice, but none mentioned pupil dilation. Thus, for both women and men, pupil dilation seemed to be an influential attraction device for interaction. Perhaps this would be no revelation to those women who, in the Middle Ages, put drops of belladonna into their eyes to enlarge their pupils, and thus to increase attractiveness, or to those expert romancers who suggest a dimly lighted meeting place.

SUMMARY

Although researchers have examined the size, color, and position of the eyes, eye rings, eyebrows, and eyespots in humans and other animals, our major concern in this chapter was with people's gaze and mutual gaze. We said that gazing serves many interpersonal functions:

1. Regulating the flow of communication, both to open the channels of communication and to assist in the turn-taking process.
2. Monitoring feedback.
3. Expressing emotion.
4. Communicating the nature of the interpersonal relationship, for example, to show variations due to status, liking, and disliking.

We also outlined a number of factors that influence the amount and duration of gaze in human relationships; for example, distance, physical characteristics, personal and personality characteristics, topics and tasks, and cultural background. From this review, we would predict *more* gazing in the following situations:

- You are discussing easy, impersonal topics.
- You are interested in your partner's reactions and are interpersonally involved.
- You like or love your partner.

- You are from a culture that emphasizes visual contact in interaction.
- You are an extravert and not shy.
- You have high affiliative or inclusion needs.
- You are dependent on your partner, and the partner has been unresponsive.
- You are listening rather than talking.
- You are female.
- You do not have a mental disorder such as depression, autism, or schizophrenia.
- You are not embarrassed, ashamed, sorrowful, sad, or trying to hide something.

The preceding list is not exhaustive. Indeed, some of the findings depend on certain important qualifications. For example, you may have less gaze and less mutual gaze when you are physically close—unless you happen to love your partner and want to get as close physically and psychologically as you can. This list is not intended to replace the qualified principles that appear in the chapter.

The last part of this chapter dealt with pupil dilation and constriction. We reviewed the findings of Eckhard Hess and others who have pursued his ideas. At this time, pupil dilation has been associated with arousal, attentiveness, mental effort, interest, and perceptual orientation. Aside from

Hess's own work, however, mixed support has been found for the idea that pupils reflect attitudinal states. Dilation occurs under conditions that seem to represent positive attitudes, but less or no support exists for the belief that constriction of pupils is associated with negative attitudes toward objects and people. Finally, we examined one study that suggests that pupil dilation may be a factor in our desire to interact with another person.

Answers to Figure 10-4: (a) happy, (b) afraid, (c) disgusted, (d) distressed, (e) guilty, (f) thoughtful, (g) flirting, (h) arrogant.

QUESTIONS FOR DISCUSSION

1. How do you use gaze in your everyday life? When are you more likely to gaze at someone for a long period of time? When are you more likely to gaze for a very short period of time?

2. Watch yourself in a mirror, and try to convey the following emotions using only your eyes and eyebrows: fear, anger, disgust, surprise, happiness, and sadness. How do your eye positions and movements change? How similar are your expressions to those you see on other people's faces every day?

3. Try to recall a time when you had a conversation with someone with a physical disability, someone on crutches or in a wheelchair, for example. Did your gazing patterns change when interacting with this person as opposed to interacting with an able-bodied person? How did your gazing patterns change?

4. As an experiment, try looking continuously at the eye region of a person you are conversing with. Is this difficult? Did the person react to this in any way—for example, by reducing gaze, moving back, or commenting?

5. People of higher status are sometimes said to gaze more and for longer periods than people of lower status. What do you think of this? Think of examples that would and would not be supportive of this theory.

6. Go to a bus or elevator that is crowded and observe how you, as well as the other people, use gaze in such a circumstance. How much, when, where, and at whom do people gaze?

BIBLIOGRAPHY

Adams, R. B., Jr., Gordon, H. L., Baird, A. A., Ambady, N., & Kleck, R. E. (2003). Effects of gaze on amygdala sensitivity to anger and fear faces. *Science, 300,* 1536.

Adams, R. B., Jr., & Kleck, R. E. (2003). Perceived gaze direction and the processing of facial displays of emotion. *Psychological Science, 14,* 644–647.

Adams, R. B., Jr., & Kleck, R. E. (2005). Effects of direct and averted gaze on the perception of facially communicated emotion. *Emotion, 5,* 3–11.

Adrien, J. L., Lenoir, P., Martineau, J., Perrot, A., Hameury, L., Larmande, C., & Sauvage, D. (1993). Blind ratings of early symptoms of autism based upon family home movies. *Journal of the American Academy of Child and Adolescent Psychiatry, 32,* 617–626.

Aiello, J. R. (1972). A test of equilibrium theory: Visual interaction in relation to orientation, distance and sex of interaction. *Psychonomic Science, 27,* 335–336.

Aiello, J. R. (1977a). Visual interaction at extended distances. *Personality and Social Psychology Bulletin, 3,* 83–86.

Aiello, J. R. (1977b). A further look at equilibrium theory: Visual interaction as a function of interpersonal distance. *Environmental Psychology and Nonverbal Behavior, 1,* 122–140.

Argyle, M., & Cook, M. (1976). *Gaze and mutual gaze.* Cambridge, UK: Cambridge University Press.

Argyle, M., & Dean, J. (1965). Eye contact, distance and affiliation. *Sociometry, 28,* 289–304.

Argyle, M., & Ingham, R. (1972). Gaze, mutual gaze and proximity. *Semiotica, 6,* 32–49.

Argyle, M., Ingham, R., Alkema, F., & McCallin, M. (1973). The different functions of gaze. *Semiotica, 7*, 19–32.

Argyle, M., Lalljee, M., & Cook, M. (1968). The effects of visibility on interaction in a dyad. *Human Relations, 21*, 3–17.

Argyle, M., Lefebvre, L., & Cook, M. (1974). The meaning of five patterns of gaze. *European Journal of Social Psychology, 4*, 125–136.

Ashear, V., & Snortum, J. R. (1971). Eye contact in children as a function of age, sex, social and intellective variables. *Developmental Psychology, 4*, 479.

Bard, K. A., Myowa-Yamakoshi, M., Tomonaga, M., Tanaka, M., Costall, A., & Matsuzawa, T. (2005). Group differences in the mutual gaze of chimpanzees *(Pan Troglodytes). Developmental Psychology, 41*, 616–624.

Barlow, J. D. (1969). Pupillary size as an index of preference in political candidates. *Perceptual and Motor Skills, 28*, 587–590.

Baron-Cohen, S., Wheelwright, S., Hill, J., Raste, Y., & Plumb, I. (2001). The "Reading the Mind in the Eyes" test revised version: A study with normal adults, and adults with Asperger syndrome or high-functioning autism. *Journal of Child Psychology & Psychiatry & Allied Disciplines, 42*, 241–251.

Baron-Cohen, S., Wheelwright, S., & Jolliffe, T. (1997). Is there a "language of the eyes"? Evidence from normal adults and adults with autism or Asperger syndrome. *Visual Cognition, 4*, 311–331.

Bavelas, J. B., Coates, L., & Johnson, T. (2002). Listener responses as a collaborative process: The role of gaze. *Journal of Communication, 52*, 566–580.

Beattie, G. W. (1978a). Sequential temporal patterns of speech and gaze in dialogue. *Semiotica, 23*, 27–52.

Beattie, G. W. (1978b). Floor apportionment and gaze in conversational dyads. *British Journal of Social and Clinical Psychology, 17*, 7–15.

Bensing, J. M., Kerssens, J. J., & van der Pasch, M. (1995). Patient-directed gaze as a tool for discovering and handling psychosocial problems in general practice. *Journal of Nonverbal Behavior, 19*, 223–242.

Bernieri, F. J., Gillis, J. S., Davis, J. M., & Grahe, J. E. (1996). Dyad rapport and the accuracy of its judgment across situations: A lens model analysis.

Journal of Personality and Social Psychology, 71, 110–129.

Berry, D. S., & Hansen, J. S. (2000). Personality, nonverbal behavior, and interaction quality in female dyads. *Personality and Social Psychology Bulletin, 26*, 278–292.

Boraston, Z. L., Corden, B., Miles, L. K., Skuse, D. H., & Blakemore, S. (2008). Perception of genuine and posed smiles by individuals with autism. *Journal of Autism and Developmental Disorders, 38*, 574–580.

Boyle, E. A., Anderson, A. H., & Newlands, A. (1994). The effects of visibility on dialogue and performance in a cooperative problem-solving task. *Language and Speech, 37*, 1–20.

Burgoon, J. K., Coker, D. A., & Coker, R. A. (1986). Communicative effects of gaze behavior: A test of two contrasting explanations. *Human Communication Research, 12*, 495–524.

Burgoon, J. K., Manusov, V., Mineo, P., & Hale, J. L. (1985). Effects of gaze on hiring, credibility, attraction and relational message interpretation. *Journal of Nonverbal Behavior, 9*, 133–146.

Burkhardt, J. C., Weider-Hatfield, D., & Hocking, J. E. (1985). Eye contact contrast effects in the employment interview. *Communication Research Reports, 2*, 5–10.

Cappella, J. N., & Greene, J. O. (1982). A discrepancy-arousal explanation of mutual influence in expressive behavior of adult–adult and infant–adult interaction. *Communication Monographs, 49*, 89–114.

Carney, D. R., Hall, J. A., & Smith LeBeau, L. (2005). Beliefs about the nonverbal expression of social power. *Journal of Nonverbal Behavior, 29*, 105–123.

Cary, M. S. (1978a). The role of gaze in the initiation of conversation. *Social Psychology, 41*, 269–271.

Cary, M. S. (1978b). Does civil inattention exist in pedestrian passing? *Journal of Personality and Social Psychology, 36*, 1185–1193.

Cheek, J. M., & Buss, A. H. (1981). Shyness and sociability. *Journal of Personality and Social Psychology, 41*, 330–339.

Cook, M., & Lalljee, M. G. (1973). Verbal substitutes for visual signals in interaction. *Semiotica, 6*, 212–221.

Cook, M., & Smith, J. M. C. (1975). The role of gaze in impression formation. *British Journal of Social and Clinical Psychology, 14,* 19–25.

Coss, R. G. (1974). Reflections on the evil eye. *Human Behavior, 3,* 16–22.

Crosby, F., Bromley, S., & Saxe, L. (1980). Recent unobtrusive studies of black and white discrimination and prejudice: A literature review. *Psychological Bulletin, 87,* 546–563.

Crosby, J. R., Monin, B., & Richardson, D. (2008). Where do we look during potentially offensive behavior? *Psychological Science, 19,* 226–228.

Dovidio, J. F., Ellyson, S. L., Keating, C. F., Heitman, K., & Brown, C. E. (1988). The relationship of social power to visual displays of dominance between men and women. *Journal of Personality and Social Psychology, 54,* 233–242.

Dovidio, J. F., Kawakami, K., Johnson, C., Johnson, B., & Howard, A. (1997). On the nature of prejudice: Automatic and controlled processes. *Journal of Experimental Social Psychology, 33,* 510–540.

Droney, J. M., & Brooks, C. I. (1993). Attributions of self-esteem as a function of duration of eye contact. *Journal of Social Psychology, 133,* 715–722.

Efran, J. S. (1968). Looking for approval: Effects on visual behavior of approbation from persons differing in importance. *Journal of Personality and Social Psychology, 10,* 21–25.

Efran, J. S., & Broughton, A. (1966). Effect of expectancies for social approval on visual behavior. *Journal of Personality and Social Psychology, 4,* 103–107.

Ehrlichman, H., & Weinberger, A. (1978). Lateral eye movements and hemispheric asymmetry: A critical review. *Psychological Bulletin, 85,* 1080–1101.

Ekman, P., & Friesen, W. V. (1975). *Unmasking the face.* Eaglewood Cliffs, NJ: Prentice-Hall.

Ekman, P., Friesen, W. V., & Tomkins, S. S. (1971). Facial Affect Scoring Technique: A first validity study. *Semiotica, 3,* 37–58.

Ellsworth, P. C., & Carlsmith, J. M. (1968). Effects of eye contact and verbal content on affective response to a dyadic interaction. *Journal of Personality and Social Psychology, 10,* 15–20.

Ellsworth, P. C., & Carlsmith, J. M. (1973). Eye contact and gaze aversion in an aggressive encounter. *Journal of Personality and Social Psychology, 28,* 280–292.

Ellsworth, P. C., Carlsmith, J. M., & Henson, A. (1972). The stare as a stimulus to flight in human subjects: A series of field experiments. *Journal of Personality and Social Psychology, 21,* 302–311.

Ellsworth, P. C., & Langer, E. J. (1976). Staring and approach: An interpretation of the stare as a non-specific activator. *Journal of Personality and Social Psychology, 33,* 117–122.

Ellsworth, P. C., & Ludwig, L. M. (1972). Visual behavior in social interaction. *Journal of Communication, 22,* 375–403.

Ellyson, S. L., Dovidio, J. F., & Fehr, B. J. (1981). Visual behavior and dominance in women and men. In C. Mayo & N. M. Henley (Eds.), *Gender and nonverbal behavior.* New York: Springer-Verlag.

Exline, R. V. (1963). Explorations in the process of person perception: Visual interaction in relation to competition, sex and need for affiliation. *Journal of Personality, 31,* 1–20.

Exline, R. V., & Eldridge, C. (1967). Effects of two patterns of a speaker's visual behavior upon the perception of the authencity of his verbal message. Paper presented at a meeting of the Eastern Psychological Association, Boston.

Exline, R. V., Ellyson, S. L., & Long, B. (1975). Visual behavior as an aspect of power role relationships. In P. Pliner, L. Krames, & T. Alloway (Eds.), *Advances in the study of communication and affect* (*Vol. 2.*) New York: Plenum.

Exline, R. V., & Fehr, B. J. (1978). Applications of semiosis to the study of visual interaction. In A. W. Siegman & S. Feldstein (Eds.), *Nonverbal behavior and communication.* Hillsdale, NJ: Erlbaum.

Exline, R. V., & Fehr, B. J. (1982). The assessment of gaze and mutual gaze. In K. R. Scherer & P. Ekman (Eds.), *Handbook of methods in nonverbal behavior research.* New York: Cambridge University Press.

Exline, R. V., Gray, D., & Schuette, D. (1965). Visual behavior in a dyad as affected by interview content and sex of respondent. *Journal of Personality and Social Psychology, 1,* 201–209.

Exline, R. V., & Messick, D. (1967). The effects of dependency and social reinforcement upon visual behavior during an interview. *British Journal of Social and Clinical Psychology, 6,* 256–266.

Exline, R. V., Thibaut, J., Hickey, C. B., & Gumpert, P. (1970). Visual interaction in relation to Machiavellianism and an unethical act. In P. Christie & F. Geis (Eds.), *Studies in Machiavellianism.* New York: Academic Press.

Exline, R. V., & Winters, L. (1965). Affective relations and mutual glances in dyads. In S. S. Tomkins & C. E. Izard (Eds.), *Affect, cognition, and personality: Empirical studies.* Oxford, UK: Springer.

Farabee, D. J., Holcom, M. L, Ramsey, S. L., & Cole, S. G. (1993). Social anxiety and speaker gaze in a persuasive atmosphere. *Journal of Research in Personality, 27,* 365–376.

Fehr, B. J., & Exline, R. V. (1987). Social visual interaction: A conceptual and literature review. In A. W. Siegman & S. Feldstein (Eds.), *Nonverbal behavior and communication* (2nd ed.). Hillsdale, NJ: Erlbaum.

Field, T. (1995). Infants of depressed mothers. *Infant Behavior and Development, 18,* 1–13.

Foddy, M. (1978). Patterns of gaze in cooperative and competitive negotiation. *Human Relations, 31,* 925–938.

Fox, E., Mathews, A., Calder, A. J., & Yiend, J. (2007). Anxiety and sensitivity to gaze direction in emotionally expressive faces. *Emotion, 7,* 478–486.

Fugita, S. S. (1974). Effects of anxiety and approval on visual interaction. *Journal of Personality and Social Psychology, 29,* 586–592.

Galin, D., & Ornstein, R. (1974). Individual differences in cognitive style: I. Reflective eye movements. *Neuropsychologia, 12,* 367–376.

Gibson, J. J., & Pick, A. D. (1963). Perception of another person's looking behavior. *American Journal of Psychology, 76,* 386–394.

Gifford, R. (1994). A lens-mapping framework for understanding the encoding and decoding of interpersonal dispositions in nonverbal behavior. *Journal of Personality and Social Psychology, 66,* 398–412.

Glenberg, A. M., Schroeder, J. L., & Robertson, D. A. (1998). Averting the gaze disengages the environment and facilitates remembering. *Memory & Cognition, 26,* 651–658.

Goffman, E. (1963). *Behavior in public places* . New York: Free Press.

Goldberg, G. N., Kiesler, C. A., & Collins, B. E. (1969). Visual behavior and face-to-face distance during interaction. *Sociometry, 32,* 43–53.

Goldwater, B. C. (1972). Psychological significance of pupillary movements. *Psychological Bulletin, 77,* 340–355.

Greene, J. O., & Frandsen, K. D. (1979). Need-fulfillment and consistency theory: Relationships between self-esteem and eye contact. *Western Journal of Speech Communication, 43,* 123–133.

Guastella, A. J., Mitchell, P. B., & Dadds, M. R. (2007). Oxytocin increases gaze to the eye region of human faces. *Biological Psychiatry, 63,* 3–5.

Guéguen, N., & Jacob, C. (2002). Direct look versus evasive glance and compliance with a request. *Journal of Social Psychology, 142,* 393–396.

Halberstadt, A. G. (1985). Race, socioeconomic status, and nonverbal behavior. In A. W. Siegman & S. Feldstein (Eds.), *Multichannel integrations of nonverbal behavior.* Hillsdale, NJ: Erlbaum.

Hall, J. A. (1984). *Nonverbal sex differences: Communication accuracy and expressive style.* Baltimore: Johns Hopkins University Press.

Hall, J. A., Coats, E. J., & Smith LeBeau, L. (2005). Nonverbal behavior and the vertical dimension of social relations: A meta-analysis. *Psychological Bulletin, 131,* 898–924.

Hall, J. A., Murphy, N. A., & Schmid Mast, M. (2007). Nonverbal self-accuracy in interpersonal interaction. *Personality and Social Psychology Bulletin, 33,* 1675–1685.

Harper, R. G., Wiens, A. N., & Matarazzo, J. D. (1978). The eye and visual behavior. In R. G. Harper, A. N. Wiens, & J. N. Matarazzo (Eds.), *Nonverbal communication: The state of the art.* New York: Wiley.

Harrison, N. A., Wilson, C. E., & Critchley, H. D. (2007). Processing of observed pupil size modulates perception of sadness and predicts empathy. *Emotion, 7,* 724–729.

Hart, H. H. (1949). The eye in symbol and symptom. *Psychoanalytic Review, 36,* 1–21.

Hatfield, E., Cacioppo, J. T., & Rapson, R. L. (1994). *Emotional contagion.* New York: Cambridge University Press.

Hays, E. R., & Plax, T. G. (1971). Pupillary response to supportive and aversive verbal messages. *Speech Monographs, 38,* 316–320.

Hearn, G. (1957). Leadership and the spatial factor in small groups. *Journal of Abnormal and Social Psychology, 54,* 269–272.

Hemsley, G. D., & Doob, A. N. (1978). The effect of looking behavior on perceptions of a communicator's credibility. *Journal of Applied Psychology, 8,* 136–144.

Henley, N. M. (1977). *Body politics: Power, sex, and nonverbal communication.* Englewood Cliffs, NJ: Prentice-Hall.

Hensley, W. E. (1990). Pupillary dilation revisited: The constriction of a nonverbal cue. *Journal of Social Behavior and Personality, 5,* 97–104.

Hess, E. H. (1975a). The role of pupil size in communication. *Scientific American, 233,* 110–112, 116–119.

Hess, E. H. (1975b). *The tell-tale eye.* New York: Van Nostrand Reinhold.

Hess, E. H., & Petrovich, S. B. (1987). Pupillary behavior in communication. In A. W. Siegman & S. Feldstein (Eds.), *Nonverbal behavior and communication* (2nd ed.). Hillsdale, NJ: Erlbaum.

Hess, E. H., & Polt, J. M. (1960). Pupil size as related to interest value of visual stimuli. *Science, 132,* 349–350.

Hess, E. H., & Polt, J. M. (1964). Pupil size in relation to mental activity during simple problem solving. *Science, 143,* 1190–1192.

Hess, E. H., Seltzer, A. L., & Shlien, J. M. (1965). Pupil response of hetero- and homosexual males to pictures of men and women: A pilot study. *Journal of Abnormal Psychology, 70,* 165–168.

Hewig, J., Trippe, R. H., Hecht, H., Straube, T., & Miltner, W. H. R. (2008). Gender differences for specific body regions when looking at men and women. *Journal of Nonverbal Behavior, 32,* 67–78.

Hindmarch, I. (1973). Eyespots and pupil dilation in nonverbal communication. In M. von Cranach & I. Vine (Eds.), *Social communication and movement.* New York: Academic Press.

Hobson, G. N., Strongman, K. T., Bull, D., & Craig, G. (1973). Anxiety and gaze aversion in dyadic encounters. *British Journal of Social and Clinical Psychology, 12,* 122–129.

Hutt, C., & Ounsted, C. (1966). The biological significance of gaze aversion with particular reference to the syndrome of infantile autism. *Behavioral Science, 11,* 346–356.

Jaffe, J., Stern, D. N., & Peery, C. (1973). "Conversational" coupling of gaze behavior in prelinguistic human development. *Journal of Psycholinguistic Research, 2,* 321–329.

Janisse, M. P. (1973). Pupil size and affect: A critical review of the literature since 1960. *Canadian Psychologist, 14,* 311–329.

Janisse, M. P., & Peavler, W. S. (1974). Pupillary research today: Emotion in the eye. *Psychology Today, 7,* 60–63.

Jellison, J. M., & Ickes, W. J. (1974). The power of the glance: Desire to see and be seen in cooperative and competitive situations. *Journal of Experimental Social Psychology, 10,* 444–450.

Kalma, A. (1992). Gazing in triads: A powerful signal in floor apportionment. *British Journal of Social Psychology, 31,* 21–39.

Kalma, A. (1993). Sociable and aggressive dominance: Personality differences in leadership style? *Leadership Quarterly, 4,* 45–64.

Kanfer, F. H. (1960). Verbal rate, eyeblink, and content in structured psychiatric interviews. *Journal of Abnormal and Social Psychology, 61,* 341–347.

Kendon, A. (1967). Some functions of gaze direction in social dinteraction. *Acta Psychologica, 26,* 22–63.

Kendon, A. (1990). *Conducting interaction: Patterns of behavior in focused encounters.* Cambridge, UK: Cambridge University Press.

Kendon, A., & Cook, M. (1969). The consistency of gaze patterns in social interaction. *British Journal of Psychology, 60,* 481–494.

Kleck, R. (1968). Physical stigma and nonverbal cues emitted in face-to-face interaction. *Human Relations, 21,* 19–28.

Kleck, R. E., & Nuessle, W. (1968). Congruence between the indicative and communicative functions of eye contact in interpersonal relations. *British Journal of Social and Clinical Psychology, 7,* 241–246.

Kleinke, C. L. (1986). Gaze and eye contact: A research review. *Psychological Bulletin, 100,* 78–100.

Kleinke, C. L., Bustos, A. A., Meeker, F. B., & Staneski, R. A. (1973). Effects of self-attributed and other-attributed gaze in interpersonal evaluations between males and females. *Journal of Experimental Social Psychology, 9,* 154–163.

Knoll, B. I., Attkiss, K. J., & Persing, J. A. (2008). The influence of forehead, brow, and periorbital aesthetics on perceived expression in the youthful face. *Plastic and Reconstructive Surgery, 121,* 1793–1802.

Koch, S. C., Baehne, C. G., Kruse, L., Zimmermann, F., & Zumbach, J. (2008). Visual dominance and visual support in groups. Manuscript submitted for publication.

Kylliäinen, A., & Hietanen, J. K. (2006). Skin conductance responses to another person's gaze in children with autism. *Journal of Autism and Developmental Disorders, 36,* 517–525.

LaFrance, M., & Mayo, C. (1976). Racial differences in gaze behavior during conversations: Two systematic observational studies. *Journal of Personality and Social Psychology, 33,* 547–552.

Leeb, R. T., & Rejskind, F. G. (2004). Here's looking at you, kid! A longitudinal study of perceived gender differences in mutual gaze behavior in young infants. *Sex Roles, 50,* 1–5.

Lefebvre, L. (1975). Encoding and decoding of ingratiation in modes of smiling and gaze. *British Journal of Social and Clinical Psychology, 14,* 33–42.

Levine, M. H., & Sutton-Smith, B. (1973). Effects of age, sex, and task on visual behavior during dyadic interaction. *Developmental Psychology, 9,* 400–405.

Libby, W. L. (1970). Eye contact and direction of looking as stable individual differences. *Journal of Experimental Research in Personality, 4,* 303–312.

Libby, W. L., & Yaklevich, D. (1973). Personality determinants of eye contact and direction of gaze aversion. *Journal of Personality and Social Psychology, 27,* 197–206.

Macrae, C. N., Hood, B. M., Milne, A. B., Rowe, A. C., & Mason, M. F. (2002). Are you looking at me? Eye gaze and person perception. *Psychological Science, 13,* 460–464.

Mansell, W., Clark, D. M., Ehlers, A., & Chen, Y. (1999). Social anxiety and attention away from emotional faces. *Cognition and Emotion, 13,* 673–690.

Mason, M. F., Tatkow, E. P., & Macrae, C. N. (2005). The look of love: Gaze shifts and person perception. *Psychological Science, 16,* 236–239.

Mathews, A., Fox, E., Yiend, J., & Calder, A. (2003). The face of fear: Effects of eye gaze and emotion on visual attention. *Visual Cognition, 10,* 823–835.

McAndrew, F. T., & Warner, J. E. (1986). Arousal seeking and the maintenance of mutual gaze in same and mixed sex dyads. *Journal of Nonverbal Behavior, 10,* 168–172.

McCauley, C., Coleman, G., & DeFusco, P. (1978). Commuters' eye contact with strangers in city and suburban train stations: Evidence of short-term adaptation to interpersonal overload in the city. *Environmental Psychology and Nonverbal Behavior, 2,* 215–225.

Mehrabian, A. (1972). *Nonverbal communication.* Chicago: Aldine/Atherton.

Mehrabian, A., & Williams, M. (1969). Nonverbal concomitants of perceived and intended persuasiveness. *Journal of Personality and Social Psychology, 13,* 37–58.

Mobbs, N. (1968). Eye contact in relation to social introversion/extroversion. *British Journal of Social and Clinical Psychology, 7,* 305–306.

Modigliani, A. (1971). Embarrassment, facework and eye-contact: Testing a theory of embarrassment. *Journal of Personality and Social Psychology, 17,* 15–24.

Mogg, K., Garner, M., & Bradley, B. P. (2007). Anxiety and orienting of gaze to angry and fearful faces. *Biological Psychology, 76,* 163–169.

Morris, D. (1967). *The naked ape.* London: Cape.

Mulac, A., Studley, L. B., Wiemann, J. M., & Bradac, J. J. (1987). Male/female gaze in same-sex and mixed-sex dyads: Gender-linked differences and mutual influence. *Human Communication Research, 13,* 323–343.

Murphy, J. D., Driscoll, D. M., & Kelly, J. R. (1999). Differences in the nonverbal behavior of men who vary in the likelihood to sexually harass. *Journal of Social Behavior and Personality, 14,* 113–128.

Murphy, N. A., Hall, J. A., & Colvin, C. R. (2003). Accurate intelligence assessments in social interaction: Mediators and gender effects. *Journal of Personality, 71,* 465–493.

Napieralski, L. P., Brooks, C. I., & Droney, J. M. (1995). The effect of duration of eye contact on American college students' attributions of state, trait, and text anxiety. *Journal of Social Psychology, 135,* 273–280.

Nevill, D. (1974). Experimental manipulation of dependency motivation and its effects on eye contact and measures of field dependency. *Journal of Personality and Social Psychology, 29,* 72–79.

Nichols, K. A., & Champness, B. G. (1969). Eye gaze and GSR. *Journal of Experimental Social Psychology, 60,* 481–494.

Noller, P. (1980). Gaze in married couples. *Journal of Nonverbal Behavior, 5,* 115–129.

Partala, T., & Surakka, V. (2003). Pupil size variation as an indication of affective processing. *International Journal of Human–Computer Studies, 59,* 185–198.

Patterson, M. L. (1976). An arousal model of interpersonal intimacy. *Psychological Review, 83,* 235–245.

Patterson, M. L., Iizuka, Y., Tubbs, M. E., Ansel, J., Tsutsumi, M., & Anson, J. (2007). Passing encounters East and West: Comparing Japanese and American pedestrian interactions. *Journal of Nonverbal Behavior, 31,* 155–166.

Patterson, M. L., & Tubbs, M. E. (2005). Through a glass darkly: Effects of smiling and visibility on recognition and avoidance in passing encounters. *Western Journal of Communication, 69,* 219–231.

Patterson, M. L., Webb, A., & Schwartz, W. (2002). Passing encounters: Patterns of recognition and avoidance in pedestrians. *Basic and Applied Social Psychology, 24,* 57–66.

Pellegrini, R. J., Hicks, R. A., & Gordon, L. (1970). The effects of an approval-seeking induction on eye contact in dyads. *British Journal of Social and Clinical Psychology, 9,* 373–374.

Pennington, D. C., & Rutter, D. R. (1981). Information or affiliation? Effects of intimacy on visual interaction. *Semiotica, 35,* 29–39.

Putnam, P., Hermans, E., & van Honk, J. (2006). Anxiety meets fear in perception of dynamic expressive gaze. *Emotion, 6,* 94–102.

Rohner, J. (2002). The time-course of visual threat processing: High traitanxious individuals eventually avert their gaze from angry faces. *Cognition & Emotion, 16,* 837–844.

Rosenberg, A., & Kagan, J. (1987). Iris pigmentation and behavioral inhibition. *Developmental Psychobiology, 20,* 377–392.

Rosse, R. B., Kendrick, K., Wyatt, R. J., Isaac, A., & Deutsch, S. I. (1994). Gaze discrimination in patients with schizophrenia: Preliminary report. *American Journal of Psychiatry, 151,* 919–921.

Rowland-Morin, P. A., Burchard, K. W., Garb, J. L., & Coe, N. P. (1991). Influence of effective communication by surgery students on their oral examination scores. *Academic Medicine, 66,* 169–171.

Rubin, Z. (1970). The measurement of romantic love. *Journal of Personality and Social Psychology, 16,* 265–273.

Rutter, D. R. (1973). Visual interaction in psychiatric patients: A review. *British Journal of Psychiatry, 123,* 193–202.

Rutter, D. R. (1984). *Looking and seeing: The role of visual communication in social interaction.* New York: Wiley.

Rutter, D. R., Morley, I. E., & Graham, J. C. (1972). Visual interaction in a group of introverts and extroverts. *European Journal of Social Psychology, 2,* 371–384.

Rutter, D. R., Stephenson, G. M., & White, P. A. (1978). The timing of looks in dyadic conversation. *British Journal of Social and Clinical Psychology, 17,* 17–21.

Schelde, T., & Hertz, M. (1994). Ethology and psychotherapy. *Ethology and Sociobiology, 15,* 383–392.

Scherwitz, L., & Helmreich, R. (1973). Interactive effects of eye contact and verbal content on interpersonal attraction in dyads. *Journal of Personality and Social Psychology, 25,* 6–14.

Schmid Mast, M. (2002). Dominance as expressed and inferred through speaking time: A meta-analysis. *Human Communication Research, 28,* 420–450.

Senju, A., Yaguchi, K., Tojo, Y., & Hasegawa, T. (2003). Eye contact does not facilitate detection in children with autism. *Cognition, 89,* B43–B51.

Simmel, G. (1921). Sociology of the senses: Visual interaction. In R. E. Park & E. W. Burgess (Eds.),

Introduction to the science of sociology. Chicago: University of Chicago Press.

Spence, D. P., & Feinberg, C. (1967). Forms of defensive looking: A naturalistic experiment. *Journal of Nervous and Mental Disorders, 145,* 261–271.

Spezio, M. L., Adolphs, R., Hurley, R. S. E., & Piven, J. (2007). Abnormal use of facial information in high-functioning autism. *Journal of Autism and Developmental Disorders, 37,* 929–939.

Stass, J. W., & Willis, F. N., Jr. (1967). Eye contact, pupil dilation, and personal preference. *Psychonomic Science, 7,* 375–376.

Stephenson, G. M., & Rutter, D. R. (1970). Eye contact, distance and affiliation: A re-evaluation. *British Journal of Psychology, 61,* 385–393.

Stephenson, G. M., Rutter, D. R., & Dore, S. R. (1973). Visual interaction and distance. *British Journal of Psychology, 64,* 251–257.

Strongman, K. T., & Champness, B. G. (1968). Dominance hierarchies and conflict in eye contact. *Acta Psychologica, 28,* 376–386.

Thayer, S. (1969). The effect of interpersonal looking duration on dominance judgments. *Journal of Social Psychology, 79,* 285–286.

Thompson, T. L. (1982). Gaze toward and avoidance of the handicapped: A field experiment. *Journal of Nonverbal Behavior, 6,* 188–196.

van Dulmen, A. M., Verhaak, P. F. M., & Bilo, H. J. G. (1997). Shifts in doctor–patient communication during a series of outpatient consultations in non–insulin-dependent diabetes mellitus. *Patient Education and Counseling, 30,* 227–237.

Vine, I. (1971). Judgment of direction of gaze: An interpretation of discrepant results. *British Journal of Social and Clinical Psychology, 10,* 320–331.

von Cranach, M., & Ellgring, J. H. (1973). Problems in the recognition of gaze direction. In M. von Cranach & I. Vine (Eds.), *Social communication and movement.* New York: Academic Press.

Walker, M. B., & Trimboli, C. (1983). The expressive function of the eye flash. *Journal of Nonverbal Behavior, 8,* 3–13.

Walters, A. S., Barrett, R. P., & Feinstein, C. (1990). Social relatedness and autism: Current research, issues, directions. *Research in Developmental Disabilities, 11,* 303–326.

Webbink, P. (1986). *The power of the eyes.* New York: Springer.

Weisz, J., & Adam, G. (1993). Hemispheric preference and lateral eye movements evoked by bilateral visual stimuli. *Neuropsychologia, 31,* 1299–1306.

Wilbur, M. P., & Roberts-Wilbur, J. (1985). Lateral eye-movement responses to visual stimuli. *Perceptual and Motor Skills, 61,* 167–177.

Williams, E. (1978). Visual interaction and speech patterns: An extension of previous results. *British Journal of Social and Clinical Psychology, 17,* 101–102.

Woodmansee, J. J. (1970). The pupil response as a measure of social attitudes. In G. F. Summers (Ed.), *Attitude measurement.* Chicago: Rand McNally.

Word, C. O., Zanna, M. P., & Cooper, J. (1974). The nonverbal mediation of self-fulfilling prophecies in interracial interaction. *Journal of Experimental Social Psychology, 10,* 109–120.

Zuckerman, M., Miserandino, M., & Bernieri, F. J. (1983). Civil inattention exists—in elevators. *Personality and Social Psychology Bulletin, 9,* 578–586.

I understand a fury in your words
But not the words.

—Shakespeare, *Othello*, Act IV

THE EFFECTS OF VOCAL CUES THAT ACCOMPANY SPOKEN WORDS

CHAPTER **11**

Ideally, this chapter would not be in written form. Instead, it would be a recording you could listen to. A recording would give you a greater appreciation of the vocal nuances that are the subject of this chapter—or, as the cliché goes, *how* something is said rather than *what* is said. But the dichotomy set up by this cliché is misleading, because *how* something is said is frequently *what* is said.

Some responses to vocal cues are elicited because we deliberately try to manipulate our voice to communicate various meanings. Robert J. McCloskey, spokesperson for the State Department during the Nixon administration, reportedly exemplified such behavior:

> McCloskey has three distinct ways of saying, "I would not speculate": spoken without accent, it means the department doesn't know for sure; emphasis on the "I" means "I wouldn't, but you may—and with some assurance"; accent on "speculate" indicates that the questioner's premise is probably wrong. (*Newsweek*, 1970, p. 106)

Most of us do the same kind of thing when we emphasize a particular part of a message. *Prosody* is the word used to describe all the variations in the voice that accompany speech and help to convey its meaning. Notice how different vocal emphases influence the interpretation of the following message:

1. *He's* giving this money to Herbie. (*He* is the one giving the money, nobody else.)
2. He's *giving* this money to Herbie. (He is *giving*, not lending, the money.)
3. He's giving *this* money to Herbie. (The money being exchanged is not from another fund or source; it is *this* money.)
4. He's giving this *money* to Herbie. (*Money* is the unit of exchange, not flowers or beads.)
5. He's giving this money to *Herbie*. (The recipient is *Herbie*, not Eric or Bill or Rod.)

We manipulate vocal pitch to indicate the end of a declarative sentence (by lowering it) or a question (by raising it). Sometimes we consciously manipulate our tone to contradict the verbal message, as in sarcasm. For instance, you can say the words "I'm having a wonderful time" so they mean "I'm having a terrible time." If you are perceived as being sarcastic, the vocal cues you have given probably superseded the verbal message.

THE RELATIVE IMPORTANCE OF CHANNELS

The assumption that vocal cues will predominate in forming attitudes based on contradictory vocal and verbal content initiated research by Mehrabian and his colleagues. In one study, the researchers presented single words previously rated as positive, neutral, or negative to listeners in positive or negative vocal tones (Mehrabian & Wiener, 1967). This experiment led to the following conclusion:

> The variability of inferences about communicator attitude on the basis of information available in content and tone combined is mainly contributed by variations in tone alone. For example, when the attitude communicated in content contradicted the attitude communicated by negative tone, the total message was judged as communicating negative attitude. (p. 109)

A similar study, pitting vocal cues against facial and verbal cues, found facial cues to be more influential (Mehrabian & Ferris, 1967). From these studies, Mehrabian devised the following formula, which illustrates the differential impact or weighting of verbal, vocal, and facial cues:

$$\text{Perceived attitude} = .07 \text{ (verbal)} + .38 \text{ (vocal)} + .55 \text{ (facial)}$$

Obviously the formula is limited by the design of Mehrabian's experiments. For instance, we do not know how the formula might change if some of the variables were manipulated more vigorously, or if more or different people did the judging; we do not know whether the formula would apply to verbal materials longer than one word; and we do not know whether these respondents were reacting to the inconsistency itself as a source of attitudinal information (see Lapakko, 1997, for a critique). The fact that respondents resolved inconsistencies by relying on nonverbal cues does not mean evaluative information is conveyed by nonverbal cues alone, or even mainly, in more realistic communication.

Indeed, Friedman (1979) found that for some kinds of messages, the words mattered more than the facial expressions. Moreover, the preference to base interpretations on words versus vocal cues changes with age: young children rely much more on verbal content, older children show a mixed pattern, and adults rely much more on nonverbal tonal qualities (Bugental, Kaswan, & Love, 1970; Morton & Trehub, 2001). When viewers are asked to guess the thoughts and feelings of people shown on videotape engaged in natural conversation, the viewers' accuracy is based far more on the words that are spoken than on the nonverbal cues, whether those cues are visual or vocal (Gesn & Ickes, 1999; Hall & Schmid Mast, 2007). However, nonverbal cues did contribute to accuracy, especially when the viewers were asked to focus on the target persons' feelings. In other situations, no doubt, nonverbal cues take on great importance, for example, when the expressors' feelings are highly aroused.

Nowadays, with text messaging and email, people rely a great deal on communication via words alone, and it is reasonable to ask what might be missed in such a medium. Kruger, Epley, Parker, and Ng (2005) found that when affective messages were conveyed through email, they were much less accurately decoded than when the same messages were conveyed in voice-to-voice and face-to-face conditions. Furthermore, adding facial cues did not improve accuracy beyond the voice-only condition. In this instance, vocal cues were crucial to fully conveying attitudinal intent.

Studies comparing impressions made by the voice to those made by the face have found the voice especially suited to conveying degrees of dominance or potency. The face has a greater impact on judgments of pleasantness or positivity (Zuckerman & Driver, 1989; Zuckerman, Amidon, Biship, & Pomerantz, 1982) and is a more effective channel than the voice by which to judge people's rapport (Grahe & Bernieri, 1999). Vocal clues to dominance include speed, tendency to interrupt, and loudness; the most obvious clue to pleasantness in the face is a smile. However, each modality can convey a wealth of other messages through more subtle variations. For example, the presence of a smile can be evident in the voice alone; in smiling, the vocal tract is shortened, with the effect of raising the resonances (Scherer, 1986). Some actors who do voice-overs on television advertisements are skilled in conveying a cheerful attitude through their voice quality alone.

Thus, even though the impact of the voice relative to other channels of communication may vary according to many factors, there is no doubt that vocal cues exert a great deal of influence on listener perceptions. Often these responses are based on stereotypes associated with various vocal qualities. Not surprisingly, the existence of such stereotypes means that some vocal qualities are preferred over others. Zuckerman and Driver (1989) documented that listeners generally agree on whether a voice is attractive or not, and also that people whose voices are considered more attractive are believed to have personality traits such as dominance, competence, industriousness, sensitivity, and warmth. Other stereotypes relating to the voice will be described later in this chapter.

THE INGREDIENTS AND METHODS OF STUDYING PARALANGUAGE

The physical mechanisms for producing nonverbal vocal qualities and sounds, also called *paralanguage*, are extremely complex (Juslin & Scherer, 2005). Figure 11-1 illustrates the many muscles and other structures involved in producing vocal sounds; these include the throat, nasal cavities, tongue, lips, mouth, and jaw. In this chapter, however, we focus on the *impact* of paralanguage rather than the mechanisms by which it is produced. Many techniques and methods have been developed for studying the role of vocal nonverbal cues in the communication process (Scherer, 2003). We provide just a short introduction here.

In one approach to studying nonverbal vocal communication, listeners are asked for their impressions or inferences about a voice sample, for example, how anxious or competent the voice sounds. Using this method, a researcher may gain insight into the social meanings of vocal cues, because listeners' impressions are based on their store of experience, knowledge, and beliefs; however, a researcher

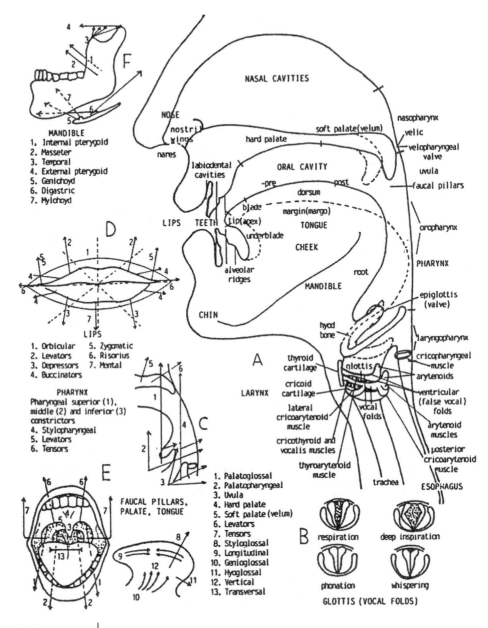

FIGURE 11-1

Muscles and structures involved in speech and paralanguage.

Source: From Fernando Poyatos. (1993). *Paralanguage: A Linguistic Approach to Interactive Speech and Sound*. Reprinted with kind permission from John Benjamins Publishing Company, Amsterdam, NL/Philadelphia. www.benjamins.com.

learns little about what specific vocal cues created a given impression, because listeners are interpreting the vocal cues in an implicit way to reach a final impression. A listener may know an angry voice when she hears one, but may not be able to pinpoint the acoustic properties that made it sound angry. (Whether their impressions are correct or not is a separate issue from the question of how the impressions are formed.)

In contrast, sometimes researchers want, and need, to measure specific vocal characteristics, also called *acoustic properties*, and for this they use automated devices or trained coders. Voice researchers use automated measurement by computers much more than do researchers who study nonvocal modalities of communication, in part because the technology exists for doing so. Some commonly measured acoustic properties are *speech rate*, or words per unit of time; *fundamental frequency* (F_0), which is the vibration rate of the vocal folds in the throat and the main contributor, along with the harmonics and resonances thus produced, to the perception of pitch; and *intensity*, which is the energy value for a speech sound, perceived as loudness. Each of these can be measured as an average value over an utterance, or over some other unit of time, or they can be described more dynamically in terms of range, variation, and contour (Scherer, 1986).

It is also possible to assess vocal nonverbal behavior at a level *between* these impressionistic and purely descriptive extremes. A listener might be asked to characterize a voice as whiny, breathy, or abrupt but not to go to the next level of subjectivity by inferring a trait or mood; for example, from the three adjectives just named, a listener might infer that the speaker is weak, sexy, or rude, respectively. You can see that the last three descriptions are further removed from the actual vocal cues and more inferential than the first three. Studying perceptions at this midway point is a crucial link in understanding the relationship between acoustic features of voices and their social impact (Scherer, 1982).

The fact that the voice has acoustic features perceived and interpreted by a listener according to his or her knowledge, stereotypes, and other cognitions is part of what is called the "lens" model of nonverbal judgment (Scherer, 2003). According to this model, a full understanding of vocal and other nonverbal phenomena must acknowledge a series of interlocking steps: A person's state or trait (A) is reflected in acoustic behavior (B), which is perceived by a listener (C), who forms an impression or attribution (D), which may then be the basis for behavioral reaction or change in the listener (E). Studies hardly ever include all of these elements. One study might document how a speaker's emotional state is reflected in acoustic changes (A–B), while another might relate acoustic properties of the voice to listeners' impressions of personality (B–D), and so forth.

All approaches for measuring vocal behavior have strengths and weaknesses. The choice depends on the questions being asked in the particular study. Hall, Roter, and Rand (1981), for example, were interested in the impact of physicians' and patients' communication of emotion during medical visits. Accordingly, they asked listeners to rate the emotions conveyed in content-masked audiotapes of doctors and patients talking during medical office visits. (Content masking obscures the verbal information while retaining nonverbal vocal properties, as explained in Chapter 3 and later in this chapter.) They found that if the physician sounded angry or anxious or contented, the patient did also, and vice versa—in other words, there was a reciprocation of expressed feelings. In that study, gathering judges' impressions made more sense than measuring acoustic properties, such as fundamental frequency or loudness, because the interest was in social impact, not the specific cues. But another researcher might focus on uncovering the relationship *between* the descriptive and impressionistic levels, that is, finding out what increased fundamental frequency, intensity, and so forth mean in terms of listeners' perceptions. For example, a voice tone we would label as "breathy" is produced by narrowing the glottis a little while letting through more air than for a normal voice and making the vocal folds vibrate without fully closing (Poyatos, 1993). Researchers studying vocal communication of emotion have been particularly active in trying to uncover what cues are used to convey different emotions.

The voice is capable of a great variety of sounds (Poyatos, 1993; Trager, 1958). The components most closely tied to speech include the three already mentioned—frequency, intensity, and speed—as well as vocal lip control, ranging from sharp to smooth transitions; articulation control, either forceful or relaxed; rhythm control, varying from smooth to jerky; and resonance, describing voice ranges from resonant to "thin." Other nonverbal vocal behaviors are less tied to speech and may even substitute for speech. These include laughing, crying, whispering, snoring, yelling, moaning, yawning, whining, sighing, and belching, along with the common "uh," "um," "mmm," "uh-huh," and other such sounds, some of which merge with our definitions of linguistic behavior. Also included as paralanguage are *nonsounds*, such as pauses between words or phrases within one person's speech and pauses when a new speaker begins, also called a *switching pause* or *speech latency*. Some related phenomena, which Mahl and Schulze (1964) placed under the broad heading of *extralinguistic phenomena*, are also relevant to any discussion of communication and vocal behavior. These include dialect or accent, nonfluencies, duration of utterance, and interaction rates.

Now that we have a sense of the ingredients of paralanguage, we can ask the next logical question: What reactions do vocal cues elicit, and how are they important in communicating?

VOCAL CUES AND SPEAKER RECOGNITION

You may have had this experience: You pick up the phone and say, "Hello." The voice on the other end says, "Hi, how ya doin'?" At this point you realize two things: (1) The greeting suggests an informality found among people who are supposed to know each other, and (2) you don't know who it is! So you try to extend the conversation without admitting your ignorance, hoping some verbal cue will be given, or that you eventually will recognize the caller's voice. As a result, you say something like, "Fine. What have you been up to?" Speaker recognition is important not only to all of us in everyday life but also to law enforcement officials and governments. Joseph Stalin assigned teams of imprisoned scientists and engineers to develop speaker-recognition technology so Stalin's police could easily identify "enemies of the state" (Hollien, 1990).

Each time you speak, you produce a complex acoustic signal. It is not exactly the same each time you speak, even if it is the same word, nor is the acoustic signal you produce exactly the same as the one produced by other speakers. The probability that greater differences will exist between the voices of two different speakers than the voice of a single speaker at two different times has led to considerable interest in the process of identifying speakers by their voices alone.

There are three primary methods for identifying speakers from the voice:

1. Listening
2. Visual comparison of spectrograms (voiceprints)
3. Recognition by computers that compare the acoustic patterns of a standard spoken message to stored versions of the same message previously spoken by the same speaker

Although machines are credited with many accomplishments in today's society, ordinary human listening compares favorably with the other two techniques for accuracy in most speaker-recognition tasks. Under certain circumstances, human beings can recognize speakers with a high degree of accuracy. In one study, a single sentence was enough to identify 8 to 10 work colleagues at more than 97 percent accuracy (van Lancker, Kreiman, & Emmorey, 1985). In another study, 83 percent accuracy for 29 familiar speakers was achieved (Ladefoged & Ladefoged, 1980). On the other hand, accuracy at recognizing voices of less familiar people is not as good, as we shall soon see.

Even when listeners accurately identify a speaker from his or her voice, they are probably not able to explain the perceptual bases for their decision. Of the many characteristics of the voice, listeners probably utilize very few in speaker recognition.

Law enforcement and judicial agencies have a special concern for identifying speakers objectively from their vocal characteristics. At the famous trial of Bruno Hauptmann, the kidnapper of Charles and Anne Morrow Lindbergh's baby, Charles Lindbergh claimed he recognized Hauptmann's voice as the voice of the kidnapper, even though it had been about 3 years since he had heard it. Skeptical about the accuracy of this identification, McGehee (1937) conducted research that found accuracy tends to drop off sharply after 3 weeks, and after 5 months, it dips to about 13 percent. Subsequent research has also found reductions in accuracy over time, but often not as dramatic as those McGehee found. Accuracy of identification by listeners also falls notably as the speech samples are made shorter, when various distortions or distractions occur—such as more speakers, disguised voices, whispering, and dialects—and when the target voice is paired with another that sounds similar to it (Hollien, 1990; Kerstholt, Jansen, van Amelsvoort, & Broeders, 2006). And, of course, accuracy varies with how many times one has heard the voice in question.

Many factors affect listening accuracy, but similar problems plague efforts to devise more "objective" methods of speaker recognition—not the least of which is the knowledge that no single set of acoustic cues reliably distinguishes speakers.

One effort to find a more objective method of speaker identification involves the *spectrogram*, also called a *voiceprint*, which is a visual picture of a person's speech. A spectrogram is a plot of vocal energy in different frequency bands as a function of time. Although some have made strong claims for the accuracy and reliability of spectrographic analysis, it seems to be quite fallible (Bolt et al., 1973). Errors in human judgment occur as interpretations of the visual data are made. The interpreter's skill becomes particularly relevant when we look at Figure 11-2. These two similar

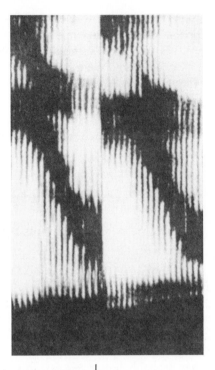

FIGURE 11-2

Similar spectrograms of the word "you" uttered by two arbitrarily selected speakers.

spectrograms of two different people uttering a single word make it sufficiently clear that we must weigh our reliance on spectrograms as evidence at trials very carefully (Hollien, 1990). Spectrograms are not like fingerprints. True, no two voices are exactly alike, but depending on the voice sample obtained and the equipment used, two different voices may appear very similar. In contrast, fingerprints, unlike voices, show little variability from one measurement to the next, unless, of course, smudges or smears have occurred. One study asked speakers to produce the same sentence using their normal voice and a number of "disguises"—speaking like an old person, using a hypernasal voice, a hoarse voice, a slow rate of speech, and a disguise of the speaker's own choosing. These voice samples were then submitted to spectrographic analysis by experts who were paid $50 if they achieved the highest accuracy of identification. Normal voices were matched with about 57 percent accuracy, but all the disguises significantly interfered with identification. The least accuracy was achieved when speakers chose their own type of disguise (Reich, Moll, & Curtis, 1976). Hollien (1990) concluded that spectrographic recognition is a still unvalidated methodology.

VOCAL CUES AND PERSONALITY

One cultural syndrome that aptly illustrates our association of vocal cues with certain personality characteristics concerns the low, deep voice associated with men and masculinity. Salespeople, radio and television announcers, lawyers, and many others try to emulate low vocal tones, which they perceive as being more sophisticated, appealing, sexy, or masculine than higher pitched voices.

Numerous research efforts have tried to determine whether certain personality traits are actually expressed in the voice and whether listeners are sensitive to these cues. It is common to find the following:

1. High agreement among judges of the voices regarding the presence of certain personality characteristics
2. Inconsistent agreement between the judges' personality perceptions and the speaker's actual score on personality tests
3. A very high correspondence between the judges' perceptions and actual criterion measures for some voices and some personality traits

We can make several points about these findings. First, the criterion measures—personality tests—are also frequently imperfect measures, meaning there might be a higher correspondence than the data seem to indicate. Furthermore, research has often ignored differences among listeners with respect to personality, culture, and developmental traits, which may profoundly impact the listener's accuracy in perceiving personality traits based on vocal cues. Research also suggests that a given personality trait may not be expressed similarly in the voices of people from different cultures.

The finding that listeners cannot always detect personality from vocal cues does not mean the voice does not contain any cues to personality. There are several lines of positive evidence on this issue. Extraversion/introversion is the trait dimension best documented in vocal cues of American speakers. Cues associated with a speaker's actual, not just perceived, extraversion, when compared to introversion, are more fluency—that is, shorter pauses when the speaking turn switches from one speaker to another, shorter silent pauses within a person's speech, and fewer hesitations—faster rate, louder speech, more dynamic contrast, higher pitch (up to a point), and more variable pitch. In addition, extraverted people have been shown to talk more, in both number of words and total speaking time (Lippa, 1998; Siegman, 1987). In light of these robust vocal manifestations of extraversion, it is not surprising that people use vocal cues such as loudness, fullness, and enunciation as a basis for judging extraversion (Lippa, 1998).

Lippa (1998) also inquired about several dimensions of masculinity and femininity relative to vocal qualities, defining the masculinity–femininity dimensions in terms of the participants' gender-typical preferences for occupations, hobbies, and other activities. Among men, those who were more "masculine" by this definition had poorer enunciation and less expressive, lower pitched, slower, and louder voices; among women, there was a correlation only for voice pitch—more "masculine" women had lower pitched voices. Listeners' perceptions partially matched these associations, with higher ratings of masculinity being given to targets whose voices were less expressive and lower pitched.

The trait of dominance also has been documented to have an associated speech style, and some of its elements overlap with those found for extraversion. Individuals who speak louder are perceived as more dominant (Harrigan, Gramata, Luck, & Margolis, 1989; Tusing & Dillard, 2000), and indeed more dominant individuals do tend to have voices that are louder than those of less dominant individuals (Hall, Coats, & Smith LeBeau, 2005; Siegman, 1987; Weaver & Anderson, 1973).

Because the stereotype and the actual behavior associated with dominance coincide, it is not surprising that Berry (1991) found that listeners were accurate in judging the personality trait of assertiveness in voices recorded while expressors recited the alphabet.

How personality is actually expressed in speech may be complex, but there is no dearth of evidence that people *believe* speech contains clues to personality. Addington (1968) conducted one of the most complete studies in this area. Male and female speakers simulated nine vocal characteristics, and judges responded to the voices by rating them on 40 personality characteristics. Judges were most reliable, meaning they agreed most with each other, in ratings of masculine–feminine, young–old, enthusiastic–apathetic, energetic–lazy, and attractive–ugly. Addington concluded that the male personality generally was perceived in terms of physical and emotional power, whereas the female personality was apparently perceived in terms of social faculties. Table 11-1 summarizes his results.

TABLE 11-1 | SIMULATED VOCAL CUES AND PERSONALITY STEREOTYPES

Simulated Vocal Cue	Speakers	Stereotyped Perceptions
Breathiness	Males	Younger, more artistic
	Females	More feminine, prettier, more petite, effervescent, high-strung, shallower
Thinness	Males	Did not alter listener's image of the speaker; no significant correlations
	Females	Increased social, physical, emotional, and mental immaturity; increased sense of humor and sensitivity
Flatness	Males	More masculine, more sluggish, colder, more withdrawn
	Females	More masculine, more sluggish, colder, more withdrawn
Nasality	Males	A wide array of socially undesirable characteristics
	Females	A wide array of socially undesirable characteristics
Tenseness	Males	Older, more unyielding, cantankerous
	Females	Younger; more emotional, feminine, high-strung; less intelligent
Throatiness	Males	Older; more realistic; mature; sophisticated; well adjusted
	Females	Less intelligent; more masculine; lazier; more boorish, unemotional, ugly, sickly, careless, inartistic, naive, humble, neurotic, quiet, uninteresting, apathetic
Increased Rate	Males	More animated and extraverted
	Females	More animated and extraverted
Increased Pitch Variety	Males	More dynamic, feminine, esthetically inclined
	Females	More dynamic and extraverted

Addington posed some interesting questions for researchers studying vocal cues and personality. To what extent are these stereotyped impressions of personality maintained in the face of conflicting personality information? And what is the relationship between a given personality impression and vocal cues? For example, Addington's research indicated that increased pitch variety led to more positive personality impressions, but is it not possible that at some point, increasing pitch variety could become so exaggerated as to evoke negative perceptions? Zuckerman's research on vocal attractiveness suggests this may be so, because extremes of pitch, pitch range, shrillness, and squeakiness produced more negative impressions.

People with more attractive voices are, in general, rated as having better personalities than people with less attractive voices, and are perceived as less neurotic, more extraverted, and more open, warm, agreeable, powerful, honest, and conscientious (Berry, 1992; Zuckerman, Hodgins, & Miyake, 1990; Zuckerman & Miyake, 1993). People with more attractive voices, as judged by independent listeners, are sexually active earlier, and have more partners, than those with less attractive voices. And, within each sex, those with more stereotypically desirable physiques—that is, those with higher shoulder-to-waist ratios for men and lower waist-to-hip ratios for women—also have more attractive voices (Hughes, Dispenza, & Gallup, 2004).

Zuckerman's research, as well as that of others (Bloom, Moore-Schoenmakers, & Masataka, 1999; Bloom, Zajac, & Titus, 1999; Riding, Lonsdale, & Brown, 2006) also uncovered the particular speech qualities that produced higher ratings on vocal attractiveness. More attractive-rated voices were more resonant; less monotonous; less nasal, even in infants; and for adult male voices, lower in pitch.

Personality stereotypes also exist about people with babyish voices. Both adults and young children with more babyish voices are perceived as more warm and honest but less powerful and competent than people with more mature-sounding voices. It seems the general qualities attributed to children are attributed to people with younger sounding voices no matter what their actual age (Berry, 1992; Berry, Hansen, Landry-Pester, & Meier, 1994).

VOCAL CUES AND GROUP PERCEPTIONS

A related line of study involves associating various characteristics with voices representative of groups of people. The study of dialects and accents is illustrative. In George Bernard Shaw's play *Pygmalion*, and its musical adaptation *My Fair Lady*, Eliza Doolittle spent considerable time and effort trying to correct her dialect so she could rise in social standing. Professor Higgins says, "Look at her—a pris'ner of the gutters; Condemned by ev'ry syllable she utters." (*My Fair Lady*, Act I, Scene 1.) Eliza's training, according to one study, was most appropriate. It suggests that if we expect a speaker to reflect a nonstandard or "lower-class" dialect, and the speaker actually presents himself or herself in accordance with standard or "upper-class" models, the evaluation will be very positive. The reverse also was true; speakers expected to speak "up" but who spoke "down" were evaluated negatively (Aboud, Clement, & Taylor, 1974). Sometimes, though, there may be a fine line between adapting to our audience and violating expectations based on our own background. If an audience thinks we are faking something or concealing who we "really are," they might judge us harshly.

Although there are some exceptions, ordinarily dialects other than the one spoken by the listener/evaluator receive less favorable evaluations than those considered standard. Generally, these negative responses occur because the listener associates the speaker's dialect with an ethnic or regional stereotype and then evaluates the voice in accordance with the stereotype.

Do regional varieties of speech in the United States differ in prestige value? Listeners in Maine, Louisiana, New York City, Arkansas, and Michigan rated 12 voice samples of American dialects and one foreign accent (Wilke & Snyder, 1941). The most unfavorably regarded were the foreign accent and so-called New Yorkese. Although this study is quite old, dialects and accent stereotypes continue to influence our judgments of speakers. Many people tested their accent stereotypes in the political realm as they evaluated the Boston Brahmin accent of John F. Kennedy, the Southern accent of Jimmy Carter, and the Austrian accent of Arnold Schwarzenegger, governor of California.

Several investigators have pursued the question of exactly how we judge the speech and dialects of others. By far the most extensive work in this direction was done by Mulac (1976). Mulac's experiments have used regional and foreign dialects, broadcasters, various speech pathologies, prose and spontaneous speech, and different modes of presentation such as written, audiotape, videotape, and sound film. This work shows we tend to respond to samples of speech along three primary dimensions:

1. *Sociointellectual status*, that is, high or low social status, blue or white collar, rich or poor, and literate or illiterate
2. *Aesthetic quality*, that is, pleasing or displeasing, nice or awful, sweet or sour, beautiful or ugly
3. *Dynamism*, that is, aggressive or unaggressive, active or passive, strong or weak, loud or soft

These results confirm studies in many other areas of perception that show we tend to see our world and the things in it according to power, evaluation, and activity dimensions.

VOCAL CUES AND JUDGMENTS OF SOCIODEMOGRAPHIC CHARACTERISTICS

Long ago, Pear (1931) did pioneering work on vocal cues and judgments of personal characteristics. Using nine speakers and over 4,000 radio listeners, he found a speaker's age could be estimated fairly accurately, the speaker's sex with remarkable accuracy, birthplace with little accuracy, and occasionally vocation with surprising accuracy. The actor and clergy were consistently identified from among the nine professionals represented. Since that time, others have been interested in judgments of such characteristics as body type, height, weight, age, occupation, status or social class, race, sex, education, and dialect region. Krauss, Freyberg, and Morsella (2002) found that a person's photograph could be matched with his or her voice with significant accuracy by naive participants. Three characteristics that are judged accurately with some consistency are sex, age, and social class or status.

SEX

Listeners who heard six recorded vowels of 20 speakers were able to identify the sex of the speaker 96 percent of the time when the tape was not altered in any way. Accuracy decreased to 91 percent for a filtered tape and to 75 percent for a whispered voice sample (Lass, Hughes, Bowyer, Waters, & Broune, 1976). These authors argued that the fundamental frequency is a more important acoustic cue in speaker gender identification than the resonance characteristics of the voices. It is certainly the case that women typically speak with a higher fundamental frequency, perceived as higher pitch, than men (Viscovich et al., 2003; Ko, Judd, & Blair, 2006). Women's voices are also more variable or expressive but less resonant than men's. Not surprisingly, these same features are used within gender when listeners make ratings of how feminine or masculine a voice sounds (Ko et al., 2006).

Social factors can, of course, qualify sex differences. For instance, males and females *interacting* with each other may manifest different vocal cues than when they present monologues or interact with a member of the same sex (Markel, Prebor, & Brandt, 1972). The topic of discussion also may affect voice production and perceptions. And if differences gradually narrow as adaptations to the social community are made, we might speculate that the vocal tones of working women in predominantly male organizations may be harder to distinguish—particularly if the sample is taken in the work milieu.

At the borderline between verbal and nonverbal behavior falls an area of study concerned with speech styles, or *speech registers*. A speech register refers to a total way of communicating through speech, which can include both nonverbal and verbal forms, and it is believed to vary systematically with social characteristics of the speakers, for example, how socially powerful a person is (Erickson, Lind, Johnson, & O'Barr, 1978). This research is pertinent to our discussion of speaker gender, because it has been suggested that certain verbal forms associated with power differentiate the speech styles of men versus women (Lakoff, 1975). Examples of less powerful speech sometimes associated with females include *tag questions* ("It's a nice day, *isn't it?*"), *hedges and qualifiers* ("sort of," "maybe"), *disclaimers* ("I don't know, *but*"), and *intensifiers* ("The puppy was *so* cute").

Interruptions, another interactional strategy that can reflect dominance, also have been hypothesized to differentiate between men and women in the direction we might expect based on stereotype. People certainly do have well-developed stereotypes about how the men and women speak, but the evidence supporting the hypothesis of gender differences in language use and interruptions is extremely mixed (Aries, 1987; Dindia, 1987; Hirschman, 1994; Irish & Hall, 1995; Kramer, 1978; Marche & Peterson, 1993; Mulac, Lundell, & Bradac, 1986; Nohara, 1992; Turner, Dindia, & Pearson, 1995). The fact that interruptions can signify enthusiastic, active participation in a conversation, rather than efforts to attain or express dominance, is probably one reason why studies are mixed as to which gender interrupts more; whereas early studies tended to find that men interrupted more, more recent studies often find no difference, and some find that females interrupt more than males.

Because interruptions can mean very different things, discussing them without drawing functional distinctions can be very misleading. For example, in a study of married and cohabiting couples, the total number of interruptions in the couples' conversations, as measured in a laboratory interaction, was not related to marital satisfaction; but interruptions that conveyed disagreement and disparagement of the other's message did predict lower satisfaction, both at the time and 2 years later—especially when the latter kind of interruption was directed from the man to the woman (Daigen & Holmes, 2000). Further evidence that the impact of interruptions might differ between men and women comes from Farley's (2008) study showing that, in general, speakers who interrupted often were less liked by listeners than speakers who did not interrupt, but that this effect was especially pronounced when the interrupter was a woman.

AGE

As we mentioned, studies show age to be fairly accurately assessed from vocal cues. In a recent study, age was judged quite accurately from the voice, and not much less so than when judgments were made from a full-length photograph (Krauss et al., 2002). Research sheds light on what kinds of cues are likely relevant to judging age from the voice. With advancing age, speech slows down, and dysfluencies and perturbations in fundamental frequency increase (Hummert, Mazloff, & Henry, 1999). Several studies have investigated voice pitch of males during infancy, childhood, adolescence, early adulthood, and middle and advanced age. There is a general lowering of pitch level from infancy through middle age, with some studies finding a reversal, such that pitch level rises slightly with advancing age. Changes in pitch flexibility, speech rate, loudness, vocal quality, articulatory control, and the like may give clues to age.

SOCIAL CLASS OR STATUS

Several studies show listeners to be amazingly accurate in judging social class or status on the basis of voice alone. Harms (1961) used a standard system to determine social class for nine speakers. Each speaker recorded a 40- to 60-second conversation in which he responded to questions and statements such as "How are you?" and "Ask for the time." Results show that listeners were not only able to identify the speakers' status, many of them said they made their decision after only 10 to 15 seconds of listening to the recording.

CHARACTERISTICS OF RECIPIENTS

So far we have been discussing ways in which a speaker's personal characteristics are reflected in his or her nonverbal speech style. But it would be very surprising if a person's speech style did not also reflect characteristics of the *other* person in an interaction. After all, we react to different kinds of people with many emotions and thoughts that may be reflected in our vocal expression, and we also have notions about how we *ought* to talk to different kinds of people.

A well-studied example of such a "target effect" is baby talk, also called *motherese*, which is the high-pitched, singsong, slow, rhythmic, repetitive, simplified way that parents around the world—fathers as well as mothers—talk to young children (Grieser & Kuhl, 1988; Snow & Ferguson, 1977; Trainor, Austin, & Desjardins, 2000). Even young children know how to talk this way to babies and pets. Furthermore, infants prefer baby talk to normal adult speech. Various purposes have been proposed for baby talk, including getting the infant's attention, promoting language development, clarifying the speaker's message, and creating an emotional bond. The last of these propositions was supported by the research of Trainor and colleagues (2000), which showed that baby talk contained more free emotional expression than typical adult-directed speech but was very similar in terms of acoustic characteristics to adult-directed speech that emphasized the communication of emotion. What makes baby talk distinctive, the authors argued, is that it contains more freely expressed emotion than typical adult-directed speech does.

Certain groups of adults who are attributed childlike qualities—or who are perceived (often erroneously) as cognitively impaired, such as the institutionalized elderly or the deaf—are also spoken to in a way that resembles baby talk. Psychologists are especially interested in this kind of "secondary" baby talk because of the possibility that it contributes to the stigmatizing of groups perceived as dependent or incompetent (Caporael, 1981).

With this in mind, DePaulo and Coleman (1986, 1987) compared the warmth of speech directed toward children, adults with mental retardation, nonnative adult speakers of English, and native adult English speakers, hypothesizing that warmth—one component of baby talk—would decrease across these four groups. The prediction was supported. In addition, when considering those with mental retardation alone, speakers displayed more vocal warmth when speaking to those with more extreme retardation. Particular ways of using the language also differed among the groups: speech to children was clearer, simpler, more attention maintaining, and had longer pauses; speech to those with retardation was very similar to this; speech to foreigners, however, was more similar to that addressed to "normal people" except for being more repetitive. Zebrowitz, Brownlow, and Olson (1992) found that the facial characteristics of children influenced how much baby talk they received from adults; those with more baby-ish faces received more baby talk than same-age children who had more mature-looking faces.

The sex of the person being spoken to also influences how we speak. Men are spoken to more loudly than women are by both men and women (Markel, Prebor, & Brandt, 1972). Similarly, in a study of people's voices on television dramas and talk shows, men were spoken to more dominantly, condescendingly, and unpleasantly than women were by both men and women (Hall & Braunwald, 1981). However, listeners who heard the speaker without knowing the gender of the person to whom they were speaking erroneously thought that women spoke meekly to men, when in fact women and men both spoke more powerfully to men.

VOCAL CUES AND EMOTION

Vocal cues are widespread among many animal species for communication about territory, relationship, identity, alarm, physical states, and emotion (Marler, Evans, & Hauser, 1992; Kitchen, Cheney, & Seyfarth, 2003). Darwin viewed the voice as a primary channel for emotional signals in both humans and animals. In this section we examine what is known about emotional expression in the human voice.

One persistent question is whether people can identify emotions in the voice. The answer is definitely "yes." There is substantial accuracy even when speakers and listeners are not from the same culture, and listeners in different cultures tend to make the same errors and confusions when judging emotions in the voice, though there appears also to be some advantage in judging voices from one's own culture (Juslin & Laukka, 2003; Scherer, 2003; Scherer, Banse, & Wallbott, 2001). Pittam and Scherer (1993) concluded that the recognition of emotion from the voice is four to five times what would be expected if listeners were simply guessing, and Juslin and Laukka (2003) concluded that across five different emotions, accuracy of judgment averaged 90 percent when calculated against a guessing rate of 50 percent.

Concerned that most emotion-judgment tasks present several negative emotions—such as anger, sadness, and fear—but typically only one positive emotion, namely happiness, Sauter and Scott (2007) presented five different positive emotions for judgment through the vocal channel. Listeners in both Great Britain and Sweden showed significant accuracy in distinguishing between amusement, contentment, sensual pleasure, achievement/triumph, and relief.

Neumann and Strack (2000) have further demonstrated that hearing voices expressing different emotions also elicits the corresponding emotional feelings, as reflected both in the listener's own voice tone and in self-ratings of mood. These, like other findings on "emotional contagion" (see Chapter 9), show that emotions can be conveyed and shared as a largely unconscious process (Chartrand & Bargh, 1999).

The notion that a listener might respond with the same kind of emotion as expressed in the speaker's voice suggests a parallel situation that we experience very often when we listen to music. Music can create potent emotional effects, and indeed experimenters often use music to induce emotions in laboratory studies. Some researchers have studied accuracy of identifying emotions in music using methods very similar to those used to study the communication of emotion in the voice. For example, a performer might be asked to play a passage on the piano so as to convey anger or happiness. Accuracy on the part of listeners can then be measured. Juslin and Laukka (2003) found, in reviewing these studies, that accuracy for judging emotions in music is very similar to accuracy in judging emotions in the voice, and furthermore that many of the same acoustic qualities account for the effects. For example, tempo and intensity increase in anger and happiness in both modalities, and variability in intensity is increased for anger and fear but is decreased for sadness and tenderness in both modalities.

You may have wondered how it is possible to separate the nonverbal voice qualities from the words being spoken in studies of vocal communication. Several methods have been used to accomplish this essential goal, and accuracy may vary somewhat depending on the method used (Juslin & Scherer, 2005). Some studies use "meaningless content," usually having the speaker say numbers or letters while trying to convey various emotional states. As early as 1959, Davitz and Davitz conducted a study of this type. Speakers were instructed to express 10 different feelings while reciting parts of the alphabet. These expressions were recorded and played to judges, who were asked to identify the emotion being expressed from the list of 10 emotions. Generally, emotions or feelings were communicated far beyond chance expectation. It is difficult to tell, of course, whether the communicators were using the same tonal or vocal cues they would use in real-life emotional reactions.

Other studies have attempted to control verbal cues by using "constant content," in which a speaker reads a standard passage while attempting to simulate different emotional states. The underlying assumption is that the passage selected is neutral in emotional tone. Another approach is to try to ignore content and focus attention on the pauses, breathing rate, and other characteristics that suggest the person's emotional state. This method is frequently used in psychotherapy to identify signs of anxiety.

Some studies have used electronic filtering to eliminate verbal content (Rogers, Scherer, & Rosenthal, 1971). A low-pass filter will hold back the higher frequencies of speech on which word recognition depends. The finished product sounds much like someone talking on the other side of a wall. One common problem with the electronically filtered technique is that some of the nonverbal vocal cues are eliminated in the filtering process, creating an artificial stimulus. Although some aspects of vocal quality may be lost in the filtering process, a listener can still adequately perceive pitch, rate, and loudness in order to judge emotional content. An advantage of the filtering method is that naturally occurring speech can be used, in contrast to the previous methods, which require the speaker to recite a standard text.

Filtered speech is the most popular method of making words unintelligible and has produced some very intriguing results, some of which we summarize here. In a study of doctors, Milmoe, Rosenthal, Blane, Chafetz, and Wolf (1967) found that the more anger was perceived in the filtered voices of doctors talking about their alcoholic patients, the less successful they were in getting those patients into therapy. Later research verified that the tone of voice used when talking *about* patients carries over into the way doctors talk *to* patients (Rosenthal, Vanicelli, & Blanck, 1984). Another study of physicians found that those who provided more medical information to their patients—and were more competent, according to technical standards for conducting a proper interview, diagnosing correctly, and so forth—were those with the lowest ratings of boredom in short, filtered clips of their voices (Hall, Roter, & Katz, 1987). It has also been found that a patient's satisfaction with a medical visit is greatest when the physician's words are rated as more pleasant and when the physician's filtered voice tone is rated as more angry and anxious. The combination of pleasant words and not-so-pleasant voice may convey a desirable message of concern and involvement in the patient's problems (Hall, Roter, & Rand, 1981). Consistent with this finding is a study (Ambady et al., 2002) that did not use filtered speech but rather ratings of surgeons' unfiltered voices talking to their patients plus statistical controls for the verbal content. That study found that surgeons whose voices were more dominant and less anxious were more likely to have been sued by patients. In the most recent study of this type, primary care physicians' voices were recorded during medical visits. Independent listeners' ratings of their filtered speech revealed that physicians whose patients were more satisfied had voices that were warm and supportive (Haskard, Williams, DiMatteo, Heritage, & Rosenthal, 2008).

Another study analyzed the filtered speech of airline passengers talking to airport agents about their lost baggage (Scherer & Ceschi, 2000). In that study, the number of "felt" and "unfelt" smiles (see Chapter 9) was counted, and judges made ratings of the passengers' filtered speech. A higher frequency of "felt" smiles indicative of genuine enjoyment (see Chapter 9), was related to less vocal anger, less worry, and less resignation and to more good humor; inauthentic or "unfelt" smiles were unrelated to the voice ratings. This and the preceding studies support the validity of filtered speech ratings as an indicator of people's feelings and as a predictor of important outcomes in real-life situations.

Although, on average, accuracy for judging emotions from the voice is very high, studies do vary in how accurately emotions are judged from voice cues. One reason for this involves the differing methods by which such observations may be made, for example, how long the voice samples are, which content-masking technique is used, or how dissimilar the response alternatives are. Another reason is that speakers and listeners vary widely in how accurately they can express and recognize different emotions (see Chapter 3). For example, in the Davitz and Davitz (1959) study, one speaker's expressions were identified correctly only 23 percent of the time, whereas another speaker communicated accurately over 50 percent of the time. In that study, like many others, accuracy was defined in terms of how well listeners could identify the emotion the speaker was asked to express. Listeners' accuracy in recognizing the intended emotion varied widely, just as the speakers' sending accuracy did.

Thus, depending on the skills that individuals bring to a communication situation, they may or may not succeed in sending and receiving vocal emotion cues well. Accuracy in judging emotions from the voice develops with age and appears to be correlated with similar psychological characteristics as is skill in judging other nonverbal cues (Baum & Nowicki, 1998; see Chapter 3). As one example, persons with autism and Asperger syndrome score lower than comparison groups on judging both vocal and facial emotion cues (Rutherford, Baron-Cohen, & Wheelwright, 2002), and the same is true for people with anorexia nervosa (Kucharska-Pietura, Nilolaou, Masiak, & Treasure, 2004). Some research questions are intrinsically more relevant to the voice than to other cue channels. For example, Thompson, Schellenberg, and Husain (2004) demonstrated that studying music helps a person's accuracy in decoding emotions conveyed in the voice.

Another qualification to any statement about the voice's overall ability to communicate emotions is that some emotions are easier to communicate than others. For example, one study found that vocal anger was identified 63 percent of the time, whereas vocal pride was identified correctly only 20 percent of the time. Another study found that joy and hate were easily recognized in the voice, but shame and love were the most difficult to recognize. In general, anger, joy, and sadness are easier to recognize in the voice than fear and disgust (Banse & Scherer, 1996; Pittam & Scherer, 1993).

In a review of studies on accuracy of judging anxiety, Harrigan, Wilson, and Rosenthal (2004) found that accuracy for judging *state anxiety*—that is, anxiety being experienced at a given moment—was higher when judgments were based on the voice alone than when they were based on video cues alone. However, for *trait anxiety*, which is a personality tendency to be anxious, this was reversed—in fact, listeners could not judge trait anxiety from the voice at all. Possibly, the immediate physiological arousal associated with state anxiety produces easily noticed vocal changes, such as tremor or speech errors.

In addition to demonstrating that emotions can be conveyed through the voice, researchers have learned a great deal about *how* the voice conveys emotion. However, one thing is clear: There is no "dictionary" of emotion cues for the voice, any more than there is for any nonverbal channel. You cannot identify key acoustic features and then look them up in a book somewhere to see which emotion is being expressed. Many factors enter into the total picture of emotional expression: contextual cues, the words being spoken, other nonverbal behaviors, individual differences in the people, and the fact that there is undoubtedly more than one way to express a given emotion. With these qualifications in mind, we now summarize key vocal cues associated with emotion.

Anxiety induced in a particular circumstance, or *state anxiety,* is often associated with nonfluencies or speech disruptions (Mahl, 1956; Siegman, 1987). Table 11-2 presents the categories of speech disturbance investigated by Cook (1965). "Non-Ah" speech errors, in categories 2 through 8, seem to increase with induced anxiety or discomfort; "Ah" errors, in category 1, do not (see the section "Hesitations, Pauses, Silence, and Speech" later in this chapter). Personality dimensions related to anxiety have also been studied in relation to the production of speech disturbances. Harrigan, Suarez, and Hartman (1994) obtained anxiety ratings of verbatim transcripts of the speech of individuals who varied in state and trait anxiety as well as in repression, which is the need to deny negative thoughts, impulses, or behaviors. Repressors' speech was judged to be the most anxious, more so even than the speech of people who were highly trait-anxious but not repressive. The authors attributed these effects to differences in the frequency of speech disturbances among groups. Although repressors do not view themselves as high on trait anxiety, their vocal behavior says otherwise. Perhaps anxious people are more aware of their anxiety and can take steps to conceal or control it, whereas repressive people are not aware of it, increasing the chances that anxiety cues will "leak out" through the voice.

TABLE 11-2 | SPEECH DISTURBANCE CATEGORIES, FREQUENCY, AND EXAMPLES

Category	% of Total	Example
1. "Er," "Ah," or "Um"	40.5	Well ... er ... when I go home
2. Sentence change	25.3	I have a book which ... the book I
3. Repetition	19.2	I often ... often work at night.
4. Stutter	7.8	It sort of l ... l ... leaves me.
5. Omission (leaving out a word or leaving it unfinished)	4.5	I went to the lib ... the Bod.
6. Sentence incompletion	1.2	He said the reason was ... anyway I
7. Tongue slip	0.7	I haven't much term [meaning time]
8. Intruding incoherent sound	1.2	I don't really know why ... dh ...

Source: From M. Cook. (1969). Anxiety, speech disturbances and speech. *British Journal of Social and Clinical Psychology*, Vol. 4, p. 107. Reprinted by permission of John Wiley and Sons.

In an experiment on therapeutic treatment for social anxiety, those patients who responded favorably to the intervention showed changes in key vocal variables when asked to give a speech in front of a group—specifically in showing a lower vocal pitch and greater continuity of speech, measured as having a smaller percentage of their speaking time spent in silence (Laukka, Linnman, Åhs et al., 2008). In general, stress from any source makes the voice rise in pitch. In one of the earliest demonstrations, Williams and Stevens (1972) analyzed recordings of the radio announcer who described, live on the air, the horrifying explosion and burning of the hydrogen-filled zeppelin *Hindenburg* at Lakehurst, New Jersey, in 1937. Comparison of his voice before and immediately after the disaster showed the fundamental frequency rose, with much less fluctuation in frequency.

Scherer's work has encompassed a broad range of emotions. In a 1974 study, he used artificial sounds, rather than spontaneous speech, to approach the question of which vocal features are associated with which emotions. Listeners rated synthesized tones on 10-point scales of pleasantness, potency, activity, and evaluation and indicated whether the stimuli could or could not be an expression of interest, sadness, fear, happiness, disgust, anger, surprise, elation, or boredom. Generally speaking, tempo and pitch variation influence a wide range of judgments about emotional expressions. Table 11-3 summarizes the results of several of Scherer's studies.

Scherer (1986) expanded his predictions to include 12 different emotions—such as irritation/cold anger, grief/desperation, elation/joy—and 18 different acoustic variables such as average fundamental frequency, variability in loudness, and speech rate. In comparing these theoretical predictions to actual research, Scherer found some impressive consistencies but also considerable variation, partly due to great differences in how the studies were conducted and the number of studies conducted. Joy/elation is well studied and is associated with higher average frequency, or *pitch*; greater frequency range; greater frequency variability; higher average intensity, or *loudness*; and faster rate. Consistent with the

TABLE 11-3 | ACOUSTIC CONCOMITANTS OF EMOTIONAL DIMENSIONS

Amplitude variation	Moderate	Pleasantness, activity, happiness
Pitch variation	Moderate	Anger, boredom, disgust, fear
Pitch contour	Down	Pleasantness, boredom, sadness
	Up	Potency, anger, fear, surprise
Pitch level	Low	Pleasantness, boredom, sadness
Tempo	Slow	Boredom, disgust, sadness
	Fast	Pleasantness, activity, potency, anger, fear
Duration (shape)	Round	Potency, boredom, disgust, fear, sadness
Filtration (lack of overtones)	Low	Sadness, pleasantness, boredom, happiness
	Moderate	Potency, activity
Tonality	Atonal	Disgust
	Tonal–minor	Anger
Rhythm	Not rhythmic	Boredom
	Rhythmic	Activity, fear, surprise

results for joy/elation, the perception of how much affection is perceived in a speaker is positively predicted by how high-pitched and expressively variable the voice is (Floyd & Ray, 2003). Anger is conveyed by higher frequency and intensity, with a greater frequency range and faster speech rate for "hot" anger. Fear is shown by higher frequency, especially high-frequency energy, and faster speech rate. Sadness—at least the quiet, resigned sort—involves lower average frequency and intensity, has downward-directed contours, and is slower (Pittam & Scherer, 1993; Scherer, Banse, Wallbott, & Goldbeck, 1991). Research is progressing on identifying emotions from acoustic variables, so that some day computers may be able to recognize vocal emotions almost as well as human listeners do (Banse & Scherer, 1996).

VOCAL CUES, COMPREHENSION, AND PERSUASION

In addition to its role in personality and emotional judgments, the voice also plays a part in retention and attitude change, which has been primarily studied in public speaking. For many years, introductory public speaking textbooks have stressed the the importance of delivery in the rhetorical situation. Delivery of the speech, rather than speech content, was perhaps the first area of rhetoric to receive quantitative examination by speech researchers. Almost every study that isolated delivery as a variable showed that delivery did matter. It had positive effects on the amount of information remembered, the amount of attitude change elicited from the audience, and the amount of credibility audience members attributed to the speaker.

Typical prescriptions for use of the voice in delivering a public speech include the following:

1. Use variety in volume, rate, pitch, and articulation. The probability of desirable outcomes is less when we use a constant rate, volume, pitch, and articulation. Being consistently overprecise may be as ineffective as being overly sloppy in articulation.
2. Base decisions concerning loud–soft, fast–slow, precise–sloppy, or high–low on what is appropriate for a given audience in a given situation.
3. Avoid excessive nonfluencies.

VOCAL CUES, COMPREHENSION, AND RETENTION

Several studies tend to support the prescriptions for vocal variety in increasing audience comprehension and retention. Woolbert (1920), in perhaps the earliest study of this type, found that large variations of rate, force, pitch, and quality produced high audience retention when compared with a no-variation condition. Glasgow (1952), using prose and poetry, established two conditions for study: "good intonation" and "mono-pitch." Multiple-choice tests, following exposure to these differing vocal samples, showed that mono-pitch decreased comprehension by more than 10 percent for both prose and poetry. Other research suggests that moderately poor vocal quality and pitch patterns, nonfluencies, mispronunciation, and even stuttering do not interfere significantly with comprehension, although listeners generally find these conditions unpleasant (Kibler & Barker, 1972; Klinger, 1959; Utzinger, 1952). All of these studies indicate that listeners are rather adaptable. It probably takes constant and extreme vocal unpleasantries to affect comprehension, and even then the listener may adapt. Poor vocal qualities probably contribute more to a listener's perception of the speaker's personality or mood than to a decrease in comprehension.

The study of speaking rate by itself yields additional evidence of listener flexibility and the lack of impact on comprehension of seemingly poor voice-related phenomena. The normal speaking rate is between 125 and 190 words per minute. Some researchers believe comprehension begins to decrease once the rate exceeds 200 words per minute, but other experts in speeded speech place the level of significant decline in comprehension at between 250 and 275 words per minute. King and Behnke (1989) point out that time-compressed speech adversely affects comprehensive listening—that is, understanding a message and remembering it for the future—but does not adversely affect short-term listening (40 seconds or less) or interpretive listening (reading between the lines) until very high levels of compression are reached, around 60 percent. Obviously, individual ability to process information at rapid rates differs widely. The inescapable conclusion from studies of speech rate, however, is that we can comprehend information at much more rapid rates than we ordinarily are exposed to. In an experiment in which individual listeners were allowed to vary the rates of presentation at will, the average choice was 1.5 times normal speed (Orr, 1968).

VOCAL CUES AND PERSUASION

What is the role of the voice in persuasive situations? It is clear we can communicate various attitudes with our voice alone, for example, friendliness, hostility, superiority, and submissiveness. Then what contribution, if any, do vocal cues make toward changing people's attitudes?

Mehrabian and Williams (1969) conducted an early series of studies on the nonverbal correlates of intended and perceived persuasiveness. The following vocal cues were associated with both "increasing intent to persuade and decoded as enhancing the persuasiveness of a communication": more speech volume, higher speech rate, and less halting speech. This early study has been followed by many studies on the relation of vocal cues to attitude change. The following vocal cues are associated with greater perceived persuasiveness, credibility, competence, or actual attitude change (Burgoon, Birk, & Pfau, 1990; Leigh & Summers, 2002). However, an upper limit to the effective range on each of these variables is likely, so that extremes would produce less, not more, credibility or persuasion.

- Fluent, nonhesitant speech
- Shorter response latencies, the pauses when speakers switch turns
- More pitch variation
- Louder voice
- Faster speech, as measured by words per minute or length of pauses

Of all these cues, faster speech has received the most attention in its relation to the persuasion process (Miller, Maruyama, Beaber, & Valone, 1976; Street, Brady,

& Lee, 1984). Why is fast speech persuasive? Possibly, faster speakers seem more credible because we assume they really know what they are talking about and truly believe it themselves. But when listening to a faster-speaking persuader, we may also be kept so busy processing the message that we have little chance to develop counterarguments in our heads. Or we may be simply distracted by noticing the faster speech, and this interferes with our ability to focus on the message and develop counterarguments (Woodall & Burgoon, 1983). It is also important to note that faster speech does not *always* produce more persuasion. Smith and Shaffer (1991) found that faster speech increased persuasion when the message was counterattitudinal—that is, when it favored a position that opposed the listener's preexisting attitude—but it decreased persuasion when the message was consistent with the listener's preexisting attitude.

At this point you may legitimately ask, "So what?" What if we know the voice's potential for eliciting various responses related to comprehension, attitude change, and speaker credibility? Obviously in real-life situations, visual and verbal cues, prior publicity and experiences with the speaker, and a multitude of other interacting factors can reduce the importance of vocal cues. In short, specific nonverbal cues do not operate in isolation in human interaction, as they do in the experiments reported here. For the most part, we do not know what their role is in context—that is, in combination with other cues and in settings outside the laboratory. DeGroot and Motowidlo's (1999) study takes us a step in that direction. These investigators asked managers in companies to let themselves be interviewed as though they were applying for their job; the managers' vocal cues were then related to their actual supervisors' performance ratings of them and also to naive observers' impressions of the taped interviews. A vocal composite that consisted of faster speech rate, more pitch variability, fewer pauses, lower pitch, and less amplitude variability was a significant predictor of both the performance ratings and the favorability of listeners' reactions, which led the authors of the study to believe that people who speak with this desirable set of vocal characteristics will be better able to perform well on the job, owing to the favorability of people's responses to them. Burgoon and colleagues (1990) also examined a wide range of different cues, vocal cues and those relating to face and body, in a study of credibility and persuasiveness. Controlling for other nonverbal behaviors, vocal fluency remained the strongest predictor of judged competence, a dimension of credibility, and it was one of the two strongest predictors of judged persuasiveness. Complementing these studies of specific vocal cues, Ambady, Krabbenhoft, and Hogan (2006) used more global ratings of electronically filtered speech to predict ratings of sales effectiveness, as made by upper management, in a sample of sales managers. Even though the sales managers' voice clips totaled only 1 minute each, ratings of qualities such as emotion, empathy, cooperation, and enthusiasm as perceived in the voice were strongly correlated with their superiors' positive evaluations of them.

VOCAL CUES AND TURN TAKING IN CONVERSATIONS

Thus far we have discussed the role of vocal cues in communicating interpersonal attitudes, emotions, and information about the speaker. Vocal cues also play an important role in managing the interaction and are part of a system of cues that helps us structure our interactions—that is, who speaks when, to whom, and for how long.

Rules for turn taking, or "floor apportionment," may have as much to do with how a conversation is perceived as does the actual verbal content of the interaction (Duncan, 1973; Wiemann & Knapp, 1975). You can probably recall instances where turn-taking rules played a significant role in your responses: for example, when a long-winded speaker would not let you get a word in edgewise; when a passive interactant refused to "take the conversational ball" you offered; when you were confronted with an "interrupter"; or those awkward moments when you and the other person started talking simultaneously. Obviously, vocal cues are only some of the signals we use to manage our turn taking (see Chapter 12). Altogether, we do a remarkable job of negotiating turn-taking through nonverbal, including vocal, cues. Only rarely do we need to explicitly verbalize this information—for example, "Okay, Lillian, I'm finished talking. Now it's your turn to talk."

Our use of these signals is mostly unconscious but conforms to definite rules of usage nonetheless. These have been described extensively by Duncan and Fiske (1977) in their analyses of two-person conversations held in a laboratory setting. Certain cues were almost invariably present when smooth turn taking took place, five of which were vocal, either verbal or nonverbal. None of these cues seems to be more important than the others; rather it seems that a smooth switch is best predicted by the sheer number of these cues. In other words, redundancy—sending several equivalent-meaning cues simultaneously—promotes smooth regulation of conversation. These cues included the speaker's pitch or a drawl at the end of a unit of speech, the grammatical completion of a unit of speech, and the use of certain routine verbal phrases. The next sections elaborate on these and other turn-regulating behaviors identified in research (Cappella, 1985; Rosenfeld, 1987).

TURN YIELDING

To yield a turn means to signal you are finished and that the other person can start talking. Sometimes we do this by asking a question, causing the pitch to rise at the end of our comment. Another unwritten rule most of us follow is that questions require, or often demand, answers. We also can drop our pitch, sometimes with a drawl on the last syllable, when finishing a declarative statement that concludes our intended turn. If the cues are not sufficient for the other person to start talking, we may have to add a trailer on the end. The trailer may be silence or may take the form of a filled pause; for example, "ya know," "so, ah," or "or something." The filled pauses reiterate the fact that you are yielding, and they fill a silence that might otherwise indicate the other's insensitivity to your signals or your own inability to make them clear.

TURN REQUESTING

We can also use vocal cues to show others that we want to say something. Although an audible inspiration of breath alone may not be a sufficient cue, it does help signal turn requesting. The mere act of interrupting or simultaneous talking may signal an impatience to get the speaking turn. Sometimes you can inject vocalizations during normal pausing of the other speaker. These "stutter starts" may be the beginning of a sentence ("I ... I ... I ...") or merely vocal buffers ("Ah ... Er ... Ah ..."). Another method for requesting a turn is to assist the other person in finishing quickly. This can be done by increasing the rapidity of our responses, much like the increased rapidity of the head nods when we are anxious to leave a situation in which another person has the floor. Normally, back-channel cues, such as "Uh-huh," "Yeah," and "Mmm-hmm," are used to encourage the other to continue speaking and to signal attentiveness. However, when these are used rapidly, the message can be "Get finished so I can talk."

Turn Maintaining

Sometimes we want to keep the floor. It may be to show our status or to avoid unpleasant feedback, or perhaps it reflects some exaggerated sense of the importance of our own words and ideas. Common vocal cues in these instances may include the following:

1. Increasing volume and rate when turn-requesting cues are sensed
2. Increasing the frequency of filled pauses
3. Decreasing the frequency and duration of silent pauses

Although Lalljee and Cook's (1969) research does not support the use of pauses for control, Rochester (1973) cites several studies that support the following conclusions:

1. More filled pauses and fewer silent pauses are found in dialogue than monologue.
2. More filled pauses and fewer silent pauses are *not* found when people want to break off speaking.
3. More filled pauses and fewer silent pauses are more likely when the speaker lacks visual means of controlling the conversation, as on the telephone.

Turn Denying

In some instances, we may want the other person to keep talking—to deny the turn when offered. The back-channel cues we noted earlier may keep the other person talking by giving reinforcement for what is being said. The rate with which these cues are delivered, however, is probably slower than when we are requesting a turn. And, of course, simply remaining silent may dramatically communicate a turn denial. Silence and pauses are the subjects of our next section.

We wish to reiterate that conversational regulation is a delicate matter involving a complex coordination of verbal behavior, vocal behavior, gaze, and body movement. Research finds that even if we would predict a turn switch based on words and voice, a switch is very unlikely if the speaker looks away from the listener during the likely switching point or engages in a hand gesture that is maintained or not returned to a resting state.

HESITATIONS, PAUSES, SILENCE, AND SPEECH

Spontaneous speech is actually highly fragmented and discontinuous. Goldman-Eisler (1968) said that even when speech is at its most fluent, two-thirds of spoken language comes in chunks of less than six words, which strongly suggests that the concept of fluency in spontaneous speech is an illusion. Pauses range in length from milliseconds to minutes. Pauses are subject to considerable variation based on individual differences, the kind of verbal task, the amount of spontaneity, and the pressures of the particular social situation.

LOCATION OR PLACEMENT OF PAUSES

Pauses are not evenly distributed throughout the speech stream. Goldman-Eisler (1968, p. 13) outlined places where pauses do occur—at both grammatical and nongrammatical junctures.

Grammatical

1. "Natural" punctuation points, for example, the end of a sentence.
2. Immediately preceding a conjunction whether (a) coordinating, such as *and, but, neither, therefore*; or (b) subordinating, such as *if, when, while, as, because*.
3. Before relative and interrogative pronouns, for example, *who, which, what, why, whose*.
4. When a question is direct or implied: "I don't know whether I will."
5. Before all adverbial clauses of time (when), manner (how), and place (where).
6. When complete parenthetical references are made: "You can tell that the house—the one on the corner—is falling into disrepair."

Nongrammatical

1. Where a gap occurs in the middle or at the end of a phrase: "In each of ... the cells of the body..."
2. Where a gap occurs between words and phrases repeated: (a) "The question of the ... of the economy" and (b) "This attitude is narrower than that ... that of many South Africans."
3. Where a gap occurs in the middle of a verbal compound: "We have ... taken issue with them and they are ... resolved to oppose us."
4. Where the structure of a sentence is disrupted by a reconsideration or a false start: "I think the problem of France is the ... what we have to remember about France is ..."

Analysis of spontaneous speech shows that only 55 percent of the pauses fall into the grammatical category, whereas oral readers of prepared texts are extremely consistent in pausing at clause and sentence junctures.

TYPES OF PAUSES

The two major types of pauses are the unfilled, silent pause and the filled pause. A *filled pause* is filled with some type of phonation such as "um" or "uh." A variety of sources associate filled pauses with a range of generally undesirable characteristics. Some people associate filled pauses and repetitions with emotional arousal; some feel that filled pauses may reduce anxiety but jam cognitive processes. Goldman-Eisler (1961) found, in four different studies, that unfilled pausing time was associated with "superior (more concise) stylistic and less probable linguistic formulations," whereas higher rates of filled pauses were linked to "inferior stylistic achievement (long-winded statement) of greater predictability." Livant (1963) found the time required to solve addition problems was significantly greater when the subject filled his pauses than when he was silent. Several experimenters reached similar conclusions: When speakers fill pauses, they also impair their performance. Thus in a heated discussion, you may maintain control of the conversation by filling the pauses, but you may also decrease the quality of your contribution. However, too many filled *or* unfilled pauses may receive negative evaluations from listeners (Christenfeld, 1995). Lalljee (1971) found that too many unfilled pauses by the speaker caused listeners to perceive the speaker as anxious, angry, or contemptuous; too many filled pauses evoked perceptions of the speaker as anxious or bored. Although these studies suggest that filled pauses are generally to be avoided, research also finds that in university lecturers, their use is correlated with more complex thought processes and use of a larger vocabulary (Schachter, Christenfeld, Ravina, & Bilous, 1991; Schachter, Rauscher, Christenfeld, & Crone, 1994).

Filled pauses show up, interestingly, much more in the speech of men than that of women (Hall, 1984). We might think of men as more assertive in general, but Siegman (1987) observed that more filled pauses are usually associated with "cautious and hesitant speech" (p. 398). Perhaps men are more socially uncomfortable than women are. It may be, however, that filled pauses are serving another function altogether—keeping the speaker's turn from being taken over by the other person, which may be of more concern for men.

REASONS WHY PAUSES OCCUR

During the course of spontaneous speech, we are confronted with situations that require decisions as to what to say and what lexical or structural form to put it in. One school of thought relates hesitancy in speech to the uncertainty of predicting the cognitive and lexical activity while speaking. The speaker may be reflecting on decisions about the immediate message or may even be projecting into the past or future—that is, "I don't think she understood what I said earlier" or "If she says no, what do I say then?" Thus the assumption is that these hesitation pauses are actually delays due to competing processes taking place in the brain. Goldman-Eisler indeed found that pause time while interpreting cartoons was twice as long as while describing them. It also was observed that with each succeeding trial (that is, with increasing reductions in spontaneity) there was a decline in pausing. Recent research continues to support the theory that longer speech latencies and a relatively large number of pauses are sometimes due to the complexity of the message being formulated (Greene & Ravizza, 1995).

Another possible explanation for some pausing behavior involves what is described as "disruption behavior." Instead of representing time for planning, the pause may indicate a disruption due to an emotional state that may have developed from negative feedback or time pressures. These disruptions may take many forms: fears about the subject matter under discussion, desire to impress the listener with verbal or intellectual skills, pressure to perform other tasks simultaneously, or pressure to produce verbal output immediately.

INFLUENCE AND COORDINATION WITHIN THE DYAD

Thus far we have considered hesitations and pauses primarily from the speaker's standpoint. Now we consider the interaction process and the effect of one person's interpersonal timing on another. For many years, Chapple (1949, 1953; Chapple & Sayles, 1961) explored the rhythms of dialogue, that is, the degree of synchrony found in the give-and-take of conversations. This involved noting who talks, when, and for how long. He developed a standardized interview in which the interviewer alternates "normal" attentive responding with silences and, later, interruptions. As you might suspect, there are many reactions. Some people respond to a nonresponse, or silence, by speeding up; others match the nonresponse; and most try some combination of the two.

Matarazzo's studies of interviewing behavior found most latencies of response were between 1 and 2 seconds, with the mean about 1.7 seconds (Matarazzo, Wiens, & Saslow, 1965). The interviewer, however, can have considerable influence on the length of the pauses. For example, when the interviewer did not respond to a statement by the interviewee, almost 65 percent of the interviewees began to talk again, but the pause was now closer to 4.5 seconds. In the same manner, Matarazzo demonstrated response matching, showing how the interviewer can also control the length of utterance by increasing the length of his own utterances. Figure 11-3

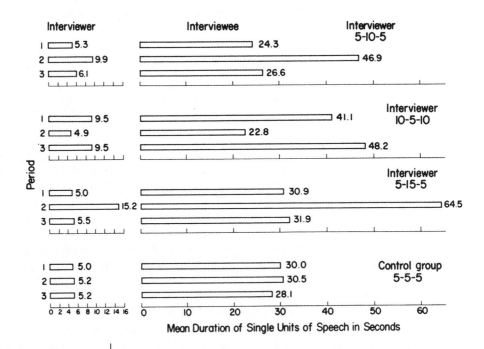

FIGURE 11-3

The influence of interviewer response duration on interviewee response duration.

Source: Addington, D. W. (1968). The relationship of selected vocal characteristics to personality perception. *Speech Monographs*, 35, 492–503. Thousand Oaks, CA: Sage Publications, Inc. Courtesy of D. W. Addington.

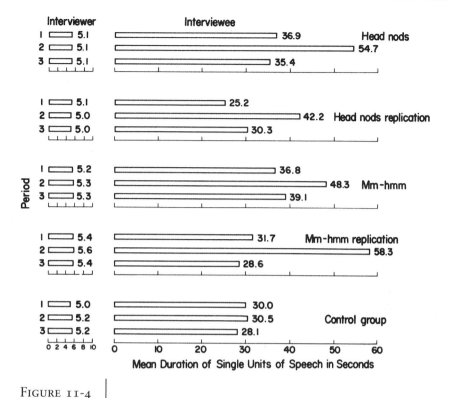

FIGURE 11-4

The influence of interviewer head nods and "Mm-hmm" on interviewee response duration.

Source: Addington, D. W. (1968). The relationship of selected vocal characteristics to personality perception. Speech Monographs, 35, 492–503. Thousand Oaks, CA: Sage Publications, Inc. Courtesy of D. W. Addington.

and Figure 11-4 show the results of several experiments involving three 15-minute segments of a 45-minute interview, with the interviewer varying his responses during different periods. As the interviewer extended the length of his responses, a corresponding increase in the length of responses from the interviewee resulted. In the same manner, there must be times when pauses beget pauses. The interviewer also can control response duration by head nodding or saying "Mmm-hmm" during the interviewee's response, as shown in Figure 11-4. This demonstrates that these back-channel responses do indeed encourage a speaker to continue speaking.

SILENCE

Most of the hesitations and pauses we have discussed are relatively short. Sometimes silences may be extended. They may be imposed by the nature of the environment, for example, in churches, libraries, courtrooms, or hospitals; they may be imposed for the duration of a given event, as at a funeral or when singing the national anthem; or they may be self-imposed, such as remaining quiet in the woods to hear other sounds, or enjoying with a lover the mutual closeness that silence may bring. Silence can mean virtually anything, and it is charged with those words that have just been exchanged; words that have been exchanged in the past; words that have not or will not be said but are fantasized; and words that may actually be said in the future. For these reasons, it would be absurd to provide a list of meanings for silence. The meaning of silence, like the meaning of words, can only be deduced after careful analysis of the communicators, subject matter, time, place, culture, and so forth.

Some of the many interpersonal functions served by silence include the following:

• Punctuation or accenting, drawing attention to certain words or ideas
• Evaluating, providing judgments of another's behavior, showing favor or disfavor, agreement or disagreement, or attacking (e.g., not responding to a comment, greeting, or letter)
• Revelation, making something known, or hiding something
• Expression of emotions: the silence of disgust, sadness, fear, anger, or love
• Mental activity, showing thoughtfulness and reflection or ignorance

(The preceding list is from Bruneau, 1973; Jaworski, 1993; and Jensen, 1973.)

SUMMARY

Generally, this chapter should leave you with the overall impression that vocal cues frequently play a major role in determining responses in human communication situations. You should be quick to challenge the cliché that vocal cues only concern how something is said—frequently they are *what* is said. What is said might be an attitude ("I like you" or "I'm superior to you"); it might be an emotion; it might be the coordination and management of the conversation; or it might be the presentation of some aspect of your personality, background, or physical features.

You should also recognize the important role vocal stereotypes play in determining responses. Whether judges are trying to estimate your occupation, sociability, race, degree of introversion, body type, or any of various other qualities about you, they will be very apt to respond to well-learned stereotypes. These stereotypes may not accurately describe you, but they will be influential in the interaction between you and others. Though research has demonstrated considerable interjudge agreement, so far it is difficult to identify many personality traits that seem to be judged with consistent accuracy. Although it is not uncommon for a person speaking a dialect other than one's own to be perceived negatively, speakers who try to correct for speech differences, and severely violate expectations for their speech, may also be perceived negatively.

Accurate judgments—that is, beyond chance levels—of age, sex, and status from vocal cues alone tend to be fairly consistently reported in the literature. Furthermore, often we are able to identify specific speakers from voice alone.

Although studies of judgments of emotions from vocal cues have used different methods, different emotions, listeners with differing sensitivity, and speakers with differing abilities for portraying emotions, the results reveal that people can make quite accurate judgments of emotions and feelings from wordless vocal messages. Some indications are that moderately poor vocal behaviors do not interfere with a listener's comprehension of a message, and that if we use variety in our volume, pitch, and rate, we may increase our chances of achieving audience comprehension in public speeches. Unchanging, constant vocal behavior, particularly at the extremes, may be less advantageous in achieving audience comprehension.

Preliminary findings also suggest that the voice may be important in some aspects of persuasion.

More fluency, higher rate, more volume, and less halting speech seem related to intent to persuade and perceived persuasiveness. We know that the credibility of the speaker plays an important role in persuasion in some situations. We now know that some decisions concerning credibility—such as dimensions of trustworthiness, dynamism, likableness, and competency—are made from word-free samples of the voice alone.

Vocal cues also help us manage the give-and-take of speaking turns. In turn yielding, turn requesting, turn maintaining, and turn denying, we use vocal cues to make our intentions clear.

We also discussed the important role of hesitations or pauses in spontaneous speech. Such pauses, ordinarily between 1 and 2 seconds long, may be greatly influenced by the other interactant, the topic being discussed, and the nature of the social situation. Pauses may be the overt manifestation of time used to make decisions about what to say and how to say it, or they may represent disruptions in the speech process.

Taken together, these findings show that vocal cues alone can give much information about a speaker, and our total reaction to another individual is at least somewhat colored by our reactions to these vocal cues. Our perceptions of verbal cues combine with other verbal and nonverbal stimuli to mold conceptions used as a basis for communicating.

QUESTIONS FOR DISCUSSION

1. Consider stereotypes you have about the voice—for example, about high or low voices, fast or slow voices, voices with different accents, and so forth. Discuss what truth you think there is to the stereotypes, based on as many real examples as you can think of.

2. Analyze the phenomenon of sarcasm in terms of the voice as well as the other cues that might be associated with it. Act out a variety of different comments in a sarcastic manner, and specify the cues you use.

3. Review the different methods for making voices free of verbal content by applying content-masking techniques. Why does the chapter argue that doing this does not free the voice of content?

4. Theorists argue that some nonverbal channels are easier than others to self-monitor and control. Compare the vocal channel to the face and body channels. How would you rank these three channels in terms of how easy they are to monitor and control? Why?

5. Spend some time paying special attention to how you use vocal cues to identify a person's characteristics, such as social class, education, sexual orientation, or personality. A good way to do this would be to sit in a public place and listen to people speaking whom you are not looking at. Or, you could listen to the television without looking at it. Analyze the cues you use. Do you have any sense of whether your judgments are correct?

BIBLIOGRAPHY

Aboud, F. E., Clement, R., & Taylor, D. M. (1974). Evaluational reactions to discrepancies between social class and language. *Sociometry, 37,* 239–250.

Addington, D. W. (1968). The relationship of selected vocal characteristics to personality perception. *Speech Monographs, 35,* 492–503.

Allport, G., & Cantril, H. (1934). Judging personality from voice. *Journal of Social Psychology, 5,* 37–54.

Ambady, N., Krabbenhoft, M. A., & Hogan, D. (2006). The 30-sec sale: Using thin-slice judgments to evaluate sales effectiveness. *Journal of Consumer Psychology, 16,* 4–13.

Ambady, N., LaPlante, D., Nguyen, T., Rosenthal, R., Chaumeton, N., & Levinson, W. (2002). Surgeons' tone of voice: A clue to malpractice history. *Surgery, 132,* 5–9.

Anisfeld, M., Bogo, N., & Lambert, W. (1962). Evaluation reactions to accented English speech. *Journal of Abnormal and Social Psychology, 65,* 223–231.

Aries, E. (1987). Gender and communication. In P. Shaver & C. Hendrick (Eds.), *Review of personality and social psychology (Vol. 7).* Newbury Park, CA: Sage.

Banse, R., & Scherer, K. R. (1996). Acoustic profiles in vocal emotion expression. *Journal of Personality and Social Psychology, 70,* 614–636.

Baum, K. M., & Nowicki, S., Jr. (1998). Perception of emotion: Measuring decoding accuracy of adult prosodic cues varying in intensity. *Journal of Nonverbal Behavior, 22,* 89–107.

Beier, E. G., & Zautra, A. (1972). Identification of vocal communication of emotions across culture. (ERIC Document Reproduction Service No. ED 056504).

Berry, D. S. (1991). Accuracy in social perception: Contributions of facial and vocal information. *Journal of Personality and Social Psychology, 61,* 298–307.

Berry, D. S. (1992). Vocal types and stereotypes: Joint effects of vocal attractiveness and vocal maturity on person perception. *Journal of Nonverbal Behavior, 16,* 41–54.

Berry, D. S., Hansen, J. S., Landry-Pester, J. C., & Meier, J. A. (1994). Vocal determinants of first impressions of young children. *Journal of Nonverbal Behavior, 18,* 187–197.

Bloom, K., Moore-Schoenmakers, K., & Masataka, N. (1999). Nasality of infant vocalizations determines gender bias in adult favorability ratings. *Journal of Nonverbal Behavior, 23,* 219–236.

Bloom, K., Zajac, D. J., & Titus, J. (1999). The influence of nasality of voice on sex-stereotyped perceptions. *Journal of Nonverbal Behavior, 23,* 271–281.

Bolt, R., Cooper, F., Davis, E., Jr., Denes, P., Pickett, J., & Stevens, K. (1973). Speaker identification by speech spectrograms. *Journal of the Acoustical Society of America, 54,* 531–537.

Boomer, D. S. (1965). Hesitation and grammatical encoding. *Language and Speech, 8,* 148–158.

Boomer, D. S., & Dittmann, A. T. (1962). Hesitation pauses and juncture pauses in speech. *Language and Speech, 5,* 215–220.

Boomer, D. S., & Dittmann, A. T. (1964). Speech rate, filled pause, and body movements in interviews. *Journal of Nervous and Mental Disease, 139,* 324–327.

Bruneau, T. J. (1973). Communicative silences: Forms and functions. *Journal of Communication, 23,* 17–46.

Buck, J. (1968). The effects of Negro and white dialectical variations upon attitudes of college students. *Speech Monographs, 35,* 181–186.

Bugental, D. E., Kaswan, J. W., & Love, L. R. (1970). Perception of contradictory meanings conveyed by verbal and nonverbal channels. *Journal of Personality and Social Psychology, 16,* 647–655.

Buller, D. B., & Aune, R. K. (1988). The effects of vocalics and nonverbal sensitivity on compliance: A speech accommodation theory explanation. *Human Communication Research, 14,* 301–332.

Buller, D. B., & Burgoon, J. K. (1986). The effects of vocalics and nonverbal sensitivity on compliance: A replication and extension. *Human Communication Research, 13,* 126–144.

Burgoon, J. K., Birk, T., & Pfau, M. (1990). Nonverbal behaviors, persuasion, and credibility. *Human Communication Research, 17,* 140–169.

Caporael, L. R. (1981). The paralanguage of caregiving: Baby talk to the institutionalized aged. *Journal of Personality and Social Psychology, 40,* 876–884.

Cappella, J. N. (1985). Controlling the floor in conversation. In A. W. Siegman & S. Feldstein (Eds.), *Multichannel integrations of nonverbal behavior.* Hillsdale, NJ: Erlbaum.

Chapple, E. D. (1949). The interaction chronograph: Its evolution and present application. *Personnel, 25,* 295–307.

Chapple, E. D. (1953). The standard experimental (stress) interview as used in interaction chronograph investigations. *Human Organizations, 12,* 23–32.

Chapple, E. D., & Sayles, L. R. (1961). *The measure of management.* New York: Macmillan.

Chartrand, T. L., & Bargh, J. A. (1999). The chameleon effect: The perception–behavior link and social interaction. *Journal of Personality and Social Psychology, 76,* 893–910.

Christenfeld, N. (1995). Does it hurt to say um? *Journal of Nonverbal Behavior, 19,* 171–186.

Cook, M. (1965). Anxiety, speech disturbances, and speech rate. *British Journal of Social and Clinical Psychology, 4,* 1–7.

Corsi, P. (1982). Speaker recognition: A survey. In J. P. Haton (Ed.), *Automatic speech analysis and recognition.* Dordrecht, Holland: Reidel.

Crosby, F., & Nyquist, L. (1977). The female register: An empirical study of Lakoff's hypothesis. *Language in Society, 6,* 313–322.

Daigen, V., & Holmes, J. G. (2000). Don't interrupt! A good rule for marriage? *Personal Relationships, 7,* 185–201.

Davitz, J. R. (1964). *The communication of emotional meaning.* New York: McGraw-Hill.

Davitz, J. R., & Davitz, L. (1959). The communication of feelings by content-free speech. *Journal of Communication, 9,* 6–13.

DeGroot, T., & Motowidlo, S. J. (1999). Why visual and vocal interview cues can affect interviewers' judgments and predict job performance. *Journal of Applied Psychology, 84,* 986–993.

DePaulo, B. M., & Coleman, L. M. (1986). Talking to children, foreigners, and retarded adults. *Journal of Personality and Social Psychology, 51,* 945–959.

DePaulo, B. M., & Coleman, L. M. (1987). Verbal and nonverbal communication of warmth to children, foreigners, and retarded adults. *Journal of Nonverbal Behavior, 11,* 75–88.

Dindia, K. (1987). The effects of sex of subject and sex of partner on interruptions. *Human Communication Research, 13,* 345–371.

Dittmann, A. T., & Llewellyn, L. G. (1967). The phonemic clause as a unit of speech decoding. *Journal of Personality and Social Psychology, 6,* 341–349.

Dittmann, A. T., & Llewellyn, L. G. (1969). Body movement and speech rhythm in social conversation. *Journal of Personality and Social Psychology, 11,* 98–106.

Doddington, G. (1985). Speaker recognition: Identifying people by their voices. *Proceedings of the IEEE, 73,* 1651–1664.

Duncan, S. (1972). Some signals and rules for taking speaking turns in conversations. *Journal of Personality and Social Psychology, 23,* 283–292.

Duncan, S. (1973). Toward a grammar for dyadic conversation. *Semiotica, 9,* 24–46.

Duncan, S., & Fiske, D. W. (1977). *Face-to-face interaction.* Hillsdale, NJ: Erlbaum.

Ellgring, H., & Scherer, K. R. (1996). Vocal indicators of mood change in depression. *Journal of Nonverbal Behavior, 20,* 83–110.

Ellis, D. S. (1967). Speech and social status in America. *Social Forces, 45,* 431–451.

Erickson, B., Lind, E. A., Johnson, B. C., & O'Barr, W. M. (1978). Speech style and impression formation in a court setting: The effects of "powerful" and "powerless" speech. *Journal of Nonverbal Behavior, 14,* 266–279.

Farley, S. (2008). Attaining status at the expense of likability: Pilfering power through conversational interruption. *Journal of Nonverbal Behavior, 32,* 241–260.

Fay, P., & Middleton, W. (1940). Judgment of occupation from the voice as transmitted over a public address system. *Sociometry, 3,* 186–191.

Floyd, K., & Ray, G. B. (2003). Human affection exchange: IV. Vocalic predictors of perceived affection in initial interactions. *Western Journal of Communication, 67,* 56–73.

Frick, R. W. (1985). Communicating emotion: The role of prosodic features. *Psychological Bulletin, 97,* 412–429.

Friedman, H. S. (1979). The interactive effects of facial expressions of emotion and verbal messages on perceptions of affective meaning. *Journal of Nonverbal Behavior, 15,* 453–469.

Gates, G. S. (1927). The role of the auditory element in the interpretation of emotions. *Psychological Bulletin, 24,* 175.

Gesn, P. R., & Ickes, W. (1999). The development of meaning contexts for empathic accuracy: Channel and sequence effects. *Journal of Personality and Social Psychology, 77,* 746–761.

Giles, H. (1971). Ethnocentrism and the evaluation of accented speech. *British Journal of Social and Clinical Psychology, 10,* 187–188.

Giles, H., & Bourhis, R. Y. (1976). Voice and racial categorization in Britain. *Communication Monographs, 43,* 108–114.

Giles, H., Henwood, K., Coupland, N., Harriman, J., & Coupland, J. (1992). Language attitudes and cognitive mediation. *Human Communication Research*, *18*, 500–527.

Giles, H., & Powesland, P. F. (1975). *Speech style and social evaluation*. New York: Academic Press.

Gill, M. M. (1994). Accent and stereotypes: Their effect on perceptions of teachers and lecture comprehension. *Journal of Applied Communication Research*, *22*, 348–361.

Glasgow, G. M. (1952). A semantic index of vocal pitch. *Speech Monographs*, *19*, 64–68.

Goldman-Eisler, F. (1961). A comparative study of two hesitation phenomena. *Language and Speech*, *4*, 18–26.

Goldman-Eisler, F. (1968). *Psycholinguistics: Experiments in spontaneous speech*. London & New York: Academic Press.

Grahe, J. E., & Bernieri, F. J. (1999). The importance of nonverbal cues in judging rapport. *Journal of Nonverbal Behavior*, *23*, 253–269.

Greene, J. O., & Ravizza, S. M. (1995). Complexity effects on temporal characteristics of speech. *Human Communication Research*, *21*, 390–421.

Grieser, D. L., & Kuhl, P. K. (1988). Maternal speech to infants in a tonal language: Support for universal prosodic features in motherese. *Developmental Psychology*, *24*, 14–20.

Hall, J. A. (1980). Voice tone and persuasion. *Journal of Personality and Social Psychology*, *38*, 924–934.

Hall, J. A. (1984). *Nonverbal sex differences: Communication accuracy and expressive style*. Baltimore: Johns Hopkins University Press.

Hall, J. A., & Braunwald, K. G. (1981). Gender cues in conversations. *Journal of Personality and Social Psychology*, *40*, 99–110.

Hall, J. A., Coats, E. J., & Smith LeBeau, L. (2005). Nonverbal behavior and the vertical dimension of social relations: A meta-analysis. *Psychological Bulletin*, *131*, 898–924.

Hall, J. A., Roter, D. L., & Katz, N. R. (1987). Task versus socioemotional behaviors in physicians. *Medical Care*, *25*, 399–412.

Hall, J. A., Roter, D. L., & Rand, C. S. (1981). Communication of affect between patient and physician. *Journal of Health and Social Behavior*, *22*, 18–30.

Hall, J. A., & Schmid Mast, M. (2007). Sources of accuracy in the empathic accuracy paradigm. *Emotion*, *7*, 438–446.

Harms, L. S. (1961). Listener judgments of status cues in speech. *Quarterly Journal of Speech*, *47*, 164–168.

Harrigan, J. A., Gramata, J. F., Luck, K. S., & Margolis, C. (1989). It's how you say it: Physicians' vocal behavior. *Social Science & Medicine*, *28*, 87–92.

Harrigan, J. A., Suarez, I., & Hartman, J. S. (1994). Effect of speech errors on observers' judgments of anxious and defensive individuals. *Journal of Research in Personality*, *28*, 505–529.

Harrigan, J. A., Wilson, K., & Rosenthal, R. (2004). Detecting state and trait anxiety from auditory and visual cues: A meta-analysis. *Personality and Social Psychology Bulletin*, *30*, 56–66.

Haskard, K. B., Williams, S. L., DiMatteo, M. R., Heritage, J., & Rosenthal, R. (2008). The provider's voice: Patient satisfaction and the content-filtered speech of nurses and physicians in primary medical care. *Journal of Nonverbal Behavior*, *32*, 1–20.

Hecker, M. H. L. (1971). Speaker recognition: An interpretive survey of the literature. *ASHA Monographs*, *16*. Washington, DC: American Speech and Hearing Association.

Hirschman, L. (1994). Female–male differences in conversational interaction. *Language in Society*, *23*, 427–442.

Hollien, H. (1990). The acoustics of crime: *The new science of forensic phonetics*. New York: Plenum.

Hughes, S. M., Dispenza, F., & Gallup, G. G., Jr. (2004). Ratings of voice attractiveness predict sexual behavior and body configuration. *Evolution and Human Behavior*, *25*, 295–304.

Hughes, S. M., Pastizzo, M. J., & Gallup, G. G., Jr. (2008). The sound of symmetry revisted: Subjective and objective analyses of voice. *Journal of Nonverbal Behavior*, *32*, 93–108.

Hummert, M. L., Mazloff, D., & Henry, C. (1999). Vocal characteristics of older adults and stereotyping. *Journal of Nonverbal Behavior*, *23*, 111–132.

Irish, J. T., & Hall, J. A. (1995). Interruptive patterns in medical visits: The effects of role, status, and gender. *Social Science & Medicine, 41,* 873–881.

Jaworski, A. (1993). *The power of silence: Social and pragmatic perspectives.* Newbury Park, CA: Sage.

Jensen, J. V. (1973). Communicative functions of silence. *ETC, 30,* 249–257.

Juslin, P. N., & Laukka, P. (2003). Communication of emotions in vocal expression and music performance: Different channels, same code? *Psychological Bulletin, 129,* 770–814.

Juslin, P. N., & Scherer, K. R. (2005). Vocal expression of affect. In J. A. Harrigan, R. Rosenthal, & K. R. Scherer (Eds.), *The new handbook of methods in nonverbal behavior research* (pp. 65–135). Oxford, UK: Oxford University Press.

Kappas, A., Hess, U., & Scherer, K. R. (1991). Voice and emotion. In R. S. Feldman & B. Rimé (Eds.), *Fundamentals of nonverbal behavior.* New York: Cambridge University Press.

Kasl, S. V., & Mahl, G. F. (1965). The relationship of disturbances and hesitations in spontaneous speech to anxiety. *Journal of Personality and Social Psychology, 1,* 425–433.

Kerstholt, J. H., Jansen, N. J. M., van Amelsvoort, A. G., & Broeders, A. P. A. (2006). Earwitnesses: Effects of accent, retention and telephone. *Applied Cognitive Psychology, 20,* 187–197.

Kibler, R. J., & Barker, L. L. (1972). Effects of selected levels of misspelling and mispronunciation on comprehension and retention. *Southern Speech Communication Journal, 37,* 361–374.

King, P. E., & Behnke, R. R. (1989). The effect of time-compressed speech on comprehensive, interpretive, and short-term listening. *Human Communication Research, 15,* 428–443.

Kitchen, D. M., Cheney, D. L., & Seyfarth, R. M. (2003). Female baboons' responses to male loud calls. *Ethology, 109,* 401–412.

Klinger, H. N. (1959). *The effects of stuttering on audience listening comprehension.* Unpublished doctoral dissertation, New York University.

Ko, S. J., Judd, C. M., & Blair, I. V. (2006). What the voice reveals: Within- and between-category stereotyping on the basis of voice. *Personality and Social Psychology Bulletin, 32,* 806–819.

Kramer, C. (1978). Female and male perceptions of female and male speech. *Language and Speech, 20,* 151–161.

Kramer, E. (1963). Judgment of personal characteristics and emotions from nonverbal properties. *Psychological Bulletin, 60,* 408–420.

Kramer, E. (1964). Personality stereotypes in voice: A reconsideration of the data. *Journal of Social Psychology, 62,* 247–251.

Krauss, R. M., Freyberg, R., & Morsella, E. (2002). Inferring speakers' physical attributes from their voices. *Journal of Experimental Social Psychology, 38,* 618–625.

Kruger, J., Epley, N., Parker, J., & Ng, Z. (2005). Egocentrism over e-mail: Can we communicate as well as we think? *Journal of Personality and Social Psychology, 89,* 925–936.

Kucharska-Pietura, K., Nilolaou, V., Masiak, M., & Treasure, J. (2004). The recognition of emotion in the faces and voice of anorexia nervosa. *International Journal of Eating Disorders, 35,* 42–47.

Ladefoged, P., & Ladefoged, J. (1980). The ability of listeners to identify voices. *UCLA Working Papers in Phonetics, 49,* 43–51.

Ladefoged, P., & Vanderslice, R. (1967). The voice-print mystique. *UCLA Working Papers in Phonetics, 7.*

Lakoff, R. (1975). *Language and women's place.* New York: Harper & Row.

Lalljee, M. G. (1971). *Disfluencies in normal English speech.* Unpublished doctoral dissertation, Oxford University, Oxford, UK.

Lalljee, M. G., & Cook, M. (1969). An experimental investigation of the filled pauses in speech. *Language and Speech, 12,* 24–28.

Lapakko, D. (1997). Three cheers for language: A closer examination of a widely cited study of nonverbal communication. *Communication Education, 46,* 63–67.

Lass, N. J., & Davis, M. (1976). An investigation of speaker height and weight identification. *Journal of the Acoustical Society of America, 60,* 700–703.

Lass, N. J., & Harvey, L. A. (1976). An investigation of speaker photograph identification. *Journal of the Acoustical Society of America, 59,* 1232–1236.

Lass, N. J., Hughes, K. R., Bowyer, M. D., Waters, L. T., & Broune, V. T. (1976). Speaker sex identification from voiced, whispered and filtered isolated vowels. *Journal of the Acoustical Society of America, 59*, 675–678.

Laukka, P. (2005). Categorical perception of vocal emotion expressions. *Emotion, 5*, 277–295.

Laukka, P., Linnman, C., Åhs, F., et al. (2008). In a nervous voice: Analysis and perception of anxiety in social phobics' speech. *Journal of Nonverbal Behavior, 32*, 195–214.

Leigh, T. W., & Summers, J. O. (2002). An initial evaluation of industrial buyers' impressions of salespersons' nonverbal cues. *Journal of Personal Selling and Sales Management, 22*, 41–53.

Levin, S., Hall, J. A., Knight, R. A., & Alpert, M. (1985). Verbal and nonverbal expression of affect in speech of schizophrenic and depressed patients. *Journal of Abnormal Psychology, 94*, 487–497.

Lippa, R. (1998). The nonverbal display and judgment of extraversion, masculinity, femininity, and gender diagnosticity: A lens model analysis. *Journal of Research in Personality, 32*, 80–107.

Livant, W. P. (1963). Antagonistic functions of verbal pauses: Filled and unfilled pauses in the solution of additions. *Language and Speech, 6*, 1–4.

Mahl, G. F. (1956). Disturbances and silences in the patient's speech in psychotherapy. *Journal of Abnormal and Social Psychology, 53*, 1–15.

Mahl, G. E., & Schulze, G. (1964). Psychological research in the extralinguistic area. In T. Sebeok, A. S. Hayes, & M. C. Bateson (Eds.), *Approaches to semiotics*. The Hague: Mouton.

Marche, T. A., & Peterson, C. (1993). The development and sex-related use of interruption behavior. *Human Communication Research, 19*, 388–408.

Markel, N. N., Meisels, M., & Houck, J. E. (1964). Judging personality from voice quality. *Journal of Abnormal and Social Psychology, 69*, 458–463.

Markel, N. N., Prebor, L. D., & Brandt, J. F. (1972). Biosocial factors in dyadic communication: Sex and speaking intensity. *Journal of Personality and Social Psychology, 23*, 11–13.

Markel, N. N., & Robin, G. L. (1965). The effect of content and sex of judge on judgments of personality from voice. *International Journal of Social Psychiatry, 11*, 295–300.

Marler, P., Evans, C. S., & Hauser, M. D. (1992). Animal signals: Motivational, referential, or both? In H. Papousek, U. Jurgens, & M. Papousek (Eds.), *Nonverbal vocal communication: Comparative and developmental approaches* (pp. 66–86). Paris: Cambridge University Press.

Matarazzo, J. D., Wiens, A. N., & Saslow, G. (1965). Studies in interview speech behavior. In L. Krasner & U. P. Ullman (Eds.), *Research in behavior modification*. New York: Holt, Rinehart & Winston.

McClone, R. E., & Hollien, H. (1963). Vocal pitch characteristics of aged women. *Journal of Speech and Hearing Research, 6*, 164–170.

McGehee, F. (1937). The reliability of the identification of the human voice. *Journal of General Psychology, 17*, 249–271.

Mehrabian, A. (1972a). Nonverbal communication. In J. Cole (Ed.), *Nebraska symposium on motivation 1971*. Lincoln: University of Nebraska Press.

Mehrabian, A. (1972b). *Silent messages*. Belmont, CA: Wadsworth.

Mehrabian, A., & Ferris, S. R. (1967). Inference of attitudes from nonverbal communication in two channels. *Journal of Counseling Psychology, 31*, 248–252.

Mehrabian, A., & Wiener, M. (1967). Decoding of inconsistent communication. *Journal of Personality and Social Psychology, 6*, 109–114.

Mehrabian, A., & Williams, M. (1969). Nonverbal concomitants of perceived and intended persuasiveness. *Journal of Personality and Social Psychology, 13*, 37–58.

Miller, D. T. (1975). The effect of dialect and ethnicity on communicator effectiveness. *Speech Monographs, 42*, 69–74.

Miller, N., Maruyama, G., Beaber, R. J., & Valone, K. (1976). Speed of speech and persuasion. *Journal of Personality and Social Psychology, 34*, 615–624.

Milmoe, S., Rosenthal, R., Blane, H. T., Chafetz, M. E., & Wolf, I. (1967). The doctor's voice: Postdictor of successful referral of alcoholic patients. *Journal of Abnormal Psychology, 72*, 78–84.

Morton, J. B., & Trehub, S. E. (2001). Children's understanding of emotions in speech. *Child Development, 72*, 834–843.

Mulac, A. (1976). Assessment and application of the revised speech dialect attitudinal scale. *Communication Monographs, 43,* 238–245.

Mulac, A., Hanley, T. D., & Prigge, D. Y. (1974). Effects of phonological speech foreignness upon three dimensions of attitude of selected American listeners. *Quarterly Journal of Speech, 60,* 411–420.

Mulac, A., Lundell, T. L., & Bradac, J. J. (1986). Male/female language differences and attributional consequences in a public speaking situation: Toward an explanation of the gender-linked language effect. *Communication Monographs, 53,* 115–129.

Neumann, R., & Strack, F. (2000). "Mood contagion": The automatic transfer of mood between persons. *Journal of Personality and Social Psychology, 79,* 211–223.

Newsweek. (1970, October 5). p. 106.

Nohara, M. (1992). Sex differences in interruption: An experimental reevaluation. *Journal of Psycholinguistic Research, 21,* 127–146.

Orr, D. B. (1968). Time compressed speech—A perspective. *Journal of Communication, 18,* 288–292.

Ostwald, P. F. (1961). The sounds of emotional disturbance. *Archives of General Psychiatry, 5,* 587–592.

O'Sullivan, M., Ekman, P., Friesen, W., & Scherer, K. (1985). What you say and how you say it: The contribution of speech content and voice quality to judgments of others. *Journal of Personality and Social Psychology, 48,* 54–62.

Pear, T. H. (1931). *Voice and personality.* London: Chapman & Hall.

Pittam, J. (1994). *Voice in social interaction: An interdisciplinary approach.* Thousand Oaks, CA: Sage.

Pittam, J., & Scherer, K. S. (1993). Vocal expression and communication of emotion. In M. Lewis & J. M. Haviland (Eds.), *Handbook of emotions.* New York: Guilford.

Poyatos, F. (1993). Paralanguage: *A linguistic and interdisciplinary approach to interactive speech and sound.* Amsterdam, NL: Benjamins.

Reich, A., & Duke, J. (1979). Effects of selected vocal disguises upon speaker identification by listening.

Journal of the Acoustical Society of America, 66, 1023–1028.

Reich, A. R., Moll, K. L., & Curtis, J. F. (1976). Effects of selected vocal disguises upon spectrographic speaker identification. *Journal of the Acoustical Society of America, 60,* 919–925.

Riding, D., Lonsdale, D., & Brown, B. (2006). The effects of average fundamental frequency and variance of fundamental frequency on male vocal attractiveness to women. *Journal of Nonverbal Behavior, 30,* 55–61.

Rochester, S. R. (1973). The significance of pauses in spontaneous speech. *Journal of Psycholinguistic Research, 2,* 51–81.

Rogers, P. L., Scherer, K. R., & Rosenthal, R. (1971). Content filtering human speech: A simple electronic system. *Behavior Research Methods and Instrumentation, 3,* 16–18.

Rosenfeld, H. M. (1987). Conversational control functions of nonverbal behavior. In A. W. Siegman & S. Feldstein (Eds.), *Nonverbal behavior and communication (2nd ed.).* Hillsdale, NJ: Erlbaum.

Rosenthal, R., Hall, J. A., DiMatteo, M. R., Rogers, P. L., & Archer, D. (1979). *Sensitivity to nonverbal communication: The PONS test.* Baltimore: Johns Hopkins University Press.

Rosenthal, R., Vanicelli, M., & Blanck, P. (1984). Speaking to and about patients: Predicting therapists' tone of voice. *Journal of Consulting and Clinical Psychology, 52,* 679–686.

Rutherford, M. D., Baron-Cohen, S., & Wheelwright, S. (2002). Reading the mind in the voice: A study with normal adults and adults with Asperger syndrome and high functioning autism. *Journal of Autism and Developmental Disorders, 32,* 189–194.

Sachs, J., Lieberman, P., & Erickson, D. (1973). Anatomic and cultural determinants of male and female speech. In R. W. Shuy & R. W. Fasold (Eds.), *Language attitudes: Current trends and prospects.* Washington, DC: Georgetown University Press.

Sauter, D. A., & Scott, S. K. (2007). More than one kind of happiness: Can we recognize vocal expressions of different positive states? *Motivation and Emotion, 31,* 192–199.

Schachter, S., Christenfeld, N., Ravina, B., & Bilous, F. (1991). Speech disfluency and the structure of knowledge. *Journal of Personality and Social Psychology, 60,* 362–367.

Schachter, S., Rauscher, F., Christenfeld, N., & Crone, K. T. (1994). The vocabularies of academia. *Psychological Science, 5,* 37–41.

Scherer, K. R. (1971). Randomized splicing: A note on a simple technique for masking speech content. *Journal of Experimental Research in Personality, 5,* 155–159.

Scherer, K. R. (1974). Acoustic concomitants of emotional dimensions: Judging affect from synthesized tone sequences. In S. Weitz (Ed.), *Nonverbal communication: Readings with commentary.* New York: Oxford University Press.

Scherer, K. R. (1979). Personality markers in speech. In K. R. Scherer & H. Giles (Eds.), *Social markers in speech.* London: Cambridge University Press.

Scherer, K. R. (1982). Methods of research on vocal communication: Paradigms and parameters. In K. R. Scherer & P. Ekman (Eds.), *Handbook of methods in nonverbal behavior research.* Cambridge, UK: Cambridge University Press.

Scherer, K. R. (1986). Vocal affect expression: A review and a model for future research. *Psychological Bulletin, 99,* 143–165.

Scherer, K. R. (2003). Vocal communication of emotion: A review of research paradigms. *Speech Communication, 40,* 227–256.

Scherer, K. R., Banse, R., & Wallbott, H. G. (2001). Emotion inferences from vocal expression correlate across languages and cultures. *Journal of Cross-Cultural Psychology, 32,* 76–92.

Scherer, K. R., Banse, R., Wallbott, H. G., & Goldbeck, T. (1991). Vocal cues in emotion encoding and decoding. *Motivation and Emotion, 15,* 123–148.

Scherer, K. R., & Ceschi, G. (2000). Criteria for emotion recognition from verbal and nonverbal expression: Studying baggage loss in the airport. *Personality and Social Psychology Bulletin, 26,* 327–339.

Scherer, K. R., Koivumaki, J., & Rosenthal, R. (1972). Minimal cues in the vocal communication of affect: Judging emotions from content-masked speech. *Journal of Psycholinguistic Research, 1,* 269–285.

Siegman, A. W. (1987). The telltale voice: Nonverbal messages of verbal communication. In A. W. Siegman & S. Feldstein (Eds.), *Nonverbal behavior and communication* (2nd ed.). Hillsdale, NJ: Erlbaum.

Smith, S. M., & Shaffer, D. R. (1991). Celerity and cajolery: Rapid speech may promote or inhibit persuasion through its impact on message elaboration. *Personality and Social Psychology Bulletin, 17,* 663–669.

Snow, C. E., & Ferguson, C. A. (Eds.). (1977). *Talking to children.* Cambridge, UK: Cambridge University Press.

Starkweather, J. A. (1961). Vocal communication of personality and human feelings. *Journal of Communication, 11,* 69.

Street, R. L., Jr. (1990). The communicative functions of paralanguage and prosody. In H. Giles & W. P. Robinson (Eds.), *Handbook of language and social psychology.* Chichester, UK: Wiley.

Street, R. L., Jr., Brady, R. M., & Lee, R. (1984). Evaluative responses to communicators: The effects of speech rate, sex, and interaction context. *Western Journal of Speech Communication, 48,* 14–27.

Thompson, W. F., Schellenberg, E. G., & Husain, G. (2004). Decoding speech prosody: Do music lessons help? *Emotion, 4,* 46–64.

Trager, G. L. (1958). Paralanguage: A first approximation. *Studies in Linguistics, 13,* 1–12.

Trainor, L. J., Austin, C. M., & Desjardins, R. N. (2000). Is infant-directed speech prosody a result of the vocal expression of emotion? *Psychological Science, 11,* 188–195.

Turner, L. H., Dindia, K., & Pearson, J. C. (1995). An investigation of female/male verbal behaviors in same-sex and mixed-sex conversations. *Communication Reports, 8,* 86–96.

Tusing, K. J., & Dillard, J. P. (2000). The sounds of dominance: Vocal precursors of perceived dominance during interpersonal influence. *Human Communication Research, 26,* 148–171.

Utzinger, V. A. (1952). *An experimental study of the effects of verbal fluency upon the listener.*

Unpublished doctoral dissertation, University of Southern California, San Diego.

van Lancker, D., Kreiman, J., & Emmorey, K. (1985). Familiar voice recognition: Patterns and parameters—Recognition of backward voices. *Journal of Phonetics, 13,* 19–38.

Viscovich, N., Borod, J., Pihan, H., Peery, S., Brickman, A. M., Tabert, M., Schmidt, M., & Spielman, J. (2003). Acoustical analysis of posed prosodic expressions: Effects of emotion and sex. *Perceptual and Motor Skills, 96,* 759–771.

Weaver, J. C., & Anderson, R. J. (1973). Voice and personality interrelationships. *Southern Speech Communication Journal, 38,* 262–278.

Weitz, S. (1972). Attitude, voice, and behavior: A repressed affect model of interracial interaction. *Journal of Personality and Social Psychology, 24,* 14–21.

Wiemann, J. M., & Knapp, M. L. (1975). Turn-taking in conversations. *Journal of Communication, 25,* 75–92.

Wilke, W., & Snyder, J. (1941). Attitudes toward American dialects. *Journal of Social Psychology, 14,* 349–362.

Williams, C. E., & Stevens, K. N. (1972). Emotions and speech: Some acoustical correlates. *Journal of the Acoustical Society of America, 52,* 1238–1250.

Williams, F. (1970). The psychological correlates of speech characteristics: On sounding "disadvantaged." *Journal of Speech and Hearing Research, 13,* 472–488.

Woodall, W. G., & Burgoon, J. K. (1983). Talking fast and changing attitudes: A critique and clarification. *Journal of Nonverbal Behavior, 8,* 126–142.

Woolbert, C. (1920). The effects of various modes of public reading. *Journal of Applied Psychology, 4,* 162–185.

Zebrowitz, L. A., Brownlow, S., & Olson, K. (1992). Baby talk to the babyfaced. *Journal of Nonverbal Behavior, 16,* 143–158.

Zuckerman, M., Amidon, M. D., Biship, S. E., & Pomerantz, S. D. (1982). Face and tone of voice in the communication of deception. *Journal of Personality and Social Psychology, 43,* 347–357.

Zuckerman, M., & Driver, R. E. (1989). What sounds beautiful is good: The vocal attractiveness stereotype. *Journal of Nonverbal Behavior, 13,* 67–82.

Zuckerman, M., Hodgins, H., & Miyake, K. (1990). The vocal attractiveness stereotype: Replication and elaboration. *Journal of Nonverbal Behavior, 14,* 97–112.

Zuckerman, M., & Miyake, K. (1993). The attractive voice: What makes it so? *Journal of Nonverbal Behavior, 17,* 119–135.

COMMUNICATING
IMPORTANT MESSAGES

Our book concludes with a discussion of how the various nonverbal signals we have discussed thus far combine as communicators pursue critical and familiar outcomes. Chapter 12 focuses on how nonverbal signals help us effectively communicate such things as intimacy, power, involvement, identity, and deception in daily interaction. Chapter 13 examines nonverbal messages in advertising, politics, education, culture, health care, and technology. Together, these two chapters show the importance of understanding nonverbal behavior to effectively manage life's most important tasks.

Nothing in nature is isolated; nothing is without connection to the whole.
—**Goethe**

USING NONVERBAL BEHAVIOR IN DAILY INTERACTION

Try to imagine yourself telling a high school student how to be a successful college student. Your approach probably would break the process into its component parts: social life, or dating and partying; intellectual life, which might include studying, taking notes, and relating to teachers; organizational life, that is, what campus and social groups to join; financial life, or how to get by with little money; and so on. As informative as your explanations and advice in these separate areas may be, you know they are not enough. You also need to point out how these parts go together to create complex situations; for example, a long-sought date has agreed to go out with you, but the date will cost a lot of money, and it will be the night before a big test.

In the same way, this book is designed to make you more knowledgeable about human interaction and about nonverbal behavior in particular. The preceding chapters focused on individual parts of the total system: eyes, face, gestures, physical appearance, voice, and so forth. In this chapter, we show how these component parts combine to achieve the various communicative outcomes we seek daily.

To fully understand any process, we continually must look at the isolated parts that make up the system and at how they combine to achieve the system's purpose. Throughout this book, we have made occasional references to multi-signal effects—for example, the role of verbal behavior in judgments of physical attractiveness and the close interrelationship of gestures with verbal behavior. Edward T. Hall, who coined the term *proxemics*, currently used to identify the study of distance and space, believed we have to consider 19 different behavioral signals to fully understand proximity in human transactions. In this chapter, we look at how various nonverbal signals help us accomplish the goals of communicating intimacy, communicating status and power, managing the interaction, communicating our identity, and deceiving others. These outcomes, along with expressing emotion and achieving understanding, seem to adequately cover the most critical interaction goals.[1]

COMMUNICATING INTIMACY

Scholars have studied nonverbal signals associated with intimacy from four different perspectives, and we will discuss each of them: the display behaviors associated with romantic courtship, courtship behaviors displayed in nonromantic situations, nonverbal behaviors that signal closeness with strangers and acquaintances, and nonverbal behaviors that signal closeness in more well-established intimate relationships.

COURTSHIP BEHAVIOR

We know that some men and women can exude such messages as "I'm available," "I'm knowledgeable," or "I want you" without saying a word. When the manifestation of these signals does not come naturally, popular books are out there to advise readers on how to do it (Strauss, 2005). These messages can be expressed by the thrust of a person's hips, touch gestures, extra-long eye contact, carefully looking at the other's body, showing excitement and desire in fleeting facial expressions, and gaining close proximity. When subtle enough, these moves will allow both parties to deny that either had committed themselves to a courtship ritual.

Academic research focusing on flirtation behavior between men and women in singles bars, hotel cocktail lounges, and bars in restaurants provides some observational data on the role of nonverbal signals in the courtship process (Grammer, Kruck, Juette, & Fink, 2000; McCormick & Jones, 1989; Moore, 1985; Perper & Weis, 1987). Most of the early signaling seems to be performed by women, and females are the "selectors" who attract attention by displaying subtle nonverbal signals that indicate a readiness for contact. The most frequently observed behaviors are three types of eye gaze: a room-encompassing glance; a short, darting glance at a specific person; and a fixed gaze of at least 3 seconds at a specific other. Other signals include smiling at a specific other person; laughing and giggling in response to

---

[1] These goals have been identified in several sources. See the following: Patterson, M. L. (1983). *Nonverbal behavior: A functional perspective.* New York: Springer-Verlag; Siegman, A. W., & Feldstein, S. (Eds.). (1985). *Multichannel integrations of nonverbal behavior.* Hillsdale, NJ: Erlbaum; Burgoon, J. K., & Hoobler, G. D. (2002) Nonverbal signals. In M. L. Knapp & J. A. Daly (Eds.), *Handbook of interpersonal communication* (pp. 240–299). Thousand Oaks, CA: Sage. The goals of communicating emotion, understanding, and persuasion are not covered in this chapter, because it would duplicate too much material in other chapters. See especially Chapter 9 and Chapter 11 for the expression of emotion; Chapter 3 and Chapter 7 for achieving understanding; and Chapter 11 for persuasion cues. For multisignal treatments of persuasion, see Burgoon, J. K., Birk, T., & Pfau, M. (1990). Nonverbal behaviors, persuasion, and credibility. *Human Communication Research, 17,* 140–169; and Burgoon, J. K. (2002). Nonverbal influence. In J. P. Dillard & M. Pfau (Eds.), *The persuasion handbook: Developments in theory and practice* (pp. 445–473). Thousands Oaks, CA: Sage. Also see: Brinol, P., & Petty. R. E. (2003). Overt head movements and persuasion: A self-validation analysis. *Journal of Personality and Social Psychology, 84,* 1123–1139.

another's comments; tossing one's head, a movement sometimes accompanied by stroking of the hair; grooming, primping, and adjusting clothes; caressing objects, such as keys or a glass; a "solitary dance," that is, keeping time to the music with visible movements; and a wide variety of "accidental" touching of some specific other. Researchers did not specifically examine the type of clothing worn in these studies, nor did they examine the tone of voice used; both are likely to be influential flirtation behaviors. In an effort to determine whether these behaviors were more likely to occur in a context where signaling interest in and attraction to others was expected, the researchers observed the behavior of women and men in snack bars, meetings, and libraries. None of these contexts revealed anything close to the number of flirting behaviors found in bars.

Are there male behaviors that increase a man's chances of being selected by a female in a context like this? A study by Renninger, Wade, and Grammer (2004) found that females gave preferential attention to males whose nonverbal behavior signaled positive intentions—interest shown by glances, openness shown by few closed-body movements—and also displayed their status, shown by maximizing the surrounding space and unreciprocated touching of other males.

Does courtship proceed according to a defined sequence of steps? Several studies suggest it does. Nielsen (1962), citing Birdwhistell, described a "courtship dance" of the American adolescent. Later, Givens (1978) and Perper (1985) described the courtship process in terms of phases. First comes the *approach* phase, in which the two people come into the same general area. The second phase involves *acknowledging* the other's attention and turning toward the other as an invitation to begin talking. Nonverbal behavior during the *interaction* phase involves an increasing amount of fleeting, nonintimate touching and a gradually increasing intensity in gaze. The *sexual arousal* phase consists of more intimate touching, kissing, and other affectionate behaviors; and the *resolution* phase is characterized by copulation. Obviously, either person can short-circuit the process or skip a step in the sequence at any point.

Morris (1971) also believes that heterosexual couples in Western culture go through a sequence of steps similar to the courtship patterns of other animals on their way to sexual intimacy. Notice the predominant nonverbal contact theme:

1. Eye to body
2. Eye to eye
3. Voice to voice
4. Hand to hand
5. Arm to shoulder
6. Arm to waist
7. Mouth to mouth
8. Hand to head
9. Hand to body
10. Mouth to breast
11. Hand to genitals
12. Genitals to genitals and/or mouth to genitals

It should be noted that any of the behaviors identified by Morris can be performed in a more or less intimate way. Mouth-to-mouth kisses, for example, may be performed with little intimacy or with a great deal of it. It should also be noted that gazing, touching, and other nonverbal behavior associated with heterosexual courtship patterns is also an important part of homosexual courtship (Delph, 1978).

QUASI-COURTSHIP BEHAVIOR

Scheflen (1965) identified some behaviors he called "quasi-courtship" behaviors, meaning they could be used during courtship, but they could also be used to communicate affiliative interest of a nonromantic type. Such behaviors may also be designed to invite affirmations of one's sexual appeal or attractiveness. Depending on the context, then, a particular cluster of behaviors could be considered friendly, flirting, or seductive. Misunderstandings associated with such behaviors are at the heart of many cases of sexual harassment and date rape. It is not uncommon, for example, for men to perceive more sexual intent in the friendly behavior of women than women see in the friendly behavior of men (Abbey & Melby, 1986; Egland, Spitzberg, & Zormeier, 1996; Koeppel, Montagne-Miller, O'Hair, & Cody, 1993; Simpson, Gangestad, & Nations, 1996).

Quasi-courtship behavior has some elements of courting, or relating to another for romantic purposes, but these behaviors are qualified by some other co-occurring behavior that says, "This is not courtship even though you see some similarities to that behavior." In some cases, quasi-courtship behaviors are used to build rapport; in some cases, it is a form of play. The overall message is one of affiliation. Scheflen (1965) made sound films of numerous therapeutic encounters, business meetings, and conferences. His content analysis of these films led him to conclude that consistent and patterned quasi-courtship behaviors were exhibited in these settings. He then developed a set of classifications for such behaviors:

- *Courtship readiness* defines a category of behaviors characterized by constant manifestations of high muscle tone, reduced eye bagginess and jowl sag, a lessening of slouch and shoulder hunching, and decreasing belly sag.
- *Preening behavior* is exemplified by such things as stroking the hair, putting on makeup, glancing in the mirror, rearranging clothes in a sketchy fashion, such as leaving buttons open, and adjusting suit coats, tugging at socks, and readjusting tie knots.
- *Positional cues* are reflected in seating arrangements that suggest, "We're not open to interaction with anyone else." Arms, legs, and torsos are arranged to inhibit others from entering conversations.
- *Actions of appeal or invitation* include flirtatious glances, gaze holding, rolling of the pelvis, crossing the legs to expose a thigh, exhibiting the wrists or palms, protruding the breasts, and others.

Others have discussed Scheflen's positional cues in terms of who is excluded and who is included. The positioning of arms and legs in Figure 12-1 clearly suggests, "We're not open to others" (in *a*) and "I'm with you—not him" (in *b*).

a    b

FIGURE 12-1

Positional cues.

LIKING BEHAVIOR, OR IMMEDIACY

In the late 1960s and early 1970s, Mehrabian (1972) conducted a number of experimental studies of what he called *immediacy*, that is, behaviors that indicate greater closeness or liking. His research identified the following cluster of signals that distinguish a positive evaluation of an interaction partner from a negative one:

- More forward lean
- Closer proximity
- More eye gaze
- More openness of arms and body
- More direct body orientation
- More touching
- More postural relaxation
- More positive facial and vocal expressions

A lower frequency of these behaviors, particularly when expected, or the manifestation of opposite behaviors tended to be associated with less intimacy or even disliking. While confirming the behaviors Mehrabian linked to immediacy, Ray and Floyd (2006) also found one form of positive vocal expression, vocal variety, primarily limited to female behavior. Some combinations of Mehrabian's immediacy behaviors also have been found when people are trying to communicate support (Trees, 2000) and politeness (Trees & Manusov, 1998). And as we note in Chapter 13, a teacher's immediacy behaviors with his or her students have been linked to positive student attitudes, toward both the instructor and the course, as well as some measures of student learning (Rodriguez, Plax, & Kearney, 1996).

BEING CLOSE IN CLOSE RELATIONSHIPS

The work by Mehrabian and others provides a useful perspective for understanding how positive and negative evaluations of interaction partners are associated with clusters of nonverbal signals. In theory, the greater the number of signals activated, the more powerful the message. Immediacy cues can instruct us on what signals to exhibit or look for in our culture during initial interactions with people we do not know very well. They do not tell us much about how people whose relationship has a history, such as how friends or lovers communicate intimacy. Close relationships to spouses, for example, cannot be accurately judged by the amount of time spent leaning forward with more direct body orientation, in close proximity with more eye gaze, and so on (Andersen, Guerrero, & Jones, 2006; Guerrero & Floyd, 2006; Manusov, Floyd, & Kerssen-Griep, 1997). Because much of this stereotypical immediacy behavior has happened early in the relationship, and it needs to be displayed only on certain occasions once the relationship is mutually agreed to be an intimate one. There are times in established relationships when it is imperative to communicate closeness with utmost clarity, for example, when the relationship has been threatened. At such times, we are likely to see again the cluster of immediacy signals by the partner or partners who wish to offset any threat to the current level of intimacy. Partners in an established close relationship also use these stereotyped signals of intimacy when they want to communicate the closeness of their intimate relationship to outsiders, who may not understand the subtle and sometimes idiosyncratic ways intimates communicate their intimacy to one another. But most everyone understands close proximity, gazing into one another's eyes, touching, and all the other signals associated with the stereotyped immediacy cluster.

Time is an important limitation of much of the work on nonverbal behavior associated with intimacy, affiliation, or liking. Mehrabian's cluster of immediacy signals is primarily limited to one-time encounters. Ongoing relationships express different levels of intimacy over time, often indicating liking and disliking in quick succession. Clore, Wiggins, and Itkin (1975a, 1975b) realized that the sequencing of immediacy behaviors may have an important influence. They first collected a large number of verbal statements describing nonverbal liking and disliking; these behaviors were limited to a female's actions toward a male. The large number of behavioral descriptions was narrowed by asking people to rate the extent to which the behavior accurately conveyed liking or disliking. Table 12.1 lists the behaviors in order, rated highest and lowest. An actress then portrayed the narrowed list of these behaviors in an interaction with a male, and the interaction was videotaped. To no one's surprise, viewers of the tape felt that "warm" behaviors would elicit greater liking from the male addressee. The interesting aspect of the studies is what happened when viewers were exposed to a combined tape in which the actress's behavior was initially warm but then turned cold, or when her behavior was initially cold but then turned warm. The reactions to these videotapes were compared with responses to videotapes showing totally warm or totally cold portrayals by the actress. People judged that the man on the videotape would be more attracted to the woman who was cold at first and warm later than he would be to the woman who was warm for the entire interaction. Further, people felt the woman whose behavior turned from warm to cold was less attractive to the man than the woman who was cold during the entire interaction. Why? It probably has to do with the extent to which the judges felt the male had responsibility for the female's change in behavior. If the man had a part in turning a cold female warm, they felt he could take credit for the change and, thereby, feel better about the interaction.

Ironically, intimates in established romantic relationships may exhibit quantitatively less nonverbal behavior typically associated with affection and intimacy than they did in forming the relationship. To establish these relationships usually means a

TABLE 12-1 | BEHAVIORS RATED AS WARM AND COLD

Warm Behaviors	Cold Behaviors
Looks into his eyes	Gives a cold stare
Touches his hand	Sneers
Moves toward him	Gives a fake yawn
Smiles frequently	Frowns
Works her eyes from his head to his toes	Moves away from him
Has a happy face	Looks at the ceiling
Smiles with mouth open	Picks her teeth
Grins	Shakes her head negatively
Sits directly facing him	Cleans her fingernails
Nods head affirmatively	Looks away
Puckers her lips	Pouts
Licks her lips	Chain smokes
Raises her eyebrows	Cracks her fingers
Has eyes wide open	Looks around the room
Uses expressive hand gestures while speaking	Picks her hands
Gives fast glances	Plays with her hair's split ends
Stretches	Smells her hair

Source: Adapted from *Journal of Consulting and Clinical Psychology*, 43, p. 493, 1975. Copyright © 1975 by the American Psychological Association. Adapted with permission.

high frequency of hugs, kisses, hand holding, and so forth; to maintain the relationship, though, it is often the quality of the act, not the frequency, that is important. Perceived sincerity, magnitude of the expression, and perfect timing are examples of qualitative factors. A hand held out to our partner at just the right moment after a fight may be the equivalent of 10 hand holdings at an earlier point in the relationship. The frequency of nonverbal acts of intimacy becomes important in established relationships when it is necessary to offset a threat to the relationship.

As intimate relationships develop, nonverbal behavior is also likely to change. To communicate a wider range of emotional states, more facial and vocal blends may occur. Sharply defined territories become more permeable. Conventionally performed nonverbal acts gradually give way to performances unique to the couple. The increasing familiarity with auditory, visual, and olfactory signals creates a condition for greater accuracy and efficiency in communicating, but it may also engender an overconfidence leading to decoding problems. More than acquaintances, intimates rely on a variety of nonverbal signals to communicate the same message. Long-term intimates are also subject to acquiring one another's facial, postural, and gestural styles, making them look more alike over time (Zajonc, Adelmann, Murphy, & Niedenthal, 1987). Intimacy brings with it exposure to more personal nonverbal acts and more talk about them. We would also expect more overt evaluations—that is, approval or disapproval of nonverbal behavior—among intimates than among acquaintances (Knapp, 1983).

In the next section, we discuss how closeness or intimacy is created by the contributions of both parties. Matching, or reciprocity, in established close relationships has the potential to differ from reciprocity among strangers or acquaintances. For example, people in established close relationships may not reciprocate the same *kind* of behavior, only its equivalent. The extent to which the behavior is equivalent to another is negotiated by the relationship partners. Thus almost any behavior can communicate intimacy in established relationships if the partners to the relationship agree that it does. Intimates also may respond either with compensation or reciprocity, but not in the same immediate time frame, which is more likely with nonintimates.

MUTUAL INFLUENCE

Whatever nonverbal behavior is used to communicate liking or disliking is inevitably the result of what both interactants do. This perspective prompted Argyle and Dean to propose *equilibrium theory* in 1965, which maintains that interactants seek an intimacy level comfortable for both of them. Eye gaze, proximity, smiling, and topic intimacy, according to this theory, signal the degree of intimacy. If the nonverbal behavior in one or more of these areas signals an increase or decrease in intimacy, the other interactant compensates by engaging in behaviors necessary to achieve equilibrium. For example, if a mere acquaintance looked at you too much, stood too close, and talked to you about intimate topics, equilibrium theory would predict that you would increase distance, look away, and try to change the topic to something less intimate. Although some attempts to test this theory found support for the predicted compensatory reactions, others found the opposite pattern—reciprocating changes in intimacy rather than offsetting them. This finding led to Patterson's (1976) *arousal-labeling model* of interpersonal intimacy, which maintained that gaze, touch, and proximity with another person creates arousal. This arousal state is then labeled either positive or negative. If it is negative—for example, dislike, embarrassment, or anxiety—the reaction will be to compensate or offset the behavior. If the arousal state is considered positive, as in liking, relief, or love, the reaction will be matching behavior, or reciprocity. Although this theory explained why we sometimes compensate for, and sometimes reciprocate, the behavior of our partner, it requires time-consuming cognitive labeling of behavior. In many encounters, these changes are too quick to involve this kind of mental processing. This consideration prompted Cappella and Greene (1982) to posit a *discrepancy-arousal theory*. This model suggests we all have expectations about other people's expressive behavior. Increases and decreases in involvement by one person that violate the other person's expectations will lead to arousal or cognitive activation. Moderate arousal results from moderate discrepancies from what had been expected; these are pleasurable, and reciprocity ensues. Large discrepancies from what had been expected are highly arousing, leading to negative affective response and compensation. Little or no discrepancy from expectations is not arousing, so we would not expect to see any compensatory or reciprocal adjustments made.

Burgoon (1978) and her colleagues proposed and tested a model specifically focused on one element of immediacy: proximity. Since then, this proximity model of expectancy violation has also been used to study and predict involvement in general (Burgoon & Hale, 1988; LePoire & Burgoon, 1994). This model is an important contribution toward our understanding of reciprocal and compensatory reactions, because it relies on both arousal and cognitive responses, and it explicates the important role of how rewarding the communicator is perceived to be.

Burgoon's *expectancy-violations model* posits that we all develop expectations for appropriate proximity in conversations: from our culture, from our personal experiences, and from our knowledge of specific interactants. When our expectations for proxemic immediacy are met, arousal is not likely to play an important role. When violations occur, too far or too close, arousal is heightened, which directs our attention to the nature of the interpersonal relationship. Interpretations then are made that guide our response. Interpretations vary, according to Burgoon's work, based on the perceptions of whether the violator is rewarding. If the person is rewarding—that is, if they have high credibility, high status, or offer positive feedback—the violation of expectations will be perceived more positively than for nonrewarding interactants.

In an elaboration of the expectancy-violations model, Burgoon and her colleagues proposed *interaction adaptation theory* (Burgoon, Stern, & Dillman, 1995). This theory assumes that each interactant enters into a conversation with requirements, expectations, and desires. Requirements are what we deem absolutely necessary, like being close enough to hear someone. Expectations are what we anticipate happening based on the norms, the people involved, and the situation. Desires are our personal goals and preferences for the interaction. This combination of what is believed to be needed, anticipated, and preferred is called an "interaction position," and it is used as the standard against which our interaction partner's behavior is judged. When our interaction partner's behavior is closely aligned with our interaction position, this theory predicts reciprocity of behavior. Reciprocity is also expected when our partner engages in major deviations that are more positive than our interaction position. However, major deviations by our interaction partner that are more negative than our interaction position are likely to make us respond with compensatory behavior. In one study, romantic partners tended to reciprocate both increases and decreases in immediacy behaviors from their partners (Guerrero, Jones, & Burgoon, 2000). Compensating behavior with romantic partners who manifest decreases in immediacy is most likely when there is a strong desire to change or neutralize the partner's decreased intimacy. Otherwise, there seems to be a natural pull to match it. Keep in mind that interaction is an ongoing, sometimes rapidly changing, process. For example, we may be surprised by a close friend who engages in more immediacy behavior than we anticipated or desired, and we may initially respond with compensatory behavior. But in a split second, our friend observes our reaction, and he or she begins acting more in line with our expectations, preferences, and desires. Then our behavior becomes more reciprocal.

What are we to make of these theories that try to predict when we reciprocate our partner's behavior and when we engage in compensatory behavior? Obviously, a simple bottom-line statement cannot take into account the many subtleties and variations associated with every human transaction, but as a general rule of thumb, we would do well to remember the following: With strangers and acquaintances, we tend to reciprocate or match their nonverbal behavior when it is perceived as generally *congruent* with our expectations and involvement preferences for that person in that situation. We tend to compensate or offset the nonverbal behavior of strangers and acquaintances when it is perceived as a *major violation* of our expectations and preferences for that person in that situation.

COMMUNICATING DOMINANCE AND STATUS

Tired of feeling weak and unimportant? Want to unlock the secrets of those who have gained authority and power? Want to know how to dominate friends, enemies, and business associates, just about anyone, with a few simple tips?

Sorry, but we cannot tell you how to do that. You can find this kind of advice in popular books on nonverbal behavior. Some "tips" from these books include the following: Put the desk between you and the person you wish to dominate. Position yourself physically higher than the other. Sit in a relaxed posture, preferably with your hands behind your head. Take up as much space as possible. Be sparing with your smiles. Press your palms firmly downwards on the table in front of you. Do not use speedy or jerky gestures, and keep your thumbs sticking out when you put your hands in your jacket pockets. Shake hands so your hand is on top of the other person's hand. The list goes on, and though there could be a germ of truth to all of this, as a general principle, you should be very skeptical of such glib advice. We can summarize the research on dominance and nonverbal behavior for you, but there are no pat answers. The desire for a simple how-to manual is great in this area, yet the research is much too complex to allow it.

Even the basic concepts are complicated. The terms *status, dominance*, and *power* are often used interchangeably, but many authors have noted their ambiguities and have offered many, and sometimes contradictory, definitions (Burgoon & Dunbar, 2006; Edinger & Patterson, 1983; Ellyson & Dovidio, 1985; Harper, 1985). The concepts are certainly related, but not perfectly: A figurehead leader has status without power, whereas a low-status member of an organization may wield considerable influence by virtue of personal contacts, shrewd insight, and social interaction skill. Status often connotes a socially valued quality that people carry with them into different situations, whereas power and dominance are more likely to be situationally defined. But dominance can also be seen as a personality trait, such as with a domineering person, in addition to a situational condition. Some researchers would say that any kind of aggressive act is dominant, but for others a behavior is dominant only if it is followed by clear evidence of submission from another individual. In research, many operational definitions have been used to represent these various concepts. The following are some illustrations of different contexts in which dominance may be considered:

- Status: attire, occupation, education, military rank, socioeconomic status, role
- Primacy: initiation of contacts, children's attempts to gain precedence in play, giving orders, boasts, not submitting to others, controlling others' behaviors, attacks
- Power: control of resources, expertise, experience, autonomy

Other issues complicate this discussion, and these must be considered before going further. One issue is whether nonverbal behaviors used to try to attain dominance or status may be different from those used by someone who has already achieved this goal (Argyle, 1988; Heslin & Patterson, 1982). Thus, acquiring and expressing dominance may not involve the same cues. Recognition of this possibility may help us sort out contradictory results. For example, research finds that more gazing is perceived as dominant, and people with more dominant personalities, people who initiate speech more in groups, and people who attain higher status in groups are also less likely to be the first to break a mutual gaze in face-to-face interaction (Dovidio & Ellyson, 1985; Kleinke, 1986; Lamb, 1981; Rosa & Mazur, 1979; Snyder & Sutker, 1977; Thayer, 1969). Many authors have noted that gaze can carry connotations of threat and coercion, and it is often assumed that higher levels of gazing are a hallmark of a dominant, powerful, or high-status individual.

We might think everything adds up—higher status people gaze more—until we also read that people with dependent personalities tend to gaze more; that people who are gazed at can feel less dominant; and that people made to feel dependent gaze longer at an experimenter (Kleinke, 1986; Mehrabian, 1972; Nevill, 1974; Thayer, 1969). These apparent contradictions may be reconciled if we consider that a person of high status or dominance may feel either secure or defensive, and a person of lower status or dominance may be struggling to gain status or may be signaling to more powerful others that he or she is no threat to that powerful other. Nonverbal behaviors, such as gaze, that people use in these different states could differ radically. For example, the person who feels out of control but is striving to gain control might engage in high levels of gaze, whereas the person who accepts a low-status role might avert his or her eyes so as not to appear threatening. Gaze, touch, and most other nonverbal behaviors take their meanings in a complex way from the situation and other co-occurring nonverbal behaviors.

Another important issue to consider in a discussion of dominance is the difference between the impression made by a particular nonverbal behavior and the actual behavior of people having different degrees of dominance, power, or status. Here are two examples: A nonsmiling face is sometimes perceived as dominant (Keating, 1985), and seeing someone touch another raises the viewer's perception of the toucher's dominance (Major & Heslin, 1982). But these findings do not necessarily mean that dominant or high-status people *actually* smile less and touch more. The evidence is mixed for both, with no overall trends either way (Hall, 1996; Hall, Coats, & Smith LeBeau, 2005; Hall & Friedman, 1999; Johnson, 1994).

In general, people have well-developed beliefs about how nonverbal behavior related to dominance, status, or power—all of which we will refer to as "dominance." Carney, Hall, and Smith LeBeau (2005) asked college students to imagine interactions among people with differing degrees of dominance, including those with either more or less dominant personalities and those with either more or less status in the workplace. A large number of beliefs were expressed by the students. The more dominant person was believed to engage in more "invasive" behaviors, to glare and gaze more, interrupt more, stand at a close distance, touch the other more, and touch themselves less, show emotions successfully, stand more erect, and pay less attention to the other person, among many other perceived dominance behaviors. Another way to examine people's beliefs is to show them nonverbal behavior—on videotape, for example—and ask them to rate how dominant the individuals seem to them. Many studies have done this, as reviewed by Hall et al. (2005). In general, the behaviors that are rated as more dominant concur with those expressed more explicitly in the Carney study.

However, for studies that related the expressors' actual degree of dominance to their nonverbal behavior, many fewer relations were found on average (Hall et al.,

2005). High actual dominance was associated with more facial expressiveness, more bodily openness, smaller interpersonal distances, better posed expression skill, less vocal variability, louder voices, more interruptions, fewer back-channel responses, fewer filled pauses, and a more relaxed-sounding voice. But many other behaviors, which are generally believed to be related to dominance, were not observed. However, as indicated above, studies vary greatly in how nonverbal behavior is related to dominance and power, sometimes showing diametrically opposed effects. This strongly suggests that the reality of dominance is complex in interesting ways.

This complex reality may have something to do with the fact that high and low dominance can have many different emotions and motives associated with it. Considering this, it may not make much sense to seek nonverbal cues that are consistently correlated with a person's dominance. For example, a person low in dominance who is feeling hostile would smile a very different amount from a low-dominant person who is feeling the need to please another person. Also the nonverbal behaviors themselves can have ambiguous meanings, and therefore it is risky to label a particular behavior as being intrinsically, or always, dominant or nondominant. For instance, although interrupting others in conversation can be a dominant behavior (Henley, 1977; Kollock, Blumstein, & Schwartz, 1985; Leffler, Gillespie, & Conaty, 1982; Robinson & Reis, 1989), we should not take this interpretation for granted. Interruption is sometimes indicative of a highly involved and participatory conversation and is not necessarily a sign of a power struggle in progress (Dindia, 1987; Kennedy & Camden, 1983).

One behavior that has consistently been associated with dominance is the visual dominance ratio (Ellyson, Dovidio, & Fehr, 1981; Exline, Ellyson, & Long, 1975). Experiments that defined status, power, and dominance in different ways found that among white college students, the higher status person gazes roughly the same percentage of the time while listening and speaking, whereas the lower status person gazes relatively more while listening. When a male and a female interact, and one is made to be the expert or is accorded higher status, that individual, regardless of sex, will engage in the visual dominance pattern. Although subtle, the visual dominance ratio does not go unnoticed. When subjects were asked to judge the relative power or potency of individuals engaging in different amounts of eye gaze, they gave higher ratings to individuals engaging in relatively more looking while speaking than to those engaging in relatively more looking while listening.

How much a person talks when in a group is also a very consistent and rather strong indicator of status or dominance, both in terms of observers' perceptions and in terms of actual status or dominance (Schmid Mast, 2002). However, even here there are exceptions. In an interview situation, the interviewee (lower power) is likely to talk more than the interviewer (higher power). And in extant groups, sometimes a person with well-established status or power can afford to sit back and say very little, knowing that others will attend fully whenever he or she chooses to speak.

Murphy, Driscoll, and Kelly (1999) connected nonverbal dominance to the likelihood that college males would engage in sexual harassment. These authors found that males who scored higher on a scale that had previously been shown to predict sexual harassment engaged in several behaviors that the authors predicted would show dominance: more open body postures, more direct eye contact, and less direct body orientation. However, nonverbal behaviors that might be construed as sexual—smiling, head tilting, and flirtatious glances—were not predicted by the scale, leading the authors to conclude that sexual harassment is more dominance related than sexuality related.

The relations of nonverbal behavior to dominance have been helpfully summarized by Burgoon and Dunbar (2006) in three major categories: effects of physical potency and energy (size and strength, expressivity), resource control (command of space, spatial precedence—who goes first), and interaction control (centrality, physical elevation, initiation, and nonreciprocation). Many findings from the literature, including many more not mentioned here, fit within this framework. However, one must remember that the relation of nonverbal communication to dominance is complex and does not lend itself to simple, formulaic approaches. Perhaps this is fortunate, in that it would be troubling if it were truly easy to dominate others through nonverbal behavior.

MANAGING THE INTERACTION

Most of the time, we do not engage in much conscious thinking about how to greet people, request a speaking turn, show our conversational partner we believe what he or she was saying, or say good-bye. We do these things to structure the interaction—to regulate the processes of coming together, the back-and-forth nature of speaking and listening, and departure. As we note later, however, these acts are also rich in content. When such acts are the subject of conscious reflection, we appreciate the importance of the messages involved.

GREETING BEHAVIOR

Greetings perform a regulatory function by signaling the beginning of an interaction. Greetings also do much more: They convey information about the relationship, reduce uncertainties, signal ways to better know the other, and structure the ensuing dialogue. Some greeting behavior follows certain conventions, like the handshake, but greetings take many forms. This was not true, however, in Germany in the 1930s, when the "Hitler salute" was imposed on the German people. This form of greeting was designed to signal one thing above all else—the greeter's willingness to follow the Nazi party's rules. It was the expected greeting in everyday administrative, commercial, political, and social situations, and it was taught to children at an early age (See Figure 12-2). The salute was a salute to Hitler, so it played no role in establishing a connection between the interacting parties. Allert (2008) argues convincingly that it wounded the sociability and connectedness among Germans of that era.

Without the imposition of any particular convention like the Hitler salute, verbal and nonverbal behavior during greetings may signal status differences, such as those between a subordinate and supervisor; degree of intimacy, as between acquaintance and lover; or it may signal a current feeling or attitude, such as aversion or interest. An emotionally charged greeting may reflect our desired involvement with the other person, or it may reflect a long absence of contact. Goffman (1971) proposed an "attenuation rule," which states that the expansiveness of a greeting with a particular person will gradually subside with continual contact

FIGURE 12-2

Children performing the Nazi salute.

with that person, for example, a co-worker at an office. Kendon and Ferber (1973) found the following six stages that characterized greetings initiated from a distance.

1. *Sighting, Orientation, and Initiation of the Approach.* A greeting, like any other transaction, requires participation by both interactants. Sometimes both will agree that acknowledgment is enough. After mutual recognition, an immediate and sustained withdrawal of attention occurs. Goffman (1963) called this common action "civil inattention." When the greeting continues, we move to stage 2.

2. *The Distant Salutation.* This is the "official ratification" that a greeting sequence has been initiated and who the participants are. A wave, smile, or call may be used for recognition. Two types of head movements were noted at this point: One, the head toss, is a fairly rapid back-and-forward tilting motion. In the other, the person tended to lower the head, hold it for a while, and then slowly raise it.

3. *The Head Dip.* Researchers have noted this movement in other contexts as a marker for transitions between activities or shifts in psychological orientation. Interestingly, this movement was not observed by Kendon and Ferber if the greeter did not continue to approach his or her partner.

4. *Approach.* As the greeting parties continued to move toward each other, several behaviors were observed. Gazing behavior probably helped signal that the participants were cleared for talking. An aversion of this gaze was seen just prior to the close salutation stage, however. Grooming behavior and one or both arms moved in front of the body were also observed at this point.

5. *Final Approach.* Participants at this stage are less than 10 feet from each other. Mutual gazing, smiling, and a positioning of the head not seen in the sequence

thus far are now seen. The palms of the hands may also be turned toward the other person.

6. *Close Salutation.* As the participants negotiate a standing position, we hear the more stereotyped, ritualistic verbalizations so characteristic of the greeting ceremony: "Hey, Steve! How ya doin'?" and so on. If the situation calls for body contact—handshakes, embraces, and the like—these will occur at this time. Even though the handshake is very common in the United States, this kind of greeting behavior is not shared in some other cultures.

The specific nature of greetings varies according to the relationship of the communicators, the setting, and the attendant verbal behavior. Our major concern here is with the nonverbal behavior. The greetings observed by Krivonos and Knapp (1975) were frequently initiated by a vertical or sideways motion of the head accompanied by eye gaze. Smiles, regardless of the degree of acquaintanceship, were also common. Perhaps the smile serves the function of setting a positive, friendly initial mood. Eye gaze signals that the communication channels are open and that an obligation to communicate exists. Other eye-related greeting behaviors included winks and the eyebrow flash (discussed in Chapter 2). The hands are often active in the greeting process with salutes, waves, handshakes (Schiffrin, 1974), handslaps, and various emblematic gestures such as the peace sign, the raised fist, or the thumbs-up gesture. Hands used in greetings have traditionally been open, but in recent years, the "fist bump" has been used by some in the United States. When fists lightly touch each other in greeting, the greeters are signaling friendliness by showing that a potentially threatening gesture is being used in a nonthreatening way. Hands also may be engaged in grooming, such as running fingers through the hair. Touching may take the form of embraces, kisses, or hitting on the hands or arm. The mouth may smile or assume an oval shape, suggesting a possible readiness for talk.

TURN-TAKING BEHAVIOR

Conversations begin and are eventually terminated. Between these two points, however, it is necessary to exchange speaking and listening roles, that is, to take turns. Without much awareness of what we are doing, we use body movements, vocalizations, and some verbal behavior that often seem to accomplish this turn taking with surprising efficiency. The act of smoothly exchanging speaking and listening turns is an extension of our discussion of interaction synchrony in Chapter 7 . And, because a number of the turn-taking cues are visual, it is understandable that we might have a harder time synchronizing our exchanges during telephone and intercom conversations.

Turn-taking behavior is not just an interesting curiosity of human behavior. We seem to base important judgments about others on how the turns are allocated and how smoothly exchanges are accomplished. Effective turn taking may elicit the perception that you and your partner "really hit it off," or that your partner is a very competent communicator; ineffective turn taking may prompt evaluations of "rude" (too many interruptions), "dominating" (not enough turn yielding), or "frustrating" (the inability to discern turn-taking cues).

The turn-taking behaviors we are about to outline have generally been derived from analyses of adult, white, and middle- and upper-class interactants. Some of these behaviors and behavior sequences may not apply to other groups. Blacks, for example, seem to gaze less than whites during interaction (Halberstadt, 1985). Other groups may develop speaking patterns with more unfilled pauses, which may communicate turn yielding to those unfamiliar with the group norm. Children who are learning turn-taking rules engage in behaviors we rarely see in adults, such as tugging at their parent's clothing and hand raising to request a speaking turn.

Speakers and listeners negotiate behaviors associated with turn taking, but speakers typically take the most responsibility for signaling two turn-taking behaviors: *turn yielding* and *turn maintaining*. Listeners typically take the most responsibility for two other types of turn-taking behaviors: *turn requesting* and *turn denying*. The behaviors associated with these acts are derived from careful analyses of both audio and visual elements enacted at junctures where interactants exchange or maintain the speaking turn (Duncan, 1975; Duncan & Fiske, 1977; Wiemann & Knapp, 1975; Wilson, Wiemann, & Zimmerman, 1984). Any individual behavior associated with speaker or listener intentions will contribute toward a smooth turn exchange; but the greater the number of signals, the greater the chances for a smooth exchange. Note, however, that a familiarity with the rules of interaction is also an important part of effective turn taking. For example, before any specific turn-taking behaviors are observed, most people enter conversations knowing that speaking roles will generally alternate in an A–B–A–B sequence, and that when one person finishes speaking, the other is generally obligated to take the conversational "ball." Cultures with different conversational rules and specialized systems of communication, such as sign language, require somewhat different turn-exchange processes, although congenitally blind and adventitiously blind communicators also display a range of vocal and bodily behaviors associated with conversational turn taking (Magnusson, 2006).

TURN YIELDING   To yield in conversation literally means you are giving up your turn and you expect the other person to start talking. As noted in Chapter 7, the termination of one's utterance can be communicated with kinesic markers (see Figure 7-14) that rise or fall with the speaker's pitch level. Questions are clearly an indication that a speaker is yielding his or her turn and expects the partner to respond. If it is a rhetorical question the speaker plans to answer, we probably will see some turn-maintaining cues; but if the listener is eager to get into the conversation, he or she may attempt to answer even a rhetorical question. Vocally, we also can indicate the end of our utterance by a decreased loudness, a slowed tempo, a drawl on the last syllable, or an utterance trailer such as "you know," "or something," or "but, uh." Naturally, an extended, unfilled pause also is used to signal turn yielding. More often than not, however, the silence becomes awkward, and the speaker adds a trailer onto the utterance. Body movements that have been accompanying the speech may also be terminated; for example, illustrative gestures come to rest, and body tenseness becomes relaxed. Gazing at the other person will also help signal the end of an utterance. If the listener does not perceive these yielding cues, and gives no turn-denying cues, the speaker may try to convey more explicit cues, such as touching the other, raising and holding the eyebrows in expectation, or saying something like "Well?"

TURN MAINTAINING If, for some reason, the speaker does not want to yield a speaking turn, we are likely to see several behaviors. Voice loudness probably will increase as turn-requesting signals are perceived in the listener. Gestures probably will not come to rest at the end of the verbal utterances, creating a gestural equivalent to the filled pause. Filled pauses probably will increase while the frequency and duration of silent pauses decrease. This minimizes the opportunities for the other person to start speaking without interrupting or to start speaking simultaneously. Sometimes we see a light touching of the other person by the speaker, which seems to say, "Hold on a little bit longer. I want to make a few more points and then you can talk." This touching is sometimes accompanied by a patting motion, as if to soothe the impatient listener. In some respects, this touch has the effect of the speaker putting his or her hand over the mouth of the would-be speaker—an act not allowed in interpersonal etiquette in our society.

TURN REQUESTING When we do not have the floor and we want to talk, we may exhibit one or more of several behaviors. An upraised index finger seems to symbolize an instrument for creating a conversational hole in the speaker's stream of words, but it also approximates a familiar, formal turn-requesting signal learned in school—a raised hand. Sometimes this upraised index finger is accompanied by an audible inspiration of breath and a straightening and tightening of posture, signaling the imminence of speech. In some cases, certain self-adaptors classified as preening behavior also may signal preparation for a new role. The very act of simultaneous talking—that is, an extended interruption—will convey your request for a speaking turn; but to make sure that request is granted, you have to speak louder than your partner, begin gesturing, and look away as if the turn were now yours. When the speaker and listener are well synchronized, the listener will anticipate the speaker's juncture for yielding and will prepare accordingly by getting the rhythm before the other person has stopped talking, much like a musician tapping his or her foot preceding a solo performance. If the requestor's rhythm does not fit the speaker's rhythm, we might observe some stutter starts—for example, "I ... I ... I was ... ." Sometimes the turn-requesting mechanism consists of efforts to speed up the speaker, realizing that the sooner one speaker has his or her say, the sooner the requestor will get his or hers. This same behavior was noted when people were anxious to terminate a conversation (Knapp, Hart, Friedrich, & Shulman, 1973). The most common method for encouraging a speaker to finish quickly is the use of rapid head nods, often accompanied by verbalizations of pseudo agreement such as "yeah," "mmm-hmm," and so forth. The requestor hopes the speaker will perceive that these comments are being given much too often, and do not follow ideas expressed logically enough, to be genuine signs of reinforcement.

TURN DENYING Sometimes we receive turn-yielding cues from the speaker, but we do not want to talk. At such times, we probably maintain a relaxed listening pose, maintain silence, or gaze intently at something in the surrounding environment. More often, we exhibit behavior that shows our continuing involvement in the content of the speaker's words but denies we are seeking a turn. This might take the form of smiling, nodding, or shaking the head; completing a sentence started by the speaker; briefly restating what the speaker just said; briefly requesting clarification of the speaker's remarks; or showing approval by appropriately placed "mmm-hmm's," "yeah's," or other noises such as the "clicking" sound that suggests "You shouldn't have said that."

The preceding repertoire of turn-taking behaviors is accurate as far as it goes, but it can be more complicated. As we noted earlier, the exchange of turns in conversation is a jointly negotiated process and not merely the display of one or more signals associated with yielding, maintaining, requesting, or denying. Sometimes, it is hard to tell who is playing the speaker role and who is playing the listener. For example, before a listener displays any requesting behavior, a speaker may provide signals that essentially project the completion of his or her turn, thereby acknowledging a request before it has occurred. Sometimes a listener uses gestures that simultaneously signal the desire for a turn, project the type of talk to ensue, and avoid disrupting the speaker's turn.

Many of the actions listeners perform during a speaker's turn are called *back-channel feedback* (Duncan, 1974; Rosenfeld, 1987; Rosenfeld & Hancks, 1980). These listener responses help regulate the flow of information and signal the energy expended in the decoding process. Listener responses can affect the type and amount of information given by the speaker, the length of his or her turn, the clarity of the speaker's content, and the extent to which the speaker communicates in a qualified or specific manner. At key points in the telling of a story, a speaker will look into the face of his or her listener—an act that is likely to produce a back-channel response such as a nod, an "mmm-hmm," or the like from the listener (Bavelas, Coates, & Johnson, 2002). Back-channel responses by the listener normally occur at the juncture of phonemic clauses by the speaker. The primary nonverbal signals are head nods, but postural changes, smiles, frowns, eyebrow flashes, and laughter (Vettin & Todt, 2004) also occur. Common verbal and vocal back-channel signals include saying "yeah," "mmm-hmm," repeating the speaker's words, asking a clarifying question, or completing a sentence for the speaker. Sometimes the listener provides these signals prior to the phonemic clause juncture, which may indicate he or she is "ahead" of the speaker. When such signals are "late," it is acknowledgment of what is being said but may also indicate a lack of full understanding. Once again, though, back-channel cues only affect the speaker if he or she is both motivated to attend to them and motivated to act on the feedback given.

LEAVE-TAKING BEHAVIOR

Having managed our way through the conversation thus far, it is now time to terminate it. Leave taking seems to serve three valuable functions in daily interaction (Knapp et al., 1973). The primary regulatory function is signaling the end of the interaction; that is, immediate physical and/or vocal contact soon will be terminated. Again, specific nonverbal manifestations of these functions vary with the relationship between the communicators, preceding dialogue, anticipated time of separation, body position—that is, whether the communicators are standing or sitting—and other factors. Decreasing eye gaze and positioning one's body toward the nearest exit were the two most frequent nonverbal behaviors observed in this study, and these seem to adequately signal impending absence. Leave-taking rituals may also summarize the substance of the discourse. This is usually accomplished verbally, but a good-night kiss may sufficiently capture the evening's pleasantries to qualify as a summarizer. Finally, departures tend to signal supportiveness, which can offset any negativity that might arise from encounter-termination signals, while simultaneously setting a positive mood for the next encounter—that is, it sends the message: "Our conversation has ended, but our relationship has not." Nonverbal supportiveness may be found in a smile, a hand-shake, touch, head nodding, and leaning forward. Because signaling supportiveness seems so important, we often use the more direct verbal signals, for example, "Thanks for your time. I'm glad we got a chance to talk."

Head nodding and leaning forward, of course, serve several simultaneous functions. Rapid head nodding toward the end of a conversation reinforces what the speaker is saying, but it is a rather empty reinforcement, because it also signals a desire to terminate the conversation. After all, if there is no apparent disagreement or lack of understanding, the speaker will feel no need to expand on his or her remarks. And although it is true that people accompany their feelings of liking by sometimes leaning toward another person, it is also necessary to lean forward to stand up in order to exit. So, like words, movements have multiple meanings and serve several functions.

Other nonverbal leave-taking behaviors include looking at a watch; placing the hands on the thighs for leverage in getting up, which also signals the other person that such a "catapult" is imminent; gathering possessions together in an orderly fashion; and accenting the departure ritual with nonvocal sounds, such as slapping the thighs when rising, stomping the floor with the feet when rising, or tapping a desk or wall with the knuckles or palm. Finally, researchers noticed that nearly all the nonverbal variables studied tended to increase in frequency during the last minute of interaction, with a peak during the 15 seconds just prior to standing. This increasing activity in at least 10 body areas just prior to the termination of an interaction may suggest why we are so frustrated when our partings "fail," that is, when our partner calls us back with "Oh, just one more thing ...." It means we have to go through the entire process of leave taking all over again!

COMMUNICATING OUR IDENTITY

The evening news shows a group of men entering a building. The narrator tells us that a fugitive sought in several states has been apprehended by the FBI. But did we need to be told? Even without the narrative, we can tell a great deal about the people and what is going on. The bearing and demeanor of some of the men have "federal agent" written all over them. They are likely to be large and burly and to wear their hair conservatively short and keep their faces closely shaved; sunglasses might be worn, and the attire is undistinguished but is likely to be a plain, dark business suit. They do not smile—indeed, they look completely humorless, erect, and controlling. And what of the suspected criminal? His posture is likely to be slumped, head bowed, the face wearing a dismal expression, with eyes averted from the camera.

You can imagine variations of this scene. The agents might be seedily dressed undercover agents or uniformed police officers; the suspect might look angry or defiant, and so forth. But we would still be able to figure out who is who, because appearance and behavior reveal significant information about people's identities—either who they are, or in many cases, who they would like to be. Identity includes social attributes, personalities, and those attitudes and roles people regard as self-defining. Thus, being a police officer is a role likely to be deeply connected to a person's self-definition, and portraying that identity appropriately is likely to be important to the person who identifies with that role. Being an arrested suspect is a more fleeting role but could be integral to the self-concept in the case of a career criminal. Sometimes it is hard to tell when behavior reflects transient emotions and roles or is part of a more enduring and deeply felt identity portrayal. A suspect's slumped or defiant posture could be either.

People have a great need to convey their identities. In previous chapters, we talked about ways in which aspects of identity such as age, occupation, culture, and personality are expressed in dress and in nonverbal behaviors. The communication of identity is, in part, self-validating: We confirm for ourselves our sense of who we are. We also show our identities for the benefit of others—both those in our group, to build solidarity and signal belonging, and those not in our group, to emphasize that they are not one of us. Michael Argyle has suggested that people want to know about others' social attributes partly to help maintain the belief that the world is a predictable place. Clues to another's identity also help us decide how to act toward that person. But direct, concrete evidence of others' identities is sometimes hard to come by, so people rely on cues and gestures (Argyle, 1988). In the case of social class, for example, a person's way of dressing tells a great deal, as do other accoutrements such as pens, briefcases, hairstyles, makeup, and jewelry. Sometimes people orchestrate these aspects of their material selves to present an "improved" version of the self in the hope of winning acceptance or approval.

Despite the efforts people make to project an image of themselves that is more socially desirable than the reality, a person's personality can still be judged with surprising accuracy from their projections. For example, Gosling and colleagues found that the looks and contents of dorm rooms and offices could provide surprisingly good clues to a person's personality (Gosling, Ko, Mannarelli, & Morris, 2002). Though some of this effect may result from a direct impact of personality on how one decorates and maintains one's environment—for example, the person low in the trait of conscientiousness may keep a sloppy room—surely a substantial portion of this effect results from deliberate efforts at self-presentation, a personal statement that says, "This is who I am."

PERSONAL IDENTITY

The concept of identity can be construed at both the personal and social levels. Personal identity consists of a unique configuration of characteristics—personality, attitudes, tastes, values, and features—that the individual perceives as personally defining. Nonverbal styles of expression can also be so distinctive that they become an aspect of identity. Davis and Dulicai (1992) provided an analysis of Adolf Hitler's movements and gestural mannerisms during public appearances. Some of Hitler's movements included finger wagging (the "scolding Dutch uncle"), forward stabs, pounding, slicing, crushing fists, and snapping punches, all of which are performed with extreme control and inward stress. Davis and Dulicai summarize the uniqueness of Hitler's movement style as follows:

> Hitler's movement is very difficult to imitate. In seminars with people who are sophisticated about movement analysis and performance such as dancers and dance therapists, most cannot even approximate the ways in which he controls the action ... and sustains such a violent intensity throughout a series of batons (pointing getures). Those who come close want to stop. It is tortured, painful, relentless, and unyielding motion. To move this way is to be at war with one's body and it is notable that, for all of the aggression that Hitler's oratory displays, it is this war with himself that stands out. (p. 161)

Personality is one of the ways we define personal identity, and personality is fairly consistent across situations and time. In many chapters of this book, we have described nonverbal behaviors displayed by people with various personality traits. Extraversion, for example, has a number of nonverbal correlates, such as faster and louder speech.

An important question is how beliefs about behavior-trait associations differ from the actual associations. People may have beliefs that are not substantiated when observational research is done. A useful way of conceptualizing this question is the "lens model," which we have mentioned in other chapters. As shown in Figure 12-3, the lens model encompasses the relation of both perceived and actual behavior to a criterion, such as a personality trait, as well as the relation between the perceived and actual trait—that is, the degree to which observers can judge which targets have the trait in question.

Table 12-2 summarizes the lens-model results of Gifford's (1994) study of 60 undergraduates videotaped in conversation. Over 20 nonverbal behaviors were coded from these tapes and then related both to the participants' self-descriptions of personality and the impressions of personality made by observers who watched the tapes with the sound turned off. Table 12-2 shows that for the trait "ambitious–dominant," there were associations between nonverbal behaviors and the personality

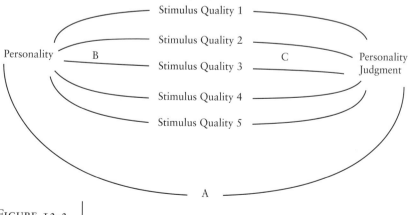

FIGURE 12-3

A diagram of a judgment lens model of social perception.

TABLE 12-2 | PERCEIVED AND ACTUAL CORRELATES OF AMBITION–DOMINANCE

Correlated with Perceived Trait Only	Correlated with Both Perceived Trait and Actual Trait	Correlated with Actual Trait Only
Head, trunk, and legs more directly facing another	More gestures	More leg lean
Head more tilted back	Legs more extended	Less object manipulation
Arms less wrapped		
More self-touching		
More headshaking		

Source: Adapted from R. Gifford (1994) *Journal of Personality and Social Psychology*, 66, p. 401.

ratings made by observers. However, actual ambition–dominance—that is, the self-ratings by those who appeared on the tapes—related to fewer behaviors, only two of which appeared on the list of behaviors correlated with observers' ratings. This suggests that observers, who were also college students, had a correct naive theory as far as these two cues were concerned but held misconceptions for all the others shown on the other side of the table; in other words, they thought that the more ambitious–dominant people would display these cues, but they were wrong The observers did, however, extract enough information to form a significantly accurate overall impression of the targets' ambition–dominance; possibly, they based their impression on additional cues that were not measured, as well as the two they used correctly. Other lens-model studies relating a wide array of nonverbal cues to perceived and actual personality traits have been done by Berry and Hansen (2000), Borkenau and Liebler (1995), Lippa (1998), and Murphy, Hall, and Colvin (2003).

Another characteristic central to our identity is our sense of how intelligent we are. There can be no doubt that intelligence, and the perception thereof, is a thing of abiding importance to people in modern society. All of us have at some point, and perhaps often, worried about how we compare to others in intelligence and in other characteristics that are related, or perceived to be related—such as SAT scores, colleges attended, and so on—and whether others will think we are as smart as we would like them to. In daily life we do a great deal of assessing others' intelligence as well as projecting our own as we would like others to see it.

Murphy, Hall, and Colvin (2003) asked what cues people look for when judging others' intelligence and whether those cues are correct. When making intelligence ratings based on 1-minute clips of conversational behavior, perceivers associated many cues with higher intelligence, including having a pleasant speech style, talking with the hands, sitting up straight, talking fast, looking at the other person while speaking, and behaving in a responsive manner. However, only a few of these were valid cues to higher intelligence, most notably looking more at the other person while speaking. Whether people higher in intelligence are aware of engaging in such behavior is not known, but certainly it is possible that if such an association is strong and constant enough, the person will incorporate that behavior into their sense of "who they are," and others will do the same.

SOCIAL IDENTITY

Race and gender are among the most salient aspects of social identity—that is, our identification with social and cultural groups—so it is not surprising that research has turned up nonverbal communication differences associated with these categories. It is, of course, an oversimplification to think of these categories as though everyone in them behaves the same. Stereotypic thinking promotes many judgment errors and undesirable behaviors. Obviously, a woman may express her womanhood differently at home than at the office—let us hope she does! Similarly, a minority student may have a different behavior style when with friends of the same social group than in a predominantly majority classroom. Also remember that distinctions such as male or female and black or white are often confounded with other distinctions, such as social class and status. Furthermore, each individual has numerous social identities: a person might be a woman *and* an Asian *and* a member of the upper crust. Furthermore, each category of social identity is often multidimensional and ambiguous. Many people cannot easily describe the complexity of their racial, ethnic, and gender identities. Thus, it can be unclear what identity factors explain a given nonverbal behavior.

At various places in this book, we have documented differences between the nonverbal behavior of blacks and whites in the United States. Although such differences in nonverbal behavior have not been studied extensively, there appear to be differences—at least in the limited populations observed—in style of walking, interpersonal distance, orientation, gaze, and conversational regulators (Burgoon, Buller, & Woodall, 1989; Halberstadt, 1985; Johnson, 1972). It is important to note that some of the findings may pertain only to subgroups and not to the larger group. For example, a distinctive walk that may be evident in urban black teenagers is probably not the same walk that would characterize black schoolteachers or executives. Keeping this in mind, research suggests that among adults, the distance maintained between interactants is typically greater, and the body orientation less direct, among African Americans than among European Americans. As an interesting contradiction to this pattern of reduced sensory involvement, studies have found African Americans to touch more than European Americans do. Perhaps the greater amount of touching reestablishes a sense of involvement.

Some research suggests that African Americans gaze less than European Americans during conversation and gaze especially little with authorities, whereas among European Americans, gaze often increases with authorities. Erickson's (1979) analysis of films of conversations pointed to distinct African-American and European-American norms for conversational turn taking and signaling attention. African-American speakers used less subtle and less frequent cues indicating that a listener should give a "listener response," a signal that the listener is paying attention. But, as listeners, African Americans employed listener responses that were more subtle and likely to be missed by a speaker from outside that group. Erickson suggested that these differences could lead to a situation in which a European-American speaker concludes an African-American interactant is either not listening or not understanding. The European American then repeats himself, which is perceived as "talking down" by the African American. Although Erickson found evidence that African-American subjects displayed bicultural competence, a kind of nonverbal bilingualism, there remained differences in conversational behavior. The potential for serious interracial misunderstanding stemming from cultural differences is obvious and has been noted by educators and others concerned with race relations.

Gender differences in nonverbal behavior also reflect the different identities of males and females, and nonverbal differences appear early in life. *Gender roles* are collections of attitudes, behaviors, and traits deemed desirable for men versus women. In our society, the male gender role, in sterotype, is exemplified by autonomy, assertiveness, dominance, and task orientation; for women, gentleness, empathy, and interpersonal orientation are stereotypical (Cross & Madson, 1997). To a great extent, nonverbal differences correspond to these role prescriptions. It is clear even from everyday observation that social displays of sexual identity and gender role have special importance. Thus we may want to show the world not only that we are men or women but that we behave as men or women are expected to behave. We discuss some of the findings from research next, and other differences have been discussed earlier in the book. Compared to women, men:

- Have less skill in sending and receiving nonverbal, especially emotional, cues
- Are less likely to notice or to be influenced by people's appearance and non-verbal behavior
- Have less expressive faces and use fewer expressive gestures
- Smile and laugh less
- Look at others less
- Keep greater distances from others

A difference involving much debate concerns interpersonal touching. When it comes to same-gender touch, the evidence is rather clear that heterosexual men are particularly averse to touching other men, except in certain prescribed settings such as team sports, both as part of the game and as expressions of team spirit. Both self-reported and observational data indicate that same-gender touching is avoided by men, at least in the United States, but is quite welcome by women. One hypothesis for men's avoidance is homophobic attitudes and the fear that touching will be seen as homosexual. Indeed, research by Roese, Olson, Borenstein, Martin, and Shores (1992) found that among men, those with the least stated liking for same-gender touching had the highest scores on a homophobia scale with items such as "Homosexuality is a sin and just plain wrong," and "Homosexual behavior disgusts me." In a second study, college students who were observed to engage in less same-gender touching in a cafeteria had stronger homophobic attitudes when surveyed by researchers, and this was found to be true for both men and women (Roese et al., 1992).

Studies on opposite-gender touching have been more widely debated (Henley, 1977; Stier & Hall, 1984), but there is some concurrence that when the individuals are young adults, or the touch is with the hand, or the arm is put around the other person, males do take the touching initiative. However, the woman is more likely to touch the man than vice versa when the couple is in their 40s or older, when the touch is either brief or involves linking her arm through the man's or initiating hand holding (Hall & Veccia, 1990), and when the couple is married rather than dating (Guerrero & Andersen, 1994; Willis & Briggs, 1992).

Although exhaustive research over the life span has not been conducted, there is reason to believe that nonverbal gender differences are especially pronounced in adolescence and the college years, when gender roles are especially salient. For example, the gender difference in smiling is not evident in young children (Dodd, Russell, & Jenkins, 1999; Hall, 1984); it peaks in adolescence and decreases after that, though never completely (LaFrance, Hecht, & Levy Paluck, 2003). Most nonverbal gender differences have been investigated among college students observed in a laboratory situation, but evidence abounds from more naturalistic settings as well. For example, male physicians interacting with patients engage in less smiling, nodding, and back-channeling (saying "mmm-hmm") than female physicians do (Hall, Irish, Roter, Ehrlich, & Miller, 1994).

The nonverbal behaviors that women engage in more than men suggest more openness, sensitivity, and involvement. In some circumstances, these traits may work to women's disadvantage (Henley, 1977). Their smiling may make them appear weak, "too nice," or even insincere; their higher levels of gazing may connote dependency; and their nonverbal style may not be distant or threatening enough to win automatic respect in the professional world. However, if this is the case, we would argue that the problem is with the stereotypic beliefs rather than with the behavior per se. Furthermore, it could also be argued that it is only because of cultural blinders that we tend to see men's behavior as "normal" and women's behavior as different or in need of correction. Because most evidence suggests that the kinds of nonverbal skills and behavior shown more by women are an asset in daily life, one could make the case that men's nonverbal behavior style and skills are a handicap in social relations.

Women's greater emotional expressivity is consistent with the stereotype that women are more emotional than men. However, several studies have found that self-reports of the intensity of emotional experience do not differ when assessed concurrently with the experience (Kring & Gordon, 1998), but studies that ask about emotional intensity in general or retrospective terms find a consistent gender difference in self-reported emotional intensity (Diener, Sanvik, & Larsen, 1985). The latter difference may be biased by the influence of gender stereotypes on self-ratings; alternatively, women may do more subsequent thinking and processing of emotional experiences, which amplifies their intensity with the passage of time. At any rate, although it is clear that women are more emotionally expressive than men, it is not clear that they are also more emotional in terms of their inner experience.

Sometimes the claim is made that women are false in their nonverbal expressions, for example, that their smiles are constant and insincere. An early study, cited often, found that women tended to smile even when their words did not contain congruently happy messages, but men's smiles were more in accord with their words (Bugental, Love, & Gianetto, 1971). Bugental called women's behavior "perfidious." The label is derogatory, but if this pattern exists it could certainly have social impact. However, a subsequent study done that tested this same hypothesis found exactly the *opposite* pattern, with women being more consistent across channels than men were (Halberstadt, Hayes, & Pike, 1988). Clearly, it is premature to conclude that inconsistent displays are the province of women.

As with race and other group differences, male and female nonverbal differences are not large in absolute terms, and we should not overestimate the size of these differences. Though some of them are large relative to other psychological differences between the sexes, they are still of modest magnitude, and even the largest nonverbal gender difference shows more similarity than difference between males and females. Stated differently, a great deal of overlap exists in the male and female repertoires. Nevertheless, there is a striking correspondence between people's beliefs about these differences and the actual magnitude of such differences (Briton & Hall, 1995; Hall & Carter, 1999), which strongly suggests that people can see these differences in daily life. Of course, societal beliefs can also translate into self-fulfilling prophecies, such that men and women come to have the behaviors that others expect them to have (Zanna & Pack, 1975).

The gender differences are also not invariant. In fact, they vary considerably as a function of setting and context, including the nature of the situation, the affective tone of an interaction, other nonverbal behaviors, and the characteristics of the other person involved (Aiello & Aiello, 1977; Hall & Halberstadt, 1986; LaFrance et al., 2003; Putnam & McCallister, 1980). As examples of this variation, the gender difference in gazing is much more evident when people are within conversational distance of one another than when they are standing farther apart. The tendency for women to smile more than men is greatest when they know they are being observed, when they are interacting with others, when they are not very familiar with the other people in the interaction, when the circumstances make them feel more anxious, and when they are Caucasian. Finally, people act in the most sex-stereotypic ways when with others of their own sex; in opposite-sex encounters, males and females often accommodate to the other's norms. So, for example, gazing is highest between females, lowest between males, and intermediate in male–female interaction (Hall, 1984; Vrugt & Kerkstra, 1984). The fact that nonverbal gender differences vary with these contextual factors demonstrates that we still have a great deal to learn about the origins of male and female behavior.

Interpretations of sex differences in gaze have concentrated on the competing themes of affiliation and warmth versus dominance and power. Because nonverbal cues do not typically have fixed meanings, this ambiguity is difficult to resolve. Smiling and gazing, for example, can have multiple meanings. However, the visual-dominance ratio described earlier in this chapter is less ambiguous than some other nonverbal behaviors, and it has been linked to differences in status, power, dominance, or expertise in a variety of studies, but to our knowledge no one has suggested that it varies with the warmth or friendliness of the interaction. Dovidio, Brown, Heltman, Ellyson, and Keating (1988) performed two experiments involving mixed-gender pairs of interactants in which the relative status of the interactants was experimentally manipulated. When a status difference was created between the interactants, the party having the higher status—whether that party was male or female—had a higher visual-dominance ratio, consistent with research already described. However, when status was *not* manipulated, men behaved in the visually dominant way that high-status communicators display, and women showed the less visually dominant behavior typical of people in low-status roles. This finding suggests a connection between dominance and gender differences in gazing patterns.

The well-established finding that women score higher on tests of judging the meanings of nonverbal cues has also been theorized to stem from dominance and status differences (Henley, 1977). In fact, little is known about why females are so often better at decoding nonverbal cues, despite much debate and discussion (Hall, 1984; Henley, 1977; Noller, 1986). So far, little evidence exists for the dominance-status interpretation (Hall et al., 2005; Hall, Halberstadt, & O'Brien, 1997). Noller (1986), like most other social psychologists, believes that females are socialized to be expert in various aspects of social interaction, including knowing the general social rules governing interpersonal relations, the general display and decoding rules appropriate to various situations, and the more specific rules governing the use of nonverbal cues in particular. It is society's expectation not only that females will be attuned to social interactions, but also that they will be responsible for how social interactions proceed. These pressures and expectations could easily produce the skill differences documented in research.

Similarly, only very limited support exists for dominance-status interpretations for gender differences in other nonverbal behaviors (Hall, 2006). Smiling, in particular, has been hypothesized to vary with dominance and status, such that the lower-power person smiles more; and it has been suggested that differences in dominance and status can explain why women smile more than men. However, research on smiling relative to dominance and status finds no overall connection between the two (Hall et al., 2005). It is likely that the amount of smiling shown by people with different degrees of dominance or status depends on other factors, such as how pleasant, ingratiating, hostile, nervous, or preoccupied they are, not on dominance and status per se.

DECEIVING OTHERS

One of the most common communicative outcomes we seek is to persuade or influence others. In previous chapters, we cited research aimed at identifying the contributions of physical attraction, distance, eye gaze, touch, and vocal cues to perceptions of authoritativeness (expertise) and character (trustworthiness)—the two central factors in the persuasive process. But the area of influence that has captured the attention of the American public and university researchers the most in recent years is the act of lying.

Three major questions drive the research in this area:

1. What behaviors distinguish liars from truth tellers?
2. What cognitive and emotional processes are at work during acts of lying?
3. How accurate are we at detecting lies?

Identifying behaviors exhibited by liars has, until recently, focused predominantly on nonverbal signals. It was incorrectly assumed that liars could manipulate their verbal behavior easily but could not or would not control their nonverbal behavior to the same extent, thereby revealing they were lying. Ekman and Friesen (1969) believed it was more likely that clues to deception would be found in the area of the feet and legs first, the hands next, and the face last. Because the face is more likely to be controlled by the liar, Ekman and Friesen argued that facial clues would be more difficult to detect. Later work by these researchers (1975), however, indicated several ways the face reveals deception, such as micromomentary expressions and the timing and location of the expression. For example, smiles made when people were trying to cover up negative feelings included traces of muscular actions associated with disgust, fear, contempt, or sadness (Ekman, Friesen, & O'Sullivan, 1988).

Attempts to develop a list of behaviors that distinguish liars from truth tellers have always faced the problem that there are many types of lies—prepared or not, short answer or extended narrative, interrogated or not—and many motivations for lying, such as to protect oneself or someone else, to get out of an obligation or promise, or to avoid conflict. For the lies that occur most in our daily interaction, people report they are not serious, are largely unplanned, and do not make them fearful of being caught (DePaulo, Kashy, Kirkendol, Wyer, & Epstein, 1996). In addition, no behavior that occurs while lying is completely unique to lying (Buck, 1984; Zuckerman, DePaulo, & Rosenthal, 1981). Ekman (1992, p. 80) put it this way: "There is no sign of deceit itself—no gesture, facial expression, or muscle twitch that in and of itself means that a person is lying." Still, attempts have been made to examine the behavioral indicators of lying regardless of how lying was operationalized. A meta-analysis of 120 studies performed by DePaulo and colleagues (2003) identified the following profile for liars when compared with truth tellers:

- *Liars are less forthcoming.* As a result, they are likely to manifest shorter responses and less elaboration; they appear to be holding back, speak at a slower rate, and have longer response latencies.
- *Liars tell stories that seem less plausible and with fewer details.* Thus, stories by liars are likely to have more discrepancies and to be less engaging—that is, they contain more word or phrase repetitions. They tend to be less direct, use fewer self-references, are more uncertain and less fluent with more hesitations, errors, and pauses, and they tend to be presented in a less active manner with fewer gestures.
- *Liars make fewer spontaneous corrections while telling their stories and are less likely to admit they cannot remember something.*
- *Liars make a more negative impression.* Overall, they seem less cooperative, make more negative statements, and use more words denoting anger and fear. They are also more likely to use offensive language, to complain more and smile less, and they seem more defensive.
- *Liars are more tense.* Their voices are likely to have a higher pitch, their pupils are more likely to be dilated for a longer period of time, and they are more likely to exhibit fidgeting.

One behavior many people expect of liars is a sharp decrease in eye gaze. Although this behavior may occur with some liars in some situations, it has become so stereotypically associated with lying in this culture that liars often consciously seek to control it. Sometimes, of course, the ability to display a normal pattern of gaze is deficient, and the liar ends up staring. And too much gazing signals that something is wrong, just as too little gazing does.

If it is difficult to find behaviors that always characterize liars, it is easier to identify behaviors associated with key underlying cognitive and emotional processes that occur during lies (Knapp, Cody, & Reardon, 1987). The two most commonly studied processes are *arousal* and *cognitive difficulty*. Nonpathological liars who know they are telling a high-stakes lie, and who know there will be important consequences if they are caught, are likely to experience one or both of these states. Nonverbally, arousal is indicated by pupil dilation, blinking, speech errors, and higher pitch. Verbally, we might see excessive responses—for example, "WHY DO YOU ALWAYS HAVE TO QUESTION ME?!" in response to a seemingly natural, nonthreatening question. Curt replies, or extremes in language usage are also seen. Obviously, people experience arousal for reasons other than lying, but aroused truth tellers and aroused liars do not seem to behave the same. Liars commonly experience cognitive difficulty as well. This may be manifested in speech hesitations, shorter responses, pupil dilation, speech errors, incongruous verbal and nonverbal behavior, and a lack of specific references.

Two other processes typical of the high-stakes lie involve *attempted control* and the *display of an affective state*. Less spontaneous, or what seems to be rehearsed behavior, would indicate attempted control. In 1991, military prisoners of war who were forced to make anti-U.S. statements on Iraqi television were reportedly trained prior to their capture to speak and behave in a wooden and mechanical manner to indicate they were lying. Indirect responses to direct questions also may signal an attempt to control one's behavior. The expected affective state is one of anxiety commonly reflected in fidgeting, stammering, and the like. But other emotional states are also relevant to deception. Anger is very common and is reflected in liars' tendencies to be negative and disaffiliative in their responses. Some liars feel enough guilt that looking away for long periods or covering their eyes with their hands is not uncommon. "Duping delight," the pleasure one may experience in deceiving another, occurs sometimes as well and may be reflected in a smile at the wrong time or a sneer of contempt.

Given what we have said about the nature of liar behavior, it should be no surprise that without the aid of any mechanical equipment such as a polygraph, people are only about 50 to 60 percent accurate in identifying whether strangers are lying to them or not. Since accuracy judgments usually combine the accuracy of people judging truthful and deceptive speakers, and since truthful speakers are usually judged with a much higher degree of accuracy, our ability to detect liars may be well below 50 percent (Levine, Park, & McCornack, 1999). Most studies assessing accuracy are based on observer judgments, not on the observations of those who are actually participating in the conversation. Some evidence suggests that participants are less accurate than observers. Higher detection rates have been obtained from professionals who are highly motivated to detect deception and reputed to be good detectors (Ekman, O'Sullivan, & Frank, 1999); people who focus on vocal cues as a good source of information about deception (Anderson, DePaulo, Ansfield, Tickle, & Green, 1999; Zuckerman, Spiegel, DePaulo, & Rosenthal, 1982); and aphasics who have poor language skills, when the detection process involves judging emotion (Etcoff, Ekman, Magee, & Frank, 2000). Analyzing both verbal and nonverbal signals may be more likely to reveal a liar than observing either type of signal alone (Vrij, Edward, Roberts, & Bull, 2000). Getting feedback during training and practice in deception detection also may improve accuracy somewhat (deTurck, 1991; deTurck, Feeley, & Roman, 1997). DePaulo and her colleagues (1988) believe liars are more likely to reveal themselves nonverbally when the lie is very important to them. They called this the *motivational impairment hypothesis*. Burgoon and Floyd (2000), however, found that liars who were highly motivated to lie often performed it more skillfully and were less apt to be uncovered through their nonverbal behavior. With all this attention given to our ability to observe liar behavior, it should be noted that this is not the way most people find out they have been lied to. Instead, they receive information about the lie from others, find physical evidence related to the deception, or the liar confesses (Park, Levine, McCornack, Morrison, & Ferrara, 2002).

Although some may bemoan the fact that our detection rate is not higher, others believe it would be undesirable to get too accurate at detecting lies. The ability to withhold information and mislead, it is argued, is just as crucial to the well-being of our society as disclosure, openness, and honesty (Knapp, 2008).

Are machines any better than human beings at detecting lies? Polygraphs, which measure various physiological indicators, such as heart rate and blood pressure, are sometimes reported to detect liars with more accuracy than most human observers. But because they too often identify truth tellers and liars incorrectly, they are barred as courtroom evidence in most states (Robinson, 1996; Vrij, 2000). Furthermore, polygraphs can be beaten. In one study, people whose lies were detected at about 80 percent were given either biofeedback or relaxation training. After they were better able to control their bodily responses, the accuracy of the polygraphs was reduced to about 20 percent (Corcoran, Lewis, & Garver, 1978). In addition to polygraphs, many products on the market claim to measure vocal microtremors. Like the polygraph, these devices are based on the assumption that liars experience anxiety, and behaviors associated with anxiety will identify them. According to Hollien (1990), these voice-stress analyzers accurately identify liars at slightly above chance—that is, not any better than most human beings could do on their own. A device that measures brain wave responses to crime-relevant words or pictures presented on a computer screen, called "brain fingerprinting," claims to have been 100 percent accurate in identifying liars in 120 tests (Farwell & Smith, 2001; Farwell & Dochin, 1991), but other researchers find the procedure to be about half as accurate and that training can help liars reduce accuracy even further (Feder, 2001; Rosenfeld, Soskins, Bosh, & Ryan, 2004). Currently, scientists are using functional magnetic resonance imaging (fMRI) in an effort to identify brain activity that would distinguish liars from truth tellers, but this process also faces serious theoretical, procedural, and accuracy problems.

What about people in close relationships? Should they not be more accurate at detecting lies? Because trust is the fundamental reason couples have close relationships, either party is likely to get away with lying quite easily at first. But once suspicion is aroused, those who know a person's behavior well are likely to be the best detectors (Comadena, 1982; McCornack & Parks, 1986). However, it is not uncommon for people in close relationships not to engage in the sort of monitoring necessary to detect deception. They may not want to confront the lie, or they may be afraid of destroying intimacy if they show distrust by their close monitoring (Knapp, 2006).

A PERSPECTIVE FOR COMMUNICATORS

Throughout this chapter, we have emphasized the idea that communicators mutually construct their reality. One person's behavior can only be understood as we see how it interacts with the behavior of another person. In the abstract, this proposition seems reasonable—one that would not be hard to memorize and recall for a test. But what does the concept of mutual influence mean in practical application to our everyday lives? Two things seem to be particularly important: First, if the outcome of any transaction is the product of behavior by both interactants, it means we must be very careful in judging and ascribing meaning to the nonverbal behavior of a single person or in generalizing a person's behavior with one person to all others. This does not suggest that people do not have a style of communicating they may carry from one encounter to another. The parts of that style that are emphasized and deemphasized, however, can change dramatically depending on whom one is interacting with. Second, if the outcome of any transaction is the product of behavior by both interactants, each must share the responsibility for the outcome. This does not mean that in some encounters one person may not take or deserve more of the responsibility than the other. It does mean that we should, perhaps more than we would like to, examine our own verbal and nonverbal behavior to determine how it contributed to the interpersonal outcome. In social life, it is rare indeed for one person to be doing everything right and the other to be doing everything wrong. Unpleasant outcomes are usually constructed mutually.

These notions return us to the self-fulfilling prophecy described in Chapter 1. The most important lessons about social life probably are these: We see what we expect to see, and what we expect of others will likely come true. Through our verbal and nonverbal behavior, we unconsciously shape other people into conformance with our expectations, in all areas of life, including educational settings (Harris & Rosenthal, 1985), psychological experiments (Rosenthal, 1976), and ordinary interpersonal relationships (Snyder, Tanke, & Berscheid, 1977; Spitz, 1997). Your nonverbal behavior does make a difference.

SUMMARY

Every day we have to accomplish goals that require the effective management and reading of nonverbal signals. This chapter identified what we know about five of those goals.

We began by discussing the various ways we manifest our liking and disliking for others. Even though certain nonverbal signals have been associated with courtship and romantic flirtation, we also know that similar behaviors occur when people are trying to communicate friendliness, interest, and playfulness. These "quasi-courtship" behaviors can lead to misunderstandings, and they remind us how important context is for interpreting nonverbal signals. The cluster of nonverbal behavior comprising immediacy or liking behavior can be usefully applied to a variety of situations in which we want to signal positive responses to strangers and acquaintances. Immediacy occurs in established close relationships, too, but mainly when it is important to be clear about one's feelings, when the relationship is threatened, or when a couple wants to communicate their closeness to outsiders. Otherwise, people in close relationships employ a more unique and varied nonverbal repertoire. We concluded this section by noting the ways people adjust the intimacy level through reciprocal or compensatory behavior.

Nonverbal behavior is also highlighted in acts of dominance and efforts to show status. Like intimacy, sometimes people will manifest different nonverbal behavior when seeking intimacy than after they have achieved it. But, again, context and individual differences are important. An aspiring executive may engage in more eye gaze while seeking the top position in the company, but another executive, equally motivated, may engage in far less eye gaze with his superiors as a sign of respect. There are a number of behaviors that have been associated with dominance and status. Some research indicates that higher status men and women tend to manifest the visual-dominance ratio, the tendency to look more while speaking than listening.

Nonverbal signals are also crucial in initiating, managing, and terminating everyday conversations. Smooth turn exchanges are negotiated when speakers signal turn-yielding cues and listeners signal turn-requesting cues. There are times, however, when listeners do not want to assume the speaking turn, and speakers do not want to give it up. These, too, are highly dependent on the manifestation of certain nonverbal signals.

We tell others and ourselves who we are when we communicate our identity through nonverbal signals. Identity may be personal, such as with individual personality, or it may be social, as in race or gender. Research has found important differences in the nonverbal behavior of men and women, for example, but often these differences are not large.

Even though we would not like to think of ourselves as deceivers, research indicates we often use deception to manage our social sphere. There is no behavior that is always associated with lying, but research shows that liars tend to be less forthcoming, provide fewer details, give off a negative impression, exhibit more tenseness, and make fewer spontaneous corrections in their speech. Arousal and cognitive difficulty often trigger the observed behaviors seen in high-stakes lying, but most of us are not very accurate, with only about a 50 to 60 percent success rate, in identifying liars whom we do not know.

QUESTIONS FOR DISCUSSION

1. Research tells us that men typically smile, laugh, and gaze at their conversational partners far less than women do. Speculate on why this is and the extent to which it is functional or dysfunctional behavior.

2. What does it mean to collaborate in a lie? Are collaborators and liars subject to similar ethical standards?

3. Identify situations in which controlling behavior is likely to be reciprocated, and when it is likely to elicit compensatory behavior. Why?

4. Try to imagine a social world in which lies could be detected accurately 99 percent of the time. Describe it.

5. Write a paragraph describing a situation in which you felt the other interactant's verbal and nonverbal behavior had little to do with your own. Exchange your description with another person who has written a similar paragraph. With additional questioning, each of you should now try to convince the other person that the episode he or she described omitted much of the partner's influence.

BIBLIOGRAPHY

INTIMACY

Abbey, A., & Melby, C. (1986). The effect of non-verbal cues on gender differences in perceptions of sexual intent. *Sex Roles, 15,* 283–298.

Afifi, W. A., & Johnson, M. L. (1999). The use and interpretation of tie signs in a public setting: Relationship and sex differences. *Journal of Social and Personal Relationships, 16,* 9–38.

Andersen, P. A. (1985). Nonverbal immediacy in interpersonal communication. In A. W. Siegman & S. Feldstein (Eds.), *Multichannel integrations of non-verbal behavior* (pp. 1–36). Hillsdale, NJ: Erlbaum.

Andersen, P. A., & Andersen, J. F. (1984). The exchange of nonverbal intimacy: A critical review of dyadic models. *Journal of Nonverbal Behavior, 8,* 327–349.

Andersen, P. A., Guerrero, L. K., Buller, D. B., & Jorgensen, P. F. (1998). An empirical comparison of three theories of nonverbal immediacy exchange. *Human Communication Research, 24,* 501–535.

Andersen, P. A., Guerrero, L. K., & Jones, S. M. (2006). Nonverbal behavior in intimate interactions and intimate relationships. In V. Manusov & M. L. Patterson (Eds.), *The Sage handbook of nonverbal communication* (pp. 259–277). Thousand Oaks, CA: Sage.

Argyle, M., & Dean, J. (1965). Eye contact, distance and affiliation. *Sociometry, 28,* 289–304.

Burgoon, J. K. (1978). A communication model of personal space violations: Explication and an initial test. *Human Communication Research, 4,* 129–142.

Burgoon, J. K., & Aho, L. (1982). Three field experiments on the effect of violations of conversation distance. *Communication Monographs, 49,* 71–88.

Burgoon, J. K., & Hale, J. L. (1988). Nonverbal expectancy violations: Model elaboration and application to immediacy behaviors. *Communication Monographs, 55,* 58–79.

Burgoon J. K., & Jones, S. B. (1976). Toward a theory of personal space expectations and their violations. *Human Communication Research, 2,* 131–146.

Burgoon, J. K., Stern, L. A., & Dillman, L. (1995). *Interpersonal adaptation: Dyadic interaction patterns.* New York: Cambridge University Press.

Cappella, J. N. (1981). Mutual influence in expressive behavior: Adult-adult and infant-adult interaction. *Psychological Bulletin, 89,* 101–132.

Cappella, J. N., & Greene, J. O. (1982). A discrepancy-arousal explanation of mutual influence in expressive behavior for adult and infant-adult interaction. *Communication Monographs, 49,* 89–114.

Clore, G. L., Wiggins, N. H., & Itkin, S. (1975a). Gain and loss in attraction: Attributions from nonverbal behavior. *Journal of Personality and Social Psychology, 31,* 706–712.

Clore, G. L., Wiggins, N. H., & Itkin, S. (1975b). Judging attraction from nonverbal behavior: The gain phenomenon. *Journal of Consulting and Clinical Psychology, 43,* 491–497.

Delph, E. W. (1978). *The silent community: Public homosexual encounters.* Beverly Hills, CA: Sage.

DePaulo, B. M., & Coleman, L. M. (1987). Verbal and nonverbal communication of warmth to children, foreigners, and retarded adults. *Journal of Nonverbal Behavior, 11,* 75–88.

Egland, K. L., Spitzberg, B. H., & Zormeier, M. M. (1996). Flirtation and conversational competence in cross-sex platonic and romantic relationships. *Communication Reports, 9,* 105–117.

Floyd, K., & Burgoon, J. K. (1999). Reacting to nonverbal expressions of liking: A test of interaction adaptation theory. *Communication Monographs, 66,* 219–239.

Givens, D. B. (1978). The nonverbal basis of attraction: Flirtation, courtship, and seduction. *Psychiatry, 41,* 346–359.

Grammer, K., Kruck, K., Juette, A., & Fink, B. (2000). Nonverbal behavior as courtship signals: The role of control and choice in selecting partners. *Evolution and Behavior, 21,* 371–390.

Guerrero. L. K., & Floyd, K. (2006). *Nonverbal communication in close relationships.* Mahwah, NJ: Erlbaum.

Guerrero, L. K., Jones, S. M., & Burgoon, J. K. (2000). Responses to nonverbal intimacy change in romantic dyads: Effects of behavioral valence and degree of behavioral change on nonverbal and verbal reactions. *Communication Monographs, 67,* 325–346.

Knapp, M. L. (1983). Dyadic relationship development. In J. M. Wiemann & R. P. Harrison (Eds.), *Nonverbal interaction* (pp. 179–207). Beverly Hills, CA: Sage.

Koeppel, L. B., Montagne-Miller, Y., O'Hair, D., & Cody, M. J. (1993). Friendly? Flirting? Wrong? In P. J. Kalbfleisch (Ed.), *Interpersonal communication: Evolving interpersonal relationships.* Hillsdale, NJ: Erlbaum.

LePoire, B. A. (1991). Orientation and defensive reactions as alternatives to arousal in theories of nonverbal reactions to changes in immediacy. *Southern Communication Journal, 56,* 138–146.

LePoire, B. A., & Burgoon, J. K. (1994). Two contrasting explanations of involvement violations: Expectancy violations theory versus discrepancy arousal theory. *Human Communication Research, 20,* 560–591.

Manusov, V., Floyd, K., & Kerssen-Griep, J. (1997). Yours, mine, and ours: Mutual attributions for nonverbal behaviors in couples' interactions. *Communication Research, 24,* 234–260.

McCormick, N. B., & Jones, A. I. (1989). Gender differences in nonverbal flirtation. *Journal of Sex Education and Therapy, 15,* 271–282.

Mehrabian, A. (1968a). Inference of attitude from the posture, orientation, and distance of a communicator. *Journal of Consulting and Clinical Psychology, 32,* 296–308.

Mehrabian, A. (1968b). Relationship of attitude to seated posture, orientation, and distance. *Journal of Personality and Social Psychology, 10,* 26–30.

Mehrabian, A. (1968c). Significance of posture and position in the communication of attitude and status relationships. *Psychological Bulletin, 71,* 359–372.

Mehrabian, A. (1972). *Nonverbal communication.* Chicago: Aldine.

Moore, M. M. (1985). Nonverbal courtship patterns in women: Content and consequences. *Ethology and Sociobiology, 6,* 237–247.

Morris, D. (1971). *Intimate behavior.* New York: Random House.

Nielsen, G. (1962). *Studies in self-confrontation.* Copenhagen: Munksgaard; Cleveland: Howard Allen.

Noller, P. (1984). *Nonverbal communication and marital interaction.* New York: Pergamon.

Patterson, M. L. (1976). An arousal model of interpersonal intimacy. *Psychological Review, 83,* 235–245.

Patterson, M. L. (1983). *Nonverbal behavior: A functional approach.* New York: Springer-Verlag.

Patterson, M. L. (Ed.). (1985). Nonverbal intimacy and exchange. *Journal of Nonverbal Behavior, 8,* 233–393.

Patterson, M. L. (2006). The evolution of theories of interactive behavior. In V. Manusov & M. L. Patterson (Eds.), *The Sage handbook of nonverbal communication* (pp. 21–39). Thousand Oaks, CA: Sage.

Patterson, M. L., Reidhead, S. M., Gooch, M. V., & Stopka, S. J. (1984). A content-classified bibliography of research on the immediacy behaviors: 1965–82. *Journal of Nonverbal Behavior, 8,* 360–393.

Perper, T. (1985). *Sex signals: The biology of love.* Philadelphia: ISI Press.

Perper, T., & Weis, D. L. (1987). Proceptive and rejective strategies of U.S. and Canadian college women. *Journal of Sex Research, 23,* 455–480.

Ray, G. B., & Floyd, K. (2006). Nonverbal expressions of liking and disliking in initial interaction: Encoding and decoding perspectives. *Southern Communication Journal, 71,* 45–65.

Reece, M., & Whitman, R. (1962). Expressive movements, warmth, and verbal reinforcement. *Journal of Abnormal and Social Psychology, 64,* 234–236.

Renninger, L. A., Wade, T. J., & Grammer, K. (2004). Getting that female glance: Patterns and consequences of male nonverbal behavior in courtship contexts. *Evolution and Human Behavior, 25,* 416–431.

Richmond, V. P., McCroskey, J. C., & Johnson, A. D. (2003). Development of the nonverbal immediacy scale (NIS): Measures of self- and other-perceived nonverbal immediacy. *Communication Quarterly, 51,* 504–517.

Rodriguez, J. I., Plax, T. G., & Kearney, P. (1996). Clarifying the relationship between teacher nonverbal immediacy and student cognitive learning: Affective learning as the central causal mediator. *Communication Education, 45,* 293–305.

Rosenfeld, H. M. (1966a). Approval-seeking and approval-inducing functions of verbal and nonverbal responses in the dyad. *Journal of Personality and Social Psychology, 4,* 597–605.

Rosenfeld, H. M. (1966b). Instrumental affiliative functions of facial and gestural expressions. *Journal of Personality and Social Psychology, 4,* 65–72.

Scheflen, A. E. (1965). Quasi-courtship behavior in psychotherapy. *Psychiatry, 28,* 245–257.

Simpson, J. A., Gangestad, S. W., & Nations, C. (1996). Sociosexuality and relationship initiation: An ethological perspective of nonverbal behavior. In G. J. O. Fletcher & J. Fitness (Eds.), *Knowledge structures in close relationships* (pp. 121–146). Mahwah, NJ: Erlbaum.

Strauss, N. (2005). *The game: Penetrating the secret society of pickup artists.* New York: ReganBooks.

Tickle-Degnen, L., & Rosenthal, R. (1990). The nature of rapport and its nonverbal correlates. *Psychological Inquiry, 1,* 285–293.

Trees, A. R. (2000). Nonverbal communication and the support process: Interactional sensitivity in interactions between mothers and young adult children. *Communication Monographs, 67,* 239–261.

Trees, A. R. & Manusov, V. (1998). Managing face concerns in criticism: Integrating nonverbal behaviors as a dimension of politeness in female friendship dyads. *Human Communication Research, 24,* 564–583.

Zajonc, R. B., Adelmann, P. K., Murphy, S. T., & Niedenthal, P. M. (1987). Convergence in the physical appearance of spouses. *Motivation and Emotion, 11,* 335–346.

DOMINANCE/STATUS

Argyle, M. (1988). *Bodily communication* (2nd ed.). London: Methuen.

Berger, J., Rosenholtz, S. J., & Zelditch, M., Jr. (1980). Status organizing processes. *Annual Review of Sociology, 6,* 479–508.

Burgoon, J. K., Buller, D. B., & Woodall, W. G. (1989). *Nonverbal communication: The unspoken dialogue.* New York: Harper & Row.

Burgoon, J. K., & Dunbar, N. E. (2006). Nonverbal expressions of dominance and power in human relationships. In V. Manusov & M. L. Patterson (Eds.), *The Sage handbook of nonverbal communication* (pp. 279–297). Thousand Oaks, CA: Sage Publications.

Burroughs, W., Schulz, W., & Aubrey, S. (1973). Quality of argument, leadership roles and eye contact in three-person leaderless groups. *Journal of Social Psychology, 90,* 89–93.

Carney, D. R., Hall, J. A., & Smith LeBeau, L. (2005). Beliefs about the nonverbal expression of social power. *Journal of Nonverbal Behavior, 29,* 105–123.

Dindia, K. (1987). The effects of sex of subject and sex of partner on interruptions. *Human Communication Research, 13,* 345–371.

Dovidio, J. F., Brown, C. E., Heltman, K., Ellyson, S. L., & Keating, C. F. (1988). Power displays between women and men in discussions of gender-linked tasks: A multichannel study. *Journal of Personality and Social Psychology, 55,* 580–587.

Dovidio, J. F., & Ellyson, S. L. (1985). Patterns of visual dominance behavior in humans. In S. L. Ellyson & J. F. Dovidio (Eds.), *Power, dominance, and nonverbal behavior* (pp. 129–149). New York: Springer-Verlag.

Dovidio, J. F., Ellyson, S. L., Keating, C. F., Heltman, K., & Brown, C. E. (1988). The relationship of social power to visual displays of dominance between men and women. *Journal of Personality and Social Psychology, 54,* 233–242.

Edinger, J. A., & Patterson, M. L. (1983). Nonverbal involvement and social control. *Psychological Bulletin, 93,* 30–56.

Ellyson, S. L., & Dovidio, J. F. (1985). Power, dominance, and nonverbal behavior: Basic concepts and issues. In S. L. Ellyson & J. F. Dovidio (Eds.), *Power, dominance, and nonverbal behavior* (pp. 1–27). New York: Springer-Verlag.

Ellyson, S. L., Dovidio, J. F., & Fehr, B. J. (1981). Visual behavior and dominance in women and men. In C. Mayo & N. M. Henley (Eds.), *Gender and nonverbal behavior.* New York: Springer-Verlag.

Exline, R. V. (1971). Visual interaction: The glances of power and preference. *Nebraska Symposium on Motivation, 19,* 163–206.

Exline, R. V., Ellyson, S. L., & Long, B. (1975). Visual behavior as an aspect of power relationships. In P. Pliner, L. Kramer, & T. Alloway (Eds.), *Nonverbal communication of aggression*. New York: Plenum.

Fehr, B. J., & Exline, R. V. (1987). Social visual interaction: A conceptual and literature review. In A. W. Siegman & S. Feldstein (Eds.), *Nonverbal behavior and communication* (2nd ed., pp. 225–326). Hillsdale, NJ: Erlbaum.

Goldstein, A. G., & Jeffords, J. (1981). Status and touching behavior. *Bulletin of the Psychonomic Society, 17*, 79–81.

Halberstadt, A. G., Dovidio, J. F., & Davidson, L. A. (1988, October). *Power, gender, and smiling*. Paper presented at the meeting of the Society of Experimental Social Psychology.

Halberstadt, A. G., & Saitta, M. B. (1987). Gender, nonverbal behavior, and perceived dominance: A test of the theory. *Journal of Personality and Social Psychology, 53*, 257–272.

Hall, J. A. (1984). *Nonverbal sex differences: Communication accuracy and expressive style*. Baltimore: Johns Hopkins University Press.

Hall, J. A. (1996). Touch, status, and gender at professional meetings. *Journal of Nonverbal Behavior, 20*, 23–44.

Hall, J. A. (2006). Women's and men's nonverbal communication: Similarities, differences, stereotypes, and origins. In V. Manusov & M. L. Patterson (Eds.), *The Sage handbook of nonverbal communication* (pp. 201–218). Thousand Oaks, CA: Sage Publications.

Hall, J. A., Coats, E. J., & Smith LeBeau, L. (2005). Nonverbal behavior and the vertical dimension of social relations: A meta-analysis. *Psychological Bulletin, 131*, 898–924.

Hall, J. A., & Friedman, G. B. (1999). Status, gender, and nonverbal behavior: A study of structured interactions between employees of a company. *Personality and Social Psychology Bulletin, 25*, 1082–1091.

Harper, R. G. (1985). Power, dominance, and nonverbal behavior: An overview. In S. L. Ellyson & J. F. Dovidio (Eds.), *Power, dominance, and nonverbal behavior* (pp. 29–48). New York: Springer-Verlag.

Henley, N. M. (1977). *Body politics: Power, sex, and nonverbal communication*. Englewood Cliffs, NJ: Prentice-Hall.

Heslin, R., & Patterson, M. L. (1982). *Nonverbal behavior and social psychology*. New York: Plenum.

Johnson, C. (1994). Gender, legitimate authority, and leader-subordinate conversations. *American Sociological Review, 59*, 122–135.

Keating, C. F. (1985). Human dominance signals: The primate in us. In S. L. Ellyson & J. F. Dovidio (Eds.), *Power, dominance, and nonverbal behavior* (pp. 89–108). New York: Springer-Verlag.

Kennedy, C. W., & Camden, C. T. (1983). A new look at interruptions. *Western Journal of Speech Communication, 47*, 45–58.

Kleinke, C. L. (1986). Gaze and eye contact: A research review. *Psychological Bulletin, 100*, 78–100.

Kollock, P., Blumstein, P., & Schwartz, P. (1985). Sex and power in interaction: Conversational privileges and duties. *American Sociological Review, 50*, 34–46.

Lamb, T. A. (1981). Nonverbal and paraverbal control in dyads and triads: Sex or power differences. *Social Psychology Quarterly, 44*, 49–53.

Latta, R. M. (1978). Relation of status incongruence to personal space. *Personality and Social Psychology Bulletin, 4*, 143–146.

Leffler, A., Gillespie, D. L., & Conaty, J. C. (1982). The effects of status differentiation on nonverbal behavior. *Social Psychology Quarterly, 45*, 153–161.

Lott, D. F., & Sommer, R. (1967). Seating arrangements and status. *Journal of Personality and Social Psychology, 7*, 90–95.

Major, B., & Heslin, R. (1982). Perceptions of cross-sex and same-sex nonreciprocal touch: It is better to give than to receive. *Journal of Nonverbal Behavior, 6*, 148–162.

Mehrabian, A. (1972). *Nonverbal communication*. Chicago: Aldine/Atherton.

Mullen, B., Salas, E., & Driskell, J. E. (1989). Salience, motivation, and artifact as contributions to the relation between participation rate and leadership. *Journal of Experimental Social Psychology, 25*, 545–559.

Murphy, J. D., Driscoll, D. M., & Kelly, J. R. (1999). Differences in nonverbal behavior of men who vary in the likelihood to sexually harass. *Journal of Social Behavior & Personality, 14*, 113–128.

Nevill, D. (1974). Experimental manipulation of dependency motivation and its effects on eye contact and measures of field dependency. *Journal of Personality and Social Psychology, 29*, 72–79.

Ridgeway, C. L. (1987). Nonverbal behavior, dominance, and the basis of status in task groups. *American Sociological Review, 52,* 683–694.

Ridgeway, C. L., Berger, J., & Smith, L. (1985). Nonverbal cues and status: An expectation states approach. *American Journal of Sociology, 90,* 955–978.

Robinson, L. F., & Reis, H. T. (1989). The effects of interruption, gender, and status on interpersonal perceptions. *Journal of Nonverbal Behavior, 13,* 141–153.

Rosa, E., & Mazur, A. (1979). Incipient status in small groups. *Social Forces, 58,* 18–37.

Schmid Mast, M. (2002). Dominance as expressed and inferred through speaking time: A meta-analysis. *Human Communication Research, 28,* 420–450.

Schwartz, B., Tesser, A., & Powell, E. (1982). Dominance cues in nonverbal behavior. *Social Psychology Quarterly, 45,* 114–120.

Siegel, S. M., Friedlander, M. L., & Heatherington, L. (1992). Nonverbal relational control in family communication. *Journal of Nonverbal Behavior, 16,* 117–139.

Snyder, R. A., & Sutker, L. W. (1977). The measurement of the construct of dominance and its relation to nonverbal behavior. *Journal of Psychology, 97,* 227–230.

Stier, D. S., & Hall, J. A. (1984). Gender differences in touch: An empirical and theoretical review. *Journal of Personality and Social Psychology, 47,* 440–459.

Thayer, S. (1969). The effect of interpersonal looking duration on dominance judgments. *Journal of Social Psychology, 79,* 285–286.

Tiedens, L. Z., & Fragale, A. R. (2003). Power moves: Complementarity in dominant and submissive nonverbal behavior. *Journal of Personality and Social Psychology, 84,* 558–568.

INTERACTION MANAGEMENT

Allert, T. (2008). *The Hitler salute: On the meaning of a gesture* (J. Chase, Trans.). New York: Metropolitan Books/Henry Holt & Co.

Ayres, J. (1975). Observers' judgments of audience members' attitudes. *Western Speech, 39,* 40–50.

Baker, C. (1977). Regulators and turn-taking in American sign language discourse. In L. A. Friedman (Ed.), *On the other hand: New perspectives on American sign language.* New York: Academic Press.

Bavelas, J. B., Coates, L., & Johnson, T. (2002). Listener responses as a collaborative process: The role of gaze. *Journal of Communication, 52,* 566–580.

Beattie, G. W. (1980). The skilled art of conversational interaction: Verbal and nonverbal signals in its regulation and management. In W. T. Singleton, P. Spurgeon, & R. B. Stammers (Eds.), *The analysis of social skill.* New York: Plenum.

Beattie, G. W. (1981). The regulation of speaker turns in face-to-face conversation: Some implications for conversation in sound-only communication channels. *Semiotica, 34,* 55–70.

Brunner, L. J. (1979). Smiles can be back channels. *Journal of Personality and Social Psychology, 37,* 728–734.

Cappella, J. N. (1985). Controlling the floor in conversation. In A. W. Siegman & S. Feldstein (Eds.), *Multichannel integrations of nonverbal behavior* (pp. 69–103). Hillsdale, NJ: Erlbaum.

Cegala, D. J., Savage, G. T., Brunner, C. C., & Conrad, A. B. (1982). An elaboration of the meaning of interaction involvement: Toward the development of a theoretical concept. *Communication Monographs, 49,* 229–248.

Coker, D. A., & Burgoon, J. K. (1987). The nature of conversational involvement and nonverbal encoding patterns. *Human Communication Research, 13,* 463–494.

Dickens, M., & Krueger, D. H. (1969). Speakers' accuracy in identifying immediate audience response during a speech. *Speech Teacher, 18,* 303–307.

Duncan, S. D., Jr. (1972). Some signals and rules for taking speaking turns in conversations. *Journal of Personality and Social Psychology, 23,* 283–292.

Duncan, S. D., Jr. (1973). Toward a grammar for dyadic conversation. *Semiotica, 9,* 29–46.

Duncan, S. D., Jr. (1974). On the structure of speaker-auditor interaction during speaking turns. *Language in Society, 2,* 161–180.

Duncan, S. D., Jr. (1975). Interaction units during speaking turns in dyadic face-to-face conversations. In A. Kendon, R. M. Harris, & M. R. Key (Eds.), *Organization of behavior in face-to-face interaction* (pp. 189–213). Chicago: Aldine.

Duncan, S. D., Jr., & Fiske, D. W. (1977). *Face-to-face interaction: Research, methods, and theory.* Hillsdale, NJ: Erlbaum.

Duncan, S. D., Jr., & Niedereche, G. (1974). On signaling that it's your turn to speak. *Journal of Experimental Social Psychology, 10,* 234–254.

Edinger, J. A., & Patterson, M. L. (1983). Nonverbal involvement and social control. *Psychological Bulletin, 93,* 30–56.

Feldstein, S., & Welkowitz, J. (1987). A chronography of conversation: In defense of an objective approach. In A. W. Siegman & S. Feldstein (Eds.), *Nonverbal behavior and communication* (2nd ed., pp. 435–499). Hillsdale, NJ: Erlbaum.

Firth, R. W. (1972). Verbal and bodily rituals of greeting and parting. In J. S. Fontaine (Ed.), *Interpretation of ritual.* London: Tavistock.

Gardiner, J. C. (1971). A synthesis of experimental studies of speech communication feedback. *Journal of Communication, 21,* 17–35.

Givens, D. (1978). Greeting a stranger: Some commonly used nonverbal signals of aversiveness. *Semiotica, 22,* 351–367.

Goffman, E. (1963). *Behavior in public places.* New York: Free Press.

Goffman, E. (1971). *Relations in public.* New York: Basic.

Greenbaum, P. E., & Rosenfeld, H. M. (1980). Varieties of touching in greetings: Sequential structure and sex-related differences. *Journal of Nonverbal Behavior, 5,* 13–25.

Halberstadt, A. G. (1985). Race, socioeconomic status, and nonverbal behavior. In A. W. Siegman & S. Feldstein (Eds.), *Multichannel integrations of nonverbal behavior* (pp. 227–266). Hillsdale, NJ: Erlbaum.

Karns, C. F. (1969). Speaker behavior to nonverbal aversive stimuli from the audience. *Speech Monographs, 36,* 26–30.

Kendon, A., & Ferber, A. (1973). A description of some human greetings. In R. P. Michael & J. H. Crook (Eds.), *Comparative ecology and behavior of primates.* London: Academic Press.

Knapp, M. L., Hart, R. P., Friedrich, G. W., & Shulman, G. M. (1973). The rhetoric of goodbye: Verbal and nonverbal correlates of human leave-taking. *Speech Monographs, 40,* 182–198.

Knuf, J. (1990/1991). Greeting and leave-taking: A bibliography of resources for the study of ritualized communication. *Research on Language and Social Interaction, 24,* 405–448.

Kraut, R., & Lewis, S. H. (1984). Some functions of feedback in conversation. In H. E. Sypher & J. L. Applegate (Eds.), *Communication by children and adults.* Beverly Hills, CA: Sage.

Krivonos, P. D., & Knapp, M. L. (1975). Initiating communication: What do you say when you say hello? *Central States Speech Journal, 26,* 115–125.

LaFrance, M., & Mayo, C. (1976). Racial differences in gaze behavior during conversations: Two systematic observational studies. *Journal of Personality and Social Psychology, 33,* 547–552.

Laver, J. (1975). Communication functions of phatic communion. In A. Kendon, R. M. Harris, & M. R. Key (Eds.), *Organization of behavior in face-to-face interaction* (pp. 215–238). Chicago: Aldine.

Leathers, D. (1979). The informational potential of the nonverbal and verbal components of feedback responses. *Southern Speech Communication Journal, 44,* 331–354.

Magnusson, A.-K. (2006). Nonverbal conversation-regulating signals of the blind adult. *Communication Studies, 57,* 421–433.

Norton, R. W., & Pettegrew, L. S. (1979). Attentiveness as a style of communication: A structural analysis. *Communication Monographs, 46,* 13–36.

O'Leary, M. J., & Gallois, C. (1985). The last ten turns: Behavior and sequencing in friends' and strangers' conversational endings. *Journal of Nonverbal Behavior, 9,* 8–27.

Pike, K. (1975). On kinesic triadic relations in turn-taking. *Semiotica, 13,* 389–394.

Rosenfeld, H. M. (1987). Conversational control functions of nonverbal behavior. In A. W. Siegman & S. Feldstein (Eds.), *Nonverbal behavior and communication* (2nd ed., pp. 563–601). Hillsdale, NJ: Erlbaum.

Rosenfeld, H. M., & Hancks, M. (1980). The nonverbal context of verbal listener responses. In M. R. Key (Ed.), *The relationship of verbal and nonverbal communication.* The Hague: Mouton.

Scheflen, A. E. (1964). Communication and regulation in psychotherapy. *Psychiatry, 27,* 126–136.

Schiffrin, D. (1974). Handwork as ceremony: The case of the handshake. *Semiotica, 12,* 189–202.

Vettin, J., & Todt, D. (2004). Laughter in conversation: Features of occurrence and acoustic structure. *Journal of Nonverbal Behavior, 28,* 93–115.

Walker, M. B., & Trimboli, C. (1982). Smooth transitions in conversational interactions. *Journal of Social Psychology, 117,* 305–306.

Walker, M. B., & Trimboli, C. (1984). The role of nonverbal signals in co-ordinating speaking turns. *Journal of Language and Social Psychology, 3,* 257–272.

Wiemann, J. M., & Knapp, M. L. (1975). Turn-taking in conversations. *Journal of Communication, 25,* 75–92.

Wilson, T. P., Wiemann, J. M., & Zimmerman, D. H. (1984). Models of turn-taking in conversational interaction. *Journal of Language and Social Psychology, 3,* 159–184.

Yngve, V. H. (1970). On getting a word in edgewise. In M. A. Campbell et al. (Eds.), *Papers from the sixth regional meeting, Chicago Linguistics Society* (pp. 567–578). Chicago: Department of Linguistics, University of Chicago.

IDENTITY

Aiello, J. R., & Aiello, T. D. (1977). Visual interaction at extended distances. *Personality and Social Psychology Bulletin, 3,* 83–86.

Argyle, M. (1988). *Bodily communication* (2nd ed.). London: Methuen.

Berry, D. S., & Hansen, J. S. (2000). Personality, nonverbal behavior, and interaction quality in female dyads. *Personality and Social Psychology Bulletin, 26,* 278–292.

Borkenau, P., & Liebler, A. (1995). Observable attributes as manifestations and cues of personality and intelligence. *Journal of Personality, 63,* 1–25.

Briton, N. J., & Hall, J. A. (1995). Beliefs about female and male nonverbal communication. *Sex Roles, 32,* 79–90.

Bugental, D. E., Love, L. R., & Gianetto, R. M. (1971). Perfidious feminine faces. *Journal of Personality and Social Psychology, 17,* 314–318.

Burgoon, J. K., Buller, D. B., & Woodall, W. G. (1989). *Nonverbal communication: The unspoken dialogue.* New York: Harper & Row.

Cross, S. E., & Madson, L. (1997). Models of the self: Self-construals and gender. *Psychological Bulletin, 122,* 5–37.

Davis, M., & Dulicai, D. (1992). Hitler's movement signature. *The Drama Review, 36,* 152–172.

Diener, E., Sandvik, E., & Larsen, R. (1985). Age and sex effects for emotional intensity. *Developmental Psychology, 21,* 542–546.

Dodd, D. K., Russell, B. L., & Jenkins, C. (1999). Smiling in school yearbook photos: Gender differences from kindergarten to adulthood. *Psychological Record, 49,* 543–554.

Dovidio, J. F., Brown, C. E., Heltman, K., Ellyson, S. L., & Keating, C. F. (1988). Power displays between women and men in discussions of gender-linked tasks: A multichannel study. *Journal of Personality and Social Psychology, 55,* 580–587.

Erickson, F. (1979). Talking down: Some cultural sources of miscommunication in interracial interviews. In A. Wolfgang (Ed.), *Nonverbal behavior: Applications and cultural implications.* New York: Academic Press.

Gifford, R. (1994). A lens-mapping framework for understanding the encoding and decoding of interpersonal dispositions in nonverbal behavior. *Journal of Personality and Social Psychology, 66,* 398–412.

Gosling, S. D., Ko, S. J., Mannarelli, T., & Morris, M. E. (2002). A room with a cue: Judgments of personality based on offices and bedrooms. *Journal of Personality and Social Psychology, 82,* 379–398.

Guerrero, L. K., & Andersen, P. A. (1994). Patterns of matching and initiation: Touch behavior and touch avoidance across romantic relationship stages. *Journal of Nonverbal Behavior, 18,* 137–153.

Halberstadt, A. G. (1985). Race, socioeconomic status, and nonverbal behavior. In A. W. Siegman & S. Feldstein (Eds.), *Multichannel integrations of nonverbal behavior.* Hillsdale, NJ: Erlbaum.

Halberstadt, A. G., Hayes, C. W., & Pike, K. M. (1988). Gender and gender role differences in smiling and communication consistency. *Sex Roles, 19,* 589–604.

Hall, J. A. (1984). *Nonverbal sex differences: Communication accuracy and expressive style.* Baltimore: Johns Hopkins University Press.

Hall, J. A. (1987). On explaining gender differences: The case of nonverbal communication. In P. Shaver & C. Hendrick (Eds.), *Review of personality and social psychology: Vol. 7* (pp. 177–200). Beverly Hills, CA: Sage.

Hall, J. A., & Carter, J. D. (1999). Gender-stereotype accuracy as an individual difference. *Journal of Personality and Social Psychology, 77,* 350–359.

Hall, J. A., Carter, J. D., & Horgan, T. G. (2000). Gender differences in nonverbal communication of emotion. In A. Fischer (Ed.), *Gender and emotion* (pp. 97–117). Paris: Cambridge University Press.

Hall, J. A., Coats, E. J., & Smith LeBeau, L. (2005). Nonverbal behavior and the vertical dimension of social relations: A meta-analysis. *Psychological Bulletin, 131,* 898–924.

Hall, J. A., & Halberstadt, A. G. (1986). Smiling and gazing. In J. S. Hyde & M. Linn (Eds.), *The psychology of gender: Advances through meta-analysis.* Baltimore: Johns Hopkins University Press.

Hall, J. A., Halberstadt, A. G., & O'Brien, C. E. (1997). "Subordination" and nonverbal sensitivity: A study and synthesis of findings based on trait measures. *Sex Roles, 37,* 295–317.

Hall, J. A., Irish, J. T., Roter, D. L., Ehrlich, C. M., & Miller, L. H. (1994). Gender in medical encounters: An analysis of physician and patient communication in a primary care setting. *Health Psychology, 13,* 384–392.

Hall, J. A., & Veccia, E. M. (1990). More "touching" observations: New insights on men, women, and interpersonal touch. *Journal of Personality and Social Psychology, 59,* 1155–1162.

Henley, N. M. (1977). *Body politics: Power, sex, and nonverbal communication.* Englewood Cliffs, NJ: Prentice-Hall.

Johnson, K. R. (1972). Black kinesics—some nonverbal communication patterns in the black culture. In L. A. Samovar & R. E. Porter (Eds.), *Intercultural communication: A reader.* Belmont, CA: Wadsworth.

Kring, A. M., & Gordon, A. H. (1998). Sex differences in emotion: Expression, experience, and physiology. *Journal of Personality and Social Psychology, 74,* 686–703.

LaFrance, M., Hecht, M. A., & Levy Paluck, E. (2003). The contingent smile: A meta-analysis of sex differences in smiling. *Psychological Bulletin, 129,* 305–334.

Lippa, R. (1998). The nonverbal display and judgment of extraversion, masculinity, femininity, and gender diagnosticity: A lens model analysis. *Journal of Research in Personality, 32,* 80–107.

Murphy, J. D., Driscoll, D. M., & Kelly, J. R. (1999). Differences in the nonverbal behavior of men who vary in the likelihood to sexually harass. *Journal of Social Behavior and Personality, 14,* 113–128.

Murphy, N. A., Hall, J. A., & Colvin, C. R. (2003). Accurate intelligence assessments in social interaction: Mediators and gender effects. *Journal of Personality, 71,* 465–493.

Noller, P. (1986). Sex differences in nonverbal communication: Advantage lost or supremacy regained? *Australian Journal of Psychology, 38,* 23–32.

Putnam, L. L., & McCallister, L. (1980). Situational effects of task and gender on nonverbal display. In D. Nimmo (Ed.), *Communication yearbook 4.* New Brunswick, NJ: Transaction.

Roese, N. J., Olson, J. M., Borenstein, M. N., Martin, A., & Shores, A. L. (1992). Same-sex touching behavior: The moderating role of homophobic attitudes. *Journal of Nonverbal Behavior, 16,* 249–259.

Rosenthal, R., & DePaulo, B. M. (1979). Sex differences in eavesdropping on nonverbal cues. *Journal of Personality and Social Psychology, 37,* 273–285.

Stier, D. S., & Hall, J. A. (1984). Gender differences in touch: An empirical and theoretical review. *Journal of Personality and Social Psychology, 47,* 440–459.

Tucker, J. S., & Friedman, H. S. (1993). Sex differences in nonverbal expressiveness: Emotional expression, personality, and impressions. *Journal of Nonverbal Behavior, 17,* 103–117.

Vrugt, A., & Kerkstra, A. (1984). Sex differences in nonverbal communication. *Semiotica, 50,* 1–41.

Willis, F. N., Jr., & Briggs, L. F. (1992). Relationship and touch in public settings. *Journal of Nonverbal Behavior, 16,* 55–63.

Zanna, M. P., & Pack, S. J. (1975). On the self-fulfilling nature of apparent sex differences in behavior. *Journal of Experimental Social Psychology, 11,* 583–591.

DECEPTION

Anderson, D. E., DePaulo, B. M., Ansfield, M. E., Tickle, J. J., & Green, E. (1999). Beliefs about cues to deception: Mindless stereotypes or untapped wisdom? *Journal of Nonverbal Behavior, 23,* 67–89.

Buck, R. (1984). *The communication of emotion.* New York: Guilford.

Burgoon, J. K., & Floyd, K. (2000). Testing for the motivational impairment effect during deceptive and truthful interaction. *Western Journal of Communication, 64,* 243–267.

Comadena, M. E. (1982). Accuracy in detecting deception: Intimate and friendship relationships. In M. Burgoon (Ed.), *Communication yearbook 6* (pp. 446–472). Newbury Park, CA: Sage.

Corcoran, J. F. T., Lewis, M. D., & Garver, R. B. (1978). Biofeedback—conditioned galvanic skin response and hypnotic suppression of arousal: A pilot study of their relation to deception. *Journal of Forensic Sciences, 23,* 155–162.

DePaulo, B. M., Kashy, D. A., Kirkendol, S. E., Wyer, M. M., & Epstein, J. A. (1996). Lying in everyday life. *Journal of Personality and Social Psychology, 70,* 979–995.

DePaulo, B. M., Kirkendol, S. E., Tang, J., & O'Brien, T. P. (1988). The motivational impairment effect in the communication of deception: Replications and extensions. *Journal of Nonverbal Behavior, 12,* 177–202.

DePaulo, B. M. Lindsay, J. J., Malone, B. E., Muhlenbruck, L., Charlton, K., & Cooper, H. (2003). Cues to deception. *Journal of Personality and Social Psychology, 129,* 74–118.

deTurck, M. A. (1991). Training observers to detect spontaneous deception: Effects of gender. *Communication Reports, 4,* 79–89.

deTurck, M. A., Feeley, T. H., & Roman, L. A. (1997). Vocal and visual cue training in behavioral lie detection. *Communication Research Reports, 14,* 249–259.

Ekman, P. (1992). *Telling lies.* (2nd ed). New York: Norton.

Ekman, P., & Friesen, W. V. (1969). Nonverbal leakage and clues to deception. *Psychiatry, 32,* 88–106.

Ekman, P., & Friesen, W. V. (1975). *Unmasking the face.* Englewood Cliffs, NJ: Prentice-Hall.

Ekman, P., Friesen, W. V., & O'Sullivan, M. (1988). Smiles when lying. *Journal of Personality and Social Psychology, 54,* 414–420.

Ekman, P., & O'Sullivan, M. (1991). Who can catch a liar? *American Psychologist, 46,* 913–920.

Ekman, P., O'Sullivan, M., & Frank, M. G. (1999). A few can catch a liar. *Psychological Science, 10,* 263–266.

Etcoff, N. L., Ekman, P., Magee, J. J., & Frank, M. G. (2000). Lie detection and language comprehension. *Nature, 405,* 139.

Farwell, L. A., & Dochin, E. (1991). The truth will out: Interrogative polygraphy ("lie detection") with event-related brain potentials. *Psychophysiology, 28,* 531–547.

Farwell, L. A., & Smith, S. S. (2001). Using brain MERMER testing to detect concealed knowledge despite efforts to conceal. *Journal of Forensic Sciences, 46,* 1–9.

Feder, B. J. (2001, October 9). Truth and justice, by the blip of a brain wave. *New York Times*, p. D3.

Feeley, T. H., & Young, M. J. (1998). Humans as lie detectors: Some more second thoughts. *Communication Quarterly, 46*, 109–126.

Hollien, H. (1990). *The acoustics of crime: The new science of forensic phonetics*. New York: Plenum.

Knapp, M. L. (2006). Lying and deception in close relationships. In A. L. Vangelisti and D. Perlman (Eds.), *The Cambridge handbook of personal relationships* (pp. 517–532). New York: Cambridge University Press.

Knapp, M. L. (2008). *Lying and deception in human interaction*. Boston: Pearson Education/Allyn & Bacon.

Knapp, M. L., Cody, M. J., & Reardon, K. K. (1987). Nonverbal signals. In C. R. Berger & S. H. Chaffee (Eds.), *Handbook of communication science* (pp. 385–418). Beverly Hills, CA: Sage.

Knapp, M. L., & Comadena, M. F. (1979). Telling it like it isn't: A review of theory and research on deceptive communications. *Human Communication Research, 5*, 270–285.

Knapp, M. L., Hart, R. P., & Dennis, H. S. (1974). An exploration of deception as a communication construct. *Human Communication Research, 1*, 15–29.

Kraut, R. E. (1978). Verbal and nonverbal cues in the perception of lying. *Journal of Personality and Social Psychology, 36*, 380–391.

Kraut, R. E., & Poe, D. (1981). Behavioral roots of person perception: Deception judgments of customs inspectors and laymen. *Journal of Personality and Social Psychology, 39*, 784–798.

Levine, T. R., Park, H. S., & McCornack, S. A. (1999). Accuracy in detecting truths and lies: Documenting the "veracity effect." *Communication Monographs, 66*, 125–144.

Lewis, M., & Saarni, C. (Eds.). (1993). *Lying and deception in everyday life*. New York: Guilford.

McCornack, S. A., & Parks, M. R. (1986). Deception detection and relationship development: The other side of trust. In M. L. McLaughlin (Ed.), *Communication yearbook 9* (pp. 377–389). Newbury Park, CA: Sage.

Mitchell, R. W., & Thompson, N. S. (Eds.). (1986). *Deception: Perspectives on human and nonhuman deceit*. Albany, NY: SUNY Press.

Nyberg, D. (1993). *The varnished truth: Truth telling and deceiving in ordinary life*. Chicago: University of Chicago Press.

Park, H. S., Levine, T. R., McCornack, S. A., Morrison, K., & Ferrara, M. (2002). How people really detect lies. *Communication Monographs, 69*, 144–157.

Robinson, W. P. (1996). *Deceit, delusion, and detection*. Thousand Oaks, CA: Sage.

Rosenfeld, J. P., Soskins, M., Bosh, G., & Ryan, A. (2004). Simple, effective countermeasures to P300-based tests of detection of concealed information. *Psychophysiology, 41*, 205–219.

Vrij, A. (2000). *Detecting lies and deceit*. New York: Wiley.

Vrij, A., Edward, K., Roberts, K. P., & Bull, R. (2000). Detecting deceit via analysis of verbal and nonverbal behavior. *Journal of Nonverbal Behavior, 24*, 239–263.

Zebrowitz, L. A., Voinescu, L., & Collins, M. A. (1996). "Wide-eyed" and "crooked-faced": Determinants of perceived and real honesty across the life span. *Personality and Social Psychology Bulletin, 22*, 1258–1269.

Zuckerman, M., DePaulo, B. M., & Rosenthal, R. (1981). Verbal and nonverbal communication of deception. In L. Berkowitz (Ed.), *Advances in experimental social psychology: Vol. 14* (pp. 1–57). New York: Academic Press.

Zuckerman, M., Spiegel, N. H., DePaulo, B. M., & Rosenthal, R. (1982). Nonverbal strategies for decoding deception. *Journal of Nonverbal Behavior, 6*, 171–187.

SELF-FULFILLING PROPHECY

Blanck, P. D. (Ed.). (1993). *Interpersonal expectations: Theory, research, and applications*. New York: Cambridge University Press.

Harris, M. J., Milich, R., Johnston, E. M., & Hoover, D. W. (1990). Effects of expectancies on children's social interactions. *Journal of Experimental Social Psychology, 26*, 1–12.

Harris, M. J., & Rosenthal, R. (1985). Mediation of interpersonal expectancy effects: 31 meta-analyses. *Psychological Bulletin, 97*, 363–386.

Rosenthal, R. (1976). *Experimenter effects in behavioral research* (enlarged ed.). New York: Irvington.

Snyder, M., Tanke, E. D., & Berscheid, E. (1977). Social perception and interpersonal behavior: On the self-fulfilling nature of social stereotypes. *Journal of Personality and Social Psychology, 35*, 656–666.

Spitz, H. H. (1997). *Nonconscious movements: From mystical messages to facilitated communication.* Mahwah, NJ: Erlbaum.

Sullins, E. S., Friedman, H. S., & Harris, M. J. (1985). Individual differences in expressive style as a mediator of expectancy communication. *Journal of Nonverbal Behavior, 9*, 229–238.

Word, C. O., Zanna, M. P., & Cooper, J. (1974). The nonverbal mediation of self-fulfilling prophecies in interracial interaction. *Journal of Experimental Social, 10*, 109–120.

The context is the frame of reference for interpreting an action.
—S. W. Littlejohn

CHAPTER **13** | NONVERBAL MESSAGES IN SPECIAL CONTEXTS

If asked what the word "fast" means, you are likely to pause, because you know the word has different meanings in different contexts. If the subject is running, fast is associated with speed; if the subject is food, fast may be associated with not eating or take-out food. Nonverbal behavior has the same multimeaning potential, and nonverbal signals may be interpreted differently in different contexts. People who are sad look down at the floor, but so do people who are submissive or shy. Knowing which meaning to attribute to a behavior requires a knowledge of the context. A smile displayed by a powerful and energetic person to a submissive and passive person may be seen as sinister, but the very same smile from the same person directed at another powerful and energetic person may be viewed as a happy smile. If any given facial expression can be interpreted in multiple ways—as delight, contentment, pleasure, approval, interest, or sexually inviting—then we need a knowledge of various contextual features to help us pinpoint the most likely meaning.

What is *context*? Those features of a social encounter that provide key markers for the meaning of any given behavior are usually identified as the context. Philippot, Feldman, and Coats (1999, p. 13) say that "nonverbal behavior can be fully understood only when considered within its social context." For example, you may feel like you understand the meaning of a particular nonverbal behavior because you are aware of certain aspects of context: 1) some personal or background characteristics of the people involved—their relationship, their age, their group membership, their gender; 2) some environmental features—the number of people involved, the accompanying lighting or noise, the time of day, the furniture configuration; 3) the expectations and norms for the situation—learning, therapy, fun; or 4) various message features—the topic, the emphasis given the behavior, what other verbal and nonverbal behavior preceded and followed the behavior in question, and so on. These features of context give meaning to nonverbal messages; but whenever we produce nonverbal messages, they have the potential to change contextual features, too.

In this chapter, we discuss nonverbal messages in the context of advertising, politics, education, culture, therapy, and technology.

ADVERTISING MESSAGES

No one in modern society needs to be told that we are surrounded by advertising. Nevertheless, people routinely underestimate the broad scope of its influence. Television, magazines, and other forms of media do far more than bombard us with direct appeals to buy products. To buy a product, you have to lay down your money; but the media exert a powerful influence on us even when nothing is bought. By immersing us in images, concepts, and associations, the media and the advertisers shape the values, attitudes, stereotypes, associations, assumptions, and expectations by which we live. Thus, advertising does far more than tell us to buy certain products. It speaks to issues that concern, and sometimes preoccupy, all people. Advertising penetrates into areas of intense personal concern for nearly everyone, such as:

- What does success mean?
- How does one define beauty?
- How should I behave in order to be socially acceptable?
- How do people belonging to different groups behave, and what do they value?
- On what should I base my self-esteem?
- What kind of a person do I want to be?

Advertising provides, in both blatant and subtle ways, answers to these questions. Furthermore, advertising does far more than just supply answers to these questions: It legitimizes the underlying premises that success, beauty, and social acceptance are the keys to happiness, and that stereotypes have validity. And it does this without our putting a penny on the counter—indeed, often without our even noticing.

Many commentators have railed at the subtle influence and the homogenizing power of the concepts and assumptions that are planted in our minds by advertising. But individuals who are exposed to advertising, which is everyone, are likely to deny advertising's influence when it comes to themselves. We are like the "fish who don't know they are wet": If these images are all we know, then that is the only reality we know—so how can we imagine an alternative? People also routinely deny social influences on themselves that they can readily see influencing others. This "I'm immune to what influences other people" fallacy is common; we see it when people deny that smoking will harm their health, that they are victims of discrimination when they obviously are, or that they engage in faulty ways of thinking about the social world, while at the same time recognizing that "other people" make these errors all the time.

Thus, we have a built-in bias against recognizing what influences us. Social psychologists have documented this in countless studies (Nisbett & Wilson, 1977; Wegner, 2002). The sheer fact that researchers can routinely conduct psychological experiments in which situational factors are manipulated to influence behavior without participants ever being aware of it proves that people's insight into the sources of their behavior is frighteningly weak.

On those occasions when we are on guard for attempted influence, we are most likely to attend to what is being *said*. Is this person telling me the truth? Are advertisers misrepresenting the product or the issues? Is the other person claiming to be better than he is? But the kinds of influence that are most likely to go unnoticed and remain out of awareness are—you guessed it—*nonverbal* in nature. In advertising, nonverbal information accounts for an overwhelming amount of the total message, especially if we include information provided by settings, backgrounds, props, possessions, clothes, hair, makeup, music, and physical and group characteristics of the people shown in addition to nonverbal behavior variables such as facial expression, tone of voice, and body movements. The unconscious conclusions we draw rest more on the nature and juxtaposition of these images and sounds than on what is actually said. As we all know, the verbal messages contained in advertisements are often silly, irrelevant, meaningless, or not likely to promote distinctive associations to the product. Yet the message can be powerful indeed.

That the influences are mainly nonverbal means that we are less guarded against their influence and less critical of their content. But to make matters worse, we are most vulnerable to such influences when we are distracted or when we are not closely attending to, or resisting, the advertiser's persuasion attempts (Petty, Cacioppo, & Schumann, 1983). When people feel a personal involvement in an issue, they attend closely to the quality of the arguments and are able to ignore irrelevant information. However, when they are not very involved—which is the state people are in when exposed to most advertising—they are prey to unconscious influence by irrelevant information, such as how sexy the model is, how charming the puppy in the ad is, how happy the people in the ad appear to be, or how wise and honest-looking the spokesperson is. Cues such as these have their influence through various psychological mechanisms, some of which have been mentioned previously in this book—for example, by associative learning, by modeling, by emotional contagion, and by inducement of mimicking; this then influences a person's emotional state, and so on. Thus, we are most vulnerable when we are in precisely those circumstances under which we experience most advertising. Furthermore, laboratory research shows that nonverbal cues that are impossible to notice consciously—that is, those presented subliminally—can serve as "primes" that influence subsequent behavior, such as behavior toward certain racial groups (Chen & Bargh, 1997). The images, associations, and stereotypes represented in advertising penetrate our minds through constant repetition and their fleeting and seemingly peripheral nature. But peripheral they are not—they *are* the message.

Empirical research is not required to show us the validity of this analysis, yet research does exist. One area of intense study has been the representation of gender in advertisements. Goffman (1979) listed several ways in which the nonverbal portrayal of women suggests demeaned status relative to men: the relative size of men versus women; how objects or people are touched or grasped; which gender appears to be in charge of the activity; the presence of ritualized subordination gestures, such as averting the eyes; "unserious" clowning or childlike poses; and the occurrence of "licensed withdrawal," when women separate themselves from the ongoing activity. Of course, one can add other specific ways in which the genders are shown stereotypically: the roles assigned to men and women—the male worker versus female homemaker, or male narrator versus female onscreen character; the distribution of products to male and female onscreen characters, such as showing men advertising life insurance, electronic products, and financial services and showing women advertising health and beauty products and retail stores; and gender disparities in body display and sexualization (Bartsch, Burnett, Diller, & Rankin-Williams, 2000; Ganahl, Prinsen, & Netzley, 2003; Goffman, 1979; Kang, 1997). Gender stereotypes are easy to detect even in television commercials aimed at children. For example, boys demonstrate or sell products more, even when the product is not gender-typed (Browne, 1998).

Specific nonverbal cues are enacted differently by males and females, too. In advertising aimed at children, boys are dominant, aggressive, effective, victorious, and likely to manipulate objects, whereas girls act shy, giggle, cover their faces, avert their eyes, lower or tilt their heads, and touch objects gently (Browne, 1998). In advertising showing adult characters, women smile more and stand in a more canted position, with weight unevenly distributed (Halberstadt & Saitta, 1987). Because such gender-stereotypical portrayals feel very normal and expected, it is difficult for us to grasp how profound the assumptions are on which they are based. Only if boys acted "like girls" and vice versa would the viewer suddenly see the stereotyping in action. One might counter that the portrayals of men and women are simply reflecting the way men and women behave in real life. Though to some extent this is true, many of the nonverbal expressions and mannerisms shown in advertising are strong exaggerations of real-life gender differences, or they show behaviors that ordinary men and women do not actually engage in.

The tendency for magazines and television to show relatively more of men's faces and relatively more of women's bodies is also well documented (Archer, Iritani, Kimes, & Barrios, 1983; Copeland, 1989; Dodd, Harcar, Foerch, & Anderson, 1989; see Chapter 9). And the disturbing, unspoken message of these depictions is that photos showing more of the face are seen as more intelligent and dominant (Schwarz & Kurz, 1989; Zuckerman, 1986). Again, a nonconscious cue manipulates our impressions of men and women.

Advertising manipulates not only how we think about products, but also how we feel emotionally, how we think about social groups, and how we think about ourselves. Images of beautiful people who seem very successful and happy simultaneously invite us to identify with them—"If I drink this beer, I can become just like them"—*and* to think we are sadly inadequate by contrast: "My boyfriend isn't as cute as the guy in the ad, my sex life doesn't seem that good, I don't have such a nice car, and my thighs will never look that good." The subtle message that the viewer is inadequate is a large part of advertising's lethal power. Even the current fad for television ads to be rapid-video montages, with many images that change so quickly you hardly know what you saw, is more than just a way to get the viewer's attention. It is a way to make viewers feel slow, dull, and excluded from the exciting, fast-paced life of the people on the screen.

Advertisers use both research and common sense in planning their strategies. No doubt a great deal of advertising research is done in-house and is never published in journals. But there is no shortage of published advertising research, some of it very early indeed. An article from 1923 asked the reasonable question, "How much smiling should an actor show for different kinds of products?" (Burtt & Clark, 1923). Research participants were shown faces with different degrees of smiling and were asked to name products that would sell best with each kind of smile. They thought that clothing would be sold best by a relatively unsmiling face, whereas toilet articles, amusements, and food would sell better if the actors smiled more.

Of course, asking people what kind of advertising messages they think would work best is not the best way to evaluate effectiveness. An advertiser would want to know about actual consumers' responses and about their purchasing choices. Current advertising researchers are especially interested in indirect methods of understanding viewers' emotional responses, and they learn about these by measuring brain activity, recording tiny electric impulses in the facial muscles associated with different emotions, and cataloguing which facial muscles move visibly (Hazlett & Hazlett, 1999; Raskin, 2003; Young, 2002; see Chapter 9 for a description of such methodologies). For example, such methods may reveal the difference between a viewer's true enjoyment smile and the polite smile of a viewer who is just saying what the researcher wants to hear. In Chapter 10 we also described early interest in using changes in pupil size as an indicator of viewers' product preferences.

The fields of selling and marketing do not concern themselves only with advertising; consumers also have face-to-face interactions with salespeople. It should come as no surprise to know that salespeople are coached in their nonverbal behavior, for example, to remember to smile at the customer. Researchers evaluate not only the impact of such coaching (Peterson, 2005) but also the relation between nonverbal decoding skill and effectiveness at being a salesperson (Byron, Terranova, & Nowicki, 2007). Indeed, salespeople who scored higher on a standard test of decoding emotional expressions in the face were more successful in both real estate and auto sales.

Should you be worried about advertising's power to exploit and manipulate you with nonverbal cues and images? Yes! But considering that you can hardly take up residence on a desert island (assuming there would be no advertising there), the best you can hope for is to arm yourself against these effects by developing your knowledge of nonverbal communication and the use of psychological tactics (Cialdini, 2007).

POLITICAL MESSAGES

Politicians have long recognized the important role of nonverbal behavior. President Lyndon Johnson is said to have been very sensitive to what nonverbal cues can communicate. He reportedly cautioned his staff not to stand in front of the windows and look across the street at the White House the day after President John F. Kennedy's assassination for fear it would appear as if they were looking for power. In journalist Bob Woodward's (2004) book about how and why President Bush and his staff initiated a preemptive attack on Iraq, he notes how members of Bush's cabinet paid close attention to Bush's body language. In the following excerpt involving General Tommy Franks, we can see that Bush, too, felt nonverbal signals played a critical role in understanding a person's reaction:

> "I'm trying to figure out what intelligent questions to ask a commander who has just impressed me in Afghanistan. I'm looking for the logic. I'm watching his body language very carefully," Bush recalled. He emphasized the body language, the eyes, the demeanor. It was more important than some of the substance. It was also why he wanted Franks there in Crawford and not as another face on a wall of screens. (p. 66)

The average American watches approximately 30 hours of television per week, which adds up to nearly 10 years by age 65. Television can highlight nonverbal signals that can influence voters, and political candidates know that the image they project on TV will affect voter choices. But biases toward candidates reflected in the facial expressions of newscasters who report on these political candidates also may play a role in voter decisions (Friedman, DiMatteo, & Mertz, 1980; Mullen, Futrell, Stairs, Rice, Baumeister, Dawson, Riordan, Radloff, Goethals, Kennedy, & Rosenfeld, 1986).

Some argue that political candidates in the United States have become so preoccupied with the image they project that their concern for arguments supporting their policies has diminished. If this is true, it is because politicians are well aware that image has the potential to trump their positions on issues (Ailes, 1988; Budescheim & DePaola, 1994). Physically unappealing candidates and candidates whose behavior does not signal energy, confidence, likeability, and a connection to voters are not likely to play well on television. Candidates whose nonverbal demeanor signals a positive relationship message on TV—facial expressions that communicate sincerity, body positions that suggest immediacy, and vocal tones that are perceived as caring—are more likely to garner voter support. Television requires what Jamieson (1988) calls "a new eloquence—a softer, warmer style of communication." This in no way minimizes the necessity of a candidate also displaying nonverbal signals that would help to communicate assertiveness and energy. How have U.S. presidential candidates fared in the image competition?

During the first of the 1960 television debates between presidential candidates Richard Nixon and John Kennedy, analysts often discussed Nixon's loss in terms of how he presented himself on television, that is, his five o'clock shadow showing through the stage makeup, lighting conditions that accentuated a tired face, a suit that blended into the background, and so forth. Nixon has been quoted as saying he spent too much time studying and not enough time on his physical appearance (Bryski & Frye, 1979–1980; Tiemens, 1978). A movement analysis by Davis (1995, p. 213) indicates Nixon's appearance was only one of his nonverbal drawbacks.

> Nixon sits with a tense, narrow posture, whereas Kennedy sits with legs crossed, hands resting easily, his weight centered. In the medium camera shots, Nixon can be seen gripping the lectern tightly and not gesticulating for long periods of time, although his head movements are clear and emphatic. And Nixon displays a disastrous pattern of hyperblinking—not just abnormally frequent (more than one per second), but at times with such rapid flutters that his eyes momentarily close. By comparison Kennedy clearly wins despite his rather ordinary and constricted showing.

It was widely reported and believed that radio listeners judged the debate a draw, whereas television viewers felt Kennedy was the winner. Even though the accuracy of this conclusion has been questioned, the belief that it was true may have been largely responsible for subsequent concern about the influence of nonverbal signals in political campaigns and debates (Kraus, 1996; Vancil & Pendell, 1987). By 1968, though, candidate Nixon felt he knew a great deal more about the role of nonverbal signals and the use of television. Joe McGinniss's (1969) book

FIGURE 13-1

One of the 2008 Presidential debates between John McCain and Barak Obama.

The Selling of the President 1968 presents a vivid, if not alarming, picture of the role nonverbal signals were expected to play in televised politics:

> Television seems particularly useful to the politician who can be charming but lacks ideas.... On television it matters less that he does not have ideas. His personality is what the viewers want to share. He need be neither statesman nor crusader; he must only show up on time. Success and failure are easily measured: how often is he invited back? Often enough and he reaches his goal—to advance from "politician" to "celebrity," a status jump bestowed by grateful viewers who feel that finally they have been given a basis for making a choice.
>
> The TV candidate, then, is measured not against his predecessors—not against a standard of performance established by two centuries of democracy—but against Mike Douglas. How well does he handle himself? Does he mumble, does he twitch, does he make me laugh? Do I feel warm inside? (pp. 29–30)
>
> The words would be the same ones Nixon always used—the words of the acceptance speech. But they would all seem fresh and lively because a series of still pictures would flash on the screen while Nixon spoke. If it were done right, it would permit Treleaven to create a Nixon image that was entirely independent of the words. Nixon would say his same old tiresome things but no one would have to listen. The words would become Muzak. Something pleasant and lulling in the background. The flashing pictures would be carefully selected to create the impression that somehow Nixon represented competence, respect for tradition, serenity, faith that the American people were better people than people anywhere else, and that all these problems others shouted about meant nothing in a land blessed with the tallest building, strongest armies, biggest factories, cutest children, and rosiest sunsets in the world. Even better: through association with these pictures, Richard Nixon could become these very things. (p. 85)

Since 1968, the strategies used to create favorable images of political candidates have become more widespread and more sophisticated. The visuals on candidate Web sites are specifically designed to develop the candidate's image in areas that are believed to help the candidate win votes—family photos or videos that imply the candidate is a person with "family values," or images of the candidate dressed casually and speaking to people who work in restaurants and factories to show the candidate's connection to voters (Verser & Wicks, 2006). The communication environment at the candidate's speeches and television appearances is carefully constructed. At a 2004 campaign speech in Indianapolis, White House aides asked people in the crowd behind President Bush to take off their ties so they would look more like the people who would benefit from his tax cut. Backdrops with pictures and slogans accompanied most of Bush's speeches and became a part of any photo of Bush, the speaker. For some who saw the photo in the newspaper the next day, the composite message of Bush and the backdrop summed up the speech completely (see Figure 13-2). When President Bush selected the site of a small shipping company to deliver a speech on how his economic plan would favor small business, his aides put up American flags and a backdrop saying "Strengthening the Economy." Boxes near the podium stamped "Made in China" were covered, and a backdrop of boxes labeled "Made in USA" was added.

Analysts of the 1976 Carter–Ford presidential debates argue that Gerald Ford's loss was attributable to less eye gaze with the camera, grimmer facial expressions, and less favorable camera angles (Tiemens, 1978). Subsequently, Jimmy Carter's

FIGURE 13-2

Bush using a backdrop to create an image.

loss to Ronald Reagan in the 1980 debate was attributed to Carter's visible tension and his inability to "coordinate his nonverbal behavior with his verbal message" (Ritter & Henry, 1990). Effective leaders are often seen as people who confidently take stock of a situation, perform smoothly, and put those around them at ease. Many saw Reagan's nonverbal behavior this way. In 1984 Reagan's expressiveness and physical attractiveness were evident, whereas his opponent, Walter Mondale, was perceived as low in expressiveness and attractiveness (Patterson, Churchill, Burger, & Powell, 1992). Expressions of fear and uncertainty may be the biggest turnoff for voters. These include looking down; hesitating; making rapid, jerky movements; or seeming to freeze, as Dan Quayle did when Lloyd Bentsen told him in the 1988 vice presidential debate, "You're no Jack Kennedy." Some even associated Walter Mondale's tense smile with a fear grimace (Masters, 1989; Sullivan, Masters, Lanzetta, McHugo, Plate, & Englis, 1991).

The fact that the faces of presidential candidates are so prominent in their campaign literature and television ads makes this feature especially important in determining voter perceptions. In one study, people looked at facial photos of the candidates vying for congressional offices from 2000 to 2004 and made a decision about which one appeared more competent. The candidates judged more competent in the U.S. Senate races won 71.6 percent of the time; the candidates judged more competent in the races for the U.S. House of Representatives won 68.8 percent of the time. A follow-up study found similar results when the judges were only allowed one second to view the photos (Todorov, Mandisodza, Goren, & Hall, 2005). When one of the candidates has a more "mature" face, and his rival is more baby faced, judgments of competence will tend to favor the more mature face (Zebrowitz, 1997). Keating, Randall, and Kendrick (1999) digitized the faces of Presidents Clinton, Reagan, and Kennedy and made them look more or less mature by altering the size of the eyes and lips. A less mature Clinton, with bigger eyes and lips, was perceived as more honest and attractive, even by those who did not support him in the 1996 election. Clinton's power ratings were not affected by his

FIGURE 13-3

Which candidate is more competent?

youthful look, but Reagan and Kennedy were seen as less powerful when their faces were made to look less mature.

Fortunately, the image advisors are not yet in control of all the variables, the least of which is the public's increasing knowledge of how political images can be molded. A carefully controlled appearance and scripted verbal behavior can readily be offset, or put in perspective, when candidates engage in spontaneous speech and interactive dialogue about substantive issues.

TEACHER–STUDENT MESSAGES

Whether it takes place in the classroom itself or not, the process of teaching and learning is a gold mine for discovering the richness and importance of nonverbal behavior (Andersen & Andersen, 1982; Babad, 1992; Philippot, Feldman, & McGee, 1992; Woolfolk & Brooks, 1983). The following are only a few reminders of the ways in which nonverbal cues play a crucial role in this context:

1. Nonverbal cues between teachers and students signal a close or distant relationship.
2. Students avoid eye gaze with teachers to avoid participation.
3. Students' body postures and facial expressions display their interest and attention in what the teacher is saying.
4. Student and teacher dress, hair length, and adornment affect classroom interaction and learning.
5. Disciplinary enactments by teachers may manifest in negative facial expressions, threatening gestures, or critical vocal tones.
6. Teachers announce they have plenty of time for student conferences, but fidget and glance at their watch when students come to see them.
7. Teachers may try to assess student comprehension and learning by visually scanning students' facial expressions.
8. Classroom design—wall colors, space between seats, size and placement of windows—effects student participation and learning.

Subtle nonverbal influences in the classroom can sometimes have dramatic results, as Rosenthal and Jacobson (1968) found. Intelligence quotient (IQ) tests were given to elementary school pupils prior to their entering for the fall term. Randomly—that is, not according to scores—some students were labeled as high scorers on an "intellectual blooming test," indicating they would show unusual intellectual development in the following year. Teachers were given this information. These students showed a sharp rise on IQ tests given at the end of the year, which experimenters attributed to teacher expectations and to the way these students were treated. Rosenthal and Jacobson had this to say:

> To summarize our speculations, we may say that by what she said, by how and when she said it, by her facial expressions, postures, and perhaps by her touch, the teacher may have communicated to the children of the experimental group that she expected improved intellectual performance. Such communications together with possible changes in teaching techniques may have helped the child learn by changing his self-concept, his expectations of his own behavior, and his motivation, as well as his cognitive style and skills. (p. 180)

In an effort to identify the cues associated with teacher expectancies, Chaikin, Sigler, and Derlega (1974) asked people to tutor a 12-year-old boy. The boy was described as either bright or dull to some, and a third group was given no information about the boy's intelligence. A 5-minute videotape of the tutoring was analyzed for behaviors indicating liking and approval. Tutors of the so-called bright boy smiled more, had more direct eye contact, leaned forward more, and nodded more than either of the other two groups. In general, then, people who expect others to do well, as compared to those who expect poor performance, seem to:

1. Create a warm socioemotional climate
2. Provide more differentiated performance feedback
3. Give more difficult material and more material
4. Give more opportunities for the performer to respond (Blanck, 1993; Rosenthal, 1985; Harris & Rosenthal, 1985)

A related line of research has examined teachers who are perceived as more and less "immediate" in their style of teaching (McCroskey & Richmond, 1992). We saw in Chapter 12 that immediacy behavior signals liking, warmth, and positive affect, and sometimes immediacy is shown when teachers move around the classroom and gain proximity to their students. Sometimes it involves more teacher smiling, facial expressions of interest when students are talking, maintaining eye gaze with students, using a friendly vocal tone, or other behaviors that students associate with liking and warmth. Research by Smythe and Hess (2005) found that student perceptions of their teacher's immediacy behavior is not always an accurate reflection of how their teacher actually behaves, but numerous studies show that when college students do associate nonverbal immediacy with a teacher, they are more likely to like the teacher and the course. There is also more teacher–student interaction in these classes, and students report that they would like to take another course from that instructor. Students feel they learn more from teachers who exhibit immediacy behavior, which is an important outcome from a motivational standpoint. But the data available at present does not provide consistent and conclusive evidence that students actually *do* learn more from teachers who exhibit more immediacy behavior (Allen, Witt, & Wheeless, 2006; Harris & Rosenthal, 2005; Witt, Wheeless, & Allen, 2004). At this point it seems reasonable to assume that perceived teacher immediacy will improve some types of student learning but not others. Nor does it seem unreasonable to assume that certain types of students will profit more or less from perceived teacher immediacy.

Even though plenty of evidence supports the conclusion that *perceived* teacher immediacy behavior has a positive impact on some important student perceptions, the exact nature of that behavior, and the way it is displayed throughout the length of the class, are not well known. For example, does a teacher have to exhibit immediacy behavior throughout every class period to be perceived as "immediate," or is the optimum style a mix of immediate and less immediate behavior? When does immediacy behavior signal that the course is "easy" or that the teacher is a "pushover"? Can a teacher be stern, strict, and businesslike and also communicate positive affect to his or her students? Woolfolk (1978) and others have found that even negative nonverbal behavior can elicit quality student performance sometimes, but it is unlikely to be an effective teaching style if used for the duration of the class. And even though we know the types of behavior associated with immediacy, it is still not clear how such behaviors should be enacted for them to be perceived as having an immediate teaching style.

Sometimes teachers treat some students better or worse than others, for example, because of race, gender, unpleasant interactions with them, and so on. Do students perceive these teacher biases even when the teachers believe they are suppressing them? Not always, but certainly much more than teachers believe. Students are often keenly aware of subtle nonverbal signals that convey messages teachers believe they are effectively masking. Babad (1992) argues that teachers need to admit their biases to themselves and recognize that such biases are likely to be perceived by others. Once that is done, more realistic goals for student–teacher communication can be developed.

Thus far we have been focusing on teacher behavior, but the classroom is a two-way street in which teachers and students mutually influence one another. As we have observed, teacher immediacy behavior elicits a number of positive outcomes from students. But students who exhibit immediacy can also elicit positive outcomes from teachers (Baringer & McCroskey, 2000). We have much to learn about the nonverbal communication of warmth and closeness in learning environments, and this knowledge will be increasingly important as distance education continues to increase (Guerrero & Miller, 1998; Mottet, 2000).

CULTURAL MESSAGES

When we learn the rules and norms people expect our behavior to match, we are learning about culture. All of us exist within several cultures—our family, our religious group, our social class, our age group, our school, our workplace, our gender, and our society. So some cultural teaching is a part of all our communication behavior. Culture in this section focuses on large groups of people, possibly millions, who vary in age, sex, gender, and social class but share a set of nonverbal behaviors that help to define them as a culture.

Any behavior identified as characteristic of a large group of people, however, does not mean that every person or every conversation in that culture will always exhibit that behavior. For example, a culture described as one in which people touch each other often may also have some members whose conversations do not involve much touching; and some conversations may be devoid of touching even though the interactants normally do a lot of touching. When touching is identified as a characteristic of a culture, it simply means that this group of people generally tends to touch each other more when compared with other groups of people.

Scholars believe cultures differ on a variety of dimensions (Gudykunst & Ting-Toomey, 1988), but three dimensions in particular are useful for examining variations in nonverbal behavior: 1) high-contact versus low-contact cultures; 2) cultures that value individualism versus cultures that value collectivism; and 3) high-context versus low-context cultures.

HIGH-CONTACT VERSUS LOW-CONTACT CULTURES

People in high-contact cultures establish close interaction distances and touch each other frequently (Hall, 1966). They enjoy the olfactory and tactile stimulation that comes with this kind of interpersonal involvement. Central and South America, southern Europe, and the Middle East are often classified as high-contact regions; Asia and northern Europe are viewed as low contact.

The United States has traditionally been labeled a low-contact culture. Informal observations by Jourard (1966) would seem to support this designation. He measured the frequency of contact between couples in cafés in various cities and reported the following contacts per hour: San Juan, Puerto Rico, 180; Paris, 110; Gainesville, Florida, 2; London, 0. Cultural habits do change, and people in the United States may be touching more now than at any time in their history (see "Touchy Topic," 2000; Willis & Rawdon, 1994). In the early 1970s, Barnlund (1975) conducted a comparative study of Japanese and U.S. touching patterns using self-reports from 120 college students in each culture. In almost every category, the amount of physical contact reported in the United States was twice that reported by the Japanese. A much more recent observational study on a U.S. campus of romantically involved cross-sex couples found that Asian couples were far less likely to walk with arms around one another than were Latino couples (Regan, Jerry, Narvaez, & Johnson, 1999). Similarly, McDaniel and Andersen (1998), in a study of cross-sex touch among travelers in a U.S. airport, found that travelers from the United States touched notably more body regions than did northeast Asians, who touched less than any group observed, including southeast Asians, Caribbean and Latin Americans, and northern Europeans. Although this study measures extent of touch, not frequency of touch, it does suggest—as do the other studies reviewed here—that whereas Asia, especially northeast Asia, may indeed have low contact as its norm, the United States seems to have norms that are further in the "contact" direction. As the U.S. population grows ever more ethnically diverse, any broad label would probably be an oversimplification.

Field (1999) speculated that patterns of touching in public might be related to cultural tendencies toward aggression. Field chose France and the United States to work with, because they differ dramatically in their rates of societal violence. Comparing French and U.S. adolescents interacting with their peers in McDonald's restaurants in Paris and Miami, she found that the U.S. sample engaged in less leaning, stroking, kissing, and hugging of their friends but more self-touching than did the French sample, consistent with France being more of a contact culture.

Classifying cultures as either high or low contact inevitably covers up differences. For example, Central and South America are both classified as "high contact," but Shuter's (1976) systematic observation of people interacting in natural settings suggests that public touching and holding decreases as one moves south from Costa Rica to Panama to Columbia. And as we noted earlier, when we label a culture as high or low contact, we should not forget that there are likely to be important variations within a culture. Halberstadt (1985), for example, reviewed race differences and nonverbal behavior and found that black Americans tend to establish larger interpersonal distances for conversation than white Americans do, but they also engage in *more* touch. As we reflect on high- and low-contact cultures, we should also recognize the importance of distinguishing between *frequency* and *meaning*. Two cultures may display different frequencies of touch, especially in public, but it is a separate question as to whether the meanings attached to those touches are different as well. Communicating intimacy through touch, for example, can be accomplished with a lot of contact or a little contact.

INDIVIDUALISM VERSUS COLLECTIVISM

Cultures have also been distinguished from one another by the extent to which they manifest individualism or collectivism (Hofstede, 2001; Triandis, 1994). Individualistic cultures emphasize things like personal rights, responsibilities, achievements, privacy, self-expression, individual initiative, and identity based on personal attributes. Regions said to typically manifest behavior aligned with this orientation include the United States, Australia, Great Britain, Canada, the Netherlands, New Zealand, Germany, Belgium, and Denmark. Nonverbal signals that support individualism may include such things as environments designed for privacy; eye gaze and vocal signals that exude confidence, strength, and dynamism; and distinctive clothing. Dion (2002) argues that stereotyping based on facial attractiveness will also be more prevalent among members of individualistic cultures, because facial attractiveness is another way to highlight distinctiveness.

Cultures with a collective orientation tend to emphasize things that show the value they put on their group membership. Of special concern would be things like interests shared with group members, collaborating for the good of the group, maintaining harmony within the group to ensure it functions well, and maintaining traditions that emphasize group values and successes. Global regions typically associated with collectivism include Venezuela, Japan, Pakistan, Peru, Taiwan, Thailand, Brazil, Kenya, and Hong Kong. Among other things, we would expect nonverbal signals in collective cultures to exhibit familiar routines, rituals, and ways of behaving that are widely known and practiced in the culture; a high frequency of deference behavior, such as bowing, gaze avoidance, and politeness routines that include the suppression of emotional displays that might offend the group; and behavior designed to avoid calling attention to the actions of an individual when it could be detrimental to the group.

HIGH-CONTEXT VERSUS LOW-CONTEXT CULTURES

According to Hall (1976), low-context cultures tend to rely on verbal messages. Words are valued because they are believed to provide information in a direct, explicit manner. Saying what you want to say as unambiguously as possible is valued, and ambiguity is not well tolerated. In contrast, high-context cultures are more likely to rely on implicit and indirect messages. Nonverbal behavior is valued, and messages gain their meaning by knowing the context. "What everyone knows" is the key to understanding, and ambiguity is better tolerated.

Effective communication in some cultures may rely more on contextual knowledge than in some other cultures, but the need to understand context is an issue that permeates any cross-cultural encounter. Ignorance of context leads to misunderstandings. "Outsiders," or people who are less knowledgeable about a culture, are less knowledgeable about contextual cues that give meaning to certain behaviors. On the other hand, the knowledge necessary to properly interpret a message comes much more easily to a cultural "insider."

SIMILARITIES ACROSS CULTURES

The fact that cultures exhibit different nonverbal behaviors gets a lot of attention. It should. These differences often lead to problematic encounters. But it is also important to understand that similarities exist across cultures as well. Some of these similarities occur because people in one or more cultures adopt a behavior exhibited in another culture. Today, information flows freely across cultures, so it is not difficult to imagine how a gesture or style of adorning the body could become a multicultural phenomenon. Information about behavior in other cultures is regularly exchanged via travelers, magazines, movies, the Internet, and other ways.

Similarities in nonverbal behavior also occur across cultures for another reason: They may be part of an inherited neurological program that members of the human species acquire. In Chapter 2, we noted that the eyebrow raise or eyebrow flash has been observed in greeting behavior in cultures around the world. Chapter 2 also reported the work of Ekman and his colleagues (Ekman, 2003; Ekman, Sorenson, & Friesen, 1969), who found people in literate and nonliterate cultures around the world who could decode six facial expressions of emotion with a high degree of accuracy; in turn, these people could make these same expressions, and these could be decoded by people from other cultures, also with a high degree of accuracy. Researchers have also found considerable cross-cultural agreement on which faces are attractive and unattractive, and some scholars speculate that this agreement occurs because it is linked to the survival of the species (Cunningham, Barbee, & Philhower, 2002; Dion, 2002; Etcoff, 1999; Rhodes, Harwood, Yoshikawa, Nishitani, McLean, 2002). The list of cross-cultural similarities in nonverbal behavior is not long, but areas that may prove fruitful to explore include meanings associated with extremes of eye gaze, caregiver touching behavior with neonates, and the need for territory. Some research on refusal and greeting sequences, reported in Chapter 2 and Chapter 12, suggests humans may even have hard-wired *patterns* of behavior.

These underlying similarities among humans are not always readily visible, because cultural teachings may direct members to mask or minimize them. For example, the *asiallinen* "matter of fact" nonverbal style in Finland demands expressive restraint in facial displays. People from more expressive cultures may view this as a nonexpression, but Finns see it as a valued expression showing emotional control. In fact, some Finnish leaders have lost credibility with their constituents by publicly showing a lack of emotional control through facial expressions that were too reflective of their feelings (Wilkins, 2005).

THERAPEUTIC SETTINGS

Anyone who has ever visited a medical doctor or a psychotherapist knows that the nonverbal cues exchanged in such a visit are important to the outcome of the visit.

In this section, we suggest four areas in which nonverbal communication is important in dealing with distress and illness, whether physical or mental:

1. *Understanding the disorder.* How do clinical professionals define different conditions, such as depression?
2. *Diagnosis.* Does the clinician reach the correct conclusions about the client's problems, states, and progress?
3. *Therapy.* Is the clinician able to help the client solve his or her problems and maintain good physical and psychological functioning?
4. *Relationship.* Do the clinician and client develop a positive and trusting interpersonal relationship?

For each of these goals, nonverbal cues play an important part (Gorawara-Bhat, Cook, & Sachs, 2007; Hall, Harrigan, & Rosenthal, 1995; Robinson, 2006; Schmid Mast, 2007). In terms of understanding a disorder, studying nonverbal behavior and skill can help researchers develop theories about the nature of the disorder. Nonverbal behavior might be part of the definition. For example, the definition of depression includes the expression of sadness, and the definition of schizophrenia includes the display of inappropriate nonverbal behavior. Similarly, autism is defined in part by the idea that such patients lack the ability to infer what's going on in someone else's head; therefore, a deficit in the ability to judge emotional expressions would be a definitional element. As summarized in previous chapters, and by Perez and Riggio (2003), many groups with psychological disorders—including depression, schizophrenia, alcoholism (Philippot, Kornreich, & Blairy, 2003), and autism (McGee & Morrier, 2003)—score lower on accuracy in judging the meanings of nonverbal cues than do control groups. At present, it is not clear to what extent the nonverbal decoding deficit so evident in impaired groups is tied uniquely to the nature of their disorders or instead reflects other factors, such as a general deficit in cognitive ability, lowered motivation to focus on experimental tasks, or the effect of medications. Studies need to include appropriate control tasks, along with the nonverbal sensitivity tests, to resolve this question.

Nonverbal cues are also important in the process of diagnosis by practicing clinicians. The process of clinical care, either by medical doctors or psychotherapists, involves expert knowledge and cognitive skills acquired through training; nevertheless, most of what clinical care consists of is interpersonal interaction. Basically, clinicians and clients talk to each other, and it is through the medium of speech that therapeutic action occurs. Naturally, nonverbal behavior is a crucial component of this interaction.

The clinician routinely studies the patient for nonverbal signs that will shed light on problems and progress. In a psychotherapy visit, the therapist's ability to read signs of emotion—especially those that signal issues not brought up verbally, those that are upsetting to clients or are denied by them—is central. In medical visits, the physician is attuned to emotional and psychosocial issues that might be causing, or be caused by, a medical condition. For instance, a patient might start experiencing depression in the aftermath of a heart attack.

Many studies have investigated the display of different nonverbal cues in relation to different psychological disorders. For example, researchers have shown that the stereotype of the depressed person as downcast and slow in response has validity. Evidence of decreased general movement; decreased expressiveness; decreased speech, gestures, eye contact, and smiling; halting speech; and a deficit in the ability to express emotions have all been documented in depressed persons (Bouhuys, 2003; Ekman & Friesen, 1974; Ellgring, 1986; Perez & Riggio, 2003; Waxer, 1976).

Some forms of schizophrenia are marked by a voice that is very flat and monotone, and an increase in very subtle muscle activation in the corrugator muscle of the face—the muscle associated with distressed-looking eyebrows—is observed compared to control participants, even when viewing positive stimuli (Kring & Earnst, 2003). Other nonverbal characteristics of schizophrenia include lack of facial expression, inappropriate affect displays, increased self-touching, and less interpersonal gazing. As discussed in Chapter 10, some nonverbal behaviors are distinctively associated with autism and related conditions such as Asperger syndrome, most notably gaze avoidance but also less smiling and gesturing (McGee & Morrier, 2003).

Another illustration of the diagnostic use of nonverbal cues is in the detection of pain. Researchers have documented the configuration of facial cues indicative of different kinds of pain in both infants and adults (Patrick, Craig, & Prkachin, 1986; Prkachin, 1992a). Some common indicators include lowering the brows, narrowing the eye openings, raising the cheeks, raising the upper lip, and wrinkling the nose. Analysis of cues may reveal information not forthcoming from self-reports provided by patients. For example, chronic and acute sufferers of temporomandibular disorder, which causes painful jaw movement, reported the same amounts of pain, but the chronic group showed more facial indications of pain both when alone and when experiencing painful procedures (LeResche, Dworkin, Wilson, & Ehrlich, 1992). Nonverbal cues can also reveal differences in the behavior of people actually experiencing pain versus those just pretending (Prkachin, 1992b).

There are also nonverbal behaviors associated with the Type A personality syndrome (a risk factor for heart attack), including loud and explosive speech and other behaviors suggestive of hostility. Indeed, many studies implicate hostility as a precursor to heart disease. In a recent study, facial expressions coded by the FACS (see Chapter 9) were associated with transient occurrences of ischemia, a condition in which there is insufficient blood supply to the muscles of the heart, a predictor of serious and even fatal coronary events. Men with known heart conditions were videotaped in interviews, and physiological measurements were made. Those experiencing episodes of ischemia showed more expressions suggestive of anger and more nonenjoyment smiles than those without ischemia (Rosenberg, Ekman, Jiang, Babyak, Coleman, Hanson, O'Connor, Waugh, & Blumenthal, 2001). Results such as these could influence physicians' care of these patients.

During medical education, there is a widespread trend to increase training and awareness of communication factors in medical care. Nevertheless, physicians typically receive only a limited amount of training in communicating with patients, including recognizing patients' states and conditions through an enhanced awareness of nonverbal cues. Clearly, physicians can use this kind of knowledge. However, it is very important that physicians not only notice cues but that they draw appropriate interpretations from them. In Chapter 10 we reviewed a study in which surgery professors erroneously thought medical students knew less if the students used averted gaze during an oral examination. Picking up on nonverbal cues is good, but it is also crucial that the correct inferences are made about them and that the physician is able to discount them if the important thing at the moment is what the patient is saying with words.

Nonverbal cues can also be tied to diagnostic judgments by considering them as an unobtrusive source of information on the patient's progress. Ellgring and Scherer (1996), Ostwald (1961), and others have found that vocal qualities, smiling, movement, and other nonverbal behaviors can change following psychotherapy.

Thus far, we have discussed ways clinicians make use of the client's cues. The client also studies the clinician for signs of understanding, interest, approval, rejection, and reassurance. The clinician's nonverbal behavior may facilitate a good relationship, a high level of trust, and a good exchange of information—what are together called the "therapeutic alliance"—or it may make the client feel disregarded and misunderstood. Hall, Horgan, Stein, and Roter (2002) found that both patients and physicians are able to judge with some, though not great, accuracy how much they are liked by the other, certainly an impression that could have far-reaching consequences. In that study, patients whose doctors liked them less were less satisfied and more likely to consider changing doctors over the following year. Greater satisfaction and attributions of empathy are associated with doctors who gaze, lean forward, nod, gesture, establish closer interpersonal distances, and have warm and enthusiastic voice quality. Sometimes certain combinations of physician cues have the best effect. Hall, Roter, and Rand (1981) found that patients were most satisfied when their physicians' voice tone was negative, such as if it was anxious, but combined with words that were positive, a mix that seemed to convey concerned positive regard. Sometimes physicians' nonverbal behaviors can signal a troubled history with patients. As noted in Chapter 11, surgeons who were sued more had voices that suggested more dominance.

Physicians who are better able to decode the meanings of nonverbal cues have patients who are more satisfied and more likely to keep their appointments (DiMatteo, Taranta, Friedman, & Prince, 1980; DiMatteo, Hays, & Prince, 1986). Those researchers also found that physicians who were more accurate at expressing nonverbal emotion cues in a posed task had more satisfied and compliant patients. So far, it is not known how these nonverbally skilled physicians put their skills into action in the medical encounter, but we can imagine that they might be good at showing empathy, creating a warm atmosphere, or picking up on the patient's unmentioned issues.

Medical educators now stress the importance of developing a good relationship with patients. It is a fallacy to think that physicians and patients are just enacting well-learned roles, or that physicians are cognitive machines that crank out professional behavior without having feelings or showing emotions. Clinicians and clients of all sorts develop relationships; they may be of a unique and highly structured kind, but they are relationships nonetheless. Therefore, all that we know about the role of nonverbal behavior in attraction, attitudes, impressions, rapport, emotions, and persuasion is relevant.

TECHNOLOGY AND NONVERBAL MESSAGES

Virtually all the research reported in this book has been designed to enhance your understanding of nonverbal behavior in face-to-face interaction. But an increasing amount of our communication is mediated by various forms of technology. Two issues emanating from this trend are especially pertinent to the study of nonverbal communication: First, does technology eliminate the role of nonverbal signals in face-to-face interaction? Second, do changes in the manifestation of nonverbal behavior mediated by technology result in less effective communication?

The answer to the first question depends on what kind of communication technology we are talking about and how it is used. Computer-mediated communication may be verbally dominant, as in texting and email; it may have verbal text with an anthropomorphic icon or photograph; it may provide ongoing visual images of interactants through videoconferencing or webcams on personal computers; and it might involve the interaction of two-dimensional animated representations of the interactants in the form of "avatars" who embody each interactant's desired behavior—including frowns, winks, smiles, and so on. Text messaging via cell phones may reduce the role of nonverbal behavior, but cell phones also have the ability to instantly complement a written message with vocal cues or a photograph. Even those forms of communication that are verbally dominant, such as text messaging and email, are not completely devoid of extraverbal signals. For example, people associate meanings with the length of time it takes a person to reply, the depth or detail of the reply, the number of spelling errors—perhaps a sign of how much care went into composing the message, or perhaps the sender's competence—and so on. The meanings associated with these and other features of the communication will no doubt vary with the nature of the interactants' relationship, their online interaction history, how important or pressing the issue is, and the like.

Will communication effectiveness suffer when people communicate in ways that eliminate or severely reduce their opportunity to see, touch, and exercise control over the interaction context? During the early stages of the technology boom, many theorists and practitioners believed that the effectiveness of human communication mediated by technology would suffer. They argued that technology could not effectively restore what would be lost by the lack of human copresence (Walther, 2006).

But human beings and the ever-increasing number of new communication technologies relate to each other in complex and diverse ways. Some messages can be effectively communicated through various technological instruments without all the nonverbal signals that might accompany the same message in face-to-face interaction. When messages are short, uncomplicated, and can be easily understood without complementary and redundant information from other channels, almost any type of mediated communication, including text and email messages, can be successful. However, email messages have been found to be less effective in accurately communicating sarcasm, humor, and certain emotions when compared to vocal and face-to-face communication. Adding to the problem is the discovery that the people who sent the email messages greatly overestimated the accuracy of their messages. Kruger, Epley, Parker, and Ng (2005), who base their conclusions on five studies, point out that it is apparently hard for the senders of email to appreciate the interpretive perspective of the receiver.

What is lost, however, is ongoing feedback and relationship information that could be used to adapt message content. Herbert and Vorauer (2003) found that evaluative feedback was more positive and more accurate in face-to-face interaction than over email. Some believe that the absence of ongoing feedback and relationship information in less personal forms of communication, like email, facilitates less sensitive, self-focused, critical, and deceptive messages (Kiesler, Siegel, & McGuire, 1984). It is not clear, however, whether less personal communication channels are also less civil. Is less civil behavior more widespread in email messages or face-to-face interactions in general? Is less civil behavior more likely in email messages but only under certain circumstances? Is less civil communication behavior more likely related to individual style than it is to the nature of the media used to communicate? We are still seeking the answers to these questions.

Interactive video often allows interactants to accomplish their communicative goals, but remote interaction via video does not seem to generate the same interpersonal impressions as face-to-face interaction. Storck and Sproull (1995) found less positive feelings among interactants who used interactive video when compared to those who interacted face-to-face.

Sometimes the introduction of nonverbal cues to computer-mediated communication can be problematic. Apparently college students already know this. In a study of 1,000 college students, Rumbaugh (2001) found that 37 percent used the Internet to meet new people, but only 11 percent posted a picture of themselves. Without a picture, students did not have to deal with visual cues that might act as a distraction or source of a stereotype—for example, weight, race, or physical attractiveness—that might hinder message credibility and relationship development. These media users want the introduction of any potentially problematic visual cues to be considered in conjunction with a history of positive interactions. When photos were introduced to partners who had been working and interacting online on several tasks, it resulted in lower ratings of affection and social attraction for their partners, but it had the opposite effect for unacquainted partners who did not have a history of interaction (Walther, Slovacek, & Tidwell, 2001). Even the introduction of dynamic nonverbal signals in videoconferencing does not guarantee more effective communication, unless the images produced fit the viewers' needs. When videoconferencing focuses on the interactants' faces, it may facilitate communication for more personal messages; but not when an object, such as a new product, is the focus of the discussion, or when the goal of the videoconference is to teach a skill, such as bike repair (Brittan, 1992; Gergle, Kraut, & Fussell, 2004; Kraut, Fussell, & Siegel, 2003). The most effective use of videoconferencing, then, would anticipate what a viewer would attend to in a face-to-face meeting. Ideally, then, the participants in a videoconference would discuss and negotiate what should be on the screen, and for how long, using face-to-face interaction as the basis for decision making.

The effectiveness of technology-mediated messages is also dependent on individual needs and preferences. Some people are more comfortable in contexts with more nonverbal cues, and some are comfortable with less. Certain groups of individuals may share a preference—for example, online dating services typically report that males are far more likely to use a photo of the potential date as the basis of a dating decision than are females (See Chapter 6).

Given the adaptable nature of human beings, it is safe to assume they will not simply be slaves to technology. Before the computer was invented, typists used capital letters, underlining, quotation marks, and parenthetical phrases like "just kidding" to offset the lack of vocal and visual cues. Computers are equipped with even more options to make a sender's message clearer and reduce uncertainties on the part of the receiver—for example, bold lettering. Emoticons such as :) for happy, or for something intended as humorous, and :(for sad are commonly used to add information to an email that might otherwise be communicated by facial or vocal expressions. But despite widespread recognition of the meaning of these two symbols, they apparently have relatively little impact on the interpretation of email messages, with one exception: frown emoticons tended to reduce the favorable or constructive ratings of positive messages (Walther & D'Addario, 2001). In addition to textual adaptations, the email message itself can be flagged as a priority, or it may be accompanied by a request for an acknowledgement of receipt. Coping also occurs when a communicator uses more than one type of technology to communicate a message, especially important and urgent ones; a text message or email, for example, that is followed by a phone call. In short, people who are striving to communicate effectively will learn how to use one or more mediated forms of communication to suit their needs and offset any deficits created by missing nonverbal cues. Different types of technology will allow differing amounts and types of nonverbal signals, but some communicators will use those systems more effectively than others.

The ability to effectively decode nonverbal cues sent in the form of computer-generated visuals will also characterize effective communicators in the digital age. Virtually anyone with a computer and some program like Photoshop has the ability to alter visual images. Given the high credibility accorded visual images in this culture, these altered images can be very persuasive, and they are easily circulated to a broad audience. Just as skilled observers of nonverbal behavior in face-to-face encounters learn what cues to attend to for effective decoding, skilled observers of online photos and videos will need to learn what features raise suspicion about an image's authenticity and what ways they can use to verify or deny those suspicions (Knapp, 2008; Lester, 2006; Messaris, 1994; Mitchell, 1992).

Technology users are not the only ones who are interested in the role of nonverbal signals and effective communication; the makers of new technologies are also looking for ways to make their instruments better reflect face-to-face interaction. The future is likely to offer a greater sophistication in the area of touching (Bailenson & Yee, 2007), smell, and three-dimensional images. The production of avatars with realistic human hair, skin, and smooth movement coordination that reflect cultural, regional, and ethnic differences are yet to be developed. But it seems likely that they will—challenging the study of nonverbal communication in ways we never envisioned.

SUMMARY

Understanding the meaning of nonverbal behavior requires an understanding of context. This chapter examined various forms of nonverbal behavior in several familiar contexts: advertising, politics, education, culture, and therapy.

Nonverbal messages embedded in advertising can be extremely influential. A wide variety of nonverbal signals including music, hairstyle, clothing, possessions, responsiveness, and such are used to influence the viewer or hearer. When the target of the ads is distracted during the processing of the ad's information, and multiple exposures to the ad occur, the impact can be even more powerful. These nonverbal signals not only help sell products, they can also influence the expectations, perceptions, and attitudes of the people exposed to them as they relate to actual daily social interaction.

It often seems as if political candidates are obsessed with creating the "right" image, and more often than not, displaying the "right" nonverbal signals is a compelling part of that image. Images of a candidate can be honed by carefully structuring the environment—the music, backdrop, others present—within which he or she is viewed. Managing how the candidate looks with the help of makeup and the appropriate clothes and hairstyles is also important, as is structuring behavior, such as having a candidate "act more assertive." On several occasions, the outcome of televised presidential debates has been attributed to nonverbal signals: calm demeanor versus tension, confidence versus uncertainty, warmth versus coldness, shortness versus height, listening with interest versus smirking, and so on.

The learning process in elementary, secondary, and college classrooms is also influenced by nonverbal messages. Students whose nonverbal signals communicate liking and warmth get positive outcomes from their teachers, and students also believe they learn more from teachers who exhibit such behaviors. Some research, however, indicates that negative nonverbal behavior by a teacher can have positive outcomes for learning in the short run.

Some nonverbal behavior is common to human beings throughout the world, but many of the behaviors we exhibit are taught to us by our culture. We explored three dimensions along which cultures vary in order to highlight cultural differences in nonverbal behavior. These dimensions focused on close versus distant behavior, behavior focused on highlighting the individual versus highlighting the group, and behavior that assumes a great deal of contextual knowledge for interpretation versus behavior that assumes little contextual knowledge. Although these broad cultural characterizations are a useful place to start, it is important to remember that variations also exist within cultures.

Therapy is another context in which nonverbal messages are crucial. Therapists and physicians rely on nonverbal signals to help them understand and diagnose depression, schizophrenia, autism, pain, and other mental and physical disorders. Equally important are nonverbal signals that occur as part of the communication between therapist and patient during therapy. Both patient and therapist are especially attuned to cues that may signal emotions being felt.

In a similar manner, physicians can learn to read nonverbal signals emanating from their patients, which can be valuable signs of an illness, fear, or how the patient feels about his or her physician. In the same way, patients can use nonverbal signals to assess how their physician feels about their illness and their relationship.

To varying degrees, nonverbal signals also play an important role in messages mediated by technology. Just as in face-to-face interaction, nonverbal signals accompanying technology may complement, repeat, substitute, accent, regulate, and conflict with verbal behavior. In some cases, however, the number and type of nonverbal signals are quite limited. Despite this, messages can be effectively communicated even though the lack of copresence often takes its toll on how the participants feel about each other. Sometimes the introduction of nonverbal cues in computer-mediated communication facilitates effectiveness; sometimes it hinders it. As technology-mediated communication increases, human beings will make adaptations with the signals available to them while seeking to approximate face-to-face interaction as much as possible. At the same time, the makers of new technology will increasingly incorporate alternatives for conveying nonverbal information that more closely approximates face-to-face interaction.

Questions for Discussion

1. Discuss how the nonverbal behavior of a patient and physician can mutually influence each other. Next time you visit a counselor or physician, try to carefully observe that person's nonverbal behavior. Is it as effective and positive as it could be?

2. You are a consultant to a vibrant, physically appealing presidential candidate who is not a deep thinker and so is unable to make good arguments for his or her platform. What would you do to get this person elected? Now reverse the situation: You are advising a person who is a deep thinker able to make good arguments for his or her platform, but this person is not dynamic and is physically unappealing. What do you do to get this person elected?

3. Suppose you were hired to advise incoming college freshmen on what nonverbal behavior they should enact to impress their teachers. What advice would you give?

4. In what ways do you think advertising influences your nonverbal behavior? How does advertising influence your perceptions of other people's nonverbal behavior? As an exercise, take careful notes on the use of nonverbal communication in television advertisements for a few hours. Did you notice things you had not noticed before?

5. Different cultures exhibit different nonverbal behavior, and sometimes these differences cause communication problems when people from those different cultures interact. But it is also true that sometimes these differences occur and there are no problems. Under what conditions do you think problems would or would not occur?

6. Select a short scene from your own life in which you were interacting with another person. Then assume you and your partner were communicating that same scene via a technology of your choice (e.g., computers, cell phones, etc.). Identify the difficulties and advantages the technology has for communicating the information in that scene.

Bibliography

Advertising Messages

Archer, D., Iritani, B., Kimes, D. D., & Barrios, M. (1983). Face-ism: Five studies of sex differences in facial prominence. *Journal of Personality and Social Psychology, 45,* 725–735.

Bartsch, R. A., Burnett, T., Diller, T. R., & Rankin-Williams, E. (2000). Gender representation in television commercials: Updating an update. *Sex Roles, 43,* 735–743.

Browne, B. A. (1998). Gender stereotypes in advertising on children's television in the 1990s: A cross-national analysis. *Journal of Advertising, 27*(1), 83–96.

Burtt, H. E., & Clark, J. C. (1923). Facial expression in advertisements. *Journal of Applied Psychology, 7,* 114–125.

Byron, K., Terranova, S., & Nowicki, S., Jr. (2007). Nonverbal emotion recognition and salespersons: Linking ability to perceived and actual success. *Journal of Applied Social Psychology, 37,* 2600–2619.

Chen, M., & Bargh, J. A. (1997). Nonconscious behavioral confirmation processes: The self-fulfilling consequences of automatic stereotype activation. *Journal of Experimental Social Psychology, 33,* 541–560.

Cialdini, R. B. (2007). *Influence: The psychology of persuasion* (Rev. ed.). New York: Collins.

Copeland, G. A. (1989). Face-ism and prime time television. *Journal of Broadcasting and Electronic Media, 33,* 209–214.

Cortese, A. J. (1999). *Provocateur: Images of women and minorities in advertising.* New York: Rowman & Littlefield.

Dodd, D. K., Harcar, V, Foerch, B. J., & Anderson, H. T. (1989). Face-ism and facial expressions of women in magazine photos. *Psychological Record, 39,* 325–331.

Ganahl, D. J., Prinsen, T. J., & Netzley, S. B. (2003). A content analysis of prime time commercials: A contextual framework of gender representation. *Sex Roles, 49,* 545–551.

Goffman, E. (1979). *Gender advertisements.* Cambridge, MA: Harvard University Press.

Halberstadt, A. G., & Saitta, M. B. (1987). Gender, nonverbal behavior, and perceived dominance: A test of the theory. *Journal of Personality and Social Psychology, 53,* 257–272.

Hazlett, R. L., & Hazlett, S. Y. (1999). Emotional response to television commercials: Facial EMG vs.

self-report. *Journal of Advertising Research, 39,* 7–23.

Kang, M. (1997). The portrayal of women's images in magazine advertisements: Goffman's gender analysis revisited. *Sex Roles, 37,* 979–996.

Nisbett, R. E., & Wilson, T. D. (1977). Telling more than we can know: Verbal reports on mental processes. *Psychological Review, 84,* 231–259.

Peterson, R. T. (2005). An examination of the relative effectiveness of training in nonverbal communication: Personal selling implications. *Journal of Marketing Education, 27,* 143–150.

Petty, R. E., Cacioppo, J. T., & Schumann, D. (1983). Central and peripheral routes to advertising effectiveness: The moderating role of involvement. *Journal of Consumer Research, 10,* 135–146.

Raskin, A. (2003). A face any business can trust. *Business 2.0, December, 58,* 60.

Schwarz, N., & Kurz, E. (1989). What's in a picture? The impact of face-ism on trait attribution. *European Journal of Social Psychology, 19,* 311–316.

Wegner, D. M. (2002). *The illusion of conscious will.* Cambridge, MA: MIT Press.

Young, C. (2002). Brain waves, picture sorts, and branding moments. *Journal of Advertising Research, 42,* 42–53.

Zuckerman, M. (1986). On the meaning and implications of facial prominence. *Journal of Nonverbal Behavior, 10,* 215–229.

POLITICAL MESSAGES

Ailes, R. (1988). *You are the message.* New York: Doubleday.

Bryski, B. G., & Frye, J. K. (1979–1980). Nonverbal communication in presidential debates. *Australian Scan, 7 and 8,* 25–31.

Budesheim, T. L., & DePaola, S. J. (1994). Beauty or the beast? The effects of appearance, personality, and issue information on evaluations of political candidates. *Personality and Social Psychology Bulletin, 20,* 339–349.

Davis, M. (1995). Presidential body politics: Movement analysis of debates and press conferences. *Semiotica, 106,* 205–244.

Friedman, H., DiMatteo, M., & Mertz, T. (1980). Nonverbal communication on television news: The

facial expression of broadcasters during coverage of a presidential election campaign. *Personality and Social Psychology Bulletin, 6,* 427–435.

Goethals, G. R. (2005). Nonverbal behavior and political leadership. In R. E. Riggio and R. S. Feldman (Eds.), *Applications of nonverbal behavior* (pp. 97–115). Mahwah, NJ: Erlbaum.

Jamieson, K. H. (1988). *Eloquence in an electronic age.* New York: Oxford University Press.

Keating, C. F., Randall, D., & Kendrick, T. (1999). Presidential physiognomies: Altered images, altered perceptions. *Political Psychology, 20,* 593–610.

Kraus, S. (1996). Winners of the first 1960 televised presidential debate between Kennedy and Nixon. *Journal of Communication, 46,* 78–94.

Masters, R. D. (1989). *The nature of politics*. New Haven, CT: Yale University Press.

McGinnis, J. (1969). *The selling of the president 1968*. New York: Simon & Schuster.

Mullen, B., Futrell, D., Stairs, D., Rice, D., Baumeister, R., Dawson, K., Riordan, C., Radloff, C., Goethals, G., Kennedy, J., & Rosenfeld, P. (1986). Newscasters' facial expressions and voting behavior of viewers: Can a smile elect a president? *Journal of Personality and Social Psychology, 51*, 291–295.

Patterson, M. L., Churchill, M. E., Burger, G. K., & Powell, J. L. (1992). Verbal and nonverbal modality effects on impressions of political candidates: Analysis from the 1984 presidential debates. *Communication Monographs, 59*, 231–242.

Ritter, K., & Henry, D. (1990). The 1980 Reagan–Carter presidential debate. In R. V. Friedenberg (Ed.), *Rhetorical studies of national political debates: 1960–1988*. New York: Praeger.

Sullivan, D. G., Masters, R. D., Lanzetta, J. T., McHugo, G. J., Plate, E., & Englis, B. G. (1991). Facial displays and political leadership. In

G. Schubert & R. Masters (Eds.), *Primate politics*. Carbondale: University of Southern Illinois Press.

Tiemens, R. K. (1978). Television's portrayal of the 1976 presidential debates: An analysis of visual content. *Communication Monographs, 45*, 362–370.

Todorov, A., Mandisodza, A. N., Goren, A., & Hall, C. C., (2005). Inferences of competence from faces predict election outcomes. *Science, 308*, 1623–1626.

Vancil, D. L., & Pendell, S. D. (1987). The myth of viewer–listener disagreement in the first Kennedy–Nixon debate. *Central States Speech Journal, 38*, 16–27.

Verser, R., & Wicks, R. H. (2006). Managing voter impressions: The use of images on presidential candidate Web sites during the 2000 campaign. *Journal of Communication, 56*, 178–197.

Woodward, B. (2004). *Plan of attack*. New York: Simon & Schuster.

Zebrowitz, L. A. (1997). *Reading faces*. Boulder, CO: Westview Press.

TEACHER–STUDENT MESSAGES

Allen, M., Witt, P. L., & Wheeless, L. R. (2006). The role of teacher immediacy as a motivational factor in student learning: Using meta-analysis to test a causal model. *Communication Education, 55*, 21–31.

Andersen, P. A., & Andersen, J. (1982). Nonverbal immediacy in instruction. In L. L. Barker (Ed.), *Communication in the classroom*. Englewood Cliffs, NJ: Prentice-Hall.

Babad, E. (1992). Teacher expectancies and nonverbal behavior. In R. S. Feldman (Ed.), *Applications of nonverbal behavioral theories and research* (pp. 167–190). Hillsdale, NJ: Erlbaum.

Baringer, D. K., & McCroskey, J. C. (2000). Immediacy in the classroom: Student immediacy. *Communication Education, 49*, 178–186.

Blanck, P. D. (Ed.). (1993). *Interpersonal expectations: Theory, research, and applications*. New York: Cambridge University Press.

Chaikin, A. L., Sigler, E., & Derlega, V. J. (1974). Nonverbal mediators of teacher expectancy effects.

Journal of Personality and Social Psychology, 30, 144–149.

Feldman, R. S. (1985). Nonverbal behavior, race, and the classroom teacher. *Theory into Practice, 24*, 45–49.

Freedman, D. P., & Holmes, M. S. (2003). *The teacher's body: Embodiment, authority, and identity in the academy*. Albany, NY: State University of New York Press.

Goldin-Meadow, S., Kim, S., & Singer, M. (1999). What the teacher's hands tell the student's mind about math. *Journal of Educational Psychology, 91*, 720–730.

Guerrero, L. K., & Miller, T. A. (1998). Associations between nonverbal behaviors and initial impressions of instructor competence and course content in videotaped distance education courses. *Communication Education, 47*, 30–42.

Harris, M. J., & Rosenthal, R. (1985). The mediation of interpersonal expectancy effects: 31 meta-analyses. *Psychological Bulletin, 97*, 363–386.

Harris, M. J., & Rosenthal, R. (2005). No more tea-chers' dirty looks: Effects of teacher nonverbal behavior on student outcomes. In R. E. Riggio & R. S. Feldman (Eds.), *Applications of nonverbal communication* (pp. 157–192). Mahwah, NJ: Erlbaum.

McCroskey, J. C., & Richmond, V. P. (1992). Increasing teacher influence through inmediacy. In V. P. Richmond & J. C. McCroskey (Eds.), *Power in the classroom: Communication, control, and concern* (pp. 101–119). Hillsdale, NJ: Erlbaum.

Mottet, T. P. (2000). Interactive television instructors' perceptions of students' nonverbal responsiveness and their influence on distance teaching. *Communication Education, 49,* 146–164.

Mottet, T. P., Beebe, S. A., Raffeld, P. C., & Paulsel, M. L. (2004). The effects of student verbal and nonverbal responsiveness on teachers' liking of students and willingness to comply with student requests. *Communication Quarterly, 52,* 27–38.

Philippot, P., Feldman, R. S., & McGee, G. (1992). Nonverbal behavioral skills in an educational context: Typical and atypical populations. In R. S. Feldman (Ed.), *Applications of nonverbal behavioral theories and research* (pp. 191–213). Hillsdale, NJ: Erlbaum.

Rosenthal, R. (1985). Nonverbal cues in the mediation of interpersonal expectancy effects. In A. W. Siegman & S. Feldstein (Eds.),

Multichannel integration of nonverbal behavior (pp. 105–128). Hillsdale, NJ: Erlbaum.

Rosenthal, R. (2002). Covert communication in classrooms, clinics, courtrooms, and cubicles. *American Psychologist, 57,* 839–849.

Rosenthal, R., & Jacobson, L. (1968). *Pygmalion in the classroom.* New York: Irvington.

Smythe, M.-J., & Hess, J. A. (2005). Are student self-reports a valid method for measuring teacher nonverbal immediacy? *Communication Education, 54,* 170–179.

Witt, P. L., Wheeless, L. R., & Allen, M. (2004). A meta-analytical review of the relationship between teacher immediacy and student learning. *Communication Monographs, 71,* 184–207.

Wolfgang, A. (Ed.). (1984). *Nonverbal behavior: Perspectives, applications, intercultural insights.* New York: Hogrefe.

Woolfolk, A. E., & Brooks, D. M. (1983). Nonverbal communication in teaching. In E. Gordon (Ed.), *Review of Research in Education, Vol. 10.* Washington, DC: American Educational Research Association.

Woolfolk, R. L. (1978). Student learning and performance under varying conditions of teacher verbal and nonverbal evaluative communication. *Journal of Educational Psychology, 70,* 87–94.

CULTURAL MESSAGES

Aiello, J. R., & Thompson, D. E. (1980). Personal space, crowding, and spatial behavior in a cultural context. In I. Altman, A. Rapoport, & J. F. Wohlwill (Eds.), *Human behavior and environment* (Vol. 4). New York: Plenum.

Altman, I., & Chemers, M. M. (1988). *Culture and environment.* New York: Cambridge University Press.

Andersen, P. A., Hecht, M. L., Hoobler, G. D., & Smallwood, M. (2002). Nonverbal communication across cultures. In W. B. Gudykunst & B. Moody (Eds.), *Handbook of international and intercultural communication* (2nd ed., pp. 89–106). Thousand Oaks, CA: Sage.

Armstrong, N., & Wagner, M. (2003). *Field guide to gestures.* Philadelphia: Quirk Books.

Barnlund, D. C. (1975). Communicative styles in two cultures: Japan and the United States. In A. Kendon, R. M. Harris, & M. R. Key (Eds.), *Organization of behavior in face-to-face interaction* (pp. 427–456). The Hague: Mouton.

Collett, P. (1971). Training Englishmen in the non-verbal behavior of Arabs: An experiment of inter-cultural communication. *International Journal of Psychology, 6,* 209–215.

Cunningham, M. R., Barbee, A. P., & Philhower, C. L. (2002). Dimensions of facial physical attractiveness: The intersection of biology and culture. In G. Rhodes & L. A. Zebrowitz (Eds.), *Facial attractiveness* (pp. 193–238). Westport, CT: Ablex.

Dion, K. K. (2002). Cultural perspectives on facial attractiveness. In G. Rhodes & L. A. Zebrowitz

(Eds.), *Facial attractiveness* (pp. 239–259). Westport, CT: Ablex.

Draper, P. (1973). Crowding among hunter-gatherers: The !Kung bushmen. *Science, 182,* 301–303.

Etcoff, N. (1999). *Survival of the prettiest.* New York: Random House.

Ekman, P. (2003). *Emotions revealed.* New York: Times Books.

Ekman, P., Sorenson, E. R., & Friesen, W. V. (1969). Pan-cultural elements in facial displays of emotions. *Science, 164,* 86–88.

Evans, G. W., Lepore, S. J., & Allen, K. M. (2000). Cross-cultural differences in tolerance for crowding: Fact or fiction? *Journal of Personality and Social Psychology, 79,* 204–210.

Field, T. (1999). American adolescents touch each other less and are more aggressive toward their peers as compared with French adolescents. *Adolescence, 34,* 753–758.

Garber, L. L., Jr., & Hyatt, E. M. (2003). Color as a tool for visual persuasion, in L. M. Scott and R. Batra (Eds.), *Persuasive imagery: A consumer response perspective* (pp. 313–336). Mahwah, NJ: Erlbaum.

Gudykunst, W. B., & Ting-Toomey, S. (1988). *Culture and interpersonal communication.* Newbury Park, CA: Sage.

Halberstadt, A. G. (1985). Race, socioeconomic status, and nonverbal behavior. In A. W. Siegman and S. Feldstein (Eds.), *Multichannel integrations of nonverbal behavior* (pp. 227–266). Hillsdale, NJ: Erlbaum.

Hall, E. T. (1966). *The hidden dimension.* New York: Doubleday Anchor.

Hall, E. T. (1976). *Beyond culture.* Garden City, NY: Doubleday Anchor.

Hofstede, G. (2001). *Culture's consequences* (2nd ed.). Thousand Oaks, CA: Sage.

Jourard, S. M. (1966). An exploratory study of body accessibility. *British Journal of Social and Clinical Psychology, 26,* 235–242.

Langlois, J. H., Roggman, L. A., & Rieser-Danner, L. A. (1990). Infants' differential social responses to attractive and unattractive faces. *Developmental Psychology, 26,* 153–159.

Lee, M. E., Matsumoto, D., Kobayashi, M., Krupp, D., Maniatis, E. F., & Roberts, W. (1992). Cultural influences on nonverbal behavior in applied settings. In R. S. Feldman (Ed.), *Applications of nonverbal behavioral theories and research* (pp. 239–261). Hillsdale, NJ: Erlbaum.

Levine, R. (1997). *A geography of time: The temporal misadventures of a social psychologist or how every culture keeps time just a little bit differently.* New York: Basic.

Matsumoto, D. (2001). Culture and emotion. In D. Matsumoto (Ed.), *The handbook of culture and psychology* (pp. 171–194). New York: Oxford University Press.

Matsumoto, D., & Yoo, S. H. (2005). Culture and applied nonverbal communication. In R. E. Riggio & R. S. Feldman (Eds.), *Applications of nonverbal communication* (pp. 255–277). Mahwah, NJ: Erlbaum.

McDaniel, E., & Andersen, P. A. (1998). International patterns of interpersonal tactile communication: A field study. *Journal of Nonverbal Behavior, 22,* 59–73.

Morris, D., Collett, P., Marsh, P., & O'Shaughnessy, M. (1980). *Gestures: Their origins and distribution.* New York: Scarborough.

Munroe, R. L., & Munroe, R. H. (1972). Population density and affective relationships in three East African societies. *Journal of Social Psychology, 88,* 15–20.

Poyatos, F. (Ed.) (1988). *Cross-cultural perspectives in nonverbal communication.* Toronto: Hogrefe.

Regan, P. C., Jerry, D., Narvaez, M., & Johnson, D. (1999). Public displays of affection among Asian and Latino heterosexual couples. *Psychological Reports, 84,* 1201–1202.

Remland, M. S., Jones, T. S., & Brinkman, H. (1991). Proxemic and haptic behavior in three European countries. *Journal of Nonverbal Behavior, 15,* 215–232.

Rhodes, G., Harwood, K., Yoshikawa, S., Nishitani, M., & McLean, I. (2002). The attractiveness of average faces: Cross-cultural evidence and possible biological basis. In G. Rhodes & L. A. Zebrowitz (Eds.), *Facial attractiveness* (pp. 35–58). Westport, CT: Ablex.

Rosenthal, R., Hall, J. A., DiMatteo, M. R., Rogers, P. L., & Archer, D. (1979). *Sensitivity to nonverbal communication:* The PONS test. Baltimore: Johns Hopkins University Press.

Shuter, R. (1976). Proxemics and tactility in Latin America. *Journal of Communication, 26,* 46–52.

Shuter, R. (1977). A field study of nonverbal communication in Germany, Italy and the United States. *Communication Monographs, 44*, 298–305.

Touchy topic: What to do when a handshake isn't enough? (2000, February 16). *Boston Globe*, pp. A1, A20.

Triandis, H. C. (1994). Theoretical and methodological approaches to the study of collectivism and individualism. In U. Kim, H. Triandis, C. Kâgitçibasi, S.-C. Choi, & G. Yoon (Eds.), *Individualism and collectivism: Theory, methods, and applications* (pp. 41–51). Thousand Oaks, CA: Sage.

Wilkins, R. (2005). The optimal form: Inadequacies and excessiveness within the *asiallinen* [matter of fact] nonverbal style in public and civic settings in Finland. *Journal of Communication, 55*, 383–400.

Willis, F. N., & Rawdon, V. A. (1994). Gender and national differences in attitudes toward same-gender touch. *Perceptual and Motor Skills, 78*, 1027–1034.

Therapeutic Settings

Ambady, N., LaPlante, D., Nguyen, T., Rosenthal, R., Chaumeton, N., & Levinson, W. (2002). Surgeons' tone of voice: A clue to malpractice history. *Surgery, 132*, 5–9.

Bensing, J. M., Kerssens, J. J., & van der Pasch, M. (1995). Patient-directed gaze as a tool for discovering and handling psychosocial problems in general practice. *Journal of Nonverbal Behavior, 19*, 223–242.

Bouhuys, A. L. (2003). Ethology and depression. In P. Philippot, R. S. Feldman, & E. J. Coats (Eds.), *Nonverbal behavior in clinical settings*. Oxford, UK: Oxford University Press.

DiMatteo, M. R., Hays, R. D., & Prince, L. M. (1986). Relationship of physicians' nonverbal communication skill to patient satisfaction, appointment noncompliance, and physician workload. *Health Psychology, 5*, 581–594.

DiMatteo, M. R., Taranta, A., Friedman, H. A., & Prince, L. M. (1980). Predicting patient satisfaction from physicians' nonverbal communication skills. *Medical Care, 18*, 376–387.

Ekman, P., & Friesen, W. V. (1974). Nonverbal behavior and psychopathology. In R. J. Friedman & M. M. Katz (Eds.), *The psychology of depression: Contemporary theory and research*. Washington, DC: Winston and Sons.

Ellgring, H. (1986). Nonverbal expression of psychological states in psychiatric patients. *European Archives of Psychiatric Neurological Science, 236*, 31–34.

Ellgring, H., & Scherer, K. R. (1996). Vocal indicators of mood change in depression. *Journal of Nonverbal Behavior, 20*, 83–110.

Gorawara-Bhat, R., Cook, M. A., & Sachs, G. A. (2007). Nonverbal communication in doctor-elderly patient transactions (NDEPT): Development of a tool. *Patient Education and Counseling, 66*, 223–234.

Griffith, C. H. III, Wilson, J. F., Langer, S., & Haist, S. A. (2003). House staff nonverbal communications skills and standardized patient satisfaction. *Journal of General Internal Medicine, 18*, 170–174.

Hall, J. A., Harrigan, J. A., & Rosenthal, R. (1995). Nonverbal behavior in clinician–patient interaction. *Applied and Preventive Psychology, 4*, 21–37.

Hall, J. A., Horgan, T. G., Stein, T. S., & Roter, D. L. (2002). Liking in the physician–patient relationship. *Patient Education and Counseling, 48*, 69–77.

Hall, J. A., Roter, D. L., & Rand, C. S. (1981). Communication of affect between patient and physician. *Journal of Health and Social Behavior, 22*, 18–30.

Haskard, K. B., Williams, S. L., DiMatteo, M. R., Heritage, J., & Rosenthal, R. (2008). The provider's voice: Patient satisfaction and the content-filtered speech of nurses and physicians in primary medical care. *Journal of Nonverbal Behavior, 32*, 1–20.

Irish, J. T., & Hall, J. A. (1995). Interruptive patterns in medical visits: The effects of role, status, and gender. *Social Science & Medicine, 41*, 873–881.

Kring, A. M., & Earnst, K. S. (2003). Nonverbal behavior in schizophrenia. In P. Philippot, R. S. Feldman, & E. J. Coats (Eds.), *Nonverbal behavior in clinical settings*. Oxford, UK: Oxford University Press.

LeResche, L., Dworkin, S. F., Wilson, L., & Ehrlich, K. J. (1992). Effect of temporomandibular disorder pain duration on facial expressions and verbal report of pain. *Pain, 51,* 289–295.

McGee, G., & Morrier, M. (2003). Clinical implications of research in nonverbal behavior of children with autism. In P. Philippot, R. S. Feldman, & E. J. Coats (Eds.), *Nonverbal behavior in clinical settings.* Oxford, UK: Oxford University Press.

Ostwald, P. F. (1961). The sounds of emotional disturbance. *Archives of General Psychiatry, 5,* 587–592.

Patrick, C. J., Craig, K. D., & Prkachin, K. M. (1986). Observer judgments of acute pain: Facial action determinants. *Journal of Personality and Social Psychology, 50,* 1291–1298.

Perez, J. E., & Riggio, R. E. (2003). Nonverbal social skills and psychopathology. In P. Philippot, R. S. Feldman, & E. J. Coats (Eds.), *Nonverbal behavior in clinical settings.* Oxford, UK: Oxford University Press.

Philippot, P., Feldman, R. S., & Coats, E. J. (Eds.). (2003). *Nonverbal behavior in clinical settings.* Oxford, UK: Oxford University Press.

Philippot, P., Kornreich, C., & Blairy, S. (2003). Nonverbal deficits and interpersonal regulation in alcoholics. In P. Philippot, R. S. Feldman, & E. J. Coats

(Eds.), *Nonverbal behavior in clinical settings.* Oxford, UK: Oxford University Press.

Prkachin, K. M. (1992a). The consistency of facial expressions of pain: A comparison across modalities. *Pain, 51,* 297–306.

Prkachin, K. M. (1992b). Dissociating spontaneous and deliberate expressions of pain: Signal detection analyses. *Pain, 51,* 57–65.

Robinson, J. D. (2006). Nonverbal communication and physician–patient interaction: Review and new directions. In V. Manusov & M. L. Patterson (Eds.), *The Sage handbook of nonverbal communication* (pp. 437–459). Thousand Oaks, CA: Sage Publications.

Rosenberg, E. L., Ekman, P., Jiang, W., Babyak, M., Coleman, R. E., Hanson, M., O'Connor, C., Waugh, R., & Blumenthal, J. A. (2001). Linkages between facial expressions of anger and transient myocardial ischemia in men with coronary artery disease. *Emotion, 1,* 107–115.

Schmid Mast, M. (2007). On the importance of nonverbal communication in the physician–patient interaction. *Patient Education and Counseling, 67,* 315–318.

Waxer, P. (1976). Nonverbal cues for depth of depression: Set versus no set. *Journal of Consulting and Clinical Psychology, 44,* 493.

TECHNOLOGY AND NONVERBAL MESSAGES

Bailenson, J. N., & Yee, N. (2007). Virtual interpersonal touch and digital chameleons. *Journal of Nonverbal Behavior, 31,* 225–242.

Brittan, D. (1992). Being there: The promise of multimedia communications. *Technology Review, 95,* 42–50.

Gergle, D., Kraut, R. E., & Fussell, S. R. (2004). Language efficiency and visual technology: Minimizing collaborative effort with visual information. Journal of Language and Social Psychology, 23, 491–517.

Herbert, B. G., & Vorauer, J. D. (2003). Seeing through the screen: Is evaluative feedback communicated more effectively in face-to-face or computer-mediated exchanges? *Computers in Human Behavior, 19,* 25–38.

Kiesler, S., Siegel, J., & McGuire, T. W. (1984). Social psychological aspects of computer-mediated

communication. *American Psychologist, 39,* 1123–1134.

Knapp, M. L. (2008). *Lying and deception in human interaction.* Boston: Pearson/Allyn & Bacon.

Kraut, R. E., Fussell, S. R., & Siegel, J. (2003). Visual information as a conversational resource in collaborative physical tasks. *Human-Computer Interaction, 18,* 13–49.

Kruger, J., Epley, N., Parker, J., & Ng, Z.-W. (2005). Egocentrism over e-mail: Can we communicate as well as we think? *Journal of Personality and Social Psychology, 89,* 925–936.

Lester, P. M. (2006). *Visual communication: Images with messages.* Belmont, CA: Wadsworth.

Messaris, P. (1994). *Visual literacy: Image, mind, and reality.* Boulder, CO: Westview Press.

Mitchell, W. J. (1992). *The reconfigured eye: Visual truth in the post-photographic era.* Cambridge, MA: MIT Press.

Rumbough, T. (2001). The development and maintenance of interpersonal relationships through computer-mediated communication. *Communication Research Reports, 18,* 223–229.

Storck, J., & Sproull, L. (1995). Through a glass darkly: What do people learn in videoconferencing? *Human Communication Research, 22,* 197–219.

Walther, J. B. (2006). Nonverbal dynamics in computer-mediated communication or :(and the net :('s with you, :) and you :) alone. In V. Manusov and M. L. Patterson, (Eds.), *The Sage handbook of nonverbal communication* (pp. 461–479). Thousand Oaks, CA: Sage.

Walther, J. B., & D'Addario, K. P. (2001). The impacts of emoticons on message interpretation in computer-mediated communication. *Social Science Computer Review, 19,* 323–345.

Walther, J. B., Slovacek, C., & Tidwell, L. C. (2001). Is a picture worth a thousand words? Photographic images in long-term and short-term virtual teams. *Communication Research, 28,* 105–134.

PHOTO CREDITS

Chapter 1 p12. Cengage Learning. p35. From I. Eibl-Eibesfeldt, "The Expressive Behavior of the Deaf-and Blind Born," in M. von Cranach and I. Vine, *Social Communication and Movement*. New York: Academic Press, 1973 and with permission from Irenāus Eibl-Eibesfeldt.

Chapter 2 p36. Filmed by I. Eibl-Eibesfeldt in T.K. Pitcairn and I. Eibl-Eibesfeldt, "Concerning the Evolution of Nonverbal Communication in Man," in M. E. Hahn and E. C. Simmel, *Communicative Behavior and Evolution*. New York: Academic Press, 1976. p37. From I. Eibl-Eibesfeldt, "The Expressive Behavior of the Deaf-and Blind Born," in M. von Cranach and I. Vine, *Social Communication and Movement*. New York: Academic Press, 1973 and with permission from Irenāus Eibl-Eibesfeldt. p38. From I. Eibl-Eibesfeldt, "The Expressive Behavior of the Deaf-and Blind Born," in M. von Cranach and I. Vine, *Social Communication and Movement*. New York: Academic Press, 1973 and with permission from Irenāus Eibl-Eibesfeldt. p40. Meltzoff, A.N., & Moore, M.K. (1977). Imitation of facial and manual gestures by human neonates. *Science, 198*, 75–78. Reprinted with permission from AAAS. p41. © Field, T., Woodson, R., Greenberg, R., & Cohen, D. (1982) Discrimination and imitation of facial expressions by neonates. *Science, 218*(8). 179–181. p43. Dr. Nancy Segal. p46. (tl) Courtesy of I. Eibl-Eibesfeldt from I. Eibl-Eibesfeldt, *Ethology: The Biology of Behavior, 2nd ed.*, New York: Holt, Rinehart & Winston, 1975, (tr) Hugo Van Lawick/National Geographic Image Collection. p47. William. K. Redican, Ph.D. 1982, San Francisco, CA. p50. William. K. Redican, Ph.D. 1982, San Francisco, CA. p50. Michael Lyster, London, 1982. p53. Filmed by I. Eibl-Eibesfeldt from I. Eibl-Eibesfeldt, Ethology: *The Biology of Behavior, 2nd ed.*, New York: Holt, Rinehart & Winston, 1975.

Chapter 3 p71. Courtesy of Judith A. Hall. p72. © Dane Archer, Ph.D., Santa Cruz, 1980. p73. © Dane Archer, Ph.D., Santa Cruz, 1980.

Chapter 4 p113. Eric Vega/istockphoto.com. p119. Joe Marquette/AP Photo. p120. Fort Worth Star–Telegram.

Chapter 5 p139. © 2010 PsychoTex/Kevin E. White. p140. Susan Stava/The New York Times/Redux Pictures. p144. Shelly Katz/Time & Life Pictures/Getty Images. p147. (t) Monkey Business Images used under license from Shutterstock, (b) Jeff Greenberg/PhotoEdit.

Chapter 6 p176. Copyright © 2002 by Ablex Publishing. Reproduced with permission of Greenwood Publishing Group, Inc. Westport, CT. p183. Copyright © 2002 by Ablex Publishing. Reproduced with permission of Greenwood Publishing Group, Inc, Westport, CT. p200. (tl, tc, tr, bl, bc) Image Source Black/Jupiter Images, (br) Serg Zastavkin/Used under license from Shutterstock. p208. RIA Novosti/Topham/The Image Works.

Chapter 7 p225. theprint/istockphoto.com. p227. Richard Hutchings/Photo Researchers. p228. Carolyn Kaster/AP Photo. p230. Reg Speller/Stringer/Getty Images. p230. Bettmann/CORBIS. p231. Bill Greenblatt/Stringer/Getty Images. p232. Matt Slocum/AP Photo. p233. (tl) Tom Costello/AP Photo, (tr) © 2010 PsychoTex/Kevin E. White. p236. AP Photo. p240. Dynamic Graphics/Creatas/Jupiter Images. p247. (t) Courtesy of Avery K. Davis, (b) Image 100/Jupiter Images. p248. AP Photo. p250. (t) Jose R. Lopez/The New York Times, (b) Cengage Learning.

Chapter 8 p269. (tl) fStop/Alamy, (tr) Alistair Berg/Digital Vision/Getty Images, (cr) Goodshot/Jupiter Images, (bl) Siri Stafford/Getty Images, (br) Blend Images/Getty Images. p277. Ron Edmonds/AP Photo. p278. Doug Mills/The New York Times/Redux. p282. (tl) Tom Morrison/Getty Images, (bc) DEX IMAGE/Getty Images, (bl, br) Courtesy of Judith A. Hall.

Chapter 9 p298. Ray Stubblebine/CORBIS. p300. Paul Ekman, Ph.D. p306. Courtesy of Veikko Surakka. p307. Paul Ekman, Ph.D. p309. Courtesy of Judith A. Hall. p313–315. Paul Ekman, Ph.D. p320. Copyright © 2009 by the American Psychological Association. Reproduced with permission. Figure 1, page 771, from Inhibiting and facilitating conditions of the human smile: A nonobtrusive test of the facial feedback hypothesis. Strack, Fritz; Martin, Leonard L.; Stepper, Sabine. *Journal of Personality and Social Psychology.* Vol 54(5), May 1988, 768–777. No further reproduction or distribution is permitted without written permission from the American Psychological Association. p323. Dr. Lawrence Ian Reed.

Chapter 10 p335. Courtesy of Mark L. Knapp. p336. Monkey Business Images used under license from Shutterstock. p341. Paul Ekman, Ph.D. p342–343. Knoll, B.I., Attkiss, K.J., & Persing, J.A. (2008). "The Influence of Forehead, Brow, and Periorbital Aesthetics on Perceived Expression in the Youthful Face. *Plastic and Reconstructive Surgery, 121*, 1793–1802. p344–345. From Baron-Cohen S.; Wheelwright S.; Jolliffe A.T. Is There a "Language of the Eyes"? Evidence from Normal Adults, and Adults with Autism or Asperger Syndrome, *Visual Cognition, Volume 4*, Number 3, 1 September 1997, pp. 311–331(21), reprinted by permission of the publisher (Taylor & Francis Group, http://www.informaworld.com). p346. With permission from Reginald B. Adams from Adams, R.B., Jr., & Kleck, R.E. (2005). Effects of direct and averted of direct and averted gaze on the perception of facially communicated emotion. *Emotion, 5*, 3–11. p357. Eckhard H. Hess, Ph.D.

Chapter 11 p374. Hollien, H. (1990). *The acoustics of crime: The new science of forensic phonetics.* Springer-Verlag New York, LLC (springer.com).

Chapter 12 p422. Hulton Archive/Getty Images.

Chapter 13 p458. Roger L. Wollenberg/UPI/Landov. p459. Charles Bennett/AP Photo. p460. Science and Capitol Advantage/AP Photo.

Name Index

SUBJECT INDEX